# Psychological and Pedagogical Considerations in Digital Textbook Use and Development

Elena Railean
*University of European Studies, Republic of Moldova & Academy of Sciences of Moldova, Republic of Moldova*

A volume in the Advances in Educational
Technologies and Instructional Design (AETID)
Book Series

| | |
|---|---|
| Managing Director: | Lindsay Johnston |
| Managing Editor: | Austin DeMarco |
| Director of Intellectual Property & Contracts: | Jan Travers |
| Acquisitions Editor: | Kayla Wolfe |
| Production Editor: | Christina Henning |
| Development Editor: | Caitlyn Martin |
| Typesetter: | Kaitlyn Kulp |
| Cover Design: | Jason Mull |

Published in the United States of America by
Information Science Reference (an imprint of IGI Global)
701 E. Chocolate Avenue
Hershey PA, USA 17033
Tel: 717-533-8845
Fax: 717-533-8661
E-mail: cust@igi-global.com
Web site: http://www.igi-global.com

Library of Congress Cataloging-in-Publication Data

Railean, Elena, 1965-
  Psychological and pedagogical considerations in digital textbook use and development / by Elena Railean.
    pages cm
  Includes bibliographical references and index.
  ISBN 978-1-4666-8300-6 (hardcover) -- ISBN 978-1-4666-8301-3 (ebook) 1. Electronic textbooks. 2. Electronic textbooks--Psychological aspects. 3. Electronic textbooks--Design. I. Title.
  LB3045.74.R34 2015
  371.33--dc23
                        2015003773

This book is published in the IGI Global book series Advances in Educational Technologies and Instructional Design (AE-TID) (ISSN: 2326-8905; eISSN: 2326-8913)

British Cataloguing in Publication Data
A Cataloguing in Publication record for this book is available from the British Library.

All work contributed to this book is new, previously-unpublished material. The views expressed in this book are those of the authors, but not necessarily of the publisher.

For electronic access to this publication, please contact: eresources@igi-global.com.

# Advances in Educational Technologies and Instructional Design (AETID) Book Series

Lawrence A. Tomei
*Robert Morris University, USA*

ISSN: 2326-8905
EISSN: 2326-8913

## MISSION

Education has undergone, and continues to undergo, immense changes in the way it is enacted and distributed to both child and adult learners. From distance education, Massive-Open-Online-Courses (MOOCs), and electronic tablets in the classroom, technology is now an integral part of the educational experience and is also affecting the way educators communicate information to students.

The **Advances in Educational Technologies & Instructional Design (AETID) Book Series** is a resource where researchers, students, administrators, and educators alike can find the most updated research and theories regarding technology's integration within education and its effect on teaching as a practice.

## COVERAGE

- Instructional Design
- Adaptive Learning
- Instructional Design Models
- Curriculum Development
- Educational Telecommunications
- Classroom Response Systems
- Hybrid Learning
- Collaboration Tools
- Bring-Your-Own-Device
- Web 2.0 and Education

IGI Global is currently accepting manuscripts for publication within this series. To submit a proposal for a volume in this series, please contact our Acquisition Editors at Acquisitions@igi-global.com or visit: http://www.igi-global.com/publish/.

# Titles in this Series

*For a list of additional titles in this series, please visit: www.igi-global.com*

*Macro-Level Learning through Massive Open Online Courses (MOOCs) Strategies and Predictions for the Future*
Elspeth McKay (RMIT University, Australia) and John Lenarcic (RMIT University, Australia)
Information Science Reference • copyright 2015 • 313pp • H/C (ISBN: 9781466683242) • US $200.00 (our price)

*Implementation and Critical Assessment of the Flipped Classroom Experience*
Abigail G. Scheg (Elizabeth City State University, USA)
Information Science Reference • copyright 2015 • 333pp • H/C (ISBN: 9781466674646) • US $175.00 (our price)

*Transforming the Future of Learning with Educational Research*
Helen Askell-Williams (Flinders University, Australia)
Information Science Reference • copyright 2015 • 381pp • H/C (ISBN: 9781466674950) • US $185.00 (our price)

*Intelligent Web-Based English Instruction in Middle Schools*
Jiyou Jia (Peking University, China)
Information Science Reference • copyright 2015 • 354pp • H/C (ISBN: 9781466666078) • US $185.00 (our price)

*Handbook of Research on Teaching Methods in Language Translation and Interpretation*
Ying Cui (Shandong University, Weihai, China) and Wei Zhao (Shandong University, Weihai, China)
Information Science Reference • copyright 2015 • 458pp • H/C (ISBN: 9781466666153) • US $325.00 (our price)

*Methodologies for Effective Writing Instruction in EFL and ESL Classrooms*
Rahma Al-Mahrooqi (Sultan Qaboos University, Oman) Vijay Singh Thakur (Dhofar University, Oman) and Adrian Roscoe (Sultan Qaboos University, Oman)
Information Science Reference • copyright 2015 • 417pp • H/C (ISBN: 9781466666191) • US $185.00 (our price)

*Student-Teacher Interaction in Online Learning Environments*
Robert D. Wright (University of North Texas, USA)
Information Science Reference • copyright 2015 • 450pp • H/C (ISBN: 9781466664616) • US $185.00 (our price)

*Cases on Technology Integration in Mathematics Education*
Drew Polly (University of North Carolina at Charlotte, USA)
Information Science Reference • copyright 2015 • 521pp • H/C (ISBN: 9781466664975) • US $200.00 (our price)

www.igi-global.com

701 E. Chocolate Ave., Hershey, PA 17033
Order online at www.igi-global.com or call 717-533-8845 x100
To place a standing order for titles released in this series, contact: cust@igi-global.com
Mon-Fri 8:00 am - 5:00 pm (est) or fax 24 hours a day 717-533-8661

# Table of Contents

## Chapter 11

## Chapter 12

# Preface

Informational globalisation has generated changes in all aspects of textbook theory, including the use and development of the digital textbooks. Postmodernist thought has found grounding in the insights of chaos theory, Godel's theorem, catastrophe theory, quantum mechanics, emerging cosmological insights, and topology theory. Technology jumps from the margins of education to the mainstream, from informal settings to formal ones and from small independently-funded projects to large-government supported initiatives, where the postmodernism values are accepted. Thus, digital textbooks are widely used in all educational systems. Dispute global challenges, teachers continue to be the main pillars of education. "Equitable, Quality Learning for All is a Dakar Consensus" (Anderson & Winthrop, 2013). This implies improving access to quality use and development of digital textbooks. While digital giants (Intel, Apple, Google and others) think about digital textbook use and development only as a technology, students prefer to fulfill certain informational and emotional needs more reliability in their own learning space. Thereupon, only few studies are available to stress the importance of the psychological and pedagogical considerations in digital textbook use and development.

In the past five decades, two development have brought textbook theory issues to the fore. First has been the increased dependence of pedagogical resources and learning tools on Information and Communication Technologies (ICT). Second, abetted by ICT, the didactic model of textbook has been transformed. Today, digital textbooks are used and developed in the most countries around the world. Among the reasons which influenced these processes are the lower cost of the digital textbooks; the availability of content; student buying and sharing trends; the continued growth of for-profit institutions and online learning; the increased popularity and availability of open digital content; an increase in digital-first publishers and open textbook movements; the textbook rental market; the growth of online retail and distribution options; the popularity and evolution of tablet devices and smartphones; the advance of e-reader software/hardware technology; format standards for digital textbooks and the growth of e-book market share in trade publishing, as was noted by Reynolds (2011, pp. 180-184).

Research in psychology and pedagogy has highlighted the relation between an informational-energetic potential for learning and the "offers" of educational technology to improve students' learning. Changing learning environments and developing technologies of programed, multimedia, hypermedia, eTexbooks and Open Source Textbooks indeed poses a number of challenges for maintaining good practice for learning. Across all discussions, there is a debate about balancing psychological and pedagogical efforts in digital learning. It is clear that a digital textbook didactic model must reflect insight and deeper learning based on behavioral actions and/or activities. Striking the balance between theory and practice in digital textbook use and development is one of the critical questions. Other tasks are simple, but not less important. For example, copyrights and plagiarism are among the world's problems. Thus, without the frontier research in pedagogy, these issues will never be solved. It is therefore necessary to review some of key concepts of modelling digital content, its structure and functionality.

## THE CHALLENGES FOR THE DIGITAL TEXTBOOK USE AND DEVELOPMENT

Each generation of textbooks' methodology addresses the challenges posed by the previous generation. In postmodernism, people have been fascinated with the idea of exploring new didactic models of textbook since the beginning of new knowledge conceptualization. Thus, postmodernism values the writerly text instead of readerly text; the mechanism for the production of knowledge derived from a dialogue pedagogy instead of narrative knowledge; quantum relativity instead of Newtonian mechanics; qualitative methods instead of quantitative methods and others, as was identified by Milovanovic (2014). Moreover, teacher-centred technologies are abominated in favor of learner-centered learning strategies. Education occurs in a variety of formal and non-formal settings allowing feedback to come from "local and real, global and virtual learning environments" (Midoro, 2005, p. 32). Unfortunately, the literature notes a number of theories relevant to digital textbook used and development. Their findings hold promise for innovative digital textbooks learning environments, but from theoretical and empirical models. And any attempt to deal with the issue of theoretical and empirical models demands an adequate understanding of the challenges that exist in the Era of Informational Globalisation and Postmodernism. Such challenges can be classified into three main categories:

- The challenge of losing a generation of artificially designed closed pedagogical systems in favour of much more natural, ubiquitous and sustainable environments with local and global, real and virtual learning environments where students are able to self-regulate their learning;
- The challenge of GAE (Globalisation, Anthropology and Existentialism) paradigm, instructional dynamic and flexible strategy, educational methodology and procedures that adequately reflect the postmodernism features and new design of globalised learning processes;
- The challenge of "digital textbooks" that are coming into global market, claiming the need to offer a textbook conceived with the digital language of the multiliteracies, offering innovative pedagogical methodology better suited for the psycho-pedagogical characteristics of the young.

Numerous studies have indicated that is a problem in managing artificially designed closed pedagogical systems especially with respect to regulating the learning needs in diversity of learning environments. Research has shown that

*…further in-depth studies are required to determine the conditions and features that users will yield positive learning results. Currently, findings on user acceptance and effectiveness are generally contradictory. While some studies on user acceptance claim that students and teachers do not prefer e-Textbooks, other studies reveal that users express satisfactory perceptions on the use of e-Textbooks over printed books. Preliminary investigation indicates that if the functions of e-Textbooks are well designed, the results of user attitude and behavior toward the use of e-Textbooks relative to traditional paper textbooks will be more encouraging. (Gu, Wu & Xu, 2014)*

There is also the challenge of establishing a new knowledge paradigm, learning strategy, educational methodology and procedures that adequately reflect the postmodernism features and new design of globalised learning processes. Such challenges exist in a multidimensional learning space and run the risk of using digital textbooks as no more than a digitalized version of printed textbook. First at an intellectual, emotional and informational-energetically student levels where it is increasingly becoming difficult for the instructional designer to develop appropriate user interfaces. Second at a real environment level, where it is becoming difficult to rely on traditional didactics to regulate behavior during formal, informal and non-formal education in rapidly changing learning environments. Clearly there are a number of pedagogical situations where it is important to use Skinner's Theory or Multimedia Learning Theory in order to keep attention or/and reinforce meaning of key curricula concepts. There are perhaps a number of other real world tasks where severe feedback control may not be the best solution.

Another challenge in the use and development of digital textbooks is related to digital textbook availability at the world level. Different types of eTextbooks and Open Source textbooks, from digitalization of learning content to utilizing interactive technologies are developed. Psychological and pedagogical concerns resulting from either the inability to affordances of such resources/tools or to specify the role of frontier research in area of pedagogy. It is indeed a challenge when dealing with global market of digital textbook use and development pedagogy and methodology. Recently literature points outs the most relevant aspects of digital textbook learning environments: intellectual autonomy, ownership of self-directed learning processes, curiosity and exploration as a natural learning mechanisms, freedom of choice, diversity, flexibility and virtual mobility, multi stimuli exposure, connectivity and personalization. What are the most relevant pedagogical strategies for digital textbooks?

## SEARCHING FOR A SOLUTION

The speed of challenges emphasizes that digital textbook isn't only an apparent phenomena, but something more that is the essential in future rounds of sustainable and durable development of human society. However, is it the greater reliance on digital infrastructure and learning platforms, even digital, in real environments? Is this statement true: "textbooks are undergoing a transformation into digital textbooks, which can offer a diverse range of supplementary digital media functions including sounds, audiovisuals, animations, 3D graphics and other state-of-the-art multimedia features" (Kim, Yoo, Park, Yoo, Byun, Cho, Ryu & Kim, 2010, p. 509)? From one point of view, this is an anthology for anyone interested in how students lean in the digital/information age. From the other point of view, this is an invitation to cross-disciplinary research.

Many innovations are around modern psychology and pedagogy. Among them are MOOCs and blended and flipped learning. However, this is only the tip of the iceberg. The increasing interest in psychological and pedagogical innovations is influenced by additional affordances of textbooks and with the increasing popularity of Open Source Textbooks. Use and development of the digital textbooks represent a strategic trend for learning (Davidson & Carliner, 2014; Evans & Rick, 2014; Panto & Comas-Quinn, 2013; Harvey, 2011; Pullen & Cole, 2010; and Kim & Jung, 2010). The meta-analysis of this literature allows coinciding that from a student's perspective to read in a portable format is more convenient, but not knowledgeable and from a teacher's perspective to have access to more pedagogical resources/tools means to have more resources and tools for better educational outcomes.

Despite the growing popularity of postmodernism philosophy and digital textbooks' use and development, a digital pedagogy is yet to be articulated. Leibovici, Bosova, Avdeeva, Rabinovici and Tarasova (2012, p.17-18) witness the following psychological and pedagogical concerns: a) difficulty of understanding; b) disconnected numbers, syllables or words; c) meaningful memorization and d) contextual surrounding of the basic information. How can these concerns be investigated? Could be the same research methodology be applied that has been built since 1960? (Talizina, 1969; Galperin, 2000). It is evident that cybernetic principles cannot be mechanically transmitted to didactic processes that triggered digital textbooks and that learning aren't t algorithms that lead from simple to complex.

During learning with digital textbooks students need to be actively engaged in processing, storing, and recovering information, as well as critical thinking and decision making processes. Since 2000 more and more publishers have developed digital textbooks and allow to construct, or/and to self-publish digital textbooks. Other companies serve as an intermediary between publishers and students, delivering the textbook in a digital format using a program for reading. In short, digital textbooks with personalized content, interactive assessments, and mediated communication provide new pathways for learning design.

Digital textbook use and development combines the power of technology with creative, innovative and metacognitive strategies. However, the multiliteracies' needs and real environments tasks require alternative psychopedagogical solutions. There are at least twelve issues, which need to be solved:

- To identify good practices of psychological and pedagogical considerations in digital textbooks' use and development to substantiate digital learning with textbooks;
- To discuss digital textbooks' terminology and to classify its diversity;
- To operate with post-modernism philosophy in order to investigate the effects of Globalisation and ICT) related to learning ideal for new educational endeavors;
- To illustrate the diversity of principles in digital textbook use and development in order to demonstrate the power of cross-principles and those norms of application in learning design;
- To differentiate digital textbooks' affordances for eight didactic systems and to identify the main features related to information/communication, learning and assessment models;
- To identify the psychological and pedagogical solutions related to elementary didactic units;
- To analyze and compare the psychological and pedagogical functions of modern teachers that could be delegated to digital textbooks in order to archive the guaranteed learning outcomes;
- To assemble the cross-principles in a new Didactical Model of Digital Textbook;
- To summarize the learning design norms of elementary didactic units common for all digital textbooks related to assessment, development and maintenance of learner's cognitive potential;
- To synthesize a model of integrated process and to prove information /communication, cognitive activity and assessment processes in digital textbook use and development;
- To summarize digital textbook' technologies and to explain the role of MetaSystems Learning Design in the ecology of learning in formal and non-formal learning environments;
- To argue and predict the features of quality indicator required by formal and non-formal, open and closed learning environments provided by the digital textbooks;
- To summarize the effects of digital plagiarism and the ways to avoid it.

All these twelve issues indicate the research problem: *What are the psychological and pedagogical considerations that would cause innovative digital textbook use and development for sustainability?*

The Era of Globalisation is shifting emphasis from Bacon's "knowledge itself is a power" to new learning ideal: *professionalism, planetary thinking and cultural pluralism*. Although many researchers, teachers and practitioners adopt this, they only tend to be more adaptive and accommodative at global challenge of using and design of digital textbooks. In practice, this is over-formalized, based on new technology, but with historical solutions software development. Such, for example is ADDIE models, used since 1960, in instructional design. Usually, these ill-conceptualized softwares have followed incorrect decisions about how digital textbook should be used and developed.

The questions listed above represent the main tasks attributed to theory and practice of textbook's use and development. One of the research directions named "MetaSystems Learning Design" was launched in PhD thesis "Psycho-pedagogical foundations of electronic textbook development". In recent positions, papers related to this thesis described the "modern pedagogy features in multi-measured space" (Rudic, 2013, p. 74); cross–principles (Railean, 2012, p. 242) and a knowledge management model (Railean, 2013a); and interdependences between MetaSystems Learning Design cross-principles and the diversity of learning environments (Railean, 2013b, 2013c). This innovative way offers solutions and recommendations in using and development of digital textbooks, emphasizing the role of post-modernism in educational philosophy, as well as principles derived from quantum and behavioural psychology, cybernetics of Open Systems, competence pedagogy, and knowledge management.

This book highlights cross-principles and seeks for innovative solutions regarding psychological and pedagogical considerations in use and development of digital textbooks. *The aim of this work is to offer a balanced coverage of related technologies that could contribute to digital textbook design focused on guaranteed learning outcomes.* Thus, the integrity of information/communication, cognitive activity and assessment mechanisms helps identify and fortifies the linkages between digital environment and learning processes. Moreover, with an emphasis on the synthesis of a new didactic model, this book addresses to usability, affordances and learnability of digital textbooks.

Establishing the cross-principles on the base of "globalisated learning processes", allows identification of laws, which are considered the first step leading to a pragmatic solutions. These principles take the form of norms for developing elementary didactic units. Either the teacher(s) or/and student(s) should be learning designers. Thus, the main condition for digital textbooks to be accepted is deeper learning. The proposed way is to use instructional dynamic and flexible strategy. Moreover, teacher(s) and student(s) play an important role in this strategy. This concerns the quality indicator in one or other environment. However, if this issue is analysed toward affordances, the focus needs to shift to developing an integrated structure of competence where the cognitive system(s) of the student(s) is the one who makes the most relevant decisions regarding what knowledge/styles is needed and in what environments. This not only moves the teaching strategies from reproductive to productive, but also ensure critical thinking about what is proposed in textbooks and what is really important for learning in a challenging environments.

The idea to diagnose psycho- pedagogical characteristics of learners before learning with software is not new. We keep this idea in our theory. In addition, it was observed that most of the proposed models describe the limited roles of teacher(s) in personalised "construction" of the content (Hong, Kim & Yoo, 2013; Zoellner & Cavanaugh, 2013; Armen & Atwoo, 2013; Lee, Messon & Yau, 2013). Apparently, the lack of meta-analysis results in increasing the probability of errors in digital textbook learning environment. Thus, this is an absolute necessity for innovative modelling.

Linear and systemical approaches in conceptualization of digital textbook(s)' use and development has also been considered as precursors of an ineffective digital learning environment, thus leading to conclusions that students prefer digital textbooks, but learn better or at the same level with printed textbooks because "on-screen reading is slower, more fatiguing, and non-comprehensive" (Wook, Michaels & Waterman, 2014, p.17). Since the learning environment provides unique solutions for architecture of integrated structure of competence, the importance of clarity in digital textbook design cannot be overstated. The proposed solution doesn't neglect the correlations between the diversity of learning environments, learners' potential and teachers' functions. Moreover, it is expected that Metasystems Learning Design is a post-modern solution, because it is based on the knowledge graph and adequate matrix, as well as on interactive and delayed feedback, integrity of information/communication, cognitive and assessment processes, and learning and behavioral actions. This allows evidencing the priority of educational outcomes based on deeper learning. In practice, this norm requires a hermeneutic dialogue between author and reader of the digital content and a new didactic model.

Analyzing digital textbooks' features in compassion with functions of teachers, it has been identified the possibilities to delegate at least six psycho-pedagogical functions of innovative teachers: information, formation, systematization, integration, cognition and self-regulation. Through promotion of "integrated flexible structure of competence" architecture, the importance of action verbs related to cognitive, affective and psychomotor activities is undisputable. This insight opens a new way for digital textbooks adoption in diversity of learning environments. Self-regulation, personalization, clarity, dynamicity and flexibility, feedback diversity and ergonomics are the keys of learning design. The meta-analysis of scientific literature and practical examples allow summarising the psycho-pedagogical norms for designing the didactic units related to teaching, learning and assessment. These norms are valid not only of their attachments to some theoretical trends or to a concrete theory, but because they are the sufficient and necessary conditions for modelling of functional learning environment. Educational technology, defined as the learning design plus personal development, represents a new culture of learning. Hence, the technological phases within the didactic model argue an innovative ecological approach, but instead reflect the main conditions for a sustainable digital textbook learning environments. All these solutions are reflected in the "quality indicator" and technology of digital textbooks.

## ORGANIZATION OF THE BOOK

The book is organized into twelve chapters. The best way to read these chapters is the following (see Figure 1).

A brief description of each of the chapters follows:

Chapter 1 identifies four good practices to substantiate digital learning with digital textbooks: visual instruction, audiovisual instruction, programmed instruction and computer aided instruction assessment. This chapter emphasizes the effectiveness of practices and concludes with a call for the future research in confusing terminology proposed during digital textbooks' use and development.

Chapter 2 summarizes the digital textbook affordances, i.e. the proprieties of digital textbooks to do what they enable to do in learner-centered learning environments related to content, feedback, social media, and desired results. The author classifies the current and future features into 8 didactic systems and identifies the main characteristics related to communication, learning and assessment.

Chapter 3 establishes the need for a comprehensive definition, as well as terminology related to digital textbook use and development. The author provides a framework for clarifying diverse initiates, exploring correlations between textbook, digital (text) book and educational software concepts and proposing a synthetic definition, derived from formal logics.

*Figure 1. The organizational structure of book*

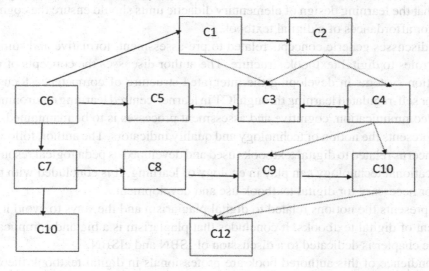

Chapter 4 presents an analysis of issues, controversies and concerns related to diversity of eTextbooks and Open Source Textbooks structures. The author identifies the common components of digital textbooks and reports them to their external and internal context. The author contends that in order to design and develop an effective structure for digital textbooks, one needs to consider the post-modernism, metacognition, feedback, competence pedagogy and knowledge management solutions.

Chapter 5 analyses the recent psycho-pedagogical functions for use and development of digital textbooks: information, formation, systematization, integration, cognition and self-regulation. It promotes the concept of integrated structure of competence that opens the way to move beyond a digitalized version of scholar print textbook toward knowledge-based-economy requirements.

Chapter 6 takes a philosophical orientation and investigates the effects of Globalisation and Information and Communication Technologies (ICT) related to learning ideal for new educational endeavors. The aim of this chapter is to elucidate the importance of challenges for teacher(s) and student(s)' role and features a meta-reflective discussion about laws of globalisated pedagogical processes and influence on psychological and pedagogical consideration in digital textbook use and development.

Chapter 7 reviews the principles of digital textbooks' design models such that thrust could be promoted in an interdisciplinary domain. The finding of this chapter is that digital textbooks need to be designed and used on the base on the following cross-principles: self-regulation; personalization; clarity; dynamicity and flexibility; feedback diversity; and ergonomics. These principles are accomplished with adequate norms of application in learner-centred learning environments.

Chapter 8 addresses the issues of Instructional Design, with particular reference to Instructional Systems Design, ADDIE and Agile models. Based on results of the pedagogical experiment, the author proposes a new didactical model that reflects both the learning design of digital textbook' context, content, environment and cognitive processes triggered by digital textbook.

Chapter 9 reviews issues surrounding the learning design of elementary didactic units common for digital textbooks. The author argues that it is possible to maintain and increase the cognitive potential of the learner with a self-regulated mechanism and hence facilitate cognition and metacognition. The author argues that the learning design of elementary didactic units should ensure the cognitive, affective and psychomotor affordances of a digital textbook.

Chapter 10 discusses generic concepts related to pre-assessment, formative and summative assessment and their roles to digital textbook structure. The author discusses the concepts of monitoring for anomaly detection systems in developing the integrated structure of competence focus on education outcomes and/or self-regulated learning through ICT in learner-centred learning environment, if integrity of information/communication, cognitive and assessment processes is to be maintained.

Chapter 11 presents the notion of technology and quality indicators. The author, following their identification of concerns related to digital textbooks used and developed as pedagogical resources, identifies the role of educational technology can play in ecology of learning. It is concluded with presentation of quality indicator necessary for digital textbook use and development.

Chapter 12 presents the notions related to digital plagiarism and the ways to avoid it for proper use and development of digital textbooks. It concludes that plagiarism is a big and complicated issue. The main part pf the chapter is dedicated to a discussion of ISBN and eISBN.

The target audience of this authored book are professionals in digital textbook theory and design. This work is a culmination of 10 years of research in interdisciplinary and trans-disciplinary areas of digital pedagogy. The book is expected to appeal to researchers in frontier investigations related to modern pedagogy but also to anyone who is interested in understanding the theme of digital textbook use and development from a metasystems learning design perspective. For a long time, the author has concentrated on different aspects of psychological and pedagogical concerns and innovative solutions in digital textbook use and development. Therefore, the author has published over 70 other publications on various aspects of learning theory and design, including the role of cognitive, quantum and artificial psychology, competence pedagogy, constructivism cybernetics and other concepts discussed here.

*Elena Railean*
*University of European Studies, Republic of Moldova & Academy of Sciences of Moldova, Republic of*
  *Moldova*

## REFERENCES

Anderson, A., & Winthrop, R. (2013). *Dakar consensus: Equitable, quality learning for all*. Brookings. Retrieved November 1, 2014 from http://www.brookings.edu/blogs/education-plus-development/posts/2013/03/25-dakar-equitable-quality-learning-anderson-winthrop

Armen, H., & Atwood, L. (2013). Creating social books. In *Proceedings of Workshop at IDC Interaction Design and Children,* (pp. 24-28). New York City. Retrieved December 1, 2013 from http://idc2013ebooks.fbk.eu/sites/idc2013ebooks.fbk.eu/files/IBooC2013.pdf#page=24

Davidson, A. L., & Carliner, S. (2014). E-Books for educational uses. In J. M. Spector, M. D. Merrill, J., Elen, & M. J. Bishop, (Eds.), *Handbook of research on educational communications and technology* (pp. 713-722). Springer New York.

Evans, M. A., & Rick, J. (2014). Supporting learning with interactive surfaces and spaces. In J. M. Spector, M. D. Merrill, J. Elen, & M. J. Bishop (Eds.), *Handbook of research on educational communications and technology* (pp. 689–701). Springer New York. doi:10.1007/978-1-4614-3185-5_55

Galperin. (2000). *Introduction in psychology* (in Russian). Moscow: University.

Gu, X., Wu, B., & Xu, X. (2014). Design, development, and learning in e-Textbooks: What we learned and where we are going. *Journal of Computers in Education*, *1*(3), article 24. Springer. Retrieved February 9, 2015, from http://link.springer.com/article/10.1007/s40692-014-0023-9/fulltext.html

Harvey, D. (2011). Analytical Chemistry 2.0: An open-access digital textbook. *Analytical and Bioanalytical Chemistry*, *399*(1), 149–152. doi:10.1007/s00216-010-4316-1 PMID:21046084

Hong, J. H., Kim, M., & Yoo, K. H. (2013). Development of a 3D digital textbook using X3D. In Y.-H. Han, D.-S. Park, W. Jia, & S.-S. Yeo (Eds.), *Ubiquitous information technologies and applications* (pp. 341–351). Springer. doi:10.1007/978-94-007-5857-5_37

Kim, J., & Jung, H. (2010). Korean Digital Textbook Project. *Computers in the Schools*, *27*(4), 247–265. doi:10.1080/07380569.2010.523887

Kim, M., Yoo, K. H., Park, C., Yoo, J. S., Byun, H., Cho, W., & Kim, N. et al. (2010). An XML-based digital textbook and its educational effectiveness. *Advances in Computer Science and Information Technology (Lecture Notes in Computer Science)*, *6059*, 509–523. doi:10.1007/978-3-642-13577-4_46

Lawrence, S. A. (2014). Exploring the use of technology, multimodal texts, and digital tools in K-12 classrooms. In S. A. Lawrence (Ed.), *Critical practice in P-12 education: Transformative teaching and learning* (pp. 24–48). Hershey, PA: Information Science Reference. doi:10.4018/978-1-4666-5059-6.ch002

Lee, H. J., Messom, C., & Yau, K. L. (2013). Can an electronic textbook be part of k-12 education? Challenges, technological solutions and open issues. *The Turkish Online Journal of Educational Technology.*, *12*(1), 32–44.

Leibovici, A. N., Bosova, L. L., Avdeeva, C. M., Rabinovici, P. D., & Tarasova, K. B. (2012). *Electronic textbooks: Recommendation for development, implementation and use of interactive multimedia electronic textbooks of a new generation for the general education based on modern mobile electronic devices* (In Russian). Moscow: The Federal Institute for Education Development.

Midoro, V. (2005). *European teachers toward the knowledge society*. Italy: Edizioni MENABO.

Milovanovic, D. (2014). *Dueling paradigms: modernist v. postmodernist thought*. Retrieved February, 9, 2015 from http://critcrim.org/critpapers/milovanovic_postmod.htm

Panto, E. & Comas-Quinn, A. (2013). The Challenge of Open Education. *Journal of e-Learning and Knowledge Society*. 9 (1), 11-22.

Pullen, D. L., & Cole, D. R. (2010). *Multiliteracies and technology enhanced education: social practice and the global classroom*. Hershey, PA: Information Science Reference. doi:10.4018/978-1-60566-673-0

Railean, E. (2012). Issues and challenges associated with the design of electronic textbook. In B. H. Khan (Ed.), *User interface design for virtual environments: Challenges and advances* (pp. 238–256). Hershey, PA: IGI Publishing.

Railean, E. (2013a). In K. K. Patel, & S. Vij (Ed.). enterprise resource planning models for the education sector: Applications and methodologies (pp.77-92). Hershey, PA: IGI Publishing.

Railean, E. (2013b). Metasystems learning design in digital textbook use and development. In *Proceedings of CAIM 2013 Conference on Applied and Industrial Mathematics* (p. 106). Bucharest, Romania: Romanian National Authority for Scientific Research. Retrieved September 2, 2013 from http://www.eapril.org/resources/EAPRIL2013/Book%20of%20abstracts_EAPRIL%202013.pdf

Railean, E. (2013c). Toward metasystems learning design theory for learning environments. In *Proceedings of EAPRIL2013 Conference*, 45. Sweeten: Bienne.

Reynolds, R. (2011). Trends influencing the growth of digital textbooks in US higher education. *Publishing Research Quarterly*, *27*(2), 178–187. doi:10.1007/s12109-011-9216-5

Rudic, G. (2013). Modern pedagogy in multi-measured space. In E. B. Assemble (Ed.), *Socrates Almanac "Science and Education"* (pp. 74–75). Oxford: Oxford Review.

Talizina. (1969). *Theoretical problems of programed learning* (in Russian). Moscow: MGU.

UNESCO. (2014). *Education. Textbook development*. Retrieved May, 24, 2014 from http://www.unesco.org/new/en/education/themes/strengthening-education-systems/languages-in-education/textbooks-development/

UNESCO. (2014). *ICT in education. Mobile learning week*. Retrieved May, 24, 2014 from http://www.unesco.org/new/en/unesco/themes/icts/m4ed/unesco-mobile-learning-week-2014/

Wook, S., Michaels, S., & Waterman, D. (2014). Print vs. electronic readings in college courses: Cost-efficiency and perceived learning. *The Internet and Higher Education*, *21*, 17–24. doi:10.1016/j.iheduc.2013.10.004

Zoellner, B., & Cavanaugh, T. (2013). Empowering pre-service science teachers to be active users of eText resources. In R. McBride & M. Searson (Eds.), *Proceedings of society for information technology & teacher education international conference* (pp. 4085–4091). Chesapeake, VA: AACE; Retrieved from http://www.editlib.org/p/48760

# Acknowledgment

First and foremost, I would like to thank my daughters Stela and Mihaela for standing beside me throughout my scientific career, writing this and other authored books in the area of modern pedagogy. I'd like to thank my parents and grandparents for allowing me to follow my ambitions throughout my childhood. All the support they have provided me over the ten years of research was the greatest gift anyone has ever given me. Thanks to all my friends and colleagues for sharing my happiness when starting this project and following with encouragement when it seemed too difficult to be completed.

Special thanks go to Professor George Rudic, director of the Centre of Modern Pedagogy and the scientific adviser for my PhD thesis, for all that he has done for me. Thank you for reading everything I've written and its revisions, for critical comments and suggestions, for guiding, coaching, tutoring, supporting and directing me over the years to hard-working for better results. I am deeply indebted for your remarkable patience and perseverance, which was indisputable in completing the works in postmodernism and practical application of MetaSystems Learning Design in digital textbook use and development. Without your support and guidelines, I may never have gotten to where I am today.

Gratitude is also expressed for the encouragement and comments offered by Professors Petru Soltan (Academy of Sciences of Moldova); Ioan Neacsu (Bucuresti University, Romania); Maia Borozan-Cojocaru, Virgil Mindacanu and Dumitru Patraşcu (Ion Creanga State Pedagogical University of Chisinau), Petru Gasin (State University of Moldova), Felix Hamza-Lup (Armstrong Atlantic State University, USA); Paivi Tynjala (Finnish Institute for Educational Research); Jose Carlos Lourenco Quadrado (ISEL, Portugal); Tiong-Thye Goh (Victoria University of Wellington, New Zeland), Giuliana Dettori (ITD-CNR, Italia); and doctors Nina Birnaz; Sergiu Cataranciuc and Gheorghe Capatina (State University of Moldova), Adelina Stefarta (Moldova University of European Studies) and Alexe Rau (director of National Library of Republic of Moldova).

Special thanks also go to the publishing team at IGI Global, whose contributions throughout the whole process from inception of the initial idea to final publication have been invaluable. In particular to Jan Travers, who assisted in keeping this project on schedule and to Allyson Gard, editorial assistant, whose enthusiasm has motivated me to proceed with my work. It has been great working with you all! Thank you very much for all your help and support!

I heartily wish to thank all the people who supported this two-year long project. Finally, I wish to thank all the authors who will read this book and find it useful and interesting. I take this opportunity to express my profound gratitude and deep regards to my listeners of conferences and workshops presented over the world.

*Elena Railean*
*University of European Studies, Republic of Moldova & Academy of Sciences of Moldova, Republic of Moldova*

# Chapter 1
# Good Practices to Substantiate Digital Learning with Textbooks

## ABSTRACT

*At the core of any learning process is a didactic triangle with three basic components: teacher, student and didactics. Globalization places the didactic triangle in an open learning environment. The "open" didactic triangle can be considered a conceptual tool for designing new learning models, including those for digital textbooks' use and development. These textbooks are more than digitalized versions of printed textbooks. Connected to the Internet/Intranet and with advanced technologies, digital textbooks offer more freedom for teaching, learning and assessment as well as connectivity, adaptivity, flexibility and interactivity. Moreover, digital textbooks have well-established psycho-pedagogical foundations. The post-modernism philosophy indicates at keeping good practices, namely visual instruction, audio-visual instruction, programmed instruction and computer aided instruction (assessment). This chapter emphasizes the effectiveness of good practices and concludes with a call for the future research of the best solutions in the area of digital textbooks use and development.*

## INTRODUCTION

The classical construct in pedagogies, known as the didactic triangle, in which student, teacher, and content form the vertices (or nodes) of a triangle, is used to conceptualize modern learning (Stenberg, Karlsson, Pitkaniemi & Maaranen, 2014; Vollstedt, Heinze, Gojdka & Rach, 2014 etc.). However, in the Age of Globalisation and Social Media the meaning of the didactical content is changing. Now, is more important the construction of the content as a personal construct. Most teachers and students have accepted this change

as unavoidable. However, research has indicated that "knowledge is growth exponentially. In many fields the life of knowledge is now measured in months and years"(Siemens, 2004). Therefore, behaviorism, cognitivism and constructivism cannot be used as a learning theory.

Globalization and Social Media "affect" the classical construction in favor of post-modern architecture. To understand the nature of learning in postmodernism, firstly should be emphases the role of design and technology. Secondly, learning is socially constructed by individuals with different intellect, power and energy to investigate the world.

DOI: 10.4018/978-1-4666-8300-6.ch001

Thirdly, the Instructional System Design ADDIE technology is rapidly changing to Learning Design. The Learning Design is inclusive of a variety of disciplines, research areas and domains including, but not limited to philosophy of learning, quantum psychology, and competence pedagogy, cybernetics and knowledge management.

The postmodernism architectural approach for learning design differs from other approaches in many fundamental ways. Now, the rationality and logics could be ignored. The knowledge have the contextual nature. The truth is not valued as much as in Industrial Age. The sustainability for educational represents the practice about how to archive personal and community goals. That is why the leadership in knowledge creation and sharing have valued more than passive listening and answering and the metacognitive strategies – valued more than cognitive intelligence. The requirements for openness witness new forms and models of teaching, assessment and learning triggered by digital textbooks. Despite the classical printed school textbook, based on fixed and pre-defined curriculum, the learning in postmodernism don't require to use the same textbooks and to process the same didactic content. Therefore, the most important thing is the *process of learning* instead of content.

On the other hand, the didactic triangle is placed in "a more learning environment" (Frick, 1998). Such environment provides the new opportunities for digital textbook use and development. The most accepted are: "autonomous, small/short, continuous, on demand, social and anywhere on ant device" (Hart, 2014). These help teachers and students to take the advantage of designing own learning. This is a case of Polyphonic Teaching. According to Edutopia (2013) in the polyphonic form, the objective is for students and teachers to gain mutual understanding and knowledge through dialogue and collaboration where both parties act as co-learners. Knowledge is created through an exchange of many different individuals' perceptions of the world, and learning is seen as the student's participation in this mutual exchange. Communication is initiated and controlled by both teacher and students. The teacher has the role of an equal collaborator with the student and share equal responsibility. Thus, to keep the didactic triangle for learning process more important is to design the processes instead of content.

It is well-known, and the research supports the assumption, that the learning alone does not deal adequately with all of the educational objectives to be achieved. It is a time for inter-, trans- and cross- disciplinary domains. Kraft (2014, p. 11) notes that the basic pedagogical operative mechanism is the incommensurable relation between pointing and learning linked together. This mechanism operates with the bodily basis; affect and emotion; special educational time; space; and social-structural conditions both materially and normatively. Furthermore, emotional intelligence represents a way of effective learning. The influence of emotional intelligence on digital learning has been widespread in the Age of Globalisation starting with Web2.0 technologies. This rapidly created a gap between what we know and what we should know in digital textbooks use and development. Such debate denotes an issue of re-conceptualization the classical didactical triangle that generate many research questions: Why are digital textbooks used and developed? How textbooks are used and developed for digital learning? What are the license issues and how can be solved? What is the main learning outcomes? etc.

This chapter is interested in exploring the key aspects of good practices to substantiate digital learning with textbooks. Oxford Dictionaries define textbook as a book used as a standard work for the study of a particular subject" (Oxford Dictionaries, 2013). In the Age of globalisation textbook must not be considered a dinosaur. It remains a vital part of learning even if it is more or less digitalized. This chapter will focus, therefore, on the role of textbooks in digital learning. The context of this discussion in limited to the good practices to substantiate digital learning with textbooks.

## BACKGROUND

Throughout time humans use textbooks as a source of knowledge. In the Age of Globalisation textbook, either printed or digital, should be also a source for inspiration, creativity, and competence development. The problem is that digital learning with textbooks becomes ubiquitous. This means that textbooks can be personalized according to students' psychological characteristics and individual learning needs and styles, being more interactive for a better understanding of complex concepts or more adaptive, if students have some gaps in knowledge and want to fill them. For this, digital textbooks provide immediate feedback, learning analytics and more other options that could increase learning.

Historically, the textbooks goes hand-in-hand with education, writing, reading, reordering, storage and disseminating technologies. The earliest meaning of paper, pen and text messages, as well as the invention of ink paralleled the introduction of papyrus, parchment, paper and, finally, digital paper. However, one of the most important innovations came with the printing press with changeable type by Gutenberg. Such textbooks were printed for the closed learning environment, known as the pedagogical system. Soon, the scientific and technological progress led to the personal computers and mobile digital devices. Some authors believes that digital textbooks is grounded in the first appearance of CDs in the middle of 1990s. Fernandes (2014) with reference to Chesser (2011) emphases that this was an initiative by publishers in order to deliver digital versions of printed materials, and in some cases multimedia-rich content, aims to make their products more competitive and more importantly offer supportive resources for teachers. Thus, digital format of textbook could be considered one of the textbooks pattern.

The first initiatives was to equip schools with computers along with the Internet connection. Such program is well-known as "one child-one computer". The second initiate is to equip schools with IPads connected to the Internet, which lead to idea of "one laptop per child". So far, including all subprograms aim to increase the number of computers in schools the content remain the same.

What is the reasons? At the beginning learning with textbooks was focused on rote memorization and the voice of the teacher and the textbook author(s) were the same. The learning activities were reading, writing and calculus. During reading in classroom students have used the same texts. Soon was observed that students aren't the same, having different learning styles and needs. Maybe for these reasons John Amos Comenius proposed the pictorial textbooks and a new teaching methodology. Later, it was advocated the object teaching – a method, in which illustrative objects are employed and each new idea is accompanied by a representation of that which it signifies. During time, Pestalozzy emphasized sensory learning, but with active learning methodologies. Moreover, Herbart opened the way to scientific pedagogy. The XVII-XVIII century's textbooks includes pictures and stores of interest to children. Using such textbooks, the teacher reads a question and the students find the answer in the text.

The other important challenges leading up to textbooks use and development is distance learning – an educational process and system in which all or a significant portion of the teaching is carried out by someone or something removed in space and time from the learner. The earliest textbooks for distance learning date back to the early 18th century. Such textbooks requires structured planning, special instructional techniques, new communication methods and the most important is changing the content.

Development of the personal computer and related technologies, used in education, leads to new methodologies. Thus, in 1936 the Scholastic Aptitude Test was first scored automatically by an IBM 805 computer. A big role began to be attributed to visual instruction and audiovisuals communications. It was observed the increasing role of technology for learning, which allows to learn individually.

The other way was proposed by Russian scientist P. Galperin. In his "Theory of the Stepwise Formation of Mental Actions", he emphasized the role of cognitive tools as auxiliary resources in thinking and promoting learning. As observed by Rezende and Valdes (2006) "Galperin criticizes the teaching models adopted by the schools and, as an alternative, he proposed the conceptual-formative model that preconizes learning through practice, not only by acting but also by understanding and then explaining why and how one acts in this or that way when faced with a certain problematic situation. The objective is to teach how to apply a scheme of conceptual references (hints) directed to the acquisition of a global method to analyze the content to be learned (basic unit). Learners must find a better way to combine all the characteristics of the action (orientation, execution, problem and context) at the same time, and make their decision about how to act to solve a problem".

However, until the middle of 1980s, a number of trends are combining to use technology for learning. Wrapped within the major social changes introduced by the personal computers and Internet, the textbook began a migration to digital learning environments. But, how can digital textbooks be used and developed in all these realities? The aim of this chapter is to identify and assemble good practices to substantiate digital learning with textbooks. This chapter is divided into a background and four sections. The background provides broad definitions and discussions of the topic and incorporates a literature review, which covers the following definitions: individual and social learning, static and mobile digital devices, e-Learning and m-learning, e-learning and m-learning platforms, e-textbooks and Open Source Textbooks. The first section deals with the main characteristics of digital learning in regards to issues, and controversies in digital textbook use and development. The next sections describe four good practices to substitute digital learning with textbooks. The last section deals with issues of using learning platforms in digital textbooks use and development.

## THE PSYCHO-PEDAGOGICAL ROOTS FOR DIGITAL TEXTBOOKS

### Issues and Controversies

There are many issues and controversies in use and development of textbooks for digital learning. One of the main issues refer to thinking about the role of didactic triangle in learning design. There are two ways to use and develop textbooks: linear and systems. Therefore:

- *Linear thinking* follows known cycles or step-by-step progression where a response to a step must be elicited before another step is taken and the probability of error during learning with textbooks can be described by a linear equation. The most used notions are: linear causality, circular causality, complexity theory and reflexivity theory.
- *Systems thinking* defines the cause-effect interdependences when learning follows a well-established algorithm or an instructional design model. The holistic approach of systems thinking means to derive understanding of parts from the behavior and proprieties of wholes rather that derive the behavior and proprieties of wholes from

those of their parts. Domains of systems thinking are systems theory, systems methods and systems practice.

Based on linear or systems thinking, the instructional designer is more interested in how to develop a system or a subject matter for memorizing instead of how to learn the proposed subject or how to view learning analytics. Usually for learning is used drill and practices techniques or/and reading strategies accomplished by the multimedia effects. The drill and practice strategy allows students to practice skills previously learned and receive corrective feedback. Thus, drill and practice goal is mastery a task or a discipline without an error. In some cases drill and practice is associated with learning by doing or some other active learning technologies. However, all these ways are based on behaviorist theories.

Postmodernism changes the vision about how people learn through recognizing, understanding and investigating the reality. Modern education is not based on the delivery the content. Thus, paraphrasing Einstein, we cannot deal with problems as effectively as possible by employing the same point of view as was used in recognizing them. In effect, digital textbooks may assume reality as a structured and organized content or as a fragmented content, which could be read or personalised by the learner. In the first case digital textbooks present only a part or an aspect of the reality, which is associated with the author(s) point of view. In the second case the proposed content encourages looking to reality from different points of view: as a reader or as a collective of readers. For this, all parts of the system are meta-connected into a metasystem in order to integrate physic with psychic.

Digital learning with textbooks also depends on digital devices features. There are two waves. In 1998-2000 ebooks devices aims to replace paper books for pleasure reading. Digital text was also available on personal computers. The second wave was in 2007, when Amazon's focus on distribution digital content through Kindle. As was noted by MacFadyen (2011, p. 5) the ebook devices are likely to follow the trajectory of mobile telephones: the device itself will become a commodity and competitive advantage will be driven by goods and services offered through the device. Dispute the changes in the technologies and services associated with ebook devices, there is considerable consistency in the ways in which the ebook reader is shaped by the observer's experience of the affordance of the printed book.

Furthermore, the concepts of postmodernism and constructivism may contribute to *behavioral design patterns*. According to definition, a behavioral design pattern represents a design pattern that identify common communication patters between learning objects and realize these patterns through increasing flexibility in carry out communication. However, to make this dream a reality the designer should take into account the potential, energy, behavior and actions of all involved into learning process. Knowledge, skills and attitudes come from systems with real learning environments. Such systems could be real or virtual, formal or non-formal, open or/and closed and all are composed from subsystems. The diversity of subsystems are enormous. Instead, linear or systems instructional design is viewed only as a process of teaching, learning and assessment. This represents the main didactic controversy in designing feasible digital textbooks.

## Four Roots toward Sustainability of Digital Textbook Use and Development

Let us analyze this idea on the base of the "system(s)" concept from philosophical, cybernetics, psychological, pedagogical and knowledge management points of view. There are two types of systems: closed and open. According to General Systems Theory the closed system is "an isolated system having no interaction with an environment" (Closed System, 2013). Besides solving a system problem for education, Frick (1998) observes that telecommunication technologies make the educational system much more open and flexible and estimates that a variety of "virtual teachers" and educational resources can be used every time and everywhere. But, according to the Systems' Theory, an open system changes its behavior in response to conditions outside its boundaries. Real Learning Systems provide more complex and changeable learning environment than all early proposed pedagogical model systems. Perhaps in attempt to solve this problem, Bronfenbrenner's Theory was proposed.

In time the main function of textbooks are not to encourage learning, but to present the content from author(s) point of view. So, for example to proceed to the next step through programed learning it is important to pass all the previous steps. But what indicators characterized the previous stages: knowledge, analytics of the learning progress, demonstrated skills or/and the attitude toward sustainability of the real life environment? On one hand, teaching and learning for a Sustainable Feature is a UNESCO program. On the other hand, the objectives of the Decade for Education Sustainable Development (ESD) are to facilitate networking linkages, exchange and interaction among stakeholders in ESD; foster increased quality of teaching and learning in ESD; help countries make progress towards and attain the Millennium Development Goals through ESD efforts and provide countries with new opportunities to incorporate ESD into education reform efforts.

How can textbook theory and design incorporate the ESD approach? Arguably, the current emphasis is placed on the communication between learner, teacher and content. Such emphasis may preclude the development of new types of resources/tools which professional bodies claim to be looking for. There are two ways: a) concentrating on changing behaviors during learning, and b) focusing on designing patterns in order to improve the didactic processes as result of learning. In both cases methodologies common

for the visual, audiovisual, and programmed and computer aided instruction (assessment) movements are used. The research seeks to address four related roots in order to explore the psychological and pedagogical considerations in digital textbook use and development:

- Visual instruction;
- Audiovisual communication;
- Programmed instruction;
- Computer aided instruction (assessment).

## VISUAL INSTRUCTION

*Visual instruction* is a term used to describe visual aids in learning. Since early 1900s, visual instruction, associated with images, techniques and behaviorist methods of teaching aims "to combat "verbalism" in the classroom" (Reiser, 2001, p. 55) and to improve education overall. It was Thomas Edison that wrote in 1912: "Our school system will be completely changed in ten years", tried to persuade teachers that silent movies would soon make books obsolete. Opinions regarding the visual content were sought from educators in new technologies. In addition to motion pictures, it was proposed to use "excursions", photographs and prints, exhibits (dioramas and taxidermic displays), graphic arts, maps and globes, stereographs and stereopticon slides. This research stand was supported by Anna Verona Dorris, who notes that visual aids are intended to complement traditional education with textbooks.

Visual instruction offers the greatest service to the early child development. Whether a specific visual aid technology enhances learning depends upon how the visual is used. Thus, there was a debate about the effectiveness of visual instruction in education. From one point of view the individual's imagination could be stimulated through the use of visual aids. However, the aids were not meant to make education easier, but only more meaningful. From other point of view, visual instruction did not obviate the need for actual "work" (textbooks and research in the library), but rather provided a stimulus for students to explore additional sources of information. The visual aids are best used in introducing new subject matter; reviewing lessons; giving concrete information for assignments and providing means for fascinating, wholesome entertainment (when supervised and managed by the school).

The motivations behind this research emerged out of a growing concern about this perceived over-reliance on school textbooks. Particularly, it has been shown that visual material should be classified by grade level and by subject matter. As was noted by Berg (2003) the "Visual Instruction Movement was concerned primarily with the use of specific media, while educational technology is oriented more towards psychological principles and the total teaching-learning process" (p. 10). It is a need to design special devices (teaching machines) to present information for understanding. Based on the behaviorism platform, those principles require instant feedback, self-pacing, and active responses to the provided stimulus, the visual instructional movement was first expected to be in harmony with new society norms. The primacy accorded to visual learning results in the wide growth of visual aids' acceptance, but the philosophical essentials stay the same for all types of learning.

However, in 1950s and 1960s, it was proposed to use *instructional television* programs, mainly of it produced locally on closed-circuit systems. Schramm, W. (1965) found that televised instruction was effective as classroom instruction when results were measured by final examinations or by standardized tests, especially in tests of critical thinking, problem solving and other nonrote aspects of learning. Moreover, research on the relation of forms of televised teaching to learning has reinforced the belief that good teaching is the same on television, film, or the lecture platform.

Much of the research on early instructional television exists in the form of reports. The four general problem areas of research are: effectiveness, appropriateness, acceptability and feasibility. It was found that those students who were taught by television not only recalled the course material equally as well at the close of semester as did those students who were though either by conventional teaching method or in TV original room but also the different groups retained approximatively the same amount after the two hundred eighteen day interval, as was observed by Carpenter & Greenhill (1958, pp. 9-12).

In a Digital Age visual instruction may be defended by appeal to Skinner's (1958) famous observation that: "behavior is what an organism is doing-or more accurately what it is observed by another organism to be going" (p. 6). This means that modern visual instruction is more about visual (mind, concept) mapping (Amadieu & Salmerón, 2014; Duan, Qiao, Yang & Ma, 2014), "meta-modeling" (Shen, Lei, Chang & Namdar, 2014) and other "visual structured tasks" (Hampshire & Hourcade, 2014). Ackman & Crair (2014, p. 167) note that visual experience is absolutely required to establish the neural circuits that produce complex visual representations in the brain.

## AUDIOVISUAL COMMUNICATION

The term "*audiovisual communication*" in learning refers to communication through a sound and a visual component. This term usually defines the medium when the use of teaching materials and techniques does not depend mainly upon the printed word through sight, and sound is used to supplement textbooks. One of the first methods of audiovisual communication in formal schooling can be considered radio. In 1930s and 1940 in many countries around the world, as was noted by Toppo (2014), thousands of classrooms tuned in each day to instructional *radio programming*, broadcast by state-sponsored "schools of the air" that were probably the most useful educational innovations of any recent period. One branch of audiovisual communication is *interactive television*. Many schools around the world have offered courses via the medium of television, because television, allows place bound students to earn credits without moving. With the television signal digitalization, there is the possibility of interactivity beyond images and sounds. This technology allows establishing an interactive dialogue.

Audiovisual communication has expanded rapidly over the last decades on computers and mobile devices. The audio-visual materials, ranging from the simple teaching devices to complex digital systems, are used in education. One of the first examples is multimedia *textbooks*.

Mayer (2014, p.171) emphasis that multimedia learning involves learning from words and pictures and includes learning from textbooks that contain text and illustrations, computer-based lessons that contain animation and narration, and face-to-face slide presentations that contain graphics and spoken word. The theories of multimedia learning tend to focus on selecting relevant information, mentally organizing the material into a coherent organization, and integrating it with relevant prior knowledge activated from long-term memory. However, an important underspecified aspect of cognitive theories concerns the role of *motivation* — that is, the internal state that initiates, maintains, and energizes the learner's effort to engage in learning processes. The motivation of using multimedia textbooks is simply: short sentences are easy to understand. In this respect, it is important to observe that fragmented text is boring for students. Highlighting essential information gives the possibility to find the most important part of the text easily. In addition, the learning analytics is important, because display of the percentages of correct/incorrect answers is the way to inform students about their progress during learning.

The second example is *two-way audio*. According to Burns (2013) the two-way audio provides instruction, content, and resources to students and teachers in isolated and hard-to-reach locations with little communication infrastructure. Moreover, the two-way audio allows back-and-forth communication between the teacher and students. In recent years the two-way radio instruction with video cameras, Internet access and interactive whiteboards enable teachers to give/to present lessons via satellite to students who have internet access. Students can watch and respond in real time via web cameras attached to their computer or via synchronous collaboration tools. In addition, students can email teachers and each other, interact with the interactive whiteboard and answer pop-up questions, participate in live group discussions. The other way is *broadcast radio* – a one-way wireless transmission over radio waves intended to reach a wide audience. This way is especially effective in cases where radio listening is a primary source of entertainment and information and television is often unavailable Not less important is *interactive radio*. The interactive radio instruction, widely used for learning and dissemination of training materials, requires only an audio device and an adult facilitator.

During the beginning of the 21$^{st}$ century, the audiovisual communication made a significant bounce in learning methodology. There are many new forms of modern audiovisual communication for examples: phones based audio-conferencing, instructional interactive television, and videoconferencing (or video teleconferencing), CD-ROM, VCDs and DVD-based materials etc. However, it took few years more before technology and infrastructure were ready and Voice over Internet Protocol solutions revolutionized pedagogical communication. This is an effective way to face-to-face communication.

Instructional television and programed radio were the most common forms of mediated communication, an alternative to classroom instruction, until in 1970s the Internet slowly evolved. Email, www, newsgroup were added in 1980 and mushroomed exponentially in 1990s. Yet, the audiovisual communication affects the learning as recognized the new behavioral patterns.

# PROGRAMMED INSTRUCTION

*Programmed instruction* is the way when technology allows students to progress at their pace with the aid of specialized features. Textbooks used for programmed instruction were defined programmed textbooks; those emphasize "that the learner's progress through the programmed material is at an individual rate" (Bartz & Darby, 1966, p. 1). In an assessment of efficiency of programmed instruction, Molenda (2012, p.12) considers how unlikely the alliance between audiovisualists and psychologists came about largely because programmed materials were initially encased inside "teaching machines", and then machines and came under the care of the audiovisual coordinator.

The history suggests that the dominant use of programed material without knowing the principles of instruction lead to ineffective and boring methods of learning. Teachers use ineffective methods of class management and present large quantities of material at once. Furthermore, it is practitioners who come to programed learning and designed self-instruction with reinforced feedback, but didn't obtain the effective learning outcomes. Fernald & Jordan (1991, p. 205) acknowledge the significant impact that programed materials have on individualized learning:

1.  **Clear Learning Objectives:** The concepts and principles to be learned and the performance criteria (e.g. recognition, recall, synthesis, and application) are clearly spelled out.
2.  **Small Steps:** The material is broken down into small steps, so the student is not burdened by having to lean too much at once.
3.  **Logical Sequence:** The material is organized so that understanding initial concepts prepares the student to grasp subsequent concepts quickly.
4.  **Active Responding:** The program requires the student to be an active learner rather than simply a passive reader, to respond frequently, and, in doing so, to construct rather than simply recognize a correct response.
5.  **Immediate Feedback:** The student receives immediate feedback about a particular response. Assuming the program is carefully prepared, the student's responses are always correct; hence, the feedback is reinforced.
6.  **Drill and Practice:** The student is given repeated opportunities, involving a variety of examples and contexts, to demonstrate correct responses.
7.  **Stimulus Fading:** Correct responses (i.e. knowledge of subject matter), initially occasioned only by the specific text of the instructional program, are transferred to the student's response repertoire through a carefully designed sequence of priming, prompting, and fading of cues.

Skinner's programs offer logical presentations of content, overt responses and presentation of immediate knowledge of correctness (a correct answer would equal positive reinforcement. However, while programmed programs were easy to produce, the success of programmed instruction suggested that machine technology and behaviorist principles were an effective combination. Instead of this, Skinner's behaviorism was based on ontological determinism and materialism, which is indirectly associated with technological determinism. This means that learning is viewed only as a technical activity and that students couldn't learn without the influence of external forces (machine stimulus). Moreover, as was noted by Paviotti, Rossi & Zarka (2012, p. 14) in the Sixties the behaviorist approach evolves toward the cognitive approach and Somon, who can be considered the father of the classical Artificial Intelligence (AI), started a movement whose work moved from the hypothesis that the human brain and the computer had common functional descriptions. Hereof a strong synergy between cognitivism in education and technological research in Intelligent Tutoring

Systems (ITS) was born. Cognitivists believe that the domain of ontology and the meta-cognition models let the teacher foresee and guide the educational process toward the solution expected by the teacher. Instead, constructivists see the technological environment as a space-time concept in which actors, supported by communication and the research potentialities provided by technologies produce knowledge finding unexpected solutions to problematic open-ended situations.

Miller & Malott (2006) argue that programmed instruction usually consists of a carefully selected and sequenced series of instructional frames, which contains a few sentences of text including a question or blank. Immediately after answering the question or filing in the blank, the student can read the correct answer (p. 112). Skinner's model involves a series of learning frames presented in a set sequence. However, each of the correct responses requires to be reinforced. Thus, within a few years of Skinner's teaching machine "it became apparent that the magic of the teaching machine was in the design of the software, not the hardware, so producers gradually shed the machines and issued their programs in the form of printed booklets and workbooks" (Molenda, 2012, p. 13).

All proposed models have limitations. So, "if the student found the material easy or familiar, he/she could "leapfrog" through a course in a minimum of lessons. However, students who needed more time and explanations found themselves directed back and forth through the total sequence of lessons until the concept was mastered" (Van Meer, 2003). Programmed Logic for Automatic Teaching Operations (PLATO) system was another one of the earliest intentions to program learning. Designed for higher learning, PLATO used a communication system between teacher and students that could be viewed as a forerunner of modern electronic mail. This was mainly a text-based independent study, sometimes with audiovisual supplements, where learners worked in isolation with seldom choices of hands-on methods. The other similar example is the TICCIT system. Instead of PLATO, this system provides built-in complex templates. The student has access to controlled keys, but the author provides information accessible behind these keys, to be displayed to the student studying some the rules and concepts for which the information provided. The system provided a map or hierarchy diagram from which the student could choose the next content with some technical help. In our days the programed instruction is more about learning content management systems and cognitive tutors. As was noted by Walling (2014, p. 19) designing innovative, effective learning, whether mediated by a stick in the dirt or a finger drawing on the touchscreen of an iPad or other tablet computer, relies on a systematic approach to connect learner to ideas and information. However, some aspects of learning may be computer-assisted, such as when students use computers to practice skills or produce media.

Furthermore, since the end of the 60's programmed instruction is influenced by cognitivism and constructivism theories of learning. Two distinct mechanisms were proposed: associative learning (repeated co-occurrence of external stimuli or memories) and insight learning (occurs suddenly when people discover new relationships within their prior knowledge as a result of reasoning or problem solving). The suggestion that programed instruction and constructivism might be combined in the creation of digital textbooks seems contradictory. Thus, programed instruction is focused on external control and reinforcement. In contrary constructivism views learning as a process in which each student constructs or build their own interpretations of external events. On the other hand, if learning with textbooks is focused on creativity and decision-making skills, then the blended use of constructivism and programed instructional methods may enable learning designers to address with the curriculum better than traditional strategies and methods of instruction. For example, programed instruction is good at helping students learn core concepts, while constructivism helps students deal with real problems.

## COMPUTER ASSISTED INSTRUCTION (ASSESSMENT)

*Computer aided (assisted, based) instruction (assessment)* represents a wide area of methods gained popularity in education in the middle of the 1960s. This concept promoted the idea that computers should assist teachers in achieving an instructional goal or in individualized learning. Technologically, the method requires an integrated hardware and software program or service, developed as application Today different instructional programs are available online from computer stores and textbook companies. In time these methods allow caring on a dialogue with students and analyzing their inputs and outputs. Instead, the design of computer assisted software has been hampered by the enormous human, hardware and software resources.

The invention of the microcomputer with a proper microprocessor paved the way of *digitalized textbooks*. This process started with the Gutenberg project and, as a result, more than 38.000 books and 600 bestsellers can be read on Kindle, Android devices, iPads, iPods in .txt, .html, .pdf, .epub. .mobi, .plucker and other formats. In addition, new instruction and assessment methods were developed. Moreover, learning comes to *hypertext and hypermedia*. As was noted by Brusilovsky, Schwarz & Weber (1996, p. 255), World Wide Web opens new ways of learning for many people, so educational programs and learning materials, installed and supported in one place, have been used by thousands of students from all over the world. However, most of the existing applications were similar with regular textbooks: *chapter by chapter, picture by picture*. Contrary to the fact that *hypermedia textbooks* are non-interactive and

non-adaptive enough, in such textbooks the text is made up of many different texts, being a combination of words written by the author, quotations, perhaps commentary, and so on. Hypermedia textbooks have audio and video, and thousands of internal linkages.

The computer aided instruction (assessment) adepts argue that the mind is not a "black box" and that the learner is an information processor with cognitive structure, schema, script, cognitive flexibility, symbol systems, subsumption etc. Gredler (2012) emphasizes, that "learning awakens a variety of developmental processes that are able to operate only when the child is interacting with people in his environment and in cooperation with his peers" (p. 116). Through instruction and learning he/she will be able to construct preconcepts (a limited understanding of a true concept or a special case of a true concept) or to develop pseudo concepts (children answer questions intended to require thinking by recalling concrete examples or concrete situations). The major shift in intellect occurs during adolescence when the mental functions of memory and thinking are inverted.

The majority of computer aided instruction (assessment) studies and programs were focused on presentation of the content and was expected that the learner will be an active participant in individual, group or collaborative learning processes. However, as most theoreticians argued the individuals learn only when new experience is related to prior knowledge, skills and attitudes and when new material is significant for them. The proposed programs often consist of drill-and-practice, where "new material is repeatedly presented in isolation and/or in context for the learner to practice until the response is automatic" (Cooke & Guzaukas, 1993). The emphasis is on immediate feedback, small steps, and the student working at his /her own rate, and working until mastery of the material is reached.

Drill-and-practice was associated with tutorials, simulations, educational games, guided discovery and problem solving. Tutorial is an activity that includes both the presentation of information and its extension into application. Educational games are on interactivity, motivation and affective learning. Simulation is software that allows to approximate reality that does not require the expense of real life or its risks. Guided discovery is software which provides a large database of information specific to a course or content area and challenges the learner to analyze, compare, infer and evaluate based on their explorations of the data. Problem solving is software which allows children to develop problem solving skills and learning strategies. The problem solving can be designed as a dynamic process in which students try to understand the situation, make a plan for the solution, select or develop methods and strategies, apply heuristics to get the solutions and check out the answers.

Advances in computer and educational technologies were penetrated by *Intelligent Tutoring Systems* – a variation of computer aided instruction such as cognitive tutors and example-tracing tutors. These programs provide a computerized learning environment that incorporates various computational models in cognitive science, computational linguistics, artificial intelligence, and mathematics. Programs take into account the pattern of errors made by an individual student over time and use this information to build a model for the education of future students. But, in 1990s computer simulation and multimedia presentations were rapidly replacing older educational tools in favor of multimedia and simulation environments. This paradigm plays a significant role in the development of Sciences of Education as an interdisciplinary domain. It offers a new way of learning powered by illustrative and interactive concepts through animation, sound and demonstration which allow students to work individually. These education programs provide immediate feedback, letting students know whether their answer is correct, partially correct or incorrect. If the answers are partially correct or incorrect,

programs offer different suggestions and guidance. This requires interactive textbooks to be used and elaborated in such a way, that learners are motivated enough to be actively engaged in individualized learning. However, teachers also need to cultivate self-directed learners.

In replicating the computer aided instruction (assessment), Sultan, Lim, MatJafri & Abdullah (2006) note that computer-assisted instruction improves instruction for students with disabilities because students receive immediate feedback and do not continue to practice the wrong skills. Many computer programs can move through instruction at the student's pace and keep track of the student's errors and progress. Computers capture the students' attention because the programs are interactive and engage the students' spirit of competitiveness to increase their scores. Also, computer-assisted instruction moves at the students' pace and usually does not move ahead until they have mastered the skill. Programs provide differentiated lessons to challenge students who are at risk, average, or gifted.

The issues of computer-aided-instruction (assessment) were analyzed using research-signed by Hendrickson et al (2013), which concluded that the following aspects affect the impact of the system:

- Design for learning (the program structure should allow the author to mirror the learning process rather than simply duplicate traditional books; the lessons should be designed around the specific subject matter and how the student may best absorb it);
- Student flexibility (the program structure must be flexible enough to accommodate a variety of student experience and styles of learning; it should allow easy re-entry to continue a particular lesson or it should have several levels of detail to handle a variety of learning needs);
- Knowledgeable authors (it is important to have authors who fully understand the

subject matter and who have the necessary communication and writing skills to present the information in an interesting and organized manner).

- Student feedback (students who are totally unfamiliar with the subject matter should be asked to critique the lesson first and their responses should be monitored and evaluated for general lesson aspects such as screen presentation, readability and user friendliness);
- Publicity and distribution (employers must be aware of the new learning tools available to them and publishing is the essence of the lessons).

While most research in computer aided instruction (assessment) is restricted to the classroom activity and to formal learning inside learning institutions, there are a number of studies which explicitly consider learning as a self-regulated activity which happens throughout life, at work, during plays and at home. Web 2.0 technologies open new doors for more effective learning strategies and have the potential to support knowledge, skills and attitude development during life-long learning. Learning management systems became a valuable tool for teachers and learners worldwide. In this system computer aided instruction (assessment) is an integral service which comes along with the learning management system or alone, because it provides many advantages to teachers and learners.

Some authors affirm that computers should not be considered as surrogate teachers controlling students' learning. Otherwise, computer should enrich the learning environment by expanding the students' control over their self-learning and by providing a better environment as a supplement to traditional methods of learning. Thus, computer-based-assessment is known more as e-assessment. Some of these concerns appear to be founded on the belief that e-assessment is limited to the indiscriminate use of multiple choice questions.

The online assessment is not seen as a panacea, but rather used only when appropriate and in balance with other types of assessment.

## Educational Platforms

In the XX-XXI centuries much attention has been given to individual learning. Individual learning refers to the capacity to learn through individual reflections on stimuli and sources and through the personal re-elaboration of individual knowledge and experience in the learning environment. Kobayashi & Wakano (2012, p. 1624) suggest that individual learning is favored over social learning in highly variable environments. Hashimoto, Warashin & Yamauchi (2010, p. 498) state that individual learning involves change of individual characters through individual experiences.

However, learning is more a social then an individual activity. Social learning refers to the transmission of knowledge, skills and attitudes through direct or indirect online or/and offline communications. Moreover, since 1960 social learning has become dependent upon devices, which could be static or/and mobile. The differences are the following:

- Static devices have a separate display screen, keyboard and could be connected to a local area network or/and Internet;
- Mobile devices are smaller and more lightweight, typically have a display screen with touch input, stylus and/or a miniature keyboard, and are connected to networks.

Learning with devices allows more flexibility in investigation of learning objects. Moreover, the *platform* bring the teaching, learning and campus experience on a device. The platform provides device security, smart connectivity, rich network options and device management. The static and mobile digital devices paved the ways to eLearning and/or mLearning. eLearning refers to the use of electronic media and ICT in education, while mLearning represents some sort of learning that happens when the learner is not at a fixed, predetermined location and can investigate the learning objects using digital technologies. Learning happens when the student accesses, analyzes and delivers resources, tools and materials at any time, from anywhere, using mobile devices. The mobile learning unlocks the users from a fixed point and put them into the more open global learning environments with the cloud computer file storage, social networking mobile interactions and personal digital devices.

Digital textbooks are used and developed mainly for the digital devices. These devices require using different eLearning and/or mLearning platforms.

- The *eLearning platform* is an integrated set of interactive online services that provide teachers, learners, parents and others involved in education with information, tools and resources to support and enhance educational delivery and management, supporting connections between learners and customization of content based on learner needs.

- The *mLearning platform* constitutes "advanced tools, delivering support in a wide range of mLearning stages – design, creation, testing, delivery, assessment, management, security etc." (Serafimov, 2013, p. 1).

Both platforms allow learners to read, write, draw, management, publishing or sketch and have the work saved. For example, during a project they can annotate an existing document and send it to classmates for peer-review. Using a Tablet PC, when attached to a digital projector with a standard VGA cable, learners can be engaged in a demonstration of their own learning outcomes or in a discussion regarding teacher/ students sketches projected on the wall.

In current web-based educational systems platforms allow personalization through different adaptive techniques in order to enhance students' learning; active participation in learning process; collaboration, annotations; modeling and other adaptive and acomodative activities, as was predicted by Piaget. Learning with educational platforms may include computers, notebooks, tablets and smartphones and other tools and devices for creating and disseminating learning aids and materials.

## FUTURE RESEARCH DIRECTIONS

Globalization and Social Media Age is focused more on learning with digital textbooks. Sustainability; polyphonic teaching, new learning strategies are only few challenges. Computers definitively change the way we learn. Learning is focused on self-regulation and predefined outcomes. The teacher is a facilitator, mentor and coach and the learner is an active participate in the learning process. The rapid development of wireless network technologies and mobile digital devices have enabled people to conveniently access the resources anytime and anywhere without the constraints of time or place. However, the research shown that even average student can reach the top of a class if he/she will have a personal tutor that can adapt teaching methods to student's style of thinking or learning. Can textbooks be developed as an effective intelligent systems? How to use visual, audiovisual, programed learning and computer-aided instruction finding? What types of digital textbook should be used and developed? This chapter intends to make a practical contribution to these issues through identification of four roots: visual learning, audio-visual learning, programmed instruction and computer aided instruction (assessment). From the results of this study, we will look into use of textbooks that influence digital learning. Through understanding the nature and functions of textbooks throughout all of the models, designers can began to develop programs that would enhance learning.

What type of digital textbooks will be used and developed in future? From one point of view the newest digital products for learning shouldn't even be called "textbooks." Certainly, it would be valuable to students to reap the benefits of textbooks in digital learning. But, is a real need in such products? What are the issues? Why should software programs be used that deliver a mix of text, videos, and homework assignments? Why should be developed customized textbooks for each student? Why textbooks should be used to grade homework? Why should be developed "personalized learning experiences"?

Unfortunately, research progress in the field of applied Learning Theory and Design has been slow. Most research over the past years has focused only on one aspect, for example on *motivation* (Compton, Campbell & Mergler, 2014); *assessment* (Wolf, 2014); *key competences* (Kuittinen, Meriläinen & Räty, 2014); *sociocnal and emotional education in primary school* (Cefai & Cavioni, 2014) etc. However, as was find by Cheng, Chou, Wang & Lin (2014, p. 20), the modified textbook promoted retention and transfer performance better than the standard textbook did and support earlier results regarding multimedia representations that increase retention and transfer of information during subsequent problem solving. From our point of view, the future research directions can go to the synthesis of metasystems. For this the Science of education needs to be rethought. But, papyrus and paper, as well as visual instruction, audiovisual instruction, programmed instruction and computer aided instruction (assessment) principles should be kept, even "adjusted" to postmodernism as a new learning paradigm, as the suitable elements for a post-modern architecture of knowledge. Thus, the networking and wireless counterparts of educational platforms will serve only as a technological innovation.

Furthermore, the synthesis of a core definition of digital textbook may serve as an indicator. Because of the enormous urgent needs for research progress in trans – and cross-disciplinary areas of digital textbook theory and practice, the psychological and pedagogical considerations in digital textbook use and development convened to fill these graphs. This research are focused on theory, methodology, and technology identifying critical issues, controversies and research problems; recognizing the most promising opportunities of new hardware, software and educational technologies and developing specific recommendations to be used in learning theory and design of digital textbooks.

## CONCLUSION

In sum, then, the literature in the relationship between visual instructions, audiovisual communication, programed learning and computer-aided instruction has certainly growth over the years and much has been learned about this interdependences. A crucial point is how to integrate hardware, software and educational technologies in digital textbooks. Zhen (2014, p.125) is convinced that textbook writers can put the audio and video materials into textbooks through network courseware and multimedia courseware or by connecting textbooks to URL. Moreover, they need to consider how to design the communicative tasks in order to increase its proportion and to give students a large number of opportunities to communicate language meaning. Merkt & Schwan (2014) add that new types of videos allow learners to decompose and annotate the presented information for deeper analysis or to navigate through videos using features enabling activities comparable to those that were shown to be efficient when processing print, Whereas avoiding cognitive overload due to the transient nature of information can be considered crucial for the optimization of videos as a source of information, information processing often starts with the localization of relevant information in a document.

As the heart of Digital Age digital textbooks are the main source and tool for exploring content of didactic triangle. This chapter has presented findings of a preliminary study of digital textbooks' roots. Trough meta-analysis of psycho-pedagogical principles and norms it was demonstrated that there are four main roots: visual, audio-visual, programmed and computer aided instruction. In time, CAI has grown in eLearning and mLearning. On the whole, these methods have been widely used for sustainability, durability and durable development of human society. But, have digital textbooks an already well-established psychological and pedagogical fundament?

Although our findings suggest that digital and digitalized textbooks' use and development are based on instructional design principles adapted from behaviorist, cognitivist, constructivist and connectionism. The limitations of this study must be acknowledged. It was employed multiple theories and models that argue the importance of visual instruction, audiovisual instruction, programmed instruction and computer aided instruction (assessment) for digital textbook use and development; therefore, it is difficult to discern the effect of each principles for content design of didactic triangle. It was observed that these principles come from epistemology of globalization; quantum and behavioral psychology, pedagogy of competence; cybernetics of open systems and knowledge management.

Moreover, designing a digital textbook should be based on modern educational ideal and not on converting printed pages into digitalized formats. Learning design of digital textbook is not only about designing the content and sequential organization of the book, but also about using and development of digital textbooks in real didactic process. The results of this chapter will be used as a starting point for future research in digital textbook area. In summary, digital textbooks' psychological and pedagogical concerns arise from dialectic, didactic and psychological contradictions between the effects of globalization and ICT on all educational systems and the requirements to design modern educational interoperable digital and cloud platforms, where students will able to connect, learn and share ideas toward sustainable and durable environment.

# REFERENCES

Bartz, W., & Darby, C. (1966). The effects of programmed textbook to achievement under three techniques of instruction. *Journal of Experimental Education*, *34*(3), 46–52. doi:10.1080/00220973.1966.11010936

Berg, G. A. (2003). Learning theory and technology: Behavioral, constructivist and adult learning approaches. In G. Berg (Ed.), *The knowledge medium: Designing effective computer-based educational learning environments* (pp. 9–27). Hershey, PA: Information Science Publishing. doi:10.4018/978-1-59140-103-2.ch002

Bronfenbrenner, U. (1977). Toward an experimental ecology of human development. *The American Psychologist*, *32*(7), 513–531. doi:10.1037/0003-066X.32.7.513

Brusilovsky, P., Schwarz, E., & Weber, G. (1997). Electronic textbooks on www: from static hypertext to interactivity and adaptivity. In B. H. Khan (Ed.), Web-based instruction: Educational technology publications (pp. 255-261). Educational Technology Publications, Inc.

Burns, M. (2011). *Distance education for teacher training: Modes, models and methods.* Retrieved October 25, 2014, from http://idd.edc.org/sites/idd.edc.org/files/Distance%20Education%20for%20Teacher%20Training%20by%20Mary%20Burns%20EDC.pdf

Carnegie Mellon. (2014). *What are clickers and how do they work?* Retrieved October 25, 2014, from http://www.cmu.edu/teaching/clickers/index.html

Carpenter, C. R., & Greenhill, I. P. (1958). An investigation of closed-circuit television for teaching university courses. instructional television research, report number two. Retrieved October 25, 2014, from http://files.eric.ed.gov/fulltext/ed014871.pdf

Cefai, C., & Cavioni, V. (2014). *Social and emotional education in primary school: Integrating theory and research into practice.* Springer Science – Business Media New York. doi:10.1007/978-1-4614-8752-4

Cooke, N. L., Guzaukas, R., Pressley, J. S., & Kerr, K. (1993). Effects of using a ratio of new items to review items during drill and practice: Three experiments. *Education & Treatment of Children*, *16*(3), 213–234.

Edutopia. (2013). *Polyphonic teaching with digital learning tools.* Retrieved October 25, 2014, from http://www.edutopia.org/blog/polyphonic-teaching-digital-learning-niels-jakob-pasgaard

Fernald, P. S., & Jordan, E. A. (1991). Programed instruction versus standard text in introductory psychology. *Teaching of Psychology*, *18*(4), 205–212. doi:10.1207/s15328023top1804_1

Frick, T. W. (1998). Restructuring education through technology. Retrieved October 25, 2014, from https://www.indiana.edu/~tedfrick/fastback/fastback326.html

Fry, E., Bryan, G., & Rigney, J. (1958). Teaching machine: An annotated bibliography. *Communication Review*, *8*(2), 1–80.

Gredler, M. (2012). Understanding Vygotsky for the classroom: Is it too late? *Educational Psychology Review*, *24*(1), 113–131. doi:10.1007/s10648-011-9183-6

Hashimoto, T., Warashin, K., & Yamauchi, H. (2010). New composite evolutionary computation algorithm using interactions among genetic evolution, individual learning and social learning. *Intelligent Data Analysis*, *14*(4), 497–514.

Hendrickson, C., Pasquale, A., Robinson, W., & Rossi-Velasco, M. (2013). *Applications of computer aided instruction.* Retrieved October 25, 2014, from http://gdi.ce.cmu.edu/docs/applications-of-computer.pdf

Kobayashi, Y., & Wakano, J. Y. (2012). Evolution of social versus individual learning in an infinite island model. *Evolution; International Journal of Organic Evolution*, *66*(5), 1624–1635. doi:10.1111/j.1558-5646.2011.01541.x PMID:22519795

Kraft, V. (2014). Constants of education. In M. Papastephanou (Ed.), Philosophical perspectives on compulsory education, (pp. 11-21). Springer. doi:10.1007/978-94-007-7311-0_2

Kuittinen, M., Meriläinen, M., & Räty, H. (2014). Professional competences of young psychologists: The dimensions of self-rated competence domains and their variation in the early years of the psychologist's career. *European Journal of Psychology of Education*, *29*(1), 63–80. doi:10.1007/s10212-013-0187-0

MacFadyen, H. (2011). *The reader's devices: The affordances of ebook readers.* Retrieved October, 25, 2014, from http://dalspace.library.dal.ca/bitstream/handle/10222/13823/MacFadyen%20-%20The%20Reader%E2%80%99s%20Devices.pdf?sequence=1

Mayer, R. (2003). The promise of multimedia learning: Using the same instructional design methods across different media. *Learning and Instruction*, *13*(2), 125–139. doi:10.1016/S0959-4752(02)00016-6

Mayer, R. E. (2014). Incorporating motivation into multimedia learning. *Learning and Instruction, 29*, 171–173. doi:10.1016/j.learninstruc.2013.04.003

Merkt, M., & Schwan, S. (2014). How does interactivity in videos affect task performance? *Computers in Human Behavior, 31*, 172–181. doi:10.1016/j.chb.2013.10.018

Miller, M. L., & Malott, R. W. (2006). Programmed Instruction: Construction responding, discrimination responding, and highlighted keywords. *Journal of Behavioral Education, 15*(2), 109–117. doi:10.1007/s10864-006-9010-1

Molenda, M. (2012). Individualized Instruction: A Recurrent Theme. *TechTrends: Linking Research and Practice to Improve Learning, 56*(6), 12–14. doi:10.1007/s11528-012-0606-0

Reiser, R. A. (2001). A history of instructional design and technology: Part I: A history of instructional media. *Educational Technology Research and Development, 49*(1), 53–64. doi:10.1007/BF02504506

Schwebel, S. L. (2014). Historical fiction, the common core, and disciplinary habits of mind. *Social Education, 78*(1), 20–24.

Serafimov, L. (2013). *The mobile platforms.* Retrieved October 25, 2014, from http://www.academia.edu/4306384/Mobile_Learning_Platforms

Shen, J., Lei, J., Chang, H. Y., & Namdar, B. (2014). Technology-enhanced, modelling-based instruction (TMBI) in science education. In J. M. Spector, M. D., Merrill, J. Elen, & M. J., Bishop (Eds.), Handbook of research on educational communication and technology (4th ed.) (pp. 529-540). New York: Springer.

Siemens, B. (2004). *Connectivism: A learning theory for the digital age.* Retrieved October 25, 2014, from http://www.elearnspace.org/Articles/connectivism.htm

Skinner, B. F. (1958). Teaching Machines. *The Sciences, 128*(3330), 969–976. doi:10.1126/science.128.3330.969 PMID:13592277

Stenberg, K., Karlsson, L., Pitkaniemi, H., & Maaranen, K. (2014). Beginning student teachers' teacher identities based on their practical theories. *European Journal of Teacher Education, 37*(2), 204–219. doi:10.1080/02619768.2014.882309

Sultan, A. S., & Lim, H. S., MatJafri, M. Z. & Abdullah, K. (2006). Developed of a computer aided instruction (CAI) package in remote sensing educational. *International Archives of the Photogrammetry, 36*(6), 29–34.

Thorndike, E. L. (1923). *Education: A first book.* New York: Macmillan Co.

Toppo, G. (2014). *Classroom technology can make learning more dangerous, and that's a good thing.* The Hechinger Report. Retrieved October 25, 2014, from http://hechingerreport.org/content/classroom-technology-can-make-learning-dangerous-thats-good-thing_17755/

Van Meer, E. (2003). PLATO: From computer-based education to corporate social responsibility. *Iterations. An Interdisciplinary Journal of Software History.* Retrieved October 25, 2014, from http://www.cbi.umn.edu/iterations/vanmeer.html

Vollstedt, M., Heinze, A., Gojdka, K., & Rach, S. (2014). Framework for examining the transformation of mathematics and mathematics learning in the transition from school to university. In S. Rezat, M. Hattermann, & A. Peter-Koop, (Eds.), Transformation: A fundamental idea of mathematics education (pp. 29-50). New York: Springer. doi:10.1007/978-1-4614-3489-4_2

Walling, D. R. (2014). Framing the learning design approach. In D. R. Walling (Ed.), *Designing learning for tablet classrooms* (pp. 19–24). Springer International Publishing. doi:10.1007/978-3-319-02420-2_4

Wolf, R. (2014). *Assessing the impact of characteristics of the test, common-items, and examinees on the preservation of equity properties in mixed-format test equating* (Doctoral dissertation). University of Pittsburgh. Retrieved October 25, 2014, from http://d-scholarship.pitt.edu/20130/

Yu, M., Zhou, C., & Xing, W. (2014). Change towards creative society: A developed knowledge model for IT in learning. In S. Li, Q. Jin, X. Jiang, & J. J. Park (Eds.), Frontier and future development of information technology in medicine and education, Vol. 286 (pp. 3373-3377). Springer Netherlands. doi:10.1007/978-94-007-7618-0_437

Zhen, W. (2014). Problems of and reflections on task design in graduate English textbooks. In *Proceedings of the International Conference on Management, Education and Social Science,* (pp. 122-126). Retrieved February 5, 2015, from http://www.atlantis-press.com/php/pub.php?publication=icmess-14&frame=http%3A//www.atlantis-press.com/php/paper-details.php%3Ffrom%3Dauthor+index%26id%3D11159%26querystr%3Dauthorstr%253DW

## ADDITIONAL READING

Alliance for Excellent Education. (2014). *Digital learning*. Retrieved October, 25, 2014, from http://all4ed.org/issues/digital-learning/

Dean, D. (2013). The Clicker Challenge: Using a Reader Response System in the (British) History Classroom. *The History Teacher, 46*(3), 455–464.

Eyal, L. (2012). Digital assessment literacy - the core role of the teacher in a digital environment. *Journal of Educational Technology & Society, 15*(2), 37–49.

Hively, W. (1959). Classroom of B. F. Skinner's "Analysis of Behavior". *Harvard Educational Review, 29*(1), 37–42.

Iliina, T. (1984). *Pedagogics*. Moscow: Prosvechenie. (in Russian)

Illina, T. (1974). *The role and place of programmed instruction in systems of tools and methods for instruction*. Moscow: МГПИ. (in Russian)

Jonassen, D. H. (2004). *Handbook of research on educational communications and technology*. Mahwah, NJ: Lawrence Erlbaum Associates.

Kang, H., & Zentall, S. (2011). Computer-generated geometry instruction: A preliminary study. *Educational Technology Research and Development, 59*(6), 783–797. doi:10.1007/s11423-011-9186-5

Keller, F. (1968). Good-bye, teacher. *Journal of Applied Behavior Analysis, 1*(1), 79–89. doi:10.1901/jaba.1968.1-79 PMID:16795164

Kendler, H. (1959). *Teaching Machines and Psychological Theory*. New York: John Wiley and Sons.

Miller, M. L., & Malott, R. W. (2006). Programmed instruction: Construction responding, discrimination responding, and highlighted keywords. [Springer.]. *Journal of Behavioral Education, 15*(2), 111–119. doi:10.1007/s10864-006-9010-1

Moszkowicz, J. (2011). Gestalt and graphic design: An exploration of the humanistic and therapeutic effects of visual organization. *Design Issues, 27*(4), 56–67. doi:10.1162/DESI_a_00105

Nicandrov, N. (1970). *Psycho-pedagogical issues in elaboration of programmed materials in works of foreign programs*. Moscow: Znanie. (in Russian)

Overvliet, K. E., Krampe, R. Th., & Wagemans, J. (2013). Grouping by Proximity in Haptic Contour Detection. *PLoS ONE, 8*(6), 1–6. doi:10.1371/journal.pone.0065412 PMID:23762364

Pask, G. (1959). The Self-Organizing Teacher. *Automated Teaching Bulletin, I,* 12.

Pinder, P. J. (2013). Utilizing instructional games as an innovative tool to improve science learning among elementary school students. *Education*, *133*(4), 434–438.

Sauter, M., Uttal, D. H., Rapp, D. N., Downing, M., & Jona, K. (2013). Getting real: The authenticity of remote labs and simulations for science learning. *Distance Education*, *34*(1), 37–47. doi:10.1080/01587919.2013.770431

Spence, K. (1959). The Relation of Learning Theory to the Technology of Education. *Harvard Educational Review*, *29*(2), 24.

Talizina, H. (1969). *Theoretical issues of programmed instruction*. Moscow: MGU. (in Russian)

Tihomirov, O. (1988). *Psychology of computing*. Kiev: Nauka. (in Russian)

van Meeuwen, L. W., Jarodzka, H., Brand-Gruwel, S., Kirschner, P. A., de Bock, J. J., & van Merriënboer, J. J. (2014). Identification of effective visual problem solving strategies in a complex visual domain. *Learning and Instruction*, *32*, 10-21. Retrieved February, 5, 2015, from http://www.sciencedirect.com/science/article/pii/S0959475214000061

Zlate, M. (2004). *Psychology of cognitive mechanisms*. Iasi: Polirom. (In Romanian)

## KEY TERMS AND DEFINITIONS

**Audiovisual Aids:** Materials using sight or sound to present information.

**Computer Assisted Instruction:** Method of using computer technology in teaching and learning. Examples of CAI applications include guided drill and practice exercises, computer visualization of complex objects, and computer-facilitated communication between students and teachers.

**Digital Learning Environment:** 1) A learning environment in a classroom, created by teachers with the use of ICT, which provide the opportunity for students to develop both academic knowledge and skills; 2) a place or a community, where Web 2.0 tools and learning technologies are used for cognitive activities and metacognition for problem solving and mobile access to campus. The activities may include social network, setting up an RSS reader etc.

**Digital Learning:** Any instructional practice that effectively uses technology to strengthen a student's learning experience.

**Programmed Textbook:** A book that in addition to instructional material contains directions on how to learn, such as how to combine visual or aural apprehension of material (reading or listening) with verification of the assimilation of knowledge and skills, how to find and eliminate discrepancies between the projected level of assimilation of knowledge and the level actually achieved.

**Textbook:** A book used as a standard work for the study of a particular subject.

**Visual Educational Movement:** A movement progressing in Britain, the United States and Australia during the 1920-1930 influenced by new audiovisual technologies and advocated by teachers, researchers, film producers, government officials, and clergy representatives as the new and improved pedagogical approach.

# Chapter 2
# Affordances in Digital Textbook Use and Development

## ABSTRACT

*The affordances of digital textbooks go beyond using textbooks in the four walls of a traditional classroom. With digital textbooks, users can swipe the text to scroll; increase/decrease size of text and images and change brightness options; view and read downloaded information; interact with 3D models and images; make notes, search topics, follow hyperlinks, take quizzes, self-regulate learning and "synthesize" own textbooks and library, etc. However, there are some constraints such as overload of working memory, depending on digital devices' functionality, etc. The correlation between affordances and constraints is analyzed through identification and description of eight didactic systems with platforms maintaining learner-centered environment, interactive feedback, social media, user interface design, and desired results. In this chapter, the concept of "affordances" as a way of strengthening eight possible models explored, called "didactic systems". The used methods are "thematic evaluation" and "comparative analysis". The conclusion and future research is provided at the end.*

## INTRODUCTION

The term *affordance* was coined by J. Gibson in 1979. This term stresses the role of human-scaled objects, attributes, events and patterns that provide effective perception of object, process or phenomena. W. Gaver (1991) extends the idea of affordance and suggests that affordance "allows us to focus not on technologies or users alone, but on the fundamental interactions between the two" (p. 83). In recent years, term has become increas-

ingly popular for a variety of contexts, including digital textbooks (Hyman, Moser & Segala, 2014; de Oliveira, Camacho & Gisbert, 2014 etc.).

What is the affordance of digital textbooks? First of all, with digital textbooks teachers and students coming from different countries, cultures, and language is able to communicate in digital learning environments. Secondly, as was emphasis by Smith, Brand & Kinash (2013, p. 814), digital textbooks offer many advantages, including portability, instant availability, integrated dictionaries,

DOI: 10.4018/978-1-4666-8300-6.ch002

translators, annotation and bookmarking tools, social sharing functions, text searching capabilities, and lower cost. Mobile devices allow digital readers to consolidate content, not having to carry heavy textbooks.

The ways to understand experiences of using and developing digital textbooks are shaped by expectations about the affordances of the print books and textbooks. While the concept of affordances rely on cognitive psychology, the term could be used to test the subtle relationships between digital textbook, as a learning object, and their users. Thus, from the cognitive perspective, affordances rely on *functional fixedness* (a term used to explain an individual's cognitive bias that limits them to using an object only in the way it is traditionally or habitually used). This means that digital textbooks may be used in the same ways as the printed textbooks, perceiving the functions of formats to be the same or with the additional function that the digital version can be read on digital device.

The digital textbook has to be considered affordable both for teachers and students. However, this statement is true, only in cases when digital textbook affordances correspond to *action*s. The actions should be analysed from philosophical, psychological, pedagogical, and cybernetic and knowledge management points of view. As was noted by Smith, Brand & Kinash (2013, pp. 816-817), affordances refer to "manipulation opportunities", that are directly perceivable and if a user encountered a completely unfamiliar artifact, the affordance would exist simply in terms of what can be done with this artifact. Educational affordances can be seen as a relationship between the learner and the technological intervention, and how learning is enabled through this interaction. From the author's point of view, the lowest level is the opportunity to read digital materials; the next level corresponds to setting exercises around words in textbooks to take advantages of on-board dictionaries and translators; manipulation to cur-

riculum and new ways of planning for a larger purpose, that are coordinated and social. In addition, e-reading devices often afford highlighting, annotations and note-taking of texts.

This chapter aims to categorize educational affordance and constrains in digital textbook use and development through summarizing the processes common for the *teacher ↔ learners'* communication. The hypothesis is: educational affordances of digital textbook mainly depends on message which flows pedagogical communication in learner-centered learning environments and change behavior. From this point of view, digital textbooks affordance correspond to *actions,* if they are perceivable in students' development. Thus, the interactions between author and reader of digital textbook are worthwhile, because digital learning occurs through more complex mechanisms than traditional learning. In the light of these considerations, is there a shift in educational affordances of the textbook? In order to answer this question, let us analyze the affordance of digital textbook in eight didactic systems.

From the design perspective, a didactic system represents a set of systems with digital learning environment in which is used direct or indirect instruction. Students receive messages using one channel or multiple channels. The communication between sender and receiver is based on technology. To this end, the textbook's affordances depends on learning design. Thus, each system can be characterized according to: a) the number of sources for communication: one $D_c$ or many $M_c$; b) the mode of receiving data stream: one $U_i$ or many $M_m$ and c) management: in an open system $O_s$ or in closed system $C_s$.

It is expected that educational organization could be analysed as a closed system and as an open system. Educational organization, viewed like a closed system, represents an artificial pedagogical system with the scope of education. The main figure is the teacher, who is the expert in the domain. However, didactical processes are modeled as instructional processes. The main pedagogical function of the teacher is to collect, communicate and manage information from one or more sources and to distribute it to one or more audiences/canals. The main sources are textbooks and/or monographs. An educational system is an open one if the systems continuously interact with its environment or surroundings in the form of information (data, knowledge), energy (skills and core competence), people (teachers, students, and administration), capital or material transfer (repositories, resources, tools).

The general perspective of the chapter is to describe the affordance of digital textbooks. Firstly, it was observed that there are eighth didactic systems. In general the term "didactic system" covers the set of open or closed hardware, software, educational and cognitive systems with traditional or/and virtual (digital) learning environments, content, context, messages and effects. Each of the systems could be characterized on the base on two-ways mode of messages provided by communicator and receiver through direct (synchronic) and non-direct (synchronic) communications to technologies working in learning environments of the closed or in an open systems with guaranteed effect.

This chapter has two main objectives. The first objective is *to describe affordances of textbooks in accordance with specific features of the analysed didactic systems*. The second objective is *to analyze the role of feedback into didactic system*. We try to answer the rhetoric question: What is the affordance of the digital textbook in modern education? The chapter is organized as follows: we begin with an examination of issues associated with digital textbooks' affordances and proceed with analysing affordances of digital textbooks in each of the didactic systems. After providing answers to these questions, in turn were draw conclusions.

## BACKGROUND

The affordances of digital textbooks aren't rely only the relationship between the learner and content, but also how learning is enabling through this interaction. Beyond this consideration, digital textbooks provide the unique opportunities for self-regulating learning, including possibility to use metacognitive strategies. In the broader sense, digital textbooks offer to students to communicate with author(s) in order to develop the knowledge base and to see learning analytics. As will became evident in subsequent of this chapter, researchers who have examined linkage between digital textbook and digital learning environment have implicitly adopted particular philosophy to explain the behavior during learning.

From one point of view, digital textbook affordances are: a) easy access to resources for *MOOC*; b) student autonomy and interaction in the *flipped classroom*; c) interaction and collaboration in *gamified classroom* and social sharing and knowledge in constructivist pedagogy (Smith, Brand and Kinash, 2013, p. 818). From other point of view, proved by Hutorskoi (2005, p. 12), the textbooks could be used and elaborated without taking into consideration the reality of the life.

This chapter aims to avoid this mistake. In fact, it is analysed the learning strategies in affordance of digital textbooks technologies to a certain extend – by tracking patterns in the ways when they may affect behavior during learning. Thus, the chapter assessable experiences in using and developing of the digital textbooks. In short, each of the didactic systems has the following characteristics:

1.  **Didactic System $D_c$-$U_i$-$C_s$:** Direct instruction, unique mode of receiving data and knowledge management in a closed pedagogical system.

2. **Didactic System $D_c$-$M_m$-$C_s$:** Direct instruction, multiple modes of analysing data and knowledge management in a closed system.
3. **Didactic System $D_c$-$U_i$-$O_s$:** Direct instruction, unique mode of analysing data and knowledge management in an open system.
4. **Didactic System $D_c$-$M_m$-$O_s$:** Direct instruction, multiple modes of analysing data and knowledge management in an open system.
5. **Didactic System $M_c$-$U_i$-$C_s$:** Indirect instruction (tutorials), unique mode of analysing data and knowledge management in a closed system.
6. **Didactic System $M_c$-$U_i$-$O_s$:** Indirect instruction (tutorials), unique mode of analysing data and knowledge management in an open system.
7. **Didactic System $M_c$-$M_m$-$C_s$:** Indirect instruction (tutorials), multiple modes of analysing data and knowledge management in closed system.
8. **Didactic System $M_c$-$M_m$-$O_s$:** Indirect instruction (tutorials), multiple modes of analysing data and knowledge management in open system.

Figure 1 depicts the integrity and name of the eight didactic systems.

Our position on this topic is proved by two methods: *thematic evaluation* and *comparative analysis*. For our case, the particular evaluation represents a review of a particular aspects of quality focusing on an experience, practice or resource that cuts across digital textbook use and development. The core of the thematic evaluation is meta-review of messages between learner, content and context. Methodology of comparative research is used to make comparisons across different models. This is the act of comparing contents and learning process with a view to analysis what teacher(s) and student(s) should do in order to receive expected outcomes. It is also a way to answer the following

*Figure 1. The eighth didactic systems for digital textbooks use and development*

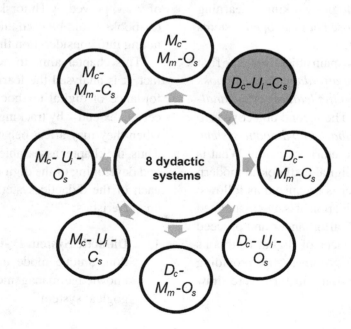

questions: 1) What is the student doing? 2) What is the teacher doing? 3) What is the content? and 4) Where is the content?

## EIGHT MODELS FOR DIDACTIC SYSTEMS WITH DIGITAL TEXTBOOK

### Didactic System $D_c$-$U_i$-$C_s$

In the first assembled didactic system the knowledge is shared through face-to-face communication, either real or virtual. This content is "deposited" in textbooks, both printed and digital. All activities are made in classrooms and are managed by innovative teacher. The teacher uses textbook(s) for reading or exploring the content and tasks. In order to do this, teacher usually recalls the content of the textbook, explaining the basic concepts. As a result, learner(s) receive(s) well-chewing content and recall(s) them when being asked for in examinations (quiz, exam or other forms of assessment). This is a teacher-centered learning environment, in which the teacher is responsible for all processes occurring in a short period of time: the transmitter of knowledge, content expert, source of all answers etc. Thus, educational outcomes with textbook will reflect short-term memory and not learning effectiveness of the process.

Indisputably, there are multiple ways to learn effectively even in traditional classroom. However, in the first model teacher explains the didactic material and prepares students for examinations. Thus, the affordance of textbooks used in this case is equal to Gaussian distribution of class results.

Usually, the teacher cannot change the order of content. Digital textbook is an alternative for *reading*. This is the case of digitized versions of printed textbooks. In many cases free digital versions resulted in increased sales pf the printed version. Students use digitized versions for assessment preparation. Digital reading may involve far more than simply decoding text as in printed textbook. In some cases this may require instructions how to take notes through highlighting, searching, bookmarking, manipulating screen resolution, understanding page orientation and text size preference setting, and turning text read-aloud features on. In the general case, the teacher presents content using a direct communication channel and the student recalls information during formal examination (Figure 2).

The main constrain of $D_c$-$U_i$-$C_s$ system relies on the fact that digitalised versions may "imitate" the structure and the format of printed textbooks and may meant the linear layout and static graphics. Students can search for content, and find definitions in the glossary, highlight passages, take notes, but not share the information for/

*Figure 2. The didactic system without immediate feedback*

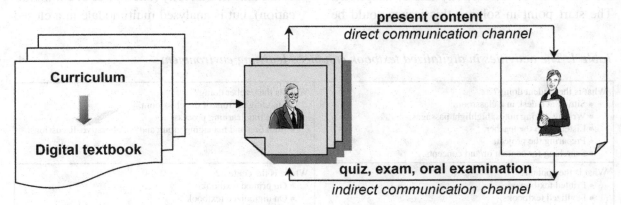

from his/her digital devices in digital learning environment. The best cases rely on successful implementation of *digitalized textbook enhanced learning* (Table 1).

The didactic system $D_c$-$U_i$-$C_s$ shows a little modernized traditional teaching. Despite the widely availability of digital devices, there are many issues in this system. This is not a surprise as it is a shared vision that a digitized textbook has to provide knowledge rather than to engage learners in self-regulated learning with textbook. For these reasons the psycho-pedagogical concerns refer to design of messages, for example: 1) How to communicate knowledge more effectively? 2) How to evaluate the knowledge?

On the contrary, in fact, the probability of errors is high. Thus:

- *The quality of the messages*, which could be transmitted and received differently (according to hardware, software, educational technologies, including cognitive systems functionality);
- *The quality of the learning environment*, which could be designed differently.
- *The minimalisation/maximalization of the immediate feedback effect* in favor of traditional assessment methodologies or assessment with multiply-choose answers.

At least, three problems need to be solved to avoid processes and outcomes errors: a) immediate feedback; b) Interactivity and c) adaptivity. The start point in solving this issues could be considered the idea proposed by Brusilovsky, Schwarz & Weber (1997): "The textbook (which is an on-line version of the normal printed LISP textbook used in the courses during the last years) is hierarchically structured into units of different level: chapters, sections, and subsections. Each unit can be presented to the student as a WWW "page" which shows the content of this unit (text and pictures) and various kinds of links from this unit to related elements of the course. All problem solving examples and problems are presented on separate "interactive" pages which use the possibilities of WWW fill-out forms" (pp. 256).

Moreover, the management of knowledge is done in a closed system. This means that digital textbooks are used in school systems with learning environments without or little interactions to other systems and when decisions are based on measure the disorders with statistics methods. Since every student has her/his learning style and preferences, we speculate that in a closed didactic system without immediate feedback the school abandon is high. According to definition, the closed systems with outputs are knowable only through their outputs. However, possible interactions between students' cognitive systems and cited didactic system have to be formalized to deeper learning.

## Didactic System $D_c$-$M_m$-$C_s$

In the second didactic system the knowledge is communicated directly (one source of communication), but is analysed multimodale in a closed

*Table 1. The activities in digitalized textbook enhanced learning environment*

| What is the student doing? | What is the teacher doing? |
|---|---|
| • Sitting at a desk in a classroom,<br>• Writing, taking notes, highlight passages,<br>• Listening to the teacher,<br>• Preparing the project,<br>• Searching for content or/and concepts. | • Standing in front of the classroom,<br>• Directing learning process,<br>• Initiating and managing group and collaborative discussions. |
| What is the content? | Where is the content? |
| • Printed textbooks.<br>• Digitized textbooks.<br>• Additional resources. | • On printed textbook.<br>• On digitalized textbook.<br>• On platform/digital environment. |

pedagogical system. This is a system in which content are based upon the knowledge, abilities and learning style of each individual learner. The core of the system is immediate feedback. The teacher(s) is responsible for planning, monitoring and assessment. He/she can use textbooks for an individual learning, for example to complete the gaps in knowledge or to enhance problem-solving skills or to develop decision making capacities. For this, digital content of textbook usually provide "tailored" content and self-assessment tasks (Figure 3).

Programed instruction was among the first, in historical significance, for system $D_c$-$M_m$-$C_s$. The authors (Jaehnig & Miller, 2007, p. 220) observe that early programs typically used small steps sized and construction responding and include:

- Antecedent stimuli that occasion a response;
- An opportunity for the learner to emit a response in the presence of the stimuli
- Outcome, consisting of information about the correctness of the response.

Frames are presented logically, although dimensions of frames differ.

Fortunately programed instruction is not the unique way for an individual learning. For example, in earlier research Keller (1968) built

a personal system of instruction. He wrote "I could have seen the clear specification of terminal skills for each course, together with the carefully grated steps leading to this end. I could have seen the demand for perfection at every level of training and for every student; the employment of classroom instructions who were little more than the successful graduates of earlier classes; the minimizing of the lecture as a teaching device and the maximalisation of student participation. I could have seen, especially, an interesting division of labor in the educational process, wherein the non-commissioned, classroom teachers were restricted to duties of guiding, clarifying, demonstrating, testing, grading, and the like, while the commissioned teacher, the training officer, dealt with matters of course logistics, the interpretation of training materials, the construction of lesson plans and guides, the evaluation of student progress, the selection of non-commissioned cadre, and the writing of reports" (pp.79-80).

Willey and Gardner (2010) demonstrate that self and peer assessment has the capacity to encourage students to take more responsibility for their own learning. Having students provide feedback improves their judgment, assessment ability and critical evaluation skills. Since students provide the feedback themselves they have to use their judgment to determine both the validity of the feedback and how they should respond, address-

*Figure 3. The didactic system Ud-Ui-Ci with immediate feedback*

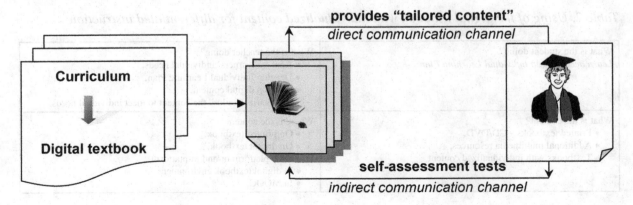

27

ing the 'incremental learner 'concerns discussed above. Feedback can be both timely, frequent and focused without undue burden. It is recommended that these learning activities be concluded with academic feedback to complete the learning cycle (pp. 429-431).

Research has shown (Kang & Zentall, 2011, pp.787-795) that a method of self-paced instruction, where participants in study geometry navigated each instructional screen by clicking either the 'Previous' or the 'Next' button with a mouse. They could proceed at their own pace to the next shape or go back to reexamine the previous image(s). Participants read the text information on the screen. The screen, each of 17, provided 'Click here' button(s), so that animation could highlight the text information. This was followed by a set of properties and the option *to click here* to view animation. The difficulty of the problems increased from the first to the 17th screen. The text information and color remained the same in each condition as presented in the first half of the lesson for the basic item. It was concluded, that students with attention problems performed better on advanced geometry problems with visually intense images than with low intense images. Those students with both hyperactivity and inattention performed even better than the comparison group in the Images-HVI condition.

The system of highly individualized learning for all students is a utopia. However, Individual Learning Plan (ILP) can help all students, including those with disabilities, create a career and academic pathway as well as compile a comprehensive, multi-media online document of their skills and experiences.

The best cases rely on successful implementation of *digital textbook with individualized content for differentiated instruction (learning)* (Table 2).

One of the examples of textbook with individualized content can be considered online textbooks, provided by CK-12 Foundation (CK-12, 2014). Here we can read the comment of Nicky: the individualized content is very helpful, because saves time instead of reading through whole textbook to read a specific concept. The other examples were reported by Schulz (2013). It was found that web-accessible, page-based custom textbook publishing system allow stitching together the electronic content, legally mixing chapters or copyrighted material online. Then, the customized textbooks can be downloaded as e-books or digitally printed, and then shipped directly to bookstores. Another type of custom textbook publishing system involves investing and storing the complete works in a centralized repository, which editors can search, update, select and organize content for delivery as customized textbooks, or fast-track the creation of new products, which can be delivered in any form.

## Didactic System $D_c$-$U_i$-$O_s$

In the third system the teacher transmits messages using direct instruction in an Open Network Learn-

*Table 2. Using of the digital textbook with individualized content for differentiated instruction*

| What is the student doing?<br>*Learn according to Individual Learning Plan* | What is the teacher doing?<br>• Analyze learners' individual needs,<br>• Develop Individual Learning Plan,<br>• Develop digital content,<br>• Summarize/"tailor" the content to meet individual needs. |
|---|---|
| What is the content?<br>• Printed textbooks +CD/DVD,<br>• Additional multimedia resources,<br>• Textbooks with individualized content. | Where is the content?<br>• On printed textbook,<br>• On digital textbook,<br>• On e-platform or/and m-platform,<br>• In digital textbook environment,<br>• In MOOC. |

ing Environments (ONLE). The ONLE represents "digital environments that empower learners to participate in creative endeavors, conduct social networking, organize/reorganize social concepts, and manage social acts by connecting people, resources, and tools by integrating Web2.0 tools to design environments that are totally transparent, or open to public view; the same architecture can be used to design the degree of openness users feel is necessary to the situation" (Tu, Sujo-Montes, Yen, Chan & Blocher, 2012). The students read the open content, protected by Creative Commons licenses or GNU-Free Document license, which allow free digital access and low-cost print options. Psychologically, it is estimated that students will receive data through visual, auditory or kinesthetic input. The role of the students is to read, hear or experiment the content. For example, exploring "Applied Discrete Structures" (Doerr & Levasseur, 2010), student can read the content, perform exercises and interactive demonstrations. In the "Introduction to psychology" (Stangor, 2010) the student can read content, do exercises and develop critical thinking abilities.

However, visual, auditory or kinesthetic input is not learning. For learning to occur is important to effectively process and recovery information. Thus, to define learning is important to understand what happens to the individual at physic and physic states. Learning can be verbal, conceptual, perceptual, motor, problem solving, emotional etc. Each student is a unique individual with intellectual skills, (meta)cognitive strategies, and attitudes, which allow analysing learning situation from different viewpoints. The student learns only from personal experience. In addition, using digital textbooks only for data input is in controversies with features of the learner-centered learning environment (Table 3).

World Wide Web makes most of the textbooks available to anyone with digital devices and Internet connection. This form of learning is anywhere and anytime. Two models attract increasing attention: a) *synchronous* (instructor-facilitated) and b) *asynchronous* (self-directed, self-paced). According to these models students can roams from one lecture topic to another. Cavanaugh (2013) describes an a textbook to be available in a few formats, providing access to the book online and through downloadable versions in ePub and AZW, that allow reading the content offline and on ebook readers and smart phones. Some didactic activities require audio conversion of printed text. In this activity student copy the section into a text-to-speech program and have it read the text aloud.

The other interesting model was described (Harrower, Robinson, Roth & Sheesely, 2009). The author pitched the idea of doing an "online textbook" because, in his opinion, teachers are frustrated with the inability of traditional textbooks to keep pace with the constant stream of new Web technologies; could not find any comprehensive online resources about web-based mapping and

*Table 3. Teacher-centred and learner-centred learning environments (adapted from Midoro, 2005)*

|  | **Teacher-Centered Learning Environment** | **Learner-Centered LEARNING Environment** |
|---|---|---|
| Classroom activity | Teacher-centered, didactic | Learner-centered, interactive |
| Teacher role | Fact teller, always expert | Collaboration, sometimes learner |
| Instruction emphasis | Facts memorization | Transformation of facts |
| Concepts of knowledge | Accumulation of facts, Quality | Quality of understanding |
| Demonstration of success | Multiple choice item | Criterion referencing, portfolios and performances |
| Technology use | Drill and practice | Communication, access, collaboration, expression |

that to make dynamic maps is necessary to span many (traditionally separate) fields from computer science to education.

Ideally, students will learn better if is used own learning style. According to the definition, provided by the Pashler, McDaniel, Rohrer & Bjork (2007, p. 106) the term *learning style* refers to the view that different people learn information in different ways. It is expected that some students seems to learn better when information is presented through words, whereas others seem to learn better through pictures. Moreover, the term *learning style* could be embraced in a number of current educational psychology textbooks, which should be accommodated by instruction tailored to individual learning styles. Is this possible? One of the possible models describes the Learning Style Questionnaire, which could be considered a component of the digital textbook design. The best cases rely on successful implementation of *digital textbook with adaptive content* (Table 4).

## Didactic System $D_c$-$M_m$-$O_s$

In this system the teacher applies direct instruction complemented with *blended learning* programs. In blended learning students learn at least in part through delivery of content and instruction via digital and online media with some elements of student control over time, place, path or pace. According to Wikipedia, there are six models of blended learning:

- *Face-to-face driver*, where the teachers drives the instruction and augments with digital tools;
- *Rotation*, where the teacher schedules students activities as an independent online study and face-to-face classroom time;
- *Flex*, where most of the curriculum is delivered via a digital platform and teachers and teachers are available for face-to-face consultation and support;
- *Labs,* where all the curriculum is delivered via a digital platform, but is a consistent physical location, usually in traditional classes;
- *Self-blend*, where students choose to augment their traditional learning with online course work;
- *Online driver*, where all curriculum and teaching is delivered via a digital platform and face-to-face meetings are schedules or made available if necessary.

There are many interesting examples of using blended learning via textbooks. Research has found (Kokkodis, Kannan & Kenthapadi, 2014) that the emergence of tablet devices, cloud computing, and abundant online multimedia content presents new opportunities to transform traditional paper-based textbooks into tablet-based electronic textbooks. Textbooks will continue to play a central role in instruction with videos enabling the additional modality to learn from.

*Table 4. Didactic activities on the base on digital textbook with adaptive content*

| What is the student doing? *Learn according to own Learning Style* | What is the teacher doing? • Develop Learning Style Questionnaire, • "Tailor" printed/digital content according to student's learning style, • Personalise the curricula, • Develop items, tasks and forms, • Formative or/and summative assessment, • Analyse learning analytics. |
|---|---|
| What is the content? • Printed textbook + adaptive tasks, • Digital textbooks with adaptive content, • Additional multimedia resources. | Where is the content? • On digital textbook environment, • On e-learning or/and m-learning platforms/portals. |

The other way show the significance of television programs in blended learning. The basic structure of the blended learning model includes pre- and post-learning processed online, where students log on to the researcher's web site from anywhere. In class, the online and/or offline activities is applied according on the content of the lesson. The researcher's personal webpage offers virtual learning space which provides American television programs related to the lessons, learning material needed in preparing for the next lesson, and assignments (Kim & Kang, 2014, p. 224).

Park (2013, p. 47) describes a didactic system in which knowledge is communicated via Web 2.0 tools (i.e., Google Docs, Blog, Twitter, and Facebook). The issues are the following: in formal education the content relies heavily on textbooks, which serves as a primary source of information. Instructors often assign weekly reading so that students can gain familiarity with a topic and thus be better prepared for class. However, these activities aren't motivating (according to *Self-Determination Theory*). To avoid this, the social media tools and digital textbooks content could be integrated in the classroom. The best cases rely on successful implementation of *textbook for blended learning activities* (Table 5).

This is a type of teaching and learning in which teachers plan the learning process as far as possible, articulate and present the content, control course by means of interventions, and guarantee results, should be particularly attracted by the opportunities provided by a digital learning environment. Drill and practice programmers are an offer in this way. Teacher plans blended activities starting with the idea that direct instruction will be considerable reduced in near future and the obtained differences will be supplemented by the digital text or bibliography list. The students will use digital learning materials "when they are out of the classroom and they can continue their face-to-face education in the blended learning environment" (Gecer, 2013, p. 362).

## Didactic System $M_c$-$U_i$-$C_s$

This system integrates an indirect instruction model, in which is presented the intelligent mode of receiving/analysing data in a "closed" pedagogical system. The content, designed and developed as a cognitive or adaptive and intelligent tutor, is provided to user via an intelligent agent or/and immediate feedback. According to definition, a cognitive tutor is a particular kind of intelligent

*Table 5. Digital textbook in blended learning activities*

| What is the student doing? (partially learn online) | What is the teacher doing? (interact with students in face-to-face sessions) |
|---|---|
| • Learn via PC or digital device, <br> • Communicate with teacher and students, <br> • Learn in part through delivery of content, <br> • Elaborate own portfolio, <br> • Present reports. | • Develop curricula/lesson plans, <br> • Monitor and manage learning, <br> • Teach students in face-to-face sessions or/and computer mediated activities, <br> • Realize and control didactic activities via digital and online media, <br> • Develop/assign online content, <br> • Formative or/and summative assessment. |
| What is the context? <br> • Textbooks, including digital, <br> • Digitalized textbook, <br> • Educational software, <br> • Multimedia or animations, <br> • Real environment. | Where is the content? <br> • Online, <br> • Offline, <br> • Online or/and offline. |

tutoring system that utilizes *a cognitive model* to provide feedback to students as they are working through problems in order to inform students about the correctness, or incorrectness of theirs actions or activities. Moreover, didactic activities are planned to be delivered in the class. Teacher defines learning outcomes and design learning process; plans activities and assessment tasks, manage learning activities etc. The processes in didactic triangle are the following (shown in Table 6).

There are many controversies in designing of on-line tutors. For example, Cognitive Tutor, developed by Carnegie learning aims to align teaching to learning to students' needs. (Carnegie, 2014). Theoretically, the pedagogical approach focuses on how students think, learn, and apply new knowledge. For this, "is accommodated" multiple learning styles, student-centered classroom infrastructure, curricula and textbook content. The most important feature is considered the thoughtful, authentic questions embedded throughout the text. Students are asked to look for patterns, estimate, predict, describe, represent, compare and contrast, calculate, solve, write a rule, generalize, and other.

The other way is *AutoTutor*, which provide a tutorial dialogue in natural language (Graesser, LI & Forsyth, 2014) in the form of ongoing conversation, with human input presented using either voice or free text input. The program accepts ad-hoc events such as learner emotions and estimates of prior knowledge from a student model, stimulate the discourse patterns of human tutors and theoretically-grounded tutoring strategies based

on cognitive learning principles. It engages in a blended dialogue while constructing the answer; speaks through an animated conversational agent and tracks the cognitive states of the learner by analysing the content of the dialogue history. The core of the AutoTutor system is the *pedagogical agent* who can interact with learners via messages, gestures, natural languages, or factual expressions. The other model is a system, where *conversation* is based on algorithms for speech recognition, and include non-verbal acts such as pointing or graphics display in addition to speech acts. Thus, the affordances of *ATLAS* (Automatically Tuned Linear Algebra Software), developed at the University of Pittsburgh; is based on assumption that engaging in a one-on-one dialogue with a tutor is more effective than listening to a lecture or reading a text.

Maybe, the main issue of $M_c$-$U_i$-$C_s$ system is the perception, interpretative strategies and affordances of the *multimodal texts,* which "present information across of variety of modes including visual images, design elements, written language and other semiotic resources. In the closed system with a learner-centered learning environment that includes a cognitive tutor students explore multimodal texts through reading or doing actions" (Jewitt & Kress, 2003). The multimodal texts conveying meanings through, at least, written language and visual image. In contrast, the primary focus in developing cognitive tutors has been on the teaching strategies and developing skills necessary for understanding writing language. Thus, the shift from a linguistic to a multimodal focus

*Table 6. Digital textbook in role of cognitive or intelligent adaptive tutor*

| What is the student doing? | What is the teacher doing? |
|---|---|
| • Interact with teacher in person, or/and<br>• Interact with online cognitive tutor,<br>• Look for patters, solve, write, answer, generalize, reasoning.<br>... | • Identify "grapes" in knowledge.<br>• Provide effective strategies/ methodologies.<br>• Develop question, lesson plan, examples. |
| What is the content?<br>• Cognitive tutor.<br>• Intelligent adaptive tutor. | Where is the content?<br>• Online (on special designed platforms). |

requires students to analyze texts and proposed tasks in new and more interactive ways and also, to use new (meta)cognitive strategies and skills.

## Didactic System $M_c$-$U_i$-$O_s$

In this didactic system are used various models, strategies and organizational forms of teaching, learning and assessment. The most recent way is Massive Open Online Courses (MOOC) with a digital or a digitalized version of a printed scholar textbook. Research describes (Clara & Barbera, 2013, pp. 129-130) the phenomena of MOOC cannot be attributed to behaviorism, cognitivism, or constructivism. Some innovative assumptions indicate to *connectivism,* as a new learning theory. However, *connectivism* aroused from the idea that the existing learning theories were unable to explain the rapid growth of knowledge, which makes knowledge itself a dynamic phenomenon; and the new kinds of production and externalization of knowledge, which multiply the perspectives embedded in knowledge.

The problem is that connectionism is only a technical branch of a postmodernism learning theory. Thus, digital textbooks, used in MOOC, usually are only the pedagogical resources, who complement videos and assessment tasks and serve as an integrated course material.

One of the possible models is *Open Source Textbook,* used and developed on the base of Creative Commons (CC) copyright licenses, which allow teachers and learners to find and incorporate free materials for reports and presentations; educators can customize textbooks and lesson plans; universities can distribute video lectures to a global audience; and publishers can adapt materials and develop services for an enhanced learning experience. These textbooks gives faculty unprecedented control over content, meaning faculty have permission to create a derivative version of any published textbook. With a simple click can be added links, rearranged chapters, edited down to the word level, and more. There are two ways to

read open digital textbooks: *as educators* and *as learners*. Educators can find and review the right textbook for their own courses, browse or search online textbook catalogue by course or topic, read the description and contents. Digital textbooks can be reviewed online or printed, customized before adoption or access to view and download supplements. Users communicate with the author and other professors using the same book through phone, chat, email, Twitter, Facebook etc.

Complementing the idea of MOOC and Open Source Textbook, many theorists believe that when is used the multimodal texts the people are associated with a wide range of a new of a new digital media conventions in the home, at school and in community based setting. For example, Mills (2011, p. 58) observes that translating of semiotic content across sign-making systems constitute a process of transmediation and note that:

- Transmediation is more than a simple reproduction of knowledge, and involves a process of knowledge transformation by degrees;
- Transmediation involves a process of continual adaptation of intentions for representing knowledge in response to the possibilities and limitations of sign-making systems, including affordances of digital systems;
- Transmediation in central to digital text production because it involves translating semiotic content via the discrete sign-making systems inherent in software interfaces.

The other way is *wikibooks,* defined as a*n open content textbooks edited individually or/in group* or a *digitalized textbook /a collection of free digitalized textbooks*. The text can be copied, co-edited modified, extended and /or redistributed if and only if the copied version is made available on the same terms to others and acknowledgment of the authors of the work used is included (a link back to the book or module is generally thought to satisfy the attribution requirement). Each of the wiki textbooks can be edited and each of edited versions can be converted into .pdf (Table 7).

Researchers (Aleven, Roll, Mclaren & Koedinger, 2010, pp. 226-227) observe that use the tutor's on-demand help facilities in an executive manner, focused on getting answers rather than understanding them. Similarly, students often did not request help in situations in which they could obviously benefit from it, such as after making multiple errors on a step. The author hypothesized that giving students feedback on their help-seeking behavior with the ITSs would help them to become better help seekers and learners. To provide this feedback it was created a context-sensitive assessment method, using a cognitive modeling approach. Thus, students should think about a step in a tutor problem before deciding whether to try the step or request a hint. If the step is familiar and they have a sense of what to do, they should try the step. If the step is not familiar, on the other hand, they should request a hint. Otherwise, students should consult the tutor's glossary. When students have made an error they request a hint. When reading hints, they spend an appropriate amount of time trying to process and understand the hint before deciding whether to request the next hint level or to try the step.

The other model describes a combination of face-to-face and distance learning. For this case the course is provided traditionally, but can include some references to MOOC. Students are required to be in a physical classroom or/and in a virtual learning environment. The schedule for each courses can be check online. The proposed example includes face-to-face and distance learning methodologies (Figure 4).

In distance learning digital textbooks supplement the course content. For example, during learning of MOOC "Introduction to Psychology" the students have access to digital workbook "Psychology", developed according to Skinner' Theory of Operant Conditioning. In this case, a digital content constitutes the integrative source of the information, which presents a logical sequence of modules, including computer based formative assessment. Learner(s) learn individually, verify understanding through testing and create new knowledge and skills with peer assessment projects.

## Didactic System $M_c$-$M_m$-$Cs$

This system is known also as *distance learning system:* a broad term encompassing a type of education, where students are registered at university, but learn on their own at home or at the office and communicate with teacher and other students via e-mail, electronic forums, videoconferencing, bulletin boards, instant messaging and other forms of computer-based communication. In a distance educational system the teacher and students can be in different systems are connected via virtual communication. Over the past several years, rhetoric and composition has come to regard digital writing as one modality among many that students, from

*Table 7. Digital textbook as Open Source textbooks*

| What is the student doing? | What is the teacher doing? |
|---|---|
| • Read open source digital content.<br>• Copy, edit, co-edit, extend content, personalize, distribute etc.<br>• Elaborate "own" learning objects. | • Develop curricula/lesson plan.<br>• Develop open digital content.<br>• Teach metacognitive strategies.<br>• Guide students how to learn.<br>• Help student to (co)edit content. |
| What is the content? | Where is the content? |
| • Free open content.<br>• Personalised learning objects. | • Online (on special designed platforms). |

*Figure 4. Integration of face-to-face and distance learning (adapted from Polat, 2005)*

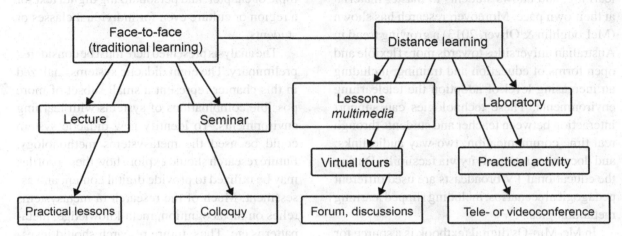

less-experienced to more advanced, can choose from when designing messages and constructing meaning. Thus, new "multiliteracies" use additional models and strategies of self-regulated learning, such as audio, video, text or digital image.

Most distance learning programs provide textbooks via an educational platform. In distance learning are used many controversial models of design. One of them is *flipped learning,* when students gain first exposure of new material outside the class, usually via textbook reading or lecture videos, Power Point presentation with voice-over or printable Power Point slides, podcasting or screencasting. These materials are created by the instructor or found online from YouTube, the Khan Academy, Coursera, MIT's OpenCourseWare etc. The class time is planned for problem-solving, discussions or debates. In terms of cognitive taxonomy flipped learning is about gaining knowledge and comprehension outside the class and focusing on higher forms of cognition in class.

## Didactic System $M_c$-$M_m$-$O_s$

Tis didactic system is developed according to *Web-Based Training* (WBT) methodology for an open system learning environment. This is an innovative approach to distance learning in which computer-based training is transforming by the technologies and methodologies of the World Wide Web, the Internet and the Intranet. Web-based training presents content in a structure allowing self-directed and self-paced instruction in any topic. Web-based training is media-rich training designed for reading, exploring and evaluating knowledge. It is a mode for delivering training via digital multimodal text, including animation and support chat, conferencing, as well as real time audio and video.

There are multiple models to deliver content including web-based training. One of these models is *flipped learning* – a form of blended learning in which students learn content online by previously watching video lectures and homework is done in class with teachers and students discussing and solving questions. Research has shown (Bergmann & Sams, 2013) that flipped learning is when educators actively transfer the responsibility and ownership of learning to their students. It happens when the teacher's lecture is delivered to students via video outside of the classroom. Then traditional class time is used for active problem solving and one-to-one or small group tutoring with the teacher. The flipped class allows teachers to have more face-to-face time with students, fosters real differentiated or personalized learning, challenges students to take responsibility for their learning, and allows students to master material at their own pace. Moreover, research has shown (McLoughlin & Oliver, 2013) a growing trend in Australian universities towards more flexible and open forms of education and training, including an increasing level of adoption the telelearning environments. These technologies can support interaction between teacher and students through real time communication; two-way audio links; and document interactivity via facsimile. During the educational TV broadcasts are used different pedagogical scenarios, including flipped learning methodologies.

In Mc-Mm-Os digital textbook is a source for Flipped Learning (Table 8).

## FUTURE RESEARCH DIRECTIONS

Recently, one has seen an unpredicted growth of digital textbooks use and development. It is expected that digital textbooks will be more than a portable document format (PDF or EPUB) versions of a hard-copy textbook. As was noted by Porter (2010, p. 152) marrying electronic textbooks with the interactive features of web-based learning can lead to a new, dynamic union–building in dictionaries, thesauri, pronunciation guides; embedding video, animations, interactive simulations; allowing tests to assess student knowledge or skills building before moving forward to a new

topic or chapter; and personalizing digital text for a region or culture even for individual classes or students.

The analysis presented here must be considered preliminary. The eight didactic systems analyzed in this chapter represent a small subset of more possible combinations of systems with learning environments. To identify new didactic system could be used the metasystems methodology. Future research should explore how these profiles may be utilized to provide digital content and assessment. Much of the research in metasystems relies on metacognition, meta-knowledge, meta-patterns etc. Thus, future research should investigate the principles and norms of metasystems learning design. Continuing the example, new research may be developed in accordance with learning processes proprieties, which indicate to an integrative information /communication, cognitive and assessment methodology.

Previous research has indicated that teacher and students do not automatically use and develop one or other didactic system. Recent report of UNESCO (2014, p. 5) points to continuing difficulties archiving quality in education for all. Dispute access to theory, technology and digital devices, 250 million children are unable to read, write, or do basic mathematics, 130 million of them are in school. Teacher need good quality learning materials. Future research is needed in identification of norms in textbooks use and development. Thus,

*Table 8. Digital textbook as source for Flipped Learning*

| What is the student doing? | What is the teacher doing? |
|---|---|
| • Watch on-line or off-line presentations, | • Browse or search in digital repository, |
| • Pause a video and rewind, | • Distribute video lectures, |
| • Re-watch the videos as many times as is needed, | • Collaborate with students, |
| • Communicate with authors, | • Help student to learn/solve task, |
| • Ask questions. | • Develop (meta)cognitive strategies. |
| What is the content? | Where is the content? |
| • eTextbook. | • On special designed platforms. |
| • Open Source Textbook. | • Digital repositories. |
| • Videos, presentations, animations etc. | • Educational TV broadcasts. |

developing specific interventions according to learning styles may improve academic outcomes. The limited use of textbooks in such interventions may have multiple causes:

- Teachers may not observe the value of textbooks in digital learning environment;
- Teachers may not use textbooks to develop a dynamic and flexible strategy of learning;
- Teachers may design a learning environment with academic outcomes;
- Teacher and students may not see total progress of learning;
- Students may not know how to learn effectively.

Future research is needed to understand what the issues of learning is; when, why and what type of textbooks are required. For these reasons to facilitate learning with textbook, four key norms need to be adhered to. First, the affordance of all type of textbooks need to be taken into account when is making decision about adopting new textbooks, not just those who meet national standards. Use and development of Open Source Textbooks may also be taking into consideration. Second, better information on behavioral and psychic characteristics of students, based on well-defined surveys/questionnaires, is needed to identify which groups of students have different learning styles and need specific textbooks. Third, information on the affordance of textbooks should be included as a part of questionnaires. Fourth, is important to identify what outcomes is needed for sustainability of the local and/or global learning environment.

## CONCLUSION

There are many factors to research the affordances of digital textbooks according to its role in different didactic systems. Much is driven by the purpose of changing from teacher-centered to learner-centered learning environments. This chapter aims to capture the affordances of digital textbook in eight didactic systems with different forms of learning, known as traditional, distance, web-based, elearning, mlearning, highly individualized, blended and flipped learning.

This chapter has examined current scientific literature and technological innovations concerning the affordance of textbook in digital learning environment. While were identified eight didactic systems in accordance with teacher and students' role in each of the didactic systems in which is used and developed textbooks, the next chapter should investigate the confusing terminology of textbooks.

## REFERENCES

Aleven, V., Roll, I., Mclaren, B. M., & Koedinger, K. R. (2010). Automated, unobtrusive, action-by-action assessment of self-regulation during learning with an Intelligent Tutoring System. *Educational Psychologist, 45*(4), 224–233. doi: 10.1080/00461520.2010.517740

Bergmann, J., & Sams, A. (2013). *Flipped classroom webinar series*. Retrieved October, 25 2014, from http://www.ascd.org/professional-development/webinars/flipped-classroom-webinars.aspx

Brusilovsky, P., Schwarz, E., & Weber, G. (1997). Electronic textbooks on www: From static hypertext to interactivity and adaptivity. In B. H. Khan (Ed.), Web-based instruction. educational technology publications (pp. 255-261). Educational Technology Publications, Inc.

Carnegie Learning. (2014). *Pedagogy. Aligned teaching to learning*. Retrieved October, 25 2014, from http://www.carnegielearning.com/learning-solutions/math-worktexts/pedagogy/

Cavanaugh, T. W. (2013). *Getting to know a digital textbook*. Retrieved October, 25 2014, from http://www.guide2digitallearning.com/teaching_learning/getting_know_digital_textbok

Center for Teaching. (2014). *Flipped the classroom*. Retrieved October, 25 2014, from http://cft.vanderbilt.edu/guides-sub-pages/flipping-the-classroom/

*CK-12*. (n. d.). Retrieved October, 25, 2014, from https://ck12.org/

Clara, M., & Barbera, E. (2013). Learning online: Massive open online courses (MOOCs), connectivism, and cultural psychology. *Distance Education, 34*(1), 129–136. doi:10.1080/015879 19.2013.770428

de Oliveira, J., Camacho, M., & Gisbert, M. (2014). Exploring student and teacher perception of e-textbooks in a primary school. *Comunicar*. Retrieved February, 5 2015, from http://eprints.rclis.org/21081/

Doerr, A., & Levasseur, K. (2010). *Applied discrete structures*. Retrieved October, 25 2014, from http://faculty.uml.edu/klevasseur/ads2/ or http://applied-discrete-structures.wiki.uml.edu/

Freedman, R., Ali, S. S., & McRoy, S. (2000). What is an Intelligent Tutoring System? *Intelligence, 11*(3), 15–16. doi:10.1145/350752.350756

Gecer, A. (2013). Lecturer-student communication in blended learning environments. *Educational Sciences: Theory and Practice, 13*(1), 362–367.

Gibson, J. J. (1986). *The ecological approach to visual perception*. USA: Lawrence Erlbaum Associate Incorporated.

Global Monitoring Report, E. F. A. (2014). *Teaching and learning: Archiving quality for all*. Retrieved October, 25 2014, from http://unesdoc.unesco.org/images/0022/002256/225660e.pdf

Graesser, A. C., Li, H., & Forsyth, C. (2014). Learning by communicating in natural language with conversational agents. *Current Directions in Psychological Science, 23*(5), 374–380. doi:10.1177/0963721414540680

Harrower, M., Robinson, A. C., Roth, R. E. & Sheesely, B. (2009). Cartography 2.0: For people who make interactive maps. *Cartographic Perspectives, 64*, 41-44.

Hutorskoi, A. B. (2005). The place of textbook in the didactic tutorial system [in Russian]. *Pedagogica, 4*, 10–18.

Hyman, J. A., Moser, M. T., & Segala, L. N. (2014). Electronic reading and digital library technologies: Understanding learner expectation and usage intent for mobile learning. *Educational Technology Research and Development, 62*(1), 35–52. doi:10.1007/s11423-013-9330-5

Jaehnig, W., & Miller, M. L. (2007). Feedback types in programmed instruction: A systematic review. *The Psychological Record, 57*(2), 219–232.

Jewitt, C., & Kress, C. (2003). *Multimodal literacy*. New York: Peter Lang.

Kang, H., & Zentall, S. (2011). Computer-generated geometry instruction: A preliminary study. *Educational Technology Research and Development, 59*(6), 783–797. doi:10.1007/s11423-011-9186-5

Keller, F. C. (1968). Good-bye, teacher.... *Journal of Applied Behavioral Annals, 1*(1), 79–89. doi:10.1901/jaba.1968.1-79 PMID:16795164

Kokkodis, M., Kannan, A., & Kenthapadi, K. (2014). Assigning videos to textbooks at appropriate granularity. In *Proceedings of the first ACM Conference on Learning@ Scale conference*, (pp. 199-200). Retrieved October, 25 2014, from http://research.microsoft.com/pubs/208441/identifyingVideoGranularityForAugmentation-las2014.pdf

McLoughlin, C., & Oliver, R. Who is in control? *Defining Interactive Learning Environments*. Retrieved October, 25 2014, from http://www.ascilite.org.au/conferences/melbourne95/smtu/paperbackup/mcloughlin.pdf

National Collaborative on Workforce and Disability for Youth. (2010). Understanding the role of individual learning plans in transition planning for youth with disabilities. *InfoBrief, 26*. Retrieved from http://www.ncwd-youth.info/sites/default/files/infobrief_issue26_0.pdf

Serafini, F. (2010). Reading multimodal texts: Perceptual, structural and ideological perspectives. *Children's Literature in Education, 41*(2), 85–104. doi:10.1007/s10583-010-9100-5

*Things you should know about flipped classrooms*. (2015). Retrieved February, 15 2015, from http://net.educause.edu/ir/library/pdf/ELI7081.pdf

Tu, C. H., Sujo-Montes, L., Yen, C. J., Chan, J. Y., & Blocher, M. (2012). The integration of personal learning environments & open network learning environments. *TechTrends: Linking Research & Practice to Improve Learning., 56*(4), 13–19. doi:10.1007/s11528-012-0571-7

Veletsianos, G., & Russell, G. S. (2014). Pedagogical agents. In *Handbook of research on educational communications and technology* (pp. 759–769). Springer New York. doi:10.1007/978-1-4614-3185-5_61

Willey, K., & Gardner, A. (2010). Investigating the capacity of self and peer assessment activities to engage students and promote learning. *European Journal of Engineering Education, 35*(4), 429–443. doi:10.1080/03043797.2010.490577

## ADDITIONAL READING

Arakelyan, A. (2014). *Sustainable Software Appropriation in the context of the future e-Textbooks of Estonia*. Retrieved October, 25, 2014 from http://www.tlu.ee/~pnormak/ISA/1-Sustainable%20Software%20Appropriation/Arman_Arakelyan_ISA_Article.pdf

Barden, O. (2014). Facebook levels the playing field: Dyslexic students learning through digital literacies. *Research in Learning Technology*. Retrieved October, 25, 2014, from http://researchinlearningtechnology.net/index.php/rlt/article/view/18535

Cangoz, B. & Altun, A. (2012). The effects of hypertext structure, presentation, and instruction types on perceived disorientation and recall performances. *Contemporary Educational Technology, 3*(2), 81-98.

Carnegie Learning. (2013). *Intelligent mathematics software that adapts to meet the needs of ALL students*. Retrieved October 25, 2014, from http://www.carnegielearning.com/specs/cognitive-tutor-overview/

Cho, M. H., & Shen, D. (2013). Self-regulation in online learning. *Distance Education, 34*(3), 290–230. doi:10.1080/01587919.2013.835770

Jirousek, C. (1997). Creating the electronic textbook. *Human Ecology, 25* (4), Retrieved October, 25, 2014, from https://www.questia.com/library/journal/1G1-20438108/creating-the-electronic-textbook

Kersaint, G., Ritzhaupt, A. D., & Liu, F. (2014). Technology to Enhance Mathematics and Science Instruction: Changes in Teacher Perceptions after Participating in a Yearlong Professional Development Program. *Journal of Computers in Mathematics and Science Teaching, 33*(1), 73–101.

Koedinger, K. R., & Aleven, V. (2007). Exploring the Assistance Dilemma in Experiments with Cognitive Tutors. *Educational Psychology Review, 19*(3), 239–264. doi:10.1007/s10648-007-9049-0

Landa, L. (1972). *Algoritmisation in learning and instruction. New Jersey*. Englewood Cliffs: Educational Technology Publications.

Lim, C., Song, H. D., & Lee, Y. (2012). Improving the usability of the user interface for a digital textbook platform for elementary-school students. *Educational Technology Research and Development*, *60*(1), 159–173. doi:10.1007/s11423-011-9222-5

Mao, J. (2014). Social media for learning: A mixed methods study on high school students' technology affordances and perspectives. *Computers in Human Behavior*, 33 (2014), 213-223, Retrieved October, 25, 2014, from http://www.sciencedirect.com/science/article/pii/S0747563214000077

Martin, J. R. (1957). Two-way educational closed-circuit television. *Electrical Engineering*, *76*(10), 921–924. doi:10.1109/EE.1957.6442778

McDonald, J. K., Yanchar, S. C., & Osguthorpe, R. T. (2005). Learning from Programmed Instruction: Examining Implications for Modern Instructional Technology. *Educational Technology Research and Development*, *53*(2), 84–98. doi:10.1007/BF02504867

McGuigan, N., Mitrovic, A., Kern, Th., & Sin, S. (2012). Transcending the Limits of Classrooms: Expanding Educational Horizons through Intelligent Tutoring. *Asian Social Science*, *8*(14), 37–48. doi:10.5539/ass.v8n14p37

Meishar-Tal, H., & Gorsky, P. (2010). Wikis: What students do and do not do when writing collaboratively. *Open Learning*, *25*(1), 25–35. doi:10.1080/02680510903482074

Radu, I. (2014). Augmented reality in education: A meta-review and cross-media analysis. *Personal and Ubiquitous Computing*, *16*(6), 1533–1543. doi:10.1007/s00779-013-0747-y

Schulz, A. C. (2013). The Next Generation of Custom Textbooks. Retrieved October 25, from, http://www.publishersweekly.com/pw/by-topic/industry-news/manufacturing/article/60309-the-next-generation-of-custom-textbooks.html

Shannon, C. E. (1948). A Mathematical Theory of Communication. *The Bell System Technical Journal*, 27, 379-423. Retrieved October, 1, 2014, from http://www.enseignement.polytechnique.fr/informatique/profs/Nicolas.Sendrier/X02/TI/shannon.pdf

Shyamala, R., Sunitha, R., & Aghila, G. (2011). Towards Learner Model Sharing Among Heterogeneous E-Learning Environments. *International Journal on Computer Science and Engineering*, *3*(5), 2034–2040.

Stirling, A., & Birt, J. (2014). An enriched multimedia eBook application to facilitate learning of anatomy. *Anatomical Sciences Education*, *7*(1), 19–27. doi:10.1002/ase.1373 PMID:23650104

Van Harmelen, H. (2008). Design trajectories: Four experiments in PLE implementation. *Interactive Learning Environments*, *16*(1), 36–46. doi:10.1080/10494820701772686

Vanlehn, K., Graesser, A. C., Jackson, G. T., Jordan, P., Olney, A., & Rose, C. P. (2007). When are tutorial dialogues more effective than reading? *Cognitive Science*, *31*(1), 3–62. doi:10.1080/03640210709336984 PMID:21635287

VanLenh, K. (2011). The relative effectiveness of human tutoring, Intelligent Tutoring Systems, and other tutoring systems. *Educational Psychologist*, *46*(4), 197–221. doi:10.1080/00461520.2011.611369

Vonderwell, S. K., & Boboc, M. (2013). Promoting Formative Assessment in Online Teaching and Learning. *TechTrends: Linking Research & Practice to Improve Learning.*, *57*(4), 22–27. doi:10.1007/s11528-013-0673-x

Wang, C. H., Shannon, D. M., & Ross, M. E. (2013). Students' characteristics, self-regulated learning, technology self-efficacy, and course outcomes in online learning. *Distance Education*, *34*(3), 302–323. doi:10.1080/01587919.2013.835779

Worm, B. S. (2013). Learning from Simple Ebooks, Online Cases or Classroom Teaching When Acquiring Complex Knowledge. A Randomized Controlled Trial in Respiratory Physiology and Pulmonology. *PLoS ONE*, *8*(9), 1–5. doi:10.1371/journal.pone.0073336 PMID:24039917

Yang, X. (2014). Teaching and Learning Fused through Digital Technologies: Activating the Power of the Crowd. In D. J. Loveless, B. Griffith, M. E. Berci, E. Ortlieb, & P. M. Sullivan, (Eds.), Academic Knowledge Construction and Multimodal Curriculum Development (pp. 71-85). Hershey PA: Information Science Reference.

## KEY TERMS AND DEFINITIONS

**Annotated Texts:** An special kind of text which serves as a guide to reading or studying. An annotated text contains 1) a copy of a published original primary source text or other established narrative, academic or literary media, available under a Wikibooks compatible license and 2) various kinds of study aids for reading, understanding, and teaching the text, like explanatory notes, introductions, summaries, questions and answers, charts, lists, indices, references, wiki links, media etc.

**Augmented Reality in Education:** "An educational medium increasingly accessible to young users such as elementary school and high school students" (Radu, 2014, p. 1883).

**Blended Learning:** A flexible learning approach, which with developing technology, assists in the maintenance of education applications which combines face-to-face classroom methods with computer-mediated activities to form an integrated instructional approach. Digital textbooks or other educational software are used to facilitate face-to-face instruction in blended learning.

**Cognitive Tutors:** A type of intelligent tutor system based on cognitive psychology theory of problem solving and learning, which provide a rich problem-solving environment with tutorial guidance in the form of step-by-step feedback, specific messages in response to common errors, and on demand instructional hints. They also select problems based on individual student performance.

**Collaborative Writing:** An activity (brainstorming, outlining, drafting, etc.), which involves the production of a document by more than one author; a complex process, involving strategies, writing activities, document control modes, roles and work modes. The collaborative writing activities are based on two main strategies: a) *longitudinal*, in which work is divided into sequential stages; and b) *parallel partitioning*, in which work is divided into segments enabling participants to work in parallel. In collaborative writing projects students can be writer, editor, reviewer, etc.

**Communication Channel:** A method of communication or access to data, information or knowledge, in which the activities of conveying and transfer of communication occurs.

**Digital Reading:** A model of reading using digital devices.

**Direct Instruction:** A term used to define explicit teaching, a skill-set using lectures or demonstrations (simulation of real world phenomena, objects and processes) of didactic material.

**Gamified Classroom:** Classroom in which game design is used to enhance non-game contexts.

**Human Tutoring:** A method of instruction, in which an adult, who is the subject-matter expert, is working synchronously with a single student.

**Indirect Instruction:** A term used to define teaching with tutorials, participatory laboratory classes, discussion, inquiry-based learning, seminars, workshops, internships etc.

**Open Educational Resources:** Digital materials that can be re-used for teaching, learning, research and more, made available free through open licenses, which allow uses of the materials that would not be easily permitted under copyright alone.

**Open Learning Environment (OLE):** A highly interactive learning learner-centered environment, in which students construct, evaluate, interpret and revise their understanding with the

help of technology. In OLE learner uses processing tools, communication tools or Web 2.0 tools in order to establish partnerships for conceptual understanding, problem-solving, decision-making, testing hypotheses etc.

**Self-Determination Theory:** A theory of human motivation based on assumptions that motivation is not a singular construct but is composed of several facets related to intrinsic or extrinsic motivation. Extrinsic motivation is composed by external, introjected, identified and integrated motivation.

**Web 2.0:** Web-based technologies in which users can contribute to content on the Internet and communicate through social media. Web 2.0 tools allows for immediate feedback on student work.

# Chapter 3
# Clarifying the Confusing Terminology of Digital Textbooks

## ABSTRACT

*Generically, a digital textbook serves as a source of knowledge in a digital learning environment. It can be taken anytime and anywhere on almost any devices optimized for digital learning. Users of digital textbooks are teacher(s) and student(s), including life-long learners who use digital devices for learning. The recent challenges indicate that digital textbook use and development have become a hot area of cross-disciplinary research. The research problems arise, first of all, from controversies between traditional curricula and access to global content, that deals with the availability of more diverse forms of information, new technologies, interactive assessment and open source textbooks. However, the "digital textbook" concept does not yet have one established meaning. Rather, multiple partly consistent, partly contradictory definitions and usages exist. This chapter provides a framework for clarifying the confusing terminology of digital textbook initiatives. To arrive at this framework, the author explores the interdependences between textbook, digital (text) book and educational software concepts and proposes a synthetic definition.*

## INTRODUCTION

A digital textbook serves as a source of knowledge in a digital learning environment. The source of knowledge relies on a *content* that can be both printed and digital. In addition to printed textbook, digital textbooks can include multimodality, interactivity and adaptability through "video clips, animation, virtual reality, etc.; and formulates them with various interactive functions for students to study according to their characteristics and academic levels" (Kim & Lee, 2012, p. 91). Digital textbooks are stored in a campus store or in e-repository. The e-repository refers to a storage location, usually in a cloud, and its use as a synonym for term "digital library". There are multiple forms: a digital repository, a virtual (digital library), and an e-store (bookstore):

DOI: 10.4018/978-1-4666-8300-6.ch003

- "A digital repository is a secure online database that houses digital versions of most authorized grades 4 to 12 student basic textbooks for language arts, mathematics, social studies and science" (Alberta, 2013).
- A virtual (digital) library is a library with multiple collections stored in a digital media format and is accessible via computers or digital devices.
- E-store (known also as online shopping, online retailing, e-shop, web-shop, web-store, online store etc.) is a form of electronic or mobile commerce, which allows buying and delivering digital textbooks over the Internet through sites, platforms or apps.

Digital textbooks can be rented or purchased. Distance education students can select and have delivered their desired textbooks online by ordering from catalogue or Textbook Option Brochure. Users have instant access to the titles on Android tablet, smartphone, iOs device and on the web. One of the most used repository is iTunes Bookstore - a software-based online digital media store operated by Apple Inc. Such libraries provide open or limited access to their resources. The examples of digital libraries with open access are LibriVox, Runiverias, Aozora Bunko, NOOK Kids Store, Children E-Book etc. On the other hand, many publishing houses provide limited access to their resources: Cambridge University Press, Oxford University Press, Springer, Elsevier, RSC Publishing, Wolters Kluwer/Ovid, Taylor, Francis etc. Rivero (2013, p. 12) argues that the leader in the digital textbook realm would be Apple, but companies like McGraw-Hill, Pearson, and Houghton Mifflin Harcourt have actually "turned the page" with multitouch available through the iBookstore. "iBooks Textbooks for iPad which provide full-screen experience filled with interactive diagrams, photos, and videos. Students can immerse themselves in images with interactive captions, 3D objects, and quiz themselves with chapter reviews. With a finger swipe, they can flip through their "books" and highlight text, take notes, run a search, locate definitions, and basically get lost in their studies".

Research has shown (Gu, Wu & Xu, 2014) that the increased widespread use of e-Textbooks in education has been anticipated because of its flexibility, accessibility, interactivity, and extensibility. However, the anticipation has not come to fruition. Although e-Textbooks have drawn wide attention, the missing standards of learning content and functionalities and barriers in the use of e-Textbooks (i.e., screen reading, licensing restrictions) are among the problems that require solutions. Also, is not clear how digital textbooks affect teaching, learning and assessment.

The chapter takes a holistic view of these challenges and looks into the current studies on terminology. The general perspective is to identify the main elements of digital textbook definitions and assemble a common synthetic definition for the term "digital textbook". The reason for this investigation is the confusing terminology concerning digital textbook use and development. Our central question concerns the optimal interdependences among terms "printed textbook", "eBook" and "educational software". Our examination, then, is from a logical perspective. The main objective is to analyse the existing terminologies of the digital textbook initiatives, to underline the affordable digital textbooks and to synthesize a general definition. Therefore, the chapter is organized into a background and three main sections. The background covers the issues of interdependences between technology and digital textbooks use and development. The first chapter considers similarities and differences between different types of digital textbooks. The section briefly covers the semantic questions of confusing terminology and presents our perspective on the issues and controversies in digital textbook terminology. The second section discusses solutions and recommendations in dealing with issues and controversies. The third chapter discusses emerging trends in terminology and provides a synthetic definition.

## BACKGROUND

The landscape of the printed textbooks used in formal, non-formal and informal education has been changing. The effectiveness of textbooks is circumscribed by the challenges of new, cutting-edge content, educational technologies and innovative strategies from anywhere and at any time. Each user can create a personal digital library on personal device or in the cloud using, for example the free tool Diido. The advantages are multiple: "immersive educational experiences will be possible; educational apps will get whole new ways to be implemented; disruptive technology may actually get more disruptive; memorization will take a backseat to problem solving and complex thinking; traditional textbooks may be replaced; classes can take place anywhere; field trips will take on a whole new dimension and glasses can remove the language barrier" (Online Universities, 2012).

Digital textbooks are taking hold to substitute the printed textbooks. Laptops, smartphones and other digital devices connected to educational platforms allow designing innovative learning environments. According to Midoro (2005) the "learning environment is a place or community in which a number of activities are accruing with the purpose of supporting learning and those actors can draw upon a number of resources when doing so. This means that digital textbooks have become accessible on interoperable learning devices and have practical applications for different learning environments. It is inappropriate to condemn printed textbooks to certain low expectations.

Printed textbooks, with their short lifespan and complex transportation ground networks may no longer be needed in the digital era" (p. 42).

The idea that textbooks are the main pedagogical resources may refer to workbooks, reference books, exercise book, casebooks, instructional manuals etc. According to dictionaries, a workbook is a paperback textbook with instruction and exercises relating to a particular subject practice problems, where the answers can be written directly in the book. The reference book is a book, such as a dictionary, atlas or encyclopaedia, intended to be consulted for information on specific matters. An exercise book (also called a version book or a copy book) is a notebook with lined, blank or squared paper, which is used in schools to copy down schoolwork, solve proposed issues and makes notes. A casebook is a type of textbook used by students in law, medicine or theatre which contain case studies, notes and some excerpts from usual cases and are focused on providing background for developing metacognitive skills. An instructional manual (or an owner's manual) is an instructional book, a book of instruction, a small handbook or booklet that is supplied with almost all technologically advanced consumer product. In some cases in a school environment the printed textbooks are used traditionally with educational software, educational media, interactive tools, or math manipulatives etc. For example, to teach mathematics at an early age the teachers can use "multi-colored bears, pattern blocks, tangram puzzles, cuisenaire rods, fraction bars, geoboards" (Morin, 2013).

Textbooks may improve learning. Given the focus of this chapter, textbook theory concerns changes in the applied learning theory and design in modern education. In terms of thinking about what content the digital textbook should cover, some results indicate that "digital version of printed textbook could be improved with educational media" (Falc, 2013; Chuilkov & Van Alstine, 2013). However, at this moment "the e-Textbook becomes an integral component of an electronic schoolbag and a main learning resource" (Gu, Wu & Xu, 2014). Concurrent to this approach, there are other ways that evidence two main concepts: "e-Textbooks" and "Open Source Textbooks". Therefore,

- E-Textbooks is "a subset of e-books" (Samuel, Grochowski & Nicholls, 2013) or "a technological innovation with need to use ICT as the medium through which textbook content is delivered" (Feldstein & Lewis, 2013, p.179).
- The Open Source Textbook is a textbook that students "can read it either online or in hard copy, and there are no restrictions on copying or printing" (Brunner, 2013, p. 6) or, "the open accessible content, which allows anyone to edit individually or collaboratively, and give it away for free reading on the Internet" (Acker, 2011, p. 47).

There are many tendencies in the use and development of digital versions of printed textbooks: digitizing the existing textbooks, developing textbooks in digital form, developing open source textbooks collaboratively, developing personal digital textbooks using authoring tools etc.

Digital textbooks are available in *virtual* or *digital learning environments*. A virtual learning environment is an e-learning system that models conventional didactic process by providing equivalent virtual or mobile access to class schedules, digital textbook content, quizzes, homework, grades, assessment and other external pedagogical resources and/or a social space where students and teachers can communicate through interactive discussions, forums of discussion, chat and other technologies. "This enables institutions to teach not only traditional full-time students but also those who cannot regularly visit the campus due to geographic or time restrictions, e. g. those on

distance learning courses, doing evening classes, or workers studying part-time" (Oxford University Press, 2013). There are two main models:

1. A local educational platform with a local server;
2. A local educational platform with an online server (a cloud system).

The first model describes the *educational platform*" with a database of members interpolated with a database of digital textbook content and a server, which is a supporting system for all digital materials. The second model describes a *cloud system*, which includes a Smart Educational Platform and a cloud of an instructional content focused on the open global market. This is a new way of provisioning classic computational resources and software applications and is "a common platform for distributing digital course materials and digital textbooks. This platform offers a common place for academics, teachers, students, content, context and digital learning environment" (Booker, 2013). Research has shown (Joo & Ahn, 2013, p. 86) about the application of the cloud computing system and tablet PC to education in South Korea. "The SMART Education Plan", approved by this country, aims to improve the school textbooks, to construct educational infrastructure facilities for cloud computing as well as development and implementation of digital textbooks. The digital textbook has been defined as a textbook for the future generation, which keeps an image of a printed textbook, contains various multimedia materials and functions, and provides or connects to Learning Management System (LMS) functions.

Students and teachers use the digital textbook anytime and anywhere through mobile devices. However, the design criteria of learning environments are changing faster. Students are encouraged to gain understanding, self-assist theirs knowledge, and demonstrate critical thinking and creativity.

But, how deeply do they need to learn? From the one hand, using an educational platform or a cloud system, the contents and the learning tool are available around the world. From the other hand, one of the recent innovation is a *digital learning environment*. As was noted by Peters (2000) "supporters of a type of teaching and learning in which the teachers plan the learning process as far as possible, articulate and present the learning content, control its course by means of interventions, and guarantee results, should be particularly attracted by the opportunities provided by a digital learning environment.". In a digital learning environment there are three main innovations: *the spoken word* (multi-sensory heteronomous presentations), the new *image of the teacher* (dynamic) and *higher levels of activity and interactivity*. One of the most impressive practical advantages of the digital learning environment is the speeding up of communication between students and teachers. This model describes the way of personalisation digital resources, including e-books and educational software. Therefore,

- The eBook (e-book, eBook, ebook, digi-talized book or textbook etc.) is a book-length publication in a digital form, consisting of text, images, or both, and pro-duced on, published through, and readable on computers or other electronic devices. The enhanced e-books (EEB) are digital publications that allow easy integration of video, audio, interactive features and mul-timodal content.
- The educational software are computer programs used for teaching and self-regu-lated learning through ICT. Most examples are drill-and-practice, educational games, educational apps, learning objects, pod-cast, digital artifacts etc.

The learning object represents any entity, digital or non-digital, that may be used or reused for learning, education or training; modular digital resources, uniquely identified and metatagged, which can support learning or any units of learn-ing, typically ranging from 2 to 15 minutes. A podcast is a type of digital media consisting of an episodic series of audio, video, PDF or ePub files subscribed to and downloaded through web syndication, or streamed online to a computer or mobile device and listened to on a portable me-dia player. Digital artifacts represent something created individually or collaboratively using Voicethread, Storify, Xtranormal, Pixton, Issuu, Storybird, Animoto, Prezi, Wikispaces, TedEd, Wordle etc. and evaluated for immediate or sub-sequent use in meaning making.

This chapter sets out to investigate the con-sequences of digital textbook terminology as a pedagogical resource and as a learning tool. It explores how the use of different approaches of digital textbooks can be summarized with par-ticular attention to changes to the specificity of content instructional design. The potential of a multimodal text for understanding the complex relationships between input, output and diversity of learning environments is generally demonstrated. Throughout the chapter the use of logical methods in defined digital textbook terminology is used as a red thread in order to answer the question: What is the "digital textbook"? It is an attempt to analyse, generalize and clarify the confusing terminology. The proposed premise is that digital textbook complex terminology could be analysed using Wenn diagrams and Formal Logics. Our assumption is that the digital textbook concept is very complex and that the diversity of its "internal structures" could be analysed through techniques that allow visualization. The diversity of concepts which construct a more complex concept as well as digital alternatives of analysed complex concepts warrants the identification of a core concept used in the learning environment equipped to commu-nicate over a wide variety of platforms.

## DIGITAL TEXTBOOK TERMINOLOGY

### Issues, Controversies and the Research Problem

The oldest meaning of digital textbooks that can be read on portable devices relates to the digitalised versions of printed textbooks (Key, 1972). Since that time many digital textbooks were used and developed. Complementing the ICT advances, researchers have been trying to define the "digital textbook" concept for more than sixty years. However, digital textbook concept is still a controversial term. The reasons are different. First, a digital learning textbook maximizes the convenience and effectiveness of learning by digitizing existing printed textbooks, to provide the advantages of printed media and multimedia learning functions such as images, audio-visuals, and 3D graphics as well as convenient functions such as navigation, but from the learning mode perspective, digital textbook is "a kind of technology-mediated learning by nature" (Chen, Gong, Yang, Yang & Huang, 2013, p. 319). Secondly, the other approach is *open online book*, which is a "free, accessible, accessible web pages that teachers and students can utilize in preparing teaching materials and exploring their interests, respectively" (Gu, Wu & Xu, 2014). Thus, the controversies between eTextbook and open online book arises the issue of digital textbook confusing terminology.

One of the main issues related to digital textbook confusing terminology is that digital devices provide a range of services far beyond the traditional pedagogy. For example, with mobile digital devices, students can take pictures and print screens, play animations and videos, send messages or emails, build their own digital library, elaborate digital portfolios etc. The other issue is that students feel "embarrassed to read". The paradox is that when digital textbooks could serve as a magnet for reading, printed textbooks are more easily to read. By nature, the digital text is multimodal and non-linear. New psychopedagogical,

energetic and affective processes are involved in processing the multimodal text. "Multimodal texts are those texts that have more than one 'mode', so that meaning is communicated through a synchronisation of modes. That is, they may incorporate spoken or written language, still or moving images, they may be produced on paper or electronic screen and may incorporate music and sound. Different types of multimodal texts that students commonly encounter in their educational environment in print form are picture books, information books, newspapers and magazines. Multimodal texts in non-print form are film, video, increasingly those texts through the electron screen such as email, the Internet and digital media, such as CD Rom and DVDs" (Walsh, 2006, p. 24).

The other issue is that digital textbooks are not designed and developed equally on the same standards (ISO/IEC JTC1 SC36 WG6, ISO/IEC JTC 1/SC 34 and others). In fact, more than a single type of textbooks with diverse learning functionality is stored on one digital device. Some digital textbooks offer little more than the printed text, while others – enhanced features. These ambitious goals lead to answering the following questions "Which technologies will be used and how every student will have access to the same information? How do we ensure that the needs of all students, including those who are physically, mentally, socially, emotionally, or financially disadvantaged, are being adequately addressed in a way that enables them to reach their fullest potential? Are educators professionally prepared to meet the needs of all students in a virtual environment? What type of professional development do they need and who will provide it?" (Jones, 2013, p. 89).

Moreover, digital reading and learning strategies differs from traditional strategies. It was observed (Serafini. 2010) that a shift from written to multimodal texts requires a parallel shift in the strategies and skills required by readers. The multimodal text includes the following semiotic systems: 1) linguistic (vocabulary, generic structure, grammar of oral and written language); 2) visual (colour, vectors, viewpoint in still and moving images); 3) audio (volume, pitch and rhythm of music, sound effects); 4) gestural (movement, speed and stillness in facial expression, body language) and 5) spatial (proximity, direction, position of layout and organisation of objects in space). (p. 85-86). Unknowing these characteristics of multimodal text led to define a confusing terminology of digital textbooks.

Furthermore, the multimodal texts convey meanings of digital textbooks through written language and visual image systems. It was observed (Serafini, 2010, p. 86) the primary focus in elementary reading education has been on the strategies and skills necessary for understanding written language. Lack of pedagogical attention to visual innovations presents serious challenges to teachers' and students' perception of digital textbooks at a time when image has begun to dominate our understanding of digital terminology. This is also a reason for confusion in digital textbook use and development terminology.

Lastly, but not the less important, is that digital textbooks trend to replace the paper textbooks. In addition, monographs have "migrated" to digital on-line courses and massive open on-line courses. The differences between digital textbooks and on-line courses became more numerous and less insignificant. This is perhaps the dominance of digital learning environments, e-learning and m-learning platforms.

There are also a lot of controversies in terminology of content. One controversy is that the table of content of digital textbooks usually includes a *hypertext*, which contains references to other texts that can be immediately accessed. The second controversy relies on individual, group, collaborative, mixed models of delivering the content. For example, "Flat World Knowledge" company allows "free reading on the Internet or purchasing a digital download or black-and-white or color-print versions of the textbook along with various study aids"(Acker, 2011, p. 47). Having little of

the tactile materiality of printed text, digital text is editable, moveable and globally accessible. Moreover, opposed to the linear text of the programed textbooks, the hypertext is multi-linear and discontinuous. Instead of this many definitions of digital textbooks are similar with definitions of programed textbooks. The other controversy is related to pedagogical methods used to deliver and assist the students' knowledge. While in programmed textbooks principles of the Theory of Operand Conditioning, proposed by Skinner, are used, the digital textbook pedagogy relies on the development of competence in different learning environments, both real and virtual. The research problem seeks to address related issues and controversies in order to explore digital textbook confusing terminology: What is the common definition of "digital textbook"?

## CONFUSING TERMINOLOGY OF DIGITAL TEXTBOOKS

The motivation behind this research emerged out of a growing concern about this perceived over-reliance on digital textbooks in university, K-12 and lifelong education, and out of another issue which has been gaining prominence in the scientific literature, namely, that digital textbook terminology has a lot in common with printed textbooks, e-books and educational software terminology. A well-established method in comparison, used to compare the following definitions:

1. "Digital version of printed textbooks" (Mardis & Everhart, 2011);
2. "Digitized forms of textbooks that will potentially replace existing paper-based textbooks in the school curriculum (Lee, Measom & Yau, 2013, p. 32).
3. A textbook, specially created for a reader like Amazon's Kindle or Apple's iPad; read-on-demand computer based textbooks like those from Google Books and Net Library;

print-on-demand e-textbooks; modular assembler of audio, visual, interactive, and text resources presented via iTunes, wikis, and digital applications (Mardis & Everhart, 2013, p. 93);

4.  A tool that "incorporate[s] a plethora of features supporting student learning, such as note-taking tools, memo pads, writing and highlighting tools, messenger services, discussion boards, navigation tools (e.g., bookmarking, page search/scroll, and course selection), screen-capture capabilities, textbook display options, and search tools" (Lim, Song & Lee, 2012, p. 160); a tool for "watch videos within their books, answer questions with immediate feedback, and explore 3D models all at the touch of their fingers on their iPads" (Encheff, 2013, p. 62).

5.  Textbooks for future inclusion of diverse materials and learning support functions such as multimedia materials (video clips, audio aids, photos, and animation), evaluation items, supplementary and deepening materials, and glossary as well as all contents in print-textbooks (Korea Institute for Curriculum and Evaluation, 2013);

6.  "The textbook of future" which provides various interaction functions with students to study anytime, anywhere and it also contains references books, workbooks, learner's dictionaries, notebooks, and existing textbooks as well (KERIS, 2014).

7.  Textbooks delivered in a digital format using a proprietary program for reading and annotating the text or a digital version of an instructor textbook, "which allow to reorganize chapters, delete or add chapters, delete or add paragraphs to individual chapters, and add their own notes, videos and images" (Harvey, 2011, p. 149).

The provided definitions allow to state that cases 1-3 refer to digital textbooks designed and used as a *pedagogical resource* and cases 4-7 refer to digital textbooks designed and used as *a learning tool*. A simple textbook in a digital format cannot be considered a digital textbook. The textbooks should meet new learning principles and be designed according to new curricula standards. One of the models is known as digital curricula, which "allow teachers the freedom and flexibility to learn and teach lessons in a way that makes sense to them, observed" (Dillon, 2008, p. 23). The other model, called "Common Core Curriculum" or "Common Core Curriculum Standards", provides a clear understanding of what students are expected to learn. This includes a clear set of shared goals and expectations for what knowledge and skills will help our students succeed.

At the level of what we perceive to be reality, the definitions of digital textbooks evidence the term "digital", which is synonymous with hardware, software and educational technologies innovations. The digital textbook concept, on the base on SWOT analyses, has strengths, weaknesses, opportunities and threats. What are digital textbooks? The widely accepted definition indicates to electronic versions of traditional printed textbooks, used in schools and colleges. The texts used at school and college are usually kept on an Internet Cloud. The textbooks and new features are available for all of the students. The students can keep all textbooks in their other digital device. The students can create their own digital textbooks and then submit them to iTunes Bookstore.

From the technological point of view, digital textbook is a pedagogical resource or a learning tool which aims to contribute to learning outcomes. From the psychopedagogical point of view a digital textbook is a kind of resource/ tool based on new learning methodologies and technologies. From the knowledge management point of view, digital textbook is a kind of pedagogical resource/ learning tool. Given this, there are important distinctions to be made between the digital textbook terminology (Figure 1).

*Figure 1. SWOT analysis of digital textbook terminology*

| Strength | Weaknesses |
|---|---|
| Extensibility of school environment<br>Multimodal text and interactive content<br>Metacognition (self-regulated learning)<br>New learning environments<br>New pedagogical functions<br>Guaranteed learning outcomes | Rapid development of technologies<br>Rapid evolution of knowledge<br>Dependence on digital device<br>Different learning theories<br>Different learning methodologies<br>Local educational policy |
| **Opportunities** | **Threats** |
| Multidimensional digital environment<br>Digital curricula (new objectives)<br>Wireless connectivity with the school<br>Reduced copy and paper costs<br>Up-to-date and personalized content<br>Individual and/or collaborative learning<br>Digital and interactive devices<br>Bookmarking, highlighting, annotating<br>Searching, viewing glossary definitions<br>Assessment (immediate/ delayed feedback)<br>Hypermedia and Web2.0 technologies | Learning design models<br>Linear and systems approaches<br>School Management (parental support)<br>Cost, data limits, coverage<br>Data management plan<br>Plan for Wi-Fi capacity<br>Outside network connections and activities<br>"Third place" for Internet access<br>Author and program licenses<br>Network design and security<br>Sustainability of education projects |

The strength column helped us to understand what is working well in digital textbook methodology. Analyzing the opportunities we looked at opportunities provided by the digital textbooks methodologies and technologies. The weaknesses helped us to answer the question: What methodologies should be improved? Threats describe obstacles we face in digital textbook use and development.

Therefore, digital textbooks are more than a digital version of the printed textbooks. For example, in her PhD thesis Barnaz (2009, p. 49) defined school textbook "a didactical tool in which educational technology aims to contribute to forming ecological competence, in a large sense, and will allow the learner to be aware and to realize purposes oriented to adaptation to constantly changing conditions of life through own intellectual potential and creativity". In addition, the instructional design of the most digital textbooks is motivated by the perceived requirement to organize knowledge in multimodal texts.

## eTextbooks, Open Source Textbooks, and Intelligent Tutoring Systems

The prediction of using new textbooks for education was made by Thorndike in *Education, A First Book*: "If, by a miracle of mechanical ingenuity, a book could be so arranged that only to him who had done what was directed on page one would page two become visible, and so on, much that now requires personal instruction could be managed by print" (Thorndike, 1912, p. 165). This idea was developed in three models: *e-Textbooks, Open Source Textbooks* and *Intelligent Tutoring Systems*. Therefore:

- eTextbooks relies on digitalized or digitalized enhanced versions of printed textbooks, usually free for instructors and up to 60% off for students, which can be read anywhere and include interactive features such as keyword, search, multicolor highlight; review digital notes etc.;
- Open Source Textbook define a textbook licensed under an open copyright license, made available online to be freely used and distributed both for instructors and students;
- Intelligent Tutoring Systems is a computer system aims to provide immediate and customized instruction or feedback to learners; contain some intelligence and is used for learning.

The main differences between e-Textbooks, Open Source Textbooks and Intelligent Tutoring Systems are in affordability, printability, accessibility, availability and other features. In addition to e-Textbooks and Intelligent Tutoring Systems, the Open Source Textbooks are free to view online, some are free to print or charge minimal fees by chapter or by the book, provide unlimited access to webpage and are downloadable in multiple formats. In both cases there are the following features: word search, copy and paste options, paper and shipping cost saving. Instead, E-Textbooks may have specific features such as: highlighting functions, matched content and page numbers, auto summarize by identification of key points in text by analyzing frequency of words in text, online dictionary and thesaurus, readability statistics: measures how easily an individual can read the text, the possibility to change the font size, background color, allowing users to use discussion forums and smartphone access.

## A COMMON DEFINITION FOR DIGITAL TEXTBOOKS

### "Digital Textbook" vs. "Printed Textbook" Concepts

Hardware, software and educational technologies have created a new level of complexity and dissemination of knowledge that extend well beyond the scope and functions of the first digitalized textbooks. Digital technologies become more accessible. Now schools and universities around the world are going paperless. "With digital textbooks book bags have gotten lighter" (Elliott, 2013). Moreover, a digital textbook could be considered a child of the printed textbook and the educational software. This allows evidencing the similar rules in editing and formatting, but, also, the differences in hardware and software technologies. The new methodology and hardware, software and educational technologies tend to impose more explicit organization on knowledge using new criteria and standards.

The similarities and differences between printed and digital textbooks are presented in Table 1.

Venn/Euler diagrams allow evidencing the possible logical relations between two sets of analysed concepts: *"printed textbooks M" and "digital textbooks ME"*. The benefits of associating apparently incongruous forms of studied concepts are in how to discern the connections that support useful interpretations. Thus, generally the "digital textbook" concept does not contain the complete text of the "printed textbook", but can contain additional features for access and dissemination (Figure 2):

The circle, named *set M*, represents all possible models of the printed textbooks and the black circle, named *set ME*, represents all possible

*Table 1. Similarities and differences between digital and printed textbook*

| | Digital Textbook | Printed Textbook |
|---|---|---|
| Unique rules for authors and editors: 1) font Times New Roman 12-14, Arial 10-12; 2) pale background; 3) logical structure of content; 4) modules (chapters, paragraphs, frames);5) assessment (formative and summative); 6) gestalt principles of perceptions (similarity, continuation, closure, proximity). | | |
| Structure | Complex structure | Simple structure: table of content, content |
| Text structure | Multimodal text (linear and non-linear) | Unimodal text (text, graphics) |
| Graphic | Digital (multimedia) | Book graphic |
| Communication | Digital/ learning environment in learner– centered learning environment | Pedagogic communication, usually in the classroom |
| Use and development | In and for the learning environments | According to the demands of educational institutions |
| Weight | Depends on digital media device | Heavier |
| Support | Web-based or cloud platforms, digital devices, computer | Paper |
| Special requirements | Installation of special computer programs (free Flash plugin, free Adobe Reader etc.) or Internet access | None |
| Accessibility | Can be zoomed to view as large or smaller text, can be accessed everywhere and every time | Might be available in an audio format or with multimedia additional features |
| Notes | Allow to highlight and write notes | None |
| Extra features | Dictionary, text-to-speech reader etc. | None |
| Lifetime | Can be updated, personalised, downloaded, disseminated, and saved infinitely | Indefinitely |

*Figure 2. Venn/Euler diagrams for printed and digital textbook sets*

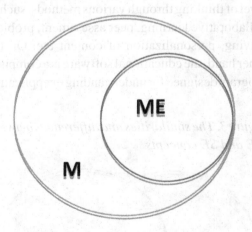

versions of digital textbooks. As can be observed, *set ME* is totally integrated in *set M*. Informally, using measure theory, *set M* is a subset of *set ME*

and the measure of *set M* is less than or equal to the measure of *set ME*. This means that digital textbooks represent a logical evolution from printed textbooks to digital textbooks. There are following advantages of digital versus printed textbooks (Dmitriy & VanAlstine, 2013):

- Lower cost;
- Easier to keep updated frequently options for customizing and updating content);
- Include new interactive mechanisms of interaction with the students;
- New ways for engaging all students in the learning process;
- Formats provide search capability and annotation features;
- Access to content may be complemented by blogs or wikis.

## "DIGITAL TEXTBOOK" VS. "EDUCATIONAL SOFTWARE" TERMINOLOGY

Digital textbooks have a lot of advantages compared to printed textbooks that rely on interactivity, addictiveness and dynamism. This allows integrating the dictionary, the text-to-speech reader, the calculator, maps, encyclopaedia, educational games or other "specialized software" (Sands & Journal, 2013). Moreover, "using digital textbooks professors know when students are skipping pages, failing to highlight significant passages, not bothering to take notes - or simply not opening the book at all" (Streitfeld, 2013). These entire features allow evidencing the compatibility between "digital textbook" and "educational software" concepts. The educational software is a type of software intended for teaching students or for self-learning in an interactive or/and adaptive environment.

Research has shown (Noveanu & Noveanu, 1994) that educational software is a learning tool based on a theoretical position, an interactive model of learning, and a program designed and used to solve a pedagogical issue in concordances with a series of pedagogical and technical coordinates.

Educational software usually came packaged with a printed textbook. Brut (2003, p. 13) states that educational software supplements the printed textbook, providing students with more interactive didactical materials. The examples of educational software are interactive dictionaries, encyclopaedias, interactive lessons, didactic games, simulations etc. All these features provide, first of all, an immediate feedback. The techniques for creating feedback associations within educational software come from the programed instruction period. The role of feedback pathways is to assist students in focusing attention on understanding the learning processes and on applying the studied rules or/and procedures. Either way, self-regulated students are exposed to a wider range of "new learning possibilities". The technological support of learning increases as students answer incorrectly.

A more radical approach to organising knowledge is to consider the possibilities provided by an instructional tool. Cucos (2006, p. 300) defines an instructional tool as a tool and an instrumental complex aimed to facilitate knowledge transmission, skills development, assessment of acquisitions, realisation of some practical applications within instructional-educational processes. The instructional tools could be divided into a) an instructional tool containing didactical messages or b) an instructional tool that facilitates transmission of didactical messages. This analysis states that digital textbooks come in a variety of technological and instructional variations.

On the other hand, the similarities between "digital textbooks" and "educational software" concepts, using Venn/Euler diagrams, are the following (Figure 3).

Set *SE* is interconnected with set *ME*. The common part represents iBook, which is an e-book authoring application by Apple Inc. for its iOS and OS X operating systems and devices. Digital textbooks push students to the highest level of thinking through various methods, such as collaborative learning, peer assessment, problem solving, personalization of content etc. On the other hand, the educational software is a computer program designed for understanding or application

*Figure 3. The similarities and differences between ME and SE concepts*

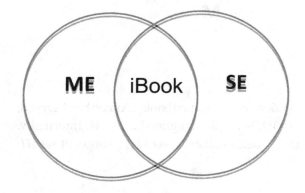

of knowledge. Moreover, the multimodal content of digital textbooks is commonly transmitted over the network or from "the cloud". That is why the "digital textbook" concept is usually associated with the "digital device" concept, defined as a device that works with discrete numbers or digits and carries either discrete information, such as numbers, letters or other individual symbols.

Moreover, digital textbook content can be open or closed. Research has shown (Petrides, Jimes, Middleton-Detzner, Walling, & Weiss, 2011, pp. 39 - 40) that open textbooks are textbooks that are made freely available online for faculty and students to use, modify and reuse through non-restrictive licensing. Open textbooks are most frequently highlighted as alternatives to traditional textbooks for their cost and accessibility benefits. Through nonrestrictive licensing and accessible technology, open textbooks – like open educational resources, more generally – are also cited for their potential to facilitate a community of users who collaborate, share, discuss, critique, use, reuse and continuously improve educational content.

## eBOOK, EDUCATIONAL SOFTWARE, AND DIGITAL TEXTBOOK: WHAT MAKES A DIFFERENCE?

An electronic book is a book-length publication in digital form, consisting of text, images, or both, readable on computers or other electronic devices (Gardiner & Ronald, 2010, p. 164). These books are produced for e-readers in PDF, ePub, txt, HTML or other formats. Electronic books are gaining popularity. Many higher education institutions around the world have ebook collections for their students. Such books should not adhere to the paper book metaphor strictly. For instance, text rich educational e books can be enhanced by adding to them dynamic, interactive visuals. Hutley (2002, p. 32) observes that electronic book may not be available as a print book and may have only been published as a book. The electronic

version of books may also not be identical to the print version, as it can have many bonus electronic features that are not possible with a print book.

Ebooks can be read online on PCs, laptops and downloaded on to Personal Digital Assistance (PDA). Technology offers information delivery 24 hours a day, 7 days a week to any place in the world with internet access; the ability to search a whole book for keywords in seconds; the ability to change text size to suit reader needs; hyperlinks to relevant web pages and the ability to continually update the content within the ebook as required. "The inclusion of multimedia and interactivity features into various eBook formats (e.g. PDF, ePub, txt and HTML) has produced a wide range of e-Textbooks formats" (Lee, Messom & Yau, 2013, p. 35).

The diversity of printed textbooks, eBooks, educational software and digital textbooks allow stating that *set SE*, common for educational software, is compatible with analysed *set ME*. The same characteristics show similarities and differences with electronic books *EB set* (Figure 4).

This figure could be interpreted as follows: *digital textbooks are a pedagogical resource or a learning tool used for teaching, learning and assessment.* The compatibility of *set ME* with *set EB* and *set EB* allow attesting that digital textbooks are indispensable attributes for digital natives -

*Figure 4. Similarities and differences between sets: ME an M, EB, SE*

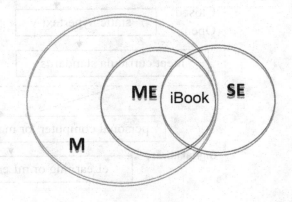

"children born after 1980 who from birth have experienced the digital world as a natural part of their daily lives and regularly access to rich resources in digital format for information and entertainment" (Houston, 2011, p. 39). Access, connectivity, adaptivity, and interactivity are essential features of a digital textbook.

## The Complexity of Studied Concept

"Digital textbook" is a complex concept that could be defined on the base on following criteria: definition, learning environment, and forms of data presentation, structure, user interface design, utilization, digital device, and learning platform. The most general definition of the digital textbook needs to include the idea of integrating workbooks, reference books, exercise books, case books or/ and instruction manuals. Much of the research concerning forms of data presentation has used "static hypertext" (Brusilovsky, Schwarz & Weber, 1996) or "multimodal text" (Anstey & Bull, 2010). The logical scheme of the digital textbook definition is the following (Figure 5).

Promising research has led to the following definition: *digital textbook is a mix of workbook, reference book, exercise book, case book and manual of instruction based on static hypertext or multimodal text, which meet curricula standards (pedagogic resources) or/and is an alternative learning tool, located in a digital library accessed through a personal computer or mobile digital device connected to Internet and directed from an educational platform.*

## THE DIVERSITY OF THE DIGITAL TEXTBOOKS INITIATIVES

The overview of digital textbook initiatives sets the stage for our discussion related to digital textbooks, elaborated as *a pedagogical resource* and *a learning tool*.

Audio textbooks aim to make reading accessible for everyone, including helping support students with learning disabilities and their families. The affordance of audio textbooks is also to allow students with visual disabilities achieve

*Figure 5. The logical structure of the "digital textbook" concept*

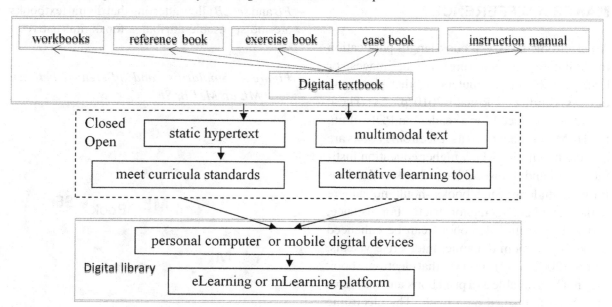

their full potential and enter the workplace. As a result, these students succeed in schooling from an early age. One of the examples is *audio textbooks* offered by Learning Ally Company. As noted on the Learning Ally Company website the mode of receiving information both visually and audibly reinforces word recognition, improves fluency, builds vocabulary and develops decoding skills. It also eases frustration, boosts confidence and makes reading much more enjoyable for those who struggle with printed text. However, it is recommended to use audio books at least 3 times for 20 minutes at a time, because this will get the child more comfortable with reading through listening. Also, it is important to set up a regular reading/listening schedule to provide adequate reading and study time that they come to expect within the rhythm of the week. The video features included into textbooks content allow students to put YouTube and other video context into a textbook without having to block or otherwise segment it away from the material.

On the other hand, following the general classification of textbooks, proposed by Bespalico (2002), digital textbooks, developed as a learn-ing tool, as well as printed textbooks could be classified on the base of the following criteria: aim *S* (pedagogic/didactic): *SPD* and *FSPD*; psycho-pedagogical criteria *C* for digital content (III. didactic, IV. declarative, V. dogmatic and VI. monographic); forms of organizing the didactic activities *F:* determined (*det.*) or unde-termined *(undet.)*; and educational technology *ET* (standard-based or unstandardized: *1, 2, …16*). In preparing digital textbook usually is used ISO/IEC JTC1/SC36 WG6 2012b standard and over 30 formats like TEXT, HTML, CHM, PDF, and EPUB. Therefore, digital textbooks can be classified as: didactic, declarative, and dogmatic and monographic (Figure 6).

The most elaborated are *monographic digital textbooks,* known as e-Textbook. These textbooks come in various forms and formats, including those created for a reader like Amazon's Kindle or Apple's iPad; Google Books and NetLibrary; print-on demand e-textbooks; modular assemblages of audio, visual, and text resources presented via iTunes, wikis and digital applications; open and free textbooks and others. "In its early stage, the e-Textbook was a supplementary multimedia

*Figure 6. The diversity of the digital textbooks designed as a learning tool*

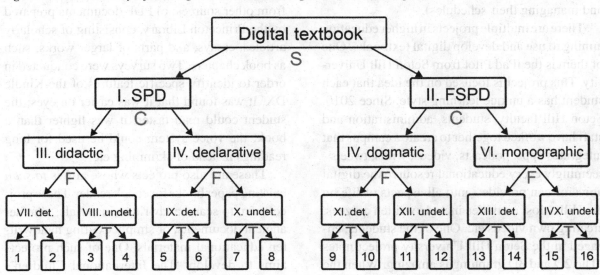

learning resource, rather than as a stand-alone replacement of printed textbooks. This type of e-textbook was developed with multimedia or html, and delivered through a website or CD-ROMs" (Gu, Wu & Xu, 2012).

## MOBILE DEVICES AND DIGITAL TEXTBOOKS

Mobile technologies are more relevant to learning with digital textbooks. Several studies have been conducted showing how mobile is exploiting the learning world (Naismith, Sharples, Vavoula & Lonsdale., 2008). In mobile learning several categories of activities are used. These categories are: a) *behaviorist activities* (presentation of a problem, feedback from the system and reinforcement); *constructivist activities* (the learner is a designer of digital simulation of new ideas and concepts); *situated activities* (the learner uses context-aware applications); *collaborative activities* (social interactions in the process of learning); *informal and lifelong activities* (the learner/teacher accesses digital news and presents them to demonstrate ideas) and *learning/teaching support activities* (provide course, reporting, reviewing student marks, access to school data, and managing their schedules).

There are multiple projects in higher education aiming to use and develop digital textbooks. One of them is the iPad Pilot from Seton Hill University. This project is focused on the idea that each student has a unique learning style. Since 2010, Seton Hill faculty, students, administration and staff have worked together to create a campus that integrates apps, podcasts, videos, wikis, tweets - seemingly every educational resource the digital universe can provide - into all aspects of life on the Hill. Most activities include written quizzes, creating own videos etc. One of the students, engaged in the Seton Hill University project notes "The 2D and 3D graphing is amazing. When the professor mentions a parabola, you know what

that looks like, but harder equations are difficult to visualize. The iPad allows you to graph equations - even to graph two equations and compare, see all sides, maybe this one goes to infinity, this one settles down to zero - so you can understand it right away". The model of individual learning through digital reading is presented in Figure 7.

The other project was running at Princeton University in 2009-2010. In final report of the project it was noted that the aim was to "gain a better understanding of the ways in which we can act to reduce student printing, to respond to students' academic needs, and to provide them with an environment that supports their academic needs as well as their desire for convenient and efficient approaches to their life and work at Princeton (p. 4)". The courses selected for the e-reader needed to meet several criteria, defined as a robust use of reserved reading materials, contents suited to e-reader delivery, and course size. Courses participating in the pilot were kept secret until enrollment was complete. Once enrollment was closed for each course, students were sent a list of guidelines that invited their participation in the Kindle pilot. The readings for the courses consisted of several types: a) books purchased from Amazon, prepared by publishers specifically for the Kindle; b) PDF documents that would have been purchased online from other sources; c) PDF documents prepared by the Princeton Library, consisting of scholarly articles, essays, and parts of larger works, such as book chapters. Two surveys were conducted in order to identify specific features of the Kindle DX. It was found that it was easier on eyes; the student could read faster; it was lighter than a book; the voice system could be used for long readings instead of skimming etc.

These are also projects whose aim is *to scan* existing paper books for ebook reader. These projects aim to scan handwritten materials, whether ancient documents, or simply existing handwritten educational materials. One of such projects aims to develop "The International Children's National Library" and allow reading the scanned

*Figure 7. Individual learning with digital textbooks*

books online. The educational value of e Books was described by Guernsey (2011): "At one end of the spectrum, there are PDFs of printed titles, while on the other end are electronic resources with animated characters, interactive quizzes, and online games that accompany texts that can be "played" while each spoken word is highlighted on the screen. With such a range of possibilities, there is not enough known yet to know what best practice is. It's frustrating to see people put money into developing something that isn't sound from a pedagogical standpoint.

Free Digital Content is another type of project which aims to produce digital textbooks in PDF format. Librarian Click is one of such projects. Wikibooks is another project that allows everyone to contribute to the development of a free library of educational textbooks. Writing New Textbooks for the open learning personal content is another type of projects. One of the examples is HS.Tutorials.Net. The aim of the project is to

develop the textbook itself. For this, it is important to find a section you have some content for (vocabulary, lesson, example problems, practice games, practice problems), then click "Edit this page", and put it in! In case of a mistake someone else will click "Edit this page" and fix it. The second aim is to develop the student user-interface using Moodle and the third is to help young people teach themselves algebra. Daytona's e-text Project aims to replace traditional textbooks with digital alternatives, including e-textbooks and open content, for the entire school. As was noted by Waters (2011) digital textbook initiative should be based on cross-platform with e-reader software that will run on any device. The devices need to work with any publisher, both proprietary content and open content. Drawing on this literature, this study seeks to add weight to and further shed light on the ways that E-textbooks as well as open textbooks could be aligned to enhanced teaching and learning.

## FUTURE RESEARCH DIRECTIONS

Future research needs to provide empirical data related to digital textbook confusing terminology. Future investigation must be related to the success of various types of hardware, software and educational technologies incorporated into different learning environments and focused on proved learning outcomes. The proposed unique definition serves as a framework for the construction of more concrete definitions in accordance to each case study or concrete situation. For example, if digital textbooks are designed and developed to complete gaps in the knowledge of science, the proposed definition will be adjusted in the following way: "digital textbook, as a tutor for science study, is a unity of workbook, exercise book and instruction manual based on multimodal text, which meets curricula standards and is an alternative interactive learning tool, located in a digital library and accessed through personal computer and/or any mobile devices, connected to Internet and directed from any of the educational platforms."

Additionally increasing complexity and diversity of learning environments need to be taken into consideration in understanding the future definitions of digital textbooks. The complexity and diversity of different learning environments provide different models of learning processes. Measuring these indicators is something problematic, however, and future work in the area of metadata must be given careful consideration. Although qualitative methods of research have predominated in psycho-pedagogics, the field is increasingly using alternative qualitative methods. These include qualitative methods of investigating the characteristics of multimodal text semiotics as well as specifics of mobile digital devices and diversity of digital textbooks.

Multiple data collection from different countries allow to state that in different countries the meaning of textbooks differs. English, for example, has only one genre: the textbook. On the other hand, Germans and French make a distinction between university books and schoolbooks. German authors define any schoolbook as a didactically prepared content. The French consider university books to be explanatory. For example, the Expository Writing Program, proposed by Kansas State University, provides students with a broad range of writing experiences in order to help them fulfill their academic, professional, and civic responsibilities. Students produce many different types of genres - evaluations, responses, analyses, reports, and proposals, among others - that they will encounter both in and outside the university. Finally, the expository writing program asks students to write for specific audiences and for specific purposes. In addition, the difference between the USA and German/French definitions doesn't exist for schoolbooks.

To sum up, the confusing terminology of digital textbooks should examine what the characteristics of learning environments are, what learning outcomes are expected to be obtained and what psycho-pedagogical characteristics of learners will conduct to guaranteed learning outcomes.

## CONCLUSION

This chapter suggested that the shift toward postmodernist ideas within the field of digital textbook use and development, as well as more generally within the social sciences and humanities, has opened up new opportunities for exploring and understanding some of the complex relationships between digital textbook terminology and complexity, or diversity of learning environments, and the importance of these for teaching, learning and assessment. This shift has involved the conceptualization of new thinking for analysing social processes and the role of personalized digital textbooks within these. The proposed definitions of authors from different parts of the world are components of these philosophical trends. This is why the digital textbook concept was defined on the base of proposed definitions, characteristics of the learning environment, and forms of data presentation, structure, user interface design, utilization, digital devices and learning platform-specific characteristics. The diversity of digital textbook initiatives was discussed. It was found that digital textbooks could be elaborated as pedagogical resources and/or as learning tools.

The differences and similarities between the concepts of digital textbooks was analysed through SWOT. It was found that the strength of digital textbooks is the extensibility of school environment, the possibility to use multimodal text and interactive content for better understanding of concepts, the possibility to use specific questions in order to develop metacognitive structures. Digital textbooks offer new learning. These ideas are particularly useful in moving towards a more process–oriented framework for analyzing principles and norms for the design and development of digital textbooks. The new ways in which students learn digitally are seen as important in proving the idea that the world is going mobile. In addition to digital versions of printed textbooks, students can use self-assessment, vocabulary etc. We concluded this chapter by focusing on ways of researching and analysing the interdependences between digital textbook use and development. In particular, we focused on the logical way in which the concept of digital textbook can be researched and theorized.

## REFERENCES

Acker, S. R. (2013). Digital textbooks. *Library Technology Reports*, *47*(8), 41–51.

Alberta (2013). *Digital repository of textbooks for students with disabilities*. Retrieved October, 25, 2014, from http://www.scholastic.com/browse/article.jsp?id=3755544

Anstey, M., & Bull, G. (2010). Helping teachers to explore multimodal texts. *Curriculum & Leadership Journal, 8*(16). Retrieved October 25, 2014 from http://www.curriculum.edu.au/leader/helping_teachers_to_explore_multimodal_texts,31522.html?issueID=12141

Bergaz. (2009). *The methodology of school textbooks* (Unpublished PhD thesis). Chisinau: Moldova State University.

Booker, E. (2013). *E-textbook pilot puts college books in cloud*. Retrieved October, 25, 2014, from http://www.informationweek.com/mobile/mobile-devices/e-textbook-pilot-puts-college-books-in-cloud/d/d-id/1108942?

Brunner, J. (2013). *Structural equation models: An open textbook*. Edition 0.07. Retrieved October 25, 2014, from http://www.utstat.utoronto.ca/~brunner/openSEM/OpenSEM_0.07f.pdf

Brusilovsky, P., Schwarz, E., & Weber, G. (1997). Electronic textbooks on www: From static hypertext to interactivity and adaptivity. In B. H. Khan (Ed.), Web-based instruction. Educational technology publications (pp. 255-261). Educational Technology Publications, Inc.

Chen, G., Gong, C., Yang, J., Yang, X., & Huang, R. (2013). The concept of eTextbooks in K- 12 Classes from the perspective of its stakeholders. *Human-Computer Interaction and Knowledge Discovery in Complex, Unstructured, Big Data (Lecture Notes in Computer Science), 7947*, 319–325. doi:10.1007/978-3-642-39146-0_29

Christiea, B. A., Millera, K., Cookea, R., White, J., & Christie, B. A. et al.. (2013). Environmental sustainability in higher education: How do academics teach? *Environmental Education Research, 19*(3), 385–414. doi:10.1080/13504622.2012.698598

Chuilkov, D. V., & VanAlstine, J. (2013). College Student choice among electronic and printed textbook options. *Journal of Education for Business, 88*(4), 216–222. doi:10.1080/08832323.2012.672936

Darrow, R. (2012). *What does it look to be a blended learning teacher?* Retrieved October 25, 2014, from http://www.slideshare.net/robdarrow/blendedlearninginacolessdarrow-dec2012v4

Dillon, N. (2008). The e-volving textbook. *The American School Board Journal, 195*(7), 20–23.

*Discovery. Create. Communicate.* (n. d.). Retrieved October 25, 2014, from http://www-2011.setonhill.edu/techadvantage/MobileLearningBrochure_CombinedFINAL.pdf

Dmitriy, V. C., & VanAlstine, J. (2013). College student choice among electronic and printed textbook options. *Journal of Education for Business, 88*(4), 216–222. doi:10.1080/08832323.2012.672936

Dziuban, C. D., Hartman, J. L., & Moskal, P. D. (2004). Blended learning. *Educause*, Issue 7. Retrieved October, 25, 2014, from https://net.educause.edu/ir/library/pdf/ERB0407.pdf

Elliott, P. (2013, March 17). Students trading textbooks for tech books. *Los Angeles Times*, A17. Retrieved 23 July 2013 from eLibrary.

Encheff, D. (2013). Creating a science e-book with fifth grade students. *TechTrends: Linking Research & Practice to Improve Learning, 57*(6), 61–72. doi:10.1007/s11528-013-0703-8

Falc, E. O. (2013). An assessment of college students' attitudes towards using an online e-textbook. *Interdisciplinary Journal of E-Learning and Learning Objects, 9*, 1-12. Retrieved October 25, 2014, from http://www.ijello.org/Volume9/IJELLOv9p001-012Falc831.pdf

Feldstein, A. P., & Lewis, R. F. (2013). Understanding slow growth in the adoption of e-textbooks: Distinguishing paper and electronic delivery of course content. *International Research in Education, 1* (1), p. 177-193. Retrieved October 25, 2014, from http://www.macrothink.org/journal/index.php/ire/article/view/4071/3542

Gu, X., Wu, B., & Xu, X. (2014). Design, development, and learning in e-Textbooks: What we learned and where we are going. *Journal of Computers in Education, 1*(3), article 24, Springer. Retrieved February 9, 2015, from http://link.springer.com/article/10.1007/s40692-014-0023-9/fulltext.html

Harvey, D. (2011). Analytical Chemistry 2.0: An open-access digital textbook. *Analytical and Bioanalytical Chemistry, 399*(1), 149–152. doi:10.1007/s00216-010-4316-1 PMID:21046084

Houston, C. (2011). Digital Books for Digital Natives. *Children & Libraries: The Journal of the Association for Library Service to Children, 9*(3), 39–42.

HS.Tutorials.Net. (2013). *OLPC - Algebra 1 in Simple English "Wiki-textbook".* Retrieved October 25, 2014, from http://www.hstutorials.net/olpcmath.htm

Hutley, S. (2002). Follow the book road: Ebooks in Australian public libraries. *APLIS, 15*(1), 32–38.

Joo, H. M., & Ahn, C. U. (2013). A study on the development of evaluation criteria for digital textbooks in Korea. In J. Herrington et al. (Eds.), *Proceedings of World Conference on Educational Multimedia, Hypermedia and Telecommunications 2013* (pp. 86-89). Chesapeake, VA: AACE. Retrieved December 15, 2013, from http://www.editlib.org/p/111935

KERIS. (2014). *Digital Textbook. School with digital textbook is everywhere*. Retrieved October 25, 2014, from. http://www.dtbook.kr/renew/english/index.htm

Key, A. (1972). *A personal computer for children of all ages*. Retrieved October 25, 2014, from http://www.mprove.de/diplom/gui/Kay72a.pdf

Kim, S. W., & Lee, M. G. (2012). Utilization of digital textbooks in Korea. In T.-T. Gon, B.-C. Seet, & P.-C.Su (Eds.). E-books & e-readers for e-learning (pp. 90-125). Orauariki: Victoria Business School.

Korea Institute for Curriculum and Evaluation. (2013). *A study on the development of evaluation criteria and process for digital textbooks*. Retrieved October, 25, 2014, from http://kice.re.kr/en/board.do?boardConfigNo=139&menuNo=410&action=vie&boardNo=31033

Lee, H. J., Messom, C., & Yau, K.-L. A. (2013). Can an electronic textbooks be part of K-12 education? Challenges, technological solutions and open issues. *The Turkish Online Journal of Educational Technology*, *12*(1), 32–44.

Lim, C., Song, H. D., & Lee, Y. (2012). Improving the usability of the user interface for a digital textbook platform for elementary-school students. *Educational Technology Research and Development*, *60*(1), 159–173. doi:10.1007/s11423-011-9222-5

Mardis, M., & Everhart, N. (2013). From paper to pixel: The promise and challenges of digital textbooks for K-12 schools. *Educational Media and Technology Yearbook*, *37*, 93–118. doi:10.1007/978-1-4614-4430-5_9

Midoro, V. (2005). *A common European framework for teachers' professional profile in ICT for education*. Italy: Edizioni MENABO Didactica.

Morin, A. (2013). *What are math manipulatives*? Retrieved October, 25, 2014, from http://childparenting.about.com/od/schoollearning/tp/what-are-math-manipulatives.htm

Naismith, L., Sharples, M., Vavoula, G., & Lonsdale, P. (2004*). Literature review in mobile technologies and learning*. Retrieved October 25, 2014, from http://telearn.archives-ouvertes.fr/docs/00/19/01/43/PDF/Naismith_2004.pdf

Noveanu, E., & Noveanu, D. (1994). The impact of new informational technologies for learning. In V. Mandacanu (Ed.), *The modern informational technologies*. (In Romanian). Chisinau: Lyceum.

Oxford University Press. (2013). *Learn about Virtual Learning Environment/Course Management System content*. Retrieved October, 25, 2014, from http://global.oup.com/uk/orc/learnvle/

Peters, O. (2000). Digital Learning Environments: New possibilities and opportunities. Retrieved October, 25, 2014, from http://www.irrodl.org/index.php/irrodl/article/view/3/336

Petrides, L., Jimes, C., Middleton-Detzner, C., Walling, J., & Weiss, S. (2011). Open textbook adoption and use: Implications for teachers and learners. *Open Learning*, *26*(1), 39–49.

Pijawka, D., Yabes, R., Frederick, C. P., & White, P. (2013). Integration of sustainability in planning and design programs in higher education: Evaluating learning outcomes. *Journal of Urbanism*, *6*(1), 24–36.

Plianram, S., & Inprasitha, M. (2012). Exploring elementary Thai teachers' use of mathematics textbook. *Creative Education*, *3*(6), 692-695. Retrieved October 25, 2014, from http://www.SciRP.org/journal/ce

Rivero, V. (2013). Digital textbooks: Show me the future! *Internet@Schools*, *20*(3), 12-16.

Rix, K. (2013). *Build your own digital textbooks*. Retrieved October 25, 2014, from http://www.scholastic.com/browse/article.jsp?id=3755544

Samuel, S., Grochowski, P., & Nicholls, N. (2013). *Students, Vendor Platforms, and E-textbooks: Using E-books as E-textbooks* (ASEE paper). Retrieved October, 25 2014, from http://deepblue.lib.umich.edu/bitstream/handle/2027.42/98430/ASEE%20paper.pdf?sequence=1

Sands, A. & Journal, E. (2013, June 26). Alberta schools prepare to turn the page to digital textbooks. *Edmonton Journal*, A1. Retrieved from eLibrary.

Serafini, F. (2010). Reading multimodal texts: Perceptual, structural and ideological perspectives. *Children's Literature in Education, 41*(2), 85–104. doi:10.1007/s10583-010-9100-5

Seton Hill University. (2013). *iPad for everyone!* Retrieved October 25, 2014, from http://www-2011.setonhill.edu/techadvantage/

Smith, R. S. (2004). *Guidelines for authors of learning objects*. MMC: The New Media Consortium. Retrieved October, 25, 2014, from http://archive2.nmc.org/guidelines/NMC%20LO%20Guidelines.pdf

Song, J. S., Kim, S. J., Byun, G. S., Song, J. H., & Lee, B. G. (2014). Comparing wireless networks for applying digital textbook. *Telecommunication Systems, 55*(1), 25–38. doi:10.1007/s11235-013-9748-4

Streitfeld. (2013, April 13). Smart textbooks monitor student engagement; Data from digital books affects how profs present material - but does it really measure learning? *Montreal Gazette.*

Tailacova, D. H. (2013). The use of technology for modelling and creating electronic textbook for the course "Mother Tongue" (in Russian). *The Young Scientist, 5*, 772-775.

*The International Children's National Library*. (2013). Retrieved October 25, 2014, from http://en.childrenslibrary.org/

The Trustees of Princeton University. (2010). *The E-reader pilot at Princeton*. Retrieved October, 25, 2014, from http://www.princeton.edu/ereaderpilot/eReaderFinalReportLong.pdf

Walsh, M. (2006). The 'textual shift': Examining the reading process with print, visual and multimodal texts. *Australian Journal of Language &Literacy., 29*(1), 24–37.

Waters, J. K. (2011). *E-textbooks: 4 keys to going all-digital*. Retrieved October, 25, 2014, from http://campustechnology.com/articles/2011/08/03/e-textbooks-4-keys-to-going-all-digital.aspx

Wiek, A., Withycombe, L., Redman, C., & Mills, S. (2011). Moving forward on competence in sustainability research and problem solving. *Environment, 53*(2), 3–13. doi:10.1080/00139157.2011.554496

## ADDITIONAL READING

Davis, M. R. (2013). English-learners going digital. *Education Week, 32*(32), 28–30.

Gopinath, R., & Geetha, B. (2013). An e-learning system based on secure data storage services in cloud computing. *International Journal of Information Technology and Web Engineering, 8*(2), 1–17. doi:10.4018/jitwe.2013040101

Husén, T. (2003). Comenius and Sweden, and Bengt Skytte's Sophopolis. *Scandinavian Journal of Educational Research, 47*(4), 387–392. doi:10.1080/00313830308592

Mann, L. (2013). *Pros and cons of digital textbooks*. Retrieved June, 1, 2014, from http://articles.chicagotribune.com/2013-08-07/features/ct-x-0807-college-kids-eyes-20130807_1_print-textbooks-digital-textbooks-computer-vision-syndrome.

Mardis, M., & Everhart, N. (2011). Digital Textbooks in Florida: Extending the Teacher Librarians' Reach. *Teacher Librarian*, *38*(3), 8–11.

Marshall, S., Kinuthia, W. & Richards, G. (2013). Open content for elearning: Cross institutional collaboration for education and training in a digital environment. *International Journal of Education and Development using ICT, 8*(3), 35-42.

Sharp, J. H. & Schultz, L. A. (2013). An exploratory study of the use of video as an instructional tool in an introductory C# programming course. *Information Systems Education Journal, 11*(6), 33-39.

Sharples, M. (1999). Electronic publication: Writing for the screen. *Journal of Adolescent & Adult Literacy*, *43*(2), 156–159.

Truong, H., Pham, T., Thoai, N., & Dustdar, S. (2012). Cloud computing for education and research in developing countries. In L. Chao (Ed.), *Cloud computing for teaching and learning: strategies for design and implementation* (pp. 64–80). Hershey, PA: Information Science Reference. doi:10.4018/978-1-4666-0957-0.ch005

## KEY TERMS AND DEFINITIONS

**Blended Learning:** A formal education program in which a student is engaged in active learning at least in part online where they have some control over the time, place, and/or pace and in part at a physical location away from home.

**Cloud Computing:** "The development and fusion of traditional computer technology and network technology such as grid computing, distributed computing, parallel computing, network storage, virtualization, and load balancing, and is a super computing model based on Internet. It distributes computing tasks to resource pools made of a large number of computers, allows all kinds of application systems to acquire the computer power, storage space, and software services according to the need" (Chen, et. al., 2013, p.192).

**Cloud System:** A knowledge management system based on the model of cloud computing and cloud computing services which offer a wide range of services to users through using Internet technologies and could be introduced in an e-learning space or developed as an e-learning cloud.

**Digital Textbook Platform:** An underlying digitalized system on which programs run, offer individual access to content through user interface, providing a framework for design, development, implementation and management of digital textbooks and other executing application tools within those textbooks.

**Educational App:** A piece of software or a self-contained program designed to fulfil a particular purpose (email, calendar, maps, create a simple document etc.), which can be downloaded by a user to a mobile device or can run on the iOS, Android, Blackberry, Windows devices or on other digital devices.

**Flipped Learning:** A model that describes a flexible learning environment, guided by teachers, which are professional educators that decide when and how to shift the direct instruction from the group to individual learning space; evaluate the content that needs to be taught directly; help students to understand the provided concepts and make activities available to students to be accessed whenever and wherever it is convenient.

**Learner-Centered Learning Environments:** A place or a community with learner-centered and interactive classroom activities, where the teacher role is changing from fact teller and omniscient expert to collaborator and sometimes learner, the concept of knowledge is defined as transformation of facts, the demonstration of success is achieved through quality of understanding, the assessment is criterion referenced, portfolios and performances, and the terminology use is proved by communication, collaboration and expression.

**Learning Environment:** A place or community in which a number of activities are accruing with the purpose of supporting learning and those actors can draw upon a number of resources when doing so. From a pedagogical methods point of view learning environment can be teacher centered or learner centered. However, from a learning designer point of view, the learning can be digital, on-line, blended.

**Learning Object:** "Any grouping of materials that is structured in a meaningful way and is tied to an educational objective. The "materials" in a learning object can be documents, pictures, simulations, movies, sounds, and so on. Structuring these in a meaningful way implies that the materials are related and are arranged in a logical order. But without a clear and measurable educational objective, the collection remains just a collection (Swit, 2004); any stand-alone resource or tool that supports student learning when surrounded by context and some instructions.

**Multimodal Text:** A text that combines two or more semiotic systems, can be delivered via different media or technologies and may be live, paper or digital electronic.

**Semiotic System:** A system that is characterized by five features. a) *Linguistic* (comprising aspects such as such vocabulary, genetic structure and the grammar of oral and written language); b) *visual* (comprising aspects such as colour, vectors and viewpoint in still and moving images); c) *audio* (comprising aspects such as volume, pitch and rhythm of music and sound effects); d) *gestural* (comprising aspects such as movement, speed and stillness in facial expression and body language) and *spatial* (comprising aspects such as proximity, direction, position of layout and organisation of objects in space), as was described by Anstey and Bull (2010).

# Chapter 4
# Structure of Digital Textbook

## ABSTRACT

*Many projects around the world aim to use and develop digital textbooks. However, differences between aims, affordances, methodologies and technologies cause many issues, controversies and concerns to arise. This chapter aims to explore the basic structure of digital textbooks. The focus is on the non-linear mechanisms of eTextbooks and Open Source Textbooks. At the beginning is investigated the current state-of-art in order to arrange the distinctive features in a hierarchical manner. Then, it assembled the digital textbook infrastructure. The proposed methodology allows identifying the common elementary components of digital textbooks through meta-analyses of proposed methodologies. To arrive at this framework, it explored the diversity of contexts, educational platforms, PC, digital devices, contents and processes. The chapter concludes with a call for future research of digital textbooks functionalities, analysing them in a diversity of four learning environments.*

## INTRODUCTION

Learning today goes beyond four walls of traditional classrooms with classic methods of teaching and printed textbooks. Digital textbooks offer a new way to explore phenomena, learning objects, processes, events, and what is more important the *information flows*. To date, they aren't only digital or digitalised imitations of printed textbooks. Digital textbooks provide many interesting features as: immediate feedback, adaptivity, multimodal text etc. Research (Kim & Park, 2014, p. 418) expect that in future, digital textbooks will elevate the learning efficiency, reduce the educational gap between different location and incomes, and the dependency on private education through the normalization of public education. In a fast-paced

world it is becoming increasingly likely that a significant portion of what students learn will be out of date by the time they finish their professional working careers. In such a world it is no longer enough for students to reproduce facts or information provided by the teacher or/and textbook. More important is being able to find, manage and evaluate new information. It was argued (Midoro, 2005, p. 52) that students learn complex subject matter best when they are engaged in the process of constructing meaning from information and from their personal experience to meet their own goals. The use of ICT should not only enhance learning, but also transform it.

We live in a knowledge-based information society where new knowledge is produced every minutes. Use and development of digital textbooks

DOI: 10.4018/978-1-4666-8300-6.ch004

has become an increasingly concept in textbook theoretical and practical studies. The growing interest in digital textbook has occurred partly in response to the changing nature of *content* and partially of *cognitive processes*. It was argued the existence of multiple ways in which cognitive and meta-cognitive processes impact attitude. For example, as was noted by Petty and Briñol (2014), emotions can serve as simple cues when elaboration is low; emotions can serve as arguments when elaboration is high; emotions can bias cognition when elaboration is high or emotions can influence the amount of thinking when elaboration is unconstrained. The impact of emotions on secondary cognition relies on happiness, anger, disgust and arousal. This way arise many legal, philosophical, pedagogic, psychological, economic, managerial, technical, and others issues. Thus, there is a dispute over the key issues in digital textbook structure. In general terms, the digital textbook structure could be developed on the base on *postmodernism* or on the base on *empiricism*. "The emergence of Digital Natives has led to change in communication methods, forms of knowledge and the way in which collective intelligence is cultivated for social education" (Jang, 2014, p. 73). The differences between the postmodernism and empirical/theoretical methods is similar to the difference between a scientific fundament with principles and trial-errors methodology aims to explain evident facts. In this way the learning design of digital textbooks should take into consideration the integration of new technologies across the curriculum and methodology of learning.

Last decade several studies have documented aspects of digital textbooks' structure, content, frameworks, text structure and learning environments (Hyman, Moser & Segala, 2014; Lawrence, 2014; Hannafin, Hill, Land & Lee, 2014; Harvey, 2011; Eppelin & Böttcher, 2011). Our research question is: *What are the key elements of the digital textbook structure?* Usually, studies aim to describe the content or/and frameworks. However, in a knowledge based society it is no longer enough to learn "fact" and "information". Being competent, have knowledge, skills, energy and attitudes to find, manage and evaluate information, time, resources, and risks. It has become evident that investigation the structure elements of digital textbooks is unprecedented. These possibilities can be attributed to easy on-line access to e-resources; registration to educational platforms and open source textbooks as well as databases with scientific articles related to use and development of digital textbooks in learning.

As many scholars have pointed out, the scientific investigation trend to SMART education, that is "a creativity focused and customised system for developing new ways to learn by using up-to-date technology like cloud computing, and enables students to study with various materials based on their aptitudes and intellectual levels using mobile Digital Textbook at anytime, anywhere and on any devices" (Jang, 2014, p. 73). Such new methodologies allow identifying, also, the common elements of textbook structures. This chapter "looks" into digital textbook structures. It is analyses the last decade challenges related to real context of the learner in concordance to digital content provided by textbooks (schoolbooks) and requirements of different learning environments.

The chapter is interested in exploring interdependences between learner's psycho-pedagogical characteristics and the real learning environment, were was radically changed. What is the learning environment with digital textbooks? What is better for a digital textbook environment: individualized (personalized); collaborative (cooperative); mastery-based or performance-based learning methods? What frames should be designed: *homogeneous* or *heterogeneous*? Homogeneous frames include text, graphic, exercises and the linear structure of text. Instead, heterogeneous frames have text, graphic, animation, spoken word and a non-linear structure that can be tailored by teacher(s) or/and students.

Our essential research question concerns *the key elements of digital textbooks' structure,* when can be used as a pedagogical resource or/ and a learning tool. The assumption is that both possible structures rely to postmodernism. First of all, the postmodernism provides a glimpse of research, which allows emphasising that Instructional Systems Design models are in contradiction with reality: "a conceptual construct, an artifacte or scientific practice" (Encyclopedia Britannica, 2014). Secondly, according to postmodernism philosophy digital textbooks have various structures, but common systems, environments and provide the similar mechanisms for human learning. Thirdly, digital textbooks' structure depends on issue(s), identified in the learning environment. Thus, "Truth" is proved by behaviourism, cognitivism, and constructivism theories. Postmodernism argues that all aspects of human psychology are socially determined. Language is semantically self-contained and that meaning of a word is not a static, but "rather a range of contrasts and differences with the meaning of other words" and not "Rene Descartes's dictum cogito, ergo sum" (Encyclopedia Britannica, 2014). Related to digital textbook these facts evidence the role of hermeneutic dialogue.

The main objective of the chapter is to identify and describe key elements of digital textbooks' structure. For the purpose of this paper, we use the terms: "pedagogical resource" and "tool for learning". Digital textbook, developed as a pedagogical resources represents any resources for teaching. The tool for learning, known also as a technical resources, are programs, that may be included in the structure of digital textbooks as educational games, worksheets, quizzes, surveys, wikis etc. All types of digital textbooks are accesses by both students and professors. These resources are often annotated or tagged by the professors who produce them.

Web2.0 and Web3.0 technologies encourages the production of new structures of digital textbooks. This is not limited to production of textbooks like pedagogical resource or/and learning tools. It was described (Jang, 2014, p.74) that

in the vision of SMART education the Korean government has initiated five flagship projects:

- Digital Textbook development and application;
- Promoting online classes and assessments;
- Creating an environment to use educational content safely;
- Building teacher's competency;
- Establishing a cloud-based education system.

Through the implementation of these projects students learn whenever and wherever they please.

The organization of the proposed chapter is as follows. The next section presents the current state-of-art with broad definitions and main concepts. The third section presents discussion on the digital textbooks structures. The final section presents discussion about future research and conclusions.

## THE CURRENT STATE-OF-ART

Informational globalization has created more opportunities for innovative textbooks focused on learning. SMART education is the next step that stand for self-directed, motivated, adapted, resource enriched and technology embedded tools. Although the growth of research in inter-disciplinary and trans-disciplinary arias of digital textbooks theory is due to a number of concerns and solutions, perhaps the most influential are psychopedagogical concerns related on the *structure' functionality*. In general terms, the structure functionality of the digital textbook is assured by three components:

- Educational system (learning system);
- Educational platform (learning platform);
- Learning environment.

*Educational system* (learning system) are naturally or artificially constructed systems for teaching, assessment and learning. Conceptually, each of the educational systems are directed by the aim and technologies. The term "aim" refers to "philosophy, philosophy of education, aim of education and personalised aim" (Rudic, 2013, p. 4). This term has different meaning for a pedagogical closed system and educational open system. Therefore, for a closed system aim refers to: *a pedagogical aim*, *a didactic aim* and/or *a personal learning aim*. Instead, for an open system aim refers, first of all, to *personalised aim*. Technology is more general term and, in case of digital textbook, integrities hardware, software and educational technologies in a functional whole. Thus, hardware refers to objects that can be actually touch, like PC, digital devices, display screen, textbook; software exists as ideas, concepts, and symbols, developed as educational platforms, knowledge management systems, content management systems, educational software, including digital textbook and educational technology is about using and development of technology in education to improve teaching, learning and assessment.

*A platform* refers to the computer system on which application program can run. The term "*educational platform*" defines the integrity of tools and services for writing, storing, disseminating of data, information and knowledge to manage didactic activities etc. The choice of an educational platform should be focused on achieving the aim, objectives, but, also, values and culture. There are different educational platforms: learning platform, digital learning platform and others. Thus, a "*learning platform*" is more specific and refers to tools and services that helps to create more effective teaching and learning experience in a colaborative or private learning environment. If the learning platform is used for digital textbook use and development, this is a *digital textbook platform*. It was argued (Lim, Song & Lee, 2012, p. 160) that a digital textbook platform is an underlying computer system on which application programs run. It

provides a framework for designing, developing, implementing and managing digital textbooks and executing application tools within those textbooks. Thus, this platform allow accessing to pedagogical resource and/or learning tool.

Students gain access to the content with digital devices and interact with other students through the *platform user interface,* which is a digital interface that should make users' interactions simple and efficient. User interface design differs, but the common elements are: design of content, design communication and educational or learning management. Access to digital textbooks is done via *digital devices* connected to *networks*. The most used digital devices in education (Rivero, 2013, p. 12) are: Google Nexus 7, Kindle Fire HD, iPad mini, Nook HD, Kobo ARC, Sony Reader and Galaxy Tablet. More of them come with Google products: Gmail, Google Chrome and Apps.

The platform create a *learning environment,* which is a complete physical, social and pedagogical context on which learning is intended to occur or "a place or community in which a number of activities are accruing with the purpose of supporting learning and those actors can draw upon a number of resources when doing so."(Midoro, 2005, p. 42). There are different types of learning environments: 1) *Desktop-Computer Assisted Learning* systems (fixed with low mobility and low level of embeddednes); 2) *Mobile Learning* environment (which hold different learning environments and enable to learn at anytime and anywhere); 3) *Pervasive Computing* environment (learner may obtain information from their learning environment via the communication between the embedded devices and environment) and 4) *Ubiquitous Learning Environment* "which enable everyone to learn at anyplace at anytime" (Joo, Park & Choi, 2014, p. 670).

The platform infrastructure, where is used digital textbooks, includes:

- Network;
- Teaching infrastructure;

- Educational software;
- Digital content.

*Network* refers to a set of computers or data network that allow computer to exchange data, information or knowledge. The everyday life of the teacher and students is changing rapidly. In modern schooling the network allows to implement the idea of "hiperconnectivity". This term is used to define modes in which life-long learners are connected through channels and networks. Through networking the teacher and the students learn how to plan, create knowledge, establish connections, being engaged in events in order to make relevant decisions.

To prevent illegal actions related to didactic process and for better security of metadata many schools around the world has developed the *school network*. Research has shown (Cornelissen, Daly, Liou, van Swet, Beijaard & Bergen, 2014) that the school network context provided both master's students and research advisors with a supportive context for collaboratively engaging in knowledge processes during research as well as after they graduated. The main advantages of school networks are the possibility to block illegal access from the outside and to prevent disclosure of the students' profiles. In a school environment is used hardware, software and educational technologies. The most innovative technology can be considered digital textbooks developed according to flexible curricula.

Teaching infrastructure is a complex endeavour in which learning has been occurred. This can use the school network as well as digital textbooks, blackboard and digital devices. All these technologies need to be connected to school network with wireless or dual-up Internet communication. In such environment the content of digital textbooks can be displayed on the screen. Because the student's digital devices will need to be used for more than four hours per day on average, additional batteries should be provided to students, and rechargers – in the classroom.

Educational software is a general term used to define programs or Apps that provide various learning support features. For example, a digital textbook structure can include a digital textbook contents viewer, a learning support system (learning device), a DataBase and a LSS (a support system in connection with digital textbooks available preference learning management). Research has shown (Song, Kim, Byun, Song & Lee, 2014, p. 5) that digital contents viewer initially ran on MS Windows only in 2008, but additional development was carried out based on the *open source*, in order to reduce the license expense of the Windows operating system and the proprietary applications (MS Office, etc.), and to prevent dependence. Currently, two versions are available. This software was redeveloped by applying international standard technology, and by integrating the two versions into a single version, and was then applied to certain schools in a pilot operation. The learning support system is composed of the web-based LMS (Learning Management System) and the LCMS (Learning Contents Management System), and supports management of assessment, learning level, and class operations.

The digital content refers to information or knowledge provided by the digital textbooks or learning tool, that allow students to read the content or/and to find, evaluate or manage information. The digital content of textbooks can be *closed* or *open*. The term "closed structure" defines the integrally written structure by author or group of authors, which could be read, easy up-dated, disseminated etc. In an increased effort from academic publishers to digitize existed textbooks, the closed structure represents PDF documents mean to be read from beginning to end. Users are able to access digital content from any device. The term "open structure" defines digital artefacts or digitized learning materials that can be assembled or personalized by users in an open learning environment. A digital artefact represents any type of items produced and stored as digital/electronic version and provided during academic work. Examples of digital artefacts include a digital/digitalized version of a learning plan, textbook etc.

In the last decade the content of digital textbook became more ubiquitous. The ubiquitous learning requires a special designed learning environment with scaffolding and mentoring system. Interaction with ubiquitous services offer valuable information. Information is expected to move freely amend the digital artifacte people use. Information is available right there and right now to support a specific activity the users is engaged in. From one point of view ubiquitous digital textbooks in middle and high school settings "vary greatly in how friendly they are to readers. Some expository texts are better than others, and some are dreadful", as was observed by Gore, 2010 (p. 105).

Research has shown (Song, Kim, Byun, Song & Lee, 2014, p. 5) that the digital textbook' content may be the same as the content of the conventional textbook, but with multimedia elements. Currently, for example, the Korea' digital textbooks inherently consist of high-quality multimedia and their size ranges from a minimum of 1 Gigabyte to a maximum of 5 Gigabytes for each subject. The entire size is 1.5 Gbytes, and if its contents for Classes provided at schools may require references to precedent contents, which are different from the way of reading books. Downloading contents for the classes may impose a heavy burden on the computer network. To resolve this problem, in digital textbook-based classes in Korea, the contents of each subject are stored in TPC, while the contents to be updated are downloaded via the network. This allows the school to provide optimal digital textbook classes at a lower cost. Students are able to search information through the Internet and use verified learning materials by Edunet, in addition to existing digital textbook contents.

In France, as was noted by Casassus (2014), the use of digital textbooks has risen sharply in the past three years. Thus, in 2014 29% of the teachers surveyed use digital textbooks; the proportion of primary teachers using digital textbooks rose to 20%, lower secondary level teachers – 36% and upper secondary – 35%. Broken down by disciplines, maths and physical sciences lead digital use (at 46%), followed by history and geography (38%), modern languages and economic and social sciences (34%), life sciences (31%) and literature (24%). Most digital usage is collective: 7% of pupils have their own digital textbooks. Digital textbooks are accessed through school computers by 25% of users, at home for 31%, and through a digital workspace – for 45% of users.

In Germany, as was noted by Knight (2014), there are some plans to complete a boring old textbook with Open Educational Resources (OER) and to reveal a new platform which would help to revolutionise the world of educational material. It was emphases that development and implementation of OER in schools is a great change for all those involved in education. The stronger use of OER including license-free learning and teaching materials in schools and the establishment of the necessary framework are declared goals of educational policy in Berlin.

## ISSUES IN DESIGN OF THE DIGITAL TEXTBOOKS' STRUCTURE

Many digital textbooks' structures have been developed. Across the educational system the practice of using and developing digital textbooks is attracted increasing attention to the extents that is now actively discussed in terms of being a problem for an innovative project. eTextbook and Open Source Textbooks has consistently registered the lower level of improvement in learning. It is also the area of debated how digital learning in postmodernism should be designed. Thus, there are three different points of view:

- From first point of view, digital textbook is a comprehensive study textbook that adds the content of various reference books to the existing printed textbook, as well as incorporating various simulations, multimedia data, and the functions of a database (assessment questions), and various management programs (Song, Kim, Byun, Song & Lee, 2014, p. 2). It is expected that such digital textbooks will maximize the learning effect and convenience by converting book-type textbooks into the electronic format to retain the strengths of the traditional book format, and by adding various multimedia study functions (e.g., animation, 3D) and other functions (e.g., search, navigation). With the appearance of digital textbooks, learners can access the latest multimedia data besides existing study materials, and use them for study in real time;

- From the second point of view, provided by OpenStax College (2014), digital textbooks are professional-quality textbooks that are free online and low-cost in print; can be customizable if the needs are different. These resources are written by one or more authors, then are peer-reviewed and backed by top-of-the line-supporting materials and may include online homework resources, online assessments and online tutorials;
- From the third point of view, there is an open textbook, licensed under an open copyright license, made available online to be freely used by students, teachers of members of the public and distributed in print, e-book or audio formats.

Thus, the first issue of digital textbook structure is *Free Open Source Digital Content*. When this first issue became available for the life-long learners, the teacher(s) and students began to have access to much more pedagogical resources than before. For example, "Principles of Microelectronics", developed by Taylor (2014), can be read live on screen or downloaded as a PDF.

However, the use and development of the free digital textbook to be read live requires new strategies for *digital reading*. There are some barriers to digital reading (Cordón-García, Gómez-Díaz, Alonso-Arévalo & Kaplan, 2014; Hyman, Moser & Segala, 2014). Research has shown (Liang & Huang, 2014, pp. 218-219) that reading patterns are a major criterion for assessing a student's overall reading situation, and may be linked to specific cognitive processes and reading outcomes. The electronic/digital learning process can be regarded, by cognitive theory, as a *multimedia learning process*. The printed words are presented visually and initially processed through the reader's eyes.

The reader may then attend to some of the incoming words and bring them into working memory, which serves as a mental workspace, where information is retrieved and integrated with incoming text. Subsequently, by mentally pronouncing the written words the reader can get them into the auditory/verbal channel. Next, the active cognitive process can take place to build the words into a coherent mental structure known as a "verbal model". Next, the reader may apply prior knowledge in the long-term memory to guide the process of integrating knowledge in working memory. Finally, after new knowledge is constructed in the working memory, it is then stored in the long-term memory, where it will serve as prior knowledge to support subsequent learning. All processes were identified in accordance with the students' patterns and reading outcomes.

The issue of digital reading arises from requirements to have reading skills. Cull (2011) observes that spending time online does not automatically lead to the development of online research or advanced reading skills. Digital reading has changed the brain functionality. There is a relationship between this low level of information literacy skills and academic performance: low-performing students typically have low information literacy skills. In addition, people generally read about 20 percent of the digital text on an average page. A typical "screen-based reading behavior" spend more time on browsing and scanning, keyword spotting, one-time reading etc. and not on in-depth reading.

The summary of the substantial differences between readings on screens online and in print are in cognitive, emotive and psychomotor activities is presented in Table 1.

The other issue of digital textbook structure is *interaction*. Tosun (2014, p. 22) notes that technology can provide enough interaction between teacher and students; can appeal to students with different learning styles in order to adjust their reading skills. However, the usage of digital reading differ from person to person, individual preferences, and subject matter. The common thing is given priority of immediate feedback. "While traditional printed books took longer to read, the research subjects who used e-books scored 9-10% higher on post-reading assessments" (Patel & Morreale, 2014, p. 21).

One more issue is *learning outcomes*. Instead of the fact that four pillars of education were established by UNESCO, in instructional design is used only the "learning to know" pillar. There are many models:

1. A "three dimensional digital textbook" with extensible format 3D (X3D) standard. The aim of textbook is to facilitate motivation and engagement with more 3D learning resources; to overcome the limitations of 2D DTs regarding multimedia features by taking full advantage of 3D graphics. As a prototype, a 3D DT was developed for the subject of general computing used in high schools in South Korea (Hong, Kim & Yoo, 2013, p. 341).

2. The "Social Book" model with a continuous scrolling page that unfolds at key points to reveal a threaded social commentary relevant to that specific content. Research has shown (Armen & Atwood, 2013, p. 25), that the social book is ideal for school texts. The original authored text remains, while the book becomes a living learning network. Students can work at own pace, self-evaluate when they think they are ready, return and review, add to the class discussion, and support co-learners. Teachers can tell from the comments and questions or pedagogical area where to apply clarifications, individual

*Table 1. Differences between digital text and printed text*

|  | **Digital Text** | **Printed Text** |
|---|---|---|
| Brain activation | Is a more cognitive and complex process<br>Requires more decisions to be made<br>The Reader uses more cognitive effort | Is a less cognitive and complex process<br>Requires less decisions to be made<br>Reader use less cognitive effort |
| Contextual environment | The context is the message<br>The paratextual ingredients of reading on a hand–held device or a computer are very different | Physical paratext |
| Cognitive focus | Personal reading on screen<br>Activities are switched every 3-10 minutes<br>Multitasking | Focused on reading |
| Comprehension | Digital technologies have a positive effect on a reader's comprehension skills | It may be easier to understand text in print |
| Reading speed | Active reading is faster<br>Requires skills of reading digital text | Requires skills of reading printed text |
| Addiction | Internet addiction | Less motivation to read |

assistance, or further group teaching and/ or exercises. Students support each other's learning and cement their own knowledge acquisition by adding examples and insights that helped them understand or retain concepts and facts.

3.  A model that describe the processes in which teacher customise and produce new content by re-purposing to suit a learner's learning style, language, skills etc. There may be some issues related to *hardware compatibility*: ability to connect different device without the use of certain equipment or software and *software compatibility:* ability of the application to run on different computers without the need to change its format. (Lee, Messon & Yau, 2013, p. 32).

These and more other issues and controversies evidence the fact that *teachers could be authors or co-authors of the content* together with their students. It was observed that both ways are not paved with stones. In order to understand digital textbooks' structure were identified three research questions:

1.  What are the elementary design units of a digital textbooks platform and learning environment?
2.  What are the elementary design units of digital textbooks device?
3.  What are the elementary design units of digital textbooks content?

## TEXTBOOK PLATFORMS AND DIVERSITY OF LEARNING ENVIRONMENTS

An educational platform may include digital textbooks. Historically, the first digital learning platform was designed by Amazon' Kindle.

Kindle device is the first that shape reading on screen. However, without the capacity of reading color text and supporting third party application, it was developed a new generation of devices, including the tablet with flat touch screen, virtual keyboard, wireless connection, and a variety of other functionalities. These devices are supported by Android OS and therefore offer a more flexible market of third-party applications.

The main characteristics of the digital textbook platforms are: learnability, effectiveness, efficiency and satisfaction. Therefore, a digital textbook platform offer different purposes related to teaching, learning and assessment. For example, *Digital Teaching Platform* provides the primary instructional environment aims to supports the teacher with tools for curriculum planning, classroom management, and student assessment in a teacher-led classroom equipped with technology that approaches one-to-one computing. In such digital learning environment, each student has a digital device with a wireless connection. As was noted by Walters, Walters & Dede (2009, p. 1-3) the teacher manages a networked workstation connected to a projector or "smart" whiteboard. Under the teacher's management, all of the interactions are facilitated by the cluster of networked computers.

A digital textbook platform serves the purpose to disseminate the e-textbooks database or to mediate interactions between teacher (content) and students. There are two main models:

1.  The closed learning platform;
2.  The open learning platform with a cloud system.

The first model describes a platform with a database of members, which interpolate with database of digital textbooks' contents, and a local server, used as supporting system for all digital materials. The second model requires a *cloud sys-*

*tem* and is focused on open global market. In the cloud system the digital textbook keeps an image of a printed textbook, but contains multimedia materials and functions, and may be connected to a Learning Management System (LMS).

Some prominent platforms for digital textbooks use and development were identified by Fernandes (2014). The most relevant data were summarized in the following table (Table 2):

*Table 2. The main relevant features of digital textbooks platforms (adapted from Fernandes, 2014)*

| Platform (Name) | Basic Features | Unique Features | Device Availability | Cost |
|---|---|---|---|---|
| Apple iBooks 2 | Highlighting; note-taking; "study cards" | Videos, 3D animations; interactive illustrations | iPad | Access to free and paid textbooks |
| Barnes & Noble NOOK Study | Highlighting; note-taking; color tags | Dual book view; "questions to instructors"; "word lookup" | Web; PC; Mac; iPad; iPone; Android | Access to free and paid textbooks |
| CafeScribe | Read, highlight, summarize search, make and share notes in assigned textbook; Snap Summary | Allows to create reading communities | Web; PC; Mac; iPad; Android | Access to free and paid textbooks |
| Cengage MindTap | Highlighting; bookmark; note-taking; "flashcards" | Google Docs Integration; learning platform (student and instructions) | PC; Mac; iPad | Paid Access; demo version by request |
| Cengage YouBook | Highlighting; bookmark; note-taking | Student discussion board; instant messaging. Instructors: embedding videos; changing text passages | PC; Mac; iPad | Paid Acces |
| CourseSmart | Highlighting; bookmark; note-taking | Students: side-by-side zooming. Instructors: edit online | Windows PC; Mac; iPad, iPhone, Kindle Fire; other browser-enabled devices | Paid Access, Free Apps |
| DynamicBooks | Highlighting; bookmark; note-taking | Students: online tests. Instructions: add animation. | Web; PC; Mac; iPad; iPhone | Free delivery services Special order: school textbooks |
| Flat World Knowledge/ MIYO | Mostly directed to instructions: exercises; upload MS Word documents; PDF files and video clips; publish in multiple formats. | | web | Free/CC license (textbooks) |
| Ingram VitalSource Bookshelf® | Highlighting; bookmark; note-taking | Online and offline environments with dedicated download apps for a full range of devices including tablets, smart phones, laptops, and desktops; vPage, Bookshelf. | Web; PC; Mac; iPad; Android | Free (Bookshelf) |
| McGram-Hill Create&Connect | Digital Learning platform: tests, quizzes, videos | | Web | Trial 21 days (Connect); free access registration (create) |
| Pageburst | Highlighting; bookmark; note-taking | Social network interaction | Web; PC; Mac; iPad | Paid Access; Free resources (Evolve) |
| Pearson MyLab | Highlighting; bookmark; note-taking | Text-to-speech; LMS integration | Web; PC; Mac | Access to free and paid textbooks |
| Wikibooks | Collaboratively writing open-content textbooks | | Web | Free/open |
| Xplana eReader | A free social learning platform | | Free mobile apps for the iPone and Android devices | |
| CK-12 | Learning objects with text, video, audio, image, quiz, interactivity | | Open-source content and technology tools for free access to high-quality, customizable educational content in multiple modalities. | |

Traditionally, a digital textbook platform provides a learning environment or is associated with a learning environment. There are two ways: teacher-centered and learner-centered learning environment. Beside the teacher-centered, in the learner-centered learning environment the teacher is a knowledge manager and the student, rather than being passive, apply, analysis, syntheses and evaluate. "For student-centered learning to take place, exemplifying, discovering, researching, and learning based on problem-solving are vital" (Cubukcu, 2012, p. 52). For example, the learner-centered digital learning environment, proposed by Wiley Plus, could features the homework management tool, algorithmic questions, interactive illustrations, guided online tutorial exercises, quizzes etc.

The difficulty, however, often lies in choosing teacher-centered or learner-centered learning environment. This decision is often influenced by specific of domain, curricula requirements etc. In addition, the textbook digital environment could be *real, virtual, blended or flipped.*

1. *The real learning environment* is common for the traditional classroom learning and can be associated also with formal and non-formal education. Using of language, interactive communication and physical learning space are three factors for real learning environments. Teachers' verbal patterns are for persuade students to learn effectively.

2. *The virtual learning environment* is "any digital learning space or environment where learning activities, opportunities, and experiences are designed on appropriate learning theories and techniques, using various attributes of digital technologies in order to create meaningful environments for diverse learners where learning is fostered and supported" (Khan, 2012, p. 2). The virtual learning environment can be *open* (own place, time and pace) or *distributed* (traditional distance learning or blended courses with a fixed schedule). Either open or distributed learning environments can be *static* (one place: a computer classroom) or *mobile* (different places: mobile digital devices).

3. *The blended learning environment* combines face-to-face and online education, which involves leveraging the Internet to afford each student a more personalised learning experience, meaning increased student control over the time, place, path, and/or pace of his or her learning. In such environments can be modelled and implemented different activities. This allow more easy access to classes schedule, digital textbooks' content, quizzes, formative and summative assessments, pedagogical resources, learning tools, processes and/or a social space where students/teachers can communicate with context, student-to-student and student-digital content through interactive discussions, forums of discussion, chat, emails etc.

4. The *flipped learning environment* is "a learning environment in which the activities traditionally completed outside of class as homework is now completed in class during instruction time. And, the activities traditionally completed in class in now completed on students' own time before class.<...> students watch a video or pre-recorded lectures before class. Then, when they arrive to class, they work through assignments or activities with their peers and the instructor"(Honeycutt & Garrett, 2014).

All ways to define the learning environment can be described as a transition from a student-centered learning environment to a learner-centered learning environment Shifting of the energy away from instructor to the learners allow using more effectively the collaborative learning strategies instead of individualised learning strategies. Moreover, in blended and/or flipped learning strategies teachers focus on higher level learning outcomes during class time and lower level outcomes outside of class.

## DIGITAL TEXTBOOK, DIGITAL DEVICES, AND USER INTERFACE DESIGN

Digital textbooks can be delivered or accessed via a number of channels. Common delivery methods are *email* or *download*, either from a repository or e-store. Digital textbooks are viewed using a digital devices or e-reader. Each of the digital textbook platforms have a collection of *windows*, known as user interfaces, which allow synchronic or a synchronic communication in human-human or human-machine modalities. The users are different: teacher, mentor, and student, and administrator, academic and administrative staff. As was noted by Khan (2012, p.3) at the heart of the user interface design is the "user" and the user is in the "driver's seat". The goal of the user interface designer is to make the user's interaction as simple and efficient as possible. This is the process of integration of content with navigational interactive controls used by learners and/or teacher to work with content.

The literature suggests that user interface design fosters a wide range of self-regulated, cognitive, affective or/and psychomotor skills. In addition, as result of widely availability of personal computer (PC) and mobile devices, the user interfaces could be accessed on different displays with different screen resolution. Screen resolution either of PC and mobile digital devices displays different sizes of texts, could be with touch or/ and mouse keyboard and equipped with Wi-Fi, Bluetooth and GPS. In addition, the quality of displays and those functionalities varies considerable. For example, touchscreens in contrast with PC allow users to highlight text and scroll through texts/ graphics with a swipe, finger or stylus. It is recommended to use 15-17 inches screen with excellent contrast ratio. The best contrast ratio is considered to be at least 200:1, especially for primary school students.

Digital textbook devices can provide different user interfaces for different users. So, the user interfaces design relies on environmental, cognitive, hardware, software, educational and psychopedagogical interoperability. The term "interoperability" defines the requirements of making different digital devices to inter-operate. One simple example of interoperability is when student interface interoperate with the smart board interface. Lee et al. (2013, p. 38) observe that using of multi-touch screen improve students' learning experience. Teachers can transmit live lessons and quizzes to students' computers during class, and students can respond on their devices using multi-touch screens.

On the other hand, the interdependencies between digital textbook, digital devices and user interface design should be based on *reliable performance* among designers and users, i.e. the designer and users should have the degree of consistency and communicate when working on learning design problem.

The lack of reliability may lead to inconvenience (Lee, Messom & Yau, 2013, p. 35). This happened when students are not able to access the material, analytics or when content or assessments are displayed with errors. Reliability relies also to rich multimedia textbooks, which require time and hardware space to be downloaded and/or updated and disseminated. One important thing is the quality and the accuracy of content: any digital content can be easily edited and displayed without any grammatical or design errors. The open access digital textbooks based should be edited as follows: one student leads the project, but the final decision should be made by teacher or expert.

Not less important is the students' health. Cognitive, social and environmental ergonomics directly influenced to this. In addition, as was noted by Lee et al. (2013, p. 36), the digital textbook content need to be *readable* (the easy than the text can be read or understood), because reading is ~ 25% - 40% slower from a screen compared to on printed page. However, students interact with a variety of digital texts. Planning activities with digital texts involves the flexible use of the different sources, including linguistic with graphic information, animation and 3D representations. Reading of digital text starts with searching and identification of individual words meaning from the digital dictionaries.

User interfaces of digital textbook offer diverse ways to access to content. The first way is *multimodal texts*. However, these texts are harder to proceed than linear texts. "To comprehend some of these texts, readers use visual literacy, which is the process of decoding texts and determining how pictures and images aid to comprehension- a continuum of reading proficiencies that move from literal to inferential/interpretation of texts" (Lawrence, 2014, p. 27). The second way is *interactive content*. In this case readers interact with the text through inserting, deleting, or replacing texts; marking passages by highlighting, underlining, or crossing out words; adding comments by inserting notes, attaching files, or recording audio comments; and manipulating the page format, text size, and screen layout.

## TOWARD THE SOLUTION FOR A COMMON DIGITAL TEXTBOOKS' CONTENT

The content of the digital textbooks is the *digital text* accessed via user interface. According to CAST (2014), digital text separates the content from the display. When content is in digital form, we can use a display device such as a computer to view it. The same content can be shown in myriad ways. With digital text we can go beyond changing font, size, and color and actually output it to a tactile display. With digital text we can go beyond the visual and tactile to an auditory display. The text can be read aloud on demand. Even more powerful is the ability to tag digital text (tags reflect the structure of the document). There are semantic or structural tags. Using different tags can be specified different ways to display parts like headers and sidebars or to specify how those elements will be displayed.

By using tagging, the learning strategies can become part of a text. There are two main formats:

- Page fidelity (or print fidelity) to the original textbook display;
- Reflowable e-textbooks.

The page/print fidelity represents the scanned pictures of the print version of the textbook. These digitalized products maintain the layout version of the paper version, mainly in. pdf or .EPUB formats. Readers access *the single page view* or *two pages view* of text. These products look like printed textbooks, having the table of contents and requires minor changes in teaching. The limitations of page fidelity products, however, allow educators and learners to switch to digital more attractive textbooks.

The *reflowable e-textbooks* format uses a flexible format system with a dynamic media and modified layouts and interactive features. Reflowable digital textbooks maintain all the content from the print textbooks, but often strip away or dynamically deal with components of page layout. They are constructed from XML source, and may have include some fluid line and page breaks. The fluid lines of text cause readers to encounter different screen sizes. A reflowable e-textbook allows users to adjust font sizes and adjust windows to their linking without causing the entire page to resize. In many cases users can designate their own preferred background colors for pages, figures, or box features. These products also allow content creators to link or embed multimedia objects directly inline in the text, thereby presenting them within the context of the given chapter of the study.

Digital textbooks with fidelity to the print textbook are most effective in environments where print and digital co-exist. As was written on CourseSmart site, the page fidelity textbooks include faithfulness to page numbers and page to page layout. Users can access both the print fidelity page images as well as a text representation accessible to screen readers and text-to-speech software. Students with disabilities have the following options: *a continuous reading mode*, which facilitates page access via scrolling instead of clicking; screen–reader access without contacting support; text–to–speech compatibility; accessible notes/ bookmarks and an outline mode to help review important topics.

There are two main initiatives in learning design of the digital textbooks: *eTextbook* and *Open Source Textbook*. eTextbooks use ICT as a medium through which digital content is developed by author(s) that follows some requirements and may easy up-dated, deposited in a digital library; purchased; rented for cost or/and compared for free or/and accessed online and delivered to be used in a distributed learning environment. The Open Source Textbooks can be read either online or in hard copy format without restrictions on copying or printing and may be edited or/and evaluated individually, in group or collaboratively and/or shared for free reading on the Internet.

Are there common elements for content of an eTextbooks and Open Source Textbooks? In order to answer this question, it is important to note that some authors/publishers try to simplify the solution of digital content and provide one general solution: the post-modernism architecture. However, according to the postmodernism approach the reality cannot be known nor described objectively; hermeneutics is only the interpretation of text from the reader's point of view and the language is only the social construct and nor the individual

characteristic of the learner. In such interpretation, critical thinking toward the solution for digital textbook content must be reflective rather than determinative. The judgment must be focused not to reproduce knowledge, but to generate new knowledge. Postmodern Hermeneutics, as the science of multimodal textual interpretation, sees the heterogeneity and diversity of the world. In Fisher's terminology this is the process of making an old text relevant to a new situation. This means that digital content can be deconstructed in visible signs, such as text, graphics, animation, etc. and visible marks for signs: speech, language, creativity, imagination, representation etc. However, decomposition of digital content in modules, sections, sub-sections, paragraphs, themes, page, sessions, frameworks etc. represents only one face of the coin. In any cases chapters contain the major component of a digital textbook. But, how should be designed the digital textbooks content? If the text is multimodal, each of the sections integrate the *elementary units for learning*. These units should include instructional and assessment activities. Research has shown (Hurwitz & Day, 2007, p. 358) that the study unit should be organized based on a) *thematic approach* or on b) *topical appro*ach. The first way allow choosing an overarching or unifying idea revealing many aspects of related concepts, events, or situations. A theme is much broader than a topic. A topical approach is a way of organizing information regarding particular subject matter. Sub-sections usually cover a concept or procedure to be learned.

## PAGE-FIDELITY AND REFLOWABLE VERSUS OPEN SOURCE TEXTBOOKS

Page-fidelity and reflowable digital textbooks are developed by many companies around the world (see *Table 3*). This trend follows the first generation of digital textbooks. The more actual is open source textbook with digital page allowing a personal construction of the multimodal text from blocs of information. The open source textbook may include a learning tool aims to provide immediate feedback and assure the adaptivity of content to students' learning style, skills, preference and level of knowledge.

Open Source Textbooks have evolved over the recent years. It was found (Wiley, Bliss & McEwen, 2014) that open textbooks have seen adoption at several levels of formal education. For example, the California Open Source Textbook Project early aims were leveraging free, already existing and widely available K-12 educational content in the public domain; better leveraging the substantial curriculum-based intellectual capital of the best K-12 and college teachers and deploying Open licenses to secure new and dominant K-12 and college textbook content that would not otherwise be made available. The main results of the implementation Open textbook in California are based on idea that Open textbooks authored to well-established K-12 State curriculum framework standards can:

1. Significantly reduce the cost of line item for K-12 printed textbooks;
2. Significantly increase the quality and range of content afforded to K-12 textbooks;
3. Put a permanent end to K-12 textbook shortages;
4. Make possible a fully portable content holdings database that scales with the introduction of new learning and classroom technologies;
5. The creation of high quality, peer-reviewed content;
6. Well-designed support standards;
7. Universal accessibility, no matter one's physical challenges;
8. Sustainable outcomes are necessary to maintain success over time.

In addition, typographical errors, minor omissions, errors, or deletions, can be quickly corrected, within hours or day; "just in time" continuous updated; can be downloaded quickly and effortlessly; can expand tools for learning and teaching that

*Table 3. eTextbooks' structure*

| Name of the Digital Textbook | | Front Matter | Table of Contents | Structure of the Chapter/Parts | Back Matter |
|---|---|---|---|---|---|
| **INFORMATICS** | Richard, M. R. (2012). Networking Fundamentals | Textbook's title, including the author's name The copyright information Preface Acknowledgments | Chapters | 1. Instructional activity<br>  1.1. Instructional objectives<br>  1.2. Key words and terms<br>  1.3. Content (text, photos, figures, tables etc.)<br>  1.4. Summary<br>  1.5. Questions<br>  1.6. Discussion Questions<br>  1.7. Interesting Web Sites for more information<br>2. Laboratory activity<br>  2.1. Instructional objectives<br>  2.2. Content: experiment, materials, procedure<br>  2.3. Questions | Appendix Glossary References Index of terms |
| | Jeffrey S. Beasley & Piyasat Nilkaew (2013). Networking Essential. | Textbook's title, including the author's name The copyright information Introduction About the author Acknowledgments | Chapters | Chapter objectives Key terms Clearly specific outline goals Content (text, illustration, photos, tables) Key terms and definitions Open-ended critical questions | Glossary of key terms Index |

*continued on following page*

*Table 3. Continued*

| Name of the Digital Textbook | Front Matter | Table of Contents | Structure of the Chapter/Parts | Back Matter |
|---|---|---|---|---|
| **CHEMISTRY** | Chemistry. (2013). Chang, Raymond & Goldsby, Kenneth. McGraw-Hill Higher Education | Textbook's title, including the author's name<br>The copyright information<br>About the author<br>Contents in brief<br>List of applications<br>List of animations<br>Preface, including description of study aids and acknowledgments | Chapters | Chapter outline<br>A Look Ahead<br>Paragraphs with<br>   1. Multimodal text (text, figures, tables)<br>   2. Review of Concepts<br>   3. "Chemistry in Action" boxes<br>   4. Examples<br>   5. Key equations<br>   6. Summary of Facts & Concepts<br>   7. Examples<br>   8. Connections to the interactive learning platform<br>   9. Questions that is dynamically change both in the level of difficulty and in content<br>   10. A note to the student | Questions & Problems<br>Summary of facts & concepts<br>Appendix<br>Chemical Mastery<br>Include eResources |
| | Burdge, Julia (2014). Chemistry. McGraw-Hill Higher Education | Textbook's title, including:<br>-the author's name<br>-the copyright information<br>-about the author<br>Brief contents<br>Preface<br>To the student<br>To the instructor, including computerizing Test Bank and Instructor's solution manual<br>Acknowledgments | Chapters | Chapters are divided into sections, which include<br>   1. Instructional objectives<br>   2. Before you begin, review these skills<br>   3. Student note<br>   4. Chapter Summary<br>   5. Key words<br>   6. Key equations<br>   7. Review questions, conceptual problems, environmental problems<br>   8. Standartized-Exam Practice Problems<br>   9. Key skills<br>Sections are divided into *themes*<br>Each theme contains:<br>   1. Title<br>   2. Figures<br>   3. Tables<br>   4. FAQ (Frequently Asked Questions)<br>   5. Animation<br>   6. Sample problem with ABC practice: Attempt, Build, Conceptualize<br>   7. Bringing chemistry to life<br>   8. Checkpoint<br>In addition, it may be included *external information* from student notes into flow of text<br>Stumbling blocks: timely warnings about common errors, reminder of important information from previous chapters, other general information. | Appendixes<br>Glossary<br>Answers to Odd-Numbered Problems |

*continued on following page*

*Table 3. Continued*

| Name of the Digital Textbook | Front Matter | Table of Contents | Structure of the Chapter/Parts | Back Matter |
|---|---|---|---|---|
| **BIOLOGY** Solomon Martin & Martin Berg (2015). Cengage Learning. | Textbook's title, including the author name The copyright information Dedication About the authors Brief content | Preface To the student Parts | Each part includes: 1. Multimodal text 2. Key Concepts Each parts are divided into sections Each section includes: 3. Learning objectives 4. Multimodal text (text+figures+tables etc.) 5. Checkpoint The section may include: 1. Key experiment | Appendixes Glossary Index |
| **MATH** Anton, Howard; Bivens, Irl C.; Davis, Stephen (2012). Calculus. John Wiley & Sons | Textbook's title, including the author name The copyright information About the authors Dedication Preface Formulas For the student Acknowledgments | Chapters | Each chapter provides: 1. an overview of what chapter is about 2. Sections (text, graphics, definition box, examples, exercises targeted with an special designed icons, technology mastery, remarks, pictures and biographical sketches, notes in the margins etc.) 3. Set of exercise in chapter, divided into: a. Quick Check b. Focus on Concepts c. True/false d. Writing 4. chapter end exercises a. Chapter Review Exercises b. Making Connections 5. Quick check exercises 6. Technology exercises 7. Chapter appendixes | Appendices Web appendices The roots of calculus The answers of odd-numbering exercise (The Student solution Supplements) |

integrate curriculum foundations, video lectures, digital images, figures and illustrations, procedural videos, interactive learning; chat rooms etc.

Assembling the structure of the digital textbooks some issues can be detected. As was noted by Tintinalli (2014, p. 74) the open source challenges as traditional e-textbooks are: validity of information; accuracy and precision; stability of information; searchability; consistency of content; and the risk of piracy. At this time, open-source content tends to be more personal than traditional textbooks, and it is not clear if there are models for modulating and balancing options. The common elements of Open Source Textbooks are presented in Table 4.

# FUTURE RESEARCH DIRECTIONS

The hierarchy and description of eTextbooks and Open Source Content Textbooks introduced in this chapter provides a guide to future research on functionality the digital content. Typically, digital textbooks functionality represents an aggregate of text and instruction mechanisms, after which research on the psychopedagogical domain will gradually move to deeper levels of quantum psychology. For example, the textbook as a pedagogical resource was initially studied at the cybernetic pedagogy node; in recent years, most research on this domain has focused on learning design mechanism design; and most recently,

*Table 4. Open source textbooks' structure*

| Name of the Digital Textbook | Table of Contents | Structure of Chapter | At the End of Chapter |
|---|---|---|---|
| Internet and the World Wide Web | Content<br>Preface<br>Chapters<br>CD with extra chapters<br>Appendixes<br>Bibliography<br>Index | Objects<br>outline (min table of content),<br>sections | Summary, terminology, self-review exercises (with/without answer), exercises. |
| New Perspectives XML Comprehensive 2end Edition | Preface, brief table of content, long table of content<br>Parts are divides into:<br>Level 1<br>Level 2 | Introduction to Level I/II<br>Tutorials<br>Chapters (called tutorials)<br>Sessions<br>Objectives<br>Appendices<br>Glossary<br>Index | Student data file<br>Case problem<br>a special reviewer/ exercising section |
| FlexBooks | Level "I am a teacher"<br>Level "I am a student"<br>(available after user is signed)<br>Table of content<br>1. Introduction<br>2. Chapter outline<br>3. Chapter summary | Read<br>Resources<br>Details<br>Reviews | Allow to create own custom online textbook that can be shared with class and other teachers through:<br>• Create a class<br>• Pick a subject or concept<br>• Practice<br>• Track progress |
| Khan Academy textbooks | 4 categories:<br>1. Devices to students<br>2. A few devices<br>3. Computer Lab<br>4. No Technology Access | Unit-driven approach<br>Gap-driven approach<br>Student-driven approach<br>Sign up new students | Personalised learning experience<br>Khan Academy Reports |

digital learning mechanism design (known as MetaSystems Learning Design) has started to be applied to these settings.

In contrast, domains that have only recently started receiving serious attention, such as neuro-psychology, quantum psychology and knowledge management, are still being studied exclusively at the level of processes outcome optimization. Hence, directions for future research include analysing new domains in the digital learning with textbooks. Additionally, in the context of functionality the mechanism of deeper learning with textbooks, it is not yet completely clear how mechanisms should be designed and evaluated. Thus, future research will also involve developing a general theory for learning design with digital textbooks.

Much research also remains to be done on topics orthogonal to the digital textbook structure. The structure of digital textbook mainly depends on how the textbook is traditionally used in the learning environment: as a pedagogical resource or/with as a learning tool. It is possible, of course, to recognize that different behavioral patterns could emerge when digital learning occur. However, there is no reason to assume that modern digital learning with textbooks would not appear, since the digital learning tools that underpin a new conceptual structure is not designed yet. As far the idea of digital textbooks are chosen by the technic personal, and not by the specialists in digital learning design, will be used and developed static textbooks like print textbooks with some innovation or improvements like virtual laboratories or simulators.

Teachers need to help students understand how to use learning tools to develop own critical thinking, problem solving and decision making skills. Although more research is needed to identify the benefits of available technologies such as networking and discrete optimisation of knowledge, firstly it is important to be explored the psychopedagogical functions of digital textbooks. The methodology of investigation should be based on postmodernism philosophy of conceptual modelling. Out future work will also seek to identify key issues within digital environments and monitor students' behavior to predict affordances of new digital textbooks. The combination of macro-, and micro-level analysis would enable police makers to identify which issues to pay more attention to in order to maintain a sustainable development of both learning communities and digital learning environments.

The emergence and rapid evolution of certain methodologies of digital textbook could be dependent on the fall of printed textbooks. Such possible correlations need future investigation of multimodal text and can support prediction of digital social community behavior and digital social community energy. On one hand, the positive users' behavior could influence learning and sustainable development of real-world communities. On the other hand, negative users' behavior badly influence the learning quality. Future research is needed in aria of digital social developed behaviors in real and virtual learning environments.

Many studies have shown that certain features (e, g. time spend for learning, learning environment, networking) influence the quality of learning. Some of these findings differ from one author to another. The mix and speed of learning design ideas is still unknown, and it is likely to be dependent on the physiological, psychological and pedagogical (learning styles) characteristics of the learners, those aim and used technology.

Digital textbook structure can influence the quality of learning. Future research is needed to investigate the correlation between physics and psychic, including quantum features of learners.

Research has shown (Janzen, Perry & Edwards, 2011) that quantum perspectives of Learning to Instructional Design eventing is connected. Connection, entanglement, and constant communication configure the basis of the quantum perspective of learning. Future, having the option to understand quantum learning on educational outcomes involve teacher(s) and students to construct own meaning through exploration of learning tools, embedded in digital textbook' structures. Out future work will explore methods to include quantum perspectives of learning in digital textbooks use and development on the base on seven research questions:

- How does learning occurs in Digital Age?
- Which factors influence learning with digital textbooks?
- What is the role of memory in digital learning?
- How does transfer of knowledge occur?
- What types of learning are best explained?
- What is the relevance to Learning Design?
- How should instruction be structured to facilitate learning?

The physical and quantum perspectives of learning rely on psychopedagogical functions of digital textbooks; human potential for learning (actions and behavioral patterns) and the didactic model for digital textbook use and development.

## CONCLUSION

In this chapter we have presented an approach to label the digital textbooks, developed as a pedagogical resource and as/with learning tool with theirs structure based on the common features they exhibit. We presented two appendixes related to eTextbook and Open Source Textbook structures in order to capture the possible common structure. There is currently no and cannot be any standards of digital textbooks structures. However, there are some common features: digital platform, digital device, and digital content and multimodal text.

The key contribution of this chapter to textbook theory is the analysis of digital textbook structures developed over the last decade. It was found that a digital textbooks structure mainly depend on issues that exist in education systems. Digital textbooks should be used and developed for different tasks, ages and socio-economic-ergonomic needs, including students with disabilities. "Students should not use textbooks that marginalize them through text, pictures or graphics. The language of the text should be age-appropriate and writing at the age – appropriate reading level. Special designed digital textbooks are useful for students with different disabilities. For example, students with sensory or motor disabilities or low cognitive abilities reading a printed textbook may seem impossible. For them, digital text is more accessible and comprehensive" (Bruhn & Hasselbring (2013, p. 3).

Technological design of the digital textbooks' structure depends on trends, learning theories, models and criteria. It can be used *2D barcodes* – an optical representation of data relating to the object to which it is attached (Uluyol & Agca, 2012; Ozdemir, 2010; Ozcelik & Acarturk, 2011; Weedon, Miller, Franco, Moorhead & Pearce, 2014; Harboe, 2013; Metcalf & Rogers, 2010; Sahu & Gonnade, 2013). 2D barcode technology, integrated into textbooks, has the potential to reduce certain types of cognitive loads, provide an easy way to access multimedia content such as audio, animation, pictures, and videos in order to support learning from textbooks. By scanning a printed barcode from a camera-equipped mobile phone, a learner can quickly access any content via the Internet. From the authors' point of view, "supporting a printed textbook with camera-equipped mobile devices and 2D barcodes linked to supplemental information, including narration to depict visuals: pictures, graphics and animations, may increase the effectiveness of learning" (Uluyol & Agca, 2012, p. 1198).

## REFERENCES

Armen, H., & Atwood, L. (2013). Creating Social Books. In *Interactive eBooks for Children. IBooC2013: Proceedings of Workshop at IDC Interaction Design and Children*, (pp. 24-28).

Booker, E. (2013). *E-textbook pilot puts college books in cloud*. Retrieved October 25, 2014, from http://www.informationweek.com/mobile/mobile-devices/e-textbook-pilot-puts-college-books-in-cloud/d/d-id/1108942?

Britanica, E. (2014). *Postmodernism and modern philosophy*. Retrieved October 25, 2014, from http://www.britannica.com/EBchecked/topic/1077292/postmodernism

California Open Source Textbook Project. (2012). Retrieved October, 25, 2014, from http://www.opensourcetext.org/

Casassus, B. (2014). French schools report sharp rise in digital textbook use. *The Bookseller*. Retrieved November 1, 2014, from http://www.thebookseller.com/news/french-schools-report-sharp-rise-digital-textbook-use

CAST. (2014). *Digital text in the classroom*. Retrieved November, 1, 2014, from http://www.cast.org/teachingeverystudent/ideas/presentations/digitaltext_slide2.cfm

Cornelissen, F., Daly, A. J., Liou, Y. H., van Swet, J., Beijaard, D., & Bergen, T. C. (2014). More than a master: Developing, sharing, and using knowledge in school–university research networks. *Cambridge Journal of Education*, *44*(1), 35–57. doi:10.1080/0305764X.2013.855170

Cubukcu, Z. (2012). Teachers' evaluation of student-centered learning environments. *Education, 133*(1), 49–66.

Cull, B. W. (2011). *Reading revolution: Online digital text and implications for reading in academe*. Retrieved October 25, 2014, from http://firstmonday.org/ojs/index.php/fm/article/view/3340/2985#author

Delors, J. (1996). *Learning: the treasure within* (Report to UNESCO of the International Commission of Education for the Twenty-first Century). UNESCO Publishing. Retrieved October 25, 2014, from http://www.unesco.org/education/pdf/15_62.pdf

Eppelin, A., & Bottcher, R. (2011). Development of a publishing framework for living open access textbooks. *Information Services & Use, 31*(3/4), 243–248.

Fernandes, L. *Digital textbooks platforms: trends and technologies*, 3191-3210. Retrieved October 25, 2014, from http://ticeduca.ie.ul.pt/atas/pdf/196.pdf

Foster, G. (2014). *The Promise of digital badges*. Retrieved October 25, 2014, from http://noctinot.com/pdf/news/techniques/Nov%202013%20%20The%20Promise%20of%20Digital%20Badges.pdf

Ghani, K. A., Noh, A. S., & Yusoff, N. (2014). Linguistic features for development of Arabic Text readability formula in Malaysia: A preliminary study. *Middle-East Journal of Scientific Research, 19*(3), 319–331.

Gore, M. C. (2010). *Promoting students' learning from the textbook. Inclusion strategies for secondary classrooms: Keys for struggling learners*. Thousand Oaks, CA: Corwin Press. doi:10.4135/9781483350424

Hallam, G. C. (2012). *Briefing paper on eTextbooks and third party eLearning products and their implications for Australian university libraries*. Retrieved October, 25, 2014, from http://eprints.qut.edu.au/55244/3/55244P.pdf

Hannafin, M. J., Hill, J. R., Land, S. M., & Lee, E. (2014). Student-centered, open learning environments: Research, theory, and practice. In J. M. Spector, M. D. Merrill, J. Elen, & M. J. Bishop. (Eds.). Handbook of research on educational communications and technology (pp. 641-651). New York: Springer.

Harvey, D. (2011). Analytical Chemistry 2.0: An open-access digital textbook. *Analytical and Bioanalytical Chemistry, 399*(1), 149–152. doi:10.1007/s00216-010-4316-1 PMID:21046084

Honeycutt, B., & Garrett, G. (2014). *Expanding the definition of a flipped learning environment*. Retrieved October 25, 2014, from http://www.facultyfocus.com/articles/instructional-design/expanding-definition-flipped-learning-environment/#sthash.zVNFRPQ0.dpuf

Hong, J. H., Kim, M., & Yoo, K. H. (2013). Development of a 3D digital textbook using X3D, ubiquitous information technologies and applications. *Lecture Notes in Electrical Engineering, 214*, 341–351. doi:10.1007/978-94-007-5857-5_37

Hyman, J. A., Moser, M. T., & Segala, L. N. (2014). Electronic reading and digital library technologies: Understanding learner expectation and usage intent for mobile learning. *Educational Technology Research and Development, 62*(1), 35–52. doi:10.1007/s11423-013-9330-5

*Introduction to postmodern philosophy*. (2014). Retrieved October 25, 2014, from http://www.postmodernpreaching.net/postmodern-philosophy.html

Jang, S. (2014). Study on service models of digital textbooks in cloud computing environment for smart education. *International Journal of U-& E-Service, Science & Technology, 7*(1), 73–82.

Janzen, K. J., Perry, B., & Edwards, M. (2011). *Aligning the quantum perspective of learning to instructional design: Exploring the seven definitive questions.* Retrieved October, 25, 2014, from http://www.irrodl.org/index.php/irrodl/article/view/1038/2024

Joo, H. M., & Ahn, C. U. (2013). A study on the development of evaluation criteria for digital textbooks in Korea. In J. Herrington et al. (Eds.), *Proceedings of World Conference on Educational Multimedia, Hypermedia and Telecommunications 2013* (pp. 86-89). Chesapeake, VA: AACE. Retrieved October, 25, 2014, from http://www.editlib.org/p/111935

Joo, K. H., Park, N. H., & Choi, J. T. (2014). An adaptive teaching and learning system for efficient ubiquitous learning. In Y.-S. Jeong, Y.-H. Park, C.-H. Hsu, J. J. Park (Eds.), Ubiquitous information technologies and applications (pp. 659-666). Springer Berlin Heidelberg. doi:10.1007/978-3-642-41671-2_84

Khan, B. (2012). Virtual learning environments: Design factors and issues. In B. Khan (Ed.), *User interface design for virtual environments: Challenges and advances* (pp. 1–15). Hershey, PA: Information Science Reference. doi:10.4018/978-1-61350-516-8.ch001

Kim, J., & Park, N. (2014). The analysis of case result and satisfaction of digital textbooks for elementary school students. *Advanced in Computer Science and its Applications (Lecture Notes in Electrical Engineering), 279,* 417–422. doi:10.1007/978-3-642-41674-3_59

Knight, D. (2014). *A textbook digital opportunity: Berlin commits to Open Education Resources (OER).* Retrieved October, 25, 2014, from http://news.siliconallee.com/2014/05/15/a-textbook-digital-opportunity-berlin-pursues-open-education-resources-oer/

Lawrence, S. A. (2014). Exploring the use of technology, multimodal texts, and digital tools in K-12 classrooms. In S. Lawrence (Ed.), *Critical practice in P-12 education: Transformative teaching and learning* (pp. 24–48). Hershey, PA: Information Science Reference. doi:10.4018/978-1-4666-5059-6.ch002

LEARN NC. (2014). *Educator's guides: North Carolina digital history. What's in a digital textbook?* Retrieved October, 25, 2014, from http://www.learnnc.org/lp/editions/nchist-eg/6628

Lee, H. J., Messom, C., & Yau, K.-L. A. (2013). Can an electronic textbook be part of K-12 education? Challenges, technological solutions and open issues. *The Turkish Online Journal of Educational Technology, 12*(1), 32–44.

Liang, T. H., & Huang, Y. M. (2014). an investigation of reading rate patterns and retrieval outcomes of elementary school students with e-books. *Journal of Educational Technology & Society, 17*(1), 218–230.

Lysenko, L. V., & Abrami, P. C. (2014). Promoting reading comprehension with the use of technology. *Computers & Education.* Retrieved October, 25, 2014, from http://www.sciencedirect.com/science/article/pii/S0360131514000207

Meshin, K., & Knoff, N. A. (2013). *A digital learning experience in tertiary design education.* Paper presented at The Teacher Academy Conference of the European League of the Institutions of Art (EUA). Retrieved October, 25, 2014, from arrow.dit.ie/aaschadocon/8/

Midoro, V. A. (2005). *A common european framework for teachers' professional profile in ICT for education*. Ortona, Italy: Edizioni MENABO DIDACTICA.

*Open Stax College*. (2014). Retrieved October 25, 2014, from https://openstaxcollege.org/books

Paxhia, S. (2011). The challenges of higher education digital publishing. *Publishing Research Quarterly*, *27*(4), 321-326.

Petty, R. E., & Brinol, P. (2014). Emotion and persuasion: Cognitive and meta-cognitive processes impact attitudes. *Cognition and Emotion*. PMID:25302943

Rivero, V. (2013). Digital textbooks: Show me the future! *Internet@Schools*, *20*(3), 12-16.

Rudic, G. (2013). Modern pedagogy in multi-measured space. In Europe Business Assemble (Ed.), Socrates Almanac "Science and Education", (pp. 74-75). Oxford: Oxford Review

Sha, L., Looi, C. K., Chen, W., & Zhang, B. H. (2012). Understanding mobile learning from the perspective of self-regulated learning. *Journal of Computer Assisted Learning*, *28*(4), 366–378. doi:10.1111/j.1365-2729.2011.00461.x

Smart, C. (2013). *Compare eTextbook*. Retrieved October, 25, 2014, from http://instructors.coursesmart.com/Compare?xmlid=9781605253565&__frompdp=1

Song, J. S., Kim, S. J., Byun, G. S., Song, J. H., & Lee, B. G. (2014). Comparing wireless networks for applying digital textbook. *Telecommunication Systems*, *55*(1), 25–38. doi:10.1007/s11235-013-9748-4

Taylor, T. (2014). *Principles of microeconomics*. Retrieved October, 28, 2014, from https://openstaxcollege.org/textbooks/principles-of-microeconomics

Tintinalli, J. E. (2014). Real textbooks or e-books: What is happening right now? *Emergency Medicine Australasia*, *26*(1), 72–75. doi:10.1111/1742-6723.12189 PMID:24495066

Tosun, N. (2014). A study on reading printed books or e-books: Reasons for student-teachers preferences. *The Turkish Online Journal of Educational Technology*, *13*(1), 21–28.

## ADDITIONAL READING

Brusilovsky, P., & Peylo, C. (2003). Adaptive and intelligent web-based educational systems. *International Journal of Artificial Intelligence in Education*, *13*(2-4), 156–172.

Brusilovsky, P., Schwarz, E., & Weber, G. (1997). Electronic textbooks on www: From static hypertext to interactivity and adaptivity. In B. H. Khan (Ed.), Web-based instruction (pp. 255-268). Englewood Cliffs, NJ: Educational Technology Publications.

Chesser, W. D. (2011). The e-textbook revolution. *Library Technology Reports*, *47*(8), 28–40.

Cordon-Garcia, J. A., Gomez-Diaz, R., Alonso-Arevalo, J., & Kaplan, N. (2014). Digital reading: Educational gaps and documentary preservation. *Information Resources Management Journal*, *27*(3), 1–11. doi:10.4018/irmj.2014070101

Davidson, A., & Carliner, S. (2014). E-books for educational uses. In: J. M. Spector, M. D. Merrill, J. Elen, & M. B. Bishop (Eds.). Handbook of research on educational communications and technology (pp. 713-722). Springer.

Dwivedi, P., & Bharadwaj, K. K. (2013). Effective trust-aware e-learning recommender system based on learning styles and knowledge levels. *Journal of Educational Technology & Society*, *16*(4), 201–216.

Hung, P. H., Hwang, G. J., Lin, Y. F., Wu, T. H., & Su, I. H. (2013). seamless connection between learning and assessment- applying progressive learning tasks in mobile ecology inquiry. *Journal of Educational Technology & Society*, *16*(1), 194–205.

Hussin, S., Manap, M. R., Amir, Z., & Krish, P. (2012). Mobile learning readiness among Malaysian students at Higher Learning Institutes. *Asian Social Science.*, *8*(12), 276–283. doi:10.5539/ass.v8n12p276

Hyman, J. A., Moser, M. T., & Segala, L. N. (2014). Electronic reading and digital library technologies: Understanding learner expectation and usage intent for mobile learning. *Educational Technology Research and Development*, *62*(1), 35–52. doi:10.1007/s11423-013-9330-5

iBooks Author. (2014). *Create and publish amazing books for iPad and Mac*. Retrieved October, 25, 2014, from http://www.apple.com/ibooks-author/

Jeng, Y. L., Wu, T. T., Huang, Y. M., Tan, Q., & Yang, S. (2010). The Add-on Impact of Mobile Applications in Learning Strategies: A Review Study. *Journal of Educational Technology & Society*, *13*(3), 3–11.

Kim, S. W., & Lee, M. G. (2012). Utilization of digital textbooks in Korea. In T.-T. Gon, B.-C. Seet, & P.-C. Su (Eds.). E-books & e-readers for e-learning (pp. 90-125). Orauariki: Victoria Business School.

Krecetnicov, K. (2002). Design of information technology tools of training [in Russian]. *Journal of Educational Technology & Society*, *5*(1), 222–243.

Larson, L. C. (2009). e-Reading and e-Responding: New tools for the next generation of readers. *Journal of Adolescent & Adult Literacy*, *53*(3), 255–258. doi:10.1598/JAAL.53.3.7

Larson, L. C. (2010). *Digital readers: The next chapter in e-book reading and response*. Retrieved February, 5, 2015, from http://citeseerx.ist.psu.edu/viewdoc/download?doi=10.1.1.363.4103&rep=rep1&type=pdf

Lim, C., Song, H. D., & Lee, Y. (2012). Improving usability of the user interface for digital textbook platform for elementary-school students. *Educational Technology Research and Development*, *60*(1), 159–173. doi:10.1007/s11423-011-9222-5

Mardis, M., & Everhart, N. (2013). From paper to pixel: The promise and challenges of digital textbooks for K-12 schools. *Educational Media and Technology Yearbook.*, *37*, 93–118. doi:10.1007/978-1-4614-4430-5_9

McCusker, S. (2014). *MacBook, Chromebook, iPads: Why schools should think beyond platforms*. Retrieved October, 25, 2014, from http://blogs.kqed.org/mindshift/2014/01/macbook-chromebook-ipads-moving-beyond-platforms/

Ozcelik, E., & Acarturk, C. (2011). Reducing the spatial distance between printed and online information sources by means of mobile technology enhances learning: Using 2D barcodes. *Computers & Education*, *57*(3), 2077–2085. doi:10.1016/j.compedu.2011.05.019

Özdemir, S. (2010). Supporting printed books with multimedia: A new way to use mobile technology for learning. *British Journal of Educational Technology*, *41*(6), 135–E138. doi:10.1111/j.1467-8535.2010.01071.x

Patel, H., & Morreale, P. (2014). Education and learning: Electronic books or traditional printed books? *Journal of Computing Sciences in Colleges*, *29*(3), 21–28.

Plus, W. (2014). Your online teaching and learning solution. Retrieved October 25, 2014, from https://www.wileyplus.com/WileyCDA/

Pon-Barry, H., Clark, B., Schultz, K., Bratt, E., Peters, S., & Haley, D. (2005). Contextualizing Reflective Dialogue in a Spoken Conversational Tutor. *Journal of Educational Technology & Society*, *8*(4), 42–51.

Porter, P. L. (2010). *Effectiveness of electronic textbooks with embedded activities on student learning*. Unpublished Ph.D. dissertation, Minnesota: Capella University.

Robbins, D. (2004). Interactive textbook. In A. Distefano, K. Rudestam, & R. Silverman (Eds.), *Encyclopedia of distributed learning* (pp. 256–258). Thousand Oaks, CA: SAGE Publications, Inc. doi:10.4135/9781412950596.n88

Sahu, S. K., & Gonnade, S. K. (2013). QR Code and Application in India. *International Journal of Recent Technology and Engineering*, *2*, 26–28.

Selemenev, S. V. (2012). What should be an electronic textbook? [in Russian]. *Computer Science Education*, *1*, 40–44.

Sengodan, V., & Iksan, Z. H. (2012). Students' Learning Styles and Intrinsic Motivation in Learning Mathematics. *Asian Social Science.*, *8*(16), 17–23. doi:10.5539/ass.v8n16p17

Simon, K. S., Cheung, K. S., Yuen, K. C., Li, E., Tsang, Y. M., & Wong, A. (2012). Open access textbooks: Opportunities and challenges. Engaging learners through emerging technologies. *Communications in Computer and Information Science*, *302*, 201–210.

Uluyol, C., & Agca, R. K. (2012). Integrating mobile multimedia into textbooks: 2D barcodes. *Computers & Education*, *59*(4), 1192–1198. doi:10.1016/j.compedu.2012.05.018

UNESCO. (2002). *ICTs and teacher education: global context and framework*. Retrieved October 25, 2014, from http://www.unescobkk.org/fileadmin/user_upload/ict/e-books/ICT_Teacher_Education/Teacher_Ed-_ChapterI.pdf

Verhoeven, L., & Perfetti, C. (2008). Advances in text comprehension: Model, process and development. *Applied Cognitive Psychology*, *22*(3), 293–300. doi:10.1002/acp.1417

Walters, G., Walters, G., & Dede, C. (2009). *Digital Teaching Platforms: A research review*. Retrieved October 25, 2014, from http://www.timetoknow.com/Data/Uploads/Digital%20Teaching%20Platform_1.pdf

Williams, J. (2012). Identity, school textbooks, and rebuilding memory. In J. Banks (Ed.), *Encyclopedia of Diversity in Education* (pp. 1119–1123). Thousand Oaks, CA: SAGE Publications, Inc. doi:10.4135/9781452218533.n352

Wook, S., Michaels, S., & Waterman, D. (2014). Print vs. electronic readings in college courses: Cost-efficiency and perceived learning. *The Internet and Higher Education*, *21*, 17–24. doi:10.1016/j.iheduc.2013.10.004

Yang, T. C., Hwang, G. J., & Yang, S. J. H. (2013). Development of an adaptive learning system with multiple perspectives based on students' learning styles and cognitive styles. *Journal of Educational Technology & Society*, *16*(4), 185–200.

## KEY TERMS AND DEFINITIONS

**Digital Library:** A collection of electronic materials with technical and user services, that is created, managed and organized for (and sometimes by) one or more user communities.

**E-Book Reader:** The device for reading in electronic/digital format or a device that can recognise the file format in which book was produced.

**Electronic Reading:** Reading in a new medium through using devices that create an electronic reading environment with computer-based test and multimedia supports.

**eReader:** An electronic personal display that is used for reading electronic books (eBooks), electronic magazines and other digital content.

**Learning Device:** Any mobile gadgets, like cell phones, tablets, and smartphones, which can actively engage students in student-centered learning environment.

**Open Network Learning Environments:** Digital environments that empower learners to participate in creative endeavors, conduct social networking, organize/reorganize social contents, and manage social acts by connecting people, resources, and tools by integrating Web 2.0 tools to design environments that are totally transparent, or open to public view; the same architecture can be used to design the degree of openness users feel is necessary to the situation (Tu, Sujo-Montes, Yen, Chan, Blocher, 2012, p. 14).

**Personal Learning Environment (PLE):** An learning environment "that allows learners to control and manage their own learning processes and provides support to set their own learning goals; manage their learning; managing both content & process; and communicate with others in the process of learning and thereby achieve learning goals" (Tu, Sujo-Montes, Yen, Chan, Blocher, 2012, p. 14).

**Ubiquitous Computing:** The new type in the information and communication world associated with a large number of small electronic devices (small computers), which have computation and communication capabilities such as smart mobile phones, smart pad, contactless smart cards, handheld terminals, sensor network nodes, Radio Frequency Identification etc., which are being used in our daily life. (Joo, Park & Choi, 2014, pp. 659-670).

**Ubiquitous Learning (U-Learning):** A new learning paradigm, which describe learning in accordance with a ubiquitous learning environment "which enable everyone to learn at anyplace at any time" (Joo, Park & Choi, 2014, p. 670).

**Usability:** The quality attribute that assesses how easy user interfaces are to use, a multi-dimensional property of a user interface, which include learnability, effectiveness etc.

**Visibility:** The quality of user interface textbooks or learning object to be visible.

# Chapter 5
# Toward More Ubiquitous Digital Textbooks Functions

## ABSTRACT

*In Digital Age the teachers' functions are completed with new attributes and roles. The focus is on adaptation and accommodation of learners in a more sustainable and durable environment and in formation of a new behavior. Some of the responsibilities are delegated to digital textbooks. Digital textbooks go beyond printed textbooks. In addition to traditional teaching and assessment through page and book graphics, it became important to diagnose the learning analytics of didactical process, the quantum state of the learning and that potential. In addition, it is important to plan activities according to meta (social) patterns; to create and co-create relevant activities; to facilitate and manage learning etc. This chapter aims to synthesize digital textbooks' functions. It promotes self-regulated learning in the open learning environment in order to open the way of Open Source Textbooks to satisfy the needs of all, including persons with learning disabilities.*

## INTRODUCTION

In less than five years to teachers' duties was added extra attributes and roles. Thus, modern teachers should know how to design an instructional program, to plan learning activities, identify the appropriate digital resources and learning tools, review the learning activities for competence development, establish work plan priorities etc. Some of responsibilities are delegated to textbooks. Thus, new textbooks have innovative or/ and interaction functions.

1. The innovative functions allow up-dating information, engaging students in activities and networks, providing immediate feedback, and dual-processing of data from multimodal text, highlighting, instant delivery of knowledge, open access to knowledge (Open Source Textbooks), flick photo galleries, rotation of 3D learning objects, tap to pop up sidebars, play video and audio, translating the content etc.

2. The interactive functionalities allow combining textbooks with reference books, work-

DOI: 10.4018/978-1-4666-8300-6.ch005

books, dictionaries and multimedia contents without the constraints of time and space. Learners can create their textbooks, underlining the important parts, taking notes, and combining the contents with high-quality, reliable knowledge that is their own.

The most recent innovation is the *ubiquitous learning environment*; i.e. that learning environment can be accessed in various contexts and situations. Moreover, as was noted by Jones and Jo (2014, p. 469), a *ubiquitous learning environment is any setting in which students can become totally immersed in the learning process*. To define:

- **Ubiquitous:** Pervasive, omnipresent, ever present, everywhere.
- **Learning:** Educational, instructive, didactic, pedagogical.
- **Environment:** Surroundings, setting, situation, atmosphere.

So, *a ubiquitous learning environment (ULE) is a situation or setting of pervasive (or omnipresent) education (or learning)*. Education is happening all around the student but the student may not even be conscious of the learning process. Source data is present in the embedded objects and students do not have to DO anything in order to learn.

Ubiquitous learning with digital textbooks has been defined in many ways. The most frequently quoted definition is: "The key is not the logic or technical specifications of the machines. Rather it is the new ways in which meaning is created, stored, delivered and accessed. This, we believe, will change the educational world in some fundamental ways – and also allow some older but good and disappointingly neglected educational ideas to work at last and work widely. The journey of ubiquitous learning is only just beginning. Along that journey we need to develop breakthrough practices and technologies that allow us to reconceive

and rebuild the content, procedures and human relationships of teaching and learning" (Cope & Kalantzis, 2008, p. 582).Ubiquitous learning contains within it two innovative concepts:

- The concept of *settings* in which student is omnipresent in the didactic process;
- The concept of *networking* imposed by ICT that meet the needs in developing of self-regulated learning abilities.

Such an innovative view requires to see the world as a *metasystem*, which is a system of systems that connect personality, time and own learning environment with the reality. The main feature of the Ubiquitous Learning Environment are:

1.  **Permanency:** Learners can never lose their work unless it is purposefully deleted. All the learning processes are recorded continuously every day.
2.  **Accessibility:** Learners have access to their documents, data, or videos from anywhere. The information is provided based on requests, but learning involved is self-directed.
3.  **Immediacy:** Wherever learners are, they can get any information immediately; solve problems quickly and may record the questions and look for the answer later.
4.  **Interactivity:** Learners can interact with experts, teachers, or peers synchronically or asynchronically. Experts are more reachable and the knowledge is more available.
5.  **Situating of Instructional Activities:** The learning could be embedded in our daily life. The problems and the knowledge required are all presented in their natural and authentic forms. It helps learners to notice the problem situations.
6.  **Adaptability:** Learners can get the right information at the right place in the right way (Alsheail, 2010, pp.16-17).

In a ubiquitous learning environment digital textbooks' functions go beyond printed textbooks. However, using digital textbooks for teaching, learning or/and assessment is not necessary a sign that ubiquitous learning has arrived. Today, in rapidly changing world, ubiquitous learning can be a need for face-to-face communication, collaborative work and decision-making. Research has shown (Kim & Jung, 2010, p. 248) that digital textbooks allow accessing content that is adaptive "tailored" to student's abilities, interests and learning style. The increasingly short life cycle of knowledge is important to be taken into account for developing such textbooks that will "carry" more information for student, but in an innovative way, as well as to increase the effectiveness of production and to distribute acquired knowledge and skills through networking. It has become important to develop textbooks by taking into account dynamic and flexible strategies, new learning tools and a new learning theory.

Learning is a personal construct and mainly depends on from what type of "blocks" were used for this construction. The own intellectual, cognitive and affective potentials reflects the capacity to process/recover information or/and to use the energy of the body. Thus, the digital learning should correspond to the physical configuration of the body and the energy. The practical application of this idea relies on (meta) cognitive learning strategies. Taking into account these concerns, the pedagogy must respond with a new integrative, dynamic and flexible concept of a learning strategy. It is not a discovery to say that scientific model has been definitively changed by the globalisation and ICT. The new science requires metacognitive thinking and a new functional mechanism, which will integrate teaching, learning and assessment in a whole. What are the functions of digital textbooks?

The general perspective of this chapter is to summarise digital textbooks' functions. It is a meta-reflection about the statement of profes-sional teacher training toward more ubiquitous learning environments. Thus, this chapter has four main purposes:

- To compose the terminology related to digital textbook' functions;
- To assemble the issues and controversies in exploring digital textbook's functions;
- To explain two categories of functions: with reference to content and to learner;
- To reconstruct the conceptual model of textbooks as meta-patterns for learning.

The main concerns of this chapter relay on psychopedagogical functions of digital textbooks use and development. The objectives are to identify and summarize digital textbooks distinctive features from technical or/and technological perspectives. It is presented an overview of functions with reference to teacher and with reference to student focusing on exploring two main concepts: ubiquitous learning and ubiquitous learning environment.

## BACKGROUND

According to dictionaries, the term "function" denotes the activities assigned to, required of, or expected of a person. The activities assigned to teachers is defines as the function of teachers. "Broadly speaking, the function of teachers is to help students learn by imparting knowledge to them and by setting up a situation in which students can and will learn effectively" (Havighurst, 2014). Moreover, the functions of teachers in face-to-face and online learning environments differ. Thus, research has shown (Alonso & Blazquez, 2009, pp. 337-338), teachers' functions in online environment relies on content, activities, interaction and design.

In modern world the teachers' functions fills with a set of attributes, roles and responsibilities performed both in the school and outside. "For teachers, the ability to apply workable solutions to individual situation and "the flexibility" to adapt to changing environments" are aspects that are becoming more and more completing" (Martin & Repetto, 2005, p. 23). In addition, the teachers' key attributes are to adapt to change, to be flexible, intuitive, innovative and persistent. They should be highly collaborative with good interpersonal skills. Teachers should be problem solving, but also, enthusiastic, creative, intellectually curious, resourceful and positive, well-organised, focused, determined and hardworking.

Dealing especially with ICT for education and new learning technologies requires a range of specific functions, attributes, roles and responsibilities to be delegated to digital textbooks. The decision about what functions could be delegated depends on pedagogical situation. Many more questions could be addressed to this issue. Besides the judgment could be summed up with a statement that *in Global Age the learning is focused on technical (ICT in education) and self-regulated learning more than ever.* Therefore:

- *Theoretically*, according to UNESCO (2014), the ICT in education can contribute to universal access to education, equality in education, the delivery of quality learning and teaching, teachers' professional development and more efficient education management, governance and administration.
- *Practically*, ICT for education provides a green way for innovations: ubiquitous learning, digital textbooks, quantum psychology, kinetic education, management etc.

There are some practical examples. As was observed by Saufa (2014), iBooks Textbooks offer iPad® users gorgeous, full screen textbooks with interactive animations, rotating 3D diagrams, flick-through photo galleries and tap-to-play videos. iBooks Textbooks don't weigh down a backpack, can be updated as events unfold and don't need to be returned. In addition, content and tools available for iPad provide teachers with new ways to customize learning, with iTunes U Course Manager Educators can share knowledge and resources directly to a global audience, to integrate their own documents as part of course curriculum as well as content from e-stores. The free iOS app gives learners access to the world's largest online catalogue of free educational content from top schools, leading universities and prominent institutions.

On the other hand, the printed textbook continue to be the primary resource for content, but in new learning environments there are also many digital versions of textbooks. These is the case of slowly shifting from teacher-centered learning environments to more learner-centered learning environments. In such environments new functions of teachers include, among others:

- *To design lesson plan* according to all requirements;
- *To integrate (to personalise) content* from different sources for real learning;
- *To motivate the student*(s) to understand, learn and self-regulate own learning;
- *To arrange conditions* which assists the growth of child's according to his/her potential;
- *To turn up the child* from assimilator of knowledge in creative and innovative being;
- *To diagnose the learning* problems and issues and give remedial;
- *To provide an coaching*, tutoring and counselling guidance;
- *To explain social and moral values*;
- *To evaluate*, record and report the learning analytics.

The delimitations of the chapter rely on psycho-pedagogical functions. The proposed position is that psycho-pedagogical functions of digital textbooks derivate from functions of innovative teachers and functions of school printed textbooks. Digital content is not only a high-enriched technological content, but also an effective tool to engage all students in learning.

## DIGITAL TEXTBOOKS FUNCTIONS

### Issues and Controversies

Traditionally, digital textbooks are mainly used and developed as *eTextbooks* and as *Open Source Textbooks*. Some authors believe that digital textbooks should have the similar structure like printed textbooks, but provide more functionality. Research has shown (Gong, Chen, Wang, Zhang & Huang, 2013) find that eTextbooks should have the similar structure and layouts as printed textbooks, but the interaction with students is more important than media rich content. In addition, note-taking and working on assignments to keep eTextbooks in classes.

However, these ideas controversies with Burrus (2014) considerations that eTextbooks provide a better-than-paper experience. Thus, with Kindle eTextbooks it is possible to read across devices; study concepts; quickly create, manage notes, get everything with a single tap, including definitions, related pages, relevant content from other sources and accesses them anytime in the Amazon cloud. In addition, it is possible to display all notes, to color the highlights, save images and bookmark it in one place. More functions were described (Grossman, 2013): "among other things, readers can search within a text for a word or phrase, bookmark pages, annotate paragraphs, and highlight key thoughts. Additionally, there is a new sepia reading mode that can ease the eyestrain that comes from staring at a screen".

In other worlds, the model used in digital textbooks functionality provide a framework for developing the technical dimension of teachers' psychopedagogical functions, such as: to integrate content from different sources for real pedagogical situations. The main functions of the teacher, according to Pandey (2010-2011) are:

- **Diagnostic Function:** Diagnose entering behavior, formulate educational objective, analyse the content, instructional material and environmental conditions.
- **Prescriptive Function:** Selection and organization of appropriate contents in appropriate sequence; selection of appropriate teaching methods, media and strategies; seeking desired cooperation from the students.
- **Evaluative Function:** Finding out the progress and outcomes of teaching.

Some more functions are: motivating the child to learn, arrange condition which assists the growth of child's mind and body; turning the child in a creative being; diagnosing learning problems and according give remedial; providing educational and vocational guidance; providing counselling; inculcating social and moral values; evaluating, recording and reporting; making curriculum material. Even if textbooks are easy damaged and their subject matter can become outdated, teacher(s) and students still prefer printed textbooks. On the other side, many companies around the word use and develop digital textbooks.

Research has shown (Rockinson-Szapkiw, Courduff, Carter & Bennett, 2013, p. 259-260) that the *nature of the textbook is changing*, because students have own laptops, tablets, smart phones, and other handheld devices and read textbooks in digital formats that can be accessed via Internet and downloaded on digital devices. Unfortunately, the educational research to support the efficacy of e-textbooks consumed via mobile devices lags behind development and adoption. There are many reasons, but many of them could be devoted "to examine the effect of e-textbooks on university students' cognitive, affective, and psychomotor learning" (p. 260).

What content is better for learning: printed or digital? In the intention to solve this issue, Daniel and Woody (2013) conduct a research in which asks participants to read a textbook chapter as *a print textbook*, *printed text pages*, *printed manuscript* in Microsoft Word, *electronic .pdf file*, or *electronic textbook*. Then, students require completing a questionnaire in order to report their perceptions of how well they remembered and understated the material and how motivated they were to play close attention to the reading and to perform well on the quiz. Results show that "there were no significant differences in this measure across media or location" (p. 20).

Research has shown (Mangen, Walgermo & Bronnick, 2013, p. 62) that the paradigm of reading is increasingly screen-based rather than paperbound. The theoretical and pedagogical implications of the ongoing digitization for reading and reading comprehension are complex and multifaceted, and a number of fundamental issues remain addressed:

- How and to what extent might comprehension of linear, narrative and non-narrative texts differ when texts are displayed on a screen as compared to being printed on paper?
- Does it impact students' reading comprehension and learning to read geography, science and history texts as PDFs on a computer screen instead of a print textbook?

The idea that digital content tends to increase the power of decision making and visual processing was definitively rejected and that this additional cognitive load, in turn, impairs reading comprehension performance. Many studies reports about the lack of empirical studies of naturalistic texts (narrative or non-narrative) and lack of significant effect for screen or paper presentation mode. With reference to Kerr and Symons (2006), the author proves that "while children, if given enough time, may be able to comprehend equal amounts

of information from paper and computer, when reading time is accounted for, children are comprehending less efficiently when reading from computer" (pp.13-14). The presentation medium on reading comprehension is also an issue for essay marking and annotation. It was evidenced a controversy that even is a shift toward assessors marking digitally scanned copies on screen rather than the original paper copies traditionally used, examiners had a weaker recall of essay quality on screen and had greater difficulty recollecting the location of details in these texts.

As was noted on KERIS site digital textbooks offer various *interactive functions*, and provide the learner with a combination of textbooks, reference books, workbooks, dictionaries, and multimedia contents such as video clips, animations, and virtual reality. Buhl (2008) observes that teachers' functions adapt to the "generation" that follow project-oriented, problem-oriented education and digital communication. However, there is a discrepancy between the functions of a teacher and their conceptions about their functions. The functions of a teacher has at one and the same time increased in complexity and had its complexity reduced. Therefore, digital Textbooks' functions can be designed so to effectively diagnose behavior and actions before, during and after learning process as well as to fit students' preferences, cognitive potential, culture, values, level of knowledge and learning styles. The main attribute of the digital textbooks is to support new media at different levels, e.g. curriculum; pedagogical situations; self-study and self-assessment; teaching activities; metacognitive strategies etc.

## TWO CATEGORIES OF FUNCTIONS: WITH REFERENCE TO TEACHER AND WITH REFERENCE TO LEARNER

Research has shown (Gerard & Roegiers (2009, p. 419) that textbooks' functions are:

- Functions with reference to the teacher
- Functions with reference to student.

Generally, these functions refer to acquisition through manual; consolidation of purchases through manual; evaluation of purchases through manual; assistance in the integration of acquisitions and the reference function. All these functions can be delegated to digital textbooks. However, this process requires some technical, methodological and psychopedagogical standards. In such consideration the functions of printed textbooks will be amplified in order to offer more possibilities to reading, writing, practice and assessment. Digital textbooks offer a digital learning environment, which can be designed as a ubiquitous digital learning environment.

Let us analyse the functions of printed textbooks in accordance with Bloom's taxonomy. Thus:

1. Acquisition → knowledge and comprehension;
2. Consolidation → application;
3. Evaluative → analysis;
4. Assistance (prescriptive) → synthesis;
5. Reference → evaluation.

Therefore, at the "knowledge" and "understand" levels the student should be able to remember previously learned information as well as to demonstrate an understanding of the facts. In order to do this, the usual printed textbooks include content, introduction, chapters, educational (learning) objectives, key words and, in some cases, bibliography. However, at the application level, the student should apply knowledge to actual situations. Printed textbooks provide text and examples used to illustrate the topic. Moreover, for analysis, the student should break down learning objects or ideas into simplest parts and find evidence to support generalisations. For this in printed textbooks is included exercises for knowledge-check or some problems.

The higher thinking skills, like synthesis and evaluation, the printed textbooks offer only assistance or/and reference functions instead of Bloom's taxonomy requirements: to compile component ideas into a new whole or to propose alternative solutions and to make and defend judgments based on internal evidence or external criteria. Traditionally, the highest order thinking levels is an aspiration of teachers (Elder & Paul, 2014). Teachers expect to make critical thinking a primary objective of their instruction and to format new attitudes and behaviors. What is the functions of digital textbooks for these objectives?

In accordance with post-modernism psychology the personal development strategies are required. One of them is self-regulation. Self-regulate learning skills is performed both by all teachers and learners. It was observed (van Beek, de Jong, Minnaert & Wubbels, 2014, p. 2) that the teachers can play an important role in developing self-regulated learning skills of students. This is a major challenge because of the diversity in curricula and cognitive levels, learning difficulties (e.g. dyslexia), students' behavioral problems and the turbulent biological, cognitive and socially challenging life stage of these students. In addition, the student's places great demands on the pedagogical practices of teachers, and it is important to gain insight to stimulate self-regulated learning. What is the role of digital textbook in self-regulation?

Authors (Coll, Rochera & de Gispert, 2014) has pointed out that the teacher's main function is to promote and facilitate collaboration between participants; to adapt it to the objectives and learning outcomes; as well as the creation, maintenance and development of online courses; providing a shared framework of rules, roles, and expectations for the group; helping participants to know if they have successfully followed the group's norms and fulfilled the expectations laid down for them; and some meta functions. There are:

- *A directive function,* when the teacher uses feedback to give the students more specific information about which aspects they need to review or how they should participate;

- *A facilitative function*, when feedback is used to give pointers, pose questions, make suggestions and offer indirect guidance that encourage the group of students to review and self-regulate both the work carried out and the learning that has been achieved.

Other functions, according to Encyclopaedia Britannica (2014), refer to mediator of learning, judge of achievement, scholar and research specialist, expert in some area of knowledge or skills, community leaders etc. In the same cases, these responsibilities are associated with ICT coordinator functions "related to the management and maintenance of schools networks, the guidance and counselling of teachers, ICT experience diffusion, and the progressive expansion of the ICT project" (Rodríguez-Miranda, Pozuelos-Estrada & León-Jariego, 2014, p. 267).

Arimoto (2014) evidences the *research function*. The author notes that modern learning requires new educational patterns with visual, vivid, adaptive and interactive teaching in order to transfer abstract knowledge to students' cognitive systems. At this time, teacher can use diverse mind maps or concept mapping techniques to summarise the content.

With the increasing usage of digital courses and deep-going practice of education the negative effects are showing (Zhang & Fan, 2014, pp.165-166). There are some main reasons:

- *Blindness used of multimedia education*, when a lot of textbooks attach teaching and digital courseware is designed as one teaching unit;
- *Teaching method over formalize* with some modern teaching method is reduced to copy of all textbook content into Power Pont presentations;
- *Weaken lecturers' leading role* when lecturers don't have the leading role in the

class and become computer manipulators or commentators;

- *The main role of students' declines* because some lecturers adopt old teaching styles or utilize modern multimedia teaching method and still insist old teaching styles and, as result, teachers play monodrama and students learn alone.

All these negative effects could be avoided if the teachers, students, content and context will form a functional whole. From this point of view, the teachers' primary function is not to provide knowledge, but to form new behaviors and attitudes. In this way, the research problems are: *How to identify new learn to lean methodologies and metacognitive strategies? What attributes and roles of modern teachers can be delegated to digital textbooks?*

Functions of a master teacher were described by Mandacanu (2009, p. 318):

- Mobilisation, research (gnoseologies);
- Communication;
- Orientation, formation;
- Information, constructive, managerial;
- Performance;
- Technical.

The comparison between functions of scholar textbook, functions of modern teacher, functions of digital textbooks and the affordance of digital textbooks is presented in Table 1.

## THE METAPATTERN FUNCTIONALITY IN A DIGITAL TEXTBOOKS MECHANISM

The learning object with the name "digital textbook" can exhibit multiple "behaviors". The behavior of the digital textbook can be estimated on the base on main function or/and on the interdependences between the main and secondary

*Table 1. Comparison of different categories of functions and affordance of digital textbooks.*

| FUNCTIONS | | | AFFORDANCE |
|---|---|---|---|
| **Scholar Textbook** | **Master Teacher** | **Digital Textbook** | |
| *with reference to learner* | | | |
| purchases through manual | mobilization, research | cognition | cognitive tutor |
| consolidation of purchases | communication | systematization | mind map, learning tool with immediate/delayed feedback |
| evaluation of purchases | orientation, formation | self-regulated learning | learning tool for formative/summative assessment with immediate/delayed feedback; intelligent interfaces with a pedagogical agent etc. |
| *with reference to teacher* | | | |
| helpful in integration of acquisitions through textbook | informational constructive managerial | information | hypermedia multimedia multimodal text |
| | performance | integration | animation audio, video blended/flipped learning |
| reference | technic | formation | hyperlinks digital text highlights searching virtual reality video clips |

functions. Let us consider the "behavior" of the digital textbook like a pattern. Any sequence of digital content that can be modelling by a main function of digital textbook can be considered a pattern. Each pattern has a complex structure. The elements of the pattern are: *an issue, a context* and *a solution*. The digital textbook patterns repeat in a predicable manner, like a lesson, and may be recognised.

Traditionally, pattern recognition is categorised according to the type of learning procedure used to generate the value. In learning with digital textbooks the pattern recognition may be categorised according to the metacognitive procedure used to generate "learning to learn" competence or the process of formation new behavior/ attitude. Thus, there are three types of learning procedures:

- Learner-centered learning procedure;
- Teacher-centered learning procedure;
- Mixed (flipped or blended) learning procedures.

As was reported in recent literature flipped teaching techniques improve student learning (Nakahara, Soga, Nakamura, Mitani & Kawana, 2014; Banister, Reinhart & Ross, 2014; Kong, 2014; Lasry, Dugdale & Charles, 2014). Can be considered flipped learning with digital textbooks in a ubiquitous learning environment a metapattern? According to general understanding a metapattern is a "pattern of patterns" with a more logical and flexible structure. Such a functionality may result from acceptance of the digital textbooks. The digital textbook assure metasystem functionality, because include the intelligent mechanism aim to rapidly diagnose *issue,* provide a *suitable context* (digital learning environment) and contribute to *solution* as result of immediate or/and immediate feedback included in a learning tool. The metapattern functionality is assured by adaptive interdependences between one main function and different functions: information *A*, integration/ formation *B,* self-regulation *C*, cognition *D*, and generalization *E* (Figure 1).

Ideally, *the condition for metapattern functionality* in a ubiquitous learning environment with digital textbook is *the integrity of action verbs related to Bloom, Simpson and Krathwohl taxonomies*. Items, used to get latent variables will be composed by these verbs and will allow to develop metacognitive thinking about own learning process. Critical thinking represents the integrity of processes and mechanisms, which include knowledge, skills and attitudes as well as sub-skills (e.g. analysis, evaluation and inference) in a whole. When the aggregate is used

appropriately the chances of producing a logical conclusion or a solution to a problem is increased. This idea is related to Table 2.

To think metacognitively individuals must be aware of their own cognitive processes and focus on self-regulated learning. However, these processes may imply inference and some learning algorithms. Metacognitive strategies should be concerned about the integrity of cognitive, affective and psychomotor processes, too. More actions verbs are provided by digital learning environments. If it is accepted that learning outcomes in a value the interdependence between input and output variables of the ubiquitous learning environment, then the quality of learning depends on how is integrated cognitive, affective and psychomotor processes in a metasystem.

On the other hand, the metacognitive thinking relies on how effectively teachers use the authoring tools to develop eTextbooks. As was noted by Gu, Wu & Xu (2014, p.123) "industries are eager to provide the authoring tools to produce e-Textbooks

*Figure 1. Interdependences between functions of digital textbooks (metapattern functionality)*

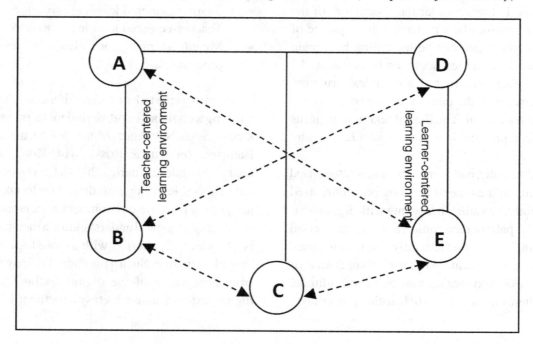

*Table 2. The integrity of actions verbs related to Bloom, Krathwohl and Simpson domains*

| N | Bloom' Cognitive Domain | Krathwohl's Affective Domain | Simpson's Psychomotor Domain |
|---|---|---|---|
| 1 | **Remember previously learned information** *Action verbs:* to arrange, to define, to describe, to duplicate, to identify, to label, to list, to match, to memorize, to name, to order, to outline, to recognize, to relate, to *recall, to repeat, to reproduce, to select, to state* | **Recovering** as being aware of sensitive of phenomena and being willing to tolerate them. *Action verbs:* asks, chooses, describes, follows, gives, holds, identifies, locates, names, points to, selects, replies, use | **Perception**: choose, describe, detect, differentiate, distinguish, identifies, isolates, relates, selects, and separates. |
| 2 | **Demonstrate an understanding of the facts.** *Action verbs:* to classify, to convert, to defend, to describe, to discuss, to distinguish, to estimate, to explain, to express, to extend, to generalized, to give example(s), to identify, to indicate, to infer, to locate, to paraphrase, to predict, to recognize, to review, to select, to summarize, to translate | | **Set**: begins, displays, explains, moves, proceeds, reacts, responds, snows, starts, volunteers |
| 3 | **Apply knowledge to actual situations.** *Action verbs:* to apply, to change, to choose, to compute, to demonstrate, to discover, to dramatize, to employ, to illustrate, to interpret, to manipulate, to modify, to operate, to practice, to predict, to prepare, to produce, to relate, to schedule, to show, to sketch, to solve, to use, to write | **Responding** is committed in some small measure to the ideas, memories, of phenomena involved by actively responding to them. *Action verbs:* answers, assists, complies, conforms, discusses, greets, helps, labels, performs, practices, presents, reads, recites, reports, selects, tells, writes | **Guided response**: assembles, builds, calibrates, constructs, dismantles, displays, dissects, fastens, fixes, grinds, heats, manipulates, measures, mends, mixes, organizes, sketches |
| 4 | | | **Mechanism:** assembles, builds, calibrates, constructs, dismantles, displays, dissects, fastens, fixes, grinds, heats, manipulates, measures, mends, mixes, organizes, sketches |
| 5 | **Analysis: Break down objects or ideas into simpler parts and find evidence to support generalizations**. *Action verbs*: to analyse, to appraise, to calculate, to categorize, to compare, to contrast, to criticize, to diagram, to differentiate, to distinguish, to experiment, to illustrate, to infer, to model, to point out, to question, to relate, to select, to separate, to subdivide, to test | **Valuing** is vialling to be perceived by others or valuing certain ideas, materials or phenomena. *Action verbs:* completes, describes, differentiates, explains, follows, forms, initiates, invites, joins, justifies, proposes, reads, reports, selects, shares, studies, works | **Complex or overt response**: assembles, builds, calibrates, constructs, dismantles, displays, dissects, fastens, fixes, grinds, heats, manipulates, measures, mends, mixes, organizes, sketches |
| 6 | **Synthesis:** compile component ideas into a new whole or propose alternative solutions. *Action verbs:* to arrange, to assemble, to categorize, to collect, to combine, to comply, to compose, to construct, to create, to develop, to devise, to explain, to formulate, to generate, to plan, to prepare, to rearrange, to reconstruct, to relate, to reorganize, to revise, to rewrite, to set up, to summarize | **Organization** is to relate to value already held and bring into a harmonised philosophy and imagine. *Action verbs:* adheres, alters, arranges, combines, compares, completes, defends, explains, generalizes, identifies, integrates, modifies, orders, organizes, prepares, relates, synthesizes | **Adaptation:** adapts, alters, changes, rearranges, reorganizes, revises, varies |
| 7 | **Evaluation: make and defend judgments based on internal evidence or external criteria.** *Action verbs: to a*ppraise, to argue, to assess, to attach, to choose, to compare, to conclude, to contrast, to defend, *to d*escribe, to discriminate, to estimate, to evaluate, to explain, to judge, to justify, to interpret, to *r*elate, to predict, to rate, to select, to summarize, to support, to value. | **Characterization by a value or value set**: acts, discriminates, displays, influences, listens, modifies, performs, practices, proposes, qualifies, questions, revises, serves, solves, uses, verifies. | **Origination:** arranges, combines, composes, constructs, creates, designs, originates |

by updating the publishing systems or platforms. These updates include functions, such as object-oriented content management and customized and device-specific layout, which facilitate the ease of creating multimedia and interactive elements. Authoring tools, such as iBooks Author and Articulate Storyline provide basic functions for end users to create e-Textbooks, whereas, several commercial products are also available for publishers or other interested parties to produce e-Textbooks, by reinventing the publishing industry.

## FUTURE RESEARCH DIRECTIONS

Teaching in a digital learning environment became a complex undertaking cognitive, affective and psychomotor activity. Research has shown (Sheehan, Tennet, Robinson & Jenkins, 2014, p. 5) that teachers should know and critically think about what is to be taught and learn; create a purposeful, responsive and safe learning environment; establish effective professional relationship with learners, colleagues and communities; engage with all learners, their prior learning experience and beliefs to support successful learning; using theory and evidence to design purposeful inclusive learning opportunities/experiences for all learners; practice ethnically and develop professionally and practice toward educational outcomes.

To sum up what we have said in this chapter, the function is define as an activity related to specific purpose and roles. There are two categories of functions: with reference to teacher (content) and with reference to learner (learning tool) and include the following functions:

- Cognition;
- Systematization;
- Self-regulated learning;
- Information;
- Integration;
- Formation.

These functions, included in five categories, defines a metapattern. Future research is need how to design and use effectively the functions of the digital textbooks toward a metapattern functionality. Comparing with the term 'software informer', the "digital textbook informer" for "cognition" function could be a safe utility designed especially for those users who care to keep their textbooks ready for any situation that might arise. Its primary aim will be to provide user with up-to-dated information, not only related to software, but, also, to psychopedagogical characteristics of learner, his/her network, professional experience etc.

The metappaterns functionality in a ubiquitous digital learning environment should be developed on the base on postmodernism philosophy. Much work needs to be done to make this model less dependent on data mining and more dependent on the professional experience, especially in inter- and trans- disciplinary areas of study or research. In this context, the concept of metapattern in needs to be modeled, developed and implemented as a continuous process of learning into changing learning environments. It is expected to develop new learning algorithms which will assure the guaranteed learning outcomes.

## CONCLUSION

The present study reveals key aspects of the way in which functions of digital textbooks can be supported in ubiquitous learning environments. Firstly, it was founded that the learning design is focused on innovative functions and interactive functions. The innovative functions assure updating information, engagement of all students in learning and self-regulated learning activities, networking, dual-processing of data from multimodal text, highlighting, instant delivery of knowledge, translating the content etc. Beside innovative functions, the interactive functions allow dating of digital content with reference books, workbooks, integrative dictionaries and multimedia contents without the constraints of time and space.

In a ubiquitous digital learning environment teacher and/or learners can create or personalise their own textbooks, underlining the important parts, taking notes, and ultimately combining the contents with high-quality, reliable knowledge and skills that is their own. Teachers' functions varies and can be categorised as an issue, context and solution. Complexity becomes even more apparent in a Ubiquitous Learning Environment with digital textbooks. Following this stream of times, digital textbooks functions should be more ubiquitous.

However, the ubiquitous learning environment requires metacognitive strategies that allow developing a deeper understanding the pattern as an issue, context and solution. Furthermore, learning processes are directed not only to intellectual development, but also to consuming/saving/keeping energy, which result from individual, group or collaborative activities and metacognitive strategies. These aspects seem to be appropriate for competence building, decision-making and problem-solving in diversity of learning environment.

One innovative way is *experiential learning*. The experiential learning has a learning impact on the whole person, including emotion (affect) and behavior in addition to cognitive stimulation. In addition, this is a methodology of education whereby structure and individual or group experiences are contrived to develop learning and perceptual capacities, to develop and reinforce cognitions, to impact on emotions and attitudes, and, importantly, to function in developing capacities to behave consistently with the insights of these processes and experiences. In a digital learning environment with textbook the experimental learning is a way to design interactive and adaptive mechanisms (Hoover, 2014, pp. 78 - 82).

## REFERENCES

Alonso, D. L., & Blazquez, E. F. (2009). Are the functions of teachers in e-learning and face-to-face learning are really different? *Journal of Educational Technology & Society, 12*(4), 331–343.

Alsheail, A. (2010). *Teaching English as a second/foreign language in a ubiquitous learning environment: a guide for ESL/EFL instructors.* Retrieved October 29, 2014 from http://csuchicodspace.calstate.edu/bitstream/handle/10211.4/184/5%209%202010%20Abdulrahman%20Alsheail.pdf?sequence=1

Amazon.com. (2014). *Study smarter with Kindle eTextbooks.* Retrieved October, 29, 2014 from http://www.amazon.com/Kindle-Textbooks/b?node=2223210011

Arimoto, A. (2014). The teaching and research nexus in the third wave age. In J.C. Shin, A. Arimoto, W. C. Cummings, & U. C. Teichler, (Eds.), Teaching and research in contemporary higher education, (pp. 15-33). Springer. doi:10.1007/978-94-007-6830-7_2

Banister, S., Reinhart, R., & Ross, C. (2014). Using digital resources to support personalized learning experiences in K-12 classrooms: The evolution of mobile devices as innovations in schools in northwest Ohio. In *Proceedings of Society for Information Technology & Teacher Education International Conference, 1*, (pp. 2715-2721).

*Bloom taxonomy.* (n. d.). Retrieved October, 25, 2014 from http://juliaec.files.wordpress.com/2011/04/blooms_taxonomy.jpg

Brophy, J. (2008). Textbook reform. In T. Good (Ed.), 21st century education: A reference handbook. (pp. 414-423). Thousand Oaks, CA: SAGE Publications, Inc. doi:10.4135/9781412964012.n45

Buhl, M. (2008). *New teacher functions in cyberspace - on technology, mass media and education, 4*(1). Retrieved October 29, 2014 from seminar.net/index.php/volume-4-issue-1-2008-previousissuesmeny-122/89-new-teacher-functions-in-cyberspace-on-technology-mass-media-and-education.

Burrus, D. (2014). *The tech trends that will disrupt, create opportunitie*s. Retrieved October 28, 2014 from http://blogs.wsj.com/cio/2014/01/16/the-tech-trends-that-will-disrupt-create-opportunities-in-2014/

Chen, N. S., & Hwang, G. J. (2014). Transforming the classrooms: Innovative digital game-based learning designs and applications. *Educational Technology Research and Development, 62*(2), 125–128.

Coll, C., Rochera, M. J., & de Gispert, I. (2014). Supporting online collaborative learning in small groups: Teacher feedback on learning content, academic task and social participation. *Computers & Education, 75*, 53–64. doi:10.1016/j.compedu.2014.01.015

Cope, B., & Kalantzis, M. (2008). Ubiquitous learning: An agenda for educational transformation. In *Proceedings of the 6th International Conference on Networked Learning*, (pp. 576-582). Retrieved November 1, 2014 from http://www.networkedlearningconference.org.uk/past/nlc2008/abstracts/PDFs/Cope_576-582.pdf

Daniel, D. B., & Woody, W. D. (2013). E-textbooks at what cost? Performance and use of electronic v. print texts. *Computers & Education, 62*, 18–23. doi:10.1016/j.compedu.2012.10.016

DeStefano, D., & LeFevre, J. A. (2007). Cognitive load in hypertext reading: A review. *Computers in Human Behavior, 23*(3), 1616–1641. doi:10.1016/j.chb.2005.08.012

Dwyer, C. P., Hogan, M. J., & Stewart, I. (2014). An integrated critical thinking framework for the 21st century. *Thinking Skills and Creativity, 12*, 43–52. doi:10.1016/j.tsc.2013.12.004

Elder, L., & Paul, R. (2014). *Critical thinking development: A stage theory. The critical thinking community*. Retrieved October 29, 2014 from http://www.criticalthinking.org/pages/critical-thinking-development-a-stage-theory/483

Gerard, F. M., & Roegiers, X. (2009). *Des manuels scolaires pour apprendre: Concevoir, évaluer, utiliser*. De Boeck Supérieur. doi:10.3917/dbu.gerar.2009.01

Gong, C., Chen, G., Wang, X., Zhang, X. & Huang, R. (2013). The functions of e-textbooks for utilizing in K-12 classes: A case study in Beijing. *Advanced Learning Technologies*, 479-480.

Grossman, S. (2013). *Google begins selling textbooks through play store*. Retrieved October 29, 2014 from http://chronicle.com/blogs/wiredcampus/google-begins-selling-textbooks-through-play-store/45367

Havighurst, R. V. (2014). Functions and roles of teachers. *Encyclopedia Britannica*. Retrieved October 29, 2014 from http://www.britannica.com/EBchecked/topic/585183/teaching/39100/Functions-and-roles-of-teachers

Jones, V., & Jo, J. H. (2014). *Ubiquitous learning environment: An adaptive teaching system using ubiquitous technology*. Retrieved November 1, 2014 from http://www.ascilite.org.au/conferences/perth04/procs/pdf/jones.pdf

KERIS. (2014). *Digital textbook. School with digital textbook is everywhere*. Retrieved October, 25, 2014 from http://www.dtbook.kr/renew/english/index.htm

Kerr, M. A., & Symons, S. E. (2006). Computerized presentation of text: Effects on children's reading of informational material. *Reading and Writing, 19*(1), 1–19. doi:10.1007/s11145-003-8128-y

Kim, J. H. Y., & Jung, H. Y. (2010). South Korean digital textbook project. *Computers in the Schools, 27*(3-4), 247-265. Retrieved October 25, 2014 from http://www.mackin.com/cms/uploads/SouthKoreanDigitalTextbookProject.pdf

Kong, S. C. (2014). Developing information literacy and critical thinking skills through domain knowledge learning in digital classrooms: An experience of practicing flipped classroom strategy. *Computers & Education, 78*, 160–173. doi:10.1016/j.compedu.2014.05.009

*Krathwohl's affective domain.* (n. d.). Retrieved October 25, 2014 from http://assessment.uconn.edu/docs/LearningTaxonomy_Affective.pdf

Kuvalja, M., Verma, M., & Whitebread, D. (2014). Patterns of co-occurring non-verbal behaviour and self-directed speech; a comparison of three methodological approaches. *Metacognition Learning.* Retrieved October 25, 2014 from http://download.springer.com/static/pdf/248/art%253A10.1007%252Fs11409-013-9106-7.pdf?auth66=1393147529_278c016eeecb7902f6ddda285adbb000&ext=.pdf

Laanpere, M., Pata, K., Normak, P., & Poldoja, H. (2014). Pedagogy-driven design of digital learning ecosystems. *Computer Science and Information Systems, 11*(1), 419–442. doi:10.2298/CSIS121204015L

Lasry, N., Dugdale, M., & Charles, E. (2014). Just in time to flip your classroom. *The Physics Teacher, 52*(1), 34–37. doi:10.1119/1.4849151

Lawrence, S. A. (2014). Exploring the use of technology, multimodal texts, and digital tools in K-12 classrooms. In S. Lawrence (Ed.), *Critical practice in P-12 education: Transformative teaching and learning* (pp. 24–48). Hershey, PA: Information Science Reference. doi:10.4018/978-1-4666-5059-6.ch002

LEARN NC. (2014). *What's in a digital textbook?* Retrieved October, 25, 2014 from http://www.learnnc.org/lp/editions/nchist-eg/6628

Mandacanu, V. (2009). *Master teacher.* Chisinau: Pontos. (in Romanian)

Mangen, A., Walgermo, B. R., & Brønnick, K. (2013). Reading linear texts on paper versus computer screen: Effects on reading comprehension. *International Journal of Educational Research, 58*, 61–68. doi:10.1016/j.ijer.2012.12.002

Martin, A., & Repetto, M. (2005). Teacher's value and attributes within a knowledge society. In V. Midoro (Ed.), A common European framework for teachers' professional profile in ICT for education (pp. 23-26). Editura Menado: Didactica.

MCC. (2014). *Textbooks for online courses.* Retrieved October 25, 2014 from http://www.mccneb.edu/elearning/textbooks.asp

Midoro, V. (2005). *A common European framework for teachers' professional profile in ICT for education.* Edizioni MENABO: Didactica.

Nakahara, T., Soga, T., Nakamura, Y., Mitani, M., & Kawana, N. (2014). Development of an e-textbook connected with a learning management system and a study of its effective use. In *World Conference on Educational Multimedia, Hypermedia and Telecommunications, 1,* (pp. 979-984).

Pandey, S. K. (2010-2011). *Teacher functions. Operations and activities in teaching.* Retrieved October, 29, 2014 from http://www.slideshare.net/pandeysk/teachers-function-operation-and-activities-in-teaching

Rockinson- Szapkiw, A. J., Courduff, J., Carter, K., & Bennett, D. (2013). Electronic versus traditional print textbooks: A comparison study on the influence of university students' learning. *Computers & Education, 63,* 259–266. doi:10.1016/j.compedu.2012.11.022

Rodríguez-Miranda, F. P., Pozuelos-Estrada, F. J., & León-Jariego, J. C. (2014). The role of ICT coordinator. Priority and time dedicated to professional functions. *Computers & Education, 72,* 262–270. doi:10.1016/j.compedu.2013.11.009

*Simpson's psychomotor domain.* (n. d.). Retrieved October, 25, 2014 from http://assessment.uconn.edu/docs/LearningTaxonomy_Psychomotor.pdf

UNESCO. (2014). *ICT in education.* Retrieved October, 29, 2014 from http://www.unesco.org/new/en/unesco/themes/icts/

van Beek, J. A., de Jong, F., Minnaert, A., & Wubbels, T. (2014). Teacher practice in secondary vocational education: Between teacher-regulated activities of student learning and student self-regulation. *Teaching and Teacher Education, 40,* 1–9. doi:10.1016/j.tate.2014.01.005

Zhang, Z., & Fan, L. (2014). *Research on negative influence and strategies of multimedia education in universities. International Conference on Education Reform and Modern Management.* Atlantis Press. doi:10.2991/ermm-14.2014.46

## ADDITIONAL READING

Dreyer, L. M. (2014). Exploring collaboration between mainstream and learning support teachers. *Education as Change, 18*(1), 179–190. doi:10.1080/16823206.2013.847018

Dwyer, K. K., & Davidson, M. M. (2013). General education oral communication assessment and student preferences for learning: E-textbook versus paper textbook. *Communication Teacher, 27*(2), 111–125. doi:10.1080/17404622.2012.752514

Falc, E. O. (2013). An assessment of college students' attitudes towards using an online e-textbook. *Interdisciplinary Journal of E-Learning and Learning Objects, 9,* 1-12. Retrieved October 25, 2014 from, http://www.ijello.org/Volume9/IJELLOv9p001-012Falc831.pdf

Lindenberger, U., & Mayr, U. (2014). Cognitive aging: Is there a dark side to environmental support? *Trends in Cognitive Sciences, 18*(1), 7–15. doi:10.1016/j.tics.2013.10.006 PMID:24210962

McLaughlin, R. L. (2013). *Comparing the readability of text presented on paper in large print with text displayed on the iPad2 for student with visual impairments* (Doctoral dissertation, California State University, Los Angeles).

Quiroga, L. (2014). *Complex systems as a basis for education and pedagogy in the 21st Century.* Retrieved October 25, 2014 from http://www.istec.org/wp-content/uploads/2012/11/Complex-Systems-as-a-Basis-for-Education-and-Pedagogy-in-the-21st-Century.pdf

Sanyal, T. A. (2014). Discourses of experience: The disciplining of identities and practices in student teaching. *Australian Journal of Teacher Education, 39*(3), article 8.

Song, J. S., Kim, S. J., Byun, G. S., Song, J. H., & Lee, B. G. (2014). Comparing wireless networks for applying digital textbook. *Telecommunication Systems, 55*(1), 25–38. doi:10.1007/s11235-013-9748-4

Uluyol, C., & Agca, R. K. (2012). Integrating mobile multimedia into textbooks: 2D barcodes. *Computers & Education, 59*(4), 1192–1198. doi:10.1016/j.compedu.2012.05.018

Vishtac, O. (2003). Criteria of development of the electronic instructional materials [in Russian]. *Pedagogy, 8,* 19–22.

Winne, P. H. (2014). Issues in researching self-regulated learning as patterns of events. *Metacognition and Learning, 9*(2), 229–237. doi:10.1007/s11409-014-9113-3

Wisse, P. (2001). METAPATTERN: Information modeling as enneadic dynamics. *Sprouts: Working Papers on Information Systems, 1*(4). Retrieved October 25, 2014 from http://sprouts.aisnet.org/1-4

## KEY TERMS AND DEFINITIONS

**Learning Analytics:** Use of intelligent data, learner-produced data, and analysis models to discover information and social connections, and to predict and advise on learning.

**Metacognition:** A relative new concept in educational psychology that define higher order thinking that involve active control and monitoring of all sorts of cognitive processes over the algorithmically developed thinking processes involved in learning.

**Metaknowledge:** The knowledge about one's own knowledge. Barr (1979, p. 1) describe metaknowledge as about other knowledge that can be either about the form of the representation scheme itself (e.g.., its syntax) or about the facts that are represented (their origin, reliability, importance etc.) The concept of meta-knowledge captures intrinsic, commonplace proprieties of human cognition.

**Metalanguage:** Any language or symbolic system used to discuss, describe, or analyze another language or symbolic system; a language the language teachers and learners use to talk about the English language, learning and teaching.

**Metavariable:** A set of abilities and rules that students use in their successful development.

**Multimedia Learning:** "The term multimedia refers to the presentation of instructional material using both words and pictures. The instructional material can be presented in verbal form, including printed or spoken text. The instructional material also can be presented in pictorial form, including static graphics, illustrations, photographs, graphs or dynamic forms such as animation or video" (Uluyol&Agca, 2012, p. 1192).

**Ubiquitous Learning:** Any kind of learning in which learners can have access to information almost anywhere/anytime in different contexts.

**Ubiquitous Learning Environment:** An environment in which learners have access to knowledge through technology and work cooperatively to learn almost anywhere at any time, regardless of their geographical location. Such environment merge eLearning with mLearning in order to provide a student with a pervasive setting in which learning can take place, even if the student or learner may not realize that he or she is learning.

**Ubiquitous Learning Materials:** Learning materials like videos, audios, PowerPoint etc. that may be transferred to mobile devices via cable or wirelessly and operated on these devices and can be transferred to and used on mobile devices.

# Chapter 6
# Educational Ideal for the New Wave of Textbooks

## ABSTRACT

*In this chapter, postmodernism features of the educational ideal (professionalism, planetary thinking and cultural pluralism) have been analysed. The general educational outcome is that the new ideal is automatically assured with a new wave of textbooks. Self-regulated learning is the primary focus of this research. It is argued that new textbooks provide more opportunities for teaching, learning and assessment. Even if the teacher is an adviser, administrator, agent provocateur, coach, moderator, observer, and the learner(s) is a knowledge worker, the new digital textbooks are not only the source of content, but also effective tools for learning. For guaranteed learning outcomes, digital textbooks should be designed according to the MetaSystem Learning Design approach. Having established this theoretical framework, the author discusses how to deal with seven laws of globalized pedagogic process. The purpose of the chapter is to elucidate the significance of new educational ideal for the new wave of digital textbooks. Conclusions and future research directions are provided at the end.*

## INTRODUCTION

Globalisation is even a modern concept to define all challenges to educational systems. As far as its impact on education is concerned, discussion of globalisation tends to consider simultaneously its effects on educational ideal, without distinguishing between educational systems and within educational systems inequalities. Moreover, the debate is often confused from a methodological point of view by the interaction between philosophy, psychology, pedagogy, cybernetics and management.

As consequence of the lack of clear theoretical and methodological approaches, the current debate is characterized by a divide between the supporters and the opponents of new educational ideal. Supports argues that globalization presents new irreversible challenges for education. Since the 80s, the world education has become increasingly "connected". The rapid diffusion of new information technologies has implied a fast downgrading of the concept of textbook, while digital textbooks use and development have risen significantly. In most countries around the world,

DOI: 10.4018/978-1-4666-8300-6.ch006

including developing countries, the current wave of digital textbooks has accompanied by increasing concerns about educational ideal.

Whatever indicators for educational ideal are chosen, the current chapter is characterized by a debate between the advocates and critics of digital textbooks use and development. While this is true even as regards distribution effects within the world, positions diverge over the impact on learning design. For instance, Bourn (2014) underline the link between increasing global dimension and promotion of digital learning and they conclude that the term 'Global Dimension' had at its central focus the promotion of learning in an interdependent world, addressing the similarities of people around the world and a belief in working towards a fairer and a more sustainable world. This term is used in relation to Global Citizenship; Sustainable Development; Social Justice; Diversity; Values and Perceptions; Interdependence; Conflict Resolution and Human Rights.

Moreover, it is suggested that a new more integrated approach is needed, one with great emphasis of the processes of learning, including critical reflection, placing learning about development at the heart of the practice of global learning, construction and application of knowledge etc. In contrast, research has shown (Aliyev, Altayev, Ismagambetova & Massanov, 2012, p. 1096) that globalisation requires a change of scenarios, attitudes to technology, and knowledge.

Globalization shifts from *instructional* system design to *learning design* (Hsieh, Lu, Lin & Lee, 2014; Lyons, Hannon & Macken, 2014; O'Rafferty, Curtis & O'Connor, 2014). As was noted by Paquette (2014, p. 14) a *basic learning design* involves three kinds of entities with relationship between them: actor's role, activities and environments grouping learning resources and activities. Activities, performed by actors are organized in a method, decomposed into alternative plays, each decomposed into a series of acts, and further decomposed into activity structures down to terminal learning or support activities.

Furthermore, the learning object paradigm has moved the focus toward aggregating resources and interactions. The learners and the facilitators use and produce learning resources. Web has been evolved to Social Web (Web2.0) and the Semantic Web (Web3.0).

A number of theories, models and approaches form the basis of the modern pedagogy (Williams & Donnellon; 2014; Rowley, 2014; Cochrane, 2014). Indeed, these theories come from debates about the relationships between globalization, educational ideal and learning. The success factors indicate to pedagogy in area of multicultural influences on child and adult development; as well as new functions of teachers and students. Essentially, it sees pedagogy as a science of the effective learning processes.

New trends in pedagogy focused on postmodernism philosophy in multi-measured spaces (Rudic, 2013) with require the b) complex behavioural metapatterns (Peregrin, 2014) and on c) emotional intelligence (D'Mello, Lehman, Pekrun & Graesser, 2014) as the ability to guide own learning, decision making thinking and behavior.

However, contrary to these predictions, the comparative analysis of the recent literature supports the idea that the globalisation impact of increasing complexity in educational systems is not necessary positive for a *developing behavior*. In particular, as was argued (Cummings & Worley, 2014, p. 8) there is an active dispute more than sixty years of research aimed at trying to understand development and developmental processes, and dispute the waning of some theories and the ascendance of others, we are no nearer attempting a systematic account of development in the context of a theoretical perspective or with an agreed –upon paradigmatic approach that when the field first acquired a semblance of scientific and academic identity. All facts indicate toward establishing a new educational ideal.

Free Meriam-Webster defines ideal as an archetypal idea, existing as a mental image or in fancy or imagination or relating to or constituting mental images, ideas, or conceptions. In such conceptualization an educational ideal can be define as an archetypal idea existing as a mental image of technological process. In such consideration, there are at least three models of educational ideal:

- Ideal of total knowledge,
- Ideal of professional knowledge,
- Professionalism, planetary thinking, cultural pluralism.

The first ideal of education, known as *ideal of total knowledge* or *Enlightenment Era*, was common until 1960. In philosophy, this period is characterized by the rejection of ontology (general metaphysics) and the Transcendental Analytic. "The use of formal concepts and principles, in abstraction from the sensible conditions under which objects can be given, cannot yield knowledge. Hence, the "transcendental" use of the understanding (its use independently of the conditions of sensibility) is considered by Kant to be dialectical, to involve erroneous applications of concepts in order to acquire knowledge of things independently of sensibility/experience. Throughout the analytic Kant elaborates on this general view, noting that the transcendental employment of the understanding, which aims towards knowledge of things independently of experience" (Grier, 2012).

During 1960-1990 it was a period of *professional knowledge and skill based teaching*. This means that in teaching were widely accepted to develop programs on the base on instructional objectives, usually structured according to Bloom's taxonomy, knowledge were presented well-structured and organized; the computers "offer" problem solving programs and intelligent tutors. It was the period of first digital textbooks, which were developed as digitalized versions of school textbooks or books. However, this learning ideal cannot be used in Era of Informational Globalisation. Here, the reference point shall be using and developing learning patterns or/and meta-patterns (Bloom &

Volk, 2012; Bod, 2014). Moreover, digitalized versions of printed textbooks "has migrated" to innovative, dynamic and flexible strategies with textbooks for the digital learning environment.

This chapter examines interdependences between globalization, new educational ideal and a new wave in digital textbooks. It is argued that teachers use and develop textbooks starting from different philosophical positions. The main argument here is that while students' roles may be established on the basic of personality or from deliberate choice, "the teacher has a variety of roles to choose from – or, rather, live up to adviser, administrator, agent provocateur, coach, moderator, observer, and more. There are roles to be played as needed of project work" (Jenseen & Heilessen, 2005, p. 63). The shifts in pedagogical functions depending on how the teacher is socially positioned in a specific context.

After reviewing the literature to elucidate understanding of current challenges, this chapter presents the issues and controversies that guided to metasystems thinking about digital textbook use and development. It is argued the differences between globalized pedagogical processes and traditional pedagogical processes. This chapter is organized into a background section and sections. The background covers broad definitions of the topic and provides arguments in favor of metasystems learning design position. The first main chapter relies to laws of globalized pedagogical processes. Staring from identification of issues, controversies and research problems have proposed to go beyond traditional pedagogical processes and emphasizes the role of dynamicity and flexibility, flexible development of personality, self-regulated learning, knowledge management and planetary culture. The second section explains the specifics of new educational ideal viewed as the learning ideal of each student. Following the idea that digital learning with textbooks is expanded with static and mobile hardware, software and educational technologies, on one side, and with the impact of networking, on the other side, this chapter provides an overview of globalized learning processes and a new educational ideal as a requirement of post-modernist philosophy for new digital learning environments.

## GLOBALISATON AND DIGITAL LEARNING ENVIRONMENT WITH TEXTBOOKS

Globalization of knowledge is, first of all, about networking and new models of information, communication, cognition and assessment moving toward hiperconnectivity. The concept of hiperconnectivity relies on *ubiquitous* forms of communication. Hiperconnectivity is used to define models in which learners are connected through channels and networks in real – virtual learning environments. They learn how to plan, model, create knowledge, establish connections, and be engaged in synchronic/asynchronic communications with other teachers and students around the word etc. In addition, growth of knowledge disseminated digital technologies and the use of digital mobile devices have heightened the awareness of new learning design principles. These principles and norms are focused on sustainability the mental structural changes and on necessity to process simultaneity information, communication, cognition and assessment tasks using at least several digital devices.

On the other hand, globalization in education refers to "cognitive shift, new relevancy spaces and new forms of subjectivities" (Macgilchrist & Christophe (2011, p. 155). Knowledge is not fixed, cut up in pieces and handed over, but rather (co)created by transacting with prior tacit knowledge, the curriculum, and other learners. It is a time to think about fundamental challengers regard a new educational ideal. There are some indicators: learning in/within global networks, where textbooks are available online, students learn anytime and anywhere. The modern students are treated as "global students" (Papastephanou, Christou & Gregoriou, 2013, p. 62). The global students are, first of all, "multiliteracies" (Pullen & Cole, 2010, p. 32). They are active in diverse cultural, social and domain-specific learning environments; use written-linguistic models and oral, visual, audio, gestural, tactile and spatial patterns of meaning. What is the fundament educational ideal for global students?

Globalization changes first of all our vision about the structure and functionality of learning environments. The evidences are: diversity of platforms, systems and patterns. Such an agglomeration of learning objects can be called "metasystems". Conceptually, as was found by Klir (1990, p. 325) meta $X$ is the name of what is observable (take place) after $X$, i.e. $X$ is prerequisite for meta $X$; meta $X$ denotes that $X$ is a background for this name; meta $X$ is used as a name thereof the above of $X$ within the meaning of more highly organized, has the higher logical type or is analyzed in a broader sense. The metasystems solution for learning outcomes was proposed by G. Pask (1968). His main argument was that different subjects use different strategies for the same skills. These strategies could be or cannot be fitted to the aspects of mental organization. From the author point of view, the adaptive metasystems is the better tool for investigation of skills as processes, focusing attention to an open system or on strategies of assimilation into a closed system (Pask, 1968, p. 4).

Research was shown (Hannafin, Hill, Land & Lee, 2014, p. 641) that new learning environment designs and frameworks are consistent with *constructivist-inspired views of learning*. Collectively, student-centered, open learning environments provide contexts wherein the individual determines learning goals, learning means, or both the learning goals and means. The individual may also establish and pursue individual learning goals with few or no external boundaries as typical during spontaneous, self-initiated learning from the Web that represent fundamentally different paradigms and philosophies. The assumption that psychological and pedagogical concerns in digital textbook use and development require a new *Learning Design* approach goes beyond linear or systemic instructional design approaches. First of all, these are relationships between student's cognitive system and digital learning environment with textbooks. Secondly, this is a *hermeneutic dialogue* between students and the author of the text. Finally, these are globalized learning processes, which require new standards.

## LAWS OF GLOBALISED PEDAGOGICAL PROCESSES

### Issues, Controversies, and the Research Problem

The synthesis of effects of globalization to educational systems and learning environments cannot be made using linear or systems thinking. Many ideas of post-modernism philosophy lead to this conclusion. Due to various definitions, prototypes and learning theories developed so far, the concept of "didactic model" is a fuzzy concept. To write the answer was *constructed* the principles of instructional design models for digital textbooks. It was observed that although conceptual modeling is a powerful approach for use and development of digital textbooks, it is difficult to figure out how to determine theirs affordance as result of instable and evolving nature of the digital textbook concept. So, the linear model, proposed by Skinner, cannot be used for digital textbook development, because is based only on *cognitive taxonomy*. The systems models provide norms for development processes of educational software and do not describe the interdependences between learner and learning objects.

Because this investigation aims to assemble the post-modernism philosophy to theory of digital textbooks use and development, the used method requires arranging learning theories and instructional design models in a hierarchy. How

are learning theories and instructional design models instantiated within digital textbook-based learning and development? In order to answer this question the issues and controversies related to design of metapattern as interdependences between the problems were identified, as well as context and contents. This allows identifying three main controversies:

- *The dialectic controversy* between digital learning in the open and closed systems;
- *The psychopedagogical controversy* between psychopedagogical characteristics of digital natives as multiliteracies and digital immigrates and;
- *The didactical controversy* between traditional learning methodologies of digitalized textbooks and knowledge management strategy required for Open Source Textbooks.

Traditionally, the learning designers use linear or systems thinking. However, while "linear thinking forces use to see one thing at a time, and to progress to whatever is next, which will in turn lead to more" (Risku & Harding, 2013, p. 113), systems thinking for centuries was overlooked. The systems thinking emphasizes looking at wholes rather than parts, addresses the role of interconnections and focused on closed interdependences. It has precise set of rules that reduced the ambiguities and miscommunications that can crop up when we talk with others about complex issues. It offers causal loop diagrams, which are rich in implications and insight. The modern systems thinking principles are: the big picture; long term, short term perspectives; measurable and no measurable data; dynamic, complex and interdependent and we are a part of system. Systems thinking offers an entirely different ways of communications and of working together more productive on understanding and solving complex problem (Lazanski, 2010, pp. 293-295).

One of main issues of linear and systems modeling are stages of educational materials development, which could include some psychopedagogical considerations. However, these stages don't take into consideration the interdependences between input, output and learning environment. In addition, pedagogical aspects of designing or using digital learning materials are much less frequently studied than technical ones. This is a serious problem also in using and development of digital textbooks. In order to solve this problem in the past six decades, learning design of digital textbooks were the object of numerous studies (Crowder, 1959; Criswell, 1989; Barker & Tucker, 1990; Bespalco, 2002; Mora, Gelman, Cervantes, MejIa & Weitzenfeld, 2003; Donovan & Bransford, 2005; Hung, 2008). It was founding that sense today "we have a large number of technological-enthusiastic teachers that try to introduce tools and functionalities without assessing first: the cognitive load, the cost, the utility, the usability, the accessibility and the psycho-pedagogical criteria that must be considered before innovate with technologies" (Agustí, Velasco & Serrano, 2011, p. 419).

Thinking about learning with digital textbooks could lead to use and development of linear or non-linear more or less algorithmic models. The linear algorithmic models describe cycles or step-by-step progression where a response to a step must be elicited before another step is taken. Instead of the linear models, the system algorithmic models describe step-by-step problem solving, with or without generation of the elementary learning objects and its analysis with immediate feedback. Getting beyond the linear sequences of the printed text, it is proposed to navigate or to search metadata in nonlinear structures of multimodal text or hypertext. It could take as a whole the proposed fragments in order to allow rising to consciousness relying to metacognition, patterns and metapatterns.

One more issue relies on students thinking styles that could be *linear or non-linear*. It was argued (Osterman & Reio, 2013) that linear thinking styles are a "preference for attending to external data and facts and processing this information through conscious logic and rational thinking to form knowledge, understanding, or a decision for guiding subsequent action. The linear thinking involves rationality, logic, and analytical thinking concentrating on external factors for comprehension and communication. Instead of this, the nonlinear thinking is related to intuition, insight, creativity, and emotions, concentrating on internal factors for comprehension and communication. The nonlinear thinking styles are a preference for attending to internal feelings, impressions, and sensations when comprehending and communicating information. This allows rewriting post-modernism thinking as that that weighs the known with unknown, learning with unknowing and conscious observations.

Three factors are essential in systems thinking: *concreteness* (as grounding in direct sensory experience), *connectedness* (refers to how integrated a piece of knowledge in both, previously learned knowledge and new information) and *practice* (Brandshow, 2005). Immediate practice is not helpful, too long delay before practice may also have negative effects: if a student cannot retrieve the material from memory and has to go back and re-learn the material, additional effort may be required when compared to practice at a moderate delay. However, from pedagogical perspective this reflect only *cognitive branch* of Bloom taxonomy. Generally speaking, learning with printed and a digitalized textbook is designed according to *prescriptive curricula requirements* and are focused on mastering new knowledge, skills, or attitude. From this reason the content of textbook is structured in lessons or study units, which are well-defined objectives, multimedia and assessment. The research problem arises as a synthesis of issues and controversies:

- What are the interdependences between globalization as a phenomenon that affects all educational systems and re-utilizable digital and non-digital learning objects?

- Is this a challenge for a new learning paradigm? Is this a need for a new learning ideal?

Critical thinking about the role of digital textbooks in diversity of the learning environments evidences the *metasystems approach*, which relies on post-modernism philosophy of learning In our point of view, the *metasystems thinking about digital textbook use and development represents an ecosystem "integrated" in the diversity of learning environments through cognitive systems and its adaptation and accommodation norms for sustainable development in order to remain viable.*

## Globalized Pedagogical Processes

Speech, speed, hyper-connectivity, and wasting of time are characteristics of the young students' behaviors. Those who have acquired some basic digital skills use them within their everyday practice. They like digital textbooks more than textbooks. Unfortunately, it is still not fully understood how to develop competence using digital textbooks, why use a digital textbook and how students learn to use different learning strategies. What is clear, however, that challenges caused by globalization affect all educational systems and all its subsystems, "constructing" a system of system.

The system of system is a *metasystem* (Klir, 1990; Fernández-Solís, Palmer & Ferris, 2007; Fletcher, 1992). As was observed (Palmer, 2002) the system of system is not unified and not totaled. Rather they provide the environment that the systems need to exist. They exist just beyond the interface of the system, either inside or outside the system. In other words the meta-system mediates between a system and its parts. The meta-system is like the glue that holds the various systems together, but its nature is not like the system, it is in fact the inverse dual of the system in every respect.

Metasystems Learning Design is based on meta-system approach. This means that outcomes of learning could be identified using Theory of Metasystem transition, proposed by B. Turchin. According to this, we can assume the concept of knowledge, described in terms of Foucauldian's terminology, as *savior*, evolve to competence, described in modern terminology as *savoir-vivre complex*. Conceptually, the boundaries of the meta-system are defined by the researcher. The most used methods are: meta-analyses and ideal type. Each of the metasystems could be meta-analyzed in order to identify similarities, differences and interdependencies between its constituent elements. One of the benefits of meta-analysis is that it can be explored in artificial defined medium and investigated using qualitative methods. For our case the framework for a metasystem investigation of Educational Ideal is considered the *Globalized Pedagogical Processes GPP*, *defined as a set of complex cognitive processes occurred in a system of systems, where are presented learning objects, inter-relations and processes, which forming an organized totality lead the student's cognitive activity at achieving specific educational outcomes. The estimated educational outcome is integrative structure of competence.*

Theoretically, each of the metasystems related to educational systems can be investigated in order to identify similarities, differences and correlational interdependences of its constituent elements. The proposed metasystems learning design methodology is focused on investigation the specific of the learning processes in correlation with learning environments characteristics for situations where the students' complex development is the starting point, center and the purpose of the didactic activities. Instead of information or knowledge the aim is to investigate the requirements for self-regulation.

The hypothesis that architecture of integrated structure of competence is the educational outcome in learning with digital textbooks, could be verified if the metasystems GPP will be analyzed in concordance with domains that investigate the concept of "competence".

The architecture of integrated structure of competence can be studied using the structural definition, proposed by F. Heylighen. According to this, the metasystem $S'$ represents an integration of a number of subsystems $S' = \{S_1, ..., S_n\}$ which are normally replicas of some template to which an unspecified self-regulated mechanism $C$ is added that controls the behavior and replication. So, the structure of metasystems represents an integration of a number of subsystems, which are normally replicas of templates (meta-patterns) to which an unspecified mechanism control the behavior and replication of the initial system. In our case, the competence template S replicates to subsystems: educational philosophy $S'$, pedagogy $S_1$, psychology $S_2$, cybernetics $S_3$, and management $S_4$. These systems correspond to domains that study the concept of competence. The transitions within and all of the systems are activated by the mechanisms of variation, selection and control, which form and maintain the functionality of studied metasystems. So, we can see the transition states from input (a priori knowledge, skills and competence) through activation of self-regulation phases.

In the Era of Informational Globalisation and Social Media, education ideal represents more than even a global social phenomenon. This means that the planetary culture has grown out of the developments in informational and communicational technologies. The base of planetary culture is complex actions in individual, colaborative, differentiated, dynamic, interactive, adaptive, innovative and mixed digital learning environments. Thus, as a result of consecutive transitions, a multilevel structure of control arises, which enables complicated forms of meta-systems behavior to occur. As a consequence, we can consider the educational ideal epistemology (S/) to be a meta-system of integrated structure of competence dynamically updated with respect to the following subsystems: pedagogy ($S^1$), psychology ($S^2$), cybernetics ($S^3$), management ($S^4$), and other domains ($S^n$) as represented in Figure 1.

From the functional point of view (Turchin & Joslyn, 1993), the metasystem transition is the case where some activity $A$, which is characteristic of the top control system of a system $S$, becomes itself controlled as a metasystem transition from $S$ to $S'$ takes place. The functional aspect of meta-system transitions can be represented by formulas of this kind:

$$\text{control of } A = A'.$$

The sequence of metasystem transitions of all integrative competence' components could be controlled by the globalization phenomena which led, starting from the appearance of *savoir-vivre* architecture of competence, to the appearance of thought:

*Figure 1. The educational ideal epistemology according to theory of metasystems transition*

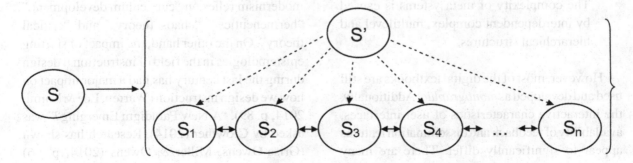

- Control of *savoir-vivre architecture of competence* = self-regulated learning outcomes;
- Control of *self-regulated learning outcomes* = interactive feedback in real environment;
- *Control of interactive feedback in real environment* = digital textbooks;
- *Control of digital textbooks* = learning design norms;
- *Control of learning design norms* = integrated savoir-vivre structure of competence.

In order to evidence the priority of integrated savoir-vivre structure of competence in new educational ideal was identified the necessary and sufficient condition of globalized pedagogical processes (GPP):

- GPP are suitable to dynamic and flexible metasystems, which have modified state and structural elements on the base on moments of time and newest situations;
- GPP is suitable to an open system, in which flows between human cognitive systems and learning environment are based on input and output characteristics. The issue of learning results from the conflicts input data and output requirements;
- GPP corresponds to a large metasystems like hyper graphs. Its subsystems have a large number of interlinked and structural elements and processes;
- GPP correspond to complex meta-systems. The complexity of metasystems is caused by interdependent complex, multilevel and hierarchical structures.

However, most of the digital textbooks are still used and developed as *monographic*. Additionally, the interactive characteristics of user interfaces, availability of feedback and dissemination features appear to significantly differ. There are many initiatives. For example, "digital textbooks allow readers to search inside of them and feature concept summaries. The interactive study materials are: flashcards and chapter outlines and quizzes to help students test their knowledge" (Apps, 2013); upper-level institutions are looking at more efficient ways for students to access their reading materials (Price, 2013); Google has launched a digital textbooks section of Books on Google Play in the U.S., available through the Play website, Android and iOS apps (Qwen, 2013). How can this dilemma been solved?

Each of the metasystem holds together systems, objects and processes, constructing a highly organized structure. This is a new culture of learning, the culture of every student which could be integrated in the planetary culture like a puzzle. The planetary culture correspond to metasystem transition from linear to metasystems thinking, is based on scientific principles and norms, and recognize the culture either of each component or a system in totality. Assessment also, has a planetary scale. This means that innovative assessment methods are individual, group and collaborative.

The meta-analysis of globalized pedagogical processes allows identifying the core concepts: dynamicity and flexibility; flexible development of personality; self-regulated learning; intrinsic motivation; integrity of cognitive, affective and psychomotor activities; knowledge management and planetary culture. These concepts were compared with concepts, identified by Podlasai (2003, p. 171) to identify the ideal type of concept. The obtained result is presented in Table 1.

Philosophy of education in context of postmodernism relies on "curriculum development," "hermeneutics," "chaos theory," and "critical theory". On the other hand, the impact of shifting epistemologies in the field of instructional design during the last century has had a major impact on how we design instruction (Warren, Lee & Najmi, 2014, p. 89). "A New Paradigm Emerging?" was asked by Crowther (2014). Research has shown (Grise-Owens, Miller & Owens (2014, p. 46)

*Table 1. Globalised pedagogical processes vs. traditional pedagogical processes*

| | Traditional Pedagogical Process | Globalisated Pedagogical Processes |
|---|---|---|
| 1 | *Law of the dynamicity*: learners actively construct their own knowledge based upon the things they have in the past. | *Law of dynamicity and flexibility*: learners actively construct their own competence passing self-regulated phases provided by local and global, real and virtual learning environments. |
| 2 | *Law of development of cognitive personality*: each learner prefers own learning style and has own genotype, readiness, motivation, strategies, thinking, methods etc. | *Law of adaptive and accommodative (flexible) development of personality*: each learner need to became a lifelong learner as an ongoing and self-motivated pursuit of own competence construction for personal reasons and needs. |
| 3 | *Law of orchestration*: each learner go through own cognitive development, which is orchestrated by the teacher. | *Law of self-regulated learning*: cognitive and metacognitive development of competence can be accelerated or slowed by the learning environment. |
| 4. | *Law of stimulation:* early teaching of any subject should emphasis basic ideas, the spiral curriculum could revise these basic ideas and provide content to build upon the full understanding them | *Law of intrinsic motivation:* the learning environment provides all necessary tools, as well as learning objects, digital artifacts, pedagogical resources and methods for cognition, metacognition and goal-oriented behavior. |
| 5 | *Law if uniqueness between emotion, logics and practices:* teaching and learning are two different psycho-pedagogical processes but guided by the similar rules: assimilation, reproduction and, rarely creativity. | *Law of uniqueness between cognitive, affective and psychomotor activities:* teaching and learning are based on internal cognitive and metacognitive processes developed by dynamic and flexible instructional strategy. |
| 6. | *Law if uniqueness between external (pedagogical) and internal (cognitive) activities:* learning is the process of accumulation facts, knowledge, skills etc. | *Law of knowledge management:* learning is the result (output) of the processes at the point when student is able to demonstrate the functionality of own performance, both in physical and virtual learning environments. |
| 7. | *Law of determinism:* the traditional learning process is "guided" by the law of inertia, law of own internal resistance to the external forces influence and the law of keeping the structural and functional integrity. | *Law of determinism to planetary culture:* learning is "guided" by the evolution of new technologies (hardware, software and education), which "half-open" the boundaries of closed pedagogical systems and linked them for planetary culture. |

that in response to increasing global challenges, the social work education adds meta-practice to traditional micro-, mezzo-, and macro-practice curriculum areas. Rudic (2013, p. 74) argued that modern pedagogy approaches needs to be conceptualized at least in 3D space. This approach reflects the holistic completed education that combines reality with virtuality, but its functionality based on synchronic interactions in real time. This new paradigm of learning relies on *transcendental pragmatism*, as a philosophy of life. Its new branch is naturalistic transcendental pragmatism (Alexander, 2014, p. 13).

Furthermore it is impossible to assemble a transcendental identity without *connectionism*. There are the following principles: "learning and knowledge rests in diversity of opinions; learning is a process of connecting specialized models of informational sources; learning may reside in non-human appliances; capacity to know more is more critical than what is currently known; nurturing and maintaining connections is needed to facilitate continual learning; ability to see connection between fields, ideas, and concepts is a core skill; currency (accurate, up-to-date knowledge) and decision – making is itself a learning process" (Mallon & Gilstrap, 2014, p. 17). The practical values of connectionism were described by Chun (2014): new media research in the field of communication and a model for the future implementation of related educational applications in classrooms connected to the Internet.

## A NEW EDUCATIONAL IDEAL

In modern world all pedagogical systems has been affected by knowledge explosions, multi diversity of input data quality, unification of learning standards, impossibility to forecast the output data in open learning environment, digital nonlinearity and multimodality of text; rapid evolution of human and non-human cognitive systems. The informational globalization has caused the transitions from:

- Closed to open educational system;
- From instructional design to learning design;
- From teacher-centered to learner-centered learning environments.

Theoretically, there is a crossing from Instructional Design to Metasystems Learning Design, which are based on core principles delivered by educational philosophy; pedagogy of integrated structure of competence; cybernetic pedagogy; quantum psychology and knowledge management principles.

The globalised education system is focused on self-regulated learning and metacognitive strategies. This is the case of the authentic learning: "the notion of learning, knowledge and skills in contexts that reflect the way the knowledge will be useful in real life" (Herrington, Reeves & Oliver, 2014). Such a way can be investigated through frontier research in pedagogy. Moreover, within any authentic learning are used authentic tasks with real-world relevance. In solving these tasks the cognitive activities match as nearly as possible the real-world issues and tasks of professionals rather than decontextualized or classroom-based tasks. But, authentic tasks usually are ill-defined, recurring students to provide their own understanding of tasks in order to complete the (meta)cognitive activities; comprise complex investigation over a sustained period of time; provide the opportunity to learn from different perspectives through collaboration, reflection and generalization. Usually, authentic tasks lead beyond domain-specific outcomes and create polished products valuable in their own right.

Educational ideal can be viewed as a learning ideal of each individual to be adaptive and acomodative in an informational globalized world with changing dynamics. Indeed, it is based on scientific methodology and, at the moment, required frontier investigation in psychological development (*informational and energy characteristics*) and pedagogical literacy (*learning analytics*). It is common for all actors of the educational system, either formal, informal or non-formal. The problem is that educational ideal is more than a priority. It is a students' need to be competitive in the global economy.

Traditionally, to achieve the educational ideal, the actors study the theory and methodology of learning and apply the finding to learning design of pedagogical resources and learning tools.

However, to set up the functionality of the educational ideal in the processes of the digital textbook use and development could be addressed even more important tasks such as:

- To illustrate the interdependences between educational ideal and learning environment in order to identify the core concept(s) in content of the digital textbook;
- To discuss the role of a new educational ideal for each student;
- To demonstrate the role of self-regulated learning for a new educational ideal;
- To evidence the role of knowledge management for digital textbook design;
- To summarize the self-directed learning from perspective of planetary culture.

The new educational ideal should be an ideal of learning for each student. However, the achievement ideal depends on interdependences between teacher(s), student(s) and content (s), respectively. The limitation of this statement is that teacher(s) could be replaced totally or partially with digital textbooks. It should be taking into account that time; speed and acceleration of knowledge production are much faster than printed and digitalized content provided. This indicates on self-regulated learning and/with metacognitive strategies as a condition for adaptation and accommodation to learning environments.

## SELF-REGULATED LEARNING AND A NEW EDUCATIONAL IDEAL

The role of self-regulated learning for a new educational ideal is indisputable. As was noted by Fuente & Lazanu (2012, p. 40) with reference to Hadwin, Winne, Stockley, Nesbit & Woszcyna (2001) self-regulated learning is by definition a *response behavior*. Self–regulated learning refers to learner's self-generated thoughts, feelings, and actions for attaining academic goals and complex interactive process involving not only cognitive self-regulation, but also motivation. The students included in the self-regulated learning processes learn to plan their actions and set specific academic goals in order to achieve them; they can anticipate problems that could prevent them from achieving their goals; they are highly self-efficacious, able to self-monitor their academic progress, and to make facilitative attributions about their performance and value model (Tanriseven & Dilmaç, 2013, p.29).

Students who use the strategies to regulate their cognition are more successful than the students who do not control and regulate their own learning. They observed that cognitive and motivational strategies are useful to predict and improve the students' learning goals social reinforcement goals, and achievement. In other words, students' self-efficacy beliefs play an important role in their academic motivation, learning and achievement (Sadi & Uyar, 2013, p. 30).

Self-regulated learning is guided by *intrinsic motivation, cognition and metacognition*. Dur-

ing internal regulation the learner specifies his/her own goals without external guidelines and chooses an effective learning strategy; in the external regulation the learners depends on others to get started or to complete a task, but in shared regulation the learner interact with environment. Clark (2012, p. 205) advances the proposition that the theory and practice of formative assessment combines cognition, social, and cultural theories which guide instructional methods and drive self-regulated strategies and lifelong learning competences among learners. It was later discussed that these theories serve as an analytic self-regulated learning model of mobile learning (Sha, Looi, Chen & Zhang, 2012). According to authors this is a conceptual framework for understanding mobile learning, in which the notion of self-regulation as agency is at the core. They found that self-regulated learning has two components: motivation and metacognition. With reference to Koriat (2007) was noted that metacognition refers to the study of what people know about their cognitive and memory processes, and how they put the metacognitive knowledge to use in regulating their information processing and behavior. Motivation, however, is a multi-faceted construct and include autonomy based on intrinsic and extrinsic motivation.

One of the most important specifics of modern educational system is the *uniqueness between cognitive, affective and psychomotor activities*. This idea could be solved as a "flexible, dynamic and instructional strategy" (Railean, 2008). This strategy indicates on powerful learning environment; in which self-regulated learning is focused on strategy of competence development through digital textbooks, which is similar to grown of perfect crystals. One can observe that "crystal" is similar to the learning outcomes. This similarity allows predicting that powerful learning environment is like a saturated solution needed at the beginning of crystal growing process. This solution need to pour over a substrate, where in our case, correspond to authentic context. Then we need to obtain a "seed crystal". In our case we will "concentrate" the main concepts in module I and, at the final phase, will add a quiz. After student wills successful pass the quiz, he/she will be engaged in active personalized learning with formative assessment and peer evaluation of project. Our "crystal" will grow! At the end of the learning process we can keep our crystal in a closed container or will "cover with a protective solution" (in our case, this is a certificate) for future exploration.

From the author point of view an electronic textbook should meet requirements following from general theory and psychology of teaching through encouragement and providing for an active cooperation with education; providing for a reciprocal feedback; simulation models; exemplary resolved problems; an adequate formulation and expression of thoughts, structure, arrangement and the way of presenting new knowledge and adaptive for an individual style. This is a knowledge management model.

In our age learning results from adaptation and accommodation at permanently changing conditions of different learning environment, which are real and virtual, global and local. It is expected that the sum of knowledge will be duplicated every two years. If this information is correct, the cognitive systems will be transited to a new *educational ideal*. As a result of meta-analyses of GPP the educational ideal was name "professionalism, planetary thinking and cultural pluralism". These educational ideal profiles appear to be powerful highlighting how learners learn and self-regulated learning in conditions of globalization of educational systems with changing learning environments.

*Professionalism* describes the standing practice or methods used by professional to perform a task. In case of education teacher's and students' roles in the instructional process is the deciding factor for the effectiveness of teaching and learning. Being professional is an ideal both for teacher(s) and student(s), because the reality requires decision-making and competitive professionals in accordance with the needs and challenges faced. Similar views were also raised by Copriady (2013, p. 177), who asserts that educational reform must begin with how students learn and how teachers teach, and not merely looking at the achievement and that is a close relationship between teacher professionalism with the act of fostering interest in learning among students.

*Planetary thinking* means that people through their actions may transform our planet. However, this transformation could be positive and negative. Education needs to absorb the global changes in culture, ergonomics and ecology of learning and to propose adequate methodologies and educational technologies. Planetary culture ideal requires thinking globally, but acting locally. The phrase "Think globally, act locally", first used in the context of environmental changes, has been used also in education. Conceptually, digital textbooks will be designed and developed internationally at global level, but used nationally at local level. The teacher(s) and student(s) around the world could develop collaborative projects regard digital textbook. Globalization and ICT offer new conceptual and methodological approach that allow making projects that couldn't even do sixty years ago.

However, in educational system come students from diverse backgrounds, learning styles and cultures. The concepts of life-long learning and adult education are more used than ever. The students with diverse background was renamed "digital natives" (Houston, 2011; Xiaoqing, Yuankun & Xiaofeng, 2013). Students with different learning styles and cultures form the *cultural pluralism,* which "highlight the subjects of cultural identity and autonomy in a world of immense power imbalances among nations and peoples" (Siame, 2012, p. 42).

The metasystems learning design could be seen as a small piece of culture of learning, which could be integrated in the planetary culture for better learning outcomes. The planetary culture defines the metasystem transition from the artificially closed pedagogical systems to the more open ones, and of the inexorable part of evolution from knowledge reproductions to knowledge worker. The planetary culture learning methodologies are focused on principles and norms balanced between "equilibrium ↔ non equilibrium". In the planetary culture the learning design of digital textbook is based on the competence methodology, where learning cannot be defined without its environment as well. But, learning environment is not unique and not static.

## FUTURE RESEARCH DIRECTIONS

Future research directions should explore how globalized learning processes and a new educational ideal may be utilized to provide understanding of the psychological and pedagogical consideration in digital textbook use and development. The ideas that emerged from globalized pedagogical processes and a new learning ideal are many and various, but tended to focus on a few key areas: metasystem configuration of digital textbook, methodology of design the elementary learning units and phases of technological projects related digital textbook use and development. There also debates about structure, functions and trends in curricula, the impact of hardware, software and educational technologies, and the need to develop the integrated structure of competence as educational outcomes. Unsurprisingly, many of these issues are revealed to be interconnected in order to be solved from philosophic, pedagogic, psychological, and cybernetic and knowledge management point of view.

The fundamental question facing instructional design of digital textbook is how psychological and pedagogical considerations in digital textbook use and development. Metasystem learning design has to anticipate demand, providing answers to

questions yet to be asked. Using a new educational ideal as a starting point helps to identify those questions: How to use available digital textbooks in order to archive the new educational ideal? How to develop digital textbooks for students in order to achieve a new educational ideal? By recognizing that emerging trends are catalysts for a positive change, metasystems learning design approach go beyond linear and instructional system design approach. In this was can drive instructional design of digital textbooks forward, demonstrating the effectiveness of metasystems learning design approach.

The future book's theme relies on analyzing metasystems learning design delimitations. From the perspective of the second chapter the issues that rely upon psychological and pedagogical considerations in digital textbook use and development will be treated through "ideal type" method. This will allow identifying the core "substrate" of philosophical, psychological, pedagogical, and cybernetic and knowledge management domains. The insight of this idea is that the core "substrate" will constitute the background for metasystems learning design principles, which could be applied for identification norms of digital textbook design as well as functions, methodologies and technologies.

## CONCLUSION

This chapter had exanimated the globalized learning processes and a new educational ideal. It identified issues as well as dialectical, psychological and didactic controversies and problems related to metasystem transition from linear design of programed textbook to metasystem learning design of modern digital textbooks. It designed the necessary and sufficient conditions of globalized pedagogical processes: a) dynamicity and flexibility; b) openness; c) hyper-connectivity and d) complex metasystem with interdependent complex, multilevel and hieratical structures.

The core concept of the metasystems approach is "metasystem". The metasystem is not a lot of systems. System of system "are not unified and not totalities. Rather they provide the environment that the system need to exist. They exist just beyond the interface of the system, either inside or outside the system. In other words the meta-system mediates between a system and its parts, just as well as it mediates between the supersystem (system of systems) and its subsystems.

The metasystem holds together interactive and interconnected objects and processes, forming a highly organized structure. Such a structure allows an intensive flux of information, data and knowledge between all internal and external systems. This means the Globalized Pedagogical Processes are guided by the following laws: dynamism and flexibility; adaptive and accommodative (flexible) development; self-regulated learning; intrinsic motivation; uniqueness between cognitive, affective and psychomotor; knowledge management and determinism to planetary culture.

The laws require understanding and achieving a new educational ideal: professionalism, planetary thinking and cultural pluralism. Being professional is an ideal both for teacher(s) and student(s). Planetary thinking and cultural pluralism defines norms of metasystems learning design focused on well-established statement: "act locally, think globally". Perhaps metasystems learning design approach is simply more efficient in digital textbook use and development than the linear and systemic ones. Multiple perspectives could be established from designing digital textbooks as pedagogical resources, as well as learning tools for developing self-regulated and metacognitive skills. It is hoped that this chapter provide guidance for researchers and educators in their design of digital textbook use and development, in their activities to archive estimated learning outcomes using digital textbooks.

## REFERENCES

Agusti, M. F., Velasco, M. R., & Serrano, M. J. (2011). E-Learning: Psycho-pedagogical utility, usability and accessibility criteria from a learner centred perspective. In F. Lazarinis, S. Green, & E. Pearson (Eds.), *Handbook of research on e-learning standards and interoperability: Frameworks and issues* (pp. 419–434). Hershey, PA: Information Science Reference. doi:10.4018/978-1-61692-789-9.ch021

Alexander, H. A. (2014). Traditions of inquiry in education: Engaging the paradigms of educational research. In A. D. Reid, E. P. Hart, & P. A. Peters (Eds.), *A companion to research in education* (pp. 13–25). Springer Netherlands. doi:10.1007/978-94-007-6809-3_2

Aliyev, S., Altayev, Z., Ismagambetova, Z., & Massanov, Y. (2012). *Philosophy of education: the challenges of globalization and innovation in the information society. Engineering & Technology., 71*, 1096–1098.

Barker, J., & Tucker, R. (1990). *The interactive learning revolution*. New York: London-Nichols Publishing.

Bespalco, V. (2002). *Teaching and learning with computers* [In Russian]. Retrieved November 1, 2014 from http://www.eusi.ru/lib/bespalko_obrasovanie/3.php

Bourn, D. (2014). *The theory and practice of global learning*. Retrieved November 1, 2014 from http://www.ioe.ac.uk/DERC_ResearchPaper11-TheTheoryAndPracticeOfGlobalLearning.pdf

Chun, L. (2014). *An exploratory study behind the implementation of computer assisted learning in classrooms connected to the internet: Hype or hope?* Retrieved November 1, 2014 http://scholarspace.manoa.hawaii.edu/bitstream/handle/10125/31454/communication005.PDF?sequence=1

Clark, I. (2012). Formative assessment: Assessment is for self-regulated learning. *Educational Psychology Review, 24*(2), 205–249. doi:10.1007/s10648-011-9191-6

Cochrane, T. D. (2014). Critical success factors for transforming pedagogy with mobile Web 2.0. *British Journal of Educational Technology, 45*(1), 65–82. doi:10.1111/j.1467-8535.2012.01384.x

Copriady, J. (2013). The implementation of lesson study programme for developing professionalism in teaching profession. *Asian Social Science, 9*(12), 176–186. doi:10.5539/ass.v9n12p176

Criswell, E. (1989). *The design of computer-based instruction.* New York: Macmillan Publishing Company.

Crowder, N. (1959). Automatic tutoring by means of intrinsic programming. In Automatic teaching: The state of the art (pp. 23–28). New York: John Wiley & Sons.

Crowther, N. A. (2014). A new paradigm emerging? Review of learning, work and practice: New understandings. *Higher Education, Skills and Work-based Learning, 4*(1), 29–49.

Cummings, T., & Worley, C. (2014). *Organization development and change.* Cengage Learning.

D'Mello, S., Lehman, B., Pekrun, R., & Graesser, A. (2014). Confusion can be beneficial for learning. *Learning and Instruction, 29,* 153–170. doi:10.1016/j.learninstruc.2012.05.003

de la Fuente, J., & Lozano, A. (2011). Design of the SEAI self-regulation assessment for young children and ethical considerations of psychological testing. In G. Dettori & D. Persico (Eds.), *Fostering self-regulated learning through ICT* (pp. 39–53). Hershey, PA: Information.

Donovan, M., & Bransford, J. (2005). *How students learn: History, mathematics, and science in the classroom.* Washington: The National Academies press.

Fernández-Solis, J., Palmer, K., & Ferris, T. (2007). *Theoretical approach to the interaction between the metasystem schemas of the artificial (built) environment and nature.* Retrieved November 1, 2014 from http://archone.tamu.edu/faculty/JSolis/Documents/014_Schema_ultra_final_21_05_07.pdf

Fletcher, J. (1992). *Individualized systems of- instruction.* Retrieved November 1, 2014 from http://www.dtic.mil/cgibin/GetTRDoc?AD=ada255960.

Grier, M. (2012). *Kant's critique of metaphysics.* Retrieved November 1, 2014 from http://plato.stanford.edu/entries/kant-metaphysics/

Grise-Owens, E., Miller, J. J., & Owens, L. W. (2014). Responding to global shifts: Meta-practice as a relevant social work practice paradigm. *Journal of Teaching in Social Work, 34*(1), 46–59. doi:10.1080/08841233.2013.866614

Hannafin, M. J., Hill, J. R., Land, S. M., & Lee, E. (2014). Student-centered, open learning environments: Research, theory, and practice. In J. M. Spector, M. D. Merrill, J. Elen, & M. J. Bishop (Eds.), *Handbook of research on educational communications and technology* (pp. 641–651). New York: Springer. doi:10.1007/978-1-4614-3185-5_51

Herrington, J., Reeves, T. C., & Oliver, R. (2014). Authentic learning environments. In J. M. Spector, M. D. Merrill, J. Elen, & M. J. Bishop (Eds.), Handbook of research on educational communications and technology (pp. 401–412). New York: Springer.

Houston, C. (2011). Digital books for digital natives. *Children & Libraries: The Journal of the Association for Library Service to Children, 9*(3), 39–42.

Hsieh, L. Y., Lu, Y. J., Lin, H. S., & Lee, Y. H. (2014). With blended learning information operational system design in response to globalized logistics talent training. In *The 2nd International Workshop on Learning Technology for Education in Cloud* (pp. 61-71). Springer Netherlands. doi:10.1007/978-94-007-7308-0_7

Hung, W. (2008). Enhancing systems-thinking skills with modelling. *British Journal of Educational Technology*, *39*(6), 1099–1120. doi:10.1111/j.1467-8535.2007.00791.x

Jenseen, S. S., & Heilessen, S. B. (2005). Time, place, and identity in project work on the net. In T. S. Roberts (Ed.), Computer-supported collaborative learning in higher education (pp. 51–75). Hershey, PA: Idea Group Publishing. doi:10.4018/978-1-59140-408-8.ch003

Klir, G. J. (1990). *Architecture of systems problem solving* [in Russian]. Moscow: Radio and Communication.

Lazanski, T. J. (2010). Systems thinking: Ancient Maya's evolution of consciousness and contemporary systems thinking. *AIP Conference Proceedings*, *1303*(1), 289–296. doi:10.1063/1.3527166

Lyons, J. P., Hannon, J., & Macken, C. (2014). Sustainable practice in embedding learning technologies: Curriculum renewal through course design intensives. In M. Gosper & D. Ifenthaler (Eds.), *Curriculum models for the 21st Century* (pp. 423–442). New York: Springer. doi:10.1007/978-1-4614-7366-4_22

Macgilchrist, F., & Christophe, B. (2011). Translating globalization theories into educational research: Thoughts on recent shifts in Holocaust education. *Discourse (Abingdon)*, *32*(1), 145–158. doi:10.1080/01596306.2011.537080

Mallon, M. N., & Gilstrap, D. L. (2014). Digital literacy and the emergence of technology-based curriculum theories. In D. J. Douglas (Ed.), Academic knowledge construction and multimodal curriculum development, (pp. 15-29). doi:10.4018/978-1-4666-4797-8.ch002

Mora, M., Gelman, O., & Cervantes, F. MejIa, M. & Weitzenfeld, A. (2003). A systemic approach for the formalization of the information systems concept: Why information systems are systems? In J. Cano (Ed.), Critical reflections on information systems: A systemic approach (pp. 1-29). Hershey, PA: Idea Group Publishing.

O'Rafferty, S., Curtis, H., & O'Connor, F. (2014). Mainstreaming sustainability in design education–a capacity building framework. *International Journal of Sustainability in Higher Education*, *15*(2), 169–187. doi:10.1108/IJSHE-05-2012-0044

Osterman, M., Reio, T. J., & Thirunarayanan, M. O. (2013). Digital literacy: A demand for nonlinear thinking styles. In M. S. Plakhotnik & S. M. Nielsen (Eds.), *Proceedings of the 12th Annual South Florida Education Research Conference SFERC 2013* (pp.149-154). Miami Florida International University. Retrieved November 2, 2014 from http://education.fiu.edu/research_conference/docs/13/SFERC202013Proceedings.pdf#page=168

Palmer, K. D. (2002). *Advanced meta-systems theory for metasystems engineers*. Retrieved November, 2, 2014 from http://holonomic.net/sd01V04.pdf

Papastephanou, M., Christou, M., & Gregoriou, Z. (2013). Globalisation, the challenge of educational synchronisation and teacher education. *Globalisation, Societies and Education*, *11*(1), 61–84. doi:10.1080/14767724.2012.690311

Paquette, G. (2014). Technology-based instructional design: Evolution and major trends. In Handbook of Research on Educational Communications and Technology (pp. 661-671). Springer New York.

Pask, G. (1968). Final scientific report 1 September 1966 to 30 November 1968. Richmond, UK: System Research. Ltd.

Peregrin, J. (2014). Rules as the impetus of cultural evolution. *Topoi*, *33*(2), 531–545. doi:10.1007/s11245-013-9219-2

Podlasai, I. (2003). *Pedagogies* (in Russian). Moscow: Vlados.

Price, K. (2013). *Does digital age mean digital textbooks*? Retrieved November 1, 2014 from http://www.hattiesburgamerican.com/article/20130811/NEWS01/308110025/Does-digital-age-mean-digital-textbooks.htm

Pullen, D., & Cole, D. (2010). *Multiliteracies and technology enhanced education: Social practice and the global classroom*. London: Information Science Reference. doi:10.4018/978-1-60566-673-0

Qwen, L. H. (2013). *Google rolls out digital textbooks, to buy and rent — but students should shop around*. Retrieved November 1, 2014 from http://gigaom.com/2013/08/09/google-rolls-out-digital-textbooks-to-buy-and-rent-but-students-should-shop-around/

Railean, E. (2008). Electronic textbooks in electronic portfolio: a new approach for the self-regulated learning. In *Proceedings of 9th International Conference on Development and Application Systems DAS 2008* (pp. 138-141). Suceava: Stefan cel Mare University of Suceava.

Railean, E. (2010). Metasystems approach to research the globalised pedagogical processes. *Annals of Spiru Haret University, Mathematics – Informatics Series* (Special issue), 31-50.

Railean, E. (2010). Self-regulated learning – condition of adaptation and accommodation of digital native to globalisated learning environments achieved through digital textbook [In Romanian]. *Romanian Journal of Education*, *1*(2), 27–38.

Railean, E. (2012). Issues and challenges associated with the design of electronic textbook. In B. H. Khan (Ed.), *User Interface Design for Virtual Environments: Challenges and Advances* (pp. 238–256). Hershey, PA: IGI Publishing. doi:10.4018/978-1-61350-516-8.ch015

Railean, E. (2013). Knowledge management model for electronic textbook design. In K. Patel & S. Vij (Eds.), *Enterprise resource planning models for the education sector: Applications and methodologies* (pp. 77–92). Hershey, PA: Information Science Reference. doi:10.4018/978-1-4666-2193-0.ch005

Risku, M. & Harding, L. (2013). A unified theory. In *Education for tomorrow: A biocentric, student-focused model for reconstructing education,* (pp. 113-134).

Rowley, J. (2014). Bridging the gap: Improving students' learning experience through shifting pedagogical practices in higher education. *International Journal of Learning and Development*, *4*(1), 28–39. doi:10.5296/ijld.v4i1.4944

Rudic, G. (2013). Modern pedagogy in multi-measured space. In E. B. Assemble (Ed.), *Socrates Almanac "Science and Education"* (pp. 74–75). Oxford: Oxford Review.

Sha, L., Looi, C. K., Chen, W., & Zhang, B. H. (2012). Understanding mobile learning from the perspective of self-regulated learning. *Journal of Computer Assisted Learning*, *28*(4), 366–378. doi:10.1111/j.1365-2729.2011.00461.x

Siame, C. N. (2012). Relativism in Berlin's cultural pluralism. *Theoria*, *59*(130), 42–58. doi:10.3167/th.2012.5913003

Tanriseven, I., & Dilmac, B. (2013). Predictive relationships between secondary school students' human values, motivational beliefs, and Self-Regulated Learning Strategies. *Educational Sciences: Theory and Practice, 13*(1), 29–36.

Turchin, V., & Joslyn, C. (1993). *The metasystems transition*. Retrieved October 12, 2014 from ftp://ftp.vub.ac.be/pub/projects/Principia_Cybernetica/PCP-Web/MST.html

Warren, S. J., Lee, J., & Najmi, A. (2014). The impact of technology and theory on instructional design since 2000. In J. M. Spector, M. D. Merrill, D. Elen, & M. J. Bishop, (Eds.), Handbook of research on educational communications and technology (pp. 89-99). Springer New York.

Williams, M. K., & Donnellon, A. (2014). Personalizing entrepreneurial learning: A pedagogy for facilitating the know why. *Entrepreneurship Research Journal, 4*(2), 167–204.

Xiaoqing, G., Yuankun, Z., & Xiaofeng, G. (2013). Meeting the "Digital Natives": Understanding the acceptance of technology in classrooms. *Journal of Educational Technology & Society, 16*(1), 392–402.

## ADDITIONAL READING

Apps. (2013). *Digital textbook platform boundless releases iPhone app*. Retrieved October, 13, 2014 from http://www.mediabistro.com/appnewser/digital-textbook-platform-boundlessreleases-iphone-app_b39398

Beetham, H., & Sharpe, R. (2013). *Rethinking pedagogy for a digital age: Designing for 21st Century learning*. Routledge. Taylor & Francis.

Bloom, J. W. & Volk, T. (2007). The use of metapatterns for research into complex systems of teaching, learning, and schooling. *An International Journal of Complexity and Education, 4*(1), Retrieved October, 13, 2014 from ualberta.ca.

Bloom, J. W., & Volk, T. (2012). Metapatterns for research into complex systems of learning. In N. M Seel (Ed.), Encyclopedia of the sciences of learning, (pp. 2243-2246).

Bocconi, S., & Repetto, F. (2005). Toward a European community of pioneer teachers. In V. Mittoro, & W. Admiral (Ed.), Pioneer Teachers (pp.43-56). Edizioni MENADO: Didactica.

Bod, R. (2014). *A new history of the humanities: The search for principles and patterns from antiquity to the present*. Oxford University Press.

Boekaerts, M. (1997). Self-regulated learning: A new concept embraced by researchers, policy makers, educators, teacher and students. *Learning and Instruction, 7*(2), 161–168. doi:10.1016/S0959-4752(96)00015-1

Boekaerts, M. (1999). Self-regulated learning: Where we are today. *International Journal of Educational Research, 31*(6), 445–457. doi:10.1016/S0883-0355(99)00014-2

Boekaerts, M. (2002). Bringing about change in the classroom: Strengths and weaknesses of the self-regulated learning approach. *Learning and Instruction, 12*(6), 589–604. doi:10.1016/S0959-4752(02)00010-5

Bolhus, S. (2003). Toward Process-oriented Teaching for Self-directed Lifelong Learning: A Multidimensional Perspective. *Learning and Instruction, 13*(3), 327–347. doi:10.1016/S0959-4752(02)00008-7

Brydges, R., Nair, P., Ma, I., Shanks, D., & Hatala, R. (2012). Directed self-regulated learning versus instructor-regulated learning in simulation training. *Medical Education*, *46*(7), 648–656. doi:10.1111/j.1365-2923.2012.04268.x PMID:22691145

Carbonneau, N., Vallerand, R., & Lafrenière, M. (2012). Toward a Tripartite Model of Intrinsic Motivation. *Journal of Personality*, *80*(5), 1147–1178. doi:10.1111/j.1467-6494.2011.00757.x PMID:22092087

Censor, N., Horovitz, S. G., & Cohen, L. G. (2014). Interference with Existing Memories Alters Offline Intrinsic Functional Brain Connectivity. *Neuron*, *81*(1), 69–76. doi:10.1016/j.neuron.2013.10.042 PMID:24411732

ERIC. (2014). *Postmodernism*. Retrieved October 12, 2014 from http://eric.ed.gov/?ti=Postmodernism

Farlex, Inc. (2013). *The free dictionary*. Retrieved October 25, 2014 from http://www.thefreedictionary.com/metapsychology

Frambach, J. M., Driessen, E. W., Chan, L. C., & van der Vleuten, C. (2012). Rethinking the globalisation of problem-based learning: How culture challenges self-directed learning. *Medical Education*, *46*(8), 738–747. doi:10.1111/j.1365-2923.2012.04290.x PMID:22803751

Fu, Q., Dienes, Z., Shang, J., & Fu, X. (2013). Who learns more? Cultural differences in implicit sequence learning. *PLoS ONE*, *8*(8), 1–11. doi:10.1371/journal.pone.0071625 PMID:23940773

Garber, I. (2010). *Meta-approach to psychology* (in Russian). Saratov: Saratov Source.

Guay, F., Chanal, J., Ratelle, C. F., Marsh, H. W., Larose, S., & Boivin, M. (2010). Intrinsic, identified, and controlled types of motivation for school subjects in young elementary school children. *The British Journal of Educational Psychology*, *80*(4), 711–735. doi:10.1348/000709910X499084 PMID:20447334

Guopeng, Z., Shen, A., & Shen, Z. (2012). Learning-by-teaching: Designing teachable agents with intrinsic motivation. *Journal of Educational Technology & Society*, *15*(4), 62–74.

Hayenga, A., & Corpus, J. (2010). Profiles of intrinsic and extrinsic motivations: A person-centered approach to motivation and achievement in middle school. *Motivation and Emotion*, *34*(4), 371–383. doi:10.1007/s11031-010-9181-x

Hjörne, E., & Saljo, R. (2014). Representing diversity in education: Student identities in contexts of learning and instruction. *International Journal of Educational Research*, *63*, 1–4. doi:10.1016/j.ijer.2012.10.001

Huba, M., & Freed, J. (2005). *Learner-centered assessment on college campuses: Shifting the focus from teaching to learning*. Needhman Heights, MA: Allyn and Bacon.

Jickling, B., & Wals, A. (2008). Globalization and environmental education: Looking beyond sustainable development. *Journal of Curriculum Studies*, *40*(1), 1–21. doi:10.1080/00220270701684667

Kalantzis, M., & Cope, B. (2008). *New learning: Elements of a science of education*. Cambridge University Press. doi:10.1017/CBO9780511811951

Landsmann, L. T. (1996). Three accounts of literacy and the role of the environment. In C. Pontecorvo, M. Orsolini, B. Burge, & L. B. Resnick, (Eds.), Children's early text construction, (pp. 101-125). Lawrence Erbaun Association, Inc.

Loertscher, D. V., & Koechlin, C. (2013). Online learning: Possibilities for a participatory culture. *Teacher Librarian*, *41*(1), 50–53.

Mayer, R. (2005). *The Cambridge handbook of multimedia learning*. New York, NJ: Cambridge University Press. doi:10.1017/CBO9780511816819

Midoro, V. (2005). *A common european framework for teachers' professional profile in ICT for education*. Ortona, Italy: Edizioni MENABO DIDACTICA.

Mihelj, M., Novak, D., Milavec, M., Ziherl, J., Olensek, A., & Munih, M. (2012). Virtual rehabilitation environment using principles of intrinsic motivation and game design. *Presence (Cambridge, Mass.)*, *21*(1), 1–15. doi:10.1162/PRES_a_00078

Moos, D. C. (2014). Setting the stage for the metacognition during hypermedia learning: What motivation constructs matter? *Computers & Education*, *70*, 128–137. doi:10.1016/j.compedu.2013.08.014

Nokelainen, P. (2006). An empirical assessment of pedagogical usability criteria for digital learning material with elementary school students. *Journal of Educational Technology & Society*, *9*(2), 178–197.

Ohler, J. (2010). *Digital community. Digital citizen*. California: Corwin.

Palfrey, J. G., & Gasser, U. (2008). *Born Digital: Understanding the first generation of digital natives*. New York: Basic Books.

Post, G. (2013). *S. Korea to pilot digital textbook program at schools next year*. Retrieved September 25, 2014 from http://www.globalpost.com/taxonomy/term/64438

Rizzardi, K. W. (2013). Redefining professionalism? Florida's code mandating the aspirational raises challenging questions. *The Florida Bar Journal*, *87*(9), 39–42.

Sadi, O., & Uyar, M. (2013). The relationship between self-efficacy, self-regulated learning strategies and achievement: A path mode. *Journal of Baltic Science Education*, *12*(1), 21–33.

Wang, Y. C. (2014). Using wikis to facilitate interaction and collaboration among EFL learners: A social constructivist approach to language teaching. *Journal of Colege Teaching and Learning*, *7*(12), 383–390.

Webster, S. (2009). *Educating for meaningful lives*. Boston: Sense Publishers.

Zimmerman, V. J. (1998). Academic studying and the development of personal skill: A self-regulatory perspective. *Educational Psychology*, *33*(2/3), 73–86. doi:10.1080/00461520.1998.9653292

## KEY TERMS AND DEFINITIONS

**Complex Behavioral "Meta-Pattern":** Meta-patterns that makes possible to grasp a pattern as something that "ought to be", i.e. that transforms the pattern into a rule.

**Digital Natives:** Children born after 1980 who from birth have experienced the digital world as a natural part of their lives and regularly access rich resources in digital format for information and entertainment. This generation uses social media to communicate and socialize, read material on the Internet for their information needs more often than traditional reference materials.

**Ideal Type:** Method of investigation in which researchers construct concepts or ideas in their pure and essential form, mostly with the intent of then comparing them against the real world.

**Intrinsic Motivation:** Motivation to engage in an activity purely for the sake of the activity itself; or engaging in a task for its own inherent rewards.

**Meta-Analyses:** Method that focus on contrasting and combining results from different studies, in the hope of identifying patterns among study results, sources of disagreement among those results, or other interesting relationships that may come to light in the context of multiple studies. The meta-analysis could be conducting as a part of systematic review.

**Metapsychology:** A philosophical inquiry and a supplement of psychology, which study some mind aspects that cannot be evaluated on the base of objective or empirical evidences.

**Person-Centered Approach:** Relationships among constructs at the level of individual are focused on particular combinations of motivational variables as they exist within individuals or groups of students, rather than taking each variable itself as the focal point.

**Postmodernism:** "A cultural, philosophical, or stylistic reaction to or successor of modernism, beginning from about 1960 - the postmodern period or approach is characterized by a relativistic or pluralistic sense that truth or reality is dependent on specific context or individual perspective" (ERIC, 2014).

**Transcendental Philosophy:** "The ongoing philosophical "research program" where its practitioners investigate "transcendental facts," or the relatively necessary conditions for the possibility of us acquiring knowledge about ourselves and our world. These facts serve as the conditions for the possibility of our experience of an objective reality, meaning that they do not require any further epistemic explanation or justification under our current cognitive practices" (Tunstall, 2014).

# Chapter 7
# Cross–Principles in Digital Textbook Use and Development

## ABSTRACT

*Recent research on digital textbook use and development suggests that principles may reflect the cross-disciplinary boundaries. There are multiple examples that evidence this idea. Therefore, the purpose of this chapter is to enrich the theoretical understanding of design and to broaden the empirical research base by adopting a cross-disciplinary focus. The chapter explores the fundamental principles of digital textbooks and describes the power of cross-principles through a new metasystems method, which allows one to synthesize a functional framework consisting from self-regulation, personalization, feedback diversity, clarity, dynamicity and flexibility and ergonomic environments. These principles are assembled from general norms derived from principles of philosophy, pedagogy, psychology, cybernetics, and knowledge management. The use of cross-principles in the learning design of digital textbooks is a relatively new phenomenon, but with great potential to achieve the guaranteed learning outcomes. Conclusions and future research directions are provided at the end.*

## INTRODUCTION

Digital textbooks, which may be exact digital recreations of physical school textbooks or may be enhanced with interactive features, are used and developed worldwide. Digital textbooks are often stored in a digital library or may be open source. Recently, there has been much debate on where principle based learning would be more efficient. For example, it was propose to use textbook as the fourth element of the didactic triangle (Vollstedt, Heinze, Gojdka & Rach, 2014, p. 29). It was hypostasis that the didactic

tetrahedron can be used for more effective design of learning. But, "knowledge is created through the action, social interaction, and reflection of students"(Mitchell, Avery, Prater & Swafford, 2014, p. 3). What principles are required for design a didactic tetrahedron?

Let us analyse what is the principle. According to the Oxford dictionaries a principle is a fundamental truth or proposition that serves as the foundation for a system of belief or behavior or for a chain of reasoning. The problem is that integration of technology in classroom traditionally was focused on deliverimg knowledge. However, the

DOI: 10.4018/978-1-4666-8300-6.ch007

desired learning outcomes must drive the *whats, hows* and *when*. To use some principles in textbook use and development, the learning designer must be innovative and creative.

The postmodernism way evidences concept map and dialogue to form a text. Mitchell (2014, p. 228) found that in postmodernism, knowledge and ideas are culturally and historically constructed through the use of knowledge and conversation, which is influenced by time, space and by the values of the community in which that knowledge is shaped. Matusov (2014, p. 1) states that postmodernism is a way of relating to reality in an age of responsibility. Dynamic learning tools and computer based assessment are for construction or assembling the content. In the center of the postmodern educational processes is the learner' psychological and physiological development for adaptivity in local-global communities.

The learning process is focused on multilateral and sustainable development of the learner. However, in digital textbooks use and development are used patterns. But, patterns is an external representation of knowledge-in-use and in collecting the knowledge of practitioners. Research has shown that (Bokhorst, Moskaliuk & Cress, 2014, pp. 153-164) that pattern forces use to structure individual contributions into pre-defined categories aim of stimulating abstraction. Each pattern describes a problem in environment, and then describes the core of the proved solution. Thus, patterns contain problem-solutions pairs, and the situation in which the solution may be useful as well as forces which contain competing requirements that influence the solution of the problem. Coherent patterns that generate an interconnected set which is used to solve problems in a specific problem domain are called a pattern language. Pattern is treated as a combination of experiences from several situations, problems that could occur in these situations and established solutions solve those problems. It is highlight that patterns promote the difficult exchange of tacit knowledge-in-use; facilitate the

recognition of solution-relevant problem features and support abstraction across similar experiences.

Can patterns represent principles for digital textbook use and development? This chapter provides a synthetic methodology based on core principles and theirs interconnections aims to response to this question. The starting point is the core principles of philosophy, psychology, pedagogy, and cybernetics and knowledge management. The multiple factors associated with these principles can be conceptualized as a pattern, which "incorporate" the cognitive, affective and psychomotor characteristics of learners and requirements of the learning environment. This "movement", devoted to challenges facing the educational system, allows to establish cross-disciplinary research. The general perspective of the chapter is to syntheses the cross-principles for digital textbook use and development and its norms of application. Therefore, the aim of the chapter is to identify and describe a functional mechanism for digital textbook use and development.

## BACKGROUND

The relationships between the most general cases, in which the area of the digital textbooks use and development are enclosed don't have the axis passing through the principles. In many cases the Instructional Design principles rely on behaviorism, cognitivism, constructivism, humanism or/ and connectionism and its norms of application for content design. We've summarized these principles:

1. Behaviorism "postulates that learning occurs through a process of events happening at the same time. It focuses primarily on the relationship between the environment and behavior and sees learning as the result of forming connections between stimuli from that environment and related responses"

(Kivunja, 2014, p. 95). The representative principles of behaviorism are: direct instruction (explicit teaching using lectures), programmed instruction (self-teaching with the aid of specialized textbooks) and social learning theory (observation, imitation and modeling), as was noted by Wu, Hsiao, Wu, Lin, & Huang (2012).

2.  Cognitivism is focused on relationship between the learner and the environment. "Individual learners' current levels of knowledge, experiences and skills have a profound impact on the way the learner makes meaning of the environment and therefore what he or she learns from his or her interaction with the environment" (Kivunja, 2014, p. 96). It was argued (as cited in Wu, Hsiao, Wu, Lin, & Huang, 2012) that in cognitivism the learners attempt to explain the world and to determine the cause of an event or behavior (attribution theory), as well as that content to be learned should be organized from simple to complex (elaboration theory); cognitive development occurs as four distinctive stages: sensorimotor, preoperational, concrete operational and formal operational; different types or levels of learning require different type of instruction (theory of conditional learning).

3.  Constructivism theories postulates that learners construct knowledge and meaning from their experience. In social constructivism is widely applied the concept of Zone of Proximal Development, developed by Vygotsky "which emphases that there is a gap between what an individual learner can archive on their own and what they can archive when their full potential is enhanced through support given by a more capable individual" (Kivunja, 2014, p. 96). The most examples of constructivist models are based on scaffold constructivism. Examples include inquiry-based learning, active learning, experiential learning, discovery learning, knowledge building and the 5E instructional model (Jobrack, 2013, p. 4). The five key elements of constructivism are: engage, explore, explain, elaborate and evaluate.

4.  Humanism focused on the freedom, value, diginity and potential of person and involves the *principle of experimental learning:* knowledge is gained through both personal and environmental experiences using four learning styles: diverge, assimilator, converger and accommodator (as cited in Wu, Hsiao, Wu, Lin, & Huang, 2012, p. 272).

5.  *Connectionism* is a theory of learning, which try to explain learning from perspective of synchronic or /and asynchronic communication; intertheoretic reduction, neuronal representation, and neuronal architecture either brain or artificial neuronal network (Khatib & Sabah, 2012; Naidu; 2012; Gayler & Levy, 2011; Glassman & Kang, 2010). Later it was argued (as was cited in Gomila, Travieso & Lobo, 2012, p. 102) that connectionist networks either implement the classical models or they fail as accounts of cognition.

On the other hand, as was mentioned by Crowder, Carbone and Friess (2014, p. 2), human neuroscience research has shown that generating new knowledge is accomplished via natural means: mental insights, scientific inquiry process, sensing, and experiencing. True learning can be a lengthy iterative process of knowledge discovery, experience, and refinement as new information is attained. The recursive refinement of knowledge and context occur as a person's cognitive systems interact, over a period of time, with their environment, where the granularity of information content results are analyzed, following by the formation of relationships and related dependences. Knowledge is attained from assimilating the information content until it reaches a threshold of decreased ambiguity and level of understanding, and is then categorized by the brain as knowledge, which act as a catalyst for decision-making. In order to understand the world we live in, humans synthesize models that enable us to reason about what we perceive, to describe and make decisions. For this, language and communication is "fuzzily" applied.

What of above mentioned theoretical trends and principles are better for digital textbook use and development? In order to answer this question let us establish the hypothesis that cognition requires one of two regimes (as was cited in Gomila, Travieso & Lobo, 2012, p. 113). These regimes are:

1. Intuitive, fast, automatic, unconscious, implicit, parallel, and associative processes;
2. Reflexive, slow, controlled, conscious, explicit, serial, rule-based processes.

From this point of view the cognitive function of language and communication depends on the activation of distributed, context-relative, coupled patterns of brain networks, which could be combined productively. One of the main tools that can activate both of these regimes to work effectively can be considered a *digital textbook*. But, what principles and norms must be followed? In the concept of post-modernist philosophy, all previously instructional design models were elaborated on the base of *linear* and *system (systemic) thinking*. However, while linear thinking is a process of thought following well-known cycles or step-by-step progression and denoting cause-effect relations, the system thinking view "problems" as parts of an overall system and potentially contribute to unintended consequences. This requires algorithmization of teaching and, as a result, a conflict with post-modernism philosophy. Unfortunately, learning design is focused on the use and development of *pedagogical resources* and *didactic tool* (Mandacanu, 2009; Ely, 1996). There are two possible solutions: a) the content is written preventively and b) the content needs to be composed by teacher or/and students. The practical examples are: e-Textbooks and Open

Source Textbook. For the second case, all corners of didactic the triangle are engaged. The use of patterns and meta-patterns in digital textbook use and development follows the cross-disciplinary principles. This means that in synthesis of the fundamental principles are involved two or more academic disciplines.

## A PRINCIPLE OR A CROSS-PRINCIPLE?

## Issues, Controversies, Problems

The Instructional Systems Design principles rely on procedure. For example, ADDLE models, which generally combine four phases: Analysis, Design, Development and implementation, and Evaluation and revision, require the following procedure:

- Specify and formulate instructional objectives using learner, learning environment and learning tasks analyses;
- Develop assessment criteria relevant to objectives;
- Design and develop instructional systems and provide arrangements and materials that enable the learner to perform as specified;
- Implement instructional plans; and
- Review the instruction based on the performance information and revise it as required (Moallem, 1998, p. 37).

This procedure is applied by the teacher in order to design content and teach it for student(s). There are two main models: a) *micro-design models*, which are prescriptive, operate within clearly defined boundaries, aim at stability except for adjustments to increase effectiveness and are externally controlled systems and b) *macro-design models*, which are open to changes in the environment as well as to changes in the systems that comprise the complex systems of education. They are continuous and dynamic, participative and interactive, and are internally controlled.

The other example is *multimedia principle,* which relies on cybernetics. Research was found (Mayer, 2014, p. 149) that adaptive problem solving involves the ability to invert solutions for problems that the problem solver has not encountered before. For this, problem solvers must adapt their existing knowledge to fit the requirements of a novel problem, including a novel problem situation that may change over time. It was proposed to solve this problem using multimedia principle. The evidence that is not the solution is the following statement "not all multimedia lessons are equally effective, so research is needed to determine evidence-based principles for effective multimedia instruction".

Nam and Smith-Jackson (2011, p. 24) showed in their previous work that web-based learning environments have been developed mainly using traditional instructional design models such as the instructional systems design, cognitive flexibility theory, and constructivist learning environment. However, many of these approaches still lack two important considerations needed for implementing learning applications based on the Web:

- Integration of the user interface design with instructional design,
- Development of the evaluation framework to improve the overall quality of Web-based learning environments.

The previous research was shown (Nonaka & Konno, 2005, p. 55) that there are two kinds of knowledge: *explicit* and *implicit.* Explicit knowledge can be expressed in words and numbers and shared in the form of data, scientific formulae, specifications, manuals etc. Tacit knowledge is highly personal and hard to formulate, and are deeply rooted in an individual's action and experience, as well as the ideas, values or emotions.

From the authors' point of view the knowledge creation is a spiralling process between explicit and tacit knowledge. However, the learning design requires four steps in knowledge creation process: *socialisation; externalisation*; *combinatio*n and internalization.

All the above mentioned examples describe the role of pedagogical, cybernetic or knowledge management principle. This conflicts with postmodernism philosophy, which emphasises the importance of relationships, personalisation and discourse in the "construction" of truth. Ideally, the principle is a belief that helps to know what is right and what is wrong. Research has found (Heylighen & Joslyn, 1994) that principles play the roles of expressing the most basic ideas in science through establishing a framework or a methodology. It is a norm to identify and describe the credible principles for digital textbook use and development. But, what is the most credible principle? The first assumption is that a credible principle is never *epistemological neural.* However, some developers of digital textbooks prefer to see instruction simply as a practical activity based on own experience, "without need to complex theoretisation" (Griffits, 2012, p. 397). There are many examples:

1.  *Transformational learning* involves creation of dynamic relationships between teachers, students, and a shared body of knowledge to promote student learning and personal growth (content). The basic principles of transformational learning are: a) facilitate students' acquisition and mastery of key concepts; b) enhance students' strategies and skills for learning and discovery and c) to promote positive learning-related attitudes, values, and beliefs in students. This is managerial norms (Slavich & Zimbardo, 2012, p. 581).

2.  *Augmented reality* (AR) is an emerging technology that utilizes mobile, context-aware devices (e.g., smartphones, tablets) that

enable participants to interact with digital information embedded within the physical environment. In the design of AR are used principles: a) enable and then challenge (challenge); b) drive by story (fantasy) and c) see the unseen (curiosity). Dunleavy (2014, p. 28) notes that these principles are used either for *location-based* or *vision-based*. The location-based learning environment presents digital media to learners as they move through a physical area with GPS and compass technologies to augment the physical environment with narrative, navigation, and/or academic information relevant to the location. The vision-based presents digital media to learners after they point the camera in their mobile device at an object or target (e.g. QR code, 2D target).

3. The *message design* in mobile learning in guided by four principles: a) design for the least common denominator; b) design for eLearning, adapt for mLearning; c) design short and "condensed" materials for smart phones and d) be creative when designing for mobile devices with 3G and 4G technologies (Wang & Shen, 2012, pp. 563-569). However, the assessment of students' practice is done both in *formal* (under the management of teacher) and *non-formal* (under self-management of learner) learning environments. In addition, this idea conflict with principles of mLearning design, generated by Theory of Multimedia: *signaling* (cue the learner on how to process information); *spatial contiguity* (align printed words near graphics); *cognitive redundancy* (avoid using the same stream for printed and spoken words) and *temporal contiguity* (present narration, keyword labels and animation together).

4. Curriculum design aims to guide students to create increasingly complex knowledge structures and to maximize the quality of learning outcomes. It was argued (Meyers

& Nulty, 2009, p. 567) that curriculum design should be a) authentic, real-world and relevant; b) constructive, sequential and interlinked; c) require students to use hither order cognitive processes and d) provide challenge, interest and motivation to learn. However, these principles controversies with future research statement (Mayes & de Freitas, 2013) that learning occurs through the process of connecting the elementary mental or behavioral units, through sequences of activity followed by feedback of some kind.

5. User *interface design* for virtual learning environments aims to makes the user's interaction as simple and efficient as possible, in terms of accomplishing users' goals. Khan (2012, p. 49) notes the following principles: *simplicity* (don't compromise usability for function); *support* (user is in control with proactive assistance); *familiarity* (build on users' prior knowledge); *obviousness* (make objects and their control visible and intuitive); *encouragement* (make actions predictable and reversible); *satisfaction* (create a feeling of progress and achievement); *accessibility* (make all objects accessible at all times); safety (keep the user out of trouble); *versatility* (support alternative interaction techniques); *personalization* (allow users to customize) and *affinity* (bring objects to life through good visual design).

All above described principles norm only one situation, for example transformational learning, augmented reality, message design, curriculum design or user interface design for virtual learning environments. Moreover, these principles derived from one academic discipline: transformational learning → pedagogics; augmented reality → informatics; message design → design etc. Understanding what principles are important in use and development of digital is, therefore, an important issue. What is more effective: a principle or a cross-principle? This question has three solutions, proposed by Hong and Sullivan (2009, p. 613):

- Learning as acquisition of knowledge;
- Learning as participation;
- Learning as knowledge creation.

From this point of view the most effective instruction design is guided by pedagogical, psychological, epistemological and socio-cultural underpinnings (Table 1):

There are also many controversies in establishing norms for use and development of digital textbooks. Advantages of digital learning with textbooks include overcoming barriers of distance, time, and up-dated content, novel learning strategies and instructional methods, while disadvantages include technical problems, dependence of digital devices, and digital competence. Digital learning with textbooks is purported to facilitate education for sustainability, but this is more vision that reality. More important, many learning designers *fail to incorporate principles for effective learning with digital textbooks.* What are the reasons? In this Digital Age learning should be focused on life-long learner, who is a real person, but was born, grew, lived and activated in diversity of real-virtual learning environments. It was demonstrated (Kelly, McCain & Jukes, 2009, p. 9) that learning styles of today's digital kids are significantly different than those for whom our high schools were originally designed. They work, think, and learn differently ... and our schools ... and instruction primarily based on teachers talking in classrooms, textbooks, memorization ... are becoming increasingly with the world around them. In addition, the real-virtual learning environments are more complex, open, and contradictory then closed pedagogical environment. However, the way to organize the instructional process in many cases was not changed.

There are many attempts to include these ideas into learning design. It was argued (Resta & Kalk, 2012, p. 397) that the structure of the learning tasks requires appropriate support, including

*Table 1. Towards an idea-centered, principle-based design approach (Hong & Sullivan, 2009, p. 615)*

| | **Learning as Acquisition** | **Learning as Participation** | **Learning as knowledge Creation** |
|---|---|---|---|
| Pedagogical underpinnings | Enhancing efficiency in knowledge appropriation as a primary instructional design goal<br>To lean in order to, potentially innovate | Facilitating participation and distributed knowing as a primary instructional design tool<br>To learn through participation | Promoting knowledge innovation or creation as primary instructional design tool<br>To innovate is to lean |
| Psychological underpinnings | Placing more emphasis on automatic processes (as ends) than controlled processes (as means) | Placing more emphasis on controlled processes (as ends) than automatic processes (as means) | Both controlled and automatic processes integrally regarded as means to progressive problem solving there is no end to this process. |
| Epistemological underpinnings | Toward more routine know-how and know-how<br>Pursuit of knowledge of promisingness not emphasized<br>Pre-determined curriculum (with clear instructional procedures) | Toward more adaptive know-how which still largely know-that<br>Pursuit of knowledge of promisingness less emphasis<br>Pre-determined curriculum (with more flexible learning process/activity) | Toward adaptive know-how and emergent know-that<br>Pursuit of knowledge of promisingness highly supported<br>Progressive curriculum necessary |
| Socio-cultural underpinnings | Community usually not emphasis<br>Social activity not necessary emphasis | Community of learners<br>Structured social activity (e.g. division of labor, scripted cooperation, reciprocal teaching, group based collaboration) | Knowledge created community<br>Emergent, opportunistically structured activity |

strong scaffolding, easy accessible resources, and effortless social connections. Poor usability creates cognitive load that interfaces with optimal learning. An optimal didactic triangle needs to reflect not only the content, but also the context of learning. The proposed model describes the learner immersed in a microsystem environment that interacts with the meso- and exo- systems. In addition, the mesosystem includes peers and mentors that interact with the learner and with each other. The exosystem shifts to a dynamic learning environment that might be online or a blended of physical and virtual spaces. The macrosystem may include more than a single society and the chronosystem includes the temporal factor of changes over time, including innovations etc. It is evident that the trend is *cross-disciplinary principles*. In order to find a solution for the dilemma: a principle or a cross-principle was identified and evaluated the research problem: *What are the cross-principles most suitable in digital textbook use and development?*

## Rational Reconstruction of Didactic Triangle and Identification of Cross-Principles

Let us begin by considering the following example:

- Digital textbooks are the source for "content" and teacher/student(s) use and develop them (Kim, & Park, 2014; Selby, Carter, & Gage, 2014; de Oliveira, Camacho, & Gisbert, 2014; Fryer, 2014; Reys, 2014; Senger, 2014).

In concept of postmodernism the cross-principles figure into reasoning by connecting input with learning outcomes. The easiest way to argue this is to consider input that can make no immediate sense to us. Thus:

Teachers $T$ and students $S$ involved in digital learning process with digital textbooks $P$ will become *competent*. To be competent means to be properly qualified. The rationality for this statement could be represented as shown in Figure 1.

The effect "competent" itself makes no sense to us because we don't know any principles concerning effectiveness of digital textbook use and development. To put it more formally, it is important to have more information or to entertain a principle like: Any teacher or student(s) who will use and develop digital textbooks will become *competent*. It can be rewritten as follows:

**P:** If teacher(s) or student(s) use and develop digital textbooks, then he/she will become *competent*.

According to the definition, the cross-principle links together two or more academic disciplines. This means that to identify the principles for digital textbook use and development we need to identify academic disciplines those object of study is "competence". The synthesis of the main ideas related to scientific literature review provides the following results:

1. *Postmodernism* (Ferri, 2014; Frias, 2014; Khasawneh, Miqdadi & Hijazi, 2014);

*Figure 1. The cause and effect in establishment of cross-principles*

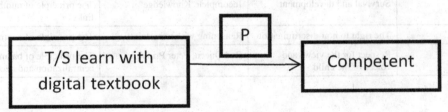

2.  *Competence pedagogy* (Laanpere, Pata, Normak & Põldoja, 2014; Knight, Shum & Littleton, 2014; Archnet, 2014);
3.  *Developmental, quantum and artificial psychology* (Boesen, Helenius, Bergqvist, Bergqvist, Lithner, Palm & Palmberg, 2014; Krabbe, 2014; Crowder, Carbone & Friess, 2014);
4.  *Cybernetic* constructivism (Boudourides, 2003; Taylor, 2014);
5.  *Management* (Kim, Williams, Rothwell & Penaloza, 2014).

The cross-principles are established on the base on MetaSystems methodology. To explore this way were proposed the following procedure:

- To identify the reference concept with respect to the related domain;
- To identify subdomains that study the proposed concept using ideal type;
- To compare main principles of each academic discipline,
- To assemble the principles in order to synthase cross-principles.

It is expected that this way will provide new opportunities for digital textbooks use and development. The result of our study is illustrated in the following table (Table 2).

The postmodernism proves the idea that learning occurs through complex, dynamic and flexible cognitive, self-regulated metacognitive and attitudinal processes.

## IMPLICATIONS AND SYNTHESIS OF CROSS-PRINCIPLES

When cross-principles connect successfully the cause to an effect, it is argued that the cause and the principle jointly *imply* the conclusion and that the cause is valid. Validity is an essential condition for correct thinking. In formal logics the valid thinking depends *on principles* of some sort. These metalinguistic principles, known as *rules of inference*, validate certain forms of critical thinking by generalizing on the norm rather than the things are referring to. The main metalinguistic principle is:

*Table 2. The synthesis of the main principles for digital textbook use and development*

| Philosophy (philosophy of postmodernism) *Closure of Knowledge principle → principle of self-regulation* *Sensitivity principle → principle of personalisati* | | | |
|---|---|---|---|
| **Psychology** | **Pedagogy** | **Cybernetics** | **Management** |
| Readiness → *principle of clarity* | Purposeful interaction | Causality | Develop own learning strategy |
| Effect | Assists students | Autocatalytic grown | Assess own learning style |
| Primacy | Support and dissonance | Selective variety | The principle of management unity |
| Recency | The right to life | Recursive Systems Construction | The principle of decision establishments |
| Intensity | Survival and development | Incomplete Knowledge | The principle of number of the chain links |
| Freedom | The right to non-discrimination | Reasoning with uncertainty | The principle of control diapason |
| Requirements | Respect for the views and voices of the child | Red Queen, Peter Principle | The principle of balance between centralization and decentralization. |

*If sentence P is true and sentence (if P, then Q is true), then Q is true.*

Taking into consideration the above mentioned norms, we could rewrite:

Teacher(s) and student(s) use and develop digital textbooks (1)

Anyone who is guided by teacher(s) and student(s) will become competent (2).

Digital textbooks use strategies focused on students' learning in order to become competent (3).

Sentence 1 correspond to P, sentence 2 correspond to (if P, then Q) and sentence 3 correspond to 1. This means that if 2 connects 1 to 3, in fact this connection depends on meta-linguistic principle 2. The logical form of these rationales is one of the valid forms of critical thinking about validity of cross-principles in digital textbook use and develop. As well as elements are composed of atoms, so the cross-principles are composed

of principles. The interdependences between the cross-principles depend on the hierarchy of interdependences, that could be 0, 1, 2, …N. In this study we will examine the level 0. This level reflects the stronger interdependences between 5 academic disciplines: philosophy, psychology, cybernetics, and pedagogy and knowledge management (Figure 2).

In such consideration the fundamental principles define the concept of digital textbook use and development as a learning object placed on any of the PC, digital device or educational cloud. Such object can include patterns or metapatterns or can be designed as a pattern. The philosophical principles represent the general norms, which denote the specifics of behaviors in diversity of the digital learning environments, ensuring all necessary conditions for achieving the integrity of well-established educational, didactic and personalized aims. The hierarchy of aims

*Figure 2. The cross-principles for digital textbook use and development*

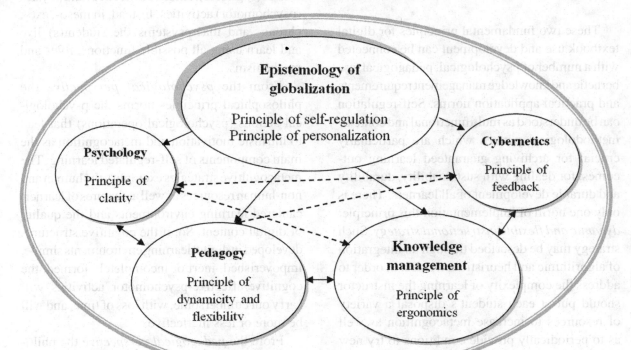

141

for concrete learner cannot be defined, because in the concept of postmodernist philosophy the aim should be established at cognitive (intellectual), affective (emotional) and psychomotor (psychic) levels. From these considerations, the fundamental principles for digital textbook use and development reflect cross-disciplinary and evidence the primary role of self-regulation and personalization. Those norms aim to develop such skills as "self-management", "self-regulation" and "self-assessment" through syntheses of the relevant patterns or/and meta-patterns as well as, using and development of the learning objects. (Persaud & Eliot, 2014; Lerner & Schmid, 2013).

- **The Principle of Self-Regulation:** To synthesize relevant patterns and meta-patterns and to assemble learning objects with metacognitive techniques, which are constituted from strategies, including psycho-pedagogical methods and cybernetics techniques, in a knowledge management model.

These two fundamental principles for digital textbook use and development can be connected with a number of psychological, pedagogical, cybernetic and knowledge management requirements and practical application norms. Self-regulation can be understood as multifunctional and context-methodological pattern which are particularly crucial for archiving guaranteed learning outcomes, for dealing with sustainability, durability and durable development of all learners. There is only one norm of implementation this principle: *dynamic and flexible instructional strategy*. Such strategy may be described through an integration of algorithmic and heuristic activities. In order to address the complexity of learning the instructor should put at each student's disposal a variety of resources to increase metacognition as well as to periodically provide conditions to try new learning methods.

- **The Principle of Personalization:** To collect, search, highlight and assemble patterns, meta-patterns as learning objects for sustainability, durability and durable development of all learners.

Based on sensitivity principle that norms "closure sometimes fails" (Becker, Black, 2012), the principle of personalisation require building of life-long personal learning environment that will include also digital textbooks. These learning objects will serve primarily as a source of understanding the phenomena and processes of permanently changing learning environment.

On the basis of metasystems learning design approach the principle of self-regulation norms the quality of learning mechanisms in relation to national cultural values integrated in planetary culture. The awareness of these values depends on the quality of bias structure, that at the microsystem generates the sustainable behavior, in cases when aim represents integrity of the intellectual (cognitive), emotive (affective) and physics (psychomotor) activities. Instead, in meso-, exo-, chrono- and macrosystems the student(s) live and learn using all possible functions, roles and mechanisms.

From the *psychological perspective* the philosophical principles norms the psychological actions (psychological operations) that lead to intrinsic motivation and metacognition as the main components of self-regulated learning. The metacognitive strategies exemplify the human and non-human resources as well as features of learner-cantered learning environments and the quality of digital content. So, if the cognitive structures developed in digital learning environments simple, impoverished, inert or incompletely formed, the cognitive-affective-psychomotor activities will carry out cumbersome, with loss of time, and will be more or less ineffective.

From the *pedagogical perspective* the philosophical principles norm the importance of learning platforms and learning strategies based on using digital textbooks as well as learning management systems and learning content management systems that incorporate portfolios and authoring tools. Their applications are guided by motivating factors: professional growth, achievement, interest etc.

From the *knowledge management perspective* the philosophical principles establish the role of knowledge management model, vital in competence development of life-long learner from a novice to professional. In the case of digital learning objects, it is important to respect cognitive ergonomic norms.

From the *cybernetic perspective* the philosophical principles norm the role of feedback and feedward loops, the possibility to determine the coefficient of assimilation as the main condition for self-regulated learning as well as the optimisation of content structure reflected in the knowledge graph.

- **The Principle of Clarity:** To write content is starting from students' understanding toward learning potential for accommodation in real and virtual, global and local learning environments. Norms of application in digital textbook use and development are as follows:
  ◦ To establish the complex aim of digital textbook use and development;
  ◦ To structure the content of digital textbook(s) on the basis of the knowledge graph;
  ◦ To clarify the structure of elementary didactic units;
  ◦ To assessable the elementary didactic units in a suitable learning object;
  ◦ To formulate items (metadata) and to identify models of its generating and analyzing;
  ◦ To plan learning analytics.

From pedagogical point of view, digital textbook use and development are normed by *pedagogy of integrated structure of competence*. The goal of such pedagogy is to develop frontier research and the practical application of innovative strategies that will enable to learn in time. This means that textbooks, as the primary teaching material, should be focused on digital reading and include not only the textual –visual representation, but also interactive reader-multimodal text techniques. The conceptual model of this idea can be characterized epistemologically and methodologically. The synthesis of epistemological – methodological approach allows stating the principle of dynamicity and flexibility.

- **The Principle of Dynamicity and Flexibility:** To apply interactive strategies, methods and techniques as requirements to identify and personalise patterns of learning objects during life, (at the macro-level) or in a short time, for example during the unit of study (at the intermediary levels). Rules of the "dynamicity and flexibility principle" are:
  ◦ To ensure the inter-, trans- and interdisciplinarity of content;
  ◦ To collect data and reconstruct the meta-concept and its derivate;
  ◦ To set up the cognitive-affective-psychomotor component of aim;
  ◦ To plan the learning strategy;
  ◦ To revise the hierarchy of behaviorist, cognitivist and constructivist tasks;
  ◦ To write the instructional objectives;
  ◦ To design the template with a metapattern and patterns.

At the metasystems level was identified the following interdependences: a) philosophy ↔ pedagogy (the personalised learning strategies); b) pedagogy ↔ psychology (the action verbs specified for cognitive-affective-psychomotor taxonomy); c) pedagogy ↔ management (the knowledge management strategy) and d) pedagogy ↔ cybernetics (feedback).

- From the cybernetic point of view, the use and development of digital textbooks are normed by feedback. However, understanding the principles of cybernetics in correlation with laws of globalised pedagogical processes using ideal methodology, allow us to evidence the role of immediate and delayed feedback in feedback loops as well as in feedward loops. The immediate feedback has the intrinsic motivation value, because it is focused on immediate analyzing the answer as correct, incorrect and partial correct. If at this closed system is added time, the number of the correctly solved tasks will increase considerably. In addition, feedback adds informational value on didactic triangle, because informs teacher/student(s) about the content through learning analytics, semantics or suggestive adaptive frameworks.

- The principle of feedback diversity norms the learning design of feedback and feedward lops with/within learning objects, patterns and metapatterns. These cross-principles allow integrating issue, context and solution(s) in networks. The cross-interdependences establish important links between: a) postmodernism philosophy ↔ cybernetics (the diversity of feedback and feedward loops in real – virtual learning environments); b) cybernetic ↔ knowledge management (the diversity of learning platforms, LMS and LMCS); c) cybernetic ↔ psychology (the Psychology of Artificial Intelligence, visual feedback, and Gestalt psychology); and cybernetic ↔ pedagogy (ebooks, e-Textbook, Open Source Textbooks etc.). The postmodernism philosophy view on feedback encourages theoreticians in Science of Education to view feedback as a necessary and sufficient condition of self-regulated learning, rather those discrete analytics indicators provided by LMS and LMCS. What are limited in the scientific literature are experimental data and practical arguments in favour or in disfavour of using interactive feedback according to Skinner' Theory of Operant Conditioning in digital textbooks.

- **The Ergonomic Principle:** To use norms of physical, cognitive and organisational ergonomics in all phases and stages of digital textbook use and development.

The "physical ergonomics, cognitive ergonomics and organisational ergonomics" (Long (2014) norms provide requirements for user interfaces design, ergonomic organisation of leaning, as well as perception, memory, reasoning, and psychomotor responses. Specific topics like mental workload, decision-making, skilled performance, human-computer interaction, human reliability, stress and training, ergonomic design of the digital learning environments through consideration of students' anthropometric and biomechanical characteristics should be respected in order to avoid the "*computer addiction*" or "*Internet addiction*". On a broad level, neglecting the ergonomic principle in digital textbook use and development leads to "computer and cyberspace addiction": an addiction to virtual realms of experience created through computer engineering. Within this board category, there may be subtypes with distinct differences. The digital nature of media is an important moment. The aura of new pedagogical resources, learning tools and virtual connections are so many today that teacher and students feel toward their personal involvement in digital learning. ICT affects all patterns of current learning activities. Moreover, in the real learning environment, the perception of information is both a spatial continuum and a temporary continuum structure.

Some ergonomic norms are already considered in digital textbook area. There are some examples: a) relative backpack weights (Bryant & Bryant, 2014, p. 19); b) robotic systems (Magallon & Weisz, 2014, p. 157), and c) dynamic geometry environments (Laborde & Laborde, 2014, p. 187). Moreover, the ergonomic design of digital textbook supports easy update content and reading of multimodal text in a new way. It was found (Serafini, 2014, p. 30) that postmodern picture books invite people to navigate and attend non-linear structures and visual representations. For this, providing students with skills and strategies for navigating and interpreting visual design elements and images, in addition to the requisite skills for making sense of writing language, it is necessary to cross the pedagogical chasm. In addition, teachers should become well informed about the types of texts being read, the learning theories, the skills, learning styles and strategies required, and the social contexts in which learning really takes place.

## FUTURE DIRECTION: CONTINUING USING THE CROSS-PRINCIPLES

The proposed cross-principles for digital textbook use and development can be brought into many didactic processes both in macro and microsystems levels. These principles show that teacher and students should take an action if, and only if, the estimated to archive the guaranteed learning outcomes. Our results show that the MetaSystems Learning Design cross-principles outperformed the multimedia learning principles, suggesting that the modified content on the basis of structure-context methodology will significantly benefit for guaranteed learning outcomes. Future research is needed in practical application of cross-principles in elementary writing, reading and arithmetic skills.

In the light of the fundamental principles of programmed textbook that favour students that use the digital textbooks, designed on the basis of Theory of Operational Learning, the concept mapping and assessment frames with immediate feedback, could be used in order to argue the finding methodology of our research. The cross-principles have been identified through own metasystems methods, that consists in the identification of the reference concept, domains that study this concept, a comparative analysis of the rules and principles and the identification of cross-principles.

The future research directions can be associated also with psychological and pedagogical considerations of *disembedding,* when ideas, books and textbooks "travel" faster than ever, and even they are located in digital repositories, their location is less important than provided content. Driven by global technological and economic changers, but also with cultural and political implications, as was noted by Eriksen (p.10), disembodying, however, also includes all manners through which social life becomes abstracted from its local and spatially fixed context. The other issues for future research could be investigation of speed, academic mobility, cultural crossboard, standardization etc.

## CONCLUSION

The chapter has detailed the issues and controversies in identification of cross-principles. It was argued that in digital textbook use and development can be applied the principles of self-regulation, personalization, feedback diversity, clarity, dynamism and flexibility and ergonomics. We hypothesis that these cross-principles will became widespread in the near future, replacing Instructional Design and Instructional Systems Design models and theories. The application of the application of MetaSystems Learning Design approach enables the development of the self-regulated learner in order to be more adaptive and accommodative at global challenges and diversity of learning environments. However, in design of the digital learning environment is very important to apply not only one or two principles, but a total integrity of cross-principles, that will lead to learning outcomes.

While learning with digital textbooks can be plan and design at different macro and micro levels, a procedure for metasystems thinking should be based on new functions and roles delegated to digital textbooks from real learning environment. In such consideration is integrated the postmodernism theoretical approach with finding of development psychology.

Ergonomic consideration for designing a learning environment with digital textbooks, taking into account psychological (cognitive), physical and organizational needs of innovative teachers and modern students, will contribute to more effective learning environment and learning outcomes. It is essential to find optimum parameters considering anthropometric, biomechanical and learning physiology parameters and associate them with students' age or cognitive levels. These parameters will determine also the effectiveness of learning design, but will also reduce stress. Since more of the ergonomic requirements are difficult to apply only for classroom environment, an integrated metasystems approach using the more "extended" version of learning environment, i.e. formal, informal and formal, has to be developed through discussion with parents.

The findings suggest that the structure, functionality and the affordances of digital textbook use and development on the basis of cross-principles guarantee the learning outcomes. This chapter has demonstrated the theoretical and applicative progress of ten years of research in the Meta-Systems Learning Design in digital textbook use and development. The cross-principles have been identified and the norms for applied cross-principles have been developed. While much research is needed to measure and profile the principles for metasystems learning design and for widely acceptance of dynamic and flexible instructional strategy, authentic assessment with immediate feedback and/or delayed feedback is a central element for a learning process that is intrinsic motivated.

# REFERENCES

Archnet, I. J. (2014). Three holy myths of architectural education in India. *International Journal of Architectural Research*, 5(1), 175–184.

Becker, K., & Black, T. (2012). *The sensitivity principle in epistemology*. Cambridge University Press. doi:10.1017/CBO9780511783630

Boesen, J., Helenius, O., Bergqvist, E., Bergqvist, T., Lithner, J., Palm, T., & Palmberg, B. (2014). Developing mathematical competence: From the intended to the enacted curriculum. *The Journal of Mathematical Behavior*, 33, 72–87. doi:10.1016/j.jmathb.2013.10.001

Bokhorst, F., Moskaliuk, J., & Cress, U. (2014). How patterns support computer-mediated exchange of knowledge-in-use. *Computers & Education*, 71, 153–164. doi:10.1016/j.compedu.2013.09.021

Boudourides, M. A. (2003). Constructivism, education, science, and technology. *Canadian Journal of Learning and Technology*, 29(3). Retrieved February 5, 2015 from http://www.cjlt.ca/index.php/cjlt/article/viewArticle/83/77

Bryant, B. P., & Bryant, J. B. (2014). Relative weights of the backpacks of elementary-aged children. *The Journal of School Nursing*, 30(1), 19–23. doi:10.1177/1059840513495417 PMID:23811534

Dautriche, I., & Chemla, E. (2014). *Cross-situational word learning in the right situations*. Retrieved November 1, 2014 from http://www.em-manuel.chemla.free.fr/Material/Dautriche-Chemla-CrossSituationalLearningRightSituations.pdf

de Oliveira, J., Camacho, M., & Gisbert, M. (2014). Exploring student and teacher perception of e-textbooks in a primary school. *Comunicar*, *21*(42), 87–95. doi:10.3916/C42-2014-08

Dunleavy, M. (2014). Design principles for augmented reality learning. *TechTrends: Linking Research & Practice to Improve Learning.*, *58*(1), 28–34. doi:10.1007/s11528-013-0717-2

Ely, D. P. (1996). Instructional technology: Contemporary frameworks. In International encyclopedia of educational technology. Oxford: Pergamon.

Eriksen, T. H. (2014). *Globalization: The key concepts*. A&C Black.

Ferri, G. (2014). Ethical communication and intercultural responsibility: A philosophical perspective. *Language and Intercultural Communication*, *14*(1), 7–23. doi:10.1080/14708477.2013.866121

Fryer, W. A. (2014). The ethic of open digital content. *Publications Archive of Wesley Fryer*. Retrieved February 5, 2015 from http://publications.wesfryer.com/index.php/archive/article/view/43/158

Glassman, M., & Kang, M. J. (2010). Pragmatism, connectionism and the Internet: A mind's perfect storm. *Computers in Human Behavior*, *26*(6), 1412–1418. doi:10.1016/j.chb.2010.04.019

Griffits, M. (2012). Is it possible to live a philosophical educational life in education, nowadays? *Journal of Philosophy of Education*, *46*(3), 397–413. doi:10.1111/j.1467-9752.2012.00861.x

International Step by Step Association. (2010). *Competent educators of the 21st Century: Principles of quality pedagogy*. Retrieved September, 1, 2014 from http://issa.nl/qrp_pedagogy.html

Internet Encyclopedia of Philosophy. (2014). *Epistemic closure principles*. Retrieved October 15, 2014 from http://www.iep.utm.edu/epis-clo/

Kelly, F. S., McCain, T., & Jukes, I. (2009). *Teaching the digital generation: No more cookie-cutter high schools*. Melbourne, Vic: Hawker Brownlow Education.

Khasawneh, O. M., Miqdadi, R. M., & Hijazi, A. Y. (2014). Implementing pragmatism and John Dewey's educational philosophy. *Journal of International Education Research*, *10*(1). Retrieved February 5, 2015 from http://cluteinstitute.com/ojs/index.php/JIER/article/view/8465/8476

Khatib, M., & Sabah, S. (2012). On major perspectives on language acquisition: Nativism, connectionism, and emergentism. *BRAIN: Broad Research in Artificial Intelligence & Neuroscience.*, *3*(4), 5–12.

Kim, J., & Park, N. (2014). The analysis of case result and satisfaction of digital textbooks for elementary school students. In H. Y. Jeong, M. S. Obaidat, N. Y. Yen, & J. J. Park, (Eds.), Advanced in Computer Science and its Applications (Lecture Notes in Electrical Engineering), vol. 279, (pp. 417-422). Springer Berlin Heidelberg. doi:10.1007/978-3-642-41674-3_59

Kim, Y., Williams, R., Rothwell, W. J., & Penaloza, P. (2014). A strategic model for technical talent management: A model based on a qualitative case study. *Performance Improvement Quarterly*, *26*(4), 93–121. doi:10.1002/piq.21159

Kivunja, C. (2014). Theoretical perspectives of how digital natives learn. *International Journal of Higher Education, 3*(1), 94-109. Retrieved September 1, 2014 from http://www.sciedu.ca/journal/index.php/ijhe/article/view/4053/2382

Knight, S., Buckingham Shum, S., & Littleton, K. (2014). Epistemology, assessment, pedagogy: where learning meets analytics in the middle space. *Journal of Learning Analytics*. Retrieved September 11, 2013 from http://oro.open.ac.uk/39226/3/JLA%202014.pdf

Krabbe, H. (2014). Digital concept mapping for formative assessment. In D. Ifenthaler & R. Hanewald (Eds.), *Digital knowledge maps in education* (pp. 275–297). Springer New York. doi:10.1007/978-1-4614-3178-7_15

Laanpere, M., Pata, K., Normak, P., & Poldoja, H. (2014). Pedagogy-driven design of digital learning ecosystems. *Computer Science and Information Systems, 11*(1), 419–442. doi:10.2298/CSIS121204015L

Laborde, C., & Laborde, J. M. (2014). Dynamic and tangible representations in mathematics education. In S. Rezat, M. Hattermann, & A. Peter-Koop, (Eds.), Transformation: A fundamental idea of mathematics education (pp. 187-202). Springer New York. doi:10.1007/978-1-4614-3489-4_10

Lerner, R. M., & Schmid, C. K. (2013). Relational developmental systems theories and the ecological validity of experimental designs. *Human Development, 56*(6), 372–380. doi:10.1159/000357179

Long, J. (2014). What is visual ergonomics? *Work: A Journal of Prevention, Assessment and Rehabilitation*. Retrieved September 11, 2014 from http://iospress.metapress.com/content/u730425263653437/fulltext.pdf

Magallon, J. C., & Weisz, G. (2014). Robotic-assisted coronary intervention. In C. A. Thompson (Ed.), *Textbook of cardiovascular intervention* (pp. 157–166). Springer London. doi:10.1007/978-1-4471-4528-8_12

Mandacanu, V. (2009). *The master teacher* (in Romanian). Chisinau: Pontos.

Matusov, E. (2015). Four ages of our relationship with the reality: An educationalist perspective. *Educational Philosophy and Theory, 47*(1), 61–83. doi:10.1080/00131857.2013.860369

Mayer, R. E. (2014). Multimedia Instruction. In J. M. Spector, M. D. Merrill, J. Elen, & M. J. Bishop, (Eds.), Handbook of research on educational communications and technology (pp. 385-399). Springer New York. doi:10.1007/978-1-4614-3185-5_31

Mayer, R. E. (2014). What problem solvers know: Cognitive readiness for adaptive problem solving. In H. F. O'Neil, R. S. Perez & E. L. Baker (Eds.), Teaching and measuring cognitive readiness (pp. 149–160). New York: Springer. doi:10.1007/978-1-4614-7579-8_8

Mayes, T., & Freitas, S. (2013). Technology–enhanced learning. In H. Beetham, & Rh. Sharpe (Eds.), Rethinking pedagogy for a digital age: Designing for 21st century learning. Taylor & Francis.

Mergel, B. (1998). *Instructional design & learning theory*. Retrieved from http://www.usask.ca/education/coursework/802papers/mergel/brenda.htm

Meyers, N. M., & Nulty, D. D. (2009). How to use (five) curriculum design principles to align authentic learning environments, assessment, students' approaches to thinking and learning outcomes. *Assessment & Evaluation in Higher Education, 34*(5), 565–577. doi:10.1080/02602930802226502

Mitchell, E. (2014). Curricula and pedagogic principles in the foundation stage (0–5). In P. Mukherji, & L. Dryden, (Eds.), Foundations of early childhood: Principles and practice, (pp. 225-143). Sage.

Mitchell, S., Avery, S., Prater, E., & Swafford, P. (2014). The impact of experiential learning on teaching quality control concepts. *Operations Management Education Review*, 8, 1–24.

Moallem, M. (1998). An expert teacher's thinking and teaching and instructional design models and principles: An ethnographic study. *Educational Technology Research and Development*, 46(2), 37–64. doi:10.1007/BF02299788

Molloy, E. K., & Boud, D. (2014). feedback models for learning, teaching and performance. In M. Spector, M. D. Merrill, J. Elen, & M. J. Bishop, (Eds.), Handbook of research on educational communications and technology (pp. 413-424). Springer New York.

Naidu, S. (2012). Connectionism. *Distance Education*, 33(3), 291–294. doi:10.1080/01587919.2012.723321

Nam, C., & Smith-Jackson, T. (2007). Web-based learning environment: A theory-based design process for development and evaluation. *Journal of Information Technology Education: Research*, 6(1), 23–43.

Nonaka, I. & Konno, N. (2005). The concept of "5, 4": building a foundation for knowledge creation. *Knowledge Management: Critical Perspectives on Business and Management, 2*(3), 53.

Persaud, N., & Eliot, M. (2014). The development and refinement of student self-regulatory strategies in online learning environments. In M. Horsley, M. Eliot, B. A. Knight, & R. Reilly, (Eds.), Current trends in eye tracking research (pp. 317-336). Springer International Publishing. doi:10.1007/978-3-319-02868-2_25

Railean, E. (2012). Issues and challenges associated with the design of electronic textbook. In B. H. Khan (Ed.), *User interface design for virtual environments: Challenges and advances* (pp. 238–256). Hershey, PA: IGI Publishing. doi:10.4018/978-1-61350-516-8.ch015

*Rational* reconstruction *II: Identifying* principles. (n. d.). Retrieved September 11, 2014 from http://www.csus.edu/indiv/m/mayesgr/phl4/tutorial/phl4rationalrecon2.htm

Resta, P., & Kalk, D. (2012). An ecological approach to instructional design: The learning synergy of interaction and context. In A. Olofsson & J. Lindberg (Eds.), *Informed design of educational technologies in higher education: Enhanced learning and teaching* (pp. 393–411). Hershey, PA: Information Science Reference.

Reys, B. J. (2014). Mathematics curriculum policies and practices in the US: The common core state standards initiative. In Y. Li & G. Lappan (Eds.), *Mathematics curriculum in school education* (pp. 35–48). Netherlands: Springer. doi:10.1007/978-94-007-7560-2_3

Rezat, S. (2006). A model of textbook use. In *Proceedings of the 30th Conference of the International Group for the Psychology of Mathematics Education, 4,* (pp. 409-416).

Rudic, G. A. (2013). *The triune aim of educational process in the present conditions, intellect, emotion and energy* [Power Point]. Presented at Republican Scientific and Practical Conference "Development Strategy of spiritual and moral education of personality in the Republic of Kazakhstan. Asthana, 29 November 2013. Retrieved October 1. 2014 from http://www.pedagogiemoderne.ru/blog

Selby, R. D., Carter, K. P., & Gage, S. H. (2014). Survey concerning electronic textbooks: Assessing student behavior and environmental considerations. *International Journal of Sustainability in Higher Education, 15*(2), 3–6.

Senger, A. J. (2014). The beneficiation of education. *Knowledge Quest*, *42*(3), 30–34.

Sims, R. (2014). Learning design or design alchemy? In R. Sims (Ed.), *Educational communication and technologies: Issues and innovations* (pp. 79–91). Springer International Publishing.

Soloman, B. A., & Felder, R. M. (2014). *Index of learning styles questionnaire*. Retrieved from http://www.engr.ncsu.edu/learningstyles/ilsweb.html

Taylor, T. (2014). Considering complexity in simple solutions: What's so complicated about Skype? *International Journal of Systems and Society*, *1*(1), 35–52. doi:10.4018/ijss.2014010104

Vollstedt, M., Heinze, A., Gojdka, K., & Rach, S. (2014). Framework for examining the transformation of mathematics and mathematics learning in the transition from school to university. In S. Rezat, M. Hattermann, & A. Peter-Koop (Eds.), *Transformation: A fundamental idea of mathematics education* (pp. 29–50). New York: Springer. doi:10.1007/978-1-4614-3489-4_2

Walling, D. R. (2014). Who's the learning designer here? In D. R. Walling (Ed.), *Designing learning for tablet classrooms: Innovation and instruction* (pp. 13–18). Springer International Publishing. doi:10.1007/978-3-319-02420-2_3

Wang, M., & Shen, R. (2012). Message design for mobile learning: Learning theories, human cognition and design principles. *British Journal of Educational Technology*, *43*(4), 561–575. doi:10.1111/j.1467-8535.2011.01214.x

Wright, M. C. (2002). Same old textbook? An evaluation metric for Web-based supplemental textbooks. *Journal of Computing in Higher Education*, *14*(1), 28–49. doi:10.1007/BF02940949

Wu, W. H., Hsiao, H. C., Wu, P. L., Lin, C. H., & Huang, S. H. (2012). Investigating the learning-theory foundations of game-based learning: A meta-analysis. *Journal of Computer Assisted Learning*, *28*(3), 235–280. doi:10.1111/j.1365-2729.2011.00437.x

Zhao, K., & Chan, C. K. (2013). Fostering collective and individual learning through knowledge building. *International Journal of Computer-Supported Collaborative Learning*, 1-33.

## ADDITIONAL READING

Aboalgasm, A., & Ward, R. (2013). *The potential roles of digital technologies in developing children's artistic ability and promoting creative activity in children aged 9–11*. Retrieved September 12, 2013 from http://www.inter-disciplinary.net/at-the-interface/wp-content/uploads/2014/01/abercrepaper.pdf

Bergman, S. D. (2014). Open source textbooks: A paradigm derived from open source software. *Publishing Research Quarterly*, *30*(1), 1–10. doi:10.1007/s12109-014-9346-7

Blandford, A., Faisal, S., & Attfield, S. (2014). Conceptual design for sensemaking. In W. Huang (Ed.), *Handbook of human centric visualization* (pp. 253–283). New York: Springer. doi:10.1007/978-1-4614-7485-2_10

Chandra, V., & Watters, J. J. (2012). Re-thinking physics teaching with web-based learning. *Computers & Education*, *58*(1), 631–640. doi:10.1016/j.compedu.2011.09.010

Chen, Y. L. (2014). A Study on Student Self-efficacy and Technology Acceptance Model within an Online Task-based Learning Environment. *Journal of Computers*, *9*(1), 34–43. doi:10.4304/jcp.9.1.34-43

Christensson, C., & Sjöström, J. (2014). Chemistry in context: Analysis of thematic chemistry videos available online. *Chemistry Education Research and Practice*, *15*(1), 59–69. doi:10.1039/C3RP00102D

Cilesiz, S., & Spector, J. M. (2014). The philosophy of science and educational technology research. In J. M. Spector, M. D. Merrill, J. Elen, & M. J. Bishop (Eds.), *Handbook of research on educational communications and technology* (pp. 875–884). New York: Springer. doi:10.1007/978-1-4614-3185-5_71

Crowder, J. A., Carbone, J. N., & Friess, S. A. (2014). The psychology of artificial intelligence. In J. A. Crowder, J. N. Carbone, & S. A. Friess (Eds.), *Artificial cognition architectures* (pp. 17–26). New York: Springer. doi:10.1007/978-1-4614-8072-3_3

Eryilmaz, E., Chiu, M. M., Thoms, B., Mary, J., & Kim, R. (2014). Design and evaluation of instructor-based and peer-oriented attention guidance functionalities in an open source anchored discussion system. *Computers & Education*, *71*, 303–321. doi:10.1016/j.compedu.2013.08.009

Fryer, W. A. (2005). The digital face of 21st century curriculum: How digital content is changing teaching and learning. *Publications Archive of Wesley Fryer*, *1*(2), 1–28.

Gombert-Courvoisier, S., Sennes, V., Ricard, M., & Ribeyre, F. (2014). Higher education for sustainable consumption: Case report on the human ecology master's course (University of Bordeaux, France). *Journal of Cleaner Production*, *62*, 82–88. doi:10.1016/j.jclepro.2013.05.032

Greenhalgh-Spencer, H. (2014). *A complex orientation to embodiment in online education: making online educational spaces more engaging and more socially just* (Doctoral dissertation). University of Illinois at Urbana-Champaign.

Hannafin, M. J., Hill, J. R., Land, S. M., & Lee, E. (2014). Student-centered, open learning environments: Research, theory, and practice. In Handbook of research on educational communications and technology (pp. 641-651). Springer New York.

Hung, W. C., Smith, T. J., & Smith, M. C. (2014). Design and usability assessment of a dialogue-based cognitive tutoring system to model expert problem solving in research design. *British Journal of Educational Technology*, *46*(1), 82–97. doi:10.1111/bjet.12125

Ifenthaler, D., & Gosper, M. (2014). Research-based learning: Connecting research and instruction. In M. Gosper & D. Ifenthaler (Eds.), *Curriculum models for the 21st Century* (pp. 73–89). New York: Springer. doi:10.1007/978-1-4614-7366-4_5

Johnson-Glenberg, M. C., Birchfield, D. A., Tolentino, L., & Koziupa, T. (2014). Collaborative embodied learning in mixed reality motion-capture environments: Two science studies. *Journal of Educational Psychology*, *106*(1), 86–104. doi:10.1037/a0034008

Jovanovic, J., & Chiong, R. (Eds.). (2014). *Technological and social environments for interactive learning*. Informing Science.

Karsh, B. T., Waterson, P., & Holden, R. J. (2014). Crossing levels in systems ergonomics: A framework to support 'mesoergonomic' inquiry. *Applied Ergonomics*, *45*(1), 45–54. doi:10.1016/j.apergo.2013.04.021 PMID:23706573

Kim, M. C., & Hannafin, M. J. (2011). Scaffolding problem solving in technology-enhanced learning environments Bridging research and theory with practice. *Computers & Education*, *56*(2), 403–417. doi:10.1016/j.compedu.2010.08.024

Kurilovas, E., Serikoviene, S., & Vuorikari, R. (2014). Expert centred vs learner centred approach for evaluating quality and reusability of learning objects. *Computers in Human Behavior, 30,* 526–534. doi:10.1016/j.chb.2013.06.047

Lee, C. B., Rooney, P., & Parada, R. H. (2014). Fostering intentional learning with systems dynamic modeling. *Australian Journal of Education, 58*(1), 89–103. doi:10.1177/0004944113517835

McKeown, C. (2014). *The cognitive science of science: explanation, discovery, and conceptual change.* MIT Press.

Norros, L. (2014). Developing human factors/ ergonomics as a design discipline. *Applied Ergonomics, 45*(1), 61–71. doi:10.1016/j.apergo.2013.04.024 PMID:23768732

Oliver, M. (2011). Teaching and learning evolution: Testing the principles of a constructivist approach through action research. *Teaching Science: The Journal of the Australian Science Teachers Association, 57*(1), 13–18.

Smith, J., & Team, A. C. (2014). *After effects CC digital classroom.* John Wiley & Sons.

Stenberg, K., Karlsson, L., Pitkaniemi, H., & Maaranen, K. (2014). Beginning student teachers' teacher identities based on their practical theories. *European Journal of Teacher Education, 37*(2), 1–16. doi:10.1080/02619768.2014.882309

Vitale, J. M., Swart, M. I., & Black, J. B. (2014). Integrating intuitive and novel grounded concepts in a dynamic geometry learning environment. *Computers & Education, 72,* 231–248. doi:10.1016/j.compedu.2013.11.004

Yeung, A. S., Tay, E. G., Hui, C., Lin, J. H. & Low Dr, E. L. (2014). Pre-service teachers' motivation in using digital technology. *Australian Journal of Teacher Education, 39*(3), 135-153.

## KEY TERMS AND DEFINITIONS

**Artificial Psychology:** A theoretical discipline, proposed by Dan Curtis (1963) that states, 1) The artificial intelligent system makes all of its decisions autonomously (without supervision or human intervention) and is capable of making decisions based on information that is new, abstract and incomplete; 2) the artificially intelligent system is capable of reprograming itself (evolving), based on new information and is capable of resolving its own programing conflicts, even in the presence of incomplete information and 3) condition 1 and 2 are met in situations that were not part of the original operational system (Crowder, Carbone & Friess, 2014, p. 18).

**Behaviorism:** A movement in philosophy of learning and psychology based upon on the idea of observable behavior.

**Cognitivism:** A theoretical framework for understanding the mind and learner as an information processor; an assumption that mental processes: thinking, language, memory, problem-solving could be explored; the idea that knowledge are schema or symbolic mental constructions.

**Connectionism:** An approach to the study of human cognition as connectionist network or artificial neuronal networks.

**Constructivism:** A philosophy of learning that emphasis the role of the knowledge construction rather that knowledge acquisition.

**Cross-Disciplinary Method:** A method that examines a subject outside the scope of its own discipline without cooperation or integration with other relevant disciplines and links together two or more academic disciplines.

**Cybernetic Constructivism:** Cybernetics of self-organisation based on the concept of autopoiesis (self-formation), which are self-contained and self-referential unities, if the following criteria are satisfied: a) the system is identifiable through its border; b) it is analyzable through its components; c) the interaction of the components obeys the general physical laws (i.e. it is a natural system); d) the boundary is self-maintained by preferential neighbourhood relation (i.e. the system can stabilize its own boundary); e) the system is contained within and producing the boundary and j) it is a self-productive system using only its own components or transformed imported material (Boudourides, 2003).

**Humanism:** A movement in philosophy that emphasis the individual and collective role of human in solving issues through concepts "freedom", "value", "diginity" and "potential of person".

**Instructional Design (ID):** "A wide range of skills and activities involved in the planning, selection, preparation, presentation, evaluation, and modification of instruction" (Moatlem, 1998, p. 37).

**Instructional Systems Design (ISD):** "A systematic model for thinking and planning that is proposed to help teachers determine both their teaching methods and what is to be taught" (Moatlem, 1998, p. 37).

**Intertheoretic Reduction:** Principle of learning based on idea that one theory that is derived from another can be reduced back to original theory in favor of more basic concepts.

**Open Source Textbooks:** Textbooks developed by author(s) using the same development model as open source software (Linux, Open Office, Apache etc.). The authors and contributors receive no direct financial compensation for their work because these works are available free for users on the internet.

**Scaffold Constructivism:** A theory of learning, developed by Bruner, which identifies the importance of providing students with enough support in the initial stages of learning a new subject. A 'scaffold' ensures that children aren't left to their own devices to understand something.

**Virtual Learning Environment:** "Any digital learning space or environment where learning activities, opportunities, and experiences are designed based in appropriate learning theories and techniques, using various attributes of digital technologies to create meaningful environments for diverse learners where learning is fostering and supported" (Khan, 2012, p. 2).

# Chapter 8
# Didactic Model of eTextbook

## ABSTRACT

*This chapter analyses the issue of effective design based on cross-principles. Based on theoretical-practical data, it proposes a new didactical model that reflects both the digital textbook' structure and the processes triggered by the digital textbook. It is argued that there are many instructional system design models, but the didactic model is a conceptualisation of processes based on postmodernism philosophy. The core of the didactical model is the processes for and of cognitive activity, designed as a pedagogical scenarios and managed through externalization, internalization, intermediation and cognition. At all knowledge management phases the personalisation of the digital content can be made on cognitive, affective and psychomotor levels. Conclusions and future research are provided at end.*

## INTRODUCTION

Digital textbooks are developed on the base on different design models. Customizable content is important part of digital textbook development. Model based design approach relies on explicit norms to describe the instructional process. Usually, eTextbooks are stored in digital libraries. Therefore, eTextbooks are on digital platforms: VitalSource CourceSmart, Classroom Voces, Discovery Education Techbook™, aPperbook, Boundless Textbooks etc. There are many sites that sell and tend textbooks: Amazon Kindle, Barnes & Noble Nook, Cengage Brain, Chegg, Coursemart, DigitalTextbooks.com, eCampus. com, Kno, Textbooks.com, Vitalsource, Zinio etc. There are some innovative apps, also. Yuzu, a digital learning platform aims to offer students next generation reading. Google Play Books offers to search within a particular word or phrase, bookmark chapters and pages, highlight and annotate key passages and get access to dictionaries, translation tools etc.

All above mentioned eTextbooks were developed based on ADDIE model, proposed in 1970s, or on most recently Agile model (known also as Agile Software Development model). Thus:

- ADDIE model represents a systemic approach for individualised and traditional *teaching materials*. It consists of five phases: Analysis, Design, Development, Implementation and Evaluation. At the Analysis is required to detail the course content, to establish objectives and to identify the learner skill level. At the Design

DOI: 10.4018/978-1-4666-8300-6.ch008

is recommended to design content, assessment instruments, exercises, subject matter and lesson planning. At the Development phase it is created the content following the design phase's blueprinted. At the Implementation phase is recommended to develop procedures for training, including curriculum, learning outcomes, delivery and testing procedures, using of software/hardware, registration etc. The Evaluation phase aims to ensure that stated goals at the first phase will meet the specified needs and issues.

- Agile model represents a type of incremental model. In case of digital textbook each step is developed in rapid life cycles software when the results in small incremental releases with each release building on previous functionality. Each step is thoroughly tested to ensure quality.

Let us analyse ADDIE and Agile models in comparison with the meaning of innovative teaching/instructing models. Teaching is a synonym of *Didactic*. Other words related to "Didactic" are: academic, cultural, informational, informative, instructive, scholarly, scholastic, tutorial etc. Conceptually, a didactic model of the digital textbook describes the interdependences between teacher, student and content. What do teachers need to know in order to teach well with digital textbooks? First of all, that teaching is not learning. First, "learning is a continual process, lasting for a lifetime. Learning and work related activities are no longer separate. In many situations, they are the same."(Siemens, 2014, p. 1). Second, the role of patterns in learning is important, but is not crucial. Third, in digital didactics a pattern may represent a concept map or a plan of instruction. It was argued (Toledano, 2002) that a pattern is the abstract representation of a good solution for a concrete, and generally frequent, problem that happens in one or more contexts. The principal objective is capturing good practices that allow us

to improve the quality of the design of systems, determining objects that support useful roles in a specific context, encapsulating complexity, and making it more flexible.

The metapattern goes beyond the pattern and represent "*the pattern which connects*" (Baterison, 1979, p. 10). The role of metappaterns is to form understanding in the underlying mechanisms of patterns and the forms in which they work, and even as a classification of patterns. The metapatterns "communicate" through hermeneutic dialogue and assemble patterns in a totality.

This chapter investigates the didactic model for digital textbook use and development. It is an attempt to synthase the generalised didactic model based on postmodernism philosophy. It is expected that a didactic model will specificity conditions dealt with digital textbook learning design.

## BACKGROUND

A generalised didactic model of digital textbook is a way to represent theory, design, implementation and assessment of digital textbook. This model describes the *conceptual modelling* of digital textbook from the perspective of postmodernism philosophy and MetaSystems Learning Design. The conceptual modelling is proved by scientific understanding of the digital learning as a process of learning activity focused on relevant decision-making and problem-solving. It requires selecting, identifying, assembling and construction of the relevant aspects of a situation in the real-virtual world.

There are many behavioural, cognitivist, constructivist and connectionism theories which could be used to describe some aspects of learning with digital textbooks. However, a model that will integrate in a whole totality use and development of digital textbook should be only a *didactic model*. Kaasboll (1998, p. 196) described in their previous work a *didactic model* for programming. Its aim is to develop a "meta-model to be taught to students, so that they can verbalize more of their learning; a model for teaching to be taught to the tutors in a course, such that they can align their activities with the lecturers, and a basis for formulating research questions for further studies of programming teaching.

The other didactic model, known as L3 model, was described by Leidig (2001) which relies on "learning-on-demand, flexible learning strategies, and collaboration between learners and tutors" (p. 2). According to this model the basic technology, consisting of methods, services, and tools, repositories, and back-office applications, is provided by a conglomerate of university research groups and software companies. The material provided through online learning must have a high didactic value, since it is primarily intended for self-paced training. Collaboration between learners or learners and trainers should be an integral part of the learning model and architecture. Not all courses can be fully self-paced. It may be that the targeted group is not large enough for an investment of the huge amounts of money it takes to prepare a course for self-study, or it may be that the nature of the learning material lends itself to collaborative learning methods such as discussion, partner exercises, or even more sophisticated collaborative forms.

Generally speaking, each of the proposed previously didactic models can be classified as *simple* or *complex*. The simple model describes the main procedures of mapping with metadata. Its main component constitutes a *teaching model*, which includes: theoretical/basic knowledge; examples, exercises/study control; open questions, problems, references; further material and maybe, a virtual laboratory. There are four access options, which can be activated alternatively: a) instructed access – learning episode; b) problem oriented access; c) selection via structure plan (sitemap, mind map) and d) selection via search/index (Loser, Grune & Hoffmann, 2002).

The complex didactic model describes the interdependences between data, information and knowledge. Its main components rely on learning based on processing, storing and disseminating data, information and knowledge of students. There are one example: based on studies in learning psychology, biology and education, the original technique Lernen durch Lehren (LdL) (German for 'learning by teaching') has been elaborated into a *meta-model* (Meta)LdL that aims at giving students a platform to acquire the competencies considered necessary for knowledge societies" (Grzega & Schoner, 2008, p. 167). Additionally, the increasing availability of digital devices, lends to use and development of *narrative* as „a privileged instrument for developing cognitive skills and organizing knowledge. This potential depends on the fact that the narrative has mostly built in an implicit form, induced by the juxtaposition of events, supporting logical links between the elements involved as a result, where each component contributes to shape the global meaning and this in turn, gives meaning to each element" (Gaeta, Loia, Mangione, Orciuoli, Ritrovato & Salerno, 2014).

The future development of digital textbooks have emerged a new way for didactic modelling of information /communication, cognitive activity and assessment processes. This way is paved by new technologies of processing text and image, delivery of content and learning materials, multi-directional communication among teachers, students and digital devices and environments. But, what is the most relevant didactic model of digital textbooks?

## MAIN FOCUS OF THE CHAPTER

### Issues, Controversies, Problems

Research has shown (Lupu & Enache, 2011) that the instructional design, as an anticipation act, foreshadowing the didactic act, allowed to conceive the didactic process from a rationalizing perspective and offer efficiency, foresight, and process rigorous attributes, overcoming the behavioural scheme from which only the entering and exiting from the educational system counts (S-R), but not taking into consideration what happens with these components (processes, mechanisms, substrata). a system of methodological operations (recommendations, prescriptions, guiding) was proposed, which will ensure the quality and efficiency of the undertaken training process. However, this system cannot be applied for digital textbook use and development. The reasons are different. First of all, because the didactic model of the digital textbook describes processes, mechanisms and substrata originated from diverse learning environments and performed by different cognitive systems.

The other idea is to develop *a didactic prototype*. It was described (Salinas, Gonzalez-Mendívil, Quintero, Ríos, Ramírez & Morales, 2013) a prototype that promotes visualization skills related to the learning of mathematical *content*. However, the goal of the project is focused only on a didactic intention of offering useful and applicable knowledge to students, in tandem with a new sense of accessibility from a cognitive point of view. In this sense the creation of a prototype that contemplates the development of cognitive abilities was proposed, used in the relation of algebraic, numeric and graphic representations of mathematical knowledge. The main function of the digital technology relies on „cognitive partner" that contributes to reflection on learning and promotion of visualisation.

The proposed didactic prototype is developing on the basis of traditional model of learning, which can be described using a classic didactic triangle. Instead of the traditional models where

learning objects aren't familiar to students, but are well familiar to teachers; in postmodern didactic models the teachers facilitate the social or professional construction of meaning (Hadzigeorgiou & Konsolas, 2001; Beckett & Gough, 2004; Marin, 2012). Of particular importance is the development of the *concept mapping* in order to engage all students in the learning process with guaranteed learning outcomes. In the concept of the postmodernism philosophy the *content* is mapped onto the methodological or/ and technological norms, express an issue and a hypothetical solution, taking into consideration the specific or the requirements of the learning environments. The solution, then, evaluated and validated in real didactic process through analytics. This model goes beyond traditional didactic model based on classical didactic triangle. It was argued (McLoughlin & Lee, 2008, p. 641) that outmoded didactic models, which place emphasis on the delivery of information by an instructor and/or from a textbook, may need to be replaced in order for student-centered learning to come to fruition.

But, in Global Age the student-centred learning is based on specific principles and norms. The controversies, however, comes from dialectic, didactic and psychopedagogical contradictions between theory and practice of *knowledge as a learning construct* and *learning in chaos of an open learning environments*. This means that classical didactic triangle has been changing (Figure 1).

The diversity of the learning environments, which, as was pointed by Midoro (2005) are global

*Figure 1. The challenges of didactic triangle, where P – professor, S – student, C- content, T-textbook*

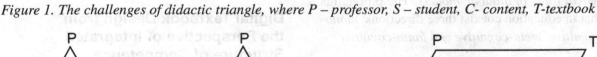
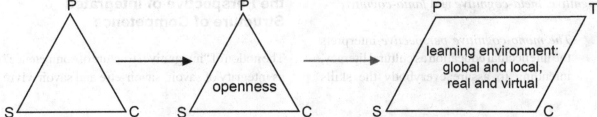

and local, real and virtual. This means that schools learning environments are not the *single providers of content*. It was evidenced (Simonneaux, 2014, p. 38) the term "Socially Acute Questions" (SAQ) to describe complex open-ended questions that bring out the uncertainties embedded in ill-structured problems, which are the heart of the problem of teaching and learning. The content is often non-stabilised and contested and includes professional and social knowledge. The authors evidence the interdependences between cognitive, affective and axiological components of education and training.

It was observed (Papastephanou, 2014, p. 178) that the educational action research has developed as a form of professional redirection of teachers toward a more substantive and decisive engagement and intervention in theoretical issues of schooling. This aim can be achieved through bringing theory with practice action research. However, despite the benefits of postmodernism philosophy and action research to education, several research problems arise with regard to digital textbook use and development. The first research problem relies on the *didactic model that describes also the role of networks (schools, professional, global classrooms etc.)*. Such a model requires at least one of the coaching styles. The powerful coaching cycle are non-linear in nature and allow constructing and reconstructing new and existing knowledge. Postmodernism is a critical style of thinking that is sensitive to the complexity of phenomena under consideration and which encourages the generation of novel ideas through little narratives (Toit, 2014, p. 114).

The second research problem relies *on theoretical topic of didactic models*. The problem is that in education coexist three directions: *mono-cognitive, meta-cognitive* and *fanta-cognitive:*

1.  *The mono-cognitive perspective* interprets the intellectual education as cultural literacy, intending to assure everybody the skills necessary to organise content, to know the words meaning and to manage the investigation tools in different disciplines.

2.  *The meta-cognitive perspective* aims at providing trainees with the "scientific thinking" methods, in order to assume, formalise and solve problems through observation, formulation of hypotheses, experimentation and assessment. In other words, it intends to enhance in a systematic way the use of direct investigation tools (attitudes, methods, techniques) allowing conceptualisation, generalisation and transferability of cultural objects.

3.  In the *fanta-cognitive perspective* the trainee can build original processes of understanding/review and discover not only new or different cultural objects, but also new or different approaches to them. They can be set up thanks to the valorisation of subjectivity.

Our proposed perspective on analysed issues, controversies and research problems is *the meta-cognitive perspective*. However, our position is based on post-modernism philosophy. In such consideration the psychological and pedagogical considerations in digital textbook use and development offer a way for implementation of cross-principles in learning design of textbooks. In these instances, the pedagogical model goes beyond of classic knowledge management model that considers four related levels: "access to information, representation of information, creation of knowledge and transference of knowledge" (Butter, Pérez & Quintana, 2014, p. 447).

## Digital Textbook Design from the Perspective of Integrated Structure of Competence

The notion of "integrative structure of competence" as integrity of savoir, savoir-etre and savoir-vivre

(Gerard & Roegiers, 2009). The observable shape of competence, according to Minder (2003, p. 32) is *performance*, which is equal to competence × capacity and correspond to expert level. The integrative structure of competence, which represents a functional construct for each learner, cannot be achieved without consideration the power of diversity of more open learning environments, in general, and of digital textbooks, in particular. In case of digital textbooks, the integrated structure of competence can be achieved only when the psycho-pedagogical functions are focused on design the specific actions related to personalized didactic activity. This allows obtaining the *performance of orientation* in new, changing and impermissible situations of real learning environments. Such a level is *savoir-vivre*. The main reason to use and develop digital textbooks is to give the teacher or/ and learner a modern resource for learning and/ or tool for construction his /her own integrated structure of competence.

The integrative structure of competence includes three main components "savoir – dire, savoir – faire and savoir – etre" (Minder, 2003). The first component represents theoretical and verbal knowledge, savoir-faire represents methods, techniques, procedures, and learning strategies, and savoir-etre represents wishes, affectivity, emotions, and motivations. It was hypnotises that savoir component can be developed on the base on Bloom cognitive taxonomy; savoir-faire – according to Simpson taxonomy and the savoir-etre – according to Krathwohl's taxonomy. This model describes the triune goal of education: "intellect, emotion, and energy" (Rudic, 2013).

The conceptual structure of integrated competence, developed through personalization of "content" in more open learning environments, is characterized by complexity, dynamicity and flexibility. The complexity represents the four stages "knowledge → integrated structure of competence → expert level" resulting from the managerial chain "information → understanding → application → evaluation" at cognitive, affective and psychomotor levels. The dynamicity is the integration of the information, understanding, application, analysis and synthesis levels (according to Bloom's taxonomy) in cognitive, affective and psychomotor activities designed on the base on suitable taxonomies. The flexibility signifies that the integrated structure of competence is a strictly cognitive-affective-psychomotor construct and can be formed only after each individual is included in a learning process.

From the three-dimensional perspectives of integrated structure of competence, the architecture of competence can be represented by the vectors OA, OB, and OC, whose maximum length corresponds to the taxonomic level that each vector represent. In a topographical plan these situations correspond to OA (6,0,0); OB (0,5,0) and OC (0,0,7). This means that the length of the vector OA equals 6 (because correspond to Bloom's taxonomy), the OB vector equals to 7 (because reflects the Simpson' taxonomy) and the length of OC is equal to 5 (which corresponds to Krathwohl's Taxonomy of Affective Domain). The resulting vector OE represent the external form of integrated structure of competence and is equal to sum of the vectors OA, OB and OC. It the ideal case the co-coordinates correspond to 6, 5, 7 dimension (Figure 2).

This interpretation describes a core concept of the new didactic model of digital textbook design: the competence needs to be developed at teacher (expert) and learner(s) levels. Digital content that is developed in line with this new didactic model reflects the postmodernism philosophy applied for the educational ideal: *professionalism, planetary thinking and cultural pluralism.*

So, we can conclude that above illustrated three-dimensional structure of competence represents a solution for achieving the educational outcomes in concordance with a new educational ideal. That is why a new didactic model of digital textbook needs to be conceptualised at the pedagogical and at the didactical levels. The rationality of this conceptualisation is the following:

*Figure 2. The dynamic and flexible structure of the competence*

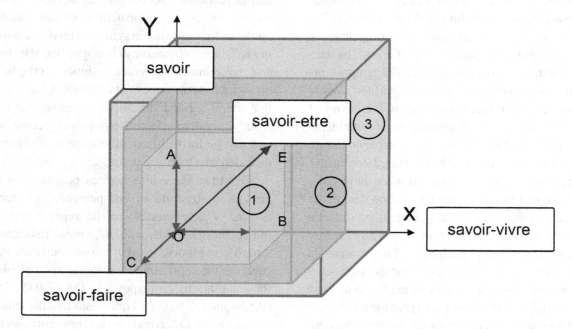

1. At the pedagogical level, the digital content is designed to form the macrostructure that represents the final form of integrated structure of competence at conceptual level, or, in other words, the self-regulated competence of the learner.
2. At the didactical level, the digital content of textbook is designed to enable the learner to achieve the curricula or/and personal objectives, as specific objectives that includes, first of all, arranging, assembling, collecting, combining, creating, designing etc.

The design of the content to achieve certain pedagogical and/or didactic levels determines the quality of knowledge managerial processes that are used to incorporate the pedagogical/didactic aims into a learner's personalized aims. These knowledge management processes are included into a functional mechanism that functions differently at two levels:

- In terms of pedagogical/didactic aims, through instructional objectives that are realized in powerful learning environments including digital or digitalised content of textbooks and computer-based formative self-assessment;
- In terms of personalized goals, through personalisation of content and solving all computer-based formative self-assessment tasks.

To be effective, the pedagogical/didactic goals are achieved through operational objectives that lead to development of integrated structure of competence. The solution for the issue of operational objectives will be presented latter. One more important issue is that operational objectives should be designed on the basis of didactic, methodological and technological criteria, but implemented through at least one of the psychopedagogical functions and according to plan of action (lesson plan, plan of study etc.), which has two main components: teaching and assessment. In such a conceptualisation the main role of the teacher is to plan and realise an effective ergonomic, by powerful learning environment, in which learner(s) are actively engaged in personalized learning process.

## The Epistemological and Methodological Dimensions

Use and development of digital textbooks according to new didactic of two dimensions: epistemological (define learning outcomes) and methodological (define operational objectives through relevant criteria, principles and functions into a concrete plan of action, that could include patterns or metapatterns). Both dimensions need to be achieved through educational dynamic and flexible strategy. A more general model describes the processes of personalisation the content through a complex of learning (teaching and assessment) strategies.

However, the most important idea of this didactic model is the establishment of the strong interdependence between *concepts*. Such structure can be useful to manage knowledge through a) *theoretical methods* (that represent the integration of scientific principles into the functional structure of student(s) cognitive system with affordance to achieve the learning outcomes or in other words methods that allow student to plan effectively a learning goal); b) *practical skills* (used by student(s) in an individual or/and collaborative learning process). For its practical application the dynamic and flexible learning strategy requires:

- *Communication/information strategies*, in which learner(s) play a central role in learning by personalisation the content, guided more or a less by the teacher-expert in domain; or/and in which teacher and students use patterns and metapatterns for the *hermeneutic dialogue*;

- *Cognitive activity* strategies, in which learner(s) build the integrated structure of competence through new ways in individual, collaborative and cooperative learning environments designed on the base on Bloom, Simpson and Krathwohl's Taxonomies;

- *Assessment strategies*, in which learner are engaged in classic and moderns forms of assessment, as well as group, collaborative and other models of environmental assessment.

The instructional dynamic and flexible strategy are guided during knowledge management phases. That is to say, communication/information strategies enable to achieve the pre-planned psychopedagogical functions of digital textbooks; cognitive activity strategies are achieved through learning activities, that represent and integrity of the cognitive, affective and psychomotor actions and assessment strategies – through assessment tasks in diversity of learning environments.

The common formula for achieved the strategies described is $Y = D(X)$, where Y represent either a pedagogical or didactic goal; X – personal goal and D indicates the learning strategies used to transfer the pedagogical/didactic goal into a personalized goal. In this formula, the role of formative self-assessment strategies is crucial. This idea is based on the assumption that computerised assessment strategies exploit the ability of the digital content to be included in feedback and/or feedward loops, to be managed through a knowledge management in order to achieve a synergistic effect and for self-regulation. Through self-regulation, the real and potential states of the human cognitive system, which are affected by interactions among external influences, can be explained. From this point of view, the nucleus of three-dimensional integrated structure of competence operates as follows:

1.  The knowledge structure provided in the digital or multimodal content acts upon the human cognitive system at the level of goal-oriented influences and based on development of intellect, emotion, and energy as cognitive, affective and psychomotor levels of competence.
2.  The incorporated tasks initiate the processes that are involved in acquiring the learning outcomes in transitory processes from the most current psychopedagogical state to the potential psychopedagogical state. The transition is equal to quantum levels: initial and final.
3.  All psychopedagogical mechanisms of each learner are involved in these processes.

Into the dynamic and flexible instructional strategy all teaching, learning and assessment processes that lead to learning outcomes represent a hierarchical dynamic and flexible construct, developed by each student that are guided by a professional teacher. This is possible because the structure of content is generated from an initial knowledge graph structure, which includes only interdependent concepts. Each author of digital textbook can build the initial structure with interdepended concepts, if he/she will use *concept mapping as* a technique for representing concepts in knowledge graphs.

The methodological dimension is represented by the way in which the didactic process is integrated into functional structures that assure the efficiency of communication/information, cognitive activity and assessment processes. The proposed model is to consider the first phase equivalent to the first module, the second phase-to the second module etc. So, the digital content of the first module incorporated from the reproductive (the content is recalled from the memory) to productive tasks (the learner synthesis a new definition, concept etc. or construct own content following concept mapping). The number of modules depends on complexity or difficulty of concepts, but, in any

case, it will serve as a fundament for designing *learning tasks* and solving it in powerful learning environments. The graphic representation of "transfer" from pedagogical/didactic aim into a personalized aim is reflected into an instructional dynamic and flexible strategy, that reflect also the system of presentation the instructional content into electronic textbook (Figure 3).

Figure 3 shows an example of strategy that ideally follows the principles presented in previous chapter. It can be observed that the content of digital textbook is divided into *modules*. There are two possible models to present digital content: *inductive* and *deductive*. As was noted by Lee and Lo (2014, p. 47), students learn effectively with either inductive or deductive methods. The content of each module is structured around information framework with formative assessment tasks and concept mapping tool. In time the number of *algorithmic activities* tasks, focused on reproductive skills, decrease in favour of *heuristic activities*. In an algorithmic method the student is presented with all data for problem-solving, context and procedures are described. The learner's decision is based on understanding and reproduction of presented algorithm. However, during heuristic activities step-by-step procedures of learning are not provided or explained explicitly. The methodology of learning was projected. In addition, different tasks were designed for formative and summative assessment using the following action verbs, proposed by Rudic (2000, p.6):

1.  **For Reproductive Skills:** To name, to list, to describe, to establish, to translate, to recall, to relate, to repeat, to conjugate (at known form).
2.  **For Cognitive skills:** To highlight, to identify, to calculate, to mean, to evaluate, to solve, to add, to transform, to conjugate (in a new form), to indicate, to change the…, to identify, to apply, to bring to …, to multiply, to decline, to divide, to extract, to change, to compare, to describe (new), to structure,

*Figure 3. The dynamic and flexible instructional strategy*

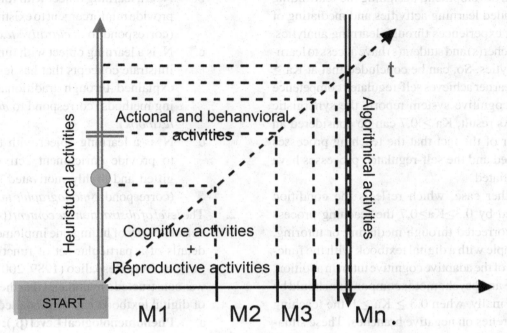

to build, to classify, to bring in increasing (describing order), to aggregate, to formulate, to build (by model), to meet, to sketch, to draw.

3. **For Actional and Behavioural Skills:** To classify, to identify, to imagine, to improvise, to analyse, to propose, to address the, to prove the opinion; to appreciate; to demonstrate; to control; to elaborate; to make an experiment; to compose (case study, divergent decision).

Particularly, cognitive skills could be "corrected" through immediate feedback.

## COMPUTER-BASED ASSESSMENT AND SYNERGISTIC EFFECT

The computer-based assessment has an important role in learning with digital textbooks. Its role is focused on obtaining the synergistic effect during self-regulated learning. In proposed approach, the synergistic effect occurred when the didactic pro-

cesses that are triggered through digital textbooks functioning together produce a result which is not independently obtainable. For this case, practically firstly was found the relevant necessary and sufficient conditions to obtain the synergistic effect. Then, we consider that learning outcomes can be ascertaining through computerised assessment. For this purpose, the assimilation coefficient was design taken into account the formula $Ka = \alpha/p$ (where Ka represents the assimilation coefficient, $\alpha$ is the number of test operations and p is the total number of test operations). It was argued (Bespalico, 1987) that one test operation is equivalent to one psychological operation needed to solve the problem within the assessment process. For example, to solve the task $2+2 = 4$ the learner will use 2 test operations, to recall the number 2 and the algebraic operation adding from long term memory, then will present the answer.

Theoretically, the formula $Ka = \alpha/p$ can be used in limits $0.7 \leq Ka \leq 1$. If the $Ka \geq 0,7$ the teaching process is equal to self-regulated learning. By teaching process we mean teaching in the zone of proximal development, designing the scaffolding and blended learning activities and mediating of learning experiences through learning analytics. Both teacher(s) and student(s) have access to learning analytics. So, can be concluded that at $Ka \geq 0,7$ the learner achieves self-regulated competence and its cognitive system reports the synergistic effect. As result, $Ka \geq 0,7$ can be considered an indicator of the fact that the teaching processes is finished and the self-regulated processes have been initiated.

In other case, which reflects the condition described by $0,3 \geq Ka \geq 0,7$ the teaching process can be corrected through mediating or tutoring, for example with a digital textbook with the functionality of the adaptive cognitive tutor. In addition, affective and psychomotor components should be added. Finally, when $0,3 \geq Ka \geq 0$ the teaching process relies on negative branches. These situations can be removed. For this situation is recommended to design special adaptive tasks tailored to unique earning styles and focused on teaching students with *learning disabilities*. Digital textbooks have the potential to teach successfully the students with learning disabilities at school and beyond (Bryant, Rao & Ok, 2014; Hildebrandt, 2014; Yellin, 2014; Codding & Martin, 2014; Hyman, Moser & Segala, 2014).

The methodological dimension can be validated, if we take into consideration the following:

1.  The diversity of learning objects, including digital textbooks diversity can be noted with $N$, where $N = \{N_1, N_2, N_3, N_4\}$. So, (Haughey & Muirhead, 2005) can be considered that:
    a.  $N_1$ is a learning object with function to introduce new concepts, extend learning by providing new means for presenting curricular material and support new types of learning opportunities not available in classroom environment (or *didactic textbook*);
    b.  $N_2$ is a learning object with function to provide reinforcement to existing skills (correspond to *declarative textbook*);
    c.  $N_3$ is a learning object with function to illustrate concepts that has less easily explained through traditional teaching methods (correspond to *dogmatic textbook*);
    d.  $N_4$ is a learning object with function to provide enrichment activities for gifted and highly motivated students (correspond to *monographic textbook*).
2.  The *level of abstraction the content* ($\beta$), which defines a way of hiding one implementation details of a particular set of functionality. Starting from Bespalico (1989, 2007) study was constructed a hypothesis that the content of digital textbook can be modelled at:
    a.  **Phenomenological Level ($\beta_1$):** Content can be personalized;
    b.  **Qualitative Level ($\beta_2$):** Concepts are presented adaptively and interactively;
    c.  **Quantitative Level ($\beta_3$):** Digital content offers possibility to self-evaluate knowledge and skills through immediate feedback and learning analytics;
    d.  **Axiomatic Level ($\beta_4$):** Digital content is part of integral structure of domain's knowledge, where the domain knowledge is either elementary or aspectual. One of the most accepted finding is learning from *concrete* to *abstract knowledge*.
3.  The *level of assimilation* ($\alpha$), which defines the level of assimilation the main concepts, represented in a knowledge graph of domain. According to Bespalico, these levels are either *reproductive* or *productive*. Therefore, the hierarchy of the assimilation levels can be:
    a.  **Level $\alpha_1$:** The learner(s) assimilates the knowledge presented in a logical man-

ner (examples: Skinner' programed textbook or academic monograph);

b. **Level $\alpha_2$:** The learner(s) is involved in learning activities related to cognitive processes, such as: remembering, understanding, applying and evaluating, including self-assessment through immediate feedback;

c. **Level $\alpha_3$:** The learner(s) is involved in learning that is guided in *instructional scaffolding* way;

d. **Level $\alpha_4$:** The learner (s) is involved in the online or/and *blended learning* activities.

4. The level of automation ($\tau$), which defines the time required to learn the concepts provided through the content of digital textbook. The level of assimilation is established in diapason: $0 \leq \tau \leq 1$ (where 0 represents the minimal time required; 1 – the maximal level (for domains that require fluency in decision-making, for example surgeon, aviator, bus driver etc.). In all other cases the coefficient of automation can be 0, 5.

5. *Assimilation awareness* ($\gamma$), which defines assimilation on the base on following criteria:

a. **Level $\gamma_1$:** Knowledge, skills and attitudes related to studied domain(s) are needed for rationalizing/reasoning with information provided;

b. **Level $\gamma_2$:** Knowledge from similar domains are needed for reasoning with data and making relevant decisions or problem solving;

c. **Level $\gamma_3$:** Interdisciplinary knowledge, skills and attitudes are needed for reasoning with data that required critical thinking, metacognition etc.;

d. **Level $\gamma_4$:** Cross-disciplinary knowledge and skills that underline and connect two or more disciplinary areas. The author of the digital monograph should provide knowledge beyond the confines of their own professional disciplines.

Beside that the analyzed diversity includes didactic, declarative, dogmatic and monographic digital textbooks, the synergistic effect can be observed only in didactic digital textbooks. So, the learning design specifications of didactic digital textbook support the use of educational technology for achievement the main pedagogical aim: cognitive development of child (i.e. the child's development in terms of information processing, psychosocial development etc.).

*objectives → content → formative assessment → summative assessment.*

Beyond printed textbook, digital textbook use and development is focused on interactivity, multimodality, adaptively, flexibility and dynamicity. To archive this aim, the instructional objectives are replaced with *learning objectives* and *learning outcomes*; printed pages (content) – to frameworks with *digitalised and multimodal text*; *formative assessment* tasks – *interactive formative assessment technologies*; *summative assessment* – interactive summative assessment technologies. The interactive assessment technologies require an integration of hardware, software and educational technologies.

The summary correlation between the topology and parameters of digital textbook use and development is represented in Table 1.

This table can be used as a norm in writing learning objectives in order to achieve learning outcomes.

## GENERALIZED DIDACTIC MODEL OF THE DIGITAL TEXTBOOK

The generalized didactic model of digital textbook describes the use and development of digital textbook according to cross-principles. The learning outcomes reflect postmodernism philosophy of developing the integrative structure of competence on the base: educational ideal → aim (pedagogi-

*Table 1. The summary correlation between the topology and parameters of digital textbooks*

| Digital Textbook Typology | N | $\beta$ | $\alpha$ | $\gamma$ | $\tau$ | $K_\alpha$ | $K\tau$ (min) |
|---|---|---|---|---|---|---|---|
| Didactic | $N_1$ | $\beta_1$-$\beta_4$ | $\alpha_4$ | $\gamma_4$ | Fluent | $1 \geq K_\alpha \geq 0.5$ | 15-20 |
| Declarative | $N_2$ | $\beta_1$-$\beta_3$ | $\alpha_3$ | $\gamma_3$ | - | $0.7 \geq K_\alpha \geq 0.3$ | - |
| Dogmatic | $N_3$ | $\beta_1$-$\beta_2$ | $\alpha_2$ | $\gamma_2$ | 0,5 | $0.7 \geq K_\alpha \geq 0.3$ | 38 |
| Monographic | $N_4$ | $\beta_2$ | $\alpha_1$ | $\gamma_1$ | - | $1 \geq K_\alpha \geq 0.7$ | - |

cal/didactical/personalized) → learning objectives → integrated structure of competence. Beside the correlation: competence → subcompetence → content → learning and assessment activities, accepted for printed school textbook development, the proposed methodological correlation for digital textbook value the role of self-regulated learning. On the basis of the didactic generalized model can be elaborated standards, syllabus, plan of actions etc.

The generalized didactic model can be read at macro level (strategies of information/communication, cognitive activity and assessment), as well as at the micro level (psychical and behavioural actions). At the macro level one of the requirements is the *integrity of pedagogical, didactic and personalized* aims. Instead of ADDIE models, the generalized didactic model describes the elaboration of the digital textbook from the perspective of functionality the primary and secondary mechanisms (cognitive, affective and psychomotor). At the micro-level the model describes the pedagogy of self–regulated learning triggered digital textbook use and development. The added value of the model is emphasizing the role of metacognition as a bridge between author of content and reader and interpreter of text (either printed or digital) established through hermeneutic dialogue (Figure 4)

The integrity of aims: pedagogical, didactic and personalized, indicates to the hierarchical structure. This means *that pedagogical design of digital textbooks can be achieved as a global model of student development through all life and* include self-regulated learning. Beside pedagogical aim, the *didactical aim* is focused on use and development of the special designed digital textbook (for example, for chemistry, mathematics, biology etc.). The *personalized aim* is focused on learners and learning for developing of the integrated structure of competence. This approach can be understood from the perspective of teacher and from the perspective of learner. From the perspective of teacher, teaching and learning are to be considered as an integrated complex process, with awareness of *contextual issues* and of learners' needs, including persons with disabilities.

The key components of personalized learning with digital textbooks are:

1. *Pre-assessment* of cognitive, affective and psychomotor norms;
2. *Teaching and learning* methods to develop the integrated structure of competence;
3. *Digital curriculum* and the choice that delivers flexible learning pathways;
4. *Learner-centered learning environment*, including digital learning environment focused on self-regulated learning and/or metacognition;
5. *Summative assessment* of integrated structure of competence in real learning environment.

The other component is "situation". In digital pedagogics this term may refer to pedagogical or teaching (learning) situations. The pedagogical situations are "situations in which one person, a teacher, chooses information for the purpose of

*Figure 4. Generalized didactic model of the digital textbook*

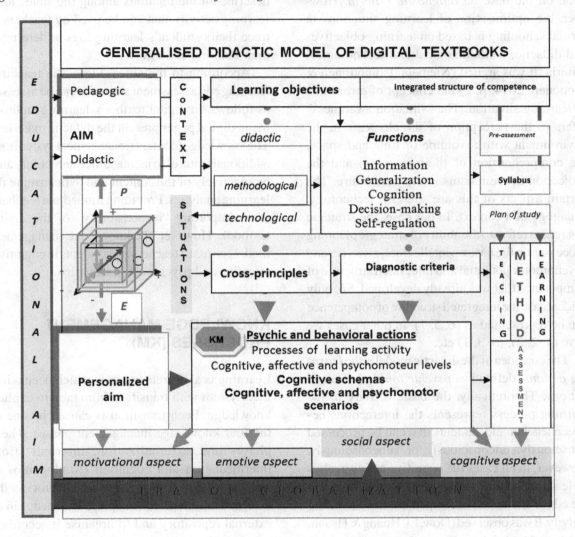

GENERALISED DIDACTIC MODEL OF DIGITAL TEXTBOOKS

helping another person, a learner, arrive at some belief. Pedagogical situations might provide uniquely powerful learning situations, especially if learners are privy to, and understand the implications of teachers' intention to help." (Shafto, Goodman, Gerstle & Ladusaw, 2014, p. 2182). However, the learning situation is the situation in which teaching or/and learning is a problem. (In this chapter only the concept of *learning situations* will be explored).

Learning with digital textbook mainly depends on situations in which students are. Ideally, in order to engage all students in digital learning, the teacher uses the best strategies and tests the functionality of the learning environment. Therefore, to optimize the students' learning firstly should be optimized the *learning situations*. In case of self-regulated learning students do individually. The optimisation of the informal learning situations is based on *cross-principles* and can be done on the base on *diagnostic criteria*. However, the optimisation of learning situations in formal schooling is based on learning objectives and didactic, methodological and technological criteria. It was argued (Niemela, Isomottonen & Lipponen, 2014, p. 2) the concept of *awareness* in learning situation. The "situation awareness" refers to the perception of the elements in the environment with a volume of time and space, the comprehension of their meaning, and the projection of their status in the near future. The certain aspects of this are strategy, technology, pedagogy and context. In our case, the strategic awareness refers to the ability of strategic planning processes on the base on intellectual, affective and psychomotor potential and integrated structure of competence that was already developed. So, only in ideal case the integrated structure of competence can be represented as (6, 5, 7). In other cases we have (4, 2, 2); (3, 3, 1) etc.

The core idea of the didactic model is the *learning actions*, defined as *psychic and behavioural actions*. Theoretically, the basic activity in the learning process represents the interactions between teacher and students that can be processed consciously, unconsciously or subconsciously. However, in all cases the cognitive activity relies on learning actions and learning states, which are the edges and nodes of the personalized learning activity. It was observed (Dow, Li, Huang & Hsuan, 2014, p. 54) that learning performance increase through learning behaviors. The *management system* allows teachers to identify student-learning activities. The process of learning activity is determined by the learning environment and is defined as a five-tuple with a finite set of activity states, that are dependent on the learning environment; a finite set of actions for the learning activity; could have one or more initial states that will initiate the learning activity and potentially trigger the learning activity; the final activity states that determine if an activity is accomplished and the transition related of the learning activity, which describe all the relations among the states for a learning activity that can be used by teachers to trace theirs student's learning logs to determine their learning activities.

According to the above ideas, the teaching, learning and assessment activities can be assessed as follows. In digital textbook learning environment, digital pages present the didactic materials. The knowledge (content) management system uses additional features to increase the interactivity and/or adaptively of the content and to determine the learning analytics. Providing immediate feedback is an important "responsibility" of the digital textbook. However, the knowledge management model can assist teachers and students in cognitive, affective and psychomotor scenarios.

## KNOWLEDGE MANAGEMENT PROCESSES (KM)

Learning is a discrete process, which occurs in a metasystem with transition from tacit to explicit knowledge. Each transition is caused by one of the four knowledge management phases. These phases are: externalization, internalization, intermediation and cognition (Koulopoulos & Frappaolo, 2000). But, for learning process the externalization means to capture knowledge in an external repository and to organise it according to selected taxonomy.

Externalisation provides the input data and metadata that inform the teacher about the psychological and pedagogical specifics of learning (knowledge, learning styles, curricula, resources, methods etc.). If digital textbooks is integrated in a knowledge management system, the externalisation phase can be accomplished by the learning analytics or/and pre-assessment interactive quiz. The diagnostic criteria should be based on psychological and pedagogical testing.

During the second phase, internalisation, the students construct their own understanding of learning subjects and continue to learn how to make relevant decisions. In a discrete knowledge management process the learning strategy can be defined for all cognitive states. However, each of the states is characterized by constant level of knowledge and variable time. The explicit knowledge is extracted from content and then is filtered and completed by the cognitive structure which is strongly individual. As more sophistically filters and systems are used, as better is result. Instead, at the end of internalisation the synergetic effect should occur.

The role of intermediation is to break tacit knowledge and to transfer it in explicit knowledge. Intermediation can be afforded through Web2.0 technologies such as chat with author of digital textbook, concept mapping of main ideas individually or in group, development a wiki project etc. cognitive and metacognitive skills could be activated through co-construction of personalized content or personalized library of digital libraries related to studied subject or theme. Problem – solving and decision – making skills, as the processes focused on guaranteed learning outcomes, can be increased in a digital textbook learning environment, as result of possibility to provide immediate feedback.

Cognition is the phase of achievement. At this phase the student should "integrate" all recent studied content in a whole functional structure (cognitive, affective and psychomotor). The result proves an effective decision-making process at the new situation provided by a sustainable environment. The proposed solution should be: *context-sensitive* (other actors are able to understand the proposed solution); *user-sensitive* (students are able to organize knowledge in the way most useful for studied domain); *flexible* (students are able to handle knowledge of any forms); *heuristic* (students learn about its users and the knowledge if processes are used); *suggestive* (students are able to deduce what knowledge needs are, represent the associations and integrate in networking).

## FUTURE RESEARCH DIRECTIONS

While modern learning is in real and virtual learning environments, more studies on postmodernism philosophy specifics are needed. Future research needs to be focused on student's actions in non-standard learning situations, in which tasks are provided by the real situations and require rapid decisions, but deeper (complex) understanding of the situation. Future research should also more extensively study the perspectives of quantum psychology to learning in order to better understand how to learn metacognitive strategies, which are "incorporated" in digital textbook content.

In this chapter the answer to the research question: *What is a didactical model for digital textbook use and development?* has been formulated: *A didactic model describes the information/communication, cognitive activity and assessment strategies used by student that is actively engaged in learning process.* Future research is needed in interdisciplinary area of digital textbook in order to understand the role of networking, immediate and delayed feedback, sketching and concept mapping.

We considered a procedure in which Bloom; Simpson and Krathwohl taxonomical action verbs can be integrated. Instead of Instructional System Design, where the instructional objective are used to indicate what an instructor and what a learner should be able to do after will be completing the unit of study; in MetaSystems learning Design the learning objectives are designed to achieve the guaranteed learning outcomes. Future research is needed to understand what methods are most effective.

The learning with digital textbook may be self-directed. The digital learning environments provide many innovative pedagogical resources and learning tools, which allow developing personalized digital textbooks or/and digital library. However, research related personalization of digital textbooks content on the base of hermeneutic dialogue is still rare. More studies is required to understand how to generate metacognitive strategies according to metasystems thinking and what strategies can be associated with innovative learning methodologies.

## CONCLUSION

This chapter provides a snapshot of how ADDIE and Agile design models are used to digital textbooks. A didactic model for digital textbook is an innovative way. It focused on how the learning is processed, stored and recovered. It has also established the importance of autonomy (pedagogic or didactic) in personalisation of digital text. This chapter has outlined how the didactic model of digital textbook has pioneered alternate linear or systems models. It has also established the importance of intrinsic motivation in learner success in digital learning environment. Our contribution has focused on synthesizing didactic model for digital textbook use and development. The model serves as a basis for future research in interdisciplinary area of textbook. We have also demonstrated how learning designers, teachers and students can work within the constructs of the didactic model to support self-regulated learning and to self-direct learning with metacognitive strategies.

## REFERENCES

Beckett, D., & Gough, J. (2004). Perceptions of professional identity: A story from paediatrics. *Studies in Continuing Education, 26*(2), 195–208. doi:10.1080/158037042000225218

Butter, M. C., Perez, L. J., & Quintana, M. G. B. (2014). School networks to promote ICT competences among teachers. Case study in intercultural schools. *Computers in Human Behavior, 30*, 442–451. doi:10.1016/j.chb.2013.06.024

Dow, C. R., Li, Y. H., Huang, L. H., & Hsuan, P. (2014). Development of activity generation and behavior observation systems for distance learning. *Computer Applications in Engineering Education, 22*(1), 52–62. doi:10.1002/cae.20528

Gaeta, M., Loia, V., Mangione, G. R., Orciuoli, F., Ritrovato, P., & Salerno, S. (2014). A methodology and an authoring tool for creating Complex Learning Objects to support interactive storytelling. *Computers in Human Behavior, 31*, 620–637. doi:10.1016/j.chb.2013.07.011

Gerard, F., & Roegiers, X. (2009). *Des manuels scolaires pour apprendre: Concevoir, évaluer, utiliser.* De Boeck Supérieur. doi:10.3917/dbu.gerar.2009.01

Grzega, J., & Schoner, M. (2008). The didactic model LdL (Lernen durch Lehren) as a way of preparing students for communication in a knowledge society. *Journal of Education for Teaching, 34*(3), 167–175. doi:10.1080/02607470802212157

Hadzigeorgiou, Y., & Konsolas, M. (2001). Global Problems and the Curriculum: Toward a humanistic and constructivist science education. *Curriculum and Teaching, 16*(2), 39–49. doi:10.7459/ct/16.2.04

Haughey, M., & Muirhead, B. (2005). Evaluating learning objects for schools. *E-Journal of Instructional Sciences and Technology, 8*(1), 229–254.

Hyman, J. A., Moser, M. T., & Segala, L. N. (2014). Electronic reading and digital library technologies: Understanding learner expectation and usage intent for mobile learning. *Educational Technology Research and Development, 62*(1), 35–52. doi:10.1007/s11423-013-9330-5

Koulopoulos, T., & Frappaolo, C. (2000). *Smart things to know about knowledge management.* Padstow, Cornwall: T. J. International Ltd.

Lee, V., & Lo, A. (2014). From theory to practice: Teaching management using films through deductive and inductive processes. *The International Journal of Management Education, 12*(1), 44–54. doi:10.1016/j.ijme.2013.05.001

Leidig, T. (2001). L3-towards an open learning environment. *Journal of Educational Resources in Computing, 1*(1), 1–11.

Lupu, E., & Enache, R. (2011). Didactic conception on the basis of cognitive and affective objectives for non-profile university-physical education. *Procedia: Social and Behavioral Sciences, 15*, 1340–1345. doi:10.1016/j.sbspro.2011.03.288

Marin, T. (2012). The professionalization of the didactic activity between "desirable" and unavoidable. *Euromentor Journal-Studies About Education, 3*(3), 22–32.

Minder, M. (2003). *The functional didactics: Objectives, strategies, assessment* (In Romanian). Chsinau: Cartier.

Niemela, P., Isomottonen, V., & Lipponen, L. (2014). Successful design of learning solutions being situation aware. *Education and Information Technologies*, 1–18.

Papastephanou, M. (2014). *Theory, practice and the philosophy of educational action research in new light. A companion to research in education.* Springer Netherlands.

Piansi, A. (2010). Learning tasks: Turning a dry subject into an engaging experience. *The Systems Thinker, 21*(2), 2-6.

Roncevic, M. (2013). Criteria for purchasing e-book platforms. *Library Technology Reports, 49*(3), 10–13.

Rudic, G. (2013). Modern pedagogy in multi-measured space. In E. B. Assemble (Ed.), *Socrates Almanac "Science and Education"* (pp. 74–75). Oxford: Oxford Review.

Salinas, P., González-Mendívil, E., Quintero, E., Ríos, H., Ramírez, H., & Morales, S. (2013). The development of a didactic prototype for the learning of mathematics through augmented reality. *Procedia Computer Science, 25*, 62–70. doi:10.1016/j.procs.2013.11.008

Sawyer, R. K. (Ed.). (2006). *The Cambridge handbook of the learning sciences, 2*(5). Cambridge: Cambridge University Press. Retrieved September 2, 2014 from http://coseenow.net/exhibit/wp-content/uploads/2009/11/science-of-learning.pdf

Shafto, P., Goodman, N. D., Gerstle, B., & Ladusaw, F. (2014). *Prior expectations in pedagogical situations*, 2182-2187. Retrieved September 2, 2014 from http://mindmodeling.org/cogsci2010/papers/0514/paper0514.pdf

Siemens, G. (2014). *Connectivism: A learning theory for the digital age.* Retrieved November 1, 2014 from http://er.dut.ac.za/bitstream/handle/123456789/69/Siemens_2005_Connectivism_A_learning_theory_for_the_digital_age.pdf?sequence=1

Simonneaux, L. (2014). Questions socialement vives and socio-scientific issues: New trends of research to meet the training needs of postmodern society. In C. Bruguière, A. Tiberghien, & P. Clement (Eds.), Topics and trends in current science education (pp. 37-54). The Netherlands: Springer.

The Digital Reader. (2014). *Barnes & Noble Launches New e-Textbook App – Yuzu.* Retrieved November 1, 2014 from http://the-digital-reader.com/2014/04/20/barnes-noble-launches-new-e-textbook-app-yuzu/#.VGt-wzSUdQE

Thoermer, A., & Williams, L. (2012). Using digital texts to promote fluent reading. *The Reading Teacher, 65*(7), 441–445. doi:10.1002/TRTR.01065

Toledano, M. (2002). *Design patterns.* Retrieved November 1, 2014 from http://www.moisesdaniel.com/wri/metapatterns.html

## ADDITIONAL READING

Albano, G., Gaeta, M., & Salerno, S. (2006). E-learning: A model and process proposal. *International Journal of Knowledge and Learning*, *2*(1), 73–88. doi:10.1504/IJKL.2006.009680

Bateson, G. (1979). *Mind and nature: A necessary unity*. New York: E. P. Dutton.

Bloom, J. (2009). *Pattern thinking, systems thinking, and complex-transferrable learning in education for sustainability*. Retrieved September 2, 2014 from http://www.jeffbloom.net/docs/b-PatternSystemThkg.pdf

Bloom, J. W. (2004). Patterns that connect: Rethinking our approach to learning, teaching, and curriculum. *Curriculum and Teaching*, *19*(1), 5–26. doi:10.7459/ct/19.1.02

Bloom, J. W., & Volk, T. (2012). Metapatterns for research into complex systems of learning. In N. M. Seel (Ed.), Encyclopedia of the sciences of learning (pp. 2243-2246).

Bruner, J. S. (2002). *Making stories: Law, literature, life*. Cambridge, MA: Harvard University Press.

Christopher, J. C., Richardson, F. C., & Christopher, S. E. (n. d.). *Philosophical Hermeneutics: A Metatheory to Transcend Dualism and Individualism in Western Psychology*. Retrieved October 2, 2014 from http://htpprints.yorku.ca/archive/00000163/02/HTP_Prints--Philosophical_Hermeneutics--A_Metatheory.htm

Classen, M. A. (2005). *A pattern language for learning* (Doctoral dissertation). University of Victoria.

Collen, A. (2012). Knowledge, management, and learning when the context of the organization is planetary. *The Learning Organization*, *19*(4), 369–382. doi:10.1108/09696471211226716

Devedzic, V., Gasevic, D., & Djuric, D. (2008). Clarifying the meta. In R. Nayak, N. Ichalkaranje, & L. C. Jain (Eds.), *Evolution of the Web in Artificial Intelligence Environments* (pp. 191–200). Springer Berlin Heidelberg. doi:10.1007/978-3-540-79140-9_8

Frank, M. S., & Dreyer, K. (2001). Beyond the electronic textbook model: Software techniques to make on-line educational content dynamic. *Journal of Digital Imaging*, *14*(2), 108–112. doi:10.1007/BF03190310 PMID:11442066

Gebru, K., Khalaf, A., & Willman, A. (2008). Outcome analysis of a research-based didactic model for education to promote culturally competent nursing care in Sweden–a questionnaire study. *Scandinavian Journal of Caring Sciences*, *22*(3), 348–356. doi:10.1111/j.1471-6712.2007.00535.x PMID:18840218

Gebru, K., & Willman, A. (2003). A research-based didactic model for education to promote culturally competent nursing care in Sweden. *Journal of Transcultural Nursing*, *14*(1), 55–61. doi:10.1177/1043659602238351 PMID:12593271

Keegan, D. J. (1980). On defining distance education. *Distance Education*, *1*(1), 13–36. doi:10.1080/0158791800010102

Laurillard, D. (1987). Computers and the emancipation of students: Giving control to the learner. *Instructional Science*, *16*(1), 3–18. doi:10.1007/BF00120002

O'Brien, D., & Voss, S. (2011). Reading Multimodally: What Is Afforded? *Journal of Adolescent & Adult Literacy*, *55*(1), 75–78.

Sternberg, R. J. (2014). *Advances in the psychology of human intelligence*. Psychology Press.

Thompson, P. W. (2002). Didactic objects and didactic models in radical constructivism. In K. Gravemeijer, R. Lehrer, B. Van Oers, & L. Verschaffel, (Eds.), Symbolizing, modelling and tool use in mathematics education (pp. 197-220). Springer Netherlands. doi:10.1007/978-94-017-3194-2_12

Uljens, M. (1997). *School didactics and learning: a school didactic model framing an analysis of pedagogical implications of learning theory.* Psychology Press. doi:10.4324/9780203304778

Volk, T., Bloom, J. W., & Richards, J. (2007). Toward a science of metapatterns: Building upon Bateson's foundation. *Kybernetes*, *36*(7/8), 1070–1080. doi:10.1108/03684920710777847

Wisse, P., & Wisse, P. (2000). *Metapattern: Context and time in information models.* Addison-Wesley Longman Publishing Co., Inc.

Wright, S., Fugett, A., & Caputa, F. (2013). Using E-readers and Internet Resources to Support Comprehension. *Journal of Educational Technology & Society*, *16*(1), 367–379.

## KEY TERMS AND DEFINITIONS

**Algorithmic Activities:** Activities in which students learn following a well-established step-by-step solution to a certain problem.

**Authentic Learning Tasks:** An approach of modelling the learning tasks based on real life tasks that integrate skills, knowledge, attitude and social context.

**Blended Learning:** "A model of learning, which combines face-to-face and online learning modalities, is a heterogeneous and steadily developing area of design and inquiry"(Halverson, Graham, Spring, Drysdale and Henrie, 2014, p. 20).

**Coaching Style:** A "meta-profession" or a style of management of training in which is used different communication skills to help students shift their perspectives and thereby discover different solutions to achieve the personal goal, ranging from their concerns in any professional or personal dimensions.

**Concept Mapping:** A techniques for representing interconnected concepts in knowledge graphs as networks of concepts, in which each of the main concepts can be a generator of personalized content.

**Didactic Model:** A representation of the didactic processes or/and didactic relationships in teaching, learning and assessment triangle.

**Didactic Process:** A complex process between teaching and assessment, planned or/modelling by teacher in order to achieve the learning outcomes.

**Hermeneutic Dialogue:** A method to understand sense of the meaning of the text, which relies on a background of meaning underlying the perspectives of the author of text and reader.

**Heuristic Activities:** Activities in which students "discover" the knowledge in a personal way that is not necessary the most optimal way.

**Instructional Scaffolding:** "support provided by a teacher/parent, peer, or a computer- or a paper-based tool that allows students to meaningfully participate in and gain skill at a task that they would be unable to complete unaided" (Belland, 2014, p. 505).

**Learning Disabilities:** An umbrella term for a wide variety of learning problems that reflect the ability to receive and process information and not the intrinsic motivation or any type of intelligence.

**Learning Process:** An individual process of learning which includes students in a range of teaching, learning and assessment activities, aims to develop new knowledge, skills and attitudes.

**Learning Task:** "A learning task is a way to structure dialogue. It is an open question put to members of a small group who have been given all the resources they need to respond or a way of engagement of learners with the new content. (Piansi, 2010).

**Narrative:** "Unique sequence of events, mental states, happenings involving human beings as characters or actors: these are its constituents. But these constituents do not, as it were, have a life or meaning of their own. Their meaning is given by their place in the overall configuration of the sequence as a whole – its plot or fabula" (Bruner, 2002).

**Taxonomy:** the practice of classification of action verbs on the base on well-established principles.

# Chapter 9
# Patterns and Metapatterns in the Elementary Didactic Units

## ABSTRACT

*The effectiveness of digital textbooks' content depends on how the brain processes, stores and recovers data (metadata), information and knowledge. This is the way to find an understanding of actions in hidden electrochemical signals, as well as the body energy and quantum relationships. It was expected that data are "synthesized" by each student on the base on hermeneutic dialogue assure the best brain structures, and, as a result, adaptation and accommodation in diversity of environments. This chapter reviews issues, contradictions and problems surrounding metasystems learning design of the elementary didactic units. The author argues that it is possible to maintain the potential of the learner (intellect, emotion and energy) with a self-regulated mechanism and, hence, facilitate cognition and metacognition. Future research directions and conclusion are provided at the end of the chapter.*

## INTRODUCTION

Education today is not about technologized teaching, but about the creation of opportunities for competence construction. More important than teaching is to monitor and guide the students' behavior and actions. It takes time before a new behavior became automatic. It is a stringent needs to educate students "driven them a deep background that go further than the mere knowledge of ideas and schemas. It is more related with a more radical actions able to improve sensibility, to mound the behavior, deeply affecting all the intellectual abilities of the human being, including the emotional one. A knowledge, or rather a state of being, able to overcome prejudices and misleading beliefs, acting also on the way a problem is faced and experienced" (Gaddi, 2014, p. 186). Thus, education is about a new technology of learning. Can digital textbooks contribute to solve these issues? Let us analyse this approach deeper.

Conceptually, beside the printed textbooks, digital textbook provides not only the content for lessons. The modern lesson, as was emphasized by Rudic (2013), is a manifestation of intellect, emotion, and energy. Furthermore, the lesson is about a modern learning technology with the effect on sustainable lives in next years. The reading text is the main focus of the modern lesson. If the teacher chooses the right methodology for reading

DOI: 10.4018/978-1-4666-8300-6.ch009

according to students' potential, time and context, the learning outcomes are guaranteed. Indeed, the mechanisms of knowledge are encoded in our brain and includes synapsis, which exchange information and ensure that the flow of data is regulated. All these processes are on the base on conscious, unconscious and subconscious programs. A program is a plan of actions aimed at accomplishing a clear business objective, with details on what work is to be done, by whom, when, and what means or resources will be used. Each program include algorithms. An algorithm is a set of rules to be following in problem-solving operations. Each algorithm has a number pf patterns and metapatterns. A pattern is a rule, which expresses a relationship between a context, a problem and a solution. A metapattern represents a pattern of patterns, which could include context and time.

The concept of pattern in learning object is not in itself a very novel idea. The research was shown (Goertzel, Pennachin & Geisweiller, 2014, p. 78) that the concept of pattern is presented in the works of Charles Peirce, Daniel Dennett, Douglas Hofstadter, Benjamin Whorf and Gregory Bateson. The meta- pattern is defined as pattern which connects. In such perspective a pattern is defined as representation as something simpler. Thus, for example, if one measure simplicity in terms of bitcount, then a program compressing an image would be a pattern in that image. But, if one uses a simplicity measure incorporated runtime as well as bot-count, then the compressed version may or not may be a pattern in the image, depending on how one's simplicity measure weights the two factors.

On the other hand, as was argued in (Toussaint & Toussaint, 2014, p. 293), without patterns life would not merely be meaningless, but would probably not exist at all. Not surprisingly the word pattern features prominently in virtually all domains of knowledge, but even so, most books and articles which contain the word assume that the reader must be familiar with its meaning, and hence do not bother to define it.

The learning environment, including the human mind, is a collection of patterns and metappaterns. Pattern thinking is the core of all human thinking because the brain functions can be view as the *pattern recognizer* (Bloom, 2009, p. 2). A fundamental view involves a recursive approach to a loosely organized sequence of recognizing patterns, analyzing those functions and/or meaning, positions in different contexts. From these perspectives the roles of patterns and metapatterns in the elementary didactic units of digital textbooks are enormous. The patterns and metapatterns ensure the mechanism of brain' functionality. Our arguments are based on Wisse (2008) reflections that the metapattern emphasis reusability and rely on multiple recursive contexts. An object may exhibit multiple behavior. Every behavior is unambiguously tied with a particular situation. With a context representing a situation and with signature as an object's bare identity, through a number of signature instances an information model represents an object in multiple contexts. Context is a recursive function of both signature and relationship between two signatures at adjacent levels in the model. Beyond pattern thinking, the MetaSystems thinking emphasis to take into account the body energy and capacity of brain to recognize, generate, analyse, assemble and summarise patterns/metapatterns for standard and non-standard life situations, both real and virtual, through comparison and synthesis with well-known features, methods, procedures and situations in order to select the most relevant activity and/or actions among several alternative possibilities. The Metasystems thinking represent our understanding of design the learning processes, following the postmodern. Indeed, MetaSystems thinking could be genetic (innate) or can be developed through innovative technologies (Table 1).

This chapter investigates the role of patterns and metapatterns in design of the *elementary didactic units*. According to definition a didactic unit is a kind of the detailed lesson plan, based on curricula. The teacher develops the didactic

*Table 1. Pattern thinking vs. MetaSystems thinking*

|  | **Pattern Thinking** | **MetaSystems Thinking** |
|---|---|---|
| Patterns | Recognizing patterns (cascading pattern extraction) | Assemble, compare and make decisions, whether we make it consciously or not |
| Relationships | Analyzing functions & meanings | Re-ordering cross-principles |
| Connections | Analyzing from multiple perspectives | Generating, combining, sintering and complying |
| Functions | Situating patterns in context | Decision-making for sustainability |
| Meanings | Locating patterns in different contexts | Reorganizing patterns in metapatterns |
| Adaptation | Evaluating & testing | Evaluation in real situations |
| Complexity | Modeling | Learning Design and Learning Analytic |
| Recursiveness | Organizing | Reorganizing (mind map) |
| Models | Categorizing | Didactic Model |
| Understandings | Associating – analogs, metaphors etc. | Summarizing – concept mapping, personalised content etc. |
| **CONCERNS** | | |
| Assumptions | Systems | MetaSystems |
| Transformative Learning | Complexity | Dynamic and flexibility |
| Context | Connects & Disconnects | Hiperconnectivity |

unit regarding knowledge, skills, attitudes, time management and the explanation given to students. The elementary didactic unit is a part of lesson plan. This may include didactic or (meta)cognitive activities, procedures, methodology, technology, thematic unit, multimedia software and practical pedagogical actions. All of these may include patterns and metapatterns.

Designing the elementary didactic units, the teacher usually has to take into account what students has to do during the class, how activities will be used and how distractors will be avoided. Each of the elementary didactic units "incorporate" at the micro-level the aim; objectives; table of contents; methodology; resources and tools; assumed knowledge of students; exercises; evaluation criteria and, possible, special resources and tools for students with specific educational needs.

The central idea of this chapter is that each pattern should be integrated in a metapattern so that they work together, forming a functional whole. The elementary didactic units can be designed according to specific cross-principles and those norms of application. Our idea is based on assumption developed by Coward (1990, pp. 7-11) that a pattern is a set of components, each of which is itself a pattern. A component can indicate positively or negatively for the presence of the patterns, and the degree of indication can vary between components. A pattern repeats when the weighted sum of identified components exceeds a threshold. This threshold can be variable. Implicit in the definition of pattern is the concept of pattern recognition as hierarchy. The components of complex patterns are generally (although not necessarily) relatively simple and are themselves composed of even more simple patterns.

## BACKGROUND

Traditionally, the elementary didactic units constitute a part of the didactic material, planed and designed according to curricula and lesson plan.

Traditionally, a didactic material represents any resource or tool used in the teaching-learning process. A good didactic material is significant, transferable, attractive, suitable and diverse. It focuses on activities and actions planned by and for students and teachers. Didactic material could be studied/produced/constructed in the classroom or can be prerecorded and studied before face-to-face teaching. This case undergoes a preparation procedure, from content design to the evaluation by experts. In science, mathematics and language the traditional developed didactic material help students to contextualize knowledge and to fill gaps left during learning. However, more and more teachers look for alternative didactic materials. Digital didactic materials are almond of them. In such conceptualization the *didactic elementary units* with digital material represent a sequence of instruction, relatively autonomous, resulting from the „analysing" the curricula from perspective of learning. Thus, a digital didactic elementary units may include a thematic unit as well as information, communication, cognitive activity and assessment processes, metacognitive strategies; procedures and resources for students with special learning needs.

The elementary didactic unit should include well defined patterns and metappaterns. Beside patterns, which express a rule according to issue, context and solution, metapatterns assure the functionality of digital learning or the "functional patterns" (Volk & Bloom, 2007, p. 25). Usually, the elementary didactic units include information units or thematic units. These are "atomic elements, self-contained and highly reusable. <...>.These elements lack associated knowledge. They need a context before they can acquire educational significance, because in themself they do not provide knowledge to the student" (Santacruz-Valencia, Navarro & Aedo (2010, p. 54). However, as was noted by Podlasai (2010, p. 208), the information unit has reminded us the "molecule" with the base information ("pure" idea), at that if it is necessary

to be added to other patterns. The brain contains all necessary patterns and the role of learning processes is only to provide the necessary conditions to process them in order to give a finite form. For example, the brain contains the "human" pattern, and the role of education is "to abrade" this pattern in order to form a self-regulated person at challenges, able to solve problems and translate the solutions into relevant decisions. In addition, the human thinking evidences the brain functions to analyze, synthesis and make decisions.

Let us think about this idea of digital elementary didactic unit with patterns from the perspective of digital textbook use and development. One of the functions of digital textbook is to provide the content/context for pedagogic communication. In concept of the postmodernism philosophy the communication includes patterns and metappaterns that should be recognized and processes by the brain in order to make relevant decisions. However, there are many issues and concerns related to *pattern recognition* during learning process (Dinsmore, Baggetta, Doyle & Loughlin, 2014; Zhang, Zhang, Ji & Guo, 2014; Bordes, Bottou, Collobert, Roth, Weston & Zettlemoyer, 2014).

It was argued (Majumdar, 2014, p. 331) that learning is a task of constructing the regions or templates in N-dimensional space in which labelled samples of the classes are contained. The pattern recognition-deriving the decision rule (learning) and using it to recognize a pattern-can be performed in two ways:

- Learning before recognition;
- Learning and recognition concurrently.

How easy can be recognized patterns in digital learning with textbooks? In order to answer this question let us think about digital textbook's terminology, proposed by Porter (2011). In his opinion an electronic textbook represents a marriage of a hardcopy book within an electronic environment with software. In this case the information is didactically prepared to be easy assimilated. But, the real world learning environments usually include complex and ill-structured data and tasks. In formal schooling elementary didactic units are associated in content unit or thematic unit. Each of the units include a pattern, defied as a rule associated with issue, context and solution) and represent the curriculum content. Learning design of digital textbooks is a complex issue. There are, at least, four areas of research:

- Learning design of digital didactic elementary units,
- Methodology of digital didactic elementary units;
- Technology of digital didactic elementary units;
- Classroom infrastructure/cloud services, including organizational ergonomics.

The elementary didactic units, as a part of digital textbook, is developed according to well-established pedagogical or didactical aim. It is expected that for guaranteed learning outcomes the elementary didactic digital units could be assembled in informational; operational and assessment frameworks. For other purposes, for example for digital reading, the operational or/and assessment frameworks can be neglected. For example, the monographic digital textbook aims to provide knowledge. The affordances of these textbooks are to be read anywhere and anytime as well to present up-dated information with multimedia/multimodal text, integrated dictionary, searching metadata etc. There are many examples of textbooks, known as eBooks or eTextbooks, which can be download from DigitalTextbook. com, Bookboon.com, Boundless CourseSmart etc. Free textbooks also include patterns and metapatterns. The most cited examples are provided by California Learning Resource Network (CLRN).

## LEARNING DESIGN OF THE ELEMENTARY DIDACTIC UNITS

### Issues and Controversies

Firstly, there seems to be some confusion related to terminology. The first issue relies to understanding the "learning unit" concept. It was argued (Beck, 2010) that a learning unit is a) any entity, digital or non-digital, that may be used for learning, education or training; b) any digital resource that can be reused to support learning; c) modular digital resource, uniquely identified and metatagged, that can be used to support learning and d) are much smaller units of learning, typically ranging from 2 to 15 minutes, self-contained, reusable, can be aggregated and tagged with metadata. However, research shows that metapatterns are the smallest functional wholes that assure guaranteed learning outcomes.

The second issue relies on a strong interdependence between the learning objects and the elementary didactic units. A learning object represents a digital piece of learning material that addresses a clearly identifiable topic or learning outcome and has the potential to be reused in different contexts. The research has shown (Cameron & Bennett, 2010, p. 898) that learning object includes: a) one or more files or modules of learning material; b) reusable in multiple settings and for multiple purposes; c) potentially usable in classrooms as components of units of work accompanied by digital and non-digital materials; and d) accessible from digital repositories, as referenced, located and accessed by metadata descriptor. The elementary didactic unit includes a functional mechanism, which assure the functionality of the digital textbook in learning environment.

All issues and controversies are examined in concept of postmodern philosophy. The heart of postmodernism is the view that reality cannot be known nor described objectively. This contrast with the modernism view that prove reality can be understood objectively. Controversies between postmodernism and modernism in design of elementary didactic units evidence the research question: What components assure the functionality of the elementary didactic units of digital textbooks? From one point of view there is a need of "incorporated motivation into multimedia learning" (Mayer, 2014), where "motivation and emotion are mediators of multimedia learning" (Leutner, 2014). From our point of view, more important is to design patterns and metapatterns that will activate the working memory patterns and metappaterns. This, data, information and knowledge are transferred from content to working memory for storing, processing and recovering.

It was demonstrated (Schweppe & Rummer (2014) that working memory stores is limited in capacity. Knowledge is constructed heir and then is integrated with each other and with prior knowledge. Once integration has occurred, the goal of learning is achieved. Moreover, a number of studies have used a dual-task paradigm to assess the role of Gestalt factors in visuospatial working memory, all studying the recall of regular patterns. It was proved that in perception, patterns that are symmetrical along the vertical axis are more salient than those with axes of symmetry in other orientation. Symmetry affects memory performance. With serial presentation, only vertical symmetry increased recall. Simultaneously presented stimuli led to an advantage or all types of symmetry when compared with asymmetrical patterns (Pieroni, Rossi-Arnaud & Baddeley, 2011, p. 145).

We had investigated this issue and decided to develop an elementary didactic units for learning calculus using Gestalt principles (Figure 1).

## From Instructional Design to MetaSystems Learning Design

Instructional design models describe processes to create teaching materials. New ways of design will likely require moving beyond a cognitive theory of multimedia learning toward one that considers learner' volition and affection as well. The elementary didactic units will serve as metapatterns with interconnected patterns. Such an innovative structure can be represented with an adequate matrix or/and a knowledge graph. For our understanding the knowledge graph is a graphical representation of the elementary didactic units' structure in case when each of the concepts represent a meta-concept and could serve as a generator of new concepts (in special learning situations).

Research has shown (Barnett, 2014, p. 9) that meta-concept is a practical concept that speaks to the student finding his or her own possibilities in a networked world. This structure is vital for learning.

There are two possible ways to include patterns/ metappaterns in the elementary didactic units:

- **Instructional Design:** "A collection of theories and models helping to understand and apply instructional methods that favor learning" (Paquette, 2014, p. 664);
- **MetaSystems Learning Design:** A postmodern approach of activities or/and actions, helping to apply self-regulated learning methods and strategies, including metacognitive strategies.

Which role gets which activities/actions at what moment in the process, is determined by the strategy.

*Figure 1. Gestalt principles and norms in elementary didactic units of "Mathematica"*

| Principle | Example of learning design |
|---|---|
| **Closure:** an object is incomplete or a space is not completely enclosed. If enough of the shape is indicated, people perceive the whole by filling in the missing information. (In our case a metappaterns "red apple" is formed by two patterns "half of red apple"). | La scăderea fracțiilor ordinare sunt posibile două situații: 1.*fracțiile au același numitor* <br> Scăderea fracțiilor cu același numitor <br> 1. scădem numărătorii și păstrăm numitorul. <br> $$1 - \frac{1}{2} = \frac{2}{2} - \frac{1}{2} = \frac{1}{2}$$ <br> *un măr minus jumătate este egal cu jumătate* |
| **Similarity:** objects look similar to one another. People often perceive them as a group or pattern (our example appears as a single unit). | $$q\frac{r}{b} = q + \frac{r}{b} = \frac{q \cdot b + r}{b}$$ |
| **Proximity:** elements are placed together and tend to be perceived as a group (the four bottles of juice form a unified whole because of their proximity). | 2. un număr zecimal este înmulțit cu un număr natural <br> *Problemă* Câți l de suc se conțin în 4 sticle de suc de 0,33 l? <br> Rezolvare: <br> Într-o sticlă se conțin 0,33 l, iar în 4 sticle de 4 ori mai mult. <br> $$0,33 \, l \times 4 = 1,32 \, l$$ <br> *la înmulțirea numărului cu un număr natural, numerele se înmulțesc între ele, iar virgu plasează de la dreapta peste atâtea cifre, câte zecimale există.* |

In our Digital Age the exponential growth of knowledge is a rule (Reich, 2014). The powerful driver of new culture of learning is activities or/and actions and not knowledge. Thus, the Instructional Design methodologies tend to ontology-based modeling. It is expected that learning environments will have a structured executable representation of the knowledge to be processed by technology in order to help users according to present and expected state of knowledge. The scenario of learning process results from activity based on educational modeling language. Knowledge-based instructional design approach focuses on the interaction between a knowledge model of a domain (usually ontology) and a process model (generally a multi-actor workflow or scenario) of the grouping tasks, resources and tools.

MetaSystems Learning Design methodologies is focused on self-regulated learning with metacognitive strategies. Based on postmodernism philosophy of Nietzsche, the MetaSystems Learning Design approach is grappled with "digital hermeneutics"(Walshaw & Duncan, 2014) and language of the digital learning or "literacy in a digital world" (Tyner, 2014). In addition to these two issues, and the answers given to them, developments in the field of digital textbook also can reinforce a postmodern view. This is to say, rather than relying on instructional system design, a self-regulated learning approach adopts a primarily theoretical-practical stance, leading on sustainable development of learner and environment. For this, the learning scenario could be managed by a teacher, but from one starting point could become self-regulated by a student. Digital textbooks are not only a source of knowledge, but, rather, the integrity of frameworks with elementary didactic units, including patterns and metappaterns. The differences between Instructional Design and MetaSystems Learning Design were identified (table 2).

According to postmodernism coherence theory of truth, we exist in the world and in relation to it. The scientific method come up in order to understand how the world works. One of this secrets is synergistic effect: the whole is more than the sum of its parts. An emergent property of a whole cannot be comprehended in terms only of sum of constituent parts. But, how to design elementary didactic units learning in order to obtain the synergistic effect in diversity of environment environments? How to engage all students in learning, when technology evolves from Web1.0 to Web3.0? How to keep intrinsic motivation during spiral learning? The answer is maybe in the classic understanding of "metasystems": meta $X_i$ is the name of things or systems, which are bigger than $X$ in sense that

it is more organized, have higher logical type or it is analyzed in more general sense.

The drive of MetaSystems thinking is to facilitate students' development on the base on generic cognitive potential. Furthermore, to assume that each of patterns or/and metappaterns are the product of the author(s) and interpreter(s). This means that the author of the digital text needs to think not only about the content, but also about the user interfaces design, communication modes and dissemination of knowledge in networks. One important issue is how to store the elementary didactic units in data base, how to identify metadata and meta-knowledge, how to generate and disseminate it. Moreover, it is important to take into account the affordances of learning platforms, as well as the power of digital devices, the consistencies of screen design, colors, formats etc. on different digital devices. The challenges provided by the ubiquitous Web, which are rapidly evolving from Social Web (Web2.0) to the Semantic Web (Web3.0) opens new ways for use and development of digital textbooks in education.

*Table 2. Main differences between Instructional System Design and MetaSystems Learning Design*

|  | **Instructional Design** | **MetaSystems Learning Design** |
|---|---|---|
| Origins | Systems theory and behaviorist psychology | Theory of open systems and pedagogy of integrated structure of competence |
| Paradigm | Soft systems paradigm: ADDIE models | GAE paradigm: metapatterns |
| Definition | Systematic process for improving instruction | Metasystems integrated processes for learning outcomes |
| Models offer | Conceptual tools to visualize, direct, and manage processes for creating high-quality teaching and learning materials | Patterns and metapatterns |
| Knowledge architecture | Cognitive architecture | Integrated structure of competence |
| Learning environment | Classroom learning environment/ classroom management | Diversity of learning environments/ knowledge management |
| Source of knowledge | principles drown from educational psychology, cognitive science, systems theory, communications, philosophy, anthropology, and organizational theory | Cross-principles drown from postmodern philosophy, quantum psychology, competence pedagogy, cybernetics, knowledge management. |
| Application | procedural guide, protocols for instructional development | Profesionalisation of teacher training on the base on postmodern philosophy |

## PATTERNS AND METAPATTERNS IN USER INTERFACES DESIGN

Instead of the paper-based textbook, "digital textbook encourages students' participation to attain the knowledge by using interactive simulation method and multimedia" (Kim, Yang, Kang & Kim, 2010, p. 405). However, even it is used in classrooms, the digital *content* is presented in the form of verbal (on-screen text or narration), pictorial (digital graphics, animation etc.) or audio (audio textbooks).

The first page is *title page*, known also as Home Page, includes the name of textbook, author(s), publish house etc. This data will serve as metadata for advanced searching in digital libraries. In some cases title page includes graphics and/or logo of the university, where the textbook was developed and/or published. The most recommended image is .jpg with the dimension 960x1280px @72dpi. Data are centered alighted. After the name of the author it is recommended to insert a page break. The next page includes the copyright notice with the sign ©, for example: © 2007 Jane Doe, then ISBN.

### Digital Table of Contents

The digital *Table of Contents* or *Contents* may follow the similar structure of printed textbook, but with hyperlinks. Usually, a table of contents is a list organized in the order in which the content appear in textbook. Instead of printed textbook, a digital textbook has a button or a special designed features in a *menu* that offer direct access to the table of contents. In some cases a table of contents is placed in the back of the digital textbook, it is interactive and deserves special treatment in every possible way. The other important distinction is the hierarchical structure of digital table of contents. Thus, a digital table of contents may present *a full table of contents* or *a short table of contents*. The full table of contents may be created automatically using PC & Word 2010 by choosing the heading styles from automatic table of contents styles. The short table of contents is created manually. Indeed, full and short table of contents is created for students with different learning styles and preferences. Moreover, the table of contents may appear after the title page or at the end of content. One of the example of digital full and short table of contents can be viewed on OpenStax College site (Appendix 1, Appendix 2).

The table of contents can be made by *hyperlinks*. The table of contents can be hyperlinked to the chapter. Hyperlink allow the user to click on any part of the table of contents and navigate directly to that page. In comparison with the printed table of contents, its digital equivalent may include extra structures. Thus, may be developed deeper tables of contents, which can be dynamically expanded and contracted in depth; guided virtual tours; bookmarks; search engine; trace of navigation etc. To develop an interactive table of content the primary text must be suited to hypertext display, being small enough to be read without scrolling. In a textual document the author should highlighting the word and then, *Insert Hyperlink*. The other way is to use concept mapping techniques. The users access content by passing from digital table of contents to page of content and vice versa via hyperlinks.

Psychological considerations in using and developing full or short table of contents refer to learning styles. Thus, it is well known that students with right-brain dominance generally are more comfortable with presentations that involve intuition (e. g. short table of contents). Instead, students with strong left-brain traits take information when is presented in a logical, linear sequence (e. g. full table of contents). Moreover, students have emotional and energetic needs. And emotion and energy plays a vital role in how students are motivated to learn and how readily students absorb ideas for future reading choosing full or short table of contents.

## Digital Page

Digital textbook content includes *digital pages*. In some cases, the hypertext medium provides similar facilities to a printed textbook. Thus, digital pages are displayed on screen and looked at on paper. A hypertext implementation of an information space allow user to navigate from page to page and from section to section, as well as to return to the table of contents, search the index, glossary or pass to cross-referenced material. Digital pages are connected via hyperlinks. Pagination is a process of arbitrary fragmentation with *Page Breaks* or *Section Breaks*. The number of breaks depends on author preference or cultural senses of which content belongs. However, for students who prefer traditional reading, may be developed the page-turning effect (This effect is a standard feature of Amazon's Kindle apps, Google Play Books software and Sony digital products!). Moreover, the digital or digitized content of digital textbooks should be easier visualized on different displays. For this, the author(s) of the digital textbook prepare a manuscript contained the tables of contents and the content of the pages, which will be digitizing or completed with digital features by specialists in informatics. The manuscript may be handwriting or prepared with word processor, even in a simultaneous collaborative way. An editor "marked-up" the manuscript and put it into the desired format. More often is used .pdf format. In order to make the text appear in a desired format, it is necessary to insert adequate commands.

The digital page can contain tables or/and figures. Tables are inserted through *Insert Table*, and figure – *Insert Figure*. Each table usually have a brief title above the table. Table footnotes are placed below the table. Each table should include not more than three rows and some columns. It is not recommended to use Bullets and Numbering. The name of the figure is placed down the figure. Figure are salved in TIF, EPS or high-resolution PDF formats. For 3D images are used U3D files.

Color image must be in RGB (red, green, blue) mode. The digital image is preferable to have 8.7 cm. Figure wider than one column should be sized to 11.4 cm or 17.8 cm wide. Numbers, letters, and symbols should be no smaller than 6 points (2 mm) and no larger than 12 pints (6 mm) after reduction and must be consistent. Composite figures must be preassembled. It is not recommended to submit figures in MS Office.

For an original figure, created in a MS Office application, using, for example, SmartArt, Chart, Screenshot or Shapes, it is not recommended to use pattern or textual files in graphics. Instead, it is recommended to use solid fills or percentage screens that will be effectively converted to vector images during file conversion (a 20% difference in percent screens is most effective for differentiation). Artwork placed within any MS Office applications should be of acceptable minimum resolution for print production: 300 dpi for halftones, 600-900 dpi for combinations, and 1000-1200 dpi for line art. Pictures and images are inserted into files. It is not recommended to use Copy/Paste or Insert Link.

Pagination is the process of divided content into discrete pages. Indeed, unlike printed pages, the digital pages can be discrete, interactive or adaptive. Discrete pages can be outputted to a printed device, being produced by digital typesetting or scanning. However, pagination on the digital devices is used for a) displaying a limited number of results on search engine results pages, or b) showing a limited dimension of page. One of the problems in digital textbook use and development can be the correct implementation of pagination. To avoid this problem it is not recommended to *Insert Page Number*.

There are numerous ways to make the page more interactive. According to definition an interactive page is such a page that in response to users' request presents choices or paths to communicate with it. The users can accordingly control or outcome of a program. The content of interactive page is written in plain html. The interactive page is created on the norms of Interactive Design: a field of study that focused on meaningful communication between through cyclical and collaborative processes between people and technology. Research was found (Campbell, 1998, p. 1) that interactivity in instructional design takes on more complex meaning. In good instruction, interactivity refers to active learning, in which the learner acts on the information to transform it into new, personal meaning. In a constructivist sense, the learner co-constructs meaning by exploring the environment, solving a problem, or applying information to a new situation that he/she helps to define.

Learning design of digital pages depends on what activities or/and actions will be carried out: *reading, hermeneutic dialogue, problem-solving, personalisation of content* (trough assembling or extending) etc. In case of reading a digitally formatted text, it may be important to demonstrate how to take-notes, highlight, search metadata, use virtual bookmarks, glossaries, manipulate screen resolution, page orientation, setup text size preference setting, turn text read-aloud features etc. There are some possibilities to differentiate, blend or flip instruction in classroom. However, instead the instructional objectives will be to integrate digital artifacts into digital formal, the focus should be on developing of patterns and metapatterns that will be easier recognized by students. While print texts are primarily informative, thedesign of digital text should be focused on developing new patterns. This is really possible because digital text can "capture" personalized digital images and videos, animation, 3D representations etc. Therefore, digital text allows engaging students in processing of new patterns.

## Digital Text

Digital text or eText is an electronic version of a written text. Comparing with printed text, digital text is more flexible. It can be searched, rearranged, condensed, annotated or read aloud by a computer. With digital text, changing, tailoring or customizing the information to meet the different needs of students is easy. It was argued (Wahl & Duffield, 2014, pp. 2-5) that different people learn differently based on individuals' ability to encode visual, auditory and other types of information. Digital technology supports for differentiation in learning. Software offer students a variety of ways to access content, work with information to develop understanding and to demonstrate what was known. There are some examples of the flexibility and adaptivity offered with digital text:

- *Text-to-speech options* can be used to read the entire speech as a preview or to read individual words.
- *The text can be changed visually*, by altering the size and color of the font or by adding more space between lines.
- *Words and phrases can be underlined, bolded or highlighted* in order to draw attention to certain facts or new vocabulary. Students can make these changes to indicate understanding, as part of assessing prior or acquired knowledge or skills.
- *The text can be reorganized* to create a summary or an outline view.
- *The text can be generated from frames* for multiplicity of the formulas.
- *The text can be placed in a box* on one side of the page with room on the other for student notes or questions.
- *Questions for students to answer or background information can be inserted close* to the relevant section of text.
- *Text can be broken into manageable chunks* with generic prompts inserted to remind students to apply a strategy (e.g., summarizing predicting, questioning, clarifying, visualizing).
- *The speech can be enhanced with a picture* of Dr. King, an audio clip of the first few lines of the speech, a timeline of the civil rights movement, or other graphics.

- *Students can copy and paste words they don't know into an online dictionary,* which will also read them aloud.
- *Students can work with the text to produce their own summary* or interpretation of the speech.
- Once enhanced, *the same documents can be used repeatedly,* with or without further modification.

Digital text is not only for reading activities. However, digital text is slowly read than the printed text. This means that digital text requires more interconnected concepts and that dimension of digital text compared to print should be reduced to 3:4. In addition, digital text font size can be adjusted at different smaller or bigger font size. It is not recommended to divide text into colons (except *ebook*s for preschool or early school children). The dimension of digital text varies 600 and 800 px. The recommended dimension for Amazon is 960-1280. Digital text is formatted in diverse formats. The most used are: HTML, ePub (version 3.0), .PDF and XML. Epub 3.0 accepts Open Type and WoFF. It is not recommended to insert *Header* and *Footer* and *Page Number*. If digital page will be displayed on different digital devices, is important to note that Kindle has 3½"x4¾" and reduce text with ¼, but *Apple iPad* is 7.31"x9.50 and display 5.81"x7.75. Digital text can be formatted at 0.5", Spacing before and after at 10 pt and margins 3-4 pixels. Each page should be separated with Breaks. The correct placement of the digital text on page is verified. The most used Font are: Serif (Times New Roman and Georgia) and Sans Serif (Arial, Trebuchet, and Verdana) and the Font Size is 10 and 12 pixels.

Digital text can be completed with visual ads. The text can be easier converted in .pdf, html and/or ePub format using *Converters*. The clarity of the digital text is achieved through modification of text size, color contrast, spacing etc. The color contrast is assured by black or dark font colors on white background. The recommended length of the sentence is 3-5 inches which include 10-12 words or 35-55 characters. Italic is used to emphasis ideas or words, but not more than 10% of paragraph.

There are multiple solutions to read digital text. One of the solutions, provided by ReadSpeaker Enterprise Highlighting, allows to better understanding online written content by speech-enabling and highlighting it at the same time. Through visual and audio format and simultaneous text highlighting while it is read, it is expected to increase student retention, comprehension, and memory. The other example is *ReadSpeaker docReader*, which allows listening to PDFs, Word documents, and a variety of other document formats through converting these documents to a web-readable format, while preserving the original layout and synchronized highlighting.

From psychopedagogical point of view, digital textbooks are more continent for deeper learning. Screens offer students experiences that paper cannot. Digital text with embedded interactive graphics, maps, timelines, animations, sound tracks and other features is more motivated. In addition, digital text provides a unique environment for comprehensive reading. Perhaps any discrepancies between paper and screen will shrink together with the attitude toward the ergonomic issues of the digital textbooks.

## Graphic Organizer

Visualization is one of the widely used technique for creating images, diagrams and animation to communicate a message both abstract and concrete. Developing a visualization application is the field of graphic. The invention of computer graphics is considered one of the most important discovery since the invention of central perspective in the Renaissance period. The use of visualization to present information or understanding in education is not a new idea. It has been used in maps, drawing, plots etc. Scientific visualization is the use of interactive, sensory representations to reinforce cognition, hypothesis building and reasoning because allow the exploration, analysis, and understanding of the data. Educational visualization is part of scientific visualization.

According to Wahl and Duffield (2014, p. 5) a graphic organizer is a visual representation of ideas of information. Calendars and maps are common examples of a graphic organizer. Such organizers are particularly suited to assessing understanding or diagnosing misunderstanding, increasing recall, designing a complex structure (e.g., long texts, large Web sites), communicating complex ideas, and incorporating both images and text. The graphic organizer can be generated electronically, using specialized software such as Kidspiration 2/Inspiration, Kid Pix, or even the graphic elements in Microsoft Word, and offers distinct advantages. Moreover, a graphic organizer can be printed out.

Interactive graphic organizer is an effective learning tool for interactive exercises and assessment.

A graphic organizer, also known as knowledge map, concept map, story map, cognitive organizer, advance organizer, or concept diagram, is a communication tool that uses visual symbols to express knowledge, concepts, thoughts, or ideas, and the relationships between them in order to provide a visual aid to facilitate learning and instruction. There are many types of graphic organizers. Some of them, developed as PDF files, can be viewed and printed from Education Oasis site.

Thinking Maps are a set of graphical organizer techniques used in primary and sensory education aim to provide a common visual language to information structure, often employed when students take notes. It is expected that Thinking Maps are ideal visual tools for learning. There are, at least, eighth types of Thinking Maps, which include 8 visual patterns linked to a specific cognitive process (Figure 2).

There are many other non-linear graphic organizes that can be used in a digital text. Among them are: *star* (to condense and organize data about multiple traits, fact, or attributes associated a single topic); *spider* (to investigate and enumerate various aspects of a single theme or topic); *fishbone* (to explore the many aspects or effects of a complex topic); *cloud* (to systematize the generation of ideas based upon a central topic); *Venn* (to visualize the relationship between two or three sets as well as to o compare and contrast the characteristics of any other item); *Pie Chart* (for displaying information about the percentages or parts of a whole); *story map* (to summarize the parts of a story) etc.

## Digital Image

Traditionally digital images are created with Adobe Illustrator, Corel Draw, GIMP, FreeHand, Logos or other equivalent software. Because digital devices have different dimensions, it is recommended: *to save images* in 300 dpi (or 300 ppi) and *to insert digital images in text* using Insert Picture and not Copy/Paste or Drag and Drop. There are two types of digital images: raster or vector based.

Sachs (1996-1999) notes that a digital image that is a rectangular array of pixels is called a bitmap. These images are: color or black and white. Digital images are composed of pixels each of which holds a single number corresponding to the gray level of the image at a particular location. Each pixel is like a tiny dot of a particular color. Each of color image holds three numbers corresponding to the primary colors Red, Green and Blue (RGB) and levels of the image at a particular location. Any color can be constructed by mixing the current amounts of red, green, and blue light. Instead of color images, binary images use only a single bit to represent each pixel. Since a bit can only exist in on or off states, every pixel in a binary image is usually black or white. Some color images are created using a full palette (three colors displayed at varying levels of intensity create

*Figure 2. Diversity of thinking maps*

| Type of Thinking Map | Purpose | Visual representation |
|---|---|---|
| Circle Map | to define in context; generate ideas; examine how you view something; brainstorm | 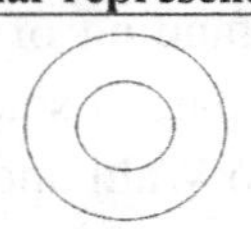 |
| Bubble Map | to describe with adjectives | 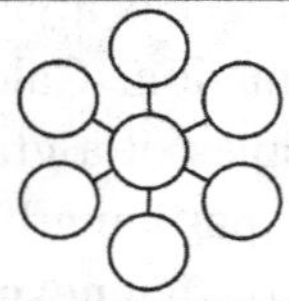 |
| Flow Map | to sequence and order information | 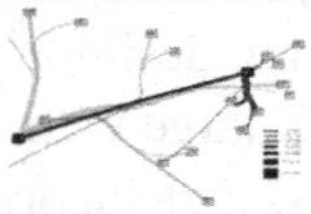 |
| Brace Map | to identify part/whole relationships | 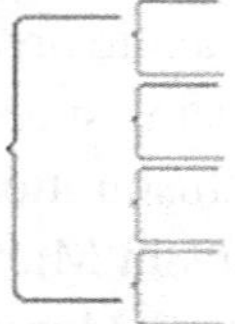 |
| Tree Map (binary, tertiary) | to classify or grouping | 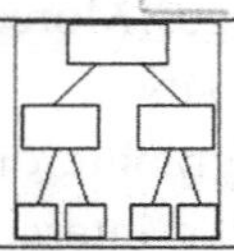 |
| Double Bubble Map | to compare and contrast | 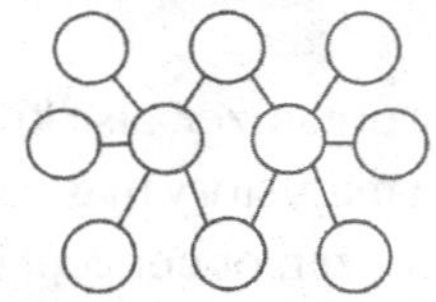 |
| Multi-flow map | to analyse causes and effects | 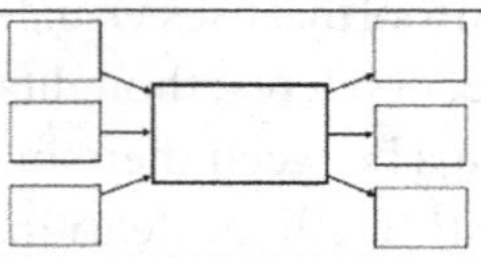 |
| Bridge Map | to illustrate analogies | 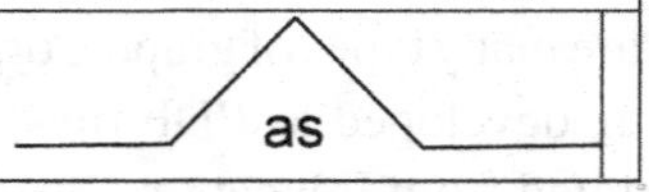 as |

over 16 million colors.), but some using a limited palette of colors, typically 256 different colors. The density of pixels in a digital image is known as *resolution*. The higher the resolution, the more information the image contains. It is not recommended to elaborate digital image larger than 600 pixels (width) x 800(height). Interior image for EPUB textbooks can be high resolution (600 dpi). A digital image should be scaled properly to fit the page. If textbook will be published in paper as well as eTextbook, the image should be elaborated with a higher resolution. As a general rule, 1200 ppi is the suggested scan resolution.

Digital images may be either raster or vector based. A raster digital image (known as bitmapped images) is often created by scanning a picture and is measure in pixels. The file types are: BMP, TIFF, GIFF, and JPEG files. A raster file is usually larger than a vector graphic image file and, as result, is usually difficult to modify without loss of information. There are some software tools that can convert a taster file into a vector file for refinement and changes. Raster images have a certain amount of pixels within each inch. For example, a 300 ppi image has 300 pixels per inch. Usually the higher the ppi, the higher the quality. If is required to use a high resolution image file, the file must have been created or scanned at both the dimension and the resolution required. E.G. if you need to print an image at 2 inches wide and 300 ppi is required, your image must be created/scanned at a minimum of 600 pixels (2in x 300dpi).

Vector based image use objects and lines (shapes) to represent image. In comparison with raster digital image, vector based images can be zoomed without losing the quality of the image. The relationship of the shapes is expressed as a mathematical equation.

Digital images are manipulated with digital pen to enhance the usability of handwriting. Digital pens look and work just like an ordinary pen but capture handwriting and drawings from paper forms and notes. Using a digital pen is a quick, easy and reliable way of capturing, searching and sending information during reading of digital text or manipulating a digital image. A digital pen can be used to fill out a form, draw a sketch, and send an exact image of the form. The digital pen (sometimes known as an electronic pen), together with normal paper overprinted with a dot pattern, captures the pen strokes with a tiny camera. It records an exact image of the handwriting and the form it was written on. The data is securely uploaded via a compatible mobile phone or by docking with a personal computer. Better yet, the digital pen can also convert handwriting to text, saving on unnecessary re-keying time.

The process of getting a digital image to look the same as in real world between two or more different media or devices is called *color manage-*

*ment*. There are many color management systems available today. The features of the color are the following:

- **Saturation:** How pure or intense the color is;
- **Brightness:** How light or dark the color is;
- **Luminance (Chrominance):** A measure of its perceived brightness.

To correctly display digital images, the user should set the brightness control on own monitor. Thus, if the level is too high, blacks will start to become grays and colors will be washed out. If the level is too low, there will be loss of shadow detail and colors will appear murky.

## Animation

One of the main forms of presentation relies on *animation*. Animation may promote deeper learning. According to the theory, students learn better with animation, if it is designed accordingly with the suitable principles. Mayer and Moreno (2002) explore different ways of multimedia learning effects and found that students learn more deeply from animation and narration than from narration along (multimedia principle); students learn more deeply when on-screen text is presented next to the portion of the animation that it describes than when on-screen text is presented far from the corresponding action in the animation (spatial continuity principle); students learn more deeply when corresponding portions of the narration and animation are presented at the same time than when they are separated in time (temporal continuity principle); students learn more deeply from animation and narration when extraneous words, sounds (including music), and video are excluded rather than included (coherence principle); students more deeply from animation and narration than from animation and on-screen text (modality principle); students learn more deeply from animation and narration than from animation, narration, and on-screen text (redundancy principle) and that students learn more deeply from animation and narration when the narration is in conversational rather than formal style (personalization principle).

The use of animation is based on interactivity: students are motivated to "interact" with digital learning objects in order to obtain impression that he/she explore the learning object, feeling to "communicate" with them and are engaged in hermeneutic dialogue toward building more sophisticated patterns. Moreover, students explore the dangerous phenomena and processes, like electrolyze, nuclear reactions etc. The potential of animation for learning requires from the possibility to capture and/or replicate learning objects from the real word context in digital learning environments. Therefore, in digital textbook content the animation can be continuous, segmented, interactive etc. In developing animation is used text, digital graphics, digital photography and special software. There are two main ways: knowledge that involves animation (movement is crucial for comprehension) and knowledge focusing on animations (movement is useful in capturing the attention of content issues).

## Content Construction

The construction of content requires well-defined authoring processes to produce the content. The most popular standard is SCORM, which allows constructing hierarchical structures to connect learning contents, schedule their delivery and communication for the client and server components of a web-based e-learning system. In addition, IMS Common Cartridge provides guidelines for content authorization, student assessment and online discussion forum, providing a more complete coverage to the pedagogical needs. However, constructing digital textbook content requires new

standards to produce, store, disseminate, purchase and rend digital textbooks according to curricula requirements.

Emerging digital technologies address this issue by allowing different modalities to find digital textbooks and to personalize digital content through multimodal text without installing Apps or other kinds of software. To take this further, all-in-one eLearning and mLearning platforms have been developed; in which teachers assume the role of producing *content* with iBook Author, CK-12 FlexBooks and Khan Academy content editor. Recently, with the availability of Web2.0 technologies, such as wiki, it became possible to develop *student-created content* during collaborative projects, in which students are editors of content. This idea can be treated as new learning methodologies that ensure students to benefit from this prior training in order to prevent them from getting confused with the unstructured characteristic of wiki.

One of the central roles in learning design should be attributed to *concept mapp*ing, which is a way to organize the information for learning. This way has been known as "a formal or semi-formal diagramming technique or a technique for representing knowledge in graphs" (Railean, 2006, p. 334). The main idea relies on core concept, which serves as pattern or metapattern for learning. It is estimated that the core concept will effectively build the *knowledge structure*. The problem of using the mind mapping in instructional design is not so easy and depends on the initial structure of instructional material. For example the instructional material can be structured in a traditional manual that can serve as the base for building the e-manual or instructional material that has been planned in course curricula. The main problems in using the mind mapping techniques in instructional design of educational software are 1) to determine the core concept around which will be built the knowledge map and 2) to find the concepts that can be associated with the core concept. These problems can be solved through applying the matrices of interactivity in which has been included the power of links.

In use and development digital textbook' content is taking into consideration that technology allow to simulate *sound* (educational radio), *vision* (interactive television) and *haptic* (haptic technologies). In addition, "participatory methods are effective at stimulating the transfer of knowledge, mutual learning and collective visioning" (De Moor, Saritas, Schuurman, Claeys, De Marez, 2014).

## Interactive 3D Technologies

Traditionally, the role of videos in digital textbooks is to motivate students. It was argued (Lau, Yen, Li & Wah, 2002, p. 192) that videos can present pre-generated learning content in motion and multimodal forms, helping students formulate and visualize abstract concepts easily. With the support of interactivity, students are allowed to proactively discover things or control the learning pace. Cognitive studies have shown that students would engage with learning material if they could easily understand abstract/difficult concepts and relate new information to what they already know. However, lack of attention and engagement results in more failing grades, more expulsions, increased dropout rates, and a lower undergraduate completion rate. Although a large set of teaching material was ported online in recent years, the learning efficiency of using such resources is reduced because of the inaccuracies in the electronic material, the paper-based way of presentation through static images and pictures, and the lack of interactivity in the applications. In such environments, the learning process is not guided; the student is lost in an "ocean" of information, and the electronic material ends-up back on the paper in a printed format. Our approach, presented in *Interactive 3D Web-Based Environments for Online Learning: Case Studies, Technologies and Challenges* focuses on the development of guided learning

experiences using a set of interactive simulators that have the capacity to pull the students in the learning process, offering enhanced motivation and intellectual stimulation. Since 3D visualization may prove critical for correct and rapid understanding of concepts, it was explore the application of 3D technologies and standards for the development of guided interactive 3D environments for online learning; the application of web-based 3D technologies in engineering, medicine, physics and chemistry. Pedagogically, the interactive 3D technologies are used in classroom equipped with an *interactive whiteboard* (an interactive display connected to a computer or/and digital devices and manipulated with a pen, finger, stylus, or other devices).

## TEXTBOOKS IN AN ALTERNATIVE FORMAT: AUDIO TEXTBOOK

The audio textbook is a textbook that is listened in an easy to understand way. In development of audio textbooks should be avoided noises caused by the narrator; wind from the narrator's mouth; audio distortion; continuity and reading too fast. The audio textbook should be recorded in 16 bit/44.1 kHz wav file format and to be saved as a 192kbps mp3. Usually, audio textbooks are recorded by:

1.  **Punch Record:** The most common, which allows easy to correct mistakes, but takes a reasonable amount of audio production experience to be able to "punch" cleanly and correctly, to achieve.
2.  **Straight Record:** Less common, which allows correcting mistakes through a simple going back and re-reading from the previous sentence or break, but it takes more time to edit.

Audio textbooks have one of the following templates:

*Template A:*
[title of audiobook]
Written by [name of author]
Narrated by [name of narrator]

*Template B:*
This has been [title of audiobook]
Written by [name of author]
Narrated by [name of narrator]
Copyright [year and name of copyright holder]
Production copyright [year it was recorded]
by [company name].

Once the audio textbook has been recorded, it should be edited as follows:

1.  Separate the audio textbooks into chapters. Each chapter can have a maximum length of 120 minutes and cannot be larger than 170MB. If a chapter exceeds that maximum length or size, it must be divided into two files at a suitable point in the narration. If the majority of the chapters are less than five minutes long and the audiobook contains over 50 chapters, can be combined up to 5 chapters per file, making sure each grouping contains the same number of files. Chapters over 5 minutes long may not be combined.

2.  Pace the read for natural sounding and flowing, as well as preserve and promote the phrasing and dramatic intent of the reader and author. Nothing is more disturbing to the listening experience than an unnatural presentation of words or phrases as well as the spaces between them. For this is recommended to sit back at the start (and then, again, at the end) of the editing process, and simply listen to a few minutes of the audiobook, while closing your eyes and asking, 'is this moving too fast? Too slowly? What pace feels right?'

3.  Verify silence or spaces of any kind. It is important to list carefully to the Room Tone and make sure that audio textbook is free of all click, pops, and background noise. All spaces between words, phrases and sentences should be void of clicks, pops, smacks or any other sounds (stomach noises, car horns, etc.) and should be replaced when necessary.

4.  Remove the breaths at the beginning of paragraphs. It is recommended to preserve breaths unless it will disturb the flow of the phrase. More breaths should be removed in an instructional reading than a dramatic reading. Breaths that seem "out of the element" of the narration, should be cut. Breaths that feel natural should be left in.

5.  **Verify Spacing:** It should be exactly 500ms (0.5 seconds) at the head of each file, and exactly 3.5 seconds at the tail. There should be exactly 2.5 seconds after the narrator announces the chapter ("chapter x").

6.  Remove as many clicks and undesirable mouth sounds from within words and phrases as time will allow. A baseline production value should be established at the beginning of the edit that is adhered to throughout the program. Care should be taken when fixing or removing any undesirable sounds around or within words so that the end result actually sounds better.

7.  Review audio textbook during Quality Control process in order to detect and repair all errors. Recording usually include misreads, omissions, mispronunciations, noises etc. This process should serve as a catch-all to correct these errors, and any other defects in the audiobook (such as a duplicated sentence, or a strip of silence).

The final stage relies on process of adjusting the sound to make it more even and "listenable". It is recommended to submit files between -23dB and -18dB RMS, with peaks hovering around -3dB and noise floor between -60dB and -50dB.

To make the audio textbook levels louder is used RMS normalization around -20db, or compression/limiting with a ratio of 3:1.

## FUTURE RESEARCH

Future research can be conducted on analysis and development of metasystem thinking about the role of pattern and metappaterns in learning environments. One issue is to identify the potential of student, including intellect, emotion and energy, and to effectively use them in modeling of digital or blended learning. This type of the architectures integrates savoir–dire, savoir–faire and savoir–etre components.

The savoir-vivre architecture for digital textbook will reflect the input and output characteristics as well as transitional states of the cognitive, affective and psychomotor systems. Behavioral states in human development should reflect dynamic integration, adaptation and accommodation in microsystem, exosystem, mezosystem and macrosystem in relationship with cronosystem. This includes the psychological, physiological and attitudinal characteristics of learner.

Adopting a process perspective on working memory requires a more general incorporation of the embedded-processes model, because working memory needs to be represented "in" the cognitive processes, where "selecting" is equivalent to activating representations in long-term memory, but "organizing" and "integrating" need to be conceptualized in one process.

## CONCLUSION

In this chapter we have presented an overview of pattern and metapatterns, highlighting the novel contributions of the patterns in elementary design units. We have also described the issues and controversies and the common requirements the authors were required to follow in order to develop personalized digital textbooks, including audio textbooks. Finally, we have assembled some requirements for use and development of digital textbooks, also providing some discussion. Modeling of the elementary didactic units represents a complex endeavor based on issues of expressiveness, reusability, adaptively and flexibility. In some cases can be used special software, for Educational Modeling Language (Caeiro, Llamas & Anido, 2014, p. 380). Future research is needed to understand the complexity of learning modeling based on MetaSystems Learning Design approach.

It can be concluded that the instructional design come down to the mechanical applications of the principles or concepts or pre-set algorithms. In our case we analyse the concept mapping technique that can be viewed as an integrative mechanism between real learning environment and brain patterns. However, the systematization and semiformal structures of the instructional context can be of significant support for digital textbook designers as they allow for using the matrices of interactivities and concept map techniques to analyze the instructional context or for building the instructional context beginning from a core concepts. This chapter can be considered a starting point for research the role of patterns and metapatterns in design of elementary didactic units.

## REFERENCES

Barnett, R. (2014). Thinking about higher education. In P., Gibbs, R. & Barnett (Eds.), Thinking about higher education, (pp. 9-22). Switzerland: Springer International Publishing. doi:10.1007/978-3-319-03254-2_2

Beck, R. J. (2010). *What are learning objects?* Retrieved July 22, 2014 from http://www4.uwm.edu/cie/learning_objects.cfm?gid=56

Bloom, J. (2009). *Pattern Thinking, systems thinking, and complex—transferrable learning in education for sustainability*. Retrieved September 1, 2014 from http://www.jeffbloom.net/docs/b-PatternSystemThkg.pdf

Bloom, J. W., & Volk, T. (2007). *The use of metapatterns for research into complex systems of teaching, learning, and schooling*. Retrieved October 3, 2014 from http://citeseerx.ist.psu.edu/viewdoc/download?doi=10.1.1.120.6165&rep=rep1&type=pdf

Bordes, A., Bottou, L., Collobert, R., Roth, D., Weston, J., & Zettlemoyer, L. (2014). Introduction to the special issue on learning semantics. *Machine Learning, 94*(2), 127–131. doi:10.1007/s10994-013-5381-4

Caeiro, M., Llamas, M., & Anido, L. (2014). PoEML: Modeling learning units through perspectives. *Computer Standards & Interfaces, 36*(2), 380–396. doi:10.1016/j.csi.2013.08.009

Cameron, T., & Bennett, S. (2010). Learning objects in practice: The integration of reusable learning objects in primary education. *British Journal of Educational Technology, 41*(6), 897–908. doi:10.1111/j.1467-8535.2010.01133.x

Campbell, K. (1998). *The Web: Design for active learning*. Retrieved September 1, 2014 from, http://www.atl.ualberta.ca/documents/articles/activeLearning001.htm

CLRN. (2014). *Electronic learning resources for California teachers*. Retrieved November 1, 2014 from http://www.clrn.org/home/

Dinsmore, D. L., Baggetta, P., Doyle, S., & Loughlin, S. M. (2014). The role of initial learning, problem features, prior knowledge, and pattern recognition on transfer success. *Journal of Experimental Education, 82*(1), 121–141. doi:10.1080/00220973.2013.835299

Eaton, S. E. (2013). *Formal, non-formal and informal learning: What are the differences?* Retrieved June, 1, 2014 from http://drsaraheaton.wordpress.com/2010/12/31/formal-non-formal-and-informal-learning-what-are-the-differences/

Lau, R. W. H., Yen, N. Y., Li, F., & Wah, B. (2014). Recent development in multimedia e-learning technologies. *World Wide Web (Bussum), 17*(2), 189–198. doi:10.1007/s11280-013-0206-8

Leutner, D. (2014). Motivation and emotion as mediators in multimedia learning. *Learning and Instruction, 29*, 174–175. doi:10.1016/j.learninstruc.2013.05.004

Majumdar, D. D. (2014). Trends in pattern recognition and machine learning. *Defence Science Journal, 35*(3), 327–351. doi:10.14429/dsj.35.6027

Mayer, R. E. (2014). Incorporating motivation into multimedia learning. *Learning and Instruction, 29*, 171–173. doi:10.1016/j.learninstruc.2013.04.003

Mayer, R. E., & Moreno, R. (2002). Animation as an aid to multimedia learning. *Educational Psychology Review, 14*(1), 87–99. doi:10.1023/A:1013184611077

Paquette, G. (2014). Technology-based instructional design: Evolution and major trends. In J. M. Spector, M. D. Merrill, J. Elen, & M. J. Bishop (Eds.), Handbook of research on educational communications and technology (pp. 661-671). Springer New York.

Pieroni, L., Rossi-Arnaud, C., & Baddeley, A. D. (2011). What can symmetry tell us about working memory? In A. Vandierendonck & A. Szmalec (Eds.), Spatial working memory (pp. 145-158). Hove: Psychology Press.

Podlasai, I. (2010). *Information-energetic pedagogy* (in Russian). Moscow: Dern Group.

Railean, E. (2006). Concept mapping in the instructional design of the educational software. In Development and Application Systems. *Proceedings of the 8th In. Conf. on Development and Application Systems* (pp. 333-338). Suceava, Romania: Stefan cel Mare University of Suceava.

Reich, Y. (2014). Year closure and a new beginning: Towards better engineering design research. *Research in Engineering Design, 25*(1), 1–2. doi:10.1007/s00163-013-0167-z

Rudic, G. (2013). Modern pedagogy in multi-measured space. In E. B. Assemble (Ed.), *Socrates Almanac "Science and Education"* (pp. 74–75). Oxford: Oxford Review.

Santacruz-Valencia, L. P., Navarro, A., Aedo, I., & Kloos, C. D. (2010). Comparison of knowledge during the assembly process of learning objects. *Journal of Intelligent Information Systems, 35*(1), 51–74. doi:10.1007/s10844-009-0088-5

Schweppe, J., & Rummer, R. (2014). Attention, working memory, and long-term memory in multimedia learning: An integrated perspective based on process models of working memory. *Educational Psychology Review, 26*(2), 285–306. doi:10.1007/s10648-013-9242-2

Shen, J., Lei, J., Chang, H. Y., & Namdar, B. (2014). Technology-enhanced, modeling-based instruction (TMBI) in science education. In J. M. Spector, M. D. Merrill, J. Elen, & M. J. Bishop (Eds.), Handbook of research on educational communications and technology (pp. 529-540). Springer New York.

Toussaint, E. R., & Toussaint, G. T. (2014). *What is a pattern?* Retrieved November, 21, 2014 from http://m.archive.bridgesmathart.org/2014/bridges2014-293.pdf

Tyner, K. (2014). *Literacy in a digital world: Teaching and learning in the age of information.* Routledge Communication Series.

Volk, T., & Bloom, J. W. (2007). The use of metapatterns for research into complex systems of teaching, learning, and schooling, Part I: Metapatterns in nature and culture. *Complicity: The International Journal of Complexity and Education, 4,* 25-43. Retrieved July 22, 2014 from http://metapatterns.wdfiles.com/local--files/members:tylervolk/ppr.Volk.Complicity1.2007.pdf

Volk, T., Bloom, J. W., & Richards, J. (2007). Toward a science of metapatterns: Building upon Bateson's foundation. *Kybernetes: The International Journal of Cybernetics, Systems, and Management Sciences, 36,* 1070-1080. Retrieved July 22, 2014 from http://metapatterns.wdfiles.com/local--files/members:tylervolk/Volk.Bateson.27Jul07.pdf

Wahl, L., & Duffield, J. (2014*). Using flexible technology to meet the needs of diverse students.* Retrieved November, 22, 2014 from http://www.wested.org/online_pubs/kn-05-01.pdf

Walshaw, M., & Duncan, W. (2014). Hermeneutics as a methodological resource for understanding empathy in on-line learning environments. *International Journal of Research & Method in Education, 1*–16. doi:10.1080/1743727X.2014.914166

Weller, M. (2007). Learning objects, learning design, and adoption through succession. *Journal of Computing in Higher Education, 19*(1), 26–47. doi:10.1007/BF03033418

Wiley, D. A. (2000). Connecting learning objects to instructional design theory: A definition, a metaphor, and a taxonomy. In D. A. Wiley (Ed.), *The instructional use of learning objects: Online version.* Retrieved from http://reusability.org/read/chapters/wiley.doc

Wisse, P. (2008). *Metapattern: Information modelling as enneadic dynamics.* Retrieved November 19, 2014 from http://sprouts.aisnet.org/156/2/R2001-04.pdf

*Writing interactive pages.* (n. d.). Retrieved November 19, 2014 from http://www.conservation-physics.org/appx/writingtec2.php

Zhang, C. X., Zhang, J. S., Ji, N. N., & Guo, G. (2014). Learning ensemble classifiers via restricted Boltzmann machines. *Pattern Recognition Letters*, *36*, 161–170. doi:10.1016/j.patrec.2013.10.009

## ADDITIONAL READING

Alonso, F., Lopez, G., Manrique, D., & Vines, J. M. (2008). Learning objects, learning objectives and learning design. *Innovations in Education and Teaching International*, *45*(4), 389–400. doi:10.1080/14703290802377265

Apps in Education. (2013). *Creating a Quiz or taking a Poll on the iPad.* Retrieved June 1, 2014 from http://appsineducation.blogspot.ro/2013/12/creating-quiz-or-taking-poll-on-ipad.html

Apps in Education. (2014). *10 Free E-Book Sites for iPad.* Retrieved June 1, 2014 from http://appsineducation.blogspot.ro/2011/10/10-free-e-book-sites-for-ipad.html

Apps in Education. (2014). *English iPad Apps.* Retrieved June 1, 2014 from http://appsineducation.blogspot.ro/p/english-ipad-apps.html

Apps in Education. (2014). *Science iPad Apps.* Retrieved June 1, 2014 from http://appsineducation.blogspot.ro/p/science-ipad-apps.html

Apps in Education. (2014). *Visual Timers for your iPad Classroom.* Retrieved June 1, 2014 from http://appsineducation.blogspot.ro/

Balatsoukas, P., Morris, A., & O'Brien, A. (2008). Learning objects update: Review and critical approach to content aggregation. *Journal of Educational Technology & Society*, *11*(2), 119–130.

Bitel, M. (2014). Flipping the equation: The need for context-focused group work education. *Social Work with Groups*, *37*(1), 48–60. doi:10.1080/01609513.2013.816916

Canaleta, X., Vernet, D., Vicent, L., & Montero, J. A. (2014). Master in teacher training: A real implementation of Active Learning. *Computers in Human Behavior*, *31*, 651–658. doi:10.1016/j.chb.2013.09.020

Churchill, D. (2005). Learning objects: An interactive representation and a mediating tool in a learning activity. *Educational Media International*, *42*(4), 333–349. doi:10.1080/09523980500237757

Churchill, D. (2011). Conceptual model learning objects and design recommendations for small screens. *Journal of Educational Technology & Society*, *14*(1), 203–216.

Coward, L. A. (1990). *Pattern thinking.* Greenwood Publishing Group.

Downey, S. (2011). i-MMOLE: Instructional framework for creating virtual world lessons. *TechTrends: Linking Research & Practice to Improve Learning*, *55*(6), 33–41.

Gellert, U. (2004). Didactic material confronted with the concept of mathematical literacy. *Educational Studies in Mathematics*, *55*(1-3), 163–179. doi:10.1023/B:EDUC.0000017693.32454.01

Greer, R. D. (1999). Is the learn unit a fundamental measure of pedagogy? *The Behavior Analyst*, *1*(22), 5–16. PMID:22478317

Hsu, I. C. (2012). Intelligent discovery for learning objects using Semantic Web technologies. *Journal of Educational Technology & Society*, *15*(1), 298–312.

Lama, M., Vidal, J. C., Otero-García, E., Bugarín, A., & Barro, S. (2012). Semantic linking of learning object repositories to DBpedia. *Journal of Educational Technology & Society*, *15*(4), 47–61.

Lowe, K., Lee, L., Schibeci, R., Cummings, R., Phillips, R., & Lake, D. (2010). Learning objects and engagement of students in Australian and New Zealand schools. *British Journal of Educational Technology*, *41*(2), 227–241. doi:10.1111/j.1467-8535.2009.00964.x

Mendonca, P. C., & Justi, R. (2014). An instrument for analyzing arguments produced in modeling-based chemistry lessons. *Journal of Research in Science Teaching*, *51*(2), 192–218. doi:10.1002/tea.21133

Meskill, C., & Anthony, N. (2014). Managing synchronous polyfocality in new media/new learning: Online language educators' instructional strategies. *System*, *42*, 177–188. doi:10.1016/j.system.2013.11.005

Noteborn, G., Dailey-Hebert, A., Carbonell, K. B., & Gijselaers, W. (2014). Essential knowledge for academic performance: Educating in the virtual world to promote active learning. *Teaching and Teacher Education*, *37*, 217–234. doi:10.1016/j.tate.2013.10.008

Ruys, I., Keer, H. V., & Aelterman, A. (2012). Examining pre-service teacher competence in lesson planning pertaining to collaborative learning. *Journal of Curriculum Studies*, *44*(3), 349–379. doi:10.1080/00220272.2012.675355

Scheiter, K., Schüler, A., Gerjets, P., Huk, T., & Hesse, F. W. (2014). Extending multimedia research: How do prerequisite knowledge and reading comprehension affect learning from text and pictures. *Computers in Human Behavior*, *31*, 73–84. doi:10.1016/j.chb.2013.09.022

Sweller, J., Van Merrienboer, J. J., & Paas, F. G. (1998). Cognitive architecture and instructional design. *Educational Psychology Review*, *10*(3), 251–296. doi:10.1023/A:1022193728205

The Gestalt principles. Retrieved November, 1, 2014 from http://graphicdesign.spokanefalls.edu/tutorials/process/gestaltprinciples/gestaltprinc.htm

Tintinalli, J. E. (2014). Real textbooks or e-books: What is happening right now? *Emergency Medicine Australasia*, *26*(1), 72–75. doi:10.1111/1742-6723.12189 PMID:24495066

Troutner, J. (2013). Lesson plans, web cams, and creation options. *Teacher Librarian*, *41*(2), 45–47.

Wareing, M. (2014). Using student lived experience to test the theoretical basis of work-based learning. *International Journal of Practice-based Learning in Health and Social Care*, *2*(1), 35–50. doi:10.11120/pblh.2013.00022

Wilhelm, P., & Wilde, R. (2005). Developing a university course for online delivery based on learning objects: From ideals to compromises. *Open Learning*, *20*(1), 65–81. doi:10.1080/0268051042000322104

Wilkerson, T., & Scheffler, A. J. (1992). Examining an assumption of linkage between lesson planning and implementation. *Education*, *113*(1), 74–80.

## KEY TERMS AND DEFINITIONS

**Bookmarks:** A collection of hypertext links established by the user.

**Conceptual Artifacts:** Designed structures or construct architectures applied in conceptual modeling.

**Conceptual Knowledge:** Relies on theories, principles and structures in a particular discipline.

**Data:** Distinct information that is formatted in a special way and exist in a variety of forms, like text on paper, digital text, bytes stored in electronic memory etc.

**Design Synthesis:** A process of organization, manipulation, pruning and filtering of data in an effort to produce information and knowledge.

**Didactic Material:** All pedagogic resources (data, information, knowledge) and learning tools, which (systems,) that allow teacher to planning, designing, developing and evaluating students' performance, evaluate and see analytics of cognitive activities (it can be gathered on the e-learning or/and m-learning platforms).

**EPUB:** The distribution and interchange format standard for digital publications and documents based on Web Standards. EPUB defines a means of representing, packaging and encoding structured and semantically enhanced Web content — including XHTML, CSS, SVG, images, and other resources — for distribution in a single-file format. EPUB allows publishers to produce and send a single digital publication file through distribution and offers consumers interoperability between software/hardware for unencrypted reflowable digital books and other publications.

**Expressiveness:** A term that define a functional language, that can be easy enough to learn that the vast majority of developers using it can be highly productive; a view into how expressive each language enables you to be in the same amount of space and equally expressive accroos nearly its entire domain of usefulness.

**Formal Education:** Organized, guided by a formal curriculum, leads to a formally recognized credential such as a high school completion diploma or a degree, and is often guided and recognized by government at some level. Teachers are usually trained as professionals in some way (Eaton, 2013).

**Generativity:** "Ability of computerized instruction to create instructional messages and interactions by combining primitive message and interaction elements rather than by storing pre-composed messages and interaction logics" (Gibbons, Nelson and Richards, 2000, p. 9).

**In-Formal Education:** No formal curriculum and no credits earned. The teacher is simply someone with more experience such as a parent, grandparent or a friend. A father teaching his child to play catch or a babysitter teaching a child their ABC's is an example of informal education (Eaton, 2013).

**Information:** Data that is accurate and timely, specific and organized for a purpose, presented within a context that gives it meaning and relevance, and can lead to an increase in understanding and descrease in incertaintly (Business dictionary, 2014).

**Instructional Objects:** Any element that can be independently drawn into a momentary assembly in order to create an instructional event. Instructional objects can include problem environments, interactive models, instructional problems or problem sets, instructional function modules, modular rouines for instructional augmentation (coaching, feedback, etc.), instructional design elements, modular rouines for representation of information, or logic modules related to instructional puroposes: management, recording, selecting etc. (Gibbons, Nelson and Richards, 2000, p. 5).

**Knowledge:** The sum or range of what has been perceived, discovered, or learned (The Free Dictionary, 2014).

**Learning Objects:** Elements of a new type of computer-based instruction grounded in the object-oriented paradigm of computer science, which values the creation of components (called "objects"); small (relative to the size of an entire course) instructional components that can be reused to be digital entities deliverable over the Internet; digital or non-digital, which can be used, re-used or referenced during technology supported learning. Examples are: multimedia content, instructional content, learning objectives, instructional software and software tools, persons, organizations, or events referenced during technology supported learning (Wiley, 2000).

**Learning:** The knowledge gained by schooling and formal, non-formal and informal education.

**Metadata:** "Data about data," or descriptive information about a resource. Metadata is stored as cataloging archived information in catalogues, digital repositories, webpages, digital libraries etc.

**Narration:** Spoken words.

**Non-Formal Learning:** Organized (even if it is only loosely organized), may or may not be guided by a formal curriculum. This type of education may be led by a qualified teacher or by a leader with more experience. Though it doesn't result in a formal degree or diploma, non-formal education is highly enriching and builds an individual's skills and capacities. Continuing education courses are an example for adults. Girl guides and boy scouts are an example for children. It is often considered more engaging, as the learner's interest is a driving force behind their participation (Eaton, 2013).

**Procedural Knowledge:** Knowledge how to do something, with a focus on skills that are transferable across multiple domains and contexts, involves possessing a skill, being able to do something, which is very different to merely knowing a collection of facts.

## APPENDIX 1

*Figure 3. Short table of contents*

**TABLE OF CONTENTS**

Preface

Functions [+]

Linear Functions [+]

Polynomial and Rational Functions [+]

Exponential and Logarithmic Functions [+]

Trigonometric Functions [+]

Periodic Functions [+]

Trigonometric Identities and Equations [+]

Further Applications of Trigonometry [+]

Systems of Equations and Inequalities [+]

Analytic Geometry [+]

Sequences, Probability and Counting Theory [+]

Introduction to Calculus [+]

Appendix

# APPENDIX 2

*Figure 4. Full table of contents*

TABLE OF CONTENTS

# Chapter 10
# Assessment in Digital Textbook Use and Development

## ABSTRACT

*Assessment with immediate feedback is an innovative strategy in digital textbook use and development. There are two forms: assessment of textbook quality and assessment of learning within the digital textbook learning environment. Digital forms of assessment ensure the speed, dynamicity and quality of students' achievement and influences how students focus and approach their learning. The purpose of this chapter is to emphasize the role of assessment for digital textbooks use and development by evidencing pre-assessment specifics, formative and summative computerized assessment. The author summarizes categories of paperless item(s), student learning patterns and functions of assessment. The role of immediate feedback for self-regulated learning is emphasized. The results indicate that MetaSystems Learning Design could be focused on immediate and delayed feedback. Lastly, after summarizing ideas, a future study topic is suggested that may promise interesting lines of research.*

## INTRODUCTION

The term "assessment" refers to any activities that teachers use to help students learn and to gauge student progress and learning analytics. Educational assessment is the process of documenting, usually in measurable terms, knowledge, skills, attitudes, and beliefs. Assessment can focus on the individual student, group, class, the textbook quality, or the educational system as a whole. There are many types of educational assessment:

- Initial, formative and summative;
- Objective and subjective;
- Criterion-referenced, norm-referenced, and ipsative;
- Informal and formal.

Educational assessment is a paved way for learning quality. However, although the growth in digital models of assessment is due to a number of factors, the most influential are based on *innovative and interactive technologies for learning in diversity of environments*. A broader range of digital tools connect assessment from platforms to on-going instruction with textbooks. These digital technologies serve students in a stringent necessity to be more competitive, adaptive and

DOI: 10.4018/978-1-4666-8300-6.ch010

accommodative in a learning environment. In addition, teachers and parents can check learning analytics. However, changing teachers' role in education requires new digital assessment tools and methods, which will place new demands on the tasks, roles and responsibilities of the student(s) or/and the teacher(s). One of these is based on using "digital concept mapping for formative assessment" (Krabbe, 2014).

As was indicated on Online Educa Berlin (2013), the most current assessment methods have a strong emphasis on knowledge and recall and do not capture the critical skills and attitudes dimension of key competence. The assessment of transversal key competences and the assessment in the context of cross-curricular work appears inadequate. What is the main cause of this effect? Maybe, the cause is "textbook continues to be a major vehicle for the transfer of knowledge" (Fryer, 2014). Or, maybe, the fact that students prefers digital reading, because "digital content is increasingly present in classrooms across the world, with a current push to increase the rate at which digital textbooks are adopted" (Choppin, Carson, Borys, Cerosaletti & Gillis, 2014, p. 11).

The digital content of textbook can incorporate different forms of assessment, allowing for conventional storage, learning analytics and summarizing the results. These evidence that students' progress during learning can be scored automatically, transmitted to the teacher and distributed as individual, group or colaborative class activity. The initial as well as the progress assessment and reports on the students' results are instantly available to the teacher, parent and student. This form could be either interactive or adaptive, and used to inform decision-making factors or to self-assist own achievements in learning.

This chapter assists that assessment is important not only to measure the students' outcomes during learning processes, but more important is to design tasks focused on adaptation and accommodation of student in real learning environments of the base on patterns and metappaterns.

It's delimited to a meta-overall framework for understanding the psychological and pedagogical concerns of assessment in digital textbook use and development. While the reliable usage of digital assessment tasks is important, it depicts the cognitive level of the students, it is just one part of a design issue. The second part is to understand what items are needed to engage all students in deeper learning with digital textbooks. And, not less important is to understand what feedback and feed-ward loops are required. Finally, what is the task's difficulty, and how to design a self-assessment quiz focusing on learning analytics?

The chapter takes a holistic view on challenges related to role of assessment in digital textbook use and development. The first section describes the background of computer based assessment and provides main definition related to assessment with digital textbooks. The literature review is incorporated into the discussion about the role and features of digital assessment, establishing the area of investigation on psychopedagogical and methodological approaches of the digital assessment's role in textbook use and development. The second section deals with assessment theories, principles, methods and techniques. In both sections we follows an outline at the particular features of digital assessment and the main issues it raises, based on MetaSystems Learning Design approach.

The general perspective of this chapter is to define psychological and methodological features of digital assessment and their roles in using and development of digital textbooks. The objectives are:

- To define the main concepts related to digital assessment with digital textbooks;
- To argue the integrity of diagnostic, formative & summative assessment for digital textbooks;
- To compare actions verbs with paperless items topology.

The postmodernism perspective helps to see assessment during digital textbook use and development as a form of evaluation aims to forms personalities that make relevant decisions regard rapidly changing conditions for a sustainable world.

## BACKGROUND

Generally speaking, digital assessment is the process of gathering, analyzing, interpreting and using information about students' progress and achievements to improve teaching and learning and include all activities that students undertake to get information in a digital learning environment. From psychopedagogical point of view, digital assessment is the process of observing student's behavior and drawing inferences about the student's knowledge and abilities, which can be focused on the individual learner (self-assessment), as well as on organized group of learners (peer, group or collaborative assessment) or on the educational system as a whole.

Digital assessment can be done with paper-pencil or paperless. Paper-pencil testing is the simplest form of digitalised assessment that requires elaborating items on computer, saving as PDF, print and disseminating in a paper-pencil environment. Paperless testing is the procedure of elaboration paperless items, digital testing, collect and interpret data in digital learning environment. There are:

- **Pre-Assessment:** A way to determine what is known about a topic before it is taught;
- **Formative Assessment:** A way to promote further improvement of student attainment;
- **Summative Assessment:** A way to summarise student's attainment at a particular time

In addition, formative assessment is carried out during the instructional process for the purpose of improving teaching or learning "by helping students internalize the features of good work, by showing them specifically how to improve, by developing habits of thinking and a sense of competency, and so forth" (Shepard, 2005). Formative assessment should be part of any digital textbook content. The psychometric properties of an online assessment are not necessarily identical to its paper and pencil original. Online assessment refers to use of ICT for any assessment-related activities. The key concept is e-*test*, which is composed from *paperless items*. The structure of the paperless item includes *stem, question* or *options*. The stem represents the beginning part of the item that presents a problem to be solved and could include a graph, a case study, a table or a detailed description which has multiple elements to it. The question is a sentence worded or expressed so as to elicit information. The options are the possible answers that need to be chosen through *correct answer* (key answer) and incorrect *answers* (called "distractors") or a form to be completed. In addition, computer based testing could be programmed to be delivered at concrete time, in a defined period of time etc. Innovative computer-based testing could represent innovative solutions for learning in digital learning environment, if it will be generated and delivered in a secure learning environment.

There are multiple forms of digital assessment, than can be integrated in any of the eight didactic systems for better results. For example, digital formative assessment is an alternative of formative assessment, but with digital tools. Using digital formats allow viewing average assignment score or per question; flags low-scoring questions; a grade distribution graph or to email each student their grade etc. What features are required for digital assessment tests efficiency during learning with digital textbooks? What are the principles and norms for learning design of digital assessment?

Assessment with digital textbooks allows immediate feedback. In addition, teacher can attach multimedia files to questions, manage classes and quizzes, access from any internet-connected computer or mobile device and allow working in individual and collaborative learning environments. The paperless item(s) are *objective, semi-objective, and subjective* or *non-standardized* (Table 1).

The easiest to be designed, programed, delivered and presented in learning analytics are the *objective items*. According to social constructivist conceptual framework, the objective items refer to the lowest levels of Bloom taxonomy: knowledge, comprehension and application. However, in concept of postmodernism philosophy and ecological systems theory the role of objective items is to create associations between student and environmental patterns at the level of macrosystem.

One of the example of using objective items in self-assessment was described by Zaiteva and Popco (2006, p. 423). It was designed an HTML textbook with a) *training mode* and b) *assessment mode*. The special mechanisms are included in structure. The theoretical material is followed by examples, questions and self-assessment tasks. The formative assessment includes quizzes and control tasks are done through summative assessment tests provided at the end of chapter (Figure 1).

The objective items require specific and predetermined answers and provide key(s). The points (or percents) are awarded only the corect answer is ticked off. The most often used are:

- *Dual choice items* requests to select one answer out of two possible answer. It include *a stem* and a *key answer* (true T-false F or yes Y-no N).
- *Check box* item allows the student to make a binary choice, i.e. a choice between one of two possible mutually exclusive options, for example checking to have correct answer (for example, Yes or True) and not checking for an incorect answer (for example No or False).
- *Pair items* require to establish correspondences/ associations between words, sentences, phases, letters or other categories of symbols which are disposed in two colums. The elements of the first colums are the premise and those in the second represent the answer.
- *Drag and drop* items require to drag and drop an object by clicking the mouse button or simply touching it with a finger and then moving the object to a new position.
- *Multiply choice* presumes the existence of a stem, a premise and of a list of options (possible sollutions). Among options one or many is correct and the others are not correct.
- *Multiple response* items require to select more than one correct answers.

*Table 1. Categories of paperless item(s)*

| Category | Objective | Semi-Objective | Subjective | Non-Standardized |
|---|---|---|---|---|
| Paperless item(s) | Dual choice items<br>Check box<br>Pair items (mathching)<br>Drag and drop<br>Multiple-choice<br>Multiple response<br>Likert scale<br>Hotspot | Short answer<br>Completion<br>Structured question<br>Fill-in-the blanks<br>Drop down list (pull-down-list)<br>Captivate simulation | Problem-situation solving<br>Essay<br>Case study<br>Project<br>Online tasks<br>Digital portfolios<br>Discussion Forum<br>Online peer assessment<br>Blogs, Wiki | True or false statements linked with a conjunction BECAUSE |

*Figure 1. The structure of electronic textbook "Learn HTML from scratch"*

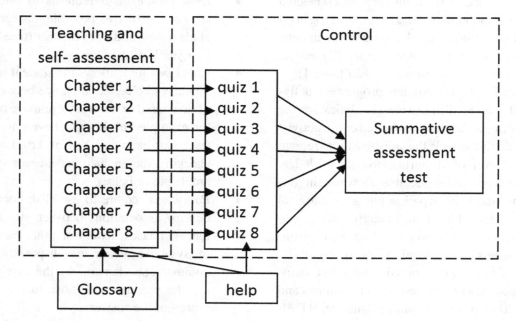

• *Likert scale* is a raiting scalewhich aims to measure attitudines or opinious by asking students to respond to a series of statements in terms of the extent to which they agree with them. It is a five or seven point scale which is used to allow the individual to express how much they agree or disagree with a particular statement.

• *Hotspot* item display an image and question and require to select the correct answer by using the cursor, stilus or finder to mark directly on a screen. It is the simplest form of a drag-and-drop question with only one "hot" area.

The objective paperless items contain alternative choices. In development of true-false items it is important to avoid: specific determinations because strongly worded statements are much more likely to be false (strongly worded statements contain *like all, always, never* and *no*); trick statements or those which appear to be true but which are really false and vice versa; double negative such as "He was not unconcerned over my disinterested

attitude"; ambiguous statements or those which have several equally plausible but incompatible interpretations; unfamiliar language; statements which are unnecessary long and difficult to follow and use of relative criteria in language (*many, old, young,* and *important*). If a statement is to test the truth or falsify a reason, the main clause should be true and the reason either true or false.

## INTEGRITY OF DIAGNOSTIC, FORMATIVE AND SUMMATIVE ASSESSMENT FOR DIGITAL TEXTBOOKS USE AND DEVELOPMENT

### Issues and Controversies

The content of assessment matches challenging subject matter. However, in order to be effective for digital textbook use and development, assessment will be focused on better measure and representation of critical thinking and problem solving skills; address learning outcomes and on-going processes; support student's learning and self-regulated learning etc. Therefore, digital assessment will be designed on the basis of cognitive and metacognitive activities of students before, during and after learning with digital textbooks, taking into account the role of patterns and metapatterns.

ICT supports learning and learning analytics. It was argued (Song, Kim, Byun, Song & Llee, 2014, p. 1) that digital textbook it a suitable medium for the provision of customized education that fits each individual's needs, and for the on-going changes in education needs such as a self-directed learning ability. To make this idea a reality, the main role should be attributed to *assessment for sustainability*. Vice versa, formative e-assessment only as the use of ICT to support the iterative process of gathering and analysing information about student learning by teachers as well as learners and of evaluating it in relation to prior achievement and attainment of intended, as well as intended learning outcomes, in a way that allows the teacher or student to adjust the learning trajectory (Pachier, Mellar, Daly, Mor, William & Laurillard, 2009, p. 1).

The effective assessment with digital textbooks requires reconceptualization of principles of learning design paperless items, its structural components, generation from data base in correlation with patterns and metapatterns or "required forms" by students etc. The assessment should help students to recognize patterns and metappaterns in real environment and adjust cognitive, behavioral and energetic potential toward a sustainable environment. Nevertheless, most studies compare *assessment of learning* and *assessment for learning* (Vonderwell & Boboc, 2013; Hargreaves, Gipps & Pickering, 2014; Bloxham & Carver, 2014; Shute & Kim, 2014; Stiggins, Chappuis & Arter, 2014; Griffin, 2014; Holmes, 2014; Veenman, Bavelaar, Wolf & Van Haaren, 2014).

Assessment of learning is focused on assigning grades, while assessment for learning is to enable students through effective feedback. Instead of the assessment of learning, the assessment for learning is formative or summative. The formative assessment aims to adapt teaching and learning to students' needs, while summative assessment aims to diagnose the learning process and to provide analytics. In formative assessment the learner is responsible for learning, been an active participant in the learning process who produce and share knowledge individually or in collaboration with others.

Assessment can be designed for learning, of learning and as learning. The assessment for learning is focused on the analysis of learner activities. The assessment of learning refers to strategies that confirm what students know at the particular moment of time and also serve to demonstrate whether or not students met curricula outcomes and the goal of individualized student programme to certify proficiency and make decisions about future programs or placement. For the assessment as learning the teacher determines the objectives, design the tasks and determine criteria for assisting performance, evaluates the students and produce constructive feedback that clarifies the strengths and weakness of the learning process. But, how well he/she knows norms to design digital assessment?

Digital assessment norms differ by paper-pencil assessment. However, the common thing is teacher-centered learning environment or student-centered learning environment. According to Midoro (2005, p. 32), the assessment in teacher-centred learning environment requires multiple choice item, while assessment in learner-centred learning environment is based on criterion referenced, portfolios and performances. Controversial topics such as students' and environmental patterning, reproductive versus productive tasking, digital assessment timing and scheduling have often been misunderstood. In learner-centered environment the student is asked not to reproduce, but to produce and share knowledge. How to make these expectations a reality in a digital textbook learning environment?

Digital assessment looks at ways of using ICT to understand the learning and patterning. For this, it is adds new features to formative and summative assessment. Alternative experiential psychopedagogical contexts for cognitive, emotional and social environments are required. These environments focused on more *immediate feedback*, which allow evidencing adaptation, interactivity, personalization and self-regulation with ICT. For this, *digital communication* allows synchronic and asynchronic hermeneutic dialogue, as well as sharing knowledge across global audiences. "Models for mental *representation* allow users to represent and share ideas in a variety of formats" (Niace, 2013).

Digital formative assessment represents a pattern for deeper learning. There are three main methods:

- **Self-Assessment:** "The process of having the learners critically reflect upon, record the progress of, and perhaps suggest grades for, their own learning" (Roberts, 2006, p. 3);
- **Peer-Assessment:** Processes of having the learners critically reflect upon, and perhaps suggest grades for, the learning of their peers. Peer assessment is distinguished from group assessment in that students assess each other's learning, even though the learning may have occurred individually, or at least outside of any formal collaborative groups" (Roberts, 2006, p. 5).
- **Group Assessment:** Process of learning in group focused on achievement of learning outcomes regarding the development of collaborative skills through collaboration and cooperation; analysing the tasks and assigning responsibility for its components; leadership, teamwork, delegation and coordination; preparation and presentation of a project etc.

Therefore, self-assessment, peer-assessment and group assessment in digital textbook environment are focused on distributed cognition, based on networking, personalization and customization of experience, multiliteracy and openness, but secured enough. Research was shown (Keppell, 2013) that students use their own technology for personalization the content. There are two main trends:

- *Student-generated content* (learners as designers);
- *Connected students* (knowledge is in the network).

Three discrete elements need to be addressed:

1. **Learning Task(s):** Patterns, metapatterns and strategies by which the learner will be engaged within an artificial learning setting and real environment, which allow to practice, apply and reflect through solving problems process, do investigations, projects, tasks, role players etc.
2. **Learning Resources:** The material containing the information, content and underprinting knowledge the learner needs to acquire to develop a strong familiarity with books, papers, articles, roles, documents, manuals, references, weblinks, case studies, lectures.
3. **Learning Supports:** The strategies and processes that assist the learner to work beyond their comfort zone which scaffolds and provides feedback, advice and provides support for reflection (schedules, instructions, procedures, announcements).

The effective learning tasks are *authentic*. However, the authentic learning tasks have real world relevance; are ill-defined, requiring students to define sub-tasks needed to complete the action; comprise complex tasks to be investigated by students over a sustained period of time; provide the opportunity for students to examine the task from different perspectives, to collaborate and to reflect. However, there remains controversy as to how transfer of patterns and metapatterns should be conceptualized and explained, what its prevalence is, what is relation to digital learning in general, and whether it exists at all. There are a wide variety of theoretical frameworks apparent in the scientific literature, which can be categorised as:

- *Authentic tasks*, "by identifying and codifying individual elements, to determine the ways in which the authenticity of an individual assessment activity might be enhanced (Ashford-Rowe, Herrington & Brown, 2014, p. 205);
- *Emotion and motivation in learning and performance,* which "influence cognitive processes" (Kim & Pekrun, 2014, p. 66);
- *The learning has also the energetic components.* Each new unit begins with new letter sound which serves as the stimulus for all activities. The new letter sound is related to a word which is related to the theme students will read about later in the lesson. Next, skills that have been previously introduced and mastered by the students are put into immediate practice through the reading of connected text (Hammond & Boltman, 2014, p. 6).

Digital textbook is an effective pedagogical resource or/and an learning tool. Numerous researchers have reached the conclusion that, in order to achieve learning, the assessment should be done through operational and evaluative frameworks with different learning tasks, resources and support.

## An Integrated Processes Model

There are many traditional forms of assessment used in digitized textbooks. For example, in open PDF textbook "Chemistry", provided by Open Education Group (http://schools.utah.gov/arc/curr/chemistryoer.pdf) is presented in form of Review Questions (Figure 2).

The other more interactive idea is provided by CK-12 (http://www.ck12.org/student/). The student can practice his/her understanding in an interactive learning environment (http://www.ck12.org/chemistry/Pure-and-Applied-Chemistry/asmtpractice/Pure-and-Applied-Chemistry-Practice/). The teacher can contribute question or create quiz. One of example is presented in figure 3.

In our point of view, the effectiveness of the digital assessment based on dynamic and flexible instructional strategy depends on how well are integrated the information/communication, cognitive and assessment strategies. The integrative structure of competence is the focus of this model. In our view, the integrative treatment is triggered

*Figure 2. The example of Review Questions in Open textbook "Chemistry"*

# REVIEW QUESTIONS

1. What is the basic unit of measurement in the metric system for length?
2. What is the basic unit of measurement in the metric system for mass?
3. Give the temperatures iin Celsius for the freezing and boiling points of water.
4. Give the temperatures iin Kelvin for the freezing and boiling points of water.
5. Would it be comfortable to swim in a swimming pool whose water temperature is 275 K? Why or why not?

*Figure 3. Example of interactive learning environment for assessment*

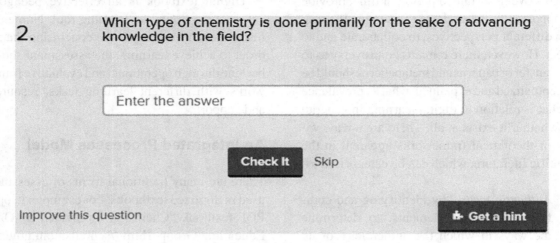

by the learning situations, which require adequate patterns for problem-solving and decision-making. This implies intellect, emotion and energy. The general outline of the proposed model is presented in Figure 4.

In short, we assert that an integrated process model of digital textbook reflect intellect, emotion and energy. The theoretical fundament of the proposed model is: cross-principles, hermeneutic dialogue and communication in digital learning environment. In the core of the model is the *personality* of the student (mE). According to a common definition, the personality refers to the sum of total qualities of character, mind (brain) and body that makes it different one from other people. The personality of the student, however, refers to the sum of intellect, emotion and energy. Therefore, in digital textbook learning environment the cognitive, affective and psychomotor levels of competence can be developed. The cognitive level results from activities focused on personalization the digital content, i.e. summering the ideas, the

*Figure 4. The model of integrated processes*

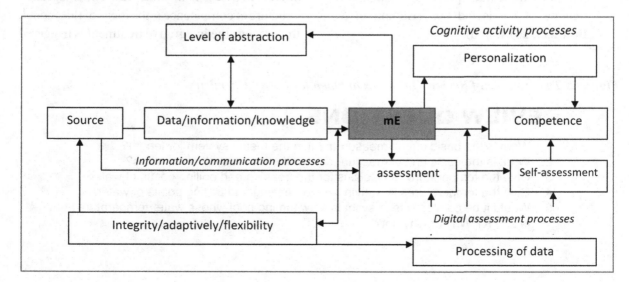

synthesis of own digital textbooks from provided content etc. The affective level, requires the synthesis of main ideas through capturing learning objects with digital devices and, then, integrating in personalised digital content of textbooks (Krathwohl taxonomy). The highest psychomotor level requires creating new movement patterns to fit a particular situation and the lowest: tasks based on hermeneutic dialogue between student and context of learning. Psychomotor assessment, designed according to Simpson taxonomy, aims to develop patterns of mind (which ensures the synaptic connections in the microsystem of the human behavior).

The assessment component environments includes the following indispensable elements:

- Learning objective associated with the national or international standards;
- A database with paperless items, adequate to the defined learning objectives;
- Calibrated assessment tools, particularly in the assessment of prognostic models;
- A system of certifying the diagnostic, prognosis, selection and/or certification of trainers.

In digital textbook learning environment teacher can use: a) *verbal messages* with the intent to persuade students, i.e. to develop or reinforce attitudes, beliefs, values or behaviors through ethos, pathos and logos (according to Aristotle); b) *nonverbal messages* with the intent to create emotional or social meaning of learning, i.e. to develop a motivation contact focused on self-regulated learning. ICT allows disseminating the pedagogic dialogue as *text* (digitalised textbook), *voice* (audiobook), or as *text, voice and context* (digital textbook with multimodal text of content). All types of messages can be disseminated online or off-line, synchronically or asynchronically. Therefore, the effectiveness of digital textbooks depends on how pedagogical communication is designed, and controlled.

## IMMEDIATE OR/AND DELAYED FEEDBACK?

Assessment in a digital textbook learning environment offers some significant improvements: immediate feedback, speech recognition and digital sound reproduction of voice, delayed feedback with detailed comments, automatic speech recognition, digital portfolios etc. However, the main specific of the digital assessment is *immediate feedback*. The immediate feedback can be integrated in a digital learning environment through different specialized programs or apps. Immediate feedback deals and adds new values to competence pedagogy. Clark (2012, p. 209-213) notes that formative assessment with immediate feedback is for self-regulated learning. There are three main aspects:

- **Formative Feedback:** Feedback aims to deeper involve students in metacognitive strategies such as personal goal-planning, monitoring, and reflection, which support self-regulated learning;
- **Asynchronous Feedback:** Feedback when there is a time interval between gathering the evidence and sharing the evidence; a time interval before gathering and sharing the evidence; or the evidence has been synthesized from historical analysis; and
- **External/Internal Feedback:** Feedback, inherent to engagement and regulation.

The role of immediate feedback differs when it is chosen to construct the valid self-assessment tool for learning with programmed textbook (in an individual learning environment) and with digital textbook (in a digital textbook learning environment). The Skinner's solution, based on Theory of Operant Conditions Theory, emphasizes the role of immediate feedback for individualised learning with reinforcement effects. This idea leads to learning-by-doing methodology.

Beside individualized learning, the modern understanding of assessment theory is personalization of content. A valid assessment tool for digital textbook generates the personalised paperless items or tests; measures the achievement of learning objectives; set up the time and provide learning analytics for teacher or/and students. The immediate feedback is important either for measure of *closed-ended questions* or *open-ended questions*. Closed-ended questions, also known as dichotomous or saturated type questions, can be answered finitely, include presuming, probing, or leading tasks, are restrictive and can be answered in a few words. Open-ended questions, also known as infinite response or unsaturated type questions, are broader; require more than one or two word responses and can be personalized (extended according to students' patterns and metapatterns). These questions solicit additional digital information to be added or provided by the student in the form of answer.

Both closed-ended and open-ended questions can be placed in instructional content or at the end of the chapter (module). However, design of the paperless items differs considerably. There are, at least, two possible ways: a) instructional design on the base on Skinner principles and b) learning design on the base on integrated structure of competence (MetaSystems Learning Design).

The first way requires "general analysis of the relevant behavioral processes, verbal and nonverbal. Specific forms of behavior are to be evoked and, through differential reinforcement, brought under the control of specific stimuli" (Skinner, 1958, p. 971). Figure 5 presents a set of frames designed to teach a third- or fourth grade pupil to spell the word "manufacture".

The first way is *rote memorization*. Arithmetic operations of adding, substation, multiplication, and division are developed before the number is reached. The pupil composes equations and expressions in a great variety of alternative forms, for example $5+4=\square$ as well as $\square+4=9$ and $5\square4=9$.

The second way is *MetaSystems Learning Design*. According to this approach, the paper-

*Figure 5. The programed procedure of rote memorization with reinforcement*

1. **Manufacture** means to make or build. *Chair factories manufacture chairs*. Copy the word here:

   □□□□□□□□□□□

2. Part of the word is like part of the word **factory**. Both parts come from an old word meaning *make* or *build*.

   m a n u □□□□ u r e

3. Part of the word is like part of the word **manual**. Both parts come from an old word for *hand*. Many things used to be made by hand.

   □□□□ f a c t u r e

4. The same letter goes in both spaces:

   m □ n u f □ c t u r e

5. The same letter goes in both spaces:

   m a n □ f a c t □ r e

6. **Chair factories** □□□□□□□□□□□ **chairs.**

less item(s) will be randomly generated from the database, which includes an infinite number of "frames" for items. The frames may include chemical or physical formulae, concentration of solutions and others. It will be presented on the digital device screen, at least, twenty-five for a limited time, but not more than twenty minutes. Instead of Skinner's reinforcement, it is proposed to generate diverse versions of same rule or to integrate rules that were learned individually or collaboratively. It is expected to arrive at the result not by rote memorization, but by "extraction" of working memory and synthesis of new patterns.

The MetaSystems Learning Design requires both immediate and delayed feedback. The role of the immediate feedback is to achieve the synergetic effect during self-regulated learning. However, the role of delayed feedback is to engage students in learning focused on guaranteed learning outcomes. Therefore, digital assessment integrates immediate and delayed feedback in feedforward and feedback loops. In feedback loops a chain of cause and effect can be designed as positive.

## FROM PURE ELECTIVE TO PURE CONSTRUCTIVE FORMS OF ANSWERS

Learning design of paperless items for digital textbook learning environment depends more of how students will process data, information or knowledge and how will answer on the proposed items. The forms of students' answer can be illustrated in 1-7 position scale. The scale, as was represented by Deatlov & Sherbacova (1975), has two extremes:

1. **Sentence:** Pure elective forms,
2. **Symbols:** Pure constructive forms of answers.

Figure 6 represents the scale of pure elective to pure constructive forms of students' answers

Therefore, number one indicates the minimal level and number seven – the maximal of formalization. Paperless items that require naming an authentic learning object is attributed to number one. This digital form of answer requires recognizing through recovering the relevant pattern from working memory and associates it with the instructional material (in our case, the formula of lime). Instead, the number seven is attributed to high formalized answers. So, in concordance with MetaSystem Learning Design approach the probability of correct response is different (Table 2).

In the first case, the student will "extract" the formula from working memory, previously recognizing it. This is the level of *knowledge* (according to Bloom's taxonomy), recommended for diagnostic of knowledge in previous assessment. In the second case the student respond to a particular situation with a specific behavioral action, that allow to "discover" the answer with the probability that formula of lime is known. This is the level of *application* (according to Bloom's taxonomy), recommended for formative assessment. In both cases the student will receive

*Figure 6. The scale of pure elective: pure constructive forms (adapted from Deatlov & Sherbacova)*

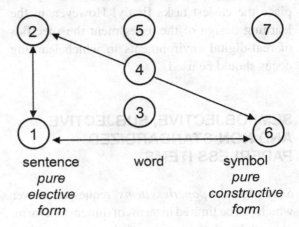

*Table 2. The differences in design of pure elective and pure constructive form of digital answer*

| Name | Form of Pure Elective Answer | Form of Pure Constructive Answer |
|---|---|---|
| *Stem* | Check the correct answer | |
| *Question* | Recognize and identify the formula of lime | The formula of slaked lime is … |
| *Options* | $CaO$<br>$CaCO_3$<br>$Ca(OH)_2$<br>$CaCO_3$ | |

an *immediate feedback*. However, in dependence of what function is realised by digital textbook: informer or self-regulation through ICT, the pure constructive answers could be completed with a hunt or without it.

The immediate feedback is commented as "Correct", "Incorrect" or "Partial Correct". To avoid learning design errors it is important to estimate the probability of all answers and forms (possible patterns). Although the digital task requires multi-level cognitive analysis, more important is to keep intrinsic motivation for learning in a digital textbook environment. For this, the mental effort of recognizing and assembling the patterns should be minimalized. Digital assessment, as an integral part of digital textbook, is focused on developing the integrated structure of competence. Arranging of paperless items cannot be done according to levels of difficulty because in real life tasks are not so arranged. Nobody will place the easiest tasks firstly! However, in the learning design of the assessment the specifics of real-digital environments in which learning occus should be used.

## SEMI-OBJECTIVE, SUBJECTIVE AND NON-STANDARDIZED PAPERLESS ITEMS

*Semi-objective paperless items* "request an answer which can be limited in terms of dimension, form, content by the structure of the stem/question; are characterized by a strongly structured task;

reduce the trainer's freedom to re-organise the received information and to formulate the answer in the wanted form' solicit the trainer to prove/demonstrate not only the knowledge but also the capacity to structure/elaborate the shortest and the most correct answer" (Project TERECoP, 2014). The most used semi-objective items are:

- *Short answer* requires to formulate the answer in the form of a short answer or phase, 1-2 words, a number, a symbol, an acronim etc.
- *Completion answer* requires to express the answer in the form of one or two words, which to match the stem and to be filled in the stem, thus the stem to become correct and complete. The task is presented in the form of an incomplete statement/sentence.
- *Structured question* requires to construct the response in a way that is between the objective items (closed items) and the subjective items (open items). A structured question could comprise texts, data, diagrams, graphics, sub-questions, suplimentary data etc.
- *Fill-in-the blank* item is often found in assessment of grammar and vocabulary. While they do require students to produce language they are rather inauthentic in terms of language use. Such items are high reliability, easier to write and limits guessing.
- *Drop-down list* (or pull-down list) item requires to choose the corect answer from

a list of options. The selected option is placed on the top of the display screen.

- *Check box* item is a box that can be click to turn an option on or off.
- *Captivate Simulation* item requires building feedback directly into a simulation, i.e. the Success, the Failure of Hint Text box and could provide the automatic report or feedback.
- *Crossword puzzle* is a grid of squares and blanks into which words crossing vertically and horizontally are written according to the clues.

Incomplete information items are writing direct questions. The student's response should have a key to the knowledge unit, e.g. concepts or principles, or a key to cognitive operations. It is important to avoid the disconnection completed through phases and spatial clues by constructing answer blanks. Answer columns should be arranged to the right of the question. The use of an unordered series of responses within the item should be avoided. A secondary key should be constructed containing all of the correct answer and acceptable alternatives. Each correctly filled blank is assigned the same value.

*Subjective paperless items* (known as non-objective or open) are relatively easy to be conceived and test the originality, creativity and the personal features of the answer. The most used are:

- **Sketch:** A rapidly executed freehand drawing that is not usually intended as a finished work; a quick, informal drawing, usually done from life.
- **Problem-Situation Solving:** An activity in which the trainer is involved in developing creativity, divergent thinking, imagination, capacity to generalize, to reframe a problem etc. There are many tecniques that may be included in a digital textbook page: brainstomimng, video or audioconferencing.

- **Essay:** An activity that requires to construct or produce an independent answer in accordsance to a set of requirements. It valorizes the ability to recall, organize and integrate the ideas, the skills to express himself/herself in writing and to interpret and apply data.
- **Case Study:** An activity that requires teacher to develop a scenario with a learning/ assessment plan and students to solve it. The scenario includes raw information that may be distributed in variois format, including email, forums, messageries etc. The learner needs to identify relevant information, seach with the case study, highlighting the words or phases or takes notes in order to answer at the case study questions.
- *Project based learning* and assessment is an active learning which places learners in situations which require authentic use of language in order to communicate through reading, writing, listening and speaking. They plan, organize, negotiate, make points, and arrive at a consensus.
- **Online Tasks:** A complex tasks that require the locating information from a variety of sources, creating instructional videos on various topics; team assignment; collaborative wring processes; research tasks; and project that ultimately yield a product.
- **Digital Portfolio:** A method of showcasing students' progress through Web2.0 and on-line tools, that may include written, recorded or visual items, homework, description of processes, tests, performance tasks, deliverables, and more.
- **Discussion Forum:** A ubiquitous commination tool or an activity taking place through online discussion groups structured in questions, statements, quotations, responses and links.

- **Online Peer Assessment:** An effective strategy to improve the learning process that allows students to reflect about the quality of learning and increase involvement of the learner in assessment while decreasing the weight of teacher's assessment.
- **Blogs:** An informational site published on the web and, possible, integrated in a course, where the student can write reflectively.
- **Wiki:** A tool for creating collaborative activities, a collection of linked web pages accessible for editing and sharing by several people together.

*Non-standardized paperless items* are used for performance, abilities, increased level of difficulty and others. These types of items require to access the value of true or false of two sentences linked by a conjunction BECAUSE and to establish a relation between them. It is appreciated the value of the statements of a stem and to identify the correlation between them. The non-standardized paperless items are homogeneous. The number of alternative answers should nearly equal the number of items to be answered. The set of items should be brief. Several relatively short matching sets are more manageable than one long one. Response alternatives should be sequenced in a logical order, if one exists. The directions should specify the basic for matching, and should indicate when the alternative answer may be used more than once. All items in a set should be placed on the same page of the test booklet.

The verbal level of items should be low, with a minimum of technical terms. Where possible, a logical sequence of items and alternative responses homogeneous in construct and form are used. It is required to have at least four alternatives per test item, but the relative length of responses should not provide a clue to the correct answer or specific determiners such as always and newer. Minimize the use of specific alternatives such as

all of these or none of the above. An alternative response should not overlap to be synonymous with other alternative responses.

## OPERATIONAL FRAMEWORK AND SELF-REGULATED LEARNING

An operational feedback is a guide to a developer' goals, procedures and design. The framework sets out the way the teacher(s) or/and learner(s) promote a culture of learning in digital textbook learning environment. It may also include principles and norms of effective learning. The role of operational framework in digital textbook assessment is to organize and manage a didactic process toward achievement of a *synergetic effect*. Experience shows that in digital textbook content can be included at least 2-5 operational frameworks, and distribute it, primarily, in the first module as a diagnostic assessment. Only after correct designed diagnostic assessment, the formative and summative tasks will measure the academic achievement of students during learning.

An operational framework is based on coefficient of assessment $K_a$. Theoretically, as was proved by Bespalico (2007), when $K_a < 0.7$, it is necessary to start with lowest level, then, move to the next level upon reaching $K_a = 0.7$ or/and $K_a > 0.7$. This is the point when the synergetic effect occurs. The number of paperless items is limited and range between 100 and 25:

$$100 > N_i > 25,$$

where Ni represents the number of items.

Therefore, the aim of operational framework is an effective design of assessment tasks as well as the differentiated knowledge management model. Ideally, after the synergetic effect the learner is an own designer of self-regulated learning process and apply metacognitive strategies. The role of the teacher is to maintain the powerful digital textbook learning environment in which students will use ICT to exchange knowledge between peers, to exercise new methodologies, and to foster a "digital dialog". He/she will assist "real connections" between digital multimodal text and learner(s) based on hermeneutic dialogue requirements and using of digital devices.

The operational framework provides tasks, which can be analysed with *immediate and delayed feedback*. The immediate feedback is more dedicated to scoring or automatizing the results, then on analysing each step in problem solving. However, the delayed feedback is for peer assessment.

The main advantage of using digital assessment in digital textbook is to engage student learning. As was noted by Karpicke, Butler & Roediger (2009, p. 471) when students have been tested on material they remember more in the long term than if they had repeatedly studied it. This phenomenon is known as the *testing effect* and shows that the act of retrieving information from memory has a potent effect on learning, enhancing long-term retention of the tested information. In relation to the e-assessment strategy, testing effect could be observed during formative assessment with immediate feedback. The literature review suggests that it is possible to obtain *a testing effect* with Open Source Textbook. It was argued (Petrides, Jimes, Middleton-Detzner, Walling & Weiss, 2011, pp. 46-47) that open textbook could be improved by adding annotation capabilities, step-by-step problem solving to the text with explanations to wrong answers that would shorten the assessment loop by quickly correcting any misunderstanding while alerting them to gaps in their knowledge. It is important the audio-component, video chapter summaries, online interactions in form of weekly.

The example of designing operation framework in digital textbook was described by us in the book chapter "Instructional Dynamic and Flexible Strategy: Integrity of Effectivity Activities for Engaging All Learners in Classrooms". It

was mentioned that the processes of the cognitive mechanism that aim to develop the functional structure of competence are based on structure-content methodology. This methodology emphasis the role of strategy, in which teacher helps students to build scheme of comprehension and to develop it from "application" through "creativity" requirements. In addition, the content of digital textbook needs to be personalized on the base of knowledge management model.

Such content cannot be prespecified, because the learner construct his/her own understanding based on a priory cognitive structure, learning potential and metacognitive capacity. That is why, according to MetaSystems Learning Design Approach, it is more important to build digital artefacts that will constitute the meta-patterns for future learning rather that to use learning objects.

Despite the fact that the extension of the cognitive structures (e.g. synapses, schemata, meta-patterns etc.) is strictly individual, the learning design of operational framework should be focused on developing the integrative structure of competence. In this case, students learn to be reflectively aware of their own knowledge construction and learn how to think like an expert and not how to reproduce or to create during assessment the similar versions of information, provided in textbooks.

In the Era of Globalisation and Social Media is a stringent need for alternative assessment methods "incorporated" in digital textbook content. The key concepts of these methods are "hiperconnectivity" that relies on ubiquitous form of communication in digital learning environment. Growth of digital content and the use of mobile devices have heightened the awareness of MetaSystems Learning Design principles. One of the first practical examples is Google Drive. The "hiperconnectivity" is a concept used to define modes in which learners are synchronically and asynchronically connected through channels and networks. They learn how to plan, create knowledge, establish connections, and be engaged in discussions, and other virtual events in order to make relevant decisions about development of own learning potential in order to be more adaptive and accommodative at changing multi-cultural, multi-languages, multi-patterns in diverse environmental settings.

What alternative assessment methods are important to be included in digital textbook? What psychological and pedagogical theories are more relevant: behaviorist, cognitivist or constructivist? The article signed by Bostock (1998, p. 225) notes that constructivism in educational environments should provide learners with personal control, authentic learning contexts and collaboration. Even if is not explicitly mentioned why traditional methods cannot achieve constructivism values with large student numbers, it was recognized that computer-based media are scaleable and may support learning. It was emphasized that constructism requires authentic assessment, student responsibility and intuitive, generative learning strategies, authentic learning contexts and cooperative support.

It was proposed an approach to the design of the learner-centered learning environments in which behaviorist, cognitivist, constructivist and humanist learning theories principles will be used hierarchically. From an interdisciplinary point of view, the proposal is based on construction of the integrated structure of competence that requires self-regulated skills. This can be done by:

- Design, production and validation phases;
- A learning environment with immediate and delayed feedback;
- Optimized graph structure of main concepts;
- Dynamic and flexible instruction strategy;
- A knowledge management model;
- New methods based on memorization and thinking;
- The clarity of tasks forms and requirements;

- Activities (cognitive, group, collaborative);
- Peer review of individual activities;
- Formative and summative assessment; and
- Action verbs based on cognitive, affective and psychomotor taxonomies.

Based on metasystems learning design approach, the pedagogical methods require epistemological and methodological dimensions. For the practical applications this means there is need to design and develop: communication/information strategies; cognitive activity strategies; and computer based assessment strategies. The learner, while engaged in communication/information strategies, will play the central role in personalization of content through hermeneutic dialogue. The learner, engaged in cognitive activities strategies will gain new knowledge, skills and competence through learning and using new constructivism methods, procedures and techniques individually, in group, collaboratively and cooperatively. Computer based assessment strategies, however, involve students either in self-assessment (pre-assessment, formative assessment, summative assessment) and innovative forms of assessment (peer review assessment, group assessment, etc.).

In addition, alternative methods of assessment should assure validity and reliability. The validity refers to how well an e-test measures what it purported to measure, while the reliability is the consistency of measure. There are three types of validity: content validity (the items in the test represent the entire range of possible items the test should cover and the questions may be drawn from a large pool of items that cover a broad range of topics and is determined by the representativeness of the items included on the final test); criterion-related validity (effectiveness is demonstrated in predicting criterion or indicators of a construct) and construct validity (an association between the scores and theoretical prediction is demonstrated).

# DIGITAL ASSESSMENT NORMS FROM THE PERSPECTIVE OF METASYSTEMS LEARNING DESIGN

The Metasystems Learning Design requires special norms, suitable for operational (formative) and evaluative (summative) frameworks, such as immediate feedback, fastening time, learning analytics, social networking, peer and collaborative assessment and other innovative forms. Compared with the past, there is now a wide range of hardware, software and educational technologies that allow developing new assessment strategies for learning. Digital textbook content for assessment may include paperless items for diagnostic, formative and summative assessment or real tasks that require digital devices. If content is "connected" to curricula, items may associated with time and learning analytics.

There are two main factors: a) measurement targets that focus on higher order, collaborative and creative thinking skills, and b) the affordances of digital textbook, in particular, the use of educational games, interactive simulations and 3D representations methods in educational assessment. It was demonstrated (Gibson, 2014) that interactive applications, many of which utilize social media methods rely on global storehouses of information, constitute a new genre of assessment performance space. Traces of a learner's problem-solving, expression or communication can now entail highly detailed computer-based documentation of the context, actions, processes and products. The performance assessment includes an evaluation of knowledge-in-action. Individuals who "generate a response" can do more than choose an answer; they can create, communicate and collaborate with others over time.

The final products and processes can be "rated for quality." However, there are some common requirements that should be respected. These norms are: a) paperless item should include, at least, one correct answer; b) it is important to avoid writing question in the following manner:

*Determine which products of reaction are formed on reduction nitric acid HNO$_3$ (d) with ZnN?*

It is evident that the un-accuracy refers to question's statement and not to proposed options. Other important condition in e-assessment for digital textbooks is to respect the time equal to 15-20 minutes that work for at least 30 operations of test. In our pedagogical experiments it was proved, that all students manifest interest to e-assessment with respect to minimal and sufficient conditions, so that all of them resolved correctly more than 70% of proposed items.

*The principle of self-regulation of learning* is ensured by dynamic and flexible instructional strategy, which allows obtaining the *synergistic effect*. However, the synergistic effect is achieved when the content of digital textbook is structured and personalized on the basis of *knowledge graph*. The knowledge graph represents a hyper-graph of main concepts, identified by teacher, "incorporated" into content, constructed by students who automatize the node taking self-regulating e-tests with condition that $K_a \geq 0.7$. The role of assessment is to provide e-items and "note" the point of self-regulation in order to automatize the cognitive side of the flexible architecture of competence. The rules are:

1. Time for e-testing should not extend 20 minutes. Each item should be presented for 90 sec.
2. The "amount of knowledge" is equivalent to 30-100 tests' operations. One test operation corresponds to one mental operation.
3. Each e-test is planned on the basis of dynamic and flexible instructional strategy. The items and the expected forms of answers could be elective or constructive. The elective items are required for first three level of Bloom' cognitive taxonomy.
4. Notation depends on proposed aim. It is applicable to select percentage points, under which can be "calculated" marks.

*The principle of personalization* requires norms to personalize both elective and constructive items. It is a brother of "personalization principle", proposed by Clark and Mayer (2011), which states "use conversational style and virtual coaches". In this case the proposed content either in form of pedagogical resource or learning tool will become significant and important for student. At the early cognitive stage the principle of personalization addresses the presentation style of proposed tasks in the form of didactic game or programming a meaning (using, for example *eToys*). In adult learning the norm is to personalize digital textbook content trough developing of his/her own portfolio. One of the examples could be considered "Digital textbook in digital portfolio" technology.

*The principle of clarity* states "write items on the base on human rationality and define clear each stem, question and option". It is argued by the following norms:

1. Paperless items have to be short presented items and in the same style;
2. Questions should not include unverified or unclear data from recital the likely occurrence of discomfort, inhibition of the student cognitive system and other negative effects;
3. In developing items should be used nomenclature and symbols familiarized for student;
4. Questions with different level of complexity and difficulty items are presented randomly.

*The principle of diversity of feedback* states "design items required elective and/or constructive answers, analyzed through immediate and delayed feedback". The norms of this principle are:

1. Design items with immediate feedback for the first three levels of Bloom's taxonomy;
2. Design items with delayed feedback for analysis, synthesis and evaluation.

Digital assessment should be considered a component of an integrated set of standards, curriculum, and professional teacher development. The paperless items reflect the knowledge, skills and attitudes students will be expected to demonstrate at the final stage of blended or digital learning. The correlation between actions verbs and paperless items topology is the following (Table 3):

Digital assessment for learning can be designed as psychological or psyho-educational. Psychological assessment measures of behavior or inteligence that are types of brain information processing through providing analytical data about the relative strengths and weakness of brain processing or potential (intelectual, emotive or/and energetic). The obtained data can be interpreted in a *norm-referenced* or in a *criterion-referenced* manner:

- Norm-referenced assessment requires to compare an individual's result with a representative sample or group norm or set of set of norms (Bell norm) and report it on the standard score (z) scale or a rescaling of it;
- Criterion-referenced assessment requires to an individual's performance to a previously specified standard of achievement (criteria).

The obtained data can be summarized and analyzed in both manners.

## FUTURE RESEARCH DIRECTIONS

The research area of this chapter is assessment in using and development of digital textbooks. The main objectives are to identify and define the main concepts related to digital assessment; to argue the integrity of diagnostic, formative &

*Table 3. The correlation between action verbs and paperless items/activities*

| | **Action Verbs** | **Paperless Items/Activities** |
|---|---|---|
| **Reproductive** | to retrieve, to recognise, to recall, to classify, to identify, to locate, to recognize, to select, to classify | dual choice items (Yes/No; Three/False etc.), multiply choice, multiple response, Likert scale, hotspot, drop-down list, check box |
| | to complete spaces, to choose, to describe in one word, to classify, to write, to reorganize, to differentiate, to recognize, to select, to label | short answer, completion answer, structured question, fill-in-the blank, drag and drop, HotSpot, pair items, crossword puzzle, captivate simulation |
| Productive | to demonstrate, to discover, to illustrate, to modify, to operate, to practice, to produce, to relate, to schedule, to sketch, to solve, to use, to write | problem-situation solving, essay, case study, non-standardized paperless items, sketch |
| | to combine, to compare, to explain, to generalize, integrate, to synthesizes, to assist, to discuss, to practice, to present, to read, to report, to select, to tell, to assemble, to display, to manipulate, to measure, to mix, to sketch | project based learning, drawing, essay, peer review assessment, chat, forum, email, virtual reality simulations, virtual simulation, virtual laboratory, videoconferencing/audioconferencing |
| | to analyse, to appraise, to calculate, to categorize, to compare, to contrast, to criticize, to diagram, to experiment, to illustrate, to model, to separate, to describe, to form, to read, to report, to display, to manipulate, to sketch | Interactive problem-solving, online tasks, essay, case study, education projects, knowledge matrix, virtual simulation, virtual laboratory, modelling, digital reading, sketch |
| | to arrange, to assemble, to categorize, to collect, to combine, to create, to explain, to formulate, to generate, to plan, to prepare, to reconstruct, to revise, to rewrite, to set up, to summarize, to integrate, to organize, to adapt, to change, to synthesizes | digital portfolio, matrix-resume, peer assessment, mind mapping, conclusion and generalisation, poster presentation |
| | to argue, to assess, to attach, to contrast, to defend, to describe, to discriminate, to estimate, to evaluate, to explain, to judge, to justify, to summarize, to display, to practice, to revise, to solve, to arrange, to combine, to compose, to construct, to create, to design | discussion forum, peer assessment, email, group discussion, blogs, Wiki, small research project, portfolios, concept mapping, education digital artefacts, virtual simulations |

summative assessment for digital textbooks and to compare action verbs with paperless items topology. This work highlights the benefits of digital assessment processes.

The literature review suggests that digital assessment represents the process of gathering, analyzing, interpreting and using information about students' progress and achievements to improve teaching and learning and include all activities that students undertake to get information.

Traditionally, a digital assessment is an integrative part of paper-pencil or paperless items for a digital learning environment. There are three options: pre-assessment, formative and summative assessment. Research was shown (Anglin, Anglin, Schumann & Kaliski, 2008) that digital assessment provides the means to capture student's knowledge in many different ways and to assess them more robustly through immediate and/or delayed feedback. Assessment based on immediate feedback for synergetic effect can be achieved during self-regulated learning with metacognitive strategies. Future research directions are to compare the *task assessment* (what the student is required to do to complete the assessment) and *the assessment of the task* (how paperless items and tasks should be designed) and how to integrate this in the diagnostic, formative or summative tasks piloted in a digital textbook learning environment.

## CONCLUSION

Assessment in a digital textbook learning environment refers to interactive processes that help students learn more effectively. Traditionally it is designed initial, formative or summative quizzes, which include objective and subjective as well as criterion-referenced, norm-referenced, and ipsative digitalised items. These items can be analysed in order to provide an immediate constructive feedback, but require a wide diversity of answers, which range from pure elective forms to pure constructive forms. Traditionally are used paperless items, which can be designed as semi-objective, subjective and non-standardized. The main examples of semi-objective items are: short answer, completion answer, structured question, fill-in-the blank, drop-down list, and check box, captivate simulation and crossword puzzle. Subjective paperless items aims to test creativity, originality and innovative solutions. In the textbook's content can be included: sketch, problem-situation solving, essay, case study, and research projects. Moreover, a digital textbook can be included in a digital portfolio, blogs, Google collaborative environment or wikis with discussion forum, and online peer assessment tasks and innovative solutions. The most interesting way is to develop into a digital textbook learning environment an operational framework, which will serve as a starting point for instructional dynamic and flexible strategy.

## REFERENCES

Anglin, L., Anglin, K., Schumann, P., & Kaliski, J. (2008). Improving the efficiency and effectiveness of grading through the use of computer-assisted grading rubrics. *Journal of Innovative Education*, *6*(1), 51–73.

Ashford-Rowe, K., Herrington, J., & Brown, C. (2014). Establishing the critical elements that determine authentic assessment. *Assessment & Evaluation in Higher Education*, *39*(2), 205–222. doi:10.1080/02602938.2013.819566

Bloxham, S., & Carver, M. (2014). Assessment for learning in higher education. *Assessment & Evaluation in Higher Education*, *39*(1), 123–126. doi:10.1080/02602938.2013.797652

Bostock, S. J. (1998). Constructivism in mass higher education: A case study. *British Journal of Educational Technology*, *29*(3), 225–240. doi:10.1111/1467-8535.00066

Choppin, J., Carson, C., Borys, Z., Cerosaletti, C., & Gillis, R. (2014). A typology for analyzing digital curricula in mathematics education. *International Journal of Education in Mathematics, Science and Technology*, *2*(1), 11–25.

Clark, I. (2012). Formative assessment: Assessment is for self-regulated learning. *Educational Psychology Review*, *24*(2), 205–249. doi:10.1007/s10648-011-9191-6

Clark, R. C., & Mayer, R. E. (2011). *E-learning and the science of instruction: Proven Guidelines for consumers and designers of multimedia learning* (3rd ed.). San Francisco, CA: John Wiley & Sons. doi:10.1002/9781118255971

Griffin, P. (2014). *Assessment for teaching*. Sage Publication Ltd.

Hammond, M., & Boltman, M. (2014). *The energy of reading project*. Retrieved October 1, 2014 from http://www.wholistichealingresearch.com/user_files/documents/ijhc/articles/HammondBotman-14-1.pdf

Hargreaves, E., Gipps, C., & Pickering, A. (2014). Assessment for learning. Formative approaches. In T. Cremin & J. Arthur (Eds.), *Learning to teach in the primary school*, (pp.313-323). Routledge.

Holmes, N. (2014). Student perceptions of their learning and engagement in response to the use of a continuous e-assessment in an undergraduate module. *Assessment & Evaluation in Higher Education, 40*(1), 1–14. doi:10.1080/02602938.2014.881978

Karpicke, J. D., Butler, A. C., & Roediger, H. L. III. (2009). Metacognitive strategies in student learning: Do students practise retrieval when they study on their own? *Memory (Hove, England), 17*(4), 471–479. doi:10.1080/09658210802647009 PMID:19358016

Keppell, M. (2013). *Designing learning-oriented assessment for a digital future.* Retrieved June 22, 2013 from www.slideshare.net/mkeppell/digital-assessment

Kim, C., & Pekrun, R. (2014). Emotions and motivation in learning and performance. In J. M. Spector, M. D. Merrill, J. Elen, & M. J. Bishop (Eds.), *Handbook of research on educational communications and technology* (pp. 66-75). Springer. doi:10.1007/978-1-4614-3185-5_6

Krabbe, H. (2014). Digital concept mapping for formative assessment. In D. Ifenthaler & R. Hanewald (Eds.), *Digital knowledge maps in education,* (pp. 275-297). Springer. doi:10.1007/978-1-4614-3178-7_15

Landa, L. (1972). *Algoritmisation in learning and instruction.* Englewood Cliffs, NJ: Educational Technology Publications.

Midoro, V. A. (2005). *Common European framework for teachers' professional profile in ICT for education.* Ortona. Italy: Edizioni MENABO DIDACTICA.

Petrides, L., Jimes, C., Middleton-Detzner, C., Walling, J., & Weiss, S. (2011). Open textbook adoption and use: Implications for teachers and learners. *Open Learning, 26*(1), 39–49.

Railean, E. (2014). Instructional dynamic and flexible strategy: Integrity of effective methods for engaging all learners in classrooms. In S. Lawrence (Ed.), *Critical practice in P-12 education: Transformative teaching and learning* (pp. 49-65). Hershey, PA: Information Science Reference.

Roberts, T. (2006). Self, peer, and group assessment in e-learning. Hershey, PA: Information Science Publishing. doi:10.4018/978-1-59140-965-6

Shute, V. J., & Kim, Y. J. (2014). Formative and stealth assessment. In J. M. Spector, M. D. Merrill, J. Elen, & M. J. Bishop (Eds.), *Handbook of research on educational communications and technology,* (pp. 311-321). Springer. doi:10.1007/978-1-4614-3185-5_25

Skinner, B. F. (1958). Teaching machines. *Sciences, 128*(3330), 969-976. Retrieved November 22, from http://apps.fischlerschool.nova.edu/toolbox/instructionalproducts/edd8124/fall11/1958-Skinner-TeachingMachines.pdf

Song, J. S., Kim, S. J., Byun, G. S., Song, J. H., & Lee, B. G. (2014). Comparing wireless networks for applying digital textbook. *Telecommunication Systems, 55*(1), 25–38. doi:10.1007/s11235-013-9748-4

Stiggins, R., Chappuis, S., & Arter, J. (2014). *Classroom assessment for student learning.* Pearson.

Veenman, M. V., Bavelaar, L., De Wolf, L., & Van Haaren, M. G. (2014). The on-line assessment of metacognitive skills in a computerized learning environment. *Learning and Individual Differences, 29,* 123–130. doi:10.1016/j.lindif.2013.01.003

Vonderwell, S., & Boboc, M. (2013). Promoting formative assessment in online teaching and learning. *TechTrends: Linking Research & Practice to Improve Learning, 57*(4), 22–27. doi:10.1007/s11528-013-0673-x

Zaiteva, L., & Popco, V. B. (2006). Development and using of electronic textbooks [in Russian]. *Journal of Educational Technology & Society*, 411–421. Retrieved from http://ifets.ieee.org/russian/depository/v9_i1/html/3.html

## ADDITIONAL READING

Arievitch, I. M., & Haepen, J. J. (2005). Connecting sociocultural theory and educational practice: Galperin's approach. *Educational Psychologist*, *40*(3), 155–165. doi:10.1207/s15326985ep4003_2

Bespaliko, V. (2002). *Education and learning with computer*. (In Russian). Moscow: State University Psychological Institute. Retrieved June 22, 2014 from http://www.eusi.ru/lib/bespalko_obrasovanie/3.php

Boesen, J., Lithner, J., & Palm, T. (2010). The relation between types of assessment tasks and the mathematical reasoning students use. *Educational Studies in Mathematics*, *75*(1), 89–105. doi:10.1007/s10649-010-9242-9

Braten, I., Anmarkrud, O., Brandmo, C., & Stromso, H. I. (2014). Developing and testing a model of direct and indirect relationships between individual differences, processing, and multiple-text comprehension. *Learning and Instruction*, *30*, 9–24. doi:10.1016/j.learninstruc.2013.11.002

Briggs, R. M., Gagne, L. J., Briggs, L. J., & Wager, W. W. (1988). *Principles of instructional design*. Holt, Rinehart, and Winston.

Clark, R. C., & Mayer, R. E. (2011). *E-learning and the science of instruction: Proven guidelines for consumers and designers of multimedia learning*. John Wiley & Sons, Incorporated. doi:10.1002/9781118255971

Code, J., & Zap, N. (2013). Assessments for learning, of learning, and as learning in 3D immersive virtual environments. In J. Herrington, . . . (Eds.), *Proceedings of world conference on educational multimedia, hypermedia and telecommunications 2013* (pp. 159–166). Chesapeake, VA: AACE. Retrieved from http://www.editlib.org/p/111949

Cuevas, J. A., Irving, M. A., & Russell, L. R. (2014). Applied cognition: Testing the effects of independent silent reading on secondary students' achievement and attribution. *Reading Psychology*, *35*(2), 127–159. doi:10.1080/02702711.2012.675419

Dirksen, J. (2011). *Design for how people learn*. Pearson Technology Group Canada.

Donovan, M., & Bransford, J. (2005). *How students learn: History, mathematics, and science in the classroom*. Washington: The National Academies press.

Eyal, L. (2012). Digital assessment literacy- the core role of the teacher in a Digital Environment. *Journal of Educational Technology & Society*, *15*(2), 37–49.

Gerard, F., & Roegiers, X. (2009). *Des manuels scolaires pour apprendre: Concevoir, évaluer, utiliser*. De Boeck Supérieur. doi:10.3917/dbu.gerar.2009.01

Gulińska, H. (2014). A textbook without pages? *International Journal of Continuing Engineering Education and Lifelong Learning*, *24*(1), 35–52. doi:10.1504/IJCEELL.2014.059333

Gurung, R. A. R., & Martin, R. C. (2011). Predicting textbook reading: The textbook assessment and usage scale. *Teaching of Psychology*, *38*(1), 22–28. doi:10.1177/0098628310390913

Horton, W. (2011). *E-learning by design*. John Wiley & Sons.

Jaehnig, W., & Miller, M. L. (2007). Feedback types in programmed instruction: A systematic review. *The Psychological Record*, 57(2), 219–232.

Landrum, R. E., Gurung, R. A., & Spann, N. (2012). Assessments of textbook usage and the relationship to student course performance. *College Teaching*, 60(1), 17–24. doi:10.1080/87567 555.2011.609573

Lembo, J. M. (1956). *The psychology of effective classroom instruction*. Columbus, Ohio: Charles E. Merrill Publishing Company.

Lim, C., Song, H. D., & Lee, Y. (2012). Improving the usability of the user interface for a digital textbook platform for elementary-school students. *Educational Technology Research and Development*, 60(1), 159–173. doi:10.1007/s11423-011-9222-5

Mayer, R. (1987). *Educational psychology. A cognitive approach*. USA: Harper Collins Publisher.

Mayer, R. (2005). *The Cambridge handbook of multimedia learning*. New York, NJ: Cambridge University Press. doi:10.1017/CBO9780511816819

Morris-Babb, M., & Henderson, S. (2012). An experiment in open-access textbook publishing: Changing the world one textbook at a Time. *Journal of Scholarly Publishing*, 43(2), 148–155.

O'Keeffe, L., & O' Donoghue, J. (2014). A role for language analysis in mathematics textbook analysis. *International Journal of Science and Mathematics Education*, 1–26.

Vonderwell, S., & Boboc, M. (2013). Promoting formative assessment in online teaching and learning. *TechTrends: Linking Research & Practice to Improve Learning*, 57(4), 22–27. doi:10.1007/s11528-013-0673-x

Wake, J. D., Dysthe, O., & Mjelstad, S. (2007). New and changing teacher roles in higher education in a digital age. *Journal of Educational Technology & Society*, 10(1), 40–51.

Waugh, C. K., & Gronlund, N. E. (2013). *Assessment of student achievement*. New Jersey: Pearson.

## KEY TERMS AND DEFINITIONS

**Digital Assessment:** Method of assessment using digital technologies that cover a variety of formats from PDF to videos that can capture and recover the student work and allow to view and access the assessment process over an extended period of time or a fixed time.

**Formal Assessment:** A form of assessment that implies a written document, such as a test, quiz, or paper.

**Formative Assessment:** Assessment carried out throughout a course or project in form of diagnostic, standardized tests, quizzes, oral question, or draft work.

**Informal Assessment:** A form of assessment that occurs in a more casual manner and may include observation, inventories, checklists, rating scales, rubrics, performance and portfolio assessments, participation, peer and self-evaluation, and discussion.

**Initial Assessment:** Pre-assessment or diagnostic assessment; conducted prior to instruction or intervention to establish a baseline from which individual student progress can be measured.

**Objective Assessment:** A form of questioning, requiring a single correct answer and may include the following types: true/false answer; multiple choice, multiple response, matching questions etc.

**Open Textbooks:** Textbooks, considered alternatives to traditional textbooks, are freely available online, disseminated through non-restrictive licensing and accessible technology can be adapted by teachers/students as result of theirs potential to facilitate a community, who collaborate, share, discuss, critique, use, reuse and continuously improve content.

**Subjective Assessment:** A form of assessment which may have more than one correct answer (or more than one way of expressing the correct answer). The types of subjective assessment are: essay, extended response questions etc.

**Summative Assessment:** Assessment generally carried out at the end of a course or project in order to summarize what the students have learned,

how they understand and can apply the outcomes in non-standard situations and to assign students a course grade and to make decisions regarding that students pass or fails the course, class etc. The forms of summative assessment are: tests, final exams, projects.

**Testing Effect:** A Research finding that "taking a test enhances long-term retention more than spending an equivalent among of time repeatedly studying" (Karpicke et al., 2009, p. 472).

# Chapter 11
# Pros and Cons of Digital Textbooks Technology

## ABSTRACT

*Students do not necessarily enjoy using textbooks. One of the main reasons is that multimodal texts are harder to process by brain patterns. Digital textbooks technology aims to reduce this pitfall, offering multimedia feedback and interactivity as the main features of the powerful learning environment. There are two ways: a) using and developing the digital textbook as a pedagogical resource and b) using and developing digital textbook as a learning tool. The first way offers speed of finding, purchasing, downloading, as well as digital reading. The second way adds the power of assembling digital content through representation in a person's own manner as well as group development of content. Educational outcomes in a digital textbook learning environment are better than in scholastic models. This chapter presents pros and cons of the digital textbook technology in concept of postmodernism philosophy. The role of the digital textbook technology for learning is proved.*

## INTRODUCTION

Mobile information technology is changing the education landscape by offering learners the opportunity to engage in asynchronous, ubiquitous instruction (Hyman, Moser & Segala, 2014, p.1). While education requires learner-centered learning environment, humans brains have the ability to recognize patterns and metappaterns and, then, transform them into concrete, actionable steps for actions or activities. Previous research was shown (Basulto, 2013) that learning results from massive, hierarchical and recursive processes. Reading is recognizing the patterns of individual

letters, then the patterns of individual words, then groups of words together, then paragraphs, then entire chapters and books.

The multimodal texts are harder to be processed by brain patters. The cause is that multimodal texts involve new forms of labour and types of patterns (Kabuto, 2014; Simon, Acosta, & Houtman, 2014; Malinowski, 2014). The digital textbook content, as a metappaterns, is used and developed as a pedagogical resource and/or as a learning tool. Its functionality is a guaranteed hardware, software and educational technologies. The sustainability of technologies is in usability, networking and interoperability (Cheng, Chou, Wang & Lin,

DOI: 10.4018/978-1-4666-8300-6.ch011

2014; Wiklund-Hornqvist, Jonsson & Nyberg, 2014; Reid, 2014 etc.). Moreover, digital textbooks are available more than ever. In addition, they influence the academic achievement (Lang et al., 2014; Moser & Segala (2014) etc.). Studies in digital textbooks area are focused on solving digital learning issues (Song, Kim, Byun, Song, & Lee, 2014; Kim & Park, 2014; Hyman, Moser & Segala; 2014; Marshall, Kinuthia & Richards, 2013 etc.).

Why is it important to research the integrity of hardware, software and educational technologies in using and development of digital textbooks? In order to solve this problem we state: Only a small part of the scientific and social knowledge is "transformed" into didactic material. The other part involuntary comes from real environment and processed unconsciously. People learn better when investigate, than read the printed text. Knowledge is a result of investigated phenomena, objects and processes, which serve as "learning objects". During life, pupils use different tools of investigation (according to theirs intellect, emotions and energetics. However, these tools are more and more sophisticated.

New digital textbook technologies impact learning because Digital Age is for Knowledge Society. Learning requires learning platforms and digital devices in order to understand how to read real-virtual signs and how to de-codify the speech and visual information from hypertext and multimodal text. In real life people solve parallel, non-linear and integrated cognitive activities, using digital to investigate world and to assemble "meaning" for non-standard solutions, visions, culture, and strategies. Pedagogics aims to develop new methods as tools for personal development in sustainable, secured and durable habitat. However, the primarily product tool and resource is *humans' capital*. This means that quality of life depends mainly on the capacity to learn and to communicate verbally and non-vernally in real-virtual learning environments. During all life we are teacher or/and students.

Global challenges to formal and non-formal education evidence the person-centric complexity, in which human adaptability is the result of the human strengths including *intellect, emotions and energetics*. In addition to these, there are really the environments' requirements about daily decisions regarding the use of the digital technologies as tools for synchronic and asynchronic communication. Digital technologies break time and place constraints give students new degrees of freedom to interact any time and place. The sense of real-virtual networking with online or/and offline activities and synchronic or/and asynchronic communications is new to the learning designer. What is, however, missing, is that there today exist no reasonable psychological and pedagogical considerations in digital textbooks' use and development that would make a change in educational technology.

However, existing eTextbook market hinges strongly with "prescribed textbooks", which may be in one university course only recommended reading, but in another not be used at all. As was noted by Hallam (2012) the eTextbook paradigm *represents a microcosm of the changes that are likely to occur, where digital pedagogies have been encouraged by a technology-enabled personalised learning environment where self-directed and inquiry-based learning can flourish*. Therefore, initially the role and potential of players in use and development of digital textbooks should be investigating. Then, not less important is to understand the methodological and technological phases for digital textbook use and development. New postmodernist learner-centric solutions focused on new learning ideal, either as sources or as learning tools are needed to better fulfilling this need.

This chapter is dedicated to technology, described in concept of the new learning ideal and postmodernism philosophy. In such approach the integrity of hardware, software and educational technologies is identified with learning design as requirements for the personal development of multiliteracies in multi-cultural setting of real-virtual learning environments. Following the concerns related to technology, will be proved the new role of technology for sustainable education.

## BACKGROUND

Research was argued (Warren, Lee & Najmi, 2014, p. 89) that impact of shifting epistemologies in the field of instructional design during the last century has had a major impact on how we design instruction. In concept of post-modernism philosophy instructional design should be focused on learning outcomes. But, what are in the reality the learning outcomes? It was observed (van Merriënboer & de Bruin (2014, p. 21) that different theories take different perspectives on learning and thus focus on other learning outcomes, other methods affecting learning processes, and other conditions under which learning takes place. Also, it is a difference of understanding the main factors that influence learning. It was evidenced that according to the perspective of Gestalt psychology, the most important factor influencing learning is insight and understanding; according to behaviorism and neo-behaviorism, it is reinforcement; according to developmental psychology, it is the learner's stage of cognitive development; according to cultural-historical theory, it is interaction with the world; according to information processing theory, it is active and deep processing of new information; according to cognitive symbolic theory, it is what the learner already knows; according to cognitive resource models, it is the limited processing capacity of the human mind, and according to social constructivism, it is the social construction of meaning.

According to definition, provided by University of Illinois at Urbana-Champaign (2014), *the learning outcomes are statements of what students will learn in a class or in a class session*. These statements should include a verb phase and an impact (in order to) phase – what students will do/be able to do and how they will

apply that skill or knowledge. In writing learning outcomes it is important to use Bloom's cognitive taxonomy and to avoid using of ambiguous verbs like understand, appreciate, know how, become familiar with, learn about, and become aware of. However, in concept of post-modernist philosophy the *learning outcomes or academic achievements represents the performance of student to solve and evaluate non-standard, non-linear, but authentic tasks that require "assembling" the solutions at intellectual, emotional and energetic levels in real-virtual learning environments*.

Methods of outcomes based education are focused on empiric measurement of formative learning outcomes through self-regulated assessment, solving tasks and viewing of learning analytics and summative learning outcomes. Let us analysis this idea starting from psychological point of view. Why should digital textbooks be used for guaranteed learning outcomes? First, it was argued (Titz & Karbach, 2014) that academic achievements have the high significance for various life outcomes, such as academic and vocational success, income, and socioeconomic status. However, to achieve elementary learning outcomes the students need to know reading and mathematics. Theoretically, the ability to read is composed of *word decoding* and *the ability to combine words and draw inferences to comprehend written text*. In solving mathematical problems students should use different strategies, like us vision-spatial sketchpad, phonological loop etc. (Cowan & Powell, 2014; Lee, Ning & Goh, 2014; Hamada & Goya, 2014; Orrantia, Munez & Tarin, 2014).

One interesting model is sketchpad. The Sketchpad is assumed to be responsible for setting up and manipulating information. Working memory distinguishes verbal processing in the phonological loop from spatial processing via the visual–spatial sketchpad (Doorn & Blokland, 2014). The sketchpad is assessed using pattern recall (St. Clair-Thompson, 2014).

Science textbooks have been an important research focus for *reading* (Cheng, Chou, Wang & Lin, 2014, p. 2). The focus of current research is devoted to the interaction of science content, cultural perspectives, and understanding of facts, concepts and processes. Therefore, consideration of text should include text structures/genres (e.g. procedures, cause–effect, problem–solution, etc.), features (e.g. headings, symbols, signs, colors, etc.), representations (e.g. visual, verbal, etc.), and cognitive and reasoning processes that are commonly found in authentic scientific work. The focus of research is on *text-visual comprehension*. However, in understanding suitable norms for print-visual texts have used dual coding theory (Paivio, 2014), generative theory of textbook design (Mayer, Steinhoff, Bower & Mars (1995), cognitive load theory (Sweller, Ayres & Kalyuga, 2011) and cognitive theory of multimedia learning (Schnotz, 2005). Our position in this topic is that before using digital textbooks in order to foster learning is important to identify what problems (psychological, physiological, pedagogical, economic etc.) should be solved only with digital technology. The examples of such tasks are the following:

1. How to motivate high achievement or Olympic students, if class have middle results?
2. How to teach student, if she or he was absent due to sickness?
3. How to engage all students in learning chemistry or mathematics for guaranteed outcomes?
4. How to motivate students to work in projects using wiki, peer assessment or portfolio?
5. How to adapt learning material for students with different knowledge and skills?
6. How to teach student(s) with learning disability in reading or mathematics?
7. How to teach student(s) with physic disability, if, for example, he or she doesn't have fingers?

This and many other problems can be solved only through implementation of digital textbooks.

## PHASES OF DIGITAL TEXTBOOK USE AND DEVELOPMENT

### Issues, Controversies, Problems

Due to the forces of globalization focused toward Knowledge Society and sustainable environments with digital textbooks use and development rely on *guaranteed learning outcomes*. Of course pressure, either direct or indirect, is extended on didactic triangle: teacher, student(s) and content. In fact, as was noted by Kautto-Koivula and Huhtaniemi (2003) knowledge always begins and ends as personal; key knowledge is scattered, and new technologies are created through intensive communication and collaboration in human networks; knowledge society is a network model, in which the smallest unit is the individual; individual knowledge is the key production value and the engine for economic growth; and knowledge differs from all other means of production in that it cannot be inherited, because it has to be acquired anew by every individual, and everyone starts out with the same total ignorance.

Instead of the above mentioned facts, the Technological Pedagogical Content Knowledge refers to knowledge about the complex relations among technology, pedagogy, and content that enable teachers to develop appropriate and context-specific teaching strategies. This framework goes beyond knowledge of content, pedagogy and technology taken individually but rather exists in a *dynamic transactional relationship* (Kereluik, Shin & Graham, 2014, p. 102). The first issue: what "elements" constitute learning and how accessible are these elements from the learning outcomes?

Digital textbook use and development requires a learning platform on digital device. There are at least two types of such platforms: eLearning and mLearning. It was find (Ally & Prieto-Blázquez,

2014) that the evolution of wireless technologies and the development of applications for mobile devices in higher education have been spectacular. The priorities of mLearning platforms are that the learner is mobile and that technology allows the learner to learn in any context. Is this statement true for any learning situations, for example in learning arithmetic, calculus, chemistry, biology or physics? What is the research problem? What type of digital textbooks should be designed for these tasks?

Turning to the term "Didactic", there is confusing understanding of terms "teaching" and "conscious learning". It is a proved fact that the students lean only when he or she is motivated to do this complex and hard activity. The basic components of Didactic Triangle, however, serve to point to a) pedagogical design patterns for instructors/designers; b) "didactic design for resource oriented education" (Bliesner, Liedtke, Welfens, Baedeker, Hasselku & Rohn, 2014, p. 1); c) instructional design for content; d) curriculum design for content-learning outcomes and e) learning design with focus on the learner's responsibility. In all this a case learning is view only as a *cognitive activity*. Akerlind, McKenzie and Lupton (2014) have tried to avoid this issue and purpose to combine phenomenographic research, and the associated variation theory of learning, with the notion of disciplinary threshold concepts. The method involves three primary stages:

- Identification of disciplinary concepts worthy of intensive curriculum design attention, using the criteria for threshold concepts;
- Action research into variation in students' understandings/misunderstandings of those concepts, using phenomenography as the research approach;
- Design of learning activities to address the poorer understandings identified in the second stage, using variation theory as a guiding framework.

The curriculum design method is inherently theory and evidence based. It was developed and trialled during a two-year project funded by the Australian Learning and Teaching Council, using physics and law disciplines as case studies. Disciplinary teachers' perceptions of the impact of the method on their teaching and understanding of student learning were profound. Attempts to measure the impact on student learning were less conclusive; teachers often unintentionally deviated from the design when putting it into practice for the first time.

*eTextbooks are available in different formats*. Nelson (2011) evidences: .Lit, .mobi, AZW, PDB, FBE, PDF, BBeB, EPUB, HTML, RB, CHM, and OEB. DRM standards include: MS reader, Adobe Adept, eReader, Mobi, Apple FairPlay, DNL, and several others. From the author's point of view, the buying decision for students to know what they are getting when they buy a particular digital book requires more education than buying a print book, because not all digital devices are created equal. In addition, as was noted by Caldwell (2012)*a*, while many popular applications offer export capabilities – which more or less corral text and images into an ePub document – proceeding from there is a challenge. Often, creators encounter troublesome CSS fragments, mismatched formats, and limited creative options within the apps. iBooks Author employs ibooks (.iba) format, that is an amalgamation of the W3C's ePub standard and CSS, with some Apple-specific code mixed in.

The other issue is *interoperability*. Caldwell (2012) observes that iBook format is incompatible with any other reader. While it is easy to use iBook template for creating new educational products, these products will not work on iPhone, for example. The author has written: "iPad-exclusivity aside, those willing to work in iBooks Author should be quite pleased. It's the best WYSIWYG ebook designer I've seen on the market so far, and formatting problems excluded, incredibly easy to work with. If you have iTunes Producer installed, you can even use the Publish button to send your finished book directly to the publishing process; you'll still need an ISBN and an iBookstore sales account to proceed, but it's a nice link to unify the process."

The other issue related to making digital textbooks is *writing apps*. Caldwell (2014) analyses Vellum 1.0 – one of the few pieces of software focused on building eBooks. So, the author of digital textbook could import the manuscript from a Word doc, as well asa style text, subhead, breaks, block quotes and verse, then – preview a live version for the iPone, Kindle, or Nook and export multiple versions with a single click. Vellum's controls are both expertly designed and easy to learn, providing the app's excellent cross-platform preview and export engine. Moreover, the app provides an array of customisation options for book style, headings, the first paragraph of a chapter etc.

## Limitations of the Printed Textbooks

Printed textbooks are not an effective medium in the context of rapidly changing the society and the increasingly short life cycle of knowledge. In addition, printed textbooks cannot contain the total volume of information required for any course. As was argued (Kim & Jung, 2010, pp. 249-254) digital textbooks can carry more information than hundreds of traditional textbooks. The multimedia based is expected to increase the effectiveness of production and distribution of information as text can be supplemented by animation and video. One of the most beneficial features of the digital textbook is its non-linear characteristic mechanism of hypertext. It was argued that a hypertext environment provides different ways to approach content; its nonlinear characteristics allow different individuals to interact with the same information through different processes. Users can create own reading structure and sequence, which change the conventional processes of structuring knowledge and understanding.

In comparison to traditional print textbooks, digital textbooks permit much more flexibility in the delivery of instruction. The flexibility offers the possibility to design a rich environment in which learners construct their integrated structure of competence. Learners can still follow paths through the subject content produced by designers, but also develop their own routes.

In a digital textbook learning environment the student "should develop personal navigation patterns whose features mirror his or her own characteristics" (Kim & Jung, 2010, pp. 254-257). Hypermedia allow an active, constructive, flexible, adaptive, and self-regulated learning. The learner can actively control and self-regulate the learning process, rather than being directed by a teacher or the argumentative structure of a textbook. The hypermedia structures enhance and stimulate a self-controlled and non-linear interaction with learning material as well as an in –depth exploration of vast amounts of information. Digital textbooks are designed to facilitate various multimedia productions such as interactive games, videos, audios, animations, 3D, and so forth. The learner's ability to generate mental representation of external information is enhanced when incoming information is presented through multiple sensory channels, when content is verbal and non-verbal.

In comparison with oriented textbooks, the digital textbooks provide interactivity and feedback. It is expected that interactivity can improve problem-solving skills. Furthermore, it is offered visibility in learning. This means that teachers and/or students are able: a) to "see" the actions that are open to them at every choice point; b) to receive immediate feedback about the actions that they have just taking and c) to get timely and insightful information about the consequences of their actions.

One of the most important pedagogical aspects of learning with digital textbook refers to combination of interactivity with feedback. It was argued that despite the ability to interact with the instructional materials (behavioral activity), learning may not occur if opportunities to obtain feedback and to reflect (cognitive activity) are absent. The interactivity is about:

- **Dialoguing:** The learner can ask a question and receive an answer, or can give an answer and receive feedback (for example, the student can click on word to receive additional data);
- **Manipulating:** The users can create and modify digital content, including setting parameters;
- **Searching:** The users seeks information by entering a query, receiving or selecting options;
- **Navigating:** The users can select from various available sources clicking on a menu etc.

Digital textbooks provide forms of online *formative assessment tools*, supplementary and in-depth learning material and allow teachers to use evaluation data to access whether study goals are achieved. The online format tests have the following advantages: can be assessed at any time, can be taken repeatedly and can provide instant feedback, which may reduce the student anxiety. Moreover, digital formative assessment can be adapted to students learning styles and to triune aim. It is important to note that digital textbook learning environment requires self-regulated learning skills.

Digital textbooks and printed textbooks differ in many ways. The types of instructional materials that printed textbooks offer are limited to text and image-centered flat, linear learning materials. Digital textbooks permit a range of multimedia learning materials. In addition, digital textbooks benefit from easy conversion of data and can reflect new facts and knowledge quickly as compared to printed textbooks. Accessing data outside of a printed textbook requires much time and expertise, while the hypertext function of the digital textbook can easily and quickly link to various educational materials or database. Digital textbook allow for differentiated instruction, where students can link to a variety of subject matter and there can be interaction among teachers, students and computers.

Various features of digital textbooks help to create learner-centered classrooms. However, there are some limitations of digital textbooks, too. Firstly, there are not clear boundaries between digital textbooks and instructional web sites particularly as regards content and structure. Secondly, the parameters of the digital textbooks were unrealistically comprehensive. Thirdly, digital textbooks tend not to provide the same kind of idiosyncratic contents and images as printed textbooks, so students still must prefer to the printed textbooks (Kim & Jung, 2010, pp. 259-260).

In addition, printed textbooks are not so convenience, whether it's using a laptop, notebook or phone. Physical storage of textbooks and didactic materials can be replaced by digital library. Digital texts can provide more current information than printed textbooks (Mann, 2013), which, hopefully, reduce "the time students take to reach a learning objective by 30-80%" (Federal Commission, 2012). Moreover, hundreds of digital textbooks and learning tools can be holding on one digital device. The average tablet contains from 8 to 64 gigabytes of storage space and can hold ~1000 textbooks! In some cases the print textbook costs more than digital textbooks, but it is taken into account the cost of class infrastructure, implementation of digital textbooks requires purchasing hardware and software, building new Wi-Fi infrastructure, and training teachers and administrators how to use the technology. With a digital text the content should update every year requiring tweaks and updates to the teacher's plans. Current content is a huge advantage for the digital text and one of the prime reasons to consider moving in this direction (Wilson, 2012).

## ADVANTAGES AND DISADVANTAGES OF DIGITAL TEXTBOOKS

There are many advantages and disadvantages in using and development of digital textbooks (table 1). At the moment, however, many studies reports about the *Computer Vision Syndrome*. It was evidenced (Bali, Neeraj & Bali, 2014) eyestrain, tired eyes, irritation, burning sensations, redness of eyes, dry eyes, blurred, and double vision, eyestrain, eye fatigue, burning sensations, irritation, redness, blurred vision, and dry eyes, among others. Maintaining a single posture over an extended period of time can cause muscular problems, including carpal tunnel syndrome, neck/shoulder pain. These problems can be omitted or minimalized, if in the processes of using and development of digital textbooks will be respected the *ergonomic principle*. In an ergonomic learning environment eyes will strain to accommodate the smaller print. It is recommended to blink more often, look at least 20 feet away from the screen every 20 minutes, for at least 20 seconds.

Ergonomically the resting point of accommodation is normally 67 cm or behind the screen. Suggestions about ergonomic positioning of the computer and its chair include the following:

- Use the computer monitor in an ergonomic position - one arm distance or 40 inches away with a downward gaze of 14° or more;
- Use a chair specially designed for computer use so that it provides necessary support to the back, legs, buttocks, and arms.

A height adjustable lumbar support can be appropriately placed to fit the lower back. The outward curve of the backrest should fit into the small of the back. The adjustment should allow the user to recline at least 15° from the vertical. The backrest should lock in place or be tension adjustable to provide adequate resistance to lower back movement. Use the keyboard in such a position that the arms and wrist are in neutral position. Avoid screen reflections, glare from window, or overhead lights.

On one hand, digital textbook can help students to learn more material faster and enrich classroom education. The brain interprets printed and digital text in different ways, digital text is read 20-30% slower than print (Noyesa & Garland, 2008). From the other point of view, reading hyper-linked text may increase the brain's "cognitive load," lowering the ability to process, store, and retain information, or "translate the new material into conceptual knowledge. Carr (2010) notes that navigating linked documents entails mental calisthenics—evaluating hyperlinks, deciding whether to click, adjusting to different formats—that are extraneous to the process of reading. Because it disrupts concentration, such activity weakens comprehension. Even though the World Wide Web has made hypertext ubiquitous and presumably less startling and unfamiliar, the cognitive problems remain (Table 1).

## SOLUTIONS AND RECOMMENDATIONS

### Key Trends Accelerating Digital Textbook Technology

Digital textbook could be used and elaborated as a *pedagogical resource* and as *a learning tool,* which allow teacher(s) and student(s) to develop personalized versions of digital textbooks and/or libraries. As a resource, digital textbooks can be read or/and listed, searching for definition, interacting with materials, resources, and experts beyond the classroom, used for solving problem or projects.

There are some major trends in *educational technology*. It was evidenced (Johnson, Adams & Cummins, 2012, p. 11) the following trends:

*Table 1. Advantages and disadvantages of digital textbooks*

| Criteria | Advantages | Disadvantages |
|---|---|---|
| Portability and access | Anywhere and anytime:<br>Learning platforms/Digital textbook platforms<br>Mobile digital devices and PC<br>Downloadable and online<br>Cloud-based platforms<br>Support for students with special needs and disabilities | Internet access, network, bandwidth<br>Storage requirements for digital devices<br>Personal relationship with print: more pleasurable, relaxing and comfortable<br>Working between multiple screens<br>Copyright and author licence |
| Availability | Instant delivery after acquisition<br>Multiple concurrent users<br>Increasing number of titles<br>Exchange sites with keyword search | Multiple platforms<br>Different formats<br>Incompatibility of some digital device |
| Currency | Up-dated information<br>Interactive animations<br>Rotating 3D diagrams<br>Flick-through photo galleries<br>Tap-to-play videos | Compatibility of educational platforms<br>Platform and digital devices costs<br>Development costs of publisher<br>Equity and ethical issues<br>Need for investment in digital skills development |
| Flexibility | Tailored (personalised) content, that allow taking notes, highlighting, conversion the formats,<br>Printed text can be listened<br>Create study cards to review later | Demands on publisher to provide more bells and whistles |
| Navigation and readability | Searchability<br>Variable fonts<br>Increasing/ decreasing text size | Less autonomy for academics<br>Requires interaction with platforms<br>Require digital devices |
| Psychology | Quantum and bioecological psychology: 1. patterns<br>2.meta-patterns | Diversity of instructional and learning design principles<br>eTextbook and Open Source Textbooks development on the base on behaviourism, cognitivism, constructivism and connectionism theories |
| Pedagogy | Energeticinformational pedagogy:<br>  1. Interactive, adaptive methods<br>  2. Student active engagement<br>  3. Independent/collaborative learning<br>  4. Self-regulated learning<br>  5. Online and offline, synchronic and asynchronic communication<br>  6. Networking, Social Media,Web3.0 etc. | Require:<br>Self-regulated learning<br>New learning methodologies<br>New instructional models<br>New pedagogical strategies<br>New learning design approach<br>New educational technologies |
| Language | Translations, Glossaries, Metadata<br>Virtual learning language academy | Multiliteracies<br>Digital natives versus digital immigrates |
| Costs and security | Potentially cheaper than print<br>Safe and secure web access | Theft of devices with access codes<br>Users may have multiple devices, but digital textbook could be accessible of one<br>Hardware: non-biodegradable, batteries. |
| Environmental solutions | No paper<br>No ink<br>No obsolete older editions<br>Ecologic solution for sustainability | Academic/publishing companies' interests |

cloud computing, mobile apps, tablet computing, game-based learning and learning analytics. Mobile apps embody the convergence of several technologies that lend themselves to educational use, including annotation tools, applications for creation and composition, and social networking tools. GPS and compasses allow sophisticated location and positioning, accelerometers and motion sensors enable the apps to be designed and used in completely new ways, digital capture and editing bring rich tools for.

However, according to NMC (2014, pp.1-4) key trends accelerating educational technology adoption in Higher Education are: a) online learning, hybrid learning, and collaborative models; b) social media use in learning; c) the creator of society; d) data-driven learning and assessment; e) Agile startup models (lean startup movement), and f) making online learning natural. On the other hand, the significant challenges impeding educational technology adoption in Higher Education is attributed to: a) low digital fluency of faculty; b) relative lack of reward for teaching; c) competitions for new models in education; d) scaling teaching innovations; e) expanding access; and f) keeping education relevant. The most important developments in educational technology for higher education are: a) Flipped Classroom; b) Learning Analytics; c) 3D Printing; d) Games and Gamification; e) Quantified Self; and Virtual Assistants. Internet-based virtual environments, such as the massively multiplayer online game "World of Warcraft" and the non-game "Second Life" are excellent environments for both capturing and emulating human personalities. It was predicted that methods related to virtual assistants can "be used to design personalized information systems or semi-autonomous artificial intelligence assistants, and perhaps even to develop new forms of education and psychotherapy that help a person evolve through improved self-emulation." (Bainbridge, 2014, p. 177).

## EDUCATIONAL AND/OR COMMERCIAL PROJECTS

However, digital textbooks are elaborated during educational and/or commercial projects. The educational projects are focused on *theoretical (fundamental)*, *applicative* or *theoretic-applicative*

investigations. Theoretical-applicative projects are developed in Research Centers and Laboratories of Universities. One of these examples is *Carnegie Learning* (2014). This is a project maintained by twenty years of research into how students think, learn and apply new knowledge in mathematics.

## Case Study 1: The Carnegie Learning High School Math Series

The Carnegie Learning High School Math Series includes *math textbooks* with collaborative classroom activities, *adaptive software* and *teacher professional development*. They can be utilized together as core curriculum or independently as a support tools. These textbooks help students understand relationships and make connections among different mathematical concepts. Learning by Doing® method help students cultivate a depth of understanding in mathematics through solving real-world problems in a collaborative, student-centered classroom. Cognitive Tutor Software® provides students with highly individualized and self-paced instruction; integrate adaptive learning technologies, assessment, and rich problem-solving activities. In addition, it is working with teachers, coaches, and leaders to build standards-based, student-centered curricula and effectively integrate technology to inform data-driven instruction. The integrity of textbook, software and teacher professional development could be achieved through three different models:

1. **Blended (Software and Textbooks):** Require students to spend three days in classroom using Carnegie Textbooks and then the remaining two days – working with Cognitive Tutor Software, which "offer the most precise method for differentiating instruction available" (Carnegie Learning, 2014b, p. 5);
2. **Software:** Can be implemented anywhere with Internet as supplemental, intervention,

SES, extended learning and support ELL, gifted, IEP, and special educational population etc.;

3. **Textbooks:** Supports a collaborative, student-centered classroom; are consumable textbooks that are updated annually; can be implemented as core, support class, double block, and more and supports ELL, gifted, IEP and special education populations.

## Case Study 2: EToys from Illinois University

EToys is a project which aims to ignite an enthusiasm for expressing ideas using the language of the computer. As was noted on Squeakland site eToys is an educational tool for teaching children powerful ideas in compelling way; a media-rich authoring environment and visual programming system and a free software program that works on almost all personal computers. The potential of EToys for digital textbook content is enormous, because it can be used as a learning tool for insight learning, critical thinking and creativity, especially in mathematics, chemistry, physics and biology. This aims "to rewrite the school's mission of technology, literacy and community (Dickinson, 2013).

## INDICATOR OF QUALITY

To accomplish the task of identification and the quality indicator of the digital textbooks, a new questionaire was created that surveyed a large number of university students. Although there are a varity of quality indicator strategies related to education in the scientific literature. The indicator of quality is used for many purposed. A good indicator of quality corresponds to the participants' capacity to engage in microtransitoions fostering teaching–and–learning as intertwinned processes. Exploiting this will require teachers and students to develop strong decision making skilss in order

to seek and be actively engaged in digital textbook learning environent (Mameli & Molinari, 2014, p. 103),).

There are many issues and contraversues related to *quality indicator* of digital textbooks. Moving from a textbook-based world to one that is digital relies on many factors, such as sustainable funding for devices, internet connectivity, up-to-date policies, prepared educators, Intellectual property and reuse rights, quality control and usability etc. Howerver, while digital content can be implemented successfully with a less advantageous ratio than 1-to-1, in order to take full advantage of what digital content can bring, each student needs to have a device fully accessible, in school and out of school. Plus, the devices can be used for a wide variety of purposes, creating efficiencies and time savings as well. Closely related to the funding devices, it is ensuring sufficient broadband in schools.

The other issue relies on copyright. Digital textbooks can be used and developed as *E-Textbooks* and *Open Textbooks*. E-textbooks, as was noted by Allen (2014), represent digitized alternatives to printed texts that students read on a laptop or tablet. Similar to PDF documents, e-textbooks enable students to annotate, highlight and search. E-textbooks, like print textbooks, use a business model based on selling individual copies of the text. To make this model of work in the digital world, e-textbooks use *copyright enforcement*, strict license terms and digital rights management (DRM) controls to lock down e-textbooks and prevent unauthorized use. These restrictions inherently short-circuit the most advantageous features of today's technology. Unlike e-textbooks, newest models of Open Textbooks use copyright to unleash, rather than to restrict, the use of content. Known as open educational resources (OERs) and open textbooks, these materials are freely distributed online under a "some rights reserved" (as opposed to "all rights reserved") copyright license that grants blanket permission to reuse, revise, remix and redistribute the content.

The developing of an online *directory of open textbooks* is curated by faculty. However, building a *library of open course materials* for the courses is a quality issue (SBCTC, 2014a). "The Open Course Library is a collection of shareable course materials, including syllabi, course activities, readings, and assessments designed by teams of college faculty, instructional designers, librarians, and other experts. Some of our materials (also called open educational resources) are paired with low cost textbooks; many of them are completely free" (SBCTC, 2014b). This issue relies on construction the survey structure and checklist and readability formulas following the digital textbook quality process.

The relationship between motivational, emotive, social and cognitive aspects of digital textbook and quality indicator has already featured in the controversies between theory and practice: digital textbooks are used and elaborated as a pedagogical resource and as a learning tool.

The other issue that may affect the quality indicator is the diversity of the licence models. Licence models can be hybrid (printed or digital options), key technology access, direct to consumer, purchase of individual chapters, 'just-in-time' access, lifetime access, purchase plus subscription for updates, site licenses, consortial licences, and rental schemes. The textbook quality itself is often an important concern (Li, Zhang and Ma, 2014, p. 305).

The quality of Open Source Textbook integrates:

- Textbook quality text;
- Digital textbook learning infrastructure;
- Production of high quality ebooks;
- Open teaching landscape.

The quality matters rubrics contain several topics that are used to evaluate the design of a course in addition to cognitive, motivational, emotive and social aspects of learning within a digital textbook learning environment. Can user-generated materials achieve the same level of quality as commercial materials? In order to answer this question,

## EXPERT AND STUDENT FORMS

There are two main forms in TELE questioner: *expert form* and *student form*.

*The expert form* includes general notes, and detailed assessment of digital textbook quality. The general notes include technological aspects, and detailed assessment – cognitive, motivational, emotive and social aspects. These aspects rely on planning, development, monitoring and assessment.

*The student form* includes the following components: Introduction, personal information, personal evaluation, evaluation self-regulated learning aspects and general assessment.

The quality of the digital textbook mainly depends on scientific-technological progress. According to digital textbook topology, some psychological and/or pedagogical aspects can be replaced or added. For example, for multimedia textbook the technological aspect will include principles and norms of multimedia learning. However, in case of digitalised textbook, the survey will include norms of digital textbook learning environment functionality. The psychological and pedagogical aspects can be kept. Conclusion arises from the idea of pedagogical design of elementary didactical units as a SCORM unit that doesn't take into account the evolution of hardware, software and educational technologies and their influences in digital textbook use and development.

Starting from postmodernism philosophy can be argued that complete survey for assessment the quality of digital textbook and identification of quality indicator for digital textbook use and development should include two main parts: TELE-EXPERT and TELE-STUDENT. The first part is structured in 1) General Notes; 2) Detailed assessment of digital textbook quality and 3)

Summative assessment of digital textbook use and development. The survey includes 2 parts: Part A and Part B. the Part A include the questions related to technological aspect of digital textbook on the base on 10 criteria, which are scaled. The Linkert Scale, i.e. a psychometric scale commonly involved in research that employs questionnaires was used. The scale was created as the simple sum of questionnaire responses over the full range of the scale.

The Likert scale was designed as a sum of responses on ten individual Likert items. Each of the items is accompanied by a horizontal line, on which a subject indicated his or her response by checking tick-marks. Therefore, the Likert item is a statement which the student were asked to evaluate according to proposed criteria. The level of agreement or disagreement is measured with equal number of positive and negative positions. In studied case were developed five statistically significant response levels. The format of each Likert items is: Strongly disagree; Disagree; neither agrees nor disagrees; Agree and strongly agree. The design of Likert scale for TELE-STUDENT was the same.

On the basis of above mentioned criteria the formula that allows to calculate the quality indicator during digital textbook use and development was elaborated. The formula includes the range made by Expert: *Expert Component* (*Ec*) and Student: *student component* (*Sc*).

It was assumed that quality indicator of digital textbook (*Ic*) constitutes an average of the ratio of the indicators established by the Expert group and Student group. The formula is:

$$Ic = \frac{\left( \dfrac{Ec_1 + Ec_2 + \ldots Ec_n}{n} + \dfrac{Sc_1 + Sc_2 + \ldots Sc_m}{m} \right)}{2}.$$

where *Ic* – quality indicator of digital textbook, *Ec*- the value established by Expert group and *Sc* – the value established by Student group, *n* –

number of experts and *m* – number of students. The data is valid, if the number of expert is at least 3; and the number of student – at least 25.

The formula for Expert component (Ec) includes assessment of technological aspect (T) and value of assessment the cognitive, motivational, emotive and social, designed at phases of pacification (P), expectation and monitoring (E) and assessment (Ev).

$$Ec = \frac{T + P + E + Ev}{4}$$

The formula for Student component includes only the assessment of cognitive, motivational, emotive and social aspects at all phases of digital textbook development.

$$Sc = \frac{P + E + Ev}{3}$$

The procedure of establishment of digital textbook quality is the following: the chestionnaries were presented to Expert and Students groups, completed. Data were collected and analysed. The Experts group is composed by, at least three independent experts. The Student group is formed by students that use or/and develop digital textbook. The forms (prototypes) were developed on the base on two models: *TELESTUDENTS-SRL* and *TELE EXPERT–SRL*. The colected data is analysed (Table 2).

The second step relies on summarizing data. This means that each value is calculated according to formula *Ec* and is presented in Table 3.

The same procedure is for tables which refer to each of student that was engaged in the digital textbook learning environment. Collected data were summarised (Table 4).

The interdependences between statistical data can be realized through different procedures and techniques. Experimentally, the quality indicator of digital textbook is equal to 4.7.

*Table 2. Quality indicator established by one expert*

| Stage | | Cognitive Aspects | Motivational Aspects | Emotive Aspects | Social Aspects |
|---|---|---|---|---|---|
| Technological aspects | 1<br>2<br>3<br>...<br>N(10) | | | | |
| Planning | | | | | |
| Execution and monitoring | | | | | |
| Assessment | | | | | |

*Table 3. Study of average values of quality indicator established by experts*

| Number of Experts | Technological Aspects | Planning | Execution and Monitoring | Assessment | Average |
|---|---|---|---|---|---|
| 1 expert | | | | | $E_c$ |
| 2 expert | | | | | $E_c$ |
| 3 expert | | | | | $E_c$ |
| .... | | | | | $E_c$ |
| N experts | | | | | $E_c$ |

*Table 4. Study of average value established by a group of students*

| Nr. | 1 | 2 | 3 | ... | 25 | Average |
|---|---|---|---|---|---|---|
| 1 student | | | | | | $S_c$ |
| 2 student | | | | | | $S_c$ |
| 3 student | | | | | | $S_c$ |
| .... | | | | | | $S_c$ |
| N students | | | | | | $S_c$ |

## FUTURE RESEARCH DIRECTIONS

Quality in digital textbook use and development is essential. Because most of the digital textbooks can be edited, improved and assambled by teachers and/or students, the quality on the development process is potentially great. Bliss (2013, pp. 9-12) reveals the key criteria: *cost, diversity, content, readability, educational impact, pedagogical aids* and *interaction.* Cost is more common at the state level. The financial constraints almost influence selection committess in K-12 contexts rather than in higher education. However, cost-effectiveness fall behind learners' needs, authenticity, ancillary materials, and communicative ability. Sensibility to diverse cultures and viewpoints is considered an unimportant criterion in textbook selection. The opinions about the importantce of content differs. Therefore, elementary science textbooks varied widely in the content they covered, but such variability is often viewed as problematic in the K-12 setting. In higher education is important to consider content accuracy in addition to content coverage. Readability is another issue. It was found that scientific textbooks had higher readability scores because they used shorter sentences and clearer, descriptive prose, but this criteria can negatively affect overall textbook quality. Educational impact explores knowledge, comprehension, motivation, learning behaviors, collaboration, grades, and assessment performance. Some authors consider pedagogical aids (e.g. illustrations, online tools, glossaries) based on theory of generative learning as a criterion for textbook selection.

Korea Institute for Curriculum and Evaluation (2013) evidences 4 domains and 17 items. The first domain "Conformance of national curriculum" reflected objects, contents, instructional methods, and evaluation in national curriculum faithfully. "Accuracy and appropriateness of instructional materials" dealt with appropriateness of the level and scopes of instructional materials; accuracy of contents; objectiveness, neutrality, fairness of contents; diverse types and sufficient amounts of instructional materials; accurate presentation of sources of instructional materials; strategies for increasing students' learning motivations and flawlessness of declaration and expressions etc. "Effects of teaching and learning support" dealt with students' self-directed learning support, effective presentation of teaching and learning support, effective presentation of interaction, and usability of external instructional materials and programs (applications). "Usability of interface" dealt with components of interface (button, menu, and icon were convenient for students to use; aesthetic appreciation of design such as colour and typography). Before making a decision about digital textbooks, it is a need for *assessment*. It was evidenced (Pasquini, 2011) things to consider from the start:

1.   *What is the learning issue*? Can technology solve it? What are the technology needs of the department or campus system? What are the long-term goals for the program? What are the learning objectives for learning? Are there gaps and needs in the current technology programs? Can these gaps and needs be addressed with digital resources?

2.   *What resources are on campus*? Who should be a member of the design/development team? What are the available resources to support the technological needs? How will online resources be researched? Who will experiment with these resources? Third, it is important to understand who will create and edit digital textbooks.

3.   *Who will be part of the team*? What roles will be assigned to the technology implementation team? What are the implementation steps for the project? What is the timeline for the project? Who must be involved in the development of the technology? Who will provide technical support? What are the desired learning outcomes? When and how will feedback be provided from the learners and the faculty?

4.   *How will you conduct a needs assessment*? Who will be the advisor group? Who will be student population? What will be the format for the feedback? Will feedback include an online survey? Focus groups?

5.   *When will you start the project*? What methods or educational outcomes needs to be changed? Will the digital resource and format meet the instructor and learner needs? Will the delivery format meet learners' needs and be applicable for subject matter? Can any technical glitches be improved? What is required to maintain the program or online resource? What is required to update the program or online resource?

6.   *Where will you go for help*/support? What are the on-going needs for this technology? Who will support the learning technology initiatives? How will assessment continue? How will the effectiveness of the program

be evaluated? Who will be on the technical support team? Who will determine the content and updates for the technology?

Future research directions are developed and empirically validated the model of digital textbook quality from the perspective of didactic model. It is the diversity of digital learning environments.

## CONCLUSION

Some quality criteria were imposed by the students. The quality textbook evaluation criteria from the students perspectives are: *human interes, learnability, pedagogical aids, text format, content coverage, overall value and pedagogical tool.* Despite the fact that readability is a useful criterion for evaluating a textbook, the human interest scores are not a reliable measure of reading appeal for most students. As was noted by Bliss (2013, pp. 17-43), digital textbook evaluation criteria, however, can use most of the textbook quality criteria. Navigability, accesibility or enhancing are also important. A digital search functionality refers to seach that is specific, simple, fast, easy to use, and has an option for advancing searching. The high quality digital textbooks have page numbers, internal linking (i.e. between chapters), and bookmarking. Access features provide multiple options for accessing digital texts, including listen to the book in audio format; exploring on multiple devices; anytime/anywhere access to digital textbooks and the right to access digital textbook even after the course had concluded. Digital textbooks can be easy to find and log in to, be compatible with diverse browsers and device operating systems, and have fast download and upload speeds. The content is clear, easy to read and use, undestandable, well-written, well-organized, up-to-date, allow for on-screen highlighting and note-taking, embedd supplementary material (i.e. links to external content, videos, and tutorials), as well as responsive quizzing with instant, directed feedback and hints.

## REFERENCES

Akerlind, G., McKenzie, J., & Lupton, M. (2014). The potential of combining phenomenography, variation theory and threshold concepts to inform curriculum design in higher education. In J. Huisman & M. Tight (Eds.), Theory and method in higher education research II (International Perspectives on Higher Education Research, 10), (pp. 227-247). doi:10.1108/S1479-3628(2014)0000010017

Ally, M., & Prieto-Blaázquez, J. (2014). What is the future of mobile learning in education? Revista de Universidad y Sociedad del Conocimiento, 11(1), 142-151.

Bainbridge, W. S. (2014). Virtual Worlds. In W. S. Bainbridge, (Ed.), Personality capture and emulation (pp. 177-203). Springer London.

Bali, J., Neeraj, N., & Bali, R. T. (2014). Computer vision syndrome: A review. *Journal of Clinical Ophthalmology and Research*, 2(1), 61.

Bell, F., Zaitseva, E., & Zakrzewska, D. (2007). Evaluation: A link in the chain of sustainability. In N. Lambropoulos & P. Zaphiris (Eds.), *User-centered design of online learning communities* (pp. 186–214). Hershey, PA: Information Science. doi:10.4018/978-1-59904-358-6.ch009

Bliesner, A., Liedtke, C., Welfens, M. J., Baedeker, C., Hasselkuß, M., & Rohn, H. (2014). "Norm-oriented interpretation learning" and resource use: The concept of "open-didactic exploration" as a contribution to raising awareness of a responsible resource use. *Resources*, 3(1), 1–30. doi:10.3390/resources3010001

Bliss, T. J. (2013). *A model of digital textbook quality from the perspective of college students* (PhD thesis). Brigham Young University. Retrieved November 25, 2014, from https://learningtomorrow. hva.nl/nl/achtergrondinformatie/Gedeelde%20 documenten/A%20model%20of%20digital%20 textbook%20quality.pdf

Caldwell, S. (2012a). *iBooks Author fashions multimedia books for the iPad.* Retrieved November 25, 2014, from http://www.macworld.com/ article/1165172/ibooks_author_fashions_multi-media_books_for_the_ipad.html

Caldwell, S. (2012b). *Hands on: iBooks Author effortless to use, but iPad-only.* Retrieved November 25, 2014, from www.macworld.com/ article/1164895/hands_on_ibooks_author_effort-less_to_use_but_ipad_only.html

Caldwell, S. (2014). *Vellum review: App offers a sleeker way to build ebooks.* Retrieved November 25, 2014, from http://www.macworld.com/ article/2084960/vellum-review-app-offers-a-sleeker-way-to-build-ebooks.html

Carnegie Learning. (2014a). *Intelligent mathematics software that adapts to meet the needs of ALL students.* Retrieved November 25, 2014, from http://www.carnegielearning.com/specs/ cognitive-tutor-overview/

Carnegie Learning. (2014b). *The high school math series. Preparing students for college, career and their future.* Retrieved November 25, 2014, from http://www.carnegielearning.com/specs/ cognitive-tutor-overview/

Carnegie Learning. (2014c). *Why is Carnegie Learning so effective? Because we are constantly doing our homework.* Retrieved November 25, 2014, from m http://www.carnegielearning.com/ research/

Carr, N. (2010) *Author Nicholas Carr: The Web shatters focus, rewires brains.* Retrieved November 25, 2014, from http://www.wired.com/ magazine/2010/05/ff_nicholas_carr/all/1

Cheng, M. C., Chou, P. I., Wang, Y. T., & Lin, C. H. (2014). Learning effects of a science textbook designed with adapted cognitive process principles on grade 5 students. *International Journal of Science and Mathematics Education, 13*(62), 1–22.

Cowan, R., & Powell, D. (2014). The contributions of domain-general and numerical factors to third-grade arithmetic skills and mathematical learning disability. *Journal of Educational Psychology, 106*(1), 214–230. doi:10.1037/a0034097 PMID:24532854

Dickinson, D. (2013). *At Kenwood, programming students to succeed.* Retrieved November 25, 2014, from http://www.news-gazette.com/ news/local/2013-12-26/kenwood-programming-students-succeed.html

Doorn, R. R., & Blokland, A. (2014). Unhindered spatial processing during route memorization is required to maximize both spatial and verbal route knowledge. *Applied Cognitive Psychology, 28*(1), 22–29. doi:10.1002/acp.2949

*eToysIllinois.org.* (2014). Retrieved November 25, 2014, from http://etoysillinois.org/

Ghani, K. A., Noh, A. S., & Yusoff, N. M. R. N. (2014). Linguistic features for development of Arabic Text readability formula in Malaysia: A preliminary study. *Middle-East Journal of Scientific Research, 19*(3), 319–331.

Hallam, G. C. (2012). *Briefing paper on eTextbooks and third party eLearning products and their implications for Australian university libraries.* Council of Australian University Libraries. Retrieved November 25, 2014, from http://eprints. qut.edu.au/55244/3/55244P.pdf

Hamada, M., & Goya, H. (2014). Influence of syllable structure on L2 auditory word learning. *Journal of Psycholinguistic Research, 44*(246), 1–17. PMID:24493208

Hyman, J. A., Moser, M. T., & Segala, L. N. (2014). Electronic reading and digital library technologies: Understanding learner expectation and usage intent for mobile learning. *Educational Technology Research and Development, 62*(1), 35–52. doi:10.1007/s11423-013-9330-5

Johnson, L., Adams, S., & Cummins, M. (2012). *The NMC Horizon Report: 2012 higher education edition.* Austin, TX: The New Media Consortium. Retrieved November 25, 2014, from http://www.nmc.org/pdf/2012-horizon-report-HE.pdf

Kabuto, B. (2014). A semiotic perspective on reading picture books: The case of *Alexander and the Wind-Up Mouse. Linguistics and Education, 25,* 12-23.

Kim, J., & Park, N. (2014). The Analysis of case result and satisfaction of digital textbooks for elementary school students. In H. Y. Jeong, M. S. Obaidat, N. Y. Yen, J. J. Park (Eds.), *Advanced in computer science and its applications* (pp. 417-422). Springer Berlin Heidelberg. doi:10.1007/978-3-642-41674-3_59

Koehler, M. J., Mishra, P., Kereluik, K., Shin, T. S., & Graham, C. R. (2014). The technological pedagogical content knowledge framework. In J. M. Spector, M. D. Merrill, J. Elen, & M. J. Bishop (Eds.), *Handbook of research on educational communications and technology* (pp. 101-111). Springer New York. doi:10.1007/978-1-4614-3185-5_9

Lang, R., Ramdoss, S., Sigafoos, J., Green, V. A., van der Meer, L., Tostanoski, A., & O'Reilly, M. F. (2014). Assistive technology for postsecondary students with disabilities. In *Assistive technologies for people with diverse abilities* (pp. 53–76). Springer New York. doi:10.1007/978-1-4899-8029-8_3

Lee, K., Ning, F., & Goh, H. C. (2014). Interaction between cognitive and non-cognitive factors: The influences of academic goal orientation and working memory on mathematical performance. *Educational Psychology, 34*(1), 73–91. doi:10.1080/01443410.2013.836158

Malinowski, D. (2014). Drawing bodies and spaces in telecollaboration: A view of research potential in synaesthesia and multimodality, from the outside. *Pedagogies, 9*(1), 63–85. doi:10.1080/1554480X.2014.877559

Mameli, C., & Molinari, L. (2014). Seeking educational quality in the unfolding of classroom discourse: A focus on microtransitions. *Language and Education, 28*(2), 103–119. doi:10.1080/09500782.2013.771654

Mann, L. (2013). *Pros and cons of digital textbooks.* Retrieved November 25, 2014, from http://articles.chicagotribune.com/2013-08-07/features/ct-x-0807-college-kids-eyes-20130807_1_print-textbooks-digital-textbooks-computer-vision-syndrome

Marshall, S., Kinuthia, W. & Richards, G. (2013). Open content for elearning: Cross institutional collaboration for education and training in a digital environment. *International Journal of Education and Development Using ICT, 8*(3), 35-42.

Mayer, R. E., Steinhoff, K., Bower, G., & Mars, R. (1995). A generative theory of textbook design: Using annotated illustrations to foster meaningful learning of science text. *Educational Technology Research and Development, 43*(1), 31–41. doi:10.1007/BF02300480

Moreno, R., & Mayer, R. E. (2007). Interactive multimodal learning environments. *Educational Psychology Review, 19*(3), 309–326. doi:10.1007/s10648-007-9047-2

NMC. (2014). *NMC Horizon Report: 2014 Higher Education Preview.* Retrieved November 25, 2014, from http://www.nmc.org/pdf/2014-horizon-he-preview.pdf

Noyesa, J. M., & Garland, K. J. (2008). Computer- vs. paper-based tasks: Are they equivalent? *Ergonomics*, *51*(9), 1352–1375http://www.twosides.info:8080/content/rsPDF_382.pdf. Retrieved November 25, 2014. doi:10.1080/00140130802170387 PMID:18802819

Orrantia, J., Múñez, D., & Tarin, J. (2014). Connecting goals and actions during reading: The role of illustrations. *Reading and Writing*, *27*(1), 153–170. doi:10.1007/s11145-013-9437-4

Paquette, G. (2014). Technology-based instructional design: Evolution and major trends. In J. M. Spector, M. D. Merrill, J. Elen, & M. J. Bishop (Eds.), *Handbook of research on educational communications and technology* (pp. 661-671). Springer New York.

ProCon.org. (2014). *Should tablets replace textbooks in K-12 schools?* Retrieved November 25, 2014, from http://tablets-textbooks.procon.org/

Railean, E. (2014). Instructional dynamic and flexible strategy: integrity of effective methods for engaging all learners in classrooms. In S. Lawrence (Ed.), *Critical practice in P-12 education: Transformative teaching and learning* (pp. 49-65). Hershey, PA: Information Science Reference.

Recio-García, J. A., Díaz-Agudo, B., & González-Calero, P. A. (2014). The COLIBRI platform: Tools, features and working examples. In S. Montani & L. C. Jain (Eds.), *Successful case-based reasoning applications-2* (pp. 55–85). Springer Berlin Heidelberg. doi:10.1007/978-3-642-38736-4_5

Reid, N. (2014). The learning of chemistry: The key role of working memory. In I. Devetak & S. A. Glažar (Eds.), *Learning with understanding in the chemistry classroom* (pp. 77–101). Springer Netherlands. doi:10.1007/978-94-007-4366-3_5

Schnotz, W. (2005). An integrated model of text and picture comprehension. In R. E. Mayer (Ed.), *The Cambridge handbook of multimedia learning* (pp. 49–70). New York: Cambridge University Press. doi:10.1017/CBO9780511816819.005

Schwartz, K. (2014). *Bypassing the textbook: Video games transform social studies curriculum.* Retrieved November 25, 2014, from http://blogs.kqed.org/mindshift/2014/01/forget-the-textbook-video-games-as-social-studies-content/

Simon, R., Acosta, A., & Houtman, E. (2014). "Memeration": Exploring academic authorship in online spaces. In R. E. Ferdig & K. E. Pytash (Eds.), *Exploring multimodal composition and digital writing* (pp. 54–67). Hershey, PA: Information Science Reference.

Song, J. S., Kim, S. J., Byun, G. S., Song, J. H., & Lee, B. G. (2014). Comparing wireless networks for applying digital textbook. *Telecommunication Systems*, *55*(1), 25–38. doi:10.1007/s11235-013-9748-4

St Clair-Thompson, H. (2014). Establishing the reliability and validity of a computerized assessment of children's working memory for use in group settings. *Journal of Psychoeducational Assessment*, *32*(1), 15–26. doi:10.1177/0734282913497344

Sweller, J. (2011). Cognitive load theory. In B. N. Ross (Ed.), *The psychology of learning and motivation. Cognition in Education* (Vol. 55). Elsevier Inc.

van Merriënboer, J. J., & de Bruin, A. B. (2014). Research paradigms and perspectives on learning. In J. M. Spector, M. D. Merrill, J. Elen, & M. J. Bishop (Eds.), *Handbook of research on educational communications and technology* (pp. 21-29). Springer New York.

Warren, S. J., Lee, J., & Najmi, A. (2014). The impact of technology and theory on instructional design since 2000. In J. M. Spector, M. D. Merrill, J. Elen, & M. J. Bishop (Eds.), *Handbook of research on educational communications and technology* (pp. 89-99). Springer New York.

Wiklund-Hörnqvist, C., Jonsson, B., & Nyberg, L. (2014). Strengthening concept learning by repeated testing. *Scandinavian Journal of Psychology*, *55*(1), 10–16. doi:10.1111/sjop.12093 PMID:24313425

Wilson, L. (2012). *Apple's iPad textbooks cost 5x more than print*. Retrieved November 25, 2014, from http://tablets-textbooks.procon.org/sourcefiles/print-vs-itext.pdf

## ADDITIONAL READING

Calibre. (2014). Retrieved November 25, 2014, from http://calibre-ebook.com/, http://calibre-ebook.com/about

Fletcher, G., Scaffhauser, D., & Levin, D. (2012). *Out of print: Reimagining the K-12 textbook in a digital age*. State Educational Technology Directors Association. (SETDA). Retrieved November 25, 2014, from http://files.eric.ed.gov/fulltext/ED536747.pdf

*Learning with Etoys: Imagine Invent Inspire*. Retrieved November 25, 2014, from http://etoysillinois.org/files/i3learning.pdf

Mayer, R. E. (2014). Incorporating motivation into multimedia learning. *Learning and Instruction*, *29*, 171–173. doi:10.1016/j.learninstruc.2013.04.003

Nelson, M. (2011). *Future of e-books or e-textbooks on college campuses*. Retrieved November 5, 2014, from Retrieved from http://thecite.blogspot.com.au/2011/02/future-of-e-books-or-e-textbooks-on.html

Paivio, A. (2014). *Mind and its evolution: A dual coding theoretical approach*. Psychology Press.

## KEY TERMS AND DEFINITIONS

**3D Printing:** Technologies that construct physical objects from three-dimensional digital content such as 3D modelling software, computer-aided design (CAD) tools, computer-aided tomography (CAT), and X-ray crystallography.

**Consumable Textbooks:** Textbooks that provide students an opportunity to take notes, solve a problem, or write complete sentences directly in the textbook's page.

**Creator Society:** A society in which occur the maker movement, i.e. user-generators videos, self-published eBooks, personalised domains etc. In a creator society higher education is "in position to shift its curricular focus to ensure learning environments align with the engagement of creator-students and foster the critical thinking skills needed to fuel a creator society"(HMC, 2014, p. 1).

**Deep Understanding:** Learning when "concepts are well represented and well connected with other concepts" (Carnegie Learning, 2014)b. Deep learning is achieved through use of real-world situations, manipulatives, graphs, diagrams and other techniques that help students to see the connections between different concepts and/or topics.

**Dual Coding Theory:** A theory of learning from image and text argued that there are two separate, but interconnected knowledge systems: verbal system and a visual imagery system.

**Flipped Classroom:** "A model of learning that rearranges how time is spending both in and out of class to shift the ownership of learning from the educators to the students. After class, students manage the content they use, the pace and style of learning, and the ways in which they demonstrate their knowledge, and the teacher becomes the guide, adapting instructional approaches to suit their learning needs and supporting their personal learning journeys. Rather than the teacher using class time to lecture to students and disperse information, that work is done by each student after class, and could take the form of watching video lectures, listening to podcasts, perusing enhancing e-book content, collaborating with their peers in online communities, and more. Students can access the wide variety of resources any time they need them. <...>. The flipped classroom model is part of a larger pedagogical movement that overlaps with blended learning; inquiry-based learning and other instructional approaches and tools that are meant to be flexible, active, and more engaging for students. It has the potential to better enable educators to design unique and quality learning opportunities, curriculum, and assessment that are more personal and relevant to students' lives" (HMC, 2014, p. 6).

**Formative Assessment:** A reflective process that promotes student learning.

**Gamification:** The integration of gaming elements, mechanics, and frameworks into non-game situations and scenarios.

**Learning Analytics:** A collection of tools used to process and analyse data stream, and to apply it to modify learning goals and strategies in real time.

**Safe Learning Environment:** "Learning environment where students feel empowered to take risks. They see both success and failure as an opportunity to learn, rather than a judgment of their inherent ability" (Carnegie Learning, 2014, p. 6)b.

**Student-Centered, Collaborative Classroom:** A classroom in which teachers facilitate learning and coach students to master math concepts and procedures, with little time spend on lectures, but "leading students in completing task-based lessons and fostering discourse where students share solutions to problems and explain their mathematical reasoning" (Carnegie Learning, 2014, p. 6)b.

**Threshold Concepts (TCs):** Concepts with the following characteristics (or attributes): a) transformative: once understood, they lead to a significant shift appears in the student's perception of the subject; b) integrative: they integrate different aspects of the subject; c) irreversible: once understood, they are difficult to unlearn; d) bounded: they delineate a particular conceptual space, and finally and e) troublesome: they are a hard to learn or grasp for the learner (Meyer and Land, 2003).

# Chapter 12
# Plagiarism, Licensing, and the Proper Use of Digital Textbooks

## ABSTRACT

*This chapter explores ways to avoid plagiarism in digital textbooks' use and development. Traditionally, the plagiarism recommendation refers to books and articles. How about textbooks? However, to avoid plagiarism it is important to make sure that licensing in digital textbooks' use and development is properly used. For licensing to be a benefit for learning, it is important to note that it may impose additional costs. This chapter reflects and includes in discussion the issue on licensing, specifically the Creative Common (CC) license of open educational resources. Secondly, it considers how the Creative Common License could improve the proper use of digital textbooks. Finally, it explores how the use of digital tools can allow students to learn more effectively.*

## INTRODUCTION

Plagiarism refers to the acts of "turning in someone else's work as your own; copying words or ideas from someone else without giving credit; failing to put a quotation in quotation marks; giving incorrect information about the source of a quotation; changing words but copying the sentence structure of a source without giving credit; copying so many words or ideas from a source that it makes up the majority of your work, whether you give credit or not" (Plagiarism.org, 2014). Oxford University defines plagiarism as "to copying or paraphrasing of other people's work or ideas without full acknowledgement" (Oxford University, 2014).

There are many types of plagiarism. On WriteCheck blog can be read that The University of Pittsburgh's undergraduate plagiarism policy (University of Pittsburgh, 2008) lists examples of plagiarism. The following are a few examples of the many manifestation of plagiarism, cited at University of Pittsburgh actual site with reference to *Gaunt, Troubadours and Irony*, Cambridge: Cambridge University Press (1989, p. 23):

- Copying the text verbatim without enclosing it is quotation marks and acknowledging the source;
- Rearranging the elements of the source text without proper acknowledgment;

DOI: 10.4018/978-1-4666-8300-6.ch012

- Selective copying elements of the source text without proper acknowledgment;
- Paraphrasing without proper acknowledgment;
- Reproducing information that is neither self-evident nor common knowledge without providing proper acknowledgment;
- Incorporating an idea brought up in conversation into your work without proper acknowledgment;
- Using in your own work ideas or material from another student's work on a similar or identical subject without proper acknowledgment;
- Asking or paying someone more proficient that yourself to vet your work without acknowledging that individual's contribution;
- Using on-line translators or interpreters, or translating or interpreting software in completing your work without proper acknowledgment;
- Asking or paying someone to produce or to complete a piece of work, or purchasing a paper from a Web-based essay service constitutes plagiarism, as does taking Web-based material in one language and translating, or having it translated, into another without proper acknowledgment.

In Harvard Guide to Using Resource (2014) can be read that it is not enough to know why plagiarism is taken so seriously in the academic world or to know how to recognize it. More important is to know how to avoid it. The best way to solve this issue is 1) to understand what it happiness when is written a paper and 2) to do follow a method that is systematic and careful. There are some guidelines:

- Keep track of your sources; print electronic sources;
- Keep sources in correct context;

- Plan ahead: budget enough time to search for sources, to take notes and to think about how to use the sources in essay;
- Don't cut and paste: file and label your sources: open a separate file on computer for each source; include the full citation for the print source or the full URL; back up to files;
- Keep your own writing and your sources separate;
- Keep your notes and your draft separate at all stages of writing process;
- Paraphrase carefully in your notes; acknowledge your sources explicitly when paraphrasing;
- Avoid reading a classmate's paper for inspiration;
- Don't save your citation for later;
- Quote your source properly: always use quotation marks for directly quoted material;
- Keep a source trail in notes and in each successive draft of essay;

This chapter is interested in exploring the key aspects of plagiarism and the ways to avoid it. This chapter will focus, therefore, on the role that licensing choice can play in terms of proper use of digital textbooks. For the purpose of this paper, it was used the term "open textbook" to mean an openly-licensed textbook offered online by its author(s) or through a non-profit or commercial open-licensed publisher. The open license sets up open textbooks apart from traditional textbooks by allowing students to read online, download, or sometimes print the book at no additional costs. Some models allow users the choice to use free online access or low-cost alternative formats such as print, audio, or e-book. Usually the open textbooks are faculty-written and peer reviewed just like printed textbooks.

## BACKGROUND

The concept of plagiarism is a relative new area of psychopedagogical research. Not ling ago, Cheung (2014) wrote: "academic writing is an important part of undergraduate study that tutors recognise as central to success in higher education. Across the academy, writing is used to access, develop and facilitate student learning. However, there are growing concerns that students appropriate written work from other sources and present it as their own, committing the academic offence of plagiarism. <…>. Recently, educators have suggested that deterring and detecting plagiarism is ineffective and described moralistic conceptualisations of plagiarism as unhelpful. These commentaries highlight the need for credible alternative approaches to plagiarism that include pedagogic aspects of academic writing. The authorial identity approach to reducing plagiarism concentrates on developing understanding of authorship in students using pedagogy". The author proposed to expand psychological knowledge concerning authorial identity in higher educational contexts and developed a new model. It was emphasized that differing from previous models by including social aspects of authorial identity, the psiho-social model informs future pedagogy development and research by outlining a robust, empirically supported theoretical framework.

One of the way to avoid plagiarism is licencing. According to Wikipedia the verb "license" or "grant license" means to give permission. A shorthand definition of a license is "an authorization (by the licensor)" to use the licensed material (by the licensee)". Any licence is granted under intellectual property laws to authorize a use. There are two types of licence: a) an open source license and b) a proprietary license. Previous research was shown (Rosen, 2004, pp. 51-71) that an open source license is the way a copyright and pattern owner grants permission to other to use his intellectual property in such a way that software freedom is protected for all. A proprietary license is the way a copyright or pattern owner grant permission to other to use his intellectual property in a restricted way, through secrecy or other limitations, so that software freedom is not protected. The open source license may be:

- **Academic Licenses:** Which are originally created by academic institutions to distribute their software to the public, allow the software to be used for any purpose whatsoever with no obligation on the part of the license to distribute the source code or derivative works;
- **Reciprocal Licenses:** Which allow software to be used for any purpose whatsoever, but they require the distributions of derivative works to distribute those works under the same license, including the requirement that the source code of those derivative works to be published;
- **Standard Licenses:** Which are designed primarily for ensuring that industry standard software and documentation be available to all for implementation of standard products;
- **Content Licenses:** Which ensure that copyrightable subject matter other than software, such as music, art, film, literacy works, and the like, be available to all for any purpose whatsoever. These licenses are used more appropriative with the Creative Common License.

Creative Common (CC) license is a free, easy-to-use copyright licenses that provide a simple, standardized way to give the public permission to share and use the creative work and allow to change the copyright terms from the default of "all rights reserved" to "some rights reserved". These licenses work alongside copyright and enable to modify the copyright terms to best suit the needs of the licenser. CC dives the flexibility and protect the people who want the right to share, freely and legally use the content without worry about the copyright infringement.

Based on these categories and for the purpose of this chapter, plagiarism in digital textbook use and development is defined as

## THE COMBINATION OF PLAGIARISM, COPYRIGHT AND LICENSING

### Issues and Controversies

Plagiarism is a complex issue in digital textbook use and development. In order to avoid this, there are many recommendations. One of them refers to licensing. Digital textbooks could be granted under all categories of licensing. However, textbooks have two distinct components, namely the *intellectual content* and its *physical embodiment*. These two components are bundled. Sold in a bundle, the publishers have no way to earn recurring revenue for its intellectual content except in the first year of the editorial cycle. As a result, it became difficult to justify new editions in a mature subject while the old editions are still perfectly usable. The price of the new textbooks is very high. But, if the intellectual content is licensing annually and separately from the physical embodiment of the textbooks, the books could be priced much lower. The online textbooks have no comparable physical embodiment. Learners pay for a semester-long password to online access. Thus, in case when the intellectual content isn't licensed collectively, students may end up paying more for online access than hard copies.

The other not less important issue is the *paraphrasing*. Using textbooks' authors paraphrase the content, by not indicate the sources at the end. As was noted on the site of School of Education of Indiana University Bloomington (2014), paraphrasing plagiarism is committed when a writer summarizes an idea taken from another source

and fails both to cite the author(s) and to provide the corresponding reference. Let us analyse this concept on the base on Free Digital Textbooks, produced by OpenStax College (2014). The user can download the full version of textbook, for free. Thus, for example, the textbook "Precalculus", written by led author Jay Abramson. It is emphasis that "Precalculus" is protected by Creative Commons Attribution 3.0 Unported License. This license allow users free *to share* (copy and transferring the material in any medium or format) and *to adapt* (remix, transform, and buid upon the material for any purpose, even commercially).

The other issue is that plagiarism includes media, ideas and idea. Technologies have changing rapidly through last 50 years, especially the ways that students discover, use and source content for writing. As was noted by AbuAli (2014, p. 1), the web evolution has made plagiarism easier to commit and originally more difficult to define. In higher education many students' acts could be considered dishonest. Dishonest practicing could include copying from previous assignments of from books, inappropriate collaboration on assignments, inappropriate reference, cheating and lying. However, from students' point of view there are some ambiguities of what plagiarism is and what is not. One of the example might include peer collaboration and knowing to what extent the collaboration.

One, not less issue is *collusion*. According to definition, provided by Brunel University London, collusion is a form of plagiarism where students work together with the intention to deceive a third party. On the University of Melbourne (2014) site collusion is noted: "Collusion is the presentation by a student of an assignment as his or her own which is in fact the result in whole or in part of unauthorized collaboration with another person or persons. Collusion involves the cooperation of two or more students in plagiarism or other forms of academic misconduct. Both the student presenting the assignment and the student(s) willingly supplying unauthorized material (colluders) are considered participants in the act of academic misconduct". Collusion may appear when students work together. Plagiarism and collusion in group work can occur when one or more students:

- Copies (or allows to be copied) from other members of a group while working in the group;
- Copies the original work, in whole or in part, of an individual who is not a member of the group, with or without the knowledge of other members of the group, and contributes the plagiarized work to a group assignment;
- Contributes less, little, or nothing to a group assignment and then claims an equal share of the work or marks;
- Discusses with other members of the group how to approach a common assessment item that requires individual submissions and relies on the same or very similar approach in the submitted assessment, without any acknowledgement of collaboration with colleagues and without the permission of the assessor.

Thus, for example, if the students work together on digital content the idea of one may become common for all group. The plagiarism is a serious problem. There are many intentions to solve this problem. One of this is copywriting. However, as is written on site of University of Melbourne (2014), copyright does not protect ideas or information, only how they are expressed in material form such as a book, journal article, image, film or sound recording. The copyright material is permitted under copyright. Copyright law requires to acknowledge any material that is used. Within the copyright context, many different *licenses* are used for a variety of purpose and/or circumstances. Different types of licenses include:

- **Statutory Licenses (for Educational Purposes):** The author of textbook can use

resources of the University Library to copy and communicate copyright material for educational purposes;

- **Licensed Databases:** The author of textbook can use University Library subscribes databases, underpinned by a license or a contract between the University and the database provider;
- **Terms and Conditions of Use:** The author of textbook should adhere to terms and conditions in using data, information or knowledge from websites, CDs, DVDs, podcasts, etc.;
- **Creative Commons:** The author of textbook allow other author/teacher/student to use the content without having to seek permissions. There are six Creative Common (CC) License. On Creative Commons Australia can be read that each of the CC licences grants certain baseline permissions to users in advance, authorizing them to use the material, provided they comply with core conditions, as well as other general terms in the licence. The core conditions are: Attribution Condition (the original creator or any other part of nominated parties must be creadited); NonCommercial (allow others to copy, distribute, display and perform the work for noncommercial purposes only); No Derivates (allow others to distribute, display and perform only verbatim copies of the work) and Share Alike (allow others to remix, adapt, and buid on the work, but only if they distribute the derivative works under the same the licence terms than govern the original work).

There are many versions of CC. The last version: Attribution-NoDerivates 4.0 International (CC BY-ND 4.0) allow users to copy and redistribute the material in any medium or format for any purpose, even commercially. In addition, the user of CC material must give the appropriate credit, provide a link to license, and indicate if changes were made. In case if the material is re-mixed, transformed, or build upon, the user may not distribute the modified material.

## INTENTIONAL AND UNINTENTIONAL PLAGIARISM

Plagiarism may be *intentional* and *unintentional*. According to Taylor (2014) intentional plagiarism refers to purposeful passing off of someone else's ideas or words as your own. Some examples of intentional plagiarism include: a) buying a pre-written research paper online; b) using a stock essay (e.g. from a fraternity or sports team paper archive); c) only changing a few words or phrases from the original source without proper citation; d) rearranging sentences and word order from the original source without proper citation and e) not giving credit (i.e. citations) to someone else's ideas. Firestone (2014) evidences that unintentional plagiarism happens when students borrow words and ideas and cite them incorrectly. There are many examples of unintentional plagiarism:

- Parts of quotes
- Long quotes without quotation marks
- Paraphrasing problems.

More specially, intentional plagiarism is produced by the author's activity when he/she know they are passing off something else work (text, media, or idea) as their own. Unintentional plagiarism is produced when the author use the work of others, but don't make reference. Both types of plagiarism can inform the readers of textbooks about some errors, but can also reduce the motivation to learn. For instance, when a teacher initiate a conversation about topic related in textbook, the students' interest is low, arguing that he/she doesn't understand the subject matter, provided in this textbook.

Some examples of intentional and unintentional plagiarism is provided by Baylor School (Table 1).

## CYBER PLAGIARISM

Cyber Plagiarism occurs when is used internet technology to locate, copy, and submit the work

*Table 1. Differences between intentional and unintentional plagiarism on the base on Baylor School examples*

| | Intentional Plagiarism | Unintentional Plagiarism |
|---|---|---|
| 1 | Passing off as one's own pre-written papers from the Internet or other sources. | Paraphrasing poorly: changing a few words without changing the sentence structure of the original, or changing the sentence structure but not the words. |
| 2 | Copying an essay or article from the Internet, on-line source, or electronic database without quoting or giving credit | Paraphrasing poorly: using words from the original that aren't part of one's vocabulary. |
| 3 | Cutting and pasting from more than one source to create a paper without quoting or giving credit. | Quoting Poorly: putting quotation marks around part of a quotation but not around all of it, or putting quotation marks around a passage that is partly paraphrased and partly quoted. |
| 4 | Allowing someone else to write the paper or do the work. | Citing Poorly: omitting an occasional citation or citing inaccurately. |
| 5 | Borrowing words or ideas from other students or sources without giving credit. | |
| 6 | Failing to put quotation marks around the words of others | |
| 7 | Fabricating a quotation or a source. | |
| 8 | Pretending that an instant translation is one's own work. | |

of another without citing the source of information. For example, Search Engines is used for finding information and placing directly in file or to download documents and to share via email, Skype etc.

Chen and Chou (2014) note that attitudes toward plagiarism may have been changed in the digital age today. In theirs studies conducted in Taiwan, aims to investigate students' perceptions of cyber-plagiarism, and were found that a) the easy of copy-paste of online resources may mainly increase students' plagiarism especially when they are under pressure of coursework; b) the college students' grade levels, gender, and disciplines are important factors influencing their perceptions of cyber-plagiarism and that c) teachers and researchers should pay attention to understand students' misinterpretation about plagiarism in order to prevent his academic misconduct.

One of the important issue of Cyber Plagiarism is *contract creating*. "Contract cheating is the process whereby students auction off the opportunity for others to complete assignments for them. It is an apparently widespread yet under-researched problem. One suggested strategy to prevent contract cheating is to shorten the turnaround time between the release of assignment details and the submission date, thus making it difficult for students to make arrangements with contractors" (Wallace & Newton, 2014, p. 233). Creating can occur at different levels. One of them is e-cheating: "used to refer to the type of academic dishonesty that utilizes some type of technology to electronically copy or use material from an unauthorized source or a source that was not cited. This can include a simple copy and paste from the Internet or some other type of electronic media" (Bain, 2014, p. 2 with reference to Jones, Reid & Bartlett, 2008) and "may also be called digital cheating and can be as broad as meaning any type of cheating using computer technology" (Bain, 2014, p. 2 with reference to Rogers, 2006).

There are many types of e-cheating, evidenced by Bain (2014, pp. 3-5). Thus,

- **E-Cheating (Inside):** Refers to use of electronic devices inside of the classroom to access unauthorized information from Internet, such as course management systems, e-mails, e-texts, electronic documents/files, text messaging, cameras, MP3 players, wireless earphones and microphones etc.;
- **E-Cheating (Outside):** Refers to use of electronic devices and many options available on-line outside of the classroom. In summary, the outside e-cheating may occurs when users copy information from the Internet or electronic media; purchase papers/documents solution/instructor manuals or tests banks from the Internet or by email; use of cheating web sites; use of Amazon's Search inside the Book; and use of Social Media to share information.

E-Cheating is a form of Cyber Plagiarism. From a psychopedagogical perspective of the digital textbook use and development, there are two levels of Cyber Plagiarism. First, Cyber Plagiarism can be focused on cutting and pasting of information from Internet, and then placing it without acknowledgement into the new work. At this level, Cyber Plagiarism includes may include paraphrasing, self-plagiarism or other traditional forms of plagiarism. Second, Cyber Plagiarism can be focused at downloading and processing of completed textbooks/courses from Smithsonian Education, Hippocampus.org, Khan Academy, Curriki or MOOC. Thus, Cyber Plagiarism is more used then other forms.

Hammond (2002) notes: "this practice is simple to do, for anyone with a basic knowledge of IT (the author has successfully tried it), and can be highly effective, if the student then links different parts together, using link sentences of their own devising. Unlike essay banks, pieces can be fitted together, to answer any relevant essay question. There is it is argued nothing wrong with using internet sits, if they are properly referenced, but often the student simply uses large chunks of web text, linked together with link sentences deliberately, as opposed to simply negligently, through poor referencing". One example of sign signs may be the students' colaborative project in developing an open digital textbook. It is clear that all students participate in project' activities planned by a teacher. But, this activities may include digital images, video or audio files that are not properly used. In such situations is more important to take own pictures. The criteria for analyses the project is not the final activity, but the processes of (meta) cognitive activities.

## DOI SYSTEM, ISBN, AND BARCODE

ISBN (an International Standard Book Number) has been used in textbook industry since 1970. Actually this a global standard to identifying titles. ISBN is used in more than 200 countries for different publishing solutions like Self-Publisher Solution, eBook Creator Solution and Cover Design Solution. There are multiple benefits of assigning and using ISBN to digital textbook. One of them, known as Direct Textbook app, is able to check prices of a new or used versions of digital textbook, if users enter the ISBN number on the free app, which is available for free download on the App Store and Google Play Store, respectively. As was wrote by DBW (2014), this app turns smartphone, tablets and other mobile devices into textbook barcode scanner; users can either scan the barcode of the textbook they need or manually enter its ISBN number into the app. The user can instantly compare digital textbook prices from hundreds of online stores.

However, according to Wikipedia ISBN issuance is country-specific, in that ISBNs are issued by the ISBN registration agency that is responsible for that country or territory regardless of the publication language. The ranges of ISBNs assigned to any particular country are based on the publishing profile of the country concerned, and so the ranges will vary depending on the number of books and the number, type, and size of publishers that are active. Research has highlighted that ISBN "is a 13-digit identification number and system, widely used in the international book trade for over 35 years and assigned through a network of international ISBN Registration Agencies. ISBNs are used to identify each unique publication whether in the form of a physical book or related materials such as eBooks, software, mixed media etc.

The DOI® System offers a persistent actionable identifier for use on digital networks. A "DOI name" refers to the syntax string within the "DOI System". The ISBN-A ("the actionable ISBN") is a service powered by DOI®, in which an existing ISBN is expressed in the DOI System." (Factsheet, 2012). Thus, for digital textbooks ISBN can be used to help users to find a textbook in bookstore, even the users are placed in different geographical areas. Usually, textbook ISBN numbers are provided as a convenience. For example, the teacher of mathematics can offer for Trigonometry (author McKeague & Turner ~ Publisher: Cengage) the following ISBN numbers:

- ISBN: 978-1-111-82685-7 (textbook only)
- ISBN: 978-1-133-53742-7 (discounted textbook with Enhanced WebAssign)
- ISBN: 978-0-538-73810-1 (eBook with Enhanced WebAssign)

The Book Industry Study Group (BISC, 2011, pp.4-5) notes that digital book as a combination of title, publisher, content, edition, file format, device applicability and usage rights. The identifier for a Book in a supply chain, physical or digital, is an ISBN. An ISBN (International Standard Book Number – ISO 2108:2005) is the identifier used for a Book, physical or digital, and other Book-like products (audio book, for example). An ISBN identifies the registrant as well as the specific title, edition and format of the Book. It is mainly used within the supply chain for ordering, listing, sales tracking and stock control purposes. The general rules for ISBN assignments are:

- **ISBNs Are Assigned:** Not created. One ISBN registration agency per country, or community, is designated by the International ISBN Agency to assign and distribute ISBNs to the publishers and self-publishers located in that area. Any number identified as an ISBN must be a valid ISBN obtained from an officially sanctioned ISBN registration agency such as R.R. Bowker, the United States ISBN Agency, or Library and Archives Canada, the Canadian ISBN Agency. At no time should a random or unsanctioned number be created and identified as an ISBN by any member of the supply chain.
- **ISBNs for Digital Books:** Should be labeled "ISBN", not "eISBN." There is no such standard as an "eISBN", nor is this the proper way to differentiate Digital Book formats.
- **Digital Books Should Never Be Identified with a Number That Is in the Same Format as an ISBN or Labeled "ISBN":** Unless that number is a legitimate ISBN issued by an official ISBN registration agency, such as R.R. Bowker in the US.
- *Digital Books should not be assigned the same ISBN as any Physical Book.*
- Digital Books of the same title but different file format (i.e., EPUB, PDF, etc.) and/or different usage rights should not be assigned or display the same ISBN:
- Identical Digital Books (i.e. an EPUB being sold on various vendor sites) should not carry different ISBNs. There must be a differentiating factor (or factors) in the Digital Book's content, file format, usage rights or metadata to justify the assignment of a unique ISBN.

It is said that "Publishers should always assign a unique ISBN to the separate Digital Books that they release into the supply chain in order to maintain a link by which metadata and sales information can be communicated back and forth provides the following guidelines for digital products" (BISC, 2011, p. 5). The Best Practice of assigning ISBN is seems to be the following:

- **Content:** If two digital books are created, one an exact textual reproduction of a Physical Book and the other an enhanced version that includes video, audio, etc., then the two Digital Books are unique and different products, and each requires a unique ISBN.
- **Format:** If an EPUB format, a PDF format and a Mobi format (among others) are created, each format should be assigned a unique ISBN. This is similar to creating a hardcover and paperback edition of a Physical Book and should follow the same rules regarding ISBN assignment.
- **Usage Rights:** If a Digital Book is made available with different usage rights in different markets (e.g. adjusting the usage settings so that printing is allowed in the version going to the education market, but not in the version going to the retail market), each version should be assigned a unique ISBN.

It is not surprising that BISC (2011, pp.7-8) guidelines have also taken advantage of ISBN users benefits when developing digital textbooks. Thus, it is assured that in case of Digital Books, the publisher determines the entity that will assign the ISBN by following one of two parts:

- If a publisher want to track ordering, listing and sales at a granular level, it is expected that the publishes *will assign a unique ISBN to each separate Digital Book* that will eventually be made available to the Consumer, regardless of whether the publisher or a trading partner is creating the final Digital Book(s);

- If a publisher wants to track ordering, listing, delivery and sales at a macro level, it is expected that the publisher *will assign a unique ISBN only to each unique Digital Book that the publisher specifically makes available to the supply chain.* The publisher must then rely on trading partners to appropriately assign and report additional unique ISBNs as needed, in conformance with this Policy Statement.

But, how to identify the adaptive, dynamic or generated digital content from clouds?

On the other hand, traditionally a textbook has a separate *barcode* on a back cover. According to a definition the barcode is an optical machine-readable code in the form of numbers and a pattern of parallel lines of varying widths, printed on a commodity and used especially for stock control. DBW (2014) wrote about the innovation (Direct Textbook barcode scanner), a mobile app which allows users to browse textbooks in a physical store and find the best price online. This practice, known also as "showrooming" is promoted by different companies that sell digital textbooks.

## FUTURE RESEARCH DIRECTIONS

This chapter outlines what is plagiarism and how to avoid it by commercial and free licensing and SBN and how to proper use of digital textbook, previously scanning the barcode with Direct Textbook app. Based on these ideas, it is clear that there are many implications for future investigations in regard to proper use of digital textbooks. One particularly intriguing area is that of using video. Wogahn (2012) wrote about that

publishing using amazon Kindle direct Publishing (KDP) or Barnes & Noble Pubit (Nook) doesn't require to assign an ISBN. In the future research was shown that "with an ever increasing interest in using multimedia elements - audio, video, animation - to enhance text and image eBooks, using the same number for different products will confuse shoppers" (Wogahn, 2013).

While digital textbook use and development can involve the use of standardized instruments, as well as ISBN numbers and barcodes, they can be seen as far removed from the trends around the use or lack of use of ISBN to identify different versions of the same textbook, written by the same author(s), but in one case using PDF version and in another the same content with interactive simulations or animations. The facts that teachers can add interactivity at own developed textbook; "assemble" digital textbooks from different contents or develop open textbooks in collaboration with students, but without to assign the ISBN number create confusion. Future research is needed how to licence digital textbooks with same content, saved in different formats. Solving this problem has the potential of upsetting digital users and ultimately creating new problems for the digital publishing industry as a whole.

Emphasis on deep internal mental processes such as thinking, memory, language, problem solving, decision making, creativity imply teacher(s) to find and explore alternative solutions to more actively engage students in learning. One of this way is interactive simulations. However, the possibilities of creating interactive simulations or capturing video, for example, with Camtasia, and inserting in licensed content been used to feel the needs for multiliteracies need to be future explored.

On the other hand, emphasis on humanistic view in psychology requires to develop collaborative projects in development of personalised digital textbooks.

## CONCLUSION

Technology provides many benefits to education and especially to learning, by providing easy access to lesson plans and digital content, including e-textbooks. However, together with this access comes the Cyber Plagiarism as improperly ways of using digital textbooks and shallow learning. Thus, "e-cheating is using this technology to commit academic dishonesty by cheating or plagiarism, regardless of when or where is happening. For traditional college courses, technology can be used in the classroom to provide students access to unauthorized resources and information. Technology can also be used outside the classroom to find answers to assessments, text for papers, and completely writing papers. The most common types of e-cheating inside the classroom focus primarily on using electronic devices to access and/or receive unauthorized information during exams" (Bain, 2014, p. 8).

There are many ways to detect plagiarism. One of them is to use technology to detect the academic work for originality. At is defined on the site of the Athabasca University plagiarism detection technology (PDT) is a product or service authorized at AU for the purpose of reviewing student work for originality. Some of these software are free to use. Usually, the plagiarism checker compare the submitted text to other documents stored in database. Top 10 free plagiarism detection tools for teachers are: Anti-Plagiarism, DupliChecker, PaperRater, Plagiarisma.net, PlagiarismChecker, Plagium, PlagTracker, Viper, SeeSources and Plagiarism Detector. The other way is to improve writing. Thus, for example Paper Rater offers two intersting tools: Grammar Checking, and Writing Suggestions focused on checking works for grammar and on providing suggestions about how to improve writing. But, for effectiveness of these ways the students should have developed own metacognitive strategies.

## REFERENCES

Bain, L. Z. (2014). How students use technology to cheat and what faculty can do about it. In *Proceedings of the Information Systems Educators Conference*, *31*(3020), pp. 1-8. Retrieved November 2, 2014 from http://proc.isecon.org/2014/pdf/3020.pdf

*Baylor School*. (2014). Retrieved November 21, 2014 from http://mail.baylorschool.org/~jstover/plagiarism/intent.htm

BISC. (2011). *BISG Policy Statement POL-1101. Best practices for identifying digital products*. Retrieved November 2, 2014 from https://www.myidentifiers.com/sites/default/files/images/BEST+PRACTICES+FOR+IDENTIFYING+DIGITAL+PRODUCTS.pdf

*Bowker. Identifier Services*. (2014). Retrieved November 21, 2014 from https://www.myidentifiers.com/Get-your-isbn-now

Chen, Y., & Chou, C. (2014). Why and who agree on copy-and-paste? Taiwan College Students' perceptions of cyber-plagiarism. In *World Conference on Educational Multimedia, Hypermedia and Telecommunications*, *1*, (pp. 937-943). Chesapeake, VA: AACE. Retrieved November 23, 2014 from http://www.editlib.org/p/147602

Cheung, K. Y. F. (2014). *Understanding the authorial writer: A mixed methods approach to the psychology of authorial identity in relation to plagiarism*. Retrieved November 21, 2014 from http://derby.openrepository.com/derby/handle/10545/324822

Creative Commons. (n. d.). *Attribution-No Derivatives 4.0 International (CC BY-ND 4.0)*. Retrieved November 21, 2014 from http://creativecommons.org/licenses/by-nd/4.0/

*Curriki*. (2014). Retrieved November 2, 2014 from http://www.curriki.org/

DBW. (2014). *New textbook app wants students to scan barcodes in stores, then buy elsewhere.* Retrieved November 2, 2014 from http://www. digitalbookworld.com/2014/new-textbook-app-wants-students-to-scan-barcodes-in-stores-then-buy-elsewhere/

Factsheet (2012). *DOI® system and the ISBN system.* Retrieved November 2, 2014 from http:// www.doi.org/factsheets/ISBN-A.html

Firestone, M. *Unintentional plagiarism: definition, examples & quiz.* Educational Portal. Retrieved November 22, 2014 from http://education-portal. com/academy/lesson/unintentional-plagiarism-definition-examples-quiz.html#lesson

Hammond. (2002). *Cyber-plagiarism: Are FE students getting away with words?* Retrieved November 2, 2014 from http://www.leeds.ac.uk/ educol/documents/00002055.htm

*Hippocampus.org.* (2014). Retrieved September 2, 2014 from http://www.hippocampus.org/

ISBN. (2014). *International ISBN agency.* Retrieved November 2, 2014 from https://www. isbn-international.org/

*Khan Academy.* (2014). Retrieved November 2, 2014 from https://www.khanacademy.org/

Plagiarim.org. (2014). *Glossary.* Retrieved November 21, 2014 from http://www.plagiarism. org/plagiarism-101/glossary

Plagiarism. (2014). *Cyber plagiarism. Plagiarism and the 21st Century Learner.* Retrieved November 21, 2014 http://plagiarism.wiki.westga.edu/ Cyber+Plagiarism

Plagiarism.org. (2014). *What is plagiarism?* Retrieved November 21, 2014 from http://www.pla-giarism.org/plagiarism-101/what-is-plagiarism/

*Smithsonian Education.* (2014). Retrieved September 2, 2014 from http://www.smithsonian-education.org/educators/

Taylor, V. (2014). *Intentional plagiarism: Definition, examples & quiz.* Educational Portal. Retrieved November 21, 2014 from http://edu-cation-portal.com/academy/lesson/intentional-plagiarism-definition-examples-quiz.html#lesson

University of Melbourne. (2014). *Academic honesty and plagiarism.* Retrieved November 21, 2014 from https://academichonesty.unimelb.edu. au/plagiarism.html

University of Pittsburgh. (2014). *Plagiarism policy.* Retrieved November 21, 2014 from http:// www.frenchanditalian.pitt.edu/undergrad/about/ plagiarism.php

Wallace, M. J., & Newton, P. M. (2014). Turn-around time and market capacity in contract cheating. *Educational Studies*, *40*(2), 233–236. doi:10.1080/03055698.2014.889597

Wogahn, D. (2012). *ISBN essentials: An FAQ for eBook publishers.* SellBox. Retrieved November 2, 2014 from http://www.sellbox.com/isbn-essentials-an-faq-for-ebook-publishers/

Wogahn, D. (2013). T*he myth of the eISBN: Why every eBook edition needs a unique number.* Retrieved November 2, 2014 from http://www. sellbox.com/myth-eisbn-every-ebook-edition-needs-unique-number/

WriteCheck. (2014). *Types of plagiarism.* Retrieved November 21, 2014 from http:// en.writecheck.com/types-of-plagiarism

## ADDITIONAL READING

Bosse, C. (2014). *Copyright & plagiarism.* Retrieved October 1, 2014 from http://fgs.athabascau.ca/ docs/Copyright_Plagiarism_2014Presentation_ Corrine.pdf/

E-Learning Industry. (2013). *Top 10 free plagiarism detection tools for teachers*. Retrieved October 1, 2014 from http://elearningindustry.com/top-10-free-plagiarism-detection-tools-for-teachers

Fryer, W. A. (2014). Strategies to address digital plagiarism. *Publications Archive of Wesley Fryer, 1*(1). Retrieved October 1, 2014 from http://www.wtvi.com/teks/04_05_articles/digital_plagiarism.html

Kier, C. A. (2014). How well do Canadian distance education students understand plagiarism? *International Review of Research in Open and Distance Learning*, *15*(1). http://www.irrodl.org/index.php/irrodl/article/view/1684/2767 Retrieved October 1, 2014

Stielow, F. (2014). *Proactive digital transformation and a virtual academic library*. The APUS Campus Guides Project. Retrieved September 1, 2014 from http://library.ifla.org/877/1/208-stielow-en.pdf

## KEY TERMS AND DEFINITIONS

**Copyright:** "A law protecting the intellectual property of individuals, giving them exclusive rights over the distribution and reproduction of that material" (Plagiarism.org, 2014).

**Intellectual Property:** "A product of the intellect, such as an expressed idea or concept that has commercial value" (Plagiarism.org, 2014).

**Paraphrase:** "A restatement of a text or passage in other words" (Plagiarism.org, 2014).

**Plagiarism:** "The reproduction or appropriation of someone else's work without proper attribution; passing off as one's own the work of someone else" (Plagiarism.org, 2014).

**Self-Plagiarism:** "Copying material you have previously produced and passing it off as a new production" (Plagiarism.org, 2014).

# Related References

To continue our tradition of advancing academic research, we have compiled a list of recommended IGI Global readings. These references will provide additional information and guidance to further enrich your knowledge and assist you with your own research and future publications.

Abdelaziz, H. A. (2013). From content engagement to cognitive engagement: Toward an immersive web-based learning model to develop self-questioning and self-study skills. *International Journal of Technology Diffusion*, 4(1), 16–32. doi:10.4018/jtd.2013010102

Acha, V., Hargiss, K. M., & Howard, C. (2013). The relationship between emotional intelligence of a leader and employee motivation to job performance. *International Journal of Strategic Information Technology and Applications*, 4(4), 80–103. doi:10.4018/ijsita.2013100105

Agrawal, P. R. (2014). Digital information management: preserving tomorrow's memory. In S. Dhamdhere (Ed.), *Cloud computing and virtualization technologies in libraries* (pp. 22–35). Hershey, PA: Information Science Reference. doi:10.4018/978-1-4666-4631-5.ch002

Akram, H. A., & Mahmood, A. (2014). Predicting personality traits, gender and psychopath behavior of Twitter users. *International Journal of Technology Diffusion*, 5(2), 1–14. doi:10.4018/ijtd.2014040101

Akyol, Z. (2013). Metacognitive development within the community of inquiry. In Z. Akyol & D. Garrison (Eds.), *Educational communities of inquiry: Theoretical framework, research and practice* (pp. 30–44). Hershey, PA: Information Science Reference. doi:10.4018/978-1-4666-2110-7.ch003

Albers, M. J. (2012). How people read. In *Human-information interaction and technical communication: Concepts and frameworks* (pp. 367–397). Hershey, PA: Information Science Reference. doi:10.4018/978-1-4666-0152-9.ch011

Albers, M. J. (2012). What people bring with them. In *Human-information interaction and technical communication: Concepts and frameworks* (pp. 61–113). Hershey, PA: Information Science Reference. doi:10.4018/978-1-4666-0152-9.ch003

Ally, M. (2012). Designing mobile learning for the user. In B. Khan (Ed.), *User interface design for virtual environments: Challenges and advances* (pp. 226–235). Hershey, PA: Information Science Reference. doi:10.4018/978-1-61350-516-8.ch014

Almeida, L., Menezes, P., & Dias, J. (2013). Augmented reality framework for the socialization between elderly people. In M. Cruz-Cunha, I. Miranda, & P. Gonçalves (Eds.), *Handbook of research on ICTs for human-centered healthcare and social care services* (pp. 430–448). Hershey, PA: Medical Information Science Reference. doi:10.4018/978-1-4666-3986-7.ch023

Alonso, E., & Mondragón, E. (2011). Computational models of learning and beyond: Symmetries of associative learning. In E. Alonso & E. Mondragón (Eds.), *Computational neuroscience for advancing artificial intelligence: Models, methods and applications* (pp. 316–332). Hershey, PA: Medical Information Science Reference. doi:10.4018/978-1-60960-021-1.ch013

Ancarani, A., & Di Mauro, C. (2013). The human side of supply chains: A behavioural perspective of supply chain risk management. In *Supply chain management: Concepts, methodologies, tools, and applications* (pp. 1453–1476). Hershey, PA: Business Science Reference. doi:10.4018/978-1-4666-2625-6.ch086

Andres, H. P. (2013). Collaborative technology and dimensions of team cognition: Test of a second-order factor model. *International Journal of Information Technology Project Management*, 4(3), 22–37. doi:10.4018/jitpm.2013070102

Arora, A. S., Raisinghani, M. S., Leseane, R., & Thompson, L. (2013). Personality scales and learning styles: Pedagogy for creating an adaptive web-based learning system. In M. Raisinghani (Ed.), *Curriculum, learning, and teaching advancements in online education* (pp. 161–182). Hershey, PA: Information Science Reference. doi:10.4018/978-1-4666-2949-3.ch012

Ashcraft, D., & Treadwell, T. (2010). The social psychology of online collaborative learning: The good, the bad, and the awkward. In Web-based education: concepts, methodologies, tools and applications (pp. 1146-1161). Hershey, PA: Information Science Reference. doi:10.4018/978-1-61520-963-7.ch078

Aston, J. (2013). Database narrative, spatial montage, and the cultural transmission of memory: An anthropological perspective. In D. Harrison (Ed.), *Digital media and technologies for virtual artistic spaces* (pp. 150–158). Hershey, PA: Information Science Reference. doi:10.4018/978-1-4666-2961-5.ch011

Asunka, S. (2013). Collaborative online learning in non-formal education settings in the developing world: A best practice framework. In V. Wang (Ed.), *Technological applications in adult and vocational education advancement* (pp. 186–201). Hershey, PA: Information Science Reference. doi:10.4018/978-1-4666-2062-9.ch015

Attia, M. (2014). The role of early learning experience in shaping teacher cognition and technology use. In P. Breen (Ed.), *Cases on teacher identity, diversity, and cognition in higher education* (pp. 1–21). Hershey, PA: Information Science Reference. doi:10.4018/978-1-4666-5990-2.ch001

Ávila, I., Menezes, E., & Braga, A. M. (2014). Strategy to support the memorization of iconic passwords. In K. Blashki & P. Isaias (Eds.), *Emerging research and trends in interactivity and the human-computer interface* (pp. 239–259). Hershey, PA: Information Science Reference. doi:10.4018/978-1-4666-4623-0.ch012

Bachvarova, Y., & Bocconi, S. (2014). Games and social networks. In T. Connolly, T. Hainey, E. Boyle, G. Baxter, & P. Moreno-Ger (Eds.), *Psychology, pedagogy, and assessment in serious games* (pp. 204–219). Hershey, PA: Information Science Reference. doi:10.4018/978-1-4666-4773-2.ch010

Bagley, C. A., & Creswell, W. H. (2013). The role of social media as a tool for learning. In E. McKay (Ed.), *ePedagogy in online learning: New developments in web mediated human computer interaction* (pp. 18–38). Hershey, PA: Information Science Reference. doi:10.4018/978-1-4666-3649-1.ch002

Balogh, Š. (2014). Forensic analysis, cryptosystem implementation, and cryptology: Methods and techniques for extracting encryption keys from volatile memory. In S. Sadkhan Al Maliky & N. Abbas (Eds.), *Multidisciplinary perspectives in cryptology and information security* (pp. 381–396). Hershey, PA: Information Science Reference. doi:10.4018/978-1-4666-5808-0.ch016

Banas, J. R., & Brown, C. A. (2012). Web 2.0 visualization tools to stimulate generative learning. In D. Polly, C. Mims, & K. Persichitte (Eds.), *Developing technology-rich teacher education programs: Key issues* (pp. 77–90). Hershey, PA: Information Science Reference. doi:10.4018/978-1-4666-0014-0.ch006

Bancroft, J., & Wang, Y. (2013). A computational simulation of the cognitive process of children knowledge acquisition and memory development. In Y. Wang (Ed.), *Cognitive informatics for revealing human cognition: Knowledge manipulations in natural intelligence* (pp. 111–127). Hershey, PA: Information Science Reference. doi:10.4018/978-1-4666-2476-4.ch008

Bartsch, R. A. (2011). Social psychology and instructional technology. In *Instructional design: Concepts, methodologies, tools and applications* (pp. 1237–1244). Hershey, PA: Information Science Reference. doi:10.4018/978-1-60960-503-2.ch508

Bertolotti, T. (2013). Facebook has it: The irresistible violence of social cognition in the age of social networking. In R. Luppicini (Ed.), *Moral, ethical, and social dilemmas in the age of technology: Theories and practice* (pp. 234–247). Hershey, PA: Information Science Reference. doi:10.4018/978-1-4666-2931-8.ch016

Berwick, R. C. (2013). Songs to syntax: Cognition, combinatorial computation, and the origin of language. In Y. Wang (Ed.), *Cognitive informatics for revealing human cognition: Knowledge manipulations in natural intelligence* (pp. 70–80). Hershey, PA: Information Science Reference. doi:10.4018/978-1-4666-2476-4.ch005

Best, C., O'Neill, B., & Gillespie, A. (2014). Assistive technology for cognition: An updated review. In G. Naik & Y. Guo (Eds.), *Emerging theory and practice in neuroprosthetics* (pp. 215–236). Hershey, PA: Medical Information Science Reference. doi:10.4018/978-1-4666-6094-6.ch011

Bhattacharya, A. (2014). Organisational justice perception: A work attitude modifier. In N. Ray & K. Chakraborty (Eds.), *Handbook of research on strategic business infrastructure development and contemporary issues in finance* (pp. 296–322). Hershey, PA: Business Science Reference. doi:10.4018/978-1-4666-5154-8.ch021

Biggiero, L. (2012). Practice vs. possession: Epistemological implications on the nature of organizational knowledge and cognition. In M. Mora, O. Gelman, A. Steenkamp, & M. Raisinghani (Eds.), *Research methodologies, innovations and philosophies in software systems engineering and information systems* (pp. 82–105). Hershey, PA: Information Science Reference. doi:10.4018/978-1-4666-0179-6.ch005

Bishop, J. (2014). The psychology of trolling and lurking: The role of defriending and gamification for increasing participation in online communities using seductive narratives. In J. Bishop (Ed.), *Gamification for human factors integration: Social, education, and psychological issues* (pp. 162–179). Hershey, PA: Information Science Reference. doi:10.4018/978-1-4666-5071-8.ch010

Blasko, D. G., Lum, H. C., White, M. M., & Drabik, H. B. (2014). Individual differences in the enjoyment and effectiveness of serious games. In T. Connolly, T. Hainey, E. Boyle, G. Baxter, & P. Moreno-Ger (Eds.), *Psychology, pedagogy, and assessment in serious games* (pp. 153–174). Hershey, PA: Information Science Reference. doi:10.4018/978-1-4666-4773-2.ch008

Borah, P. (2014). Interaction of incivility and news frames in the political blogosphere: Consequences and psychological mechanisms. In A. Solo (Ed.), *Handbook of research on political activism in the information age* (pp. 407–424). Hershey, PA: Information Science Reference. doi:10.4018/978-1-4666-6066-3.ch024

Borri, D., & Camarda, D. (2011). Spatial ontologies in multi-agent environmental planning. In J. Yearwood & A. Stranieri (Eds.), *Technologies for supporting reasoning communities and collaborative decision making: Cooperative approaches* (pp. 272–295). Hershey, PA: Information Science Reference. doi:10.4018/978-1-60960-091-4.ch015

Boukhobza, J. (2013). Flashing in the cloud: Shedding some light on NAND flash memory storage systems. In D. Kyriazis, A. Voulodimos, S. Gogouvitis, & T. Varvarigou (Eds.), *Data intensive storage services for cloud environments* (pp. 241–266). Hershey, PA: Business Science Reference. doi:10.4018/978-1-4666-3934-8.ch015

Boyle, E. (2014). Psychological aspects of serious games. In T. Connolly, T. Hainey, E. Boyle, G. Baxter, & P. Moreno-Ger (Eds.), *Psychology, pedagogy, and assessment in serious games* (pp. 1–18). Hershey, PA: Information Science Reference. doi:10.4018/978-1-4666-4773-2.ch001

Boyle, E., Terras, M. M., Ramsay, J., & Boyle, J. M. (2014). Executive functions in digital games. In T. Connolly, T. Hainey, E. Boyle, G. Baxter, & P. Moreno-Ger (Eds.), *Psychology, pedagogy, and assessment in serious games* (pp. 19–46). Hershey, PA: Information Science Reference. doi:10.4018/978-1-4666-4773-2.ch002

Breen, P. (2014). Philosophies, traditional pedagogy, and new technologies: A report on a case study of EAP teachers' integration of technology into traditional practice. In P. Breen (Ed.), *Cases on teacher identity, diversity, and cognition in higher education* (pp. 317–341). Hershey, PA: Information Science Reference. doi:10.4018/978-1-4666-5990-2.ch013

Buchanan, A. (2014). Protective factors in family relationships. In M. Merviö (Ed.), *Contemporary social issues in east Asian societies: Examining the spectrum of public and private spheres* (pp. 76–85). Hershey, PA: Information Science Reference. doi:10.4018/978-1-4666-5031-2.ch004

Burke, M. E., & Speed, C. (2014). Knowledge recovery: Applications of technology and memory. In M. Michael & K. Michael (Eds.), *Uberveillance and the social implications of microchip implants: Emerging technologies* (pp. 133–142). Hershey, PA: Information Science Reference. doi:10.4018/978-1-4666-4582-0.ch005

Burusic, J., & Karabegovic, M. (2014). The role of students' personality traits in the effective use of social networking sites in the educational context. In G. Mallia (Ed.), *The social classroom: Integrating social network use in education* (pp. 224–243). Hershey, PA: Information Science Reference. doi:10.4018/978-1-4666-4904-0.ch012

Caixinha, A., Magalhães, V., & Alexandre, I. M. (2013). Do you remember, or have you forgotten? In R. Martinho, R. Rijo, M. Cruz-Cunha, & J. Varajão (Eds.), *Information systems and technologies for enhancing health and social care* (pp. 136–146). Hershey, PA: Medical Information Science Reference. doi:10.4018/978-1-4666-3667-5.ch009

Carbonaro, N., Cipresso, P., Tognetti, A., Anania, G., De Rossi, D., Pallavicini, F., & Riva, G. et al. (2014). Psychometric assessment of cardio-respiratory activity using a mobile platform. [IJHCR]. *International Journal of Handheld Computing Research*, 5(1), 13–29. doi:10.4018/ijhcr.2014010102

Castellani, M. (2011). Cognitive tools for group decision making: The repertory grid approach revisited. In J. Yearwood & A. Stranieri (Eds.), *Technologies for supporting reasoning communities and collaborative decision making: Cooperative approaches* (pp. 172–192). Hershey, PA: Information Science Reference. doi:10.4018/978-1-60960-091-4.ch010

Cawthon, S. W., Harris, A., & Jones, R. (2010). Cognitive apprenticeship in an online research lab for graduate students in psychology. *International Journal of Web-Based Learning and Teaching Technologies*, 5(1), 1–15. doi:10.4018/jwltt.2010010101

Cederborg, T., & Oudeyer, P. (2014). Learning words by imitating. In *Computational linguistics: Concepts, methodologies, tools, and applications* (pp. 1674–1704). Hershey, PA: Information Science Reference. doi:10.4018/978-1-4666-6042-7.ch084

Cervantes, J., Rodríguez, L., López, S., Ramos, F., & Robles, F. (2013). Cognitive process of moral decision-making for autonomous agents. *International Journal of Software Science and Computational Intelligence*, 5(4), 61–76. doi:10.4018/ijssci.2013100105

Chadwick, D. D., Fullwood, C., & Wesson, C. J. (2014). Intellectual disability, identity, and the internet. In *Assistive technologies: Concepts, methodologies, tools, and applications* (pp. 198–223). Hershey, PA: Information Science Reference. doi:10.4018/978-1-4666-4422-9.ch011

Chan, E. C., Baciu, G., & Mak, S. C. (2010). Cognitive location-aware information retrieval by agent-based semantic matching. [IJSSCI]. *International Journal of Software Science and Computational Intelligence*, 2(3), 21–31. doi:10.4018/jssci.2010070102

Chen, C. (2014). Differences between visual style and verbal style learners in learning English. [IJDET]. *International Journal of Distance Education Technologies*, 12(1), 91–104. doi:10.4018/ijdet.2014010106

Chen, K., & Barthès, J. A. (2012). Giving personal assistant agents a case-based memory. In Y. Wang (Ed.), *Developments in natural intelligence research and knowledge engineering: Advancing applications* (pp. 287–304). Hershey, PA: Information Science Reference. doi:10.4018/978-1-4666-1743-8.ch021

Chen, S., Tai, C., Wang, T., & Wang, S. G. (2011). Social simulation with both human agents and software agents: An investigation into the impact of cognitive capacity on their learning behavior. In S. Chen, Y. Kambayashi, & H. Sato (Eds.), *Multi-agent applications with evolutionary computation and biologically inspired technologies: Intelligent techniques for ubiquity and optimization* (pp. 95–117). Hershey, PA: Medical Information Science Reference. doi:10.4018/978-1-60566-898-7.ch006

Chiriacescu, V., Soh, L., & Shell, D. F. (2013). Understanding human learning using a multi-agent simulation of the unified learning model. *International Journal of Cognitive Informatics and Natural Intelligence*, 7(4), 1–25. doi:10.4018/ijcini.2013100101

Christen, M., Alfano, M., Bangerter, E., & Lapsley, D. (2013). Ethical issues of 'morality mining': Moral identity as a focus of data mining. In H. Rahman & I. Ramos (Eds.), *Ethical data mining applications for socio-economic development* (pp. 1–21). Hershey, PA: Information Science Reference. doi:10.4018/978-1-4666-4078-8.ch001

Cipresso, P., Serino, S., Gaggioli, A., & Riva, G. (2014). Modeling the diffusion of psychological stress. In J. Rodrigues (Ed.), *Advancing medical practice through technology: Applications for healthcare delivery, management, and quality* (pp. 178–204). Hershey, PA: Medical Information Science Reference. doi:10.4018/978-1-4666-4619-3.ch010

Code, J. (2013). Agency and identity in social media. In S. Warburton & S. Hatzipanagos (Eds.), *Digital identity and social media* (pp. 37–57). Hershey, PA: Information Science Reference. doi:10.4018/978-1-4666-1915-9.ch004

Combs, R. M., & Mazur, J. (2014). 3D modeling in a high school computer visualization class: Enacting a productive, distributed social learning environment. In *K-12 education: Concepts, methodologies, tools, and applications* (pp. 1020–1040). Hershey, PA: Information Science Reference. doi:10.4018/978-1-4666-4502-8.ch061

Cook, R. G., & Sutton, R. (2014). Administrators' assessments of online courses and student retention in higher education: Lessons learned. In S. Mukerji & P. Tripathi (Eds.), *Handbook of research on transnational higher education* (pp. 138–150). Hershey, PA: Information Science Reference. doi:10.4018/978-1-4666-4458-8.ch008

Correa, T., Bachmann, I., Hinsley, A. W., & Gil de Zúñiga, H. (2013). Personality and social media use. In E. Li, S. Loh, C. Evans, & F. Lorenzi (Eds.), *Organizations and social networking: Utilizing social media to engage consumers* (pp. 41–61). Hershey, PA: Business Science Reference. doi:10.4018/978-1-4666-4026-9.ch003

Cowell, R. A., Bussey, T. J., & Saksida, L. M. (2011). Using computational modelling to understand cognition in the ventral visual-perirhinal pathway. In E. Alonso & E. Mondragón (Eds.), *Computational neuroscience for advancing artificial intelligence: Models, methods and applications* (pp. 15–45). Hershey, PA: Medical Information Science Reference. doi:10.4018/978-1-60960-021-1.ch002

Crespo, R. G., Martíne, O. S., Lovelle, J. M., García-Bustelo, B. C., Díaz, V. G., & Ordoñez de Pablos, P. (2014). Improving cognitive load on students with disabilities through software aids. In *Assistive technologies: Concepts, methodologies, tools, and applications* (pp. 1255–1268). Hershey, PA: Information Science Reference. doi:10.4018/978-1-4666-4422-9.ch066

Cró, M. D., Andreucci, L., Pinho, A. M., & Pereira, A. (2013). Resilience and psychomotricity in preschool education: A study with children that are socially, culturally, and economically disadvantaged. In M. Cruz-Cunha, I. Miranda, & P. Gonçalves (Eds.), *Handbook of research on ICTs for human-centered healthcare and social care services* (pp. 366–378). Hershey, PA: Medical Information Science Reference. doi:10.4018/978-1-4666-3986-7.ch019

Cummings, J. J., & Ross, T. L. (2013). Optimizing the psychological benefits of choice: information transparency and heuristic use in game environments. In R. Ferdig (Ed.), *Design, utilization, and analysis of simulations and game-based educational worlds* (pp. 142–157). Hershey, PA: Information Science Reference. doi:10.4018/978-1-4666-4018-4.ch009

Curumsing, M. K., Pedell, S., & Vasa, R. (2014). Designing an evaluation tool to measure emotional goals. [IJPOP]. *International Journal of People-Oriented Programming*, *3*(1), 22–43. doi:10.4018/ijpop.2014010102

Cuzzocrea, F., Murdaca, A. M., & Oliva, P. (2013). Using precision teaching method to improve foreign language and cognitive skills in university students. In A. Cartelli (Ed.), *Fostering 21st century digital literacy and technical competency* (pp. 201–211). Hershey, PA: Information Science Reference. doi:10.4018/978-1-4666-2943-1.ch014

DaCosta, B., & Seok, S. (2010). Human cognition in the design of assistive technology for those with learning disabilities. In S. Seok, E. Meyen, & B. DaCosta (Eds.), *Handbook of research on human cognition and assistive technology: Design, accessibility and transdisciplinary perspectives* (pp. 1–20). Hershey, PA: Medical Information Science Reference. doi:10.4018/978-1-61520-817-3.ch001

DaCosta, B., & Seok, S. (2010). Multimedia design of assistive technology for those with learning disabilities. In S. Seok, E. Meyen, & B. DaCosta (Eds.), *Handbook of research on human cognition and assistive technology: Design, accessibility and transdisciplinary perspectives* (pp. 43–60). Hershey, PA: Medical Information Science Reference. doi:10.4018/978-1-61520-817-3.ch003

Danielsson, U., & Öberg, K. D. (2011). Psychosocial life environment and life roles in interaction with daily use of information communication technology boundaries between work and leisure. In D. Haftor & A. Mirijamdotter (Eds.), *Information and communication technologies, society and human beings: Theory and framework (Festschrift in honor of Gunilla Bradley)* (pp. 266–282). Hershey, PA: Information Science Reference. doi:10.4018/978-1-60960-057-0.ch020

Daradoumis, T., & Lafuente, M. M. (2014). Studying the suitability of discourse analysis methods for emotion detection and interpretation in computer-mediated educational discourse. In H. Lim & F. Sudweeks (Eds.), *Innovative methods and technologies for electronic discourse analysis* (pp. 119–143). Hershey, PA: Information Science Reference. doi:10.4018/978-1-4666-4426-7.ch006

De Simone, C., Marquis, T., & Groen, J. (2013). Optimizing conditions for learning and teaching in K-20 education. In V. Wang (Ed.), *Handbook of research on teaching and learning in K-20 education* (pp. 535–552). Hershey, PA: Information Science Reference. doi:10.4018/978-1-4666-4249-2.ch031

Deka, G. C. (2014). Significance of in-memory computing for real-time big data analytics. In P. Raj & G. Deka (Eds.), *Handbook of research on cloud infrastructures for big data analytics* (pp. 352–369). Hershey, PA: Information Science Reference. doi:10.4018/978-1-4666-5864-6.ch014

Demirbilek, M. (2010). Cognitive load and disorientation issues in hypermedia as assistive technology. In S. Seok, E. Meyen, & B. DaCosta (Eds.), *Handbook of research on human cognition and assistive technology: Design, accessibility and transdisciplinary perspectives* (pp. 109–120). Hershey, PA: Medical Information Science Reference. doi:10.4018/978-1-61520-817-3.ch007

Derrick, M. G. (2013). The inventory of learner persistence. In M. Bocarnea, R. Reynolds, & J. Baker (Eds.), *Online instruments, data collection, and electronic measurements: Organizational advancements* (pp. 271–290). Hershey, PA: Information Science Reference. doi:10.4018/978-1-4666-2172-5.ch016

Doolittle, P. E., McNeill, A. L., Terry, K. P., & Scheer, S. B. (2011). Multimedia, cognitive load, and pedagogy. In *Instructional design: Concepts, methodologies, tools and applications* (pp. 1564–1585). Hershey, PA: Information Science Reference. doi:10.4018/978-1-60960-503-2.ch706

Dourlens, S., & Ramdane-Cherif, A. (2013). Cognitive memory for semantic agents architecture in robotic interaction. In Y. Wang (Ed.), *Cognitive informatics for revealing human cognition: Knowledge manipulations in natural intelligence* (pp. 82–97). Hershey, PA: Information Science Reference. doi:10.4018/978-1-4666-2476-4.ch006

Dubbels, B. (2011). Cognitive ethnography: A methodology for measure and analysis of learning for game studies. [IJGCMS]. *International Journal of Gaming and Computer-Mediated Simulations*, *3*(1), 68–78. doi:10.4018/jgcms.2011010105

Dunbar, N. E., Wilson, S. N., Adame, B. J., Elizondo, J., Jensen, M. L., Miller, C. H., & Burgoon, J. K. et al. (2013). MACBETH: Development of a training game for the mitigation of cognitive bias. [IJGBL]. *International Journal of Game-Based Learning*, *3*(4), 7–26. doi:10.4018/ijgbl.2013100102

Dunham, A. H., & Burt, C. D. (2012). Mentoring and the transfer of organizational memory within the context of an aging workforce: Cultural implications for competitive advantage. In *Organizational learning and knowledge: Concepts, methodologies, tools and applications* (pp. 3076–3099). Hershey, PA: Business Science Reference. doi:10.4018/978-1-60960-783-8.ch817

Durrington, V. A., & Du, J. (2013). Learning tasks, peer interaction, and cognition process an online collaborative design model. [IJICTE]. *International Journal of Information and Communication Technology Education*, *9*(1), 38–50. doi:10.4018/jicte.2013010104

Duțu, A. (2014). Understanding consumers' behaviour change in uncertainty conditions: A psychological perspective. In F. Musso & E. Druica (Eds.), *Handbook of research on retailer-consumer relationship development* (pp. 45–69). Hershey, PA: Business Science Reference. doi:10.4018/978-1-4666-6074-8.ch004

Dwyer, P. (2013). Measuring collective cognition in online collaboration venues. In N. Kock (Ed.), *Interdisciplinary applications of electronic collaboration approaches and technologies* (pp. 46–61). Hershey, PA: Information Science Reference. doi:10.4018/978-1-4666-2020-9.ch004

Egan, R. G., & Zhou, M. (2011). Re-conceptualizing calibration using trace methodology. In G. Dettori & D. Persico (Eds.), *Fostering self-regulated learning through ICT* (pp. 71–88). Hershey, PA: Information Science Reference. doi:10.4018/978-1-61692-901-5.ch005

El-Farargy, N. (2013). Refresher training in clinical psychology supervision: A blended learning approach. In A. Benson, J. Moore, & S. Williams van Rooij (Eds.), *Cases on educational technology planning, design, and implementation: A project management perspective* (pp. 295–317). Hershey, PA: Information Science Reference. doi:10.4018/978-1-4666-4237-9.ch016

El Louadi, M., & Tounsi, I. (2010). Do organizational memory and information technology interact to affect organizational information needs and provision? In M. Jennex (Ed.), *Ubiquitous developments in knowledge management: Integrations and trends* (pp. 1–20). Hershey, PA: Information Science Reference. doi:10.4018/978-1-60566-954-0.ch001

Estrada-Hernández, N., & Stachowiak, J. R. (2010). Evaluating systemic assistive technology needs. In S. Seok, E. Meyen, & B. DaCosta (Eds.), *Handbook of research on human cognition and assistive technology: Design, accessibility and transdisciplinary perspectives* (pp. 239–250). Hershey, PA: Medical Information Science Reference. doi:10.4018/978-1-61520-817-3.ch016

Fitzpatrick, M., & Theoharis, R. (2010). Assistive technology for deaf and hard of hearing students. In S. Seok, E. Meyen, & B. DaCosta (Eds.), *Handbook of research on human cognition and assistive technology: Design, accessibility and transdisciplinary perspectives* (pp. 179–191). Hershey, PA: Medical Information Science Reference. doi:10.4018/978-1-61520-817-3.ch012

Francis, A. G. Jr, Mehta, M., & Ram, A. (2012). Emotional memory and adaptive personalities. In *Machine learning: Concepts, methodologies, tools and applications* (pp. 1292–1313). Hershey, PA: Information Science Reference. doi:10.4018/978-1-60960-818-7.ch507

Gagliardi, F. (2014). A cognitive machine-learning system to discover syndromes in erythematosquamous diseases. In J. Rodrigues (Ed.), *Advancing medical practice through technology: Applications for healthcare delivery, management, and quality* (pp. 66–101). Hershey, PA: Medical Information Science Reference. doi:10.4018/978-1-4666-4619-3.ch005

Gaines, B. R., & Shaw, M. L. (2013). Sociocognitive inquiry. In *Data mining: Concepts, methodologies, tools, and applications* (pp. 1688–1708). Hershey, PA: Information Science Reference. doi:10.4018/978-1-4666-2455-9.ch088

Gardner, M. K., & Hill, R. D. (2013). Training older adults to improve their episodic memory: Three different approaches to enhancing numeric memory. In R. Zheng, R. Hill, & M. Gardner (Eds.), *Engaging older adults with modern technology: Internet use and information access needs* (pp. 191–211). Hershey, PA: Information Science Reference. doi:10.4018/978-1-4666-1966-1.ch010

Ghili, S., Nazarian, S., Tavana, M., Keyvanshokouhi, S., & Isaai, M. T. (2013). A complex systems paradox of organizational learning and knowledge management. [IJKBO]. *International Journal of Knowledge-Based Organizations*, *3*(3), 53–72. doi:10.4018/ijkbo.2013070104

Gibson, D. (2012). Designing a computational model of learning. In *Machine learning: Concepts, methodologies, tools and applications* (pp. 147–174). Hershey, PA: Information Science Reference. doi:10.4018/978-1-60960-818-7.ch203

Gibson, M., Renaud, K., Conrad, M., & Maple, C. (2013). Music is the key: Using our enduring memory for songs to help users log on. In *IT policy and ethics: Concepts, methodologies, tools, and applications* (pp. 1018–1037). Hershey, PA: Information Science Reference. doi:10.4018/978-1-4666-2919-6.ch046

Godine, N., & Barnett, J. E. (2013). The use of telepsychology in clinical practice: Benefits, effectiveness, and issues to consider. *International Journal of Cyber Behavior, Psychology and Learning*, *3*(4), 70–83. doi:10.4018/ijcbpl.2013100105

Gökçay, D. (2011). Emotional axes: Psychology, psychophysiology and neuroanatomical correlates. In D. Gökçay & G. Yildirim (Eds.), *Affective computing and interaction: Psychological, cognitive and neuroscientific perspectives* (pp. 56–73). Hershey, PA: Information Science Reference. doi:10.4018/978-1-61692-892-6.ch003

Goswami, R., Jena, R. K., & Mahapatro, B. B. (2013). Psycho-social impact of shift work: A study of ferro-alloy industries in Orissa. In P. Ordóñez de Pablos (Ed.), *Business, technology, and knowledge management in Asia: Trends and innovations* (pp. 166–174). Hershey, PA: Business Science Reference. doi:10.4018/978-1-4666-2652-2.ch013

Graff, M. (2011). Can cognitive style predict how individuals use web-based learning environments? In *Instructional design: Concepts, methodologies, tools and applications* (pp. 1553–1563). Hershey, PA: Information Science Reference. doi:10.4018/978-1-60960-503-2.ch705

Griffiths, M., Kuss, D. J., & Ortiz de Gortari, A. B. (2013). Videogames as therapy: A review of the medical and psychological literature. In M. Cruz-Cunha, I. Miranda, & P. Gonçalves (Eds.), *Handbook of research on ICTs and management systems for improving efficiency in healthcare and social care* (pp. 43–68). Hershey, PA: Medical Information Science Reference. doi:10.4018/978-1-4666-3990-4.ch003

Guger, C., Sorger, B., Noirhomme, Q., Naci, L., Monti, M. M., & Real, R. ... Cincotti, F. (2014). Brain-computer interfaces for assessment and communication in disorders of consciousness. In G. Naik & Y. Guo (Eds.), Emerging theory and practice in neuroprosthetics (pp. 181-214). Hershey, PA: Medical Information Science Reference. doi:10.4018/978-1-4666-6094-6.ch010

Güngör, H. (2014). Adolescent suicides as a chaotic phenomenon. In Ş. Erçetin & S. Banerjee (Eds.), *Chaos and complexity theory in world politics* (pp. 306–324). Hershey, PA: Information Science Reference. doi:10.4018/978-1-4666-6070-0.ch022

Hai-Jew, S. (2013). Interpreting "you" and "me": Personal voices, PII, biometrics, and imperfect/perfect electronic memory in a democracy. In C. Akrivopoulou & N. Garipidis (Eds.), *Digital democracy and the impact of technology on governance and politics: New globalized practices* (pp. 20–37). Hershey, PA: Information Science Reference. doi:10.4018/978-1-4666-3637-8.ch003

Hainey, T., Connolly, T. M., Chaudy, Y., Boyle, E., Beeby, R., & Soflano, M. (2014). Assessment integration in serious games. In T. Connolly, T. Hainey, E. Boyle, G. Baxter, & P. Moreno-Ger (Eds.), *Psychology, pedagogy, and assessment in serious games* (pp. 317–341). Hershey, PA: Information Science Reference. doi:10.4018/978-1-4666-4773-2.ch015

Hainey, T., Soflano, M., & Connolly, T. M. (2014). A randomised controlled trial to evaluate learning effectiveness using an adaptive serious game to teach SQL at higher education level. In T. Connolly, T. Hainey, E. Boyle, G. Baxter, & P. Moreno-Ger (Eds.), *Psychology, pedagogy, and assessment in serious games* (pp. 270–291). Hershey, PA: Information Science Reference. doi:10.4018/978-1-4666-4773-2.ch013

Haque, J., Erturk, M., Arslan, H., & Moreno, W. (2011). Cognitive aeronautical communication system. *International Journal of Interdisciplinary Telecommunications and Networking*, *3*(1), 20–35. doi:10.4018/jitn.2011010102

Hauge, J. B., Boyle, E., Mayer, I., Nadolski, R., Riedel, J. C., Moreno-Ger, P., & Ritchie, J. et al. (2014). Study design and data gathering guide for serious games' evaluation. In T. Connolly, T. Hainey, E. Boyle, G. Baxter, & P. Moreno-Ger (Eds.), *Psychology, pedagogy, and assessment in serious games* (pp. 394–419). Hershey, PA: Information Science Reference. doi:10.4018/978-1-4666-4773-2.ch018

Haykin, S. (2013). Cognitive dynamic systems. In Y. Wang (Ed.), *Cognitive informatics for revealing human cognition: Knowledge manipulations in natural intelligence* (pp. 250–260). Hershey, PA: Information Science Reference. doi:10.4018/978-1-4666-2476-4.ch016

Henderson, A. M., & Sabbagh, M. A. (2014). Learning words from experience: An integrated framework. In *Computational linguistics: Concepts, methodologies, tools, and applications* (pp. 1705–1727). Hershey, PA: Information Science Reference. doi:10.4018/978-1-4666-6042-7.ch085

Hendrick, H. W. (2011). Cognitive and organizational complexity and behavior: Implications for organizational design and leadership. In D. Haftor & A. Mirijamdotter (Eds.), *Information and communication technologies, society and human beings: Theory and framework (Festschrift in honor of Gunilla Bradley)* (pp. 147–159). Hershey, PA: Information Science Reference. doi:10.4018/978-1-60960-057-0.ch013

Henrie, K. M., & Miller, D. W. (2013). An examination of mediation: Insights into the role of psychological mediators in the use of persuasion knowledge. In R. Eid (Ed.), *Managing customer trust, satisfaction, and loyalty through information communication technologies* (pp. 106–117). Hershey, PA: Business Science Reference. doi:10.4018/978-1-4666-3631-6.ch007

Ho, W. C., Dautenhahn, K., Lim, M., Enz, S., Zoll, C., & Watson, S. (2012). Towards learning 'self' and emotional knowledge in social and cultural human-agent interactions. In *Virtual learning environments: Concepts, methodologies, tools and applications* (pp. 1426–1445). Hershey, PA: Information Science Reference. doi:10.4018/978-1-4666-0011-9.ch705

Holt, L., & Ziegler, M. F. (2013). Promoting team learning in the classroom. In V. Wang (Ed.), *Technological applications in adult and vocational education advancement* (pp. 94–105). Hershey, PA: Information Science Reference. doi:10.4018/978-1-4666-2062-9.ch008

Honey, R. C., & Grand, C. S. (2011). Application of connectionist models to animal learning: Interactions between perceptual organization and associative processes. In E. Alonso & E. Mondragón (Eds.), *Computational neuroscience for advancing artificial intelligence: Models, methods and applications* (pp. 1–14). Hershey, PA: Medical Information Science Reference. doi:10.4018/978-1-60960-021-1.ch001

Hoppenbrouwers, S., Schotten, B., & Lucas, P. (2012). Towards games for knowledge acquisition and modeling. In R. Ferdig & S. de Freitas (Eds.), *Interdisciplinary advancements in gaming, simulations and virtual environments: Emerging trends* (pp. 281–299). Hershey, PA: Information Science Reference. doi:10.4018/978-1-4666-0029-4.ch018

Huang, C., Liang, C., & Lin, E. (2014). A study on emotion releasing effect with music and color. In F. Cipolla-Ficarra (Ed.), *Advanced research and trends in new technologies, software, human-computer interaction, and communicability* (pp. 23–31). Hershey, PA: Information Science Reference. doi:10.4018/978-1-4666-4490-8.ch003

Huang, W. D., & Tettegah, S. Y. (2014). Cognitive load and empathy in serious games: A conceptual framework. In J. Bishop (Ed.), *Gamification for human factors integration: Social, education, and psychological issues* (pp. 17–30). Hershey, PA: Information Science Reference. doi:10.4018/978-1-4666-5071-8.ch002

Huijnen, C. (2011). The use of assistive technology to support the wellbeing and independence of people with memory impairments. In J. Soar, R. Swindell, & P. Tsang (Eds.), *Intelligent technologies for bridging the grey digital divide* (pp. 65–79). Hershey, PA: Information Science Reference. doi:10.4018/978-1-61520-825-8.ch005

Huseyinov, I. N. (2014). Fuzzy linguistic modelling in multi modal human computer interaction: Adaptation to cognitive styles using multi level fuzzy granulation method. In *Assistive technologies: Concepts, methodologies, tools, and applications* (pp. 1481–1496). Hershey, PA: Information Science Reference. doi:10.4018/978-1-4666-4422-9.ch077

Hussey, H. D., Fleck, B. K., & Richmond, A. S. (2014). Promoting active learning through a flipped course design. In J. Keengwe, G. Onchwari, & J. Oigara (Eds.), *Promoting active learning through the flipped classroom model* (pp. 23–46). Hershey, PA: Information Science Reference. doi:10.4018/978-1-4666-4987-3.ch002

Ilin, R., & Perlovsky, L. (2010). Cognitively inspired neural network for recognition of situations. *International Journal of Natural Computing Research*, *1*(1), 36–55. doi:10.4018/jncr.2010010102

Ilin, R., & Perlovsky, L. (2011). Cognitive based distributed sensing, processing, and communication. In B. Igelnik (Ed.), *Computational modeling and simulation of intellect: Current state and future perspectives* (pp. 131–161). Hershey, PA: Information Science Reference. doi:10.4018/978-1-60960-551-3.ch006

Jenkins, J. L., Durcikova, A., & Burns, M. B. (2013). Simplicity is bliss: Controlling extraneous cognitive load in online security training to promote secure behavior. *Journal of Organizational and End User Computing*, *25*(3), 52–66. doi:10.4018/joeuc.2013070104

Jennings, D. J., Alonso, E., Mondragón, E., & Bonardi, C. (2011). Temporal uncertainty during overshadowing: A temporal difference account. In E. Alonso & E. Mondragón (Eds.), *Computational neuroscience for advancing artificial intelligence: Models, methods and applications* (pp. 46–55). Hershey, PA: Medical Information Science Reference. doi:10.4018/978-1-60960-021-1.ch003

Jin, S., DaCosta, B., & Seok, S. (2014). Social skills development for children with autism spectrum disorders through the use of interactive storytelling games. In B. DaCosta & S. Seok (Eds.), *Assistive technology research, practice, and theory* (pp. 144–159). Hershey, PA: Medical Information Science Reference. doi:10.4018/978-1-4666-5015-2.ch010

Johnson, R. D., De Ridder, D., & Gillett, G. (2014). Neurosurgery to enhance brain function: Ethical dilemmas for the neuroscientist and society. In S. Thompson (Ed.), *Global issues and ethical considerations in human enhancement technologies* (pp. 96–118). Hershey, PA: Medical Information Science Reference. doi:10.4018/978-1-4666-6010-6.ch006

Johnson, V., & Price, C. (2010). A longitudinal case study on the use of assistive technology to support cognitive processes across formal and informal educational settings. In S. Seok, E. Meyen, & B. DaCosta (Eds.), *Handbook of research on human cognition and assistive technology: Design, accessibility and transdisciplinary perspectives* (pp. 192–198). Hershey, PA: Medical Information Science Reference. doi:10.4018/978-1-61520-817-3.ch013

Kalyuga, S. (2012). Cognitive load aspects of text processing. In C. Boonthum-Denecke, P. McCarthy, & T. Lamkin (Eds.), *Cross-disciplinary advances in applied natural language processing: Issues and approaches* (pp. 114–132). Hershey, PA: Information Science Reference. doi:10.4018/978-1-61350-447-5.ch009

Kammler, D., Witte, E. M., Chattopadhyay, A., Bauwens, B., Ascheid, G., Leupers, R., & Meyr, H. (2012). Automatic generation of memory interfaces for ASIPs. In S. Virtanen (Ed.), *Innovations in embedded and real-time systems engineering for communication* (pp. 79–100). Hershey, PA: Information Science Reference. doi:10.4018/978-1-4666-0912-9.ch005

Khan, T. M. (2011). Theory of mind in autistic children: multimedia based support. In P. Ordóñez de Pablos, J. Zhao, & R. Tennyson (Eds.), *Technology enhanced learning for people with disabilities: Approaches and applications* (pp. 167–179). Hershey, PA: Information Science Reference. doi:10.4018/978-1-61520-923-1.ch012

Khetrapal, N. (2010). Cognition meets assistive technology: Insights from load theory of selective attention. In S. Seok, E. Meyen, & B. DaCosta (Eds.), *Handbook of research on human cognition and assistive technology: Design, accessibility and transdisciplinary perspectives* (pp. 96–108). Hershey, PA: Medical Information Science Reference. doi:10.4018/978-1-61520-817-3.ch006

Khetrapal, N. (2010). Cognitive science helps formulate games for moral education. In K. Schrier & D. Gibson (Eds.), *Ethics and game design: Teaching values through play* (pp. 181–196). Hershey, PA: Information Science Reference. doi:10.4018/978-1-61520-845-6.ch012

Kickmeier-Rust, M. D., Mattheiss, E., Steiner, C., & Albert, D. (2011). A psycho-pedagogical framework for multi-adaptive educational games. *International Journal of Game-Based Learning*, *1*(1), 45–58. doi:10.4018/ijgbl.2011010104

Kiel, L. D., & McCaskill, J. (2013). Cognition and complexity: An agent-based model of cognitive capital under stress. In S. Banerjee (Ed.), *Chaos and complexity theory for management: Nonlinear dynamics* (pp. 254–268). Hershey, PA: Business Science Reference. doi:10.4018/978-1-4666-2509-9.ch012

Kiili, K., & Perttula, A. (2013). A design framework for educational exergames. In S. de Freitas, M. Ott, M. Popescu, & I. Stanescu (Eds.), *New pedagogical approaches in game enhanced learning: Curriculum integration* (pp. 136–158). Hershey, PA: Information Science Reference. doi:10.4018/978-1-4666-3950-8.ch008

Kiliç, F. (2011). Structuring of knowledge and cognitive load. In G. Kurubacak & T. Yuzer (Eds.), *Handbook of research on transformative online education and liberation: Models for social equality* (pp. 370–382). Hershey, PA: Information Science Reference. doi:10.4018/978-1-60960-046-4.ch020

Kim, E. B. (2011). Student personality and learning outcomes in e-learning: An introduction to empirical research. In S. Eom & J. Arbaugh (Eds.), *Student satisfaction and learning outcomes in e-learning: An introduction to empirical research* (pp. 294–315). Hershey, PA: Information Science Reference. doi:10.4018/978-1-60960-615-2.ch013

Kinsell, C. (2010). Investigating assistive technologies using computers to simulate basic curriculum for individuals with cognitive impairments. In S. Seok, E. Meyen, & B. DaCosta (Eds.), *Handbook of research on human cognition and assistive technology: Design, accessibility and transdisciplinary perspectives* (pp. 61–75). Hershey, PA: Medical Information Science Reference. doi:10.4018/978-1-61520-817-3.ch004

Kirwan, G., & Power, A. (2012). Can forensic psychology contribute to solving the problem of cybercrime? In G. Kirwan & A. Power (Eds.), *The psychology of cyber crime: Concepts and principles* (pp. 18–36). Hershey, PA: Information Science Reference. doi:10.4018/978-1-61350-350-8.ch002

Klippel, A., Richter, K., & Hansen, S. (2013). Cognitively ergonomic route directions. In *Geographic information systems: Concepts, methodologies, tools, and applications* (pp. 250–257). Hershey, PA: Information Science Reference. doi:10.4018/978-1-4666-2038-4.ch017

Knafla, B., & Champandard, A. J. (2012). Behavior trees: Introduction and memory-compact implementation. In A. Kumar, J. Etheredge, & A. Boudreaux (Eds.), *Algorithmic and architectural gaming design: Implementation and development* (pp. 40–66). Hershey, PA: Information Science Reference. doi:10.4018/978-1-4666-1634-9.ch003

Kokkinos, C. M., Antoniadou, N., Dalara, E., Koufogazou, A., & Papatziki, A. (2013). Cyber-bullying, personality and coping among pre-adolescents. *International Journal of Cyber Behavior, Psychology and Learning, 3*(4), 55–69. doi:10.4018/ijcbpl.2013100104

Konrath, S. (2013). The empathy paradox: Increasing disconnection in the age of increasing connection. In R. Luppicini (Ed.), *Handbook of research on technoself: Identity in a technological society* (pp. 204–228). Hershey, PA: Information Science Reference. doi:10.4018/978-1-4666-2211-1.ch012

Kopp, B., & Mandl, H. (2012). Supporting virtual collaborative learning using collaboration scripts and content schemes. In *Virtual learning environments: Concepts, methodologies, tools and applications* (pp. 470–487). Hershey, PA: Information Science Reference. doi:10.4018/978-1-4666-0011-9.ch303

Kumar, S., Singhal, D., & Murthy, G. R. (2013). Doubly cognitive architecture based cognitive wireless sensor networks. In N. Chilamkurti (Ed.), *Security, design, and architecture for broadband and wireless network technologies* (pp. 121–126). Hershey, PA: Information Science Reference. doi:10.4018/978-1-4666-3902-7.ch009

Kutaula, S., & Talwar, V. (2014). Integrating psychological contract and service-related outcomes in emerging economies: A proposed conceptual framework. In A. Goyal (Ed.), *Innovations in services marketing and management: Strategies for emerging economies* (pp. 291–306). Hershey, PA: Business Science Reference. doi:10.4018/978-1-4666-4671-1.ch016

Kyriakaki, G., & Matsatsinis, N. (2014). Pedagogical evaluation of e-learning websites with cognitive objectives. In D. Yannacopoulos, P. Manolitzas, N. Matsatsinis, & E. Grigoroudis (Eds.), *Evaluating websites and web services: Interdisciplinary perspectives on user satisfaction* (pp. 224–240). Hershey, PA: Information Science Reference. doi:10.4018/978-1-4666-5129-6.ch013

Kyritsis, M., Gulliver, S. R., & Morar, S. (2014). Cognitive and environmental factors influencing the process of spatial knowledge acquisition within virtual reality environments. *International Journal of Artificial Life Research*, 4(1), 43–58. doi:10.4018/ijalr.2014010104

Laffey, J., Stichter, J., & Schmidt, M. (2010). Social orthotics for youth with ASD to learn in a collaborative 3D VLE. In S. Seok, E. Meyen, & B. DaCosta (Eds.), *Handbook of research on human cognition and assistive technology: Design, accessibility and transdisciplinary perspectives* (pp. 76–95). Hershey, PA: Medical Information Science Reference. doi:10.4018/978-1-61520-817-3.ch005

Lai, S., & Han, H. (2014). Behavioral planning theory. In J. Wang (Ed.), *Encyclopedia of business analytics and optimization* (pp. 265–272). Hershey, PA: Business Science Reference. doi:10.4018/978-1-4666-5202-6.ch025

Lawson, D. (2013). Analysis and use of the life styles inventory 1 and 2 by human synergistics international. In M. Bocarnea, R. Reynolds, & J. Baker (Eds.), *Online instruments, data collection, and electronic measurements: Organizational advancements* (pp. 76–96). Hershey, PA: Information Science Reference. doi:10.4018/978-1-4666-2172-5.ch005

Lee, L., & Hung, J. C. (2011). Effect of teaching using whole brain instruction on accounting learning. In Q. Jin (Ed.), *Distance education environments and emerging software systems: New technologies* (pp. 261–282). Hershey, PA: Information Science Reference. doi:10.4018/978-1-60960-539-1.ch016

Levin, I., & Kojukhov, A. (2013). Personalization of learning environments in a post-industrial class. In M. Pătruţ & B. Pătruţ (Eds.), *Social media in higher education: Teaching in web 2.0* (pp. 105–123). Hershey, PA: Information Science Reference. doi:10.4018/978-1-4666-2970-7.ch006

Li, A., Li, H., Guo, R., & Zhu, T. (2013). MobileSens: A ubiquitous psychological laboratory based on mobile device. [IJCBPL]. *International Journal of Cyber Behavior, Psychology and Learning*, 3(2), 47–55. doi:10.4018/ijcbpl.2013040104

Li, R. (2013). Traditional to hybrid: Social media's role in reshaping instruction in higher education. In A. Sigal (Ed.), *Advancing library education: Technological innovation and instructional design* (pp. 65–90). Hershey, PA: Information Science Reference. doi:10.4018/978-1-4666-3688-0.ch005

Li, X., Lin, Z., & Wu, J. (2014). Language processing in the human brain of literate and illiterate subjects. In *Computational linguistics: Concepts, methodologies, tools, and applications* (pp. 1391–1400). Hershey, PA: Information Science Reference. doi:10.4018/978-1-4666-6042-7.ch068

Li, X., Ouyang, Z., & Luo, Y. (2013). The cognitive load affects the interaction pattern of emotion and working memory. *International Journal of Cognitive Informatics and Natural Intelligence*, 6(2), 68–81. doi:10.4018/jcini.2012040104

Lin, T., Li, X., Wu, Z., & Tang, N. (2013). Automatic cognitive load classification using high-frequency interaction events: An exploratory study. *International Journal of Technology and Human Interaction*, 9(3), 73–88. doi:10.4018/jthi.2013070106

Linek, S. B. (2011). As you like it: What media psychology can tell us about educational game design. In P. Felicia (Ed.), *Handbook of research on improving learning and motivation through educational games: Multidisciplinary approaches* (pp. 606–632). Hershey, PA: Information Science Reference. doi:10.4018/978-1-60960-495-0.ch029

Linek, S. B., Marte, B., & Albert, D. (2014). Background music in educational games: Motivational appeal and cognitive impact. In J. Bishop (Ed.), *Gamification for human factors integration: Social, education, and psychological issues* (pp. 259–271). Hershey, PA: Information Science Reference. doi:10.4018/978-1-4666-5071-8.ch016

Logeswaran, R. (2011). Neural networks in medicine. In *Clinical technologies: Concepts, methodologies, tools and applications* (pp. 744–765). Hershey, PA: Medical Information Science Reference. doi:10.4018/978-1-60960-561-2.ch308

Low, R. (2011). Cognitive architecture and instructional design in a multimedia context. In *Instructional design: Concepts, methodologies, tools and applications* (pp. 496–510). Hershey, PA: Information Science Reference. doi:10.4018/978-1-60960-503-2.ch301

Low, R., Jin, P., & Sweller, J. (2014). Instructional design in digital environments and availability of mental resources for the aged subpopulation. In *Assistive technologies: Concepts, methodologies, tools, and applications* (pp. 1131–1154). Hershey, PA: Information Science Reference. doi:10.4018/978-1-4666-4422-9.ch059

Lu, J., & Peng, Y. (2014). Brain-computer interface for cyberpsychology: Components, methods, and applications. *International Journal of Cyber Behavior, Psychology and Learning*, 4(1), 1–14. doi:10.4018/ijcbpl.2014010101

Ludvig, E. A., Bellemare, M. G., & Pearson, K. G. (2011). A primer on reinforcement learning in the brain: Psychological, computational, and neural perspectives. In E. Alonso & E. Mondragón (Eds.), *Computational neuroscience for advancing artificial intelligence: Models, methods and applications* (pp. 111–144). Hershey, PA: Medical Information Science Reference. doi:10.4018/978-1-60960-021-1.ch006

Lützenberger, M. (2014). A driver's mind: Psychology runs simulation. In D. Janssens, A. Yasar, & L. Knapen (Eds.), *Data science and simulation in transportation research* (pp. 182–205). Hershey, PA: Information Science Reference. doi:10.4018/978-1-4666-4920-0.ch010

Mancha, R., Yoder, C. Y., & Clark, J. G. (2013). Dynamics of affect and cognition in simulated agents: Bridging the gap between experimental and simulation research. *International Journal of Agent Technologies and Systems*, 5(2), 78–96. doi:10.4018/jats.2013040104

Manchiraju, S. (2014). Predicting behavioral intentions toward sustainable fashion consumption: A comparison of attitude-behavior and value-behavior consistency models. In H. Kaufmann & M. Panni (Eds.), *Handbook of research on consumerism in business and marketing: Concepts and practices* (pp. 225–243). Hershey, PA: Business Science Reference. doi:10.4018/978-1-4666-5880-6.ch011

Mancilla, R. L. (2013). Getting smart about split attention. In B. Zou, M. Xing, Y. Wang, M. Sun, & C. Xiang (Eds.), *Computer-assisted foreign language teaching and learning: Technological advances* (pp. 210–229). Hershey, PA: Information Science Reference. doi:10.4018/978-1-4666-2821-2.ch012

Manrique-de-Lara, P. Z. (2013). Does discretionary internet-based behavior of instructors contribute to student satisfaction? An empirical study on 'cybercivism'. [IJCBPL]. *International Journal of Cyber Behavior, Psychology and Learning*, 3(1), 50–66. doi:10.4018/ijcbpl.2013010105

Markov, K., Vanhoof, K., Mitov, I., Depaire, B., Ivanova, K., Velychko, V., & Gladun, V. (2013). Intelligent data processing based on multi-dimensional numbered memory structures. In X. Naidenova & D. Ignatov (Eds.), *Diagnostic test approaches to machine learning and commonsense reasoning systems* (pp. 156–184). Hershey, PA: Information Science Reference. doi:10.4018/978-1-4666-1900-5.ch007

Martin, J. N. (2014). How can we incorporate relevant findings from psychology into systems methods? *International Journal of Systems and Society, 1*(1), 1–11. doi:10.4018/ijss.2014010101

Mayer, I., Bekebrede, G., Warmelink, H., & Zhou, Q. (2014). A brief methodology for researching and evaluating serious games and game-based learning. In T. Connolly, T. Hainey, E. Boyle, G. Baxter, & P. Moreno-Ger (Eds.), *Psychology, pedagogy, and assessment in serious games* (pp. 357–393). Hershey, PA: Information Science Reference. doi:10.4018/978-1-4666-4773-2.ch017

Mazumdar, B. D., & Mishra, R. B. (2011). Cognitive parameter based agent selection and negotiation process for B2C e-commerce. In V. Sugumaran (Ed.), *Intelligent, adaptive and reasoning technologies: New developments and applications* (pp. 181–203). Hershey, PA: Information Science Reference. doi:10.4018/978-1-60960-595-7.ch010

McLaren, I. (2011). APECS: An adaptively parameterised model of associative learning and memory. In E. Alonso & E. Mondragón (Eds.), *Computational neuroscience for advancing artificial intelligence: Models, methods and applications* (pp. 145–164). Hershey, PA: Medical Information Science Reference. doi:10.4018/978-1-60960-021-1.ch007

McMurray, B., Zhao, L., Kucker, S. C., & Samuelson, L. K. (2013). Pushing the envelope of associative learning: Internal representations and dynamic competition transform association into development. In L. Gogate & G. Hollich (Eds.), *Theoretical and computational models of word learning: Trends in psychology and artificial intelligence* (pp. 49–80). Hershey, PA: Information Science Reference. doi:10.4018/978-1-4666-2973-8.ch003

Mena, R. J. (2014). The quest for a massively multiplayer online game that teaches physics. In T. Connolly, T. Hainey, E. Boyle, G. Baxter, & P. Moreno-Ger (Eds.), *Psychology, pedagogy, and assessment in serious games* (pp. 292–316). Hershey, PA: Information Science Reference. doi:10.4018/978-1-4666-4773-2.ch014

Misra, S. (2011). Cognitive complexity measures: An analysis. In A. Dogru & V. Biçer (Eds.), *Modern software engineering concepts and practices: Advanced approaches* (pp. 263–279). Hershey, PA: Information Science Reference. doi:10.4018/978-1-60960-215-4.ch011

Mok, J. (2010). Social and distributed cognition in collaborative learning contexts. In S. Dasgupta (Ed.), *Social computing: Concepts, methodologies, tools, and applications* (pp. 1838–1854). Hershey, PA: Information Science Reference. doi:10.4018/978-1-60566-984-7.ch121

Moore, J. E., & Love, M. S. (2013). An examination of prestigious stigma: The case of the technology geek. In B. Medlin (Ed.), *Integrations of technology utilization and social dynamics in organizations* (pp. 48–73). Hershey, PA: Information Science Reference. doi:10.4018/978-1-4666-1948-7.ch004

Moore, M. J., Nakano, T., Suda, T., & Enomoto, A. (2013). Social interactions and automated detection tools in cyberbullying. In L. Caviglione, M. Coccoli, & A. Merlo (Eds.), *Social network engineering for secure web data and services* (pp. 67–87). Hershey, PA: Information Science Reference. doi:10.4018/978-1-4666-3926-3.ch004

Moseley, A. (2014). A case for integration: Assessment and games. In T. Connolly, T. Hainey, E. Boyle, G. Baxter, & P. Moreno-Ger (Eds.), *Psychology, pedagogy, and assessment in serious games* (pp. 342–356). Hershey, PA: Information Science Reference. doi:10.4018/978-1-4666-4773-2.ch016

Mpofu, S. (2014). Memory, national identity, and freedom of expression in the information age: Discussing the taboo in the Zimbabwean public sphere. In A. Solo (Ed.), *Handbook of research on political activism in the information age* (pp. 114–128). Hershey, PA: Information Science Reference. doi:10.4018/978-1-4666-6066-3.ch007

Mulvey, F., & Heubner, M. (2014). Eye movements and attention. In *Assistive technologies: Concepts, methodologies, tools, and applications* (pp. 1030–1054). Hershey, PA: Information Science Reference. doi:10.4018/978-1-4666-4422-9.ch053

Munipov, V. (2011). Psychological and social problems of automation and computerization. In D. Haftor & A. Mirijamdotter (Eds.), *Information and communication technologies, society and human beings: Theory and framework (Festschrift in honor of Gunilla Bradley)* (pp. 136–146). Hershey, PA: Information Science Reference. doi:10.4018/978-1-60960-057-0.ch012

Najjar, M., & Mayers, A. (2012). A cognitive computational knowledge representation theory. In *Machine learning: Concepts, methodologies, tools and applications* (pp. 1819–1838). Hershey, PA: Information Science Reference. doi:10.4018/978-1-60960-818-7.ch708

Nakamura, H. (2011). Cognitive decline in patients with Alzheimer's disease: A six-year longitudinal study of mini-mental state examination scores. In J. Wu (Ed.), *Early detection and rehabilitation technologies for dementia: Neuroscience and biomedical applications* (pp. 107–111). Hershey, PA: Medical Information Science Reference. doi:10.4018/978-1-60960-559-9.ch013

Nankee, C. (2010). Switch technologies. In S. Seok, E. Meyen, & B. DaCosta (Eds.), *Handbook of research on human cognition and assistive technology: Design, accessibility and transdisciplinary perspectives* (pp. 157–168). Hershey, PA: Medical Information Science Reference. doi:10.4018/978-1-61520-817-3.ch010

Nap, H. H., & Diaz-Orueta, U. (2014). Rehabilitation gaming. In J. Bishop (Ed.), *Gamification for human factors integration: Social, education, and psychological issues* (pp. 122–147). Hershey, PA: Information Science Reference. doi:10.4018/978-1-4666-5071-8.ch008

Naranjo-Saucedo, A. B., Suárez-Mejías, C., Parra-Calderón, C. L., González-Aguado, E., Böckel-Martínez, F., & Yuste-Marco, A. … Marco, A. (2014). Interactive games with robotic and augmented reality technology in cognitive and motor rehabilitation. In Robotics: Concepts, methodologies, tools, and applications (pp. 1233-1254). Hershey, PA: Information Science Reference. doi:10.4018/978-1-4666-4607-0.ch059

Ndinguri, E., Machtmes, K., Hatala, J. P., & Coco, M. L. (2014). Learning through immersive virtual environments: An organizational context. In J. Keengwe, G. Schnellert, & K. Kungu (Eds.), *Cross-cultural online learning in higher education and corporate training* (pp. 185–199). Hershey, PA: Information Science Reference. doi:10.4018/978-1-4666-5023-7.ch010

Ninaus, M., Witte, M., Kober, S. E., Friedrich, E. V., Kurzmann, J., & Hartsuiker, E. … Wood, G. (2014). Neurofeedback and serious games. In T. Connolly, T. Hainey, E. Boyle, G. Baxter, & P. Moreno-Ger (Eds.), Psychology, pedagogy, and assessment in serious games (pp. 82-110). Hershey, PA: Information Science Reference. doi:10.4018/978-1-4666-4773-2.ch005

Nobre, F. S. (2012). The roles of cognitive machines in customer-centric organizations: Towards innovations in computational organizational management networks. In F. Nobre, D. Walker, & R. Harris (Eds.), *Technological, managerial and organizational core competencies: Dynamic innovation and sustainable development* (pp. 653–674). Hershey, PA: Business Science Reference. doi:10.4018/978-1-61350-165-8.ch035

Norris, S. E. (2014). Transformative curriculum design and program development: Creating effective adult learning by leveraging psychological capital and self-directedness through the exercise of human agency. In V. Wang & V. Bryan (Eds.), *Andragogical and pedagogical methods for curriculum and program development* (pp. 118–141). Hershey, PA: Information Science Reference. doi:10.4018/978-1-4666-5872-1.ch007

Norris, S. E., & Porter, T. H. (2013). Self-monitoring scale. In M. Bocarnea, R. Reynolds, & J. Baker (Eds.), *Online instruments, data collection, and electronic measurements: Organizational advancements* (pp. 118–133). Hershey, PA: Information Science Reference. doi:10.4018/978-1-4666-2172-5.ch007

O'Connell, R. M. (2014). Mind mapping for critical thinking. In L. Shedletsky & J. Beaudry (Eds.), *Cases on teaching critical thinking through visual representation strategies* (pp. 354–386). Hershey, PA: Information Science Reference. doi:10.4018/978-1-4666-5816-5.ch014

Okrigwe, B. N. (2010). Cognition and learning. In S. Seok, E. Meyen, & B. DaCosta (Eds.), *Handbook of research on human cognition and assistive technology: Design, accessibility and transdisciplinary perspectives* (pp. 388–400). Hershey, PA: Medical Information Science Reference. doi:10.4018/978-1-61520-817-3.ch027

Ong, E. H., & Khan, J. Y. (2013). Cognitive cooperation in wireless networks. In M. Ku & J. Lin (Eds.), *Cognitive radio and interference management: Technology and strategy* (pp. 179–204). Hershey, PA: Information Science Reference. doi:10.4018/978-1-4666-2005-6.ch010

Orlova, M. (2014). Social psychology of health as a social-psychological situation. In Ş. Erçetin & S. Banerjee (Eds.), *Chaos and complexity theory in world politics* (pp. 331–335). Hershey, PA: Information Science Reference. doi:10.4018/978-1-4666-6070-0.ch024

Orr, K., & McGuinness, C. (2014). What is the "learning" in games-based learning? In T. Connolly, T. Hainey, E. Boyle, G. Baxter, & P. Moreno-Ger (Eds.), Psychology, pedagogy, and assessment in serious games (pp. 221-242). Hershey, PA: Information Science Reference. doi:10.4018/978-1-4666-4773-2.ch011

Ortiz Zezzatti, C. A., Martínez, J., Castillo, N., González, S., & Hernández, P. (2012). Improve card collection from memory alpha using sociolinguistics and Japanese puzzles. In C. Ortiz Zezzatti, C. Chira, A. Hernandez, & M. Basurto (Eds.), *Logistics management and optimization through hybrid artificial intelligence systems* (pp. 310–326). Hershey, PA: Information Science Reference. doi:10.4018/978-1-4666-0297-7.ch012

Ota, N., Maeshima, S., Osawa, A., Kawarada, M., & Tanemura, J. (2011). Prospective memory impairment in remembering to remember in mild cognitive impairment and healthy subjects. In J. Wu (Ed.), *Early detection and rehabilitation technologies for dementia: Neuroscience and biomedical applications* (pp. 98–106). Hershey, PA: Medical Information Science Reference. doi:10.4018/978-1-60960-559-9.ch012

Ouwehand, K., van Gog, T., & Paas, F. (2013). The use of gesturing to facilitate older adults' learning from computer-based dynamic visualizations. In R. Zheng, R. Hill, & M. Gardner (Eds.), *Engaging older adults with modern technology: Internet use and information access needs* (pp. 33–58). Hershey, PA: Information Science Reference. doi:10.4018/978-1-4666-1966-1.ch003

Özel, S. (2012). Utilizing cognitive resources in user interface designs. In B. Khan (Ed.), *User interface design for virtual environments: Challenges and advances* (pp. 115–123). Hershey, PA: Information Science Reference. doi:10.4018/978-1-61350-516-8.ch007

Parsons, T. D., & Courtney, C. G. (2011). Neurocognitive and psychophysiological interfaces for adaptive virtual environments. In M. Ziefle & C. Röcker (Eds.), *Human-centered design of e-health technologies: Concepts, methods and applications* (pp. 208–233). Hershey, PA: Medical Information Science Reference. doi:10.4018/978-1-60960-177-5.ch009

Peden, B. F., & Tiry, A. M. (2013). Using web surveys for psychology experiments: A case study in new media technology for research. In N. Sappleton (Ed.), *Advancing research methods with new technologies* (pp. 70–99). Hershey, PA: Information Science Reference. doi:10.4018/978-1-4666-3918-8.ch005

Perakslis, C. (2014). Willingness to adopt RFID implants: Do personality factors play a role in the acceptance of uberveillance? In M. Michael & K. Michael (Eds.), *Uberveillance and the social implications of microchip implants: Emerging technologies* (pp. 144–168). Hershey, PA: Information Science Reference. doi:10.4018/978-1-4666-4582-0.ch006

Pereira, G., Brisson, A., Dias, J., Carvalho, A., Dimas, J., & Mascarenhas, S. ... Paiva, A. (2014). Non-player characters and artificial intelligence. In T. Connolly, T. Hainey, E. Boyle, G. Baxter, & P. Moreno-Ger (Eds.), Psychology, pedagogy, and assessment in serious games (pp. 127-152). Hershey, PA: Information Science Reference. doi:10.4018/978-1-4666-4773-2.ch007

Pereira, R., Hornung, H., & Baranauskas, M. C. (2014). Cognitive authority revisited in web social interaction. In M. Pańkowska (Ed.), *Frameworks of IT prosumption for business development* (pp. 142–157). Hershey, PA: Business Science Reference. doi:10.4018/978-1-4666-4313-0.ch010

Phebus, A. M., Gitlin, B., Shuffler, M. L., & Wildman, J. L. (2014). Leading global virtual teams: The supporting role of trust and team cognition. In E. Nikoi & K. Boateng (Eds.), *Collaborative communication processes and decision making in organizations* (pp. 177–200). Hershey, PA: Business Science Reference. doi:10.4018/978-1-4666-4478-6.ch010

Plunkett, D., Banerjee, R., & Horn, E. (2010). Supporting early childhood outcomes through assistive technology. In S. Seok, E. Meyen, & B. DaCosta (Eds.), *Handbook of research on human cognition and assistive technology: Design, accessibility and transdisciplinary perspectives* (pp. 339–359). Hershey, PA: Medical Information Science Reference. doi:10.4018/978-1-61520-817-3.ch024

Prakash, S., Vaish, A., Coul, N., Saravana, G. K., Srinidhi, T. N., & Botsa, J. (2014). Child security in cyberspace through moral cognition. In *Cyber behavior: Concepts, methodologies, tools, and applications* (pp. 1946–1958). Hershey, PA: Information Science Reference. doi:10.4018/978-1-4666-5942-1.ch102

Prescott, J., & Bogg, J. (2013). Self, career, and gender issues: A complex interplay of internal/external factors. In *Gendered occupational differences in science, engineering, and technology careers* (pp. 79–111). Hershey, PA: Information Science Reference. doi:10.4018/978-1-4666-2107-7.ch004

Prescott, J., & Bogg, J. (2013). Stereotype, attitudes, and identity: Gendered expectations and behaviors. In *Gendered occupational differences in science, engineering, and technology careers* (pp. 112–135). Hershey, PA: Information Science Reference. doi:10.4018/978-1-4666-2107-7.ch005

Pressey, A., Salciuviene, L., & Barnes, S. (2013). Uncovering relationships between emotional states and higher-order needs: Enhancing consumer emotional experiences in computer-mediated environment. *International Journal of Online Marketing*, *3*(1), 31–46. doi:10.4018/ijom.2013010103

Qin, X., Li, C., Chen, H., Qin, B., Du, X., & Wang, S. (2014). In memory data processing systems. In J. Wang (Ed.), *Encyclopedia of business analytics and optimization* (pp. 1182–1191). Hershey, PA: Business Science Reference. doi:10.4018/978-1-4666-5202-6.ch109

Ramos, I., & Oliveira e Sá, J. (2014). Organizational memory: The role of business intelligence to leverage the application of collective knowledge. In H. Rahman & R. de Sousa (Eds.), *Information systems and technology for organizational agility, intelligence, and resilience* (pp. 206–223). Hershey, PA: Business Science Reference. doi:10.4018/978-1-4666-5970-4.ch010

Ratten, V. (2013). The development of social e-enterprises, mobile communication and social networks: A social cognitive perspective of technological innovation. [JECO]. *Journal of Electronic Commerce in Organizations*, *11*(3), 68–77. doi:10.4018/jeco.2013070104

Reddy, Y. B. (2013). Nanocomputing in cognitive radio networks to improve the performance. In N. Meghanathan & Y. Reddy (Eds.), *Cognitive radio technology applications for wireless and mobile ad hoc networks* (pp. 173–193). Hershey, PA: Information Science Reference. doi:10.4018/978-1-4666-4221-8.ch010

Redien-Collot, R., & Lefebvre, M. R. (2014). SMEs' leaders: Building collective cognition and competences to trigger positive strategic outcomes. In K. Todorov & D. Smallbone (Eds.), *Handbook of research on strategic management in small and medium enterprises* (pp. 143–158). Hershey, PA: Business Science Reference. doi:10.4018/978-1-4666-5962-9.ch008

Remmele, B., & Whitton, N. (2014). Disrupting the magic circle: The impact of negative social gaming behaviours. In T. Connolly, T. Hainey, E. Boyle, G. Baxter, & P. Moreno-Ger (Eds.), *Psychology, pedagogy, and assessment in serious games* (pp. 111–126). Hershey, PA: Information Science Reference. doi:10.4018/978-1-4666-4773-2.ch006

Renaud, P., Chartier, S., Fedoroff, P., Bradford, J., & Rouleau, J. L. (2011). The use of virtual reality in clinical psychology research. In *Clinical technologies: Concepts, methodologies, tools and applications* (pp. 2073–2093). Hershey, PA: Medical Information Science Reference. doi:10.4018/978-1-60960-561-2.ch805

Revett, K. (2012). Cognitive biometrics: A novel approach to continuous person authentication. In I. Traore & A. Ahmed (Eds.), *Continuous authentication using biometrics: Data, models, and metrics* (pp. 105–136). Hershey, PA: Information Science Reference. doi:10.4018/978-1-61350-129-0.ch006

Rødseth, I. (2011). A motive analysis as a first step in designing technology for the use of intuition in criminal investigation. In A. Mesquita (Ed.), *Sociological and philosophical aspects of human interaction with technology: Advancing concepts* (pp. 276–298). Hershey, PA: Information Science Reference. doi:10.4018/978-1-60960-575-9.ch015

Rothblatt, M. (2014). Mindclone technoselves: Multi-substrate legal identities, cyber-psychology, and biocyberethics. In *Cyber behavior: Concepts, methodologies, tools, and applications* (pp. 1199–1216). Hershey, PA: Information Science Reference. doi:10.4018/978-1-4666-5942-1.ch062

Rückemann, C. (2013). Integrated information and computing systems for advanced cognition with natural sciences. In C. Rückemann (Ed.), *Integrated information and computing systems for natural, spatial, and social sciences* (pp. 1–26). Hershey, PA: Information Science Reference. doi:10.4018/978-1-4666-2190-9.ch001

Rudnianski, M., & Kravcik, M. (2014). The road to critical thinking and intelligence analysis. In T. Connolly, T. Hainey, E. Boyle, G. Baxter, & P. Moreno-Ger (Eds.), *Psychology, pedagogy, and assessment in serious games* (pp. 47–61). Hershey, PA: Information Science Reference. doi:10.4018/978-1-4666-4773-2.ch003

Rufer, R., & Adams, R. H. (2012). Adapting three-dimensional-virtual world to reach diverse learners in an MBA program. In H. Yang & S. Yuen (Eds.), *Handbook of research on practices and outcomes in virtual worlds and environments* (pp. 606–619). Hershey, PA: Information Science Reference. doi:10.4018/978-1-60960-762-3.ch033

Saadé, R. G. (2010). Cognitive mapping decision support for the design of web-based learning environments. *International Journal of Web-Based Learning and Teaching Technologies*, 5(3), 36–53. doi:10.4018/jwltt.2010070103

Saeed, N., & Sinnappan, S. (2014). Comparing learning styles and technology acceptance of two culturally different groups of students. In T. Issa, P. Isaias, & P. Kommers (Eds.), *Multicultural awareness and technology in higher education: Global perspectives* (pp. 244–264). Hershey, PA: Information Science Reference. doi:10.4018/978-1-4666-5876-9.ch012

Samuelson, L. K., Spencer, J. P., & Jenkins, G. W. (2013). A dynamic neural field model of word learning. In L. Gogate & G. Hollich (Eds.), *Theoretical and computational models of word learning: Trends in psychology and artificial intelligence* (pp. 1–27). Hershey, PA: Information Science Reference. doi:10.4018/978-1-4666-2973-8.ch001

Sanjram, P. K., & Gupta, M. (2013). Task difficulty and time constraint in programmer multitasking: An analysis of prospective memory performance and cognitive workload. *International Journal of Green Computing*, 4(1), 35–57. doi:10.4018/jgc.2013010103

Sato, Y., Ji, Z., & van Dijk, S. (2013). I think I have heard that one before: Recurrence-based word learning with a robot. In L. Gogate & G. Hollich (Eds.), *Theoretical and computational models of word learning: Trends in psychology and artificial intelligence* (pp. 327–349). Hershey, PA: Information Science Reference. doi:10.4018/978-1-4666-2973-8.ch014

Scalzone, F., & Zontini, G. (2013). Thinking animals and thinking machines in psychoanalysis and beyond. In F. Orsucci & N. Sala (Eds.), *Complexity science, living systems, and reflexing interfaces: New models and perspectives* (pp. 44–68). Hershey, PA: Information Science Reference. doi:10.4018/978-1-4666-2077-3.ch003

Schafer, S. B. (2013). Fostering psychological coherence: With ICTs. In M. Cruz-Cunha, I. Miranda, & P. Gonçalves (Eds.), *Handbook of research on ICTs for human-centered healthcare and social care services* (pp. 29–47). Hershey, PA: Medical Information Science Reference. doi:10.4018/978-1-4666-3986-7.ch002

Scheiter, K., Wiebe, E., & Holsanova, J. (2011). Theoretical and instructional aspects of learning with visualizations. In *Instructional design: Concepts, methodologies, tools and applications* (pp. 1667–1688). Hershey, PA: Information Science Reference. doi:10.4018/978-1-60960-503-2.ch710

Seo, K. K., Byk, A., & Collins, C. (2011). Cognitive apprenticeship inspired simulations. In *Gaming and simulations: Concepts, methodologies, tools and applications* (pp. 346–358). Hershey, PA: Information Science Reference. doi:10.4018/978-1-60960-195-9.ch202

Serenko, N. (2014). Informational, physical, and psychological privacy as determinants of patient behaviour in health care. In V. Michell, D. Rosenorn-Lanng, S. Gulliver, & W. Currie (Eds.), *Handbook of research on patient safety and quality care through health informatics* (pp. 1–20). Hershey, PA: Medical Information Science Reference. doi:10.4018/978-1-4666-4546-2.ch001

Shibata, T. (2013). A human-like cognitive computer based on a psychologically inspired VLSI brain model. In J. Wu (Ed.), *Technological advancements in biomedicine for healthcare applications* (pp. 247–266). Hershey, PA: Medical Information Science Reference. doi:10.4018/978-1-4666-2196-1.ch027

Shirkhodaee, M., & Rezaee, S. (2013). Evaluating the persuasive and memory effects of viral advertising. *International Journal of Online Marketing*, *3*(3), 51–61. doi:10.4018/ijom.2013070104

Simzar, R., & Domina, T. (2014). Attending to student motivation through critical practice: A recommendation for improving accelerated mathematical learning. In S. Lawrence (Ed.), *Critical practice in P-12 education: Transformative teaching and learning* (pp. 66–116). Hershey, PA: Information Science Reference. doi:10.4018/978-1-4666-5059-6.ch004

Smart, P. R., Engelbrecht, P. C., Braines, D., Strub, M., & Giammanco, C. (2010). The network-extended mind. In D. Verma (Ed.), *Network science for military coalition operations: Information exchange and interaction* (pp. 191–236). Hershey, PA: Information Science Reference. doi:10.4018/978-1-61520-855-5.ch010

Smith, M. A. (2011). Functions of unconscious and conscious emotion in the regulation of implicit and explicit motivated behavior. In D. Gökçay & G. Yildirim (Eds.), *Affective computing and interaction: Psychological, cognitive and neuroscientific perspectives* (pp. 25–55). Hershey, PA: Information Science Reference. doi:10.4018/978-1-61692-892-6.ch002

Soliman, F. (2014). Could knowledge, learning, and innovation gaps be spiralling? In F. Soliman (Ed.), *Learning models for innovation in organizations: Examining roles of knowledge transfer and human resources management* (pp. 1–29). Hershey, PA: Business Science Reference. doi:10.4018/978-1-4666-4884-5.ch001

Somyürek, S. (2012). Interactive learning in workplace training. In J. Jia (Ed.), *Educational stages and interactive learning: From kindergarten to workplace training* (pp. 498–514). Hershey, PA: Information Science Reference. doi:10.4018/978-1-4666-0137-6.ch027

Spadaro, L., Timpano, F., Marino, S., & Bramanti, P. (2013). Telemedicine and Alzheimer disease: ICT-based services for people with Alzheimer disease and their caregivers. In V. Gulla, A. Mori, F. Gabbrielli, & P. Lanzafame (Eds.), *Telehealth networks for hospital services: New methodologies* (pp. 191–206). Hershey, PA: Medical Information Science Reference. doi:10.4018/978-1-4666-2979-0.ch013

Spiegel, T. (2014). An overview of cognition roles in decision-making. In J. Wang (Ed.), *Encyclopedia of business analytics and optimization* (pp. 74–84). Hershey, PA: Business Science Reference. doi:10.4018/978-1-4666-5202-6.ch008

Stachon, Z., & Šašinka, C. (2012). Human cognition: People in the world and world in their minds. In T. Podobnikar & M. Čeh (Eds.), *Universal ontology of geographic space: Semantic enrichment for spatial data* (pp. 97–122). Hershey, PA: Information Science Reference. doi:10.4018/978-1-4666-0327-1.ch005

Stefurak, J. R., Surry, D. W., & Hayes, R. L. (2011). Technology in the supervision of mental health professionals: Ethical, interpersonal, and epistemological implications. In D. Surry, R. Gray Jr, & J. Stefurak (Eds.), *Technology integration in higher education: Social and organizational aspects* (pp. 114–131). Hershey, PA: Information Science Reference. doi:10.4018/978-1-60960-147-8.ch009

Stieglitz, S. (2014). The American memory project. In J. Krueger (Ed.), *Cases on electronic records and resource management implementation in diverse environments* (pp. 106–116). Hershey, PA: Information Science Reference. doi:10.4018/978-1-4666-4466-3.ch006

Suárez, M. G., & Gumiel, C. G. (2014). The use of sensorial marketing in stores: Attracting clients through their senses. In F. Musso & E. Druica (Eds.), *Handbook of research on retailer-consumer relationship development* (pp. 258–274). Hershey, PA: Business Science Reference. doi:10.4018/978-1-4666-6074-8.ch014

Sugiura, M. (2013). A cognitive neuroscience approach to self and mental health. In J. Wu (Ed.), *Biomedical engineering and cognitive neuroscience for healthcare: Interdisciplinary applications* (pp. 1–10). Hershey, PA: Medical Information Science Reference. doi:10.4018/978-1-4666-2113-8.ch001

Sujo-Montes, L. E., Armfield, S. W., Yen, C., & Tu, C. (2014). The use of ubiquitous learning for children with Down Syndrome. In F. Neto (Ed.), *Technology platform innovations and forthcoming trends in ubiquitous learning* (pp. 160–176). Hershey, PA: Information Science Reference. doi:10.4018/978-1-4666-4542-4.ch009

Tamba, H. (2013). Workers' mental health problems and future perspectives in Japan: Psychological job stress research. In J. Wu (Ed.), *Biomedical engineering and cognitive neuroscience for healthcare: Interdisciplinary applications* (pp. 370–379). Hershey, PA: Medical Information Science Reference. doi:10.4018/978-1-4666-2113-8.ch038

Tatachari, S., Manikandan, K. S., & Gunta, S. (2014). A synthesis of organizational learning and knowledge management literatures. In M. Chilton & J. Bloodgood (Eds.), *Knowledge management and competitive advantage: Issues and potential solutions* (pp. 122–147). Hershey, PA: Information Science Reference. doi:10.4018/978-1-4666-4679-7.ch008

Taxén, L. (2010). Cognitive grounding. In L. Taxen (Ed.), *Using activity domain theory for managing complex systems* (pp. 108–124). Hershey, PA: Information Science Reference. doi:10.4018/978-1-60566-192-6.ch006

Te'eni, D. (2012). Knowledge for communicating knowledge. In *Organizational learning and knowledge: Concepts, methodologies, tools and applications* (pp. 1656–1665). Hershey, PA: Business Science Reference. doi:10.4018/978-1-60960-783-8.ch501

Terras, M. M., & Ramsay, J. (2014). E-learning, mobility, and time: A psychological framework. In E. Barbera & P. Reimann (Eds.), *Assessment and evaluation of time factors in online teaching and learning* (pp. 63–90). Hershey, PA: Information Science Reference. doi:10.4018/978-1-4666-4651-3.ch003

Thapa, A. (2013). A study on worker's perceptions of psychological capital on their earnings. *International Journal of Applied Behavioral Economics*, 2(3), 27–42. doi:10.4018/ijabe.2013070103

Thatcher, A., & Ndabeni, M. (2013). A psychological model to understand e-adoption in the context of the digital divide. In *Digital literacy: Concepts, methodologies, tools, and applications* (pp. 1402–1424). Hershey, PA: Information Science Reference. doi:10.4018/978-1-4666-1852-7.ch074

Thompson, K., & Markauskaite, L. (2014). Identifying group processes and affect in learners: A holistic approach to assessment in virtual worlds in higher education. In S. Kennedy-Clark, K. Everett, & P. Wheeler (Eds.), *Cases on the assessment of scenario and game-based virtual worlds in higher education* (pp. 175–210). Hershey, PA: Information Science Reference. doi:10.4018/978-1-4666-4470-0.ch006

Titus, C. S. (2013). The use of developmental psychology in ethics: Beyond Kohlberg and Seligman? In F. Doridot, P. Duquenoy, P. Goujon, A. Kurt, S. Lavelle, N. Patrignani, & A. Santuccio et al. (Eds.), *Ethical governance of emerging technologies development* (pp. 266–286). Hershey, PA: Information Science Reference. doi:10.4018/978-1-4666-3670-5.ch018

Tiwary, U. S., & Siddiqui, T. J. (2014). Working together with computers: Towards a general framework for collaborative human computer interaction. In *Assistive technologies: Concepts, methodologies, tools, and applications* (pp. 141–162). Hershey, PA: Information Science Reference. doi:10.4018/978-1-4666-4422-9.ch008

Tomono, A. (2013). Display technology of images with scents and its psychological evaluation. In T. Nakamoto (Ed.), *Human olfactory displays and interfaces: Odor sensing and presentation* (pp. 429–445). Hershey, PA: Information Science Reference. doi:10.4018/978-1-4666-2521-1.ch022

Torres, G., Jaime, K., & Ramos, F. (2013). Brain architecture for visual object identification. *International Journal of Cognitive Informatics and Natural Intelligence*, 7(1), 75–97. doi:10.4018/jcini.2013010104

Trajkovski, G., Stojanov, G., Collins, S., Eidelman, V., Harman, C., & Vincenti, G. (2011). Cognitive robotics and multiagency in a fuzzy modeling framework. In G. Trajkovski (Ed.), *Developments in intelligent agent technologies and multi-agent systems: Concepts and applications* (pp. 132–152). Hershey, PA: Information Science Reference. doi:10.4018/978-1-60960-171-3.ch009

Tran, B. (2014). Rhetoric of play: Utilizing the gamer factor in selecting and training employees. In T. Connolly, T. Hainey, E. Boyle, G. Baxter, & P. Moreno-Ger (Eds.), *Psychology, pedagogy, and assessment in serious games* (pp. 175–203). Hershey, PA: Information Science Reference. doi:10.4018/978-1-4666-4773-2.ch009

Tran, B. (2014). The psychology of consumerism in business and marketing: The macro and micro behaviors of Hofstede's cultural consumers. In H. Kaufmann & M. Panni (Eds.), *Handbook of research on consumerism in business and marketing: Concepts and practices* (pp. 286–308). Hershey, PA: Business Science Reference. doi:10.4018/978-1-4666-5880-6.ch014

Travica, B. (2014). Homo informaticus. In *Examining the informing view of organization: Applying theoretical and managerial approaches* (pp. 34–66). Hershey, PA: Business Science Reference. doi:10.4018/978-1-4666-5986-5.ch002

Twomey, K. E., Horst, J. S., & Morse, A. F. (2013). An embodied model of young children's categorization and word learning. In L. Gogate & G. Hollich (Eds.), *Theoretical and computational models of word learning: Trends in psychology and artificial intelligence* (pp. 172–196). Hershey, PA: Information Science Reference. doi:10.4018/978-1-4666-2973-8.ch008

Ursyn, A. (2014). Cognitive processes involved in visual thought. In *Perceptions of knowledge visualization: Explaining concepts through meaningful images* (pp. 131–173). Hershey, PA: Information Science Reference. doi:10.4018/978-1-4666-4703-9.ch005

Ursyn, A. (2014). Communication through many senses. In *Perceptions of knowledge visualization: Explaining concepts through meaningful images* (pp. 25–60). Hershey, PA: Information Science Reference. doi:10.4018/978-1-4666-4703-9.ch002

Ursyn, A. (2014). Four trapped in an elevator. In *Computational solutions for knowledge, art, and entertainment: Information exchange beyond text* (pp. 322–329). Hershey, PA: Information Science Reference. doi:10.4018/978-1-4666-4627-8.ch016

Usart, M., & Romero, M. (2014). Time factor assessment in game-based learning: Time perspective and time-on-task as individual differences between players. In T. Connolly, T. Hainey, E. Boyle, G. Baxter, & P. Moreno-Ger (Eds.), *Psychology, pedagogy, and assessment in serious games* (pp. 62–81). Hershey, PA: Information Science Reference. doi:10.4018/978-1-4666-4773-2.ch004

Usoro, A., Majewski, G., & Bloom, L. (2012). Individual and collaborative approaches in e-learning design. In *Virtual learning environments: Concepts, methodologies, tools and applications* (pp. 1110–1130). Hershey, PA: Information Science Reference. doi:10.4018/978-1-4666-0011-9.ch514

van den Brink, J. C. (2014). How positive psychology can support sustainable project management. In *Sustainable practices: Concepts, methodologies, tools and applications* (pp. 958–973). Hershey, PA: Information Science Reference. doi:10.4018/978-1-4666-4852-4.ch053 van der Helden, J., & Bekkering, H. (2014). The role of implicit and explicit feedback in learning and the implications for distance education techniques. In T. Yuzer & G. Eby (Eds.), *Handbook of research on emerging priorities and trends in distance education: Communication, pedagogy, and technology* (pp. 367–384). Hershey, PA: Information Science Reference. doi:10.4018/978-1-4666-5162-3.ch025

van Mierlo, C. M., Jarodzka, H., Kirschner, F., & Kirschner, P. A. (2012). Cognitive load theory in e-learning. In Z. Yan (Ed.), *Encyclopedia of cyber behavior* (pp. 1178–1211). Hershey, PA: Information Science Reference. doi:10.4018/978-1-4666-0315-8.ch097

van Rosmalen, P., Wilson, A., & Hummel, H. G. (2014). Games for and by teachers and learners. In T. Connolly, T. Hainey, E. Boyle, G. Baxter, & P. Moreno-Ger (Eds.), *Psychology, pedagogy, and assessment in serious games* (pp. 243–269). Hershey, PA: Information Science Reference. doi:10.4018/978-1-4666-4773-2.ch012

Vega, J., Perdices, E., & Cañas, J. M. (2014). Attentive visual memory for robot localization. In Robotics: Concepts, methodologies, tools, and applications (pp. 785-811). Hershey, PA: Information Science Reference. doi:10.4018/978-1-4666-4607-0.ch038

Vinther, J. (2012). Cognitive skills through CALL-enhanced teacher training. In F. Zhang (Ed.), *Computer-enhanced and mobile-assisted language learning: Emerging issues and trends* (pp. 158–187). Hershey, PA: Information Science Reference. doi:10.4018/978-1-61350-065-1.ch008

Vogel, E. H., & Ponce, F. P. (2011). Empirical issues and theoretical mechanisms of Pavlovian conditioning. In E. Alonso & E. Mondragón (Eds.), *Computational neuroscience for advancing artificial intelligence: Models, methods and applications* (pp. 81–110). Hershey, PA: Medical Information Science Reference. doi:10.4018/978-1-60960-021-1.ch005

Vragov, R. (2013). Detecting behavioral biases in mixed human-proxy online auction markets. *International Journal of Strategic Information Technology and Applications*, 4(4), 60–79. doi:10.4018/ijsita.2013100104

Wagner, C. L., & Delisi, J. (2010). Multi-sensory environments and augmentative communication tools. In S. Seok, E. Meyen, & B. DaCosta (Eds.), *Handbook of research on human cognition and assistive technology: Design, accessibility and transdisciplinary perspectives* (pp. 121–131). Hershey, PA: Medical Information Science Reference. doi:10.4018/978-1-61520-817-3.ch008

Walk, A. M., & Conway, C. M. (2014). Two distinct sequence learning mechanisms for syntax acquisition and word learning. In *Computational linguistics: Concepts, methodologies, tools, and applications* (pp. 540–560). Hershey, PA: Information Science Reference. doi:10.4018/978-1-4666-6042-7.ch025

Wang, H. (2014). A guide to assistive technology for teachers in special education. In *Assistive technologies: Concepts, methodologies, tools, and applications* (pp. 12–25). Hershey, PA: Information Science Reference. doi:10.4018/978-1-4666-4422-9.ch002

Wang, J. (2012). Organizational learning and technology. In V. Wang (Ed.), *Encyclopedia of e-leadership, counseling and training* (pp. 154–170). Hershey, PA: Information Science Reference. doi:10.4018/978-1-61350-068-2.ch012

Wang, K. Y. (2014). Mixing metaphors: Sociological and psychological perspectives on virtual communities. In *Cross-cultural interaction: Concepts, methodologies, tools and applications* (pp. 116–132). Hershey, PA: Information Science Reference. doi:10.4018/978-1-4666-4979-8.ch008

Wang, Y. (2013). Neuroinformatics models of human memory: Mapping the cognitive functions of memory onto neurophysiological structures of the brain. *International Journal of Cognitive Informatics and Natural Intelligence, 7*(1), 98–122. doi:10.4018/jcini.2013010105

Wang, Y. (2013). The cognitive mechanisms and formal models of consciousness. *International Journal of Cognitive Informatics and Natural Intelligence, 6*(2), 23–40. doi:10.4018/jcini.2012040102

Wang, Y. (2013). Towards the synergy of cognitive informatics, neural informatics, brain informatics, and cognitive computing. In Y. Wang (Ed.), *Cognitive informatics for revealing human cognition: Knowledge manipulations in natural intelligence* (pp. 1–19). Hershey, PA: Information Science Reference. doi:10.4018/978-1-4666-2476-4.ch001

Wang, Y., Berwick, R. C., Haykin, S., Pedrycz, W., Kinsner, W., & Baciu, G. … Gavrilova, M. L. (2013). Cognitive informatics and cognitive computing in year 10 and beyond. In Y. Wang (Ed.), Cognitive informatics for revealing human cognition: Knowledge manipulations in natural intelligence (pp. 140-157). Hershey, PA: Information Science Reference. doi:10.4018/978-1-4666-2476-4.ch010

Wang, Y., Fariello, G., Gavrilova, M. L., Kinsner, W., Mizoguchi, F., Patel, S., & Tsumoto, S. et al. (2013). Perspectives on cognitive computers and knowledge processors. *International Journal of Cognitive Informatics and Natural Intelligence, 7*(3), 1–24. doi:10.4018/ijcini.2013070101

Wang, Y., Patel, S., & Patel, D. (2013). The cognitive process and formal models of human attentions. *International Journal of Software Science and Computational Intelligence, 5*(1), 32–50. doi:10.4018/ijssci.2013010103

Wang, Y., Pedrycz, W., Baciu, G., Chen, P., Wang, G., & Yao, Y. (2012). Perspectives on cognitive computing and applications. In Y. Wang (Ed.), *Breakthroughs in software science and computational intelligence* (pp. 1–12). Hershey, PA: Information Science Reference. doi:10.4018/978-1-4666-0264-9.ch001

Wang, Y., Widrow, B. C., Zhang, B., Kinsner, W., Sugawara, K., Sun, F., & Zhang, D. et al. (2013). Perspectives on the field of cognitive informatics and its future development. In Y. Wang (Ed.), *Cognitive informatics for revealing human cognition: Knowledge manipulations in natural intelligence* (pp. 20–34). Hershey, PA: Information Science Reference. doi:10.4018/978-1-4666-2476-4.ch002

Was, C. A., & Woltz, D. J. (2013). Implicit memory and aging: Adapting technology to utilize preserved memory functions. In R. Zheng, R. Hill, & M. Gardner (Eds.), *Engaging older adults with modern technology: Internet use and information access needs* (pp. 1–19). Hershey, PA: Information Science Reference. doi:10.4018/978-1-4666-1966-1.ch001

Wei, H. (2013). A neural dynamic model based on activation diffusion and a micro-explanation for cognitive operations. *International Journal of Cognitive Informatics and Natural Intelligence*, *6*(2), 1–22. doi:10.4018/jcini.2012040101

Wexler, R. H., & Roff-Wexler, S. (2013). The evolution and development of self in virtual worlds. *International Journal of Cyber Behavior, Psychology and Learning*, *3*(1), 1–6. doi:10.4018/ijcbpl.2013010101

Wickramasinghe, N. (2012). Knowledge economy for innovating organizations. In *Organizational learning and knowledge: Concepts, methodologies, tools and applications* (pp. 2298–2309). Hershey, PA: Business Science Reference. doi:10.4018/978-1-60960-783-8.ch616

Widrow, B. C., & Aragon, J. (2012). Cognitive memory: Human like memory. In Y. Wang (Ed.), *Breakthroughs in software science and computational intelligence* (pp. 84–99). Hershey, PA: Information Science Reference. doi:10.4018/978-1-4666-0264-9.ch006

Widyanto, L., & Griffiths, M. (2013). An empirical study of problematic internet use and self-esteem. In R. Zheng (Ed.), *Evolving psychological and educational perspectives on cyber behavior* (pp. 82–95). Hershey, PA: Information Science Reference. doi:10.4018/978-1-4666-1858-9.ch006

Wilson, M. S., & Pascoe, J. (2010). Using software to deliver language intervention in inclusionary settings. In S. Seok, E. Meyen, & B. DaCosta (Eds.), *Handbook of research on human cognition and assistive technology: Design, accessibility and transdisciplinary perspectives* (pp. 132–156). Hershey, PA: Medical Information Science Reference. doi:10.4018/978-1-61520-817-3.ch009

Wilson, S., & Haslam, N. (2013). Reasoning about human enhancement: Towards a folk psychological model of human nature and human identity. In R. Luppicini (Ed.), *Handbook of research on technoself: Identity in a technological society* (pp. 175–188). Hershey, PA: Information Science Reference. doi:10.4018/978-1-4666-2211-1.ch010

Wilson, S. G. (2014). Enhancement and identity: A social psychological perspective. In S. Thompson (Ed.), *Global issues and ethical considerations in human enhancement technologies* (pp. 241–256). Hershey, PA: Medical Information Science Reference. doi:10.4018/978-1-4666-6010-6.ch014

Winsor, D. L. (2012). The epistemology of young children. In S. Blake, D. Winsor, & L. Allen (Eds.), *Child development and the use of technology: Perspectives, applications and experiences* (pp. 21–44). Hershey, PA: Information Science Reference. doi:10.4018/978-1-61350-317-1.ch002

Winsor, D. L., & Blake, S. (2012). Socrates and Descartes meet the E*Trade baby: The impact of early technology on children's developing beliefs about knowledge and knowing. In S. Blake, D. Winsor, & L. Allen (Eds.), *Child development and the use of technology: Perspectives, applications and experiences* (pp. 1–20). Hershey, PA: Information Science Reference. doi:10.4018/978-1-61350-317-1.ch001

Yakavenka, H. (2012). Developing professional competencies through international peer learning communities. In V. Dennen & J. Myers (Eds.), *Virtual professional development and informal learning via social networks* (pp. 134–154). Hershey, PA: Information Science Reference. doi:10.4018/978-1-4666-1815-2.ch008

Yamaguchi, M., & Shetty, V. (2013). Evaluating the psychobiologic effects of fragrances through salivary biomarkers. In T. Nakamoto (Ed.), *Human olfactory displays and interfaces: Odor sensing and presentation* (pp. 359–369). Hershey, PA: Information Science Reference. doi:10.4018/978-1-4666-2521-1.ch017

Yan, Z., & Zheng, R. Z. (2013). Growing from childhood into adolescence: The science of cyber behavior. In R. Zheng (Ed.), *Evolving psychological and educational perspectives on cyber behavior* (pp. 1–14). Hershey, PA: Information Science Reference. doi:10.4018/978-1-4666-1858-9.ch001

Yildirim, G., & Gökçay, D. (2011). Problems associated with computer-mediated communication cognitive psychology and neuroscience perspectives. In D. Gökçay & G. Yildirim (Eds.), *Affective computing and interaction: Psychological, cognitive and neuroscientific perspectives* (pp. 244–261). Hershey, PA: Information Science Reference. doi:10.4018/978-1-61692-892-6.ch011

Younan, Y., Joosen, W., Piessens, F., & Van den Eynden, H. (2012). Improving memory management security for C and C. In K. Khan (Ed.), *Security-aware systems applications and software development methods* (pp. 190–216). Hershey, PA: Information Science Reference. doi:10.4018/978-1-4666-1580-9.ch011

Yu, C., & Smith, L. B. (2013). A sensory-motor solution to early word-referent learning. In L. Gogate & G. Hollich (Eds.), *Theoretical and computational models of word learning: Trends in psychology and artificial intelligence* (pp. 133–152). Hershey, PA: Information Science Reference. doi:10.4018/978-1-4666-2973-8.ch006

Yu, J., Chen, Z., Lu, J., Liu, T., Zhou, L., Liu, X., . . . Chui, D. (2013). The important role of lipids in cognitive impairment. In Bioinformatics: Concepts, methodologies, tools, and applications (pp. 268-272). Hershey, PA: Medical Information Science Reference. doi:10.4018/978-1-4666-3604-0.ch014

Yu, Y., Yang, J., & Wu, J. (2013). Cognitive functions and neuronal mechanisms of tactile working memory. In J. Wu (Ed.), *Biomedical engineering and cognitive neuroscience for healthcare: Interdisciplinary applications* (pp. 89–98). Hershey, PA: Medical Information Science Reference. doi:10.4018/978-1-4666-2113-8.ch010

Zelinski, E. M. (2013). How interventions might improve cognition in healthy older adults. *International Journal of Gaming and Computer-Mediated Simulations*, *5*(3), 72–82. doi:10.4018/jgcms.2013070105

Zhang, J., Luo, X., Lu, L., & Liu, W. (2013). An acquisition model of deep textual semantics based on human reading cognitive process. *International Journal of Cognitive Informatics and Natural Intelligence*, *6*(2), 82–103. doi:10.4018/jcini.2012040105

Zheng, R. Z. (2013). Effective online learning for older people: A heuristic design approach. In R. Zheng, R. Hill, & M. Gardner (Eds.), *Engaging older adults with modern technology: Internet use and information access needs* (pp. 142–159). Hershey, PA: Information Science Reference. doi:10.4018/978-1-4666-1966-1.ch008

Zhou, M., & Xu, Y. (2013). Challenges to use recommender systems to enhance meta-cognitive functioning in online learners. In *Data mining: Concepts, methodologies, tools, and applications* (pp. 1916–1935). Hershey, PA: Information Science Reference. doi:10.4018/978-1-4666-2455-9.ch099

Ziaeehezarjeribi, Y., & Graves, I. (2013). Behind the MASK: Motivation through avatar skills and knowledge. In R. Ferdig (Ed.), *Design, utilization, and analysis of simulations and game-based educational worlds* (pp. 225–239). Hershey, PA: Information Science Reference. doi:10.4018/978-1-4666-4018-4.ch014

Zoss, A. M. (2014). Cognitive processes and traits related to graphic comprehension. In M. Huang & W. Huang (Eds.), *Innovative approaches of data visualization and visual analytics* (pp. 94–110). Hershey, PA: Information Science Reference. doi:10.4018/978-1-4666-4309-3.ch005

# Compilation of References

Acker, S. R. (2013). Digital textbooks. *Library Technology Reports, 47*(8), 41–51.

Agusti, M. F., Velasco, M. R., & Serrano, M. J. (2011). E-Learning: Psycho-pedagogical utility, usability and accessibility criteria from a learner centred perspective. In F. Lazarinis, S. Green, & E. Pearson (Eds.), *Handbook of research on e-learning standards and interoperability: Frameworks and issues* (pp. 419–434). Hershey, PA: Information Science Reference. doi:10.4018/978-1-61692-789-9.ch021

Akerlind, G., McKenzie, J., & Lupton, M. (2014). The potential of combining phenomenography, variation theory and threshold concepts to inform curriculum design in higher education. In J. Huisman &M. Tight (Eds.), Theory and method in higher education research II (International Perspectives on Higher Education Research, 10), (pp. 227-247). doi:10.1108/S1479-3628(2014)0000010017

Alberta (2013). *Digital repository of textbooks for students with disabilities*. Retrieved October, 25, 2014, from http://www.scholastic.com/browse/article.jsp?id=3755544

Aleven, V., Roll, I., Mclaren, B. M., & Koedinger, K. R. (2010). Automated, unobtrusive, action-by-action assessment of self-regulation during learning with an Intelligent Tutoring System. *Educational Psychologist, 45*(4), 224–233. doi:10.1080/00461520.2010.517740

Alexander, H. A. (2014). Traditions of inquiry in education: Engaging the paradigms of educational research. In A. D. Reid, E. P. Hart, & P. A. Peters (Eds.), *A companion to research in education* (pp. 13–25). Springer Netherlands. doi:10.1007/978-94-007-6809-3_2

Aliyev, S., Altayev, Z., Ismagambetova, Z., & Massanov, Y. (2012). *Philosophy of education: the challenges of globalization and innovation in the information society. Engineering& Technology., 71*, 1096–1098.

Ally, M., & Prieto-Blaázquez, J. (2014). What is the future of mobile learning in education? Revista de Universidad y Sociedad del Conocimiento, 11(1), 142-151.

Alonso, D. L., & Blazquez, E. F. (2009). Are the functions of teachers in e-learning and face-to-face learning are really different? *Journal of Educational Technology & Society, 12*(4), 331–343.

Alsheail, A. (2010). *Teaching English as a second/foreign language in a ubiquitous learning environment: a guide for ESL/EFL instructors*. Retrieved October 29, 2014 from http://csuchicodspace.calstate.edu/bitstream/handle/10211.4/184/5%209%202010%20Abdulrahman%20Alsheail.pdf?sequence=1

Amazon.com. (2014). *Study smarter with Kindle eTextbooks*. Retrieved October, 29, 2014 from http://www.amazon.com/Kindle-Textbooks/b?node=2223210011

Anderson, A., & Winthrop, R. (2013). *Dakar consensus: Equitable, quality learning for all*. Brookings. Retrieved November 1, 2014 from http://www.brookings.edu/blogs/education-plus-development/posts/2013/03/25-dakar-equitable-quality-learning-anderson-winthrop

Anglin, L., Anglin, K., Schumann, P., & Kaliski, J. (2008). Improving the efficiency and effectiveness of grading through the use of computer-assisted grading rubrics. *Journal of Innovative Education, 6*(1), 51–73.

Anstey, M., & Bull, G. (2010). Helping teachers to explore multimodal texts. *Curriculum & Leadership Journal, 8*(16). Retrieved October 25, 2014 from http://www.curriculum.edu.au/leader/helping_teachers_to_explore_multimodal_texts,31522.html?issueID=12141

Archnet, I. J. (2014). Three holy myths of architectural education in India. *International Journal of Architectural Research, 5*(1), 175–184.

Arimoto, A. (2014). The teaching and research nexus in the third wave age. In J.C. Shin, A. Arimoto, W. C. Cummings, & U. C. Teichler, (Eds.), Teaching and research in contemporary higher education, (pp. 15-33). Springer. doi:10.1007/978-94-007-6830-7_2

Armen, H., & Atwood, L. (2013). Creating Social Books. In *Interactive eBooks for Children. IBooC2013: Proceedings of Workshop at IDC Interaction Design and Children*, (pp. 24-28).

Ashford-Rowe, K., Herrington, J., & Brown, C. (2014). Establishing the critical elements that determine authentic assessment. *Assessment & Evaluation in Higher Education, 39*(2), 205–222. doi:10.1080/02602938.2013.819566

Bain, L. Z. (2014). How students use technology to cheat and what faculty can do about it. In *Proceedings of the Information Systems Educators Conference, 31*(3020), pp. 1-8. Retrieved November 2, 2014 from http://proc.isecon.org/2014/pdf/3020.pdf

Bainbridge, W. S. (2014). Virtual Worlds. In W. S. Bainbridge, (Ed.), Personality capture and emulation (pp. 177-203). Springer London.

Bali, J., Neeraj, N., & Bali, R. T. (2014). Computer vision syndrome: A review. *Journal of Clinical Ophthalmology and Research, 2*(1), 61.

Banister, S., Reinhart, R., & Ross, C. (2014). Using digital resources to support personalized learning experiences in K-12 classrooms: The evolution of mobile devices as innovations in schools in northwest Ohio. In *Proceedings of Society for Information Technology & Teacher Education International Conference, 1*, (pp. 2715-2721).

Barker, J., & Tucker, R. (1990). *The interactive learning revolution.* New York: London-Nichols Publishing.

Barnett, R. (2014). Thinking about higher education. In P., Gibbs, R. & Barnett (Eds.), Thinking about higher education, (pp. 9-22). Switzerland: Springer International Publishing. doi:10.1007/978-3-319-03254-2_2

Bartz, W., & Darby, C. (1966). The effects of programmed textbook to achievement under three techniques of instruction. *Journal of Experimental Education, 34*(3), 46–52. doi:10.1080/00220973.1966.11010936

*Baylor School.* (2014). Retrieved November 21, 2014 from http://mail.baylorschool.org/~jstover/plagiarism/intent.htm

Beck, R. J. (2010). *What are learning objects?* Retrieved July 22, 2014 from http://www4.uwm.edu/cie/learning_objects.cfm?gid=56

Becker, K., & Black, T. (2012). *The sensitivity principle in epistemology.* Cambridge University Press. doi:10.1017/CBO9780511783630

Beckett, D., & Gough, J. (2004). Perceptions of professional identity: A story from paediatrics. *Studies in Continuing Education, 26*(2), 195–208. doi:10.1080/158037042000225218

Bell, F., Zaitseva, E., & Zakrzewska, D. (2007). Evaluation: A link in the chain of sustainability. In N. Lambropoulos & P. Zaphiris (Eds.), *User-centered design of online learning communities* (pp. 186–214). Hershey, PA: Information Science. doi:10.4018/978-1-59904-358-6.ch009

Bergaz. (2009). *The methodology of school textbooks* (Unpublished PhD thesis). Chisinau: Moldova State University.

Berg, G. A. (2003). Learning theory and technology: Behavioral, constructivist and adult learning approaches. In G. Berg (Ed.), *The knowledge medium: Designing effective computer-based educational learning environments* (pp. 9–27). Hershey, PA: Information Science Publishing. doi:10.4018/978-1-59140-103-2.ch002

Bergmann, J., & Sams, A. (2013). *Flipped classroom webinar series.* Retrieved October, 25 2014, from http://www.ascd.org/professional-development/webinars/flipped-classroom-webinars.aspx

Bespalco, V. (2002). *Teaching and learning with computers* [In Russian]. Retrieved November 1, 2014 from http://www.eusi.ru/lib/bespalko_obrasovanie/3.php

BISC. (2011). *BISG Policy Statement POL-1101. Best practices for identifying digital products.* Retrieved November 2, 2014 from https://www.myidentifiers.com/sites/default/files/images/BEST+PRACTICES+FOR+IDENTIFYING+DIGITAL+PRODUCTS.pdf

Bliesner, A., Liedtke, C., Welfens, M. J., Baedeker, C., Hasselkuß, M., & Rohn, H. (2014). "Norm-oriented interpretation learning" and resource use: The concept of "open-didactic exploration" as a contribution to raising awareness of a responsible resource use. *Resources, 3*(1), 1–30. doi:10.3390/resources3010001

Bliss, T. J. (2013). *A model of digital textbook quality from the perspective of college students* (PhD thesis). Brigham Young University. Retrieved November 25, 2014, from https://learningtomorrow.hva.nl/nl/achtergrondinformatie/Gedeelde%20documenten/A%20model%20of%20digital%20textbook%20quality.pdf

*Bloom taxonomy.* (n. d.). Retrieved October, 25, 2014 from http://juliaec.files.wordpress.com/2011/04/blooms_taxonomy.jpg

Bloom, J. (2009). *Pattern Thinking, systems thinking, and complex—transferrable learning in education for sustainability.* Retrieved September 1, 2014 from http://www.jeffbloom.net/docs/b-PatternSystemThkg.pdf

Bloom, J. W., & Volk, T. (2007). *The use of metapatterns for research into complex systems of teaching, learning, and schooling.* Retrieved October 3, 2014 from http://citeseerx.ist.psu.edu/viewdoc/download?doi=10.1.1.120.6165&rep=rep1&type=pdf

Bloxham, S., & Carver, M. (2014). Assessment for learning in higher education. *Assessment & Evaluation in Higher Education, 39*(1), 123–126. doi:10.1080/02602938.2013.797652

Boesen, J., Helenius, O., Bergqvist, E., Bergqvist, T., Lithner, J., Palm, T., & Palmberg, B. (2014). Developing mathematical competence: From the intended to the enacted curriculum. *The Journal of Mathematical Behavior, 33*, 72–87. doi:10.1016/j.jmathb.2013.10.001

Bokhorst, F., Moskaliuk, J., & Cress, U. (2014). How patterns support computer-mediated exchange of knowledge-in-use. *Computers & Education, 71*, 153–164. doi:10.1016/j.compedu.2013.09.021

Booker, E. (2013). *E-textbook pilot puts college books in cloud.* Retrieved October, 25, 2014, from http://www.informationweek.com/mobile/mobile-devices/e-textbook-pilot-puts-college-books-in-cloud/d/d-id/1108942?

Bordes, A., Bottou, L., Collobert, R., Roth, D., Weston, J., & Zettlemoyer, L. (2014). Introduction to the special issue on learning semantics. *Machine Learning, 94*(2), 127–131. doi:10.1007/s10994-013-5381-4

Bostock, S. J. (1998). Constructivism in mass higher education: A case study. *British Journal of Educational Technology, 29*(3), 225–240. doi:10.1111/1467-8535.00066

Boudourides, M. A. (2003). Constructivism, education, science, and technology. *Canadian Journal of Learning and Technology, 29*(3). Retrieved February 5, 2015 from http://www.cjlt.ca/index.php/cjlt/article/viewArticle/83/77

Bourn, D. (2014). *The theory and practice of global learning.* Retrieved November 1, 2014 from http://www.ioe.ac.uk/DERC_ResearchPaper11-TheTheoryAndPracticeOfGlobalLearning.pdf

*Bowker. Identifier Services.* (2014). Retrieved November 21, 2014 from https://www.myidentifiers.com/Get-your-isbn-now

Britanica, E. (2014). *Postmodernism and modern philosophy.* Retrieved October 25, 2014, from http://www.britannica.com/EBchecked/topic/1077292/postmodernism

Bronfenbrenner, U. (1977). Toward an experimental ecology of human development. *The American Psychologist, 32*(7), 513–531. doi:10.1037/0003-066X.32.7.513

Brophy, J. (2008). Textbook reform. In T. Good (Ed.), 21st century education: A reference handbook. (pp. 414-423). Thousand Oaks, CA: SAGE Publications, Inc. doi:10.4135/9781412964012.n45

Brunner, J. (2013). *Structural equation models: An open textbook.* Edition 0.07. Retrieved October 25, 2014, from http://www.utstat.utoronto.ca/~brunner/openSEM/OpenSEM_0.07f.pdf

Brusilovsky, P., Schwarz, E., & Weber, G. (1997). Electronic textbooks on www: From static hypertext to interactivity and adaptivity. In B. H. Khan (Ed.), Web-based instruction. Educational technology publications (pp. 255-261). Educational Technology Publications, Inc.

Bryant, B. P., & Bryant, J. B. (2014). Relative weights of the backpacks of elementary-aged children. *The Journal of School Nursing*, *30*(1), 19–23. doi:10.1177/1059840513495417 PMID:23811534

Buhl, M. (2008). *New teacher functions in cyberspace - on technology, mass media and education*, *4*(1). Retrieved October 29, 2014 from seminar.net/index.php/volume-4-issue-1-2008-previousissuesmeny-122/89-new-teacher-functions-in-cyberspace-on-technology-mass-media-and-education.

Burns, M. (2011). *Distance education for teacher training: Modes, models and methods*. Retrieved October 25, 2014, from http://idd.edc.org/sites/idd.edc.org/files/Distance%20Education%20for%20Teacher%20Training%20by%20Mary%20Burns%20EDC.pdf

Burrus, D. (2014). *The tech trends that will disrupt, create opportunities*. Retrieved October 28, 2014 from http://blogs.wsj.com/cio/2014/01/16/the-tech-trends-that-will-disrupt-create-opportunities-in-2014/

Butter, M. C., Perez, L. J., & Quintana, M. G. B. (2014). School networks to promote ICT competences among teachers. Case study in intercultural schools. *Computers in Human Behavior*, *30*, 442–451. doi:10.1016/j.chb.2013.06.024

Caeiro, M., Llamas, M., & Anido, L. (2014). PoEML: Modeling learning units through perspectives. *Computer Standards & Interfaces*, *36*(2), 380–396. doi:10.1016/j.csi.2013.08.009

Caldwell, S. (2012a). *iBooks Author fashions multimedia books for the iPad*. Retrieved November 25, 2014, from http://www.macworld.com/article/1165172/ibooks_author_fashions_multimedia_books_for_the_ipad.html

Caldwell, S. (2012b). *Hands on: iBooks Author effortless to use, but iPad-only*. Retrieved November 25, 2014, from www.macworld.com/article/1164895/hands_on_ibooks_author_effortless_to_use_but_ipad_only.html

Caldwell, S. (2014). *Vellum review: App offers a sleeker way to build ebooks*. Retrieved November 25, 2014, from http://www.macworld.com/article/2084960/vellum-review-app-offers-a-sleeker-way-to-build-ebooks.html

California Open Source Textbook Project. (2012). Retrieved October, 25, 2014, from http://www.open-sourcetext.org/

Cameron, T., & Bennett, S. (2010). Learning objects in practice: The integration of reusable learning objects in primary education. *British Journal of Educational Technology*, *41*(6), 897–908. doi:10.1111/j.1467-8535.2010.01133.x

Campbell, K. (1998). *The Web: Design for active learning*. Retrieved September 1, 2014 from, http://www.atl.ualberta.ca/documents/articles/activeLearning001.htm

Carnegie Learning. (2014). *Pedagogy. Aligned teaching to learning*. Retrieved October, 25 2014, from http://www.carnegielearning.com/learning-solutions/math-worktexts/pedagogy/

Carnegie Learning. (2014a). *Intelligent mathematics software that adapts to meet the needs of ALL students*. Retrieved November 25, 2014, from http://www.carnegie-learning.com/specs/cognitive-tutor-overview/

Carnegie Learning. (2014b). *The high school math series. Preparing students for college, career and their future*. Retrieved November 25, 2014, from http://www.carnegielearning.com/specs/cognitive-tutor-overview/

Carnegie Learning. (2014c). *Why is Carnegie Learning so effective? Because we are constantly doing our homework*. Retrieved November 25, 2014, from m http://www.carnegielearning.com/research/

Carnegie Mellon. (2014). *What are clickers and how do they work?* Retrieved October 25, 2014, from http://www.cmu.edu/teaching/clickers/index.html

Carpenter, C. R., & Greenhill, I. P. (1958). An investigation of closed-circuit television for teaching university courses. instructional television research, report number two. Retrieved October 25, 2014, from http://files.eric.ed.gov/fulltext/ed014871.pdf

Carr, N. (2010) *Author Nicholas Carr: The Web shatters focus, rewires brains.* Retrieved November 25, 2014, from http://www.wired.com/magazine/2010/05/ff_nicholas_carr/all/1

Casassus, B. (2014). French schools report sharp rise in digital textbook use. *The Bookseller.* Retrieved November 1, 2014, from http://www.thebookseller.com/news/french-schools-report-sharp-rise-digital-textbook-use

CAST. (2014). *Digital text in the classroom.* Retrieved November, 1, 2014, from http://www.cast.org/teachingeverystudent/ideas/presentations/digitaltext_slide2.cfm

Cavanaugh, T. W. (2013). *Getting to know a digital textbook.* Retrieved October, 25 2014, from http://www.guide2digitallearning.com/teaching_learning/getting_know_digital_textbok

Cefai, C., & Cavioni, V. (2014). *Social and emotional education in primary school: Integrating theory and research into practice.* Springer Science – Business Media New York. doi:10.1007/978-1-4614-8752-4

Center for Teaching. (2014). *Flipped the classroom.* Retrieved October, 25 2014, from http://cft.vanderbilt.edu/guides-sub-pages/flipping-the-classroom/

Chen, Y., & Chou, C. (2014). Why and who agree on copy-and-paste? Taiwan College Students' perceptions of cyber-plagiarism. In *World Conference on Educational Multimedia, Hypermedia and Telecommunications, 1,* (pp. 937-943). Chesapeake, VA: AACE. Retrieved November 23, 2014 from http://www.editlib.org/p/147602

Chen, G., Gong, C., Yang, J., Yang, X., & Huang, R. (2013). The concept of eTextbooks in K- 12 Classes from the perspective of its stakeholders. *Human-Computer Interaction and Knowledge Discovery in Complex, Unstructured, Big Data (Lecture Notes in Computer Science), 7947,* 319–325. doi:10.1007/978-3-642-39146-0_29

Cheng, M. C., Chou, P. I., Wang, Y. T., & Lin, C. H. (2014). Learning effects of a science textbook designed with adapted cognitive process principles on grade 5 students. *International Journal of Science and Mathematics Education, 13*(62), 1–22.

Chen, N. S., & Hwang, G. J. (2014). Transforming the classrooms: Innovative digital game-based learning designs and applications. *Educational Technology Research and Development, 62*(2), 125–128.

Cheung, K. Y. F. (2014). *Understanding the authorial writer: A mixed methods approach to the psychology of authorial identity in relation to plagiarism.* Retrieved November 21, 2014 from http://derby.openrepository.com/derby/handle/10545/324822

Choppin, J., Carson, C., Borys, Z., Cerosaletti, C., & Gillis, R. (2014). A typology for analyzing digital curricula in mathematics education. *International Journal of Education in Mathematics, Science and Technology, 2*(1), 11–25.

Christiea, B. A., Millera, K., Cookea, R., White, J., & Christie, B. A. et al.. (2013). Environmental sustainability in higher education: How do academics teach? *Environmental Education Research, 19*(3), 385–414. doi:10.1080/13504622.2012.698598

Chuilkov, D. V., & VanAlstine, J. (2013). College Student choice among electronic and printed textbook options. *Journal of Education for Business, 88*(4), 216–222. doi:10.1080/08832323.2012.672936

Chun, L. (2014). *An exploratory study behind the implementation of computer assisted learning in classrooms connected to the internet: Hype or hope?* Retrieved November 1, 2014 http://scholarspace.manoa.hawaii.edu/bitstream/handle/10125/31454/communication005.PDF?sequence=1

*CK-12.* (n. d.). Retrieved October, 25, 2014, from https://ck12.org/

Clara, M., & Barbera, E. (2013). Learning online: Massive open online courses (MOOCs), connectivism, and cultural psychology. *Distance Education, 34*(1), 129–136. doi:10.1080/01587919.2013.770428

Clark, I. (2012). Formative assessment: Assessment is for self-regulated learning. *Educational Psychology Review, 24*(2), 205–249. doi:10.1007/s10648-011-9191-6

Clark, R. C., & Mayer, R. E. (2011). *E-learning and the science of instruction: Proven Guidelines for consumers and designers of multimedia learning* (3rd ed.). San Francisco, CA: John Wiley & Sons. doi:10.1002/9781118255971

CLRN. (2014). *Electronic learning resources for California teachers*. Retrieved November 1, 2014 from http://www.clrn.org/home/

Cochrane, T. D. (2014). Critical success factors for transforming pedagogy with mobile Web 2.0. *British Journal of Educational Technology*, *45*(1), 65–82. doi:10.1111/j.1467-8535.2012.01384.x

Coll, C., Rochera, M. J., & de Gispert, I. (2014). Supporting online collaborative learning in small groups: Teacher feedback on learning content, academic task and social participation. *Computers & Education*, *75*, 53–64. doi:10.1016/j.compedu.2014.01.015

Cooke, N. L., Guzaukas, R., Pressley, J. S., & Kerr, K. (1993). Effects of using a ratio of new items to review items during drill and practice: Three experiments. *Education & Treatment of Children*, *16*(3), 213–234.

Cope, B., & Kalantzis, M. (2008). Ubiquitous learning: An agenda for educational transformation. In *Proceedings of the 6th International Conference on Networked Learning*, (pp. 576-582). Retrieved November 1, 2014 from http://www.networkedlearningconference.org.uk/past/nlc2008/abstracts/PDFs/Cope_576-582.pdf

Copriady, J. (2013). The implementation of lesson study programme for developing professionalism in teaching profession. *Asian Social Science*, *9*(12), 176–186. doi:10.5539/ass.v9n12p176

Cornelissen, F., Daly, A. J., Liou, Y. H., van Swet, J., Beijaard, D., & Bergen, T. C. (2014). More than a master: Developing, sharing, and using knowledge in school–university research networks. *Cambridge Journal of Education*, *44*(1), 35–57. doi:10.1080/0305764X.2013.855170

Cowan, R., & Powell, D. (2014). The contributions of domain-general and numerical factors to third-grade arithmetic skills and mathematical learning disability. *Journal of Educational Psychology*, *106*(1), 214–230. doi:10.1037/a0034097 PMID:24532854

Creative Commons. (n. d.). *Attribution-No Derivatives 4.0 International (CC BY-ND 4.0)*. Retrieved November 21, 2014 from http://creativecommons.org/licenses/by-nd/4.0/

Criswell, E. (1989). *The design of computer-based instruction*. New York: Macmillan Publishing Company.

Crowder, N. (1959). Automatic tutoring by means of intrinsic programming. In Automatic teaching: The state of the art (pp. 23–28). New York: John Wiley & Sons.

Crowther, N. A. (2014). A new paradigm emerging? Review of learning, work and practice: New understandings. *Higher Education, Skills and Work-based Learning*, *4*(1), 29–49.

Cubukcu, Z. (2012). Teachers' evaluation of student-centered learning environments. *Education*, *133*(1), 49–66.

Cull, B. W. (2011). *Reading revolution: Online digital text and implications for reading in academe*. Retrieved October 25, 2014, from http://firstmonday.org/ojs/index.php/fm/article/view/3340/2985#author

Cummings, T., & Worley, C. (2014). *Organization development and change*. Cengage Learning.

*Curriki*. (2014). Retrieved November 2, 2014 from http://www.curriki.org/

D'Mello, S., Lehman, B., Pekrun, R., & Graesser, A. (2014). Confusion can be beneficial for learning. *Learning and Instruction*, *29*, 153–170. doi:10.1016/j.learninstruc.2012.05.003

Daniel, D. B., & Woody, W. D. (2013). E-textbooks at what cost? Performance and use of electronic v. print texts. *Computers & Education*, *62*, 18–23. doi:10.1016/j.compedu.2012.10.016

Darrow, R. (2012). *What does it look to be a blended learning teacher?* Retrieved October 25, 2014, from http://www.slideshare.net/robdarrow/blendedlearninginacolessdarrow-dec2012v4

Dautriche, I., & Chemla, E. (2014). *Cross-situational word learning in the right situations*. Retrieved November 1, 2014 from http://www.emmanuel.chemla.free.fr/Material/Dautriche-Chemla-CrossSituationalLearningRightSituations.pdf

Davidson, A. L., & Carliner, S. (2014). E-Books for educational uses. In J. M. Spector, M. D. Merrill, J., Elen, & M. J. Bishop, (Eds.), Handbook of research on educational communications and technology (pp. 713-722). Springer New York.

DBW. (2014). *New textbook app wants students to scan barcodes in stores, then buy elsewhere*. Retrieved November 2, 2014 from http://www.digitalbookworld.com/2014/new-textbook-app-wants-students-to-scan-barcodes-in-stores-then-buy-elsewhere/

de la Fuente, J., & Lozano, A. (2011). Design of the SEAI self-regulation assessment for young children and ethical considerations of psychological testing. In G. Dettori & D. Persico (Eds.), *Fostering self-regulated learning through ICT* (pp. 39–53). Hershey, PA: Information.

de Oliveira, J., Camacho, M., & Gisbert, M. (2014). Exploring student and teacher perception of e-textbooks in a primary school. *Comunicar*. Retrieved February, 5 2015, from http://eprints.rclis.org/21081/

de Oliveira, J., Camacho, M., & Gisbert, M. (2014). Exploring student and teacher perception of e-textbooks in a primary school. *Comunicar, 21*(42), 87–95. doi:10.3916/C42-2014-08

Delors, J. (1996). *Learning: the treasure within* (Report to UNESCO of the International Commission of Education for the Twenty-first Century). UNESCO Publishing. Retrieved October 25, 2014, from http://www.unesco.org/education/pdf/15_62.pdf

DeStefano, D., & LeFevre, J. A. (2007). Cognitive load in hypertext reading: A review. *Computers in Human Behavior, 23*(3), 1616–1641. doi:10.1016/j.chb.2005.08.012

Dickinson, D. (2013). *At Kenwood, programming students to succeed*. Retrieved November 25, 2014, from http://www.news-gazette.com/news/local/2013-12-26/kenwood-programming-students-succeed.html

Dillon, N. (2008). The e-volving textbook. *The American School Board Journal, 195*(7), 20–23.

Dinsmore, D. L., Baggetta, P., Doyle, S., & Loughlin, S. M. (2014). The role of initial learning, problem features, prior knowledge, and pattern recognition on transfer success. *Journal of Experimental Education, 82*(1), 121–141. doi:10.1080/00220973.2013.835299

Discovery. Create. Communicate. (n. d.). Retrieved October 25, 2014, from http://www-2011.setonhill.edu/techadvantage/MobileLearningBrochure_CombinedFINAL.pdf

Doerr, A., & Levasseur, K. (2010). *Applied discrete structures*. Retrieved October, 25 2014, from http://faculty.uml.edu/klevasseur/ads2/ or http://applied-discrete-structures.wiki.uml.edu/

Donovan, M., & Bransford, J. (2005). *How students learn: History, mathematics, and science in the classroom*. Washington: The National Academies press.

Doorn, R. R., & Blokland, A. (2014). Unhindered spatial processing during route memorization is required to maximize both spatial and verbal route knowledge. *Applied Cognitive Psychology, 28*(1), 22–29. doi:10.1002/acp.2949

Dow, C. R., Li, Y. H., Huang, L. H., & Hsuan, P. (2014). Development of activity generation and behavior observation systems for distance learning. *Computer Applications in Engineering Education, 22*(1), 52–62. doi:10.1002/cae.20528

Dunleavy, M. (2014). Design principles for augmented reality learning. *TechTrends: Linking Research & Practice to Improve Learning., 58*(1), 28–34. doi:10.1007/s11528-013-0717-2

Dwyer, C. P., Hogan, M. J., & Stewart, I. (2014). An integrated critical thinking framework for the 21st century. *Thinking Skills and Creativity, 12*, 43–52. doi:10.1016/j.tsc.2013.12.004

Dziuban, C. D., Hartman, J. L., & Moskal, P. D. (2004). Blended learning. *Educause*, Issue 7. Retrieved October, 25, 2014, from https://net.educause.edu/ir/library/pdf/ERB0407.pdf

Eaton, S. E. (2013). *Formal, non-formal and informal learning: What are the differences?* Retrieved June, 1, 2014 from http://drsaraheaton.wordpress.com/2010/12/31/formal-non-formal-and-informal-learning-what-are-the-differences/

Edutopia. (2013). *Polyphonic teaching with digital learning tools*. Retrieved October 25, 2014, from http://www.edutopia.org/blog/polyphonic-teaching-digital-learning-niels-jakob-pasgaard

Elder, L., & Paul, R. (2014). *Critical thinking development: A stage theory. The critical thinking community.* Retrieved October 29, 2014 from http://www.criticalthinking.org/pages/critical-thinking-development-a-stage-theory/483

Elliott, P. (2013, March 17). Students trading textbooks for tech books. *Los Angeles Times*, A17. Retrieved 23 July 2013 from eLibrary.

Ely, D. P. (1996). Instructional technology: Contemporary frameworks. In International encyclopedia of educational technology. Oxford: Pergamon.

Encheff, D. (2013). Creating a science e-book with fifth grade students. *TechTrends: Linking Research & Practice to Improve Learning, 57*(6), 61–72. doi:10.1007/s11528-013-0703-8

Eppelin, A., & Bottcher, R. (2011). Development of a publishing framework for living open access textbooks. *Information Services & Use, 31*(3/4), 243–248.

Eriksen, T. H. (2014). *Globalization: The key concepts.* A&C Black.

*eToysIllinois.org.* (2014). Retrieved November 25, 2014, from http://etoysillinois.org/

Evans, M. A., & Rick, J. (2014). Supporting learning with interactive surfaces and spaces. In J. M. Spector, M. D. Merrill, J. Elen, & M. J. Bishop (Eds.), *Handbook of research on educational communications and technology* (pp. 689–701). Springer New York. doi:10.1007/978-1-4614-3185-5_55

Factsheet (2012). *DOI® system and the ISBN system.* Retrieved November 2, 2014 from http://www.doi.org/factsheets/ISBN-A.html

Falc, E. O. (2013). An assessment of college students' attitudes towards using an online e-textbook. *Interdisciplinary Journal of E-Learning and Learning Objects, 9,* 1-12. Retrieved October 25, 2014, from http://www.ijello.org/Volume9/IJELLOv9p001-012Falc831.pdf

Feldstein, A. P., & Lewis, R. F. (2013). Understanding slow growth in the adoption of e-textbooks: Distinguishing paper and electronic delivery of course content. *International Research in Education, 1* (1), p. 177-193. Retrieved October 25, 2014, from http://www.macrothink.org/journal/index.php/ire/article/view/4071/3542

Fernald, P. S., & Jordan, E. A. (1991). Programed instruction versus standard text in introductory psychology. *Teaching of Psychology, 18*(4), 205–212. doi:10.1207/s15328023top1804_1

Fernandes, L. *Digital textbooks platforms: trends and technologies,* 3191-3210. Retrieved October 25, 2014, from http://ticeduca.ie.ul.pt/atas/pdf/196.pdf

Fernández-Solis, J., Palmer, K., & Ferris, T. (2007). *Theoretical approach to the interaction between the metasystem schemas of the artificial (built) environment and nature.* Retrieved November 1, 2014 from http://archone.tamu.edu/faculty/JSolis/Documents/014_Schema_ultra_final_21_05_07.pdf

Ferri, G. (2014). Ethical communication and intercultural responsibility: A philosophical perspective. *Language and Intercultural Communication, 14*(1), 7–23. doi:10.1080/14708477.2013.866121

Firestone, M. *Unintentional plagiarism: definition, examples & quiz.* Educational Portal. Retrieved November 22, 2014 from http://education-portal.com/academy/lesson/unintentional-plagiarism-definition-examples-quiz.html#lesson

Fletcher, J. (1992). *Individualized systems of- instruction.* Retrieved November 1, 2014 from http://www.dtic.mil/cgibin/GetTRDoc?AD=ada255960.

Foster, G. (2014). *The Promise of digital badges.* Retrieved October 25, 2014, from http://noctinot.com/pdf/news/techniques/Nov%202013%20%20The%20Promise%20of%20Digital%20Badges.pdf

Freedman, R., Ali, S. S., & McRoy, S. (2000). What is an Intelligent Tutoring System? *Intelligence*, *11*(3), 15–16. doi:10.1145/350752.350756

Frick, T. W. (1998). Restructuring education through technology. Retrieved October 25, 2014, from https://www.indiana.edu/~tedfrick/fastback/fastback326.html

Fry, E., Bryan, G., & Rigney, J. (1958). Teaching machine: An annotated bibliography. *Communication Review*, *8*(2), 1–80.

Fryer, W. A. (2014). The ethic of open digital content. *Publications Archive of Wesley Fryer*. Retrieved February 5, 2015 from http://publications.wesfryer.com/index.php/archive/article/view/43/158

Gaeta, M., Loia, V., Mangione, G. R., Orciuoli, F., Ritrovato, P., & Salerno, S. (2014). A methodology and an authoring tool for creating Complex Learning Objects to support interactive storytelling. *Computers in Human Behavior*, *31*, 620–637. doi:10.1016/j.chb.2013.07.011

Galperin. (2000). *Introduction in psychology* (in Russian). Moscow: University.

Gecer, A. (2013). Lecturer-student communication in blended learning environments. *Educational Sciences: Theory and Practice*, *13*(1), 362–367.

Gerard, F. M., & Roegiers, X. (2009). *Des manuels scolaires pour apprendre: Concevoir, évaluer, utiliser*. De Boeck Supérieur. doi:10.3917/dbu.gerar.2009.01

Ghani, K. A., Noh, A. S., & Yusoff, N. (2014). Linguistic features for development of Arabic Text readability formula in Malaysia: A preliminary study. *Middle-East Journal of Scientific Research*, *19*(3), 319–331.

Gibson, J. J. (1986). *The ecological approach to visual perception*. USA: Lawrence Erlbaum Associate Incorporated.

Glassman, M., & Kang, M. J. (2010). Pragmatism, connectionism and the Internet: A mind's perfect storm. *Computers in Human Behavior*, *26*(6), 1412–1418. doi:10.1016/j.chb.2010.04.019

Global Monitoring Report, E. F. A. (2014). *Teaching and learning: Archiving quality for all*. Retrieved October, 25 2014, from http://unesdoc.unesco.org/images/0022/002256/225660e.pdf

Gong, C., Chen, G., Wang, X., Zhang, X. & Huang, R. (2013). The functions of e-textbooks for utilizing in K-12 classes: A case study in Beijing. *Advanced Learning Technologies*, 479-480.

Gore, M. C. (2010). *Promoting students' learning from the textbook. Inclusion strategies for secondary classrooms: Keys for struggling learners*. Thousand Oaks, CA: Corwin Press. doi:10.4135/9781483350424

Graesser, A. C., Li, H., & Forsyth, C. (2014). Learning by communicating in natural language with conversational agents. *Current Directions in Psychological Science*, *23*(5), 374–380. doi:10.1177/0963721414540680

Gredler, M. (2012). Understanding Vygotsky for the classroom: Is it too late? *Educational Psychology Review*, *24*(1), 113–131. doi:10.1007/s10648-011-9183-6

Grier, M. (2012). *Kant's critique of metaphysics*. Retrieved November 1, 2014 from http://plato.stanford.edu/entries/kant-metaphysics/

Griffin, P. (2014). *Assessment for teaching*. Sage Publication Ltd.

Griffits, M. (2012). Is it possible to live a philosophical educational life in education, nowadays? *Journal of Philosophy of Education*, *46*(3), 397–413. doi:10.1111/j.1467-9752.2012.00861.x

Grise-Owens, E., Miller, J. J., & Owens, L. W. (2014). Responding to global shifts: Meta-practice as a relevant social work practice paradigm. *Journal of Teaching in Social Work*, *34*(1), 46–59. doi:10.1080/08841233.2013.866614

Grossman, S. (2013). *Google begins selling textbooks through play store*. Retrieved October 29, 2014 from http://chronicle.com/blogs/wiredcampus/google-begins-selling-textbooks-through-play-store/45367

Grzega, J., & Schoner, M. (2008). The didactic model LdL (Lernen durch Lehren) as a way of preparing students for communication in a knowledge society. *Journal of Education for Teaching*, *34*(3), 167–175. doi:10.1080/02607470802212157

Gu, X., Wu, B., & Xu, X. (2014). Design, development, and learning in e-Textbooks: What we learned and where we are going. *Journal of Computers in Education, 1*(3), article 24, Springer. Retrieved February 9, 2015, from http://link.springer.com/article/10.1007/s40692-014-0023-9/fulltext.html

Hadzigeorgiou, Y., & Konsolas, M. (2001). Global Problems and the Curriculum: Toward a humanistic and constructivist science education. *Curriculum and Teaching, 16*(2), 39–49. doi:10.7459/ct/16.2.04

Hallam, G. C. (2012). *Briefing paper on eTextbooks and third party eLearning products and their implications for Australian university libraries.* Council of Australian University Libraries. Retrieved November 25, 2014, from http://eprints.qut.edu.au/55244/3/55244P.pdf

Hamada, M., & Goya, H. (2014). Influence of syllable structure on L2 auditory word learning. *Journal of Psycholinguistic Research, 44*(246), 1–17. PMID:24493208

Hammond. (2002). *Cyber-plagiarism: Are FE students getting away with words?* Retrieved November 2, 2014 from http://www.leeds.ac.uk/educol/documents/00002055.htm

Hammond, M., & Boltman, M. (2014). *The energy of reading project.* Retrieved October 1, 2014 from http://www.wholistichealingresearch.com/user_files/documents/ijhc/articles/HammondBotman-14-1.pdf

Hannafin, M. J., Hill, J. R., Land, S. M., & Lee, E. (2014). Student-centered, open learning environments: Research, theory, and practice. In J. M. Spector, M. D. Merrill, J. Elen, & M. J. Bishop. (Eds.). Handbook of research on educational communications and technology (pp. 641-651). New York: Springer.

Hannafin, M. J., Hill, J. R., Land, S. M., & Lee, E. (2014). Student-centered, open learning environments: Research, theory, and practice. In J. M. Spector, M. D. Merrill, J. Elen, & M. J. Bishop (Eds.), *Handbook of research on educational communications and technology* (pp. 641–651). New York: Springer. doi:10.1007/978-1-4614-3185-5_51

Hargreaves, E., Gipps, C., & Pickering, A. (2014). Assessment for learning. Formative approaches. In T. Cremin & J. Arthur (Eds.), *Learning to teach in the primary school,* (pp.313-323). Routledge.

Harrower, M., Robinson, A. C., Roth, R. E. & Sheesely, B. (2009). Cartography 2.0: For people who make interactive maps. *Cartographic Perspectives, 64*, 41-44.

Harvey, D. (2011). Analytical Chemistry 2.0: An open-access digital textbook. *Analytical and Bioanalytical Chemistry, 399*(1), 149–152. doi:10.1007/s00216-010-4316-1 PMID:21046084

Hashimoto, T., Warashin, K., & Yamauchi, H. (2010). New composite evolutionary computation algorithm using interactions among genetic evolution, individual learning and social learning. *Intelligent Data Analysis, 14*(4), 497–514.

Haughey, M., & Muirhead, B. (2005). Evaluating learning objects for schools. *E-Journal of Instructional Sciences and Technology, 8*(1), 229–254.

Havighurst, R. V. (2014). Functions and roles of teachers. *Encyclopedia Britannica.* Retrieved October 29, 2014 from http://www.britannica.com/EBchecked/topic/585183/teaching/39100/Functions-and-roles-of-teachers

Hendrickson, C., Pasquale, A., Robinson, W., & Rossi-Velasco, M. (2013). *Applications of computer aided instruction.* Retrieved October 25, 2014, from http://gdi.ce.cmu.edu/docs/applications-of-computer.pdf

Herrington, J., Reeves, T. C., & Oliver, R. (2014). Authentic learning environments. In J. M. Spector, M. D. Merrill, J. Elen, & M. J. Bishop (Eds.), Handbook of research on educational communications and technology (pp. 401–412). New York: Springer.

*Hippocampus.org.* (2014). Retrieved September 2, 2014 from http://www.hippocampus.org/

Holmes, N. (2014). Student perceptions of their learning and engagement in response to the use of a continuous e-assessment in an undergraduate module. *Assessment & Evaluation in Higher Education, 40*(1), 1–14. doi:10.1080/02602938.2014.881978

Honeycutt, B., & Garrett, G. (2014). *Expanding the definition of a flipped learning environment.* Retrieved October 25, 2014, from http://www.facultyfocus.com/articles/instructional-design/expanding-definition-flipped-learning-environment/#sthash.zVNFRPQ0.dpuf

Hong, J. H., Kim, M., & Yoo, K. H. (2013). Development of a 3D digital textbook using X3D. ubiquitous information technologies and applications. *Lecture Notes in Electrical Engineering, 214,* 341–351. doi:10.1007/978-94-007-5857-5_37

Houston, C. (2011). Digital books for digital natives. *Children & Libraries: The Journal of the Association for Library Service to Children, 9*(3), 39–42.

HS.Tutorials.Net. (2013). *OLPC - Algebra 1 in Simple English "Wiki-textbook"*. Retrieved October 25, 2014, from http://www.hstutorials.net/olpcmath.htm

Hsieh, L. Y., Lu, Y. J., Lin, H. S., & Lee, Y. H. (2014). With blended learning information operational system design in response to globalized logistics talent training. In *The 2nd International Workshop on Learning Technology for Education in Cloud* (pp. 61-71). Springer Netherlands. doi:10.1007/978-94-007-7308-0_7

Hung, W. (2008). Enhancing systems-thinking skills with modelling. *British Journal of Educational Technology, 39*(6), 1099–1120. doi:10.1111/j.1467-8535.2007.00791.x

Hutley, S. (2002). Follow the book road: Ebooks in Australian public libraries. *APLIS, 15*(1), 32–38.

Hutorskoi, A. B. (2005). The place of textbook in the didactic tutorial system [in Russian]. *Pedagogica, 4,* 10–18.

Hyman, J. A., Moser, M. T., & Segala, L. N. (2014). Electronic reading and digital library technologies: Understanding learner expectation and usage intent for mobile learning. *Educational Technology Research and Development, 62*(1), 35–52. doi:10.1007/s11423-013-9330-5

International Step by Step Association. (2010). *Competent educators of the 21ˢᵗ Century: Principles of quality pedagogy*. Retrieved September, 1, 2014 from http://issa.nl/qrp_pedagogy.html

Internet Encyclopedia of Philosophy. (2014). *Epistemic closure principles*. Retrieved October 15, 2014 from http://www.iep.utm.edu/epis-clo/

*Introduction to postmodern philosophy*. (2014). Retrieved October 25, 2014, from http://www.postmodernpreaching.net/postmodern-philosophy.html

ISBN. (2014). *International ISBN agency*. Retrieved November 2, 2014 from https://www.isbn-international.org/

Jaehnig, W., & Miller, M. L. (2007). Feedback types in programmed instruction: A systematic review. *The Psychological Record, 57*(2), 219–232.

Jang, S. (2014). Study on service models of digital textbooks in cloud computing environment for smart education. *International Journal of U-& E-Service, Science & Technology, 7*(1), 73–82.

Janzen, K. J., Perry, B., & Edwards, M. (2011). *Aligning the quantum perspective of learning to instructional design: Exploring the seven definitive questions*. Retrieved October, 25, 2014, from http://www.irrodl.org/index.php/irrodl/article/view/1038/2024

Jenseen, S. S., & Heilessen, S. B. (2005). Time, place, and identity in project work on the net. In T. S. Roberts (Ed.), *Computer-supported collaborative learning in higher education* (pp. 51–75). Hershey, PA: Idea Group Publishing. doi:10.4018/978-1-59140-408-8.ch003

Jewitt, C., & Kress, C. (2003). *Multimodal literacy*. New York: Peter Lang.

Johnson, L., Adams, S., & Cummins, M. (2012). *The NMC Horizon Report: 2012 higher education edition*. Austin, TX: The New Media Consortium. Retrieved November 25, 2014, from http://www.nmc.org/pdf/2012-horizon-report-HE.pdf

Jones, V., & Jo, J. H. (2014). *Ubiquitous learning environment: An adaptive teaching system using ubiquitous technology*. Retrieved November 1, 2014 from http://www.ascilite.org.au/conferences/perth04/procs/pdf/jones.pdf

Joo, H. M., & Ahn, C. U. (2013). A study on the development of evaluation criteria for digital textbooks in Korea. In J. Herrington et al. (Eds.), *Proceedings of World Conference on Educational Multimedia, Hypermedia and Telecommunications 2013* (pp. 86-89). Chesapeake, VA: AACE. Retrieved December 15, 2013, from http://www.editlib.org/p/111935

Joo, K. H., Park, N. H., & Choi, J. T. (2014). An adaptive teaching and learning system for efficient ubiquitous learning. In Y.-S. Jeong, Y.-H. Park, C.-H. Hsu, J. J. Park (Eds.), Ubiquitous information technologies and applications (pp. 659-666). Springer Berlin Heidelberg. doi:10.1007/978-3-642-41671-2_84

Kabuto, B. (2014). A semiotic perspective on reading picture books: The case of *Alexander and the Wind-Up Mouse. Linguistics and Education, 25,* 12-23.

Kang, H., & Zentall, S. (2011). Computer-generated geometry instruction: A preliminary study. *Educational Technology Research and Development, 59*(6), 783–797. doi:10.1007/s11423-011-9186-5

Karpicke, J. D., Butler, A. C., & Roediger, H. L., III. (2009). Metacognitive strategies in student learning: Do students practise retrieval when they study on their own? *Memory (Hove, England), 17*(4), 471–479. doi:10.1080/09658210802647009

Keller, F. C. (1968). Good-bye, teacher.... *Journal of Applied Behavioral Annals, 1*(1), 79–89. doi:10.1901/jaba.1968.1-79 PMID:16795164

Kelly, F. S., McCain, T., & Jukes, I. (2009). *Teaching the digital generation: No more cookie-cutter high schools.* Melbourne, Vic: Hawker Brownlow Education.

Keppell, M. (2013). *Designing learning-oriented assessment for a digital future.* Retrieved June 22, 2013 from www.slideshare.net/mkeppell/digital-assessment

KERIS. (2014). *Digital textbook. School with digital textbook is everywhere.* Retrieved October, 25, 2014 from http://www.dtbook.kr/renew/english/index.htm

Kerr, M. A., & Symons, S. E. (2006). Computerized presentation of text: Effects on children's reading of informational material. *Reading and Writing, 19*(1), 1–19. doi:10.1007/s11145-003-8128-y

Key, A. (1972). *A personal computer for children of all ages.* Retrieved October 25, 2014, from http://www.mprove.de/diplom/gui/Kay72a.pdf

Khan Academy. (2014). Retrieved November 2, 2014 from https://www.khanacademy.org/

Khan, B. (2012). Virtual learning environments: Design factors and issues. In B. Khan (Ed.), *User interface design for virtual environments: Challenges and advances* (pp. 1–15). Hershey, PA: Information Science Reference. doi:10.4018/978-1-61350-516-8.ch001

Khasawneh, O. M., Miqdadi, R. M., & Hijazi, A. Y. (2014). Implementing pragmatism and John Dewey's educational philosophy. *Journal of International Education Research, 10*(1). Retrieved February 5, 2015 from http://cluteinstitute.com/ojs/index.php/JIER/article/view/8465/8476

Khatib, M., & Sabah, S. (2012). On major perspectives on language acquisition: Nativism, connectionism, and emergentism. *BRAIN: Broad Research in Artificial Intelligence & Neuroscience., 3*(4), 5–12.

Kim, J. H. Y., & Jung, H. Y. (2010). South Korean digital textbook project. *Computers in the Schools, 27*(3-4), 247-265. Retrieved October 25, 2014 from http://www.mackin.com/cms/uploads/SouthKoreanDigitalTextbookProject.pdf

Kim, S. W., & Lee, M. G. (2012). Utilization of digital textbooks in Korea. In T.-T. Gon, B.-C. Seet, & P.-C.Su (Eds.). E-books & e-readers for e-learning (pp. 90-125). Orauariki: Victoria Business School.

Kim, J., & Jung, H. (2010). Korean Digital Textbook Project. *Computers in the Schools, 27*(4), 247–265. doi: 10.1080/07380569.2010.523887

Kim, C., & Pekrun, R. (2014). Emotions and motivation in learning and performance. In J. M. Spector, M. D. Merrill, J. Elen, & M. J. Bishop (Eds.), *Handbook of research on educational communications and technology* (pp. 66-75). Springer. doi:10.1007/978-1-4614-3185-5_6

Kim, J., & Park, N. (2014). The analysis of case result and satisfaction of digital textbooks for elementary school students. *Advanced in Computer Science and its Applications (Lecture Notes in Electrical Engineering), 279,* 417–422. doi:10.1007/978-3-642-41674-3_59

Kim, M., Yoo, K. H., Park, C., Yoo, J. S., Byun, H., Cho, W., & Kim, N. et al. (2010). An XML-based digital textbook and its educational effectiveness. *Advances in Computer Science and Information Technology (Lecture Notes in Computer Science)*, *6059*, 509–523. doi:10.1007/978-3-642-13577-4_46

Kim, Y., Williams, R., Rothwell, W. J., & Penaloza, P. (2014). A strategic model for technical talent management: A model based on a qualitative case study. *Performance Improvement Quarterly*, *26*(4), 93–121. doi:10.1002/piq.21159

Kivunja, C. (2014). Theoretical perspectives of how digital natives learn. *International Journal of Higher Education*, *3*(1), 94-109. Retrieved September 1, 2014 from http://www.sciedu.ca/journal/index.php/ijhe/article/view/4053/2382

Klir, G. J. (1990). *Architecture of systems problem solving* [in Russian]. Moscow: Radio and Communication.

Knight, D. (2014). *A textbook digital opportunity: Berlin commits to Open Education Resources (OER)*. Retrieved October, 25, 2014, from http://news.siliconallee.com/2014/05/15/a-textbook-digital-opportunity-berlin-pursues-open-education-resources-oer/

Knight, S., Buckingham Shum, S., & Littleton, K. (2014). Epistemology, assessment, pedagogy: where learning meets analytics in the middle space. *Journal of Learning Analytics*. Retrieved September 11, 2013 from http://oro.open.ac.uk/39226/3/JLA%202014.pdf

Kobayashi, Y., & Wakano, J. Y. (2012). Evolution of social versus individual learning in an infinite island model. *Evolution; International Journal of Organic Evolution*, *66*(5), 1624–1635. doi:10.1111/j.1558-5646.2011.01541.x PMID:22519795

Koehler, M. J., Mishra, P., Kereluik, K., Shin, T. S., & Graham, C. R. (2014). The technological pedagogical content knowledge framework. In J. M. Spector, M. D. Merrill, J. Elen, & M. J. Bishop (Eds.), Handbook of research on educational communications and technology (pp. 101-111). Springer New York. doi:10.1007/978-1-4614-3185-5_9

Kokkodis, M., Kannan, A., & Kenthapadi, K. (2014). Assigning videos to textbooks at appropriate granularity. In *Proceedings of the first ACM Conference on Learning@ Scale conference,* (pp. 199-200). Retrieved October, 25 2014, from http://research.microsoft.com/pubs/208441/identifyingVideoGranularityForAugmentation-las2014.pdf

Kong, S. C. (2014). Developing information literacy and critical thinking skills through domain knowledge learning in digital classrooms: An experience of practicing flipped classroom strategy. *Computers & Education*, *78*, 160–173. doi:10.1016/j.compedu.2014.05.009

Korea Institute for Curriculum and Evaluation. (2013). *A study on the development of evaluation criteria and process for digital textbooks*. Retrieved October, 25, 2014, from http://kice.re.kr/en/board.do?boardConfigNo=139&menuNo=410&action=vie&boardNo=31033

Koulopoulos, T., & Frappaolo, C. (2000). *Smart things to know about knowledge management*. Padstow, Cornwall: T. J. International Ltd.

Krabbe, H. (2014). Digital concept mapping for formative assessment. In D. Ifenthaler & R. Hanewald (Eds.), *Digital knowledge maps in education* (pp. 275–297). Springer New York. doi:10.1007/978-1-4614-3178-7_15

Kraft, V. (2014). Constants of education. In M. Papastephanou (Ed.), Philosophical perspectives on compulsory education, (pp. 11-21). Springer. doi:10.1007/978-94-007-7311-0_2

*Krathwohl's affective domain*. (n. d.). Retrieved October 25, 2014 from http://assessment.uconn.edu/docs/LearningTaxonomy_Affective.pdf

Kuittinen, M., Meriläinen, M., & Räty, H. (2014). Professional competences of young psychologists: The dimensions of self-rated competence domains and their variation in the early years of the psychologist's career. *European Journal of Psychology of Education*, *29*(1), 63–80. doi:10.1007/s10212-013-0187-0

Kuvalja, M., Verma, M., & Whitebread, D. (2014). Patterns of co-occurring non-verbal behaviour and self-directed speech; a comparison of three methodological approaches. *Metacognition Learning*. Retrieved October 25, 2014 from http://download.springer.com/static/pdf/248/art%253A1 0.1007%252Fs11409-013-9106-7.pdf?auth66=1393147 529_278c016eeecb7902f6ddda285adbb000&ext=.pdf

Laanpere, M., Pata, K., Normak, P., & Poldoja, H. (2014). Pedagogy-driven design of digital learning ecosystems. *Computer Science and Information Systems*, *11*(1), 419–442. doi:10.2298/CSIS121204015L

Laborde, C., & Laborde, J. M. (2014). Dynamic and tangible representations in mathematics education. In S. Rezat, M. Hattermann, & A. Peter-Koop, (Eds.), Transformation: A fundamental idea of mathematics education (pp. 187-202). Springer New York. doi:10.1007/978-1-4614-3489-4_10

Landa, L. (1972). *Algoritmisation in learning and instruction*. Englewood Cliffs, NJ: Educational Technology Publications.

Lang, R., Ramdoss, S., Sigafoos, J., Green, V. A., van der Meer, L., Tostanoski, A., & O'Reilly, M. F. (2014). Assistive technology for postsecondary students with disabilities. In *Assistive technologies for people with diverse abilities* (pp. 53–76). Springer New York. doi:10.1007/978-1-4899-8029-8_3

Lasry, N., Dugdale, M., & Charles, E. (2014). Just in time to flip your classroom. *The Physics Teacher*, *52*(1), 34–37. doi:10.1119/1.4849151

Lau, R. W. H., Yen, N. Y., Li, F., & Wah, B. (2014). Recent development in multimedia e-learning technologies. *World Wide Web (Bussum)*, *17*(2), 189–198. doi:10.1007/s11280-013-0206-8

Lawrence, S. A. (2014). Exploring the use of technology, multimodal texts, and digital tools in K-12 classrooms. In S. Lawrence (Ed.), *Critical practice in P-12 education: Transformative teaching and learning* (pp. 24–48). Hershey, PA: Information Science Reference. doi:10.4018/978-1-4666-5059-6.ch002

Lazanski, T. J. (2010). Systems thinking: Ancient Maya's evolution of consciousness and contemporary systems thinking. *AIP Conference Proceedings*, *1303*(1), 289–296. doi:10.1063/1.3527166

LEARN NC. (2014). *Educator's guides: North Carolina digital history. What's in a digital textbook?* Retrieved October, 25, 2014, from http://www.learnnc.org/lp/editions/nchist-eg/6628

LEARN NC. (2014). *What's in a digital textbook?* Retrieved October, 25, 2014 from http://www.learnnc.org/lp/editions/nchist-eg/6628

Lee, H. J., Messom, C., & Yau, K.-L. A. (2013). Can an electronic textbooks be part of K-12 education? Challenges, technological solutions and open issues. *The Turkish Online Journal of Educational Technology*, *12*(1), 32–44.

Lee, K., Ning, F., & Goh, H. C. (2014). Interaction between cognitive and non-cognitive factors: The influences of academic goal orientation and working memory on mathematical performance. *Educational Psychology*, *34*(1), 73–91. doi:10.1080/01443410.2013.836158

Lee, V., & Lo, A. (2014). From theory to practice: Teaching management using films through deductive and inductive processes. *The International Journal of Management Education*, *12*(1), 44–54. doi:10.1016/j.ijme.2013.05.001

Leibovici, A. N., Bosova, L. L., Avdeeva, C. M., Rabinovici, P. D., & Tarasova, K. B. (2012). *Electronic textbooks: Recommendation for development, implementation and use of interactive multimedia electronic textbooks of a new generation for the general education based on modern mobile electronic devices* (In Russian).Moscow: The Federal Institute for Education Development.

Leidig, T. (2001). L3-towards an open learning environment. *Journal of Educational Resources in Computing*, *1*(1), 1–11.

Lerner, R. M., & Schmid, C. K. (2013). Relational developmental systems theories and the ecological validity of experimental designs. *Human Development*, *56*(6), 372–380. doi:10.1159/000357179

Leutner, D. (2014). Motivation and emotion as mediators in multimedia learning. *Learning and Instruction*, *29*, 174–175. doi:10.1016/j.learninstruc.2013.05.004

Liang, T. H., & Huang, Y. M. (2014). an investigation of reading rate patterns and retrieval outcomes of elementary school students with e-books. *Journal of Educational Technology & Society*, *17*(1), 218–230.

Lim, C., Song, H. D., & Lee, Y. (2012). Improving the usability of the user interface for a digital textbook platform for elementary-school students. *Educational Technology Research and Development, 60*(1), 159–173. doi:10.1007/s11423-011-9222-5

Long, J. (2014). What is visual ergonomics? *Work: A Journal of Prevention, Assessment and Rehabilitation*. Retrieved September 11, 2014 from http://iospress.metapress.com/content/u730425263653437/fulltext.pdf

Lupu, E., & Enache, R. (2011). Didactic conception on the basis of cognitive and affective objectives for non-profile university-physical education. *Procedia: Social and Behavioral Sciences, 15*, 1340–1345. doi:10.1016/j.sbspro.2011.03.288

Lyons, J. P., Hannon, J., & Macken, C. (2014). Sustainable practice in embedding learning technologies: Curriculum renewal through course design intensives. In M. Gosper & D. Ifenthaler (Eds.), *Curriculum models for the 21st Century* (pp. 423–442). New York: Springer. doi:10.1007/978-1-4614-7366-4_22

Lysenko, L. V., & Abrami, P. C. (2014). Promoting reading comprehension with the use of technology. *Computers & Education*. Retrieved October, 25, 2014, from http://www.sciencedirect.com/science/article/pii/S0360131514000207

MacFadyen, H. (2011). *The reader's devices: The affordances of ebook readers*. Retrieved October, 25, 2014, from http://dalspace.library.dal.ca/bitstream/handle/10222/13823/MacFadyen%20-%20The%20Reader%E2%80%99s%20Devices.pdf?sequence=1

Macgilchrist, F., & Christophe, B. (2011). Translating globalization theories into educational research: Thoughts on recent shifts in Holocaust education. *Discourse (Abingdon), 32*(1), 145–158. doi:10.1080/01596306.2011.537080

Magallon, J. C., & Weisz, G. (2014). Robotic-assisted coronary intervention. In C. A. Thompson (Ed.), *Textbook of cardiovascular intervention* (pp. 157–166). Springer London. doi:10.1007/978-1-4471-4528-8_12

Majumdar, D. D. (2014). Trends in pattern recognition and machine learning. *Defence Science Journal, 35*(3), 327–351. doi:10.14429/dsj.35.6027

Malinowski, D. (2014). Drawing bodies and spaces in telecollaboration: A view of research potential in synaesthesia and multimodality, from the outside. *Pedagogies, 9*(1), 63–85. doi:10.1080/1554480X.2014.877559

Mallon, M. N., & Gilstrap, D. L. (2014). Digital literacy and the emergence of technology-based curriculum theories. In D. J. Douglas (Ed.), Academic knowledge construction and multimodal curriculum development, (pp. 15-29). doi:10.4018/978-1-4666-4797-8.ch002

Mameli, C., & Molinari, L. (2014). Seeking educational quality in the unfolding of classroom discourse: A focus on microtransitions. *Language and Education, 28*(2), 103–119. doi:10.1080/09500782.2013.771654

Mandacanu, V. (2009). *The master teacher* (in Romanian). Chisinau: Pontos.

Mangen, A., Walgermo, B. R., & Brønnick, K. (2013). Reading linear texts on paper versus computer screen: Effects on reading comprehension. *International Journal of Educational Research, 58*, 61–68. doi:10.1016/j.ijer.2012.12.002

Mann, L. (2013). *Pros and cons of digital textbooks*. Retrieved November 25, 2014, from http://articles.chicagotribune.com/2013-08-07/features/ct-x-0807-college-kids-eyes-20130807_1_print-textbooks-digital-textbooks-computer-vision-syndrome

Mardis, M., & Everhart, N. (2013). From paper to pixel: The promise and challenges of digital textbooks for K-12 schools. *Educational Media and Technology Yearbook, 37*, 93–118. doi:10.1007/978-1-4614-4430-5_9

Marin, T. (2012). The professionalization of the didactic activity between "desirable" and unavoidable. *Euromentor Journal-Studies About Education, 3*(3), 22–32.

Marshall, S., Kinuthia, W. & Richards, G. (2013). Open content for elearning: Cross institutional collaboration for education and training in a digital environment. *International Journal of Education and Development Using ICT, 8*(3), 35-42.

Martin, A., & Repetto, M. (2005). Teacher's value and attributes within a knowledge society. In V. Midoro (Ed.), A common European framework for teachers' professional profile in ICT for education (pp. 23-26). Editura Menado: Didactica.

Matusov, E. (2015). Four ages of our relationship with the reality: An educationalist perspective. *Educational Philosophy and Theory*, *47*(1), 61–83. doi:10.1080/00131857.2013.860369

Mayer, R. E. (2014). Multimedia Instruction. In J. M. Spector, M. D. Merrill, J. Elen, & M. J. Bishop, (Eds.), Handbook of research on educational communications and technology (pp. 385-399). Springer New York. doi:10.1007/978-1-4614-3185-5_31

Mayer, R. E. (2014). What problem solvers know: Cognitive readiness for adaptive problem solving. In H. F. O'Neil, R. S. Perez & E. L. Baker (Eds.), Teaching and measuring cognitive readiness (pp. 149–160). New York: Springer. doi:10.1007/978-1-4614-7579-8_8

Mayer, R. (2003). The promise of multimedia learning: Using the same instructional design methods across different media. *Learning and Instruction*, *13*(2), 125–139. doi:10.1016/S0959-4752(02)00016-6

Mayer, R. E. (2014). Incorporating motivation into multimedia learning. *Learning and Instruction*, *29*, 171–173. doi:10.1016/j.learninstruc.2013.04.003

Mayer, R. E., & Moreno, R. (2002). Animation as an aid to multimedia learning. *Educational Psychology Review*, *14*(1), 87–99. doi:10.1023/A:1013184611077

Mayer, R. E., Steinhoff, K., Bower, G., & Mars, R. (1995). A generative theory of textbook design: Using annotated illustrations to foster meaningful learning of science text. *Educational Technology Research and Development*, *43*(1), 31–41. doi:10.1007/BF02300480

Mayes, T., & Freitas, S. (2013). Technology–enhanced learning. In H. Beetham, & Rh. Sharpe (Eds.), Rethinking pedagogy for a digital age: Designing for 21st century learning. Taylor & Francis.

MCC. (2014). *Textbooks for online courses*. Retrieved October 25, 2014 from http://www.mccneb.edu/elearning/textbooks.asp

McLoughlin, C., & Oliver, R. Who is in control? *Defining Interactive Learning Environments*. Retrieved October, 25 2014, from http://www.ascilite.org.au/conferences/melbourne95/smtu/paperbackup/mcloughlin.pdf

Mergel, B. (1998). *Instructional design & learning theory*. Retrieved from http://www.usask.ca/education/coursework/802papers/mergel/brenda.htm

Merkt, M., & Schwan, S. (2014). How does interactivity in videos affect task performance? *Computers in Human Behavior*, *31*, 172–181. doi:10.1016/j.chb.2013.10.018

Meshin, K., & Knoff, N. A. (2013). *A digital learning experience in tertiary design education*. Paper presented at The Teacher Academy Conference of the European League of the Institutions of Art (EUA). Retrieved October, 25, 2014, from arrow.dit.ie/aaschadocon/8/

Meyers, N. M., & Nulty, D. D. (2009). How to use (five) curriculum design principles to align authentic learning environments, assessment, students' approaches to thinking and learning outcomes. *Assessment & Evaluation in Higher Education*, *34*(5), 565–577. doi:10.1080/02602930802226502

Midoro, V. (2005). *A common European framework for teachers' professional profile in ICT for education*. Italy: Edizioni MENABO Didactica.

Midoro, V. (2005). *European teachers toward the knowledge society*. Italy: Edizioni MENABO.

Miller, M. L., & Malott, R. W. (2006). Programmed Instruction: Construction responding, discrimination responding, and highlighted keywords. *Journal of Behavioral Education*, *15*(2), 109–117. doi:10.1007/s10864-006-9010-1

Milovanovic, D. (2014). *Dueling paradigms: modernist v. postmodernist thought*. Retrieved February, 9, 2015 from http://critcrim.org/critpapers/milovanovic_postmod.htm

Minder, M. (2003). *The functional didactics: Objectives, strategies, assessment* (In Romanian). Chsinau: Cartier.

Mitchell, E. (2014). Curricula and pedagogic principles in the foundation stage (0–5). In P. Mukherji, & L. Dryden, (Eds.), Foundations of early childhood: Principles and practice, (pp. 225-143). Sage.

Mitchell, S., Avery, S., Prater, E., & Swafford, P. (2014). The impact of experiential learning on teaching quality control concepts. *Operations Management Education Review*, *8*, 1–24.

Moallem, M. (1998). An expert teacher's thinking and teaching and instructional design models and principles: An ethnographic study. *Educational Technology Research and Development, 46*(2), 37–64. doi:10.1007/BF02299788

Molenda, M. (2012). Individualized Instruction: A Recurrent Theme. *TechTrends: Linking Research and Practice to Improve Learning, 56*(6), 12–14. doi:10.1007/s11528-012-0606-0

Molloy, E. K., & Boud, D. (2014). feedback models for learning, teaching and performance. In M. Spector, M. D. Merrill, J. Elen, & M. J. Bishop, (Eds.), Handbook of research on educational communications and technology (pp. 413-424). Springer New York.

Mora, M., Gelman, O., & Cervantes, F. MejIa, M. & Weitzenfeld, A. (2003). A systemic approach for the formalization of the information systems concept: Why information systems are systems? In J. Cano (Ed.), Critical reflections on information systems: A systemic approach (pp. 1-29). Hershey, PA: Idea Group Publishing.

Moreno, R., & Mayer, R. E. (2007). Interactive multimodal learning environments. *Educational Psychology Review, 19*(3), 309–326. doi:10.1007/s10648-007-9047-2

Morin, A. (2013). *What are math manipulatives?* Retrieved October, 25, 2014, from http://childparenting.about.com/od/schoollearning/tp/what-are-math-manipulatives.htm

Naidu, S. (2012). Connectionism. *Distance Education, 33*(3), 291–294. doi:10.1080/01587919.2012.723321

Naismith, L., Sharples, M., Vavoula, G., & Lonsdale, P. (2004). *Literature review in mobile technologies and learning.* Retrieved October 25, 2014, from http://telearn.archives-ouvertes.fr/docs/00/19/01/43/PDF/Naismith_2004.pdf

Nakahara, T., Soga, T., Nakamura, Y., Mitani, M., & Kawana, N. (2014). Development of an e-textbook connected with a learning management system and a study of its effective use. In *World Conference on Educational Multimedia, Hypermedia and Telecommunications, 1*, (pp. 979-984).

Nam, C., & Smith-Jackson, T. (2007). Web-based learning environment: A theory-based design process for development and evaluation. *Journal of Information Technology Education: Research, 6*(1), 23–43.

National Collaborative on Workforce and Disability for Youth. (2010). Understanding the role of individual learning plans in transition planning for youth with disabilities. *InfoBrief, 26.* Retrieved from http://www.ncwd-youth.info/sites/default/files/infobrief_issue26_0.pdf

Niemela, P., Isomottonen, V., & Lipponen, L. (2014). Successful design of learning solutions being situation aware. *Education and Information Technologies*, 1–18.

NMC. (2014). *NMC Horizon Report: 2014 Higher Education Preview.* Retrieved November 25, 2014, from http://www.nmc.org/pdf/2014-horizon-he-preview.pdf

Nonaka, I. & Konno, N. (2005). The concept of "5, 4": building a foundation for knowledge creation. *Knowledge Management: Critical Perspectives on Business and Management, 2*(3), 53.

Noveanu, E., & Noveanu, D. (1994). The impact of new informational technologies for learning. In V. Mandacanu (Ed.), *The modern informational technologies.* (In Romanian).Chisinau: Lyceum.

Noyesa, J. M., & Garland, K. J. (2008). Computer- vs. paper-based tasks: Are they equivalent? *Ergonomics, 51*(9), 1352–1375http://www.twosides.info:8080/content/rsPDF_382.pdf. Retrieved November 25, 2014. doi:10.1080/00140130802170387 PMID:18802819

*Open Stax College.* (2014). Retrieved October 25, 2014, from https://openstaxcollege.org/books

O'Rafferty, S., Curtis, H., & O'Connor, F. (2014). Mainstreaming sustainability in design education–a capacity building framework. *International Journal of Sustainability in Higher Education, 15*(2), 169–187. doi:10.1108/IJSHE-05-2012-0044

Orrantia, J., Múñez, D., & Tarin, J. (2014). Connecting goals and actions during reading: The role of illustrations. *Reading and Writing, 27*(1), 153–170. doi:10.1007/s11145-013-9437-4

Osterman, M., Reio, T. J., & Thirunarayanan, M. O. (2013). Digital literacy: A demand for nonlinear thinking styles. In M. S. Plakhotnik & S. M. Nielsen (Eds.), *Proceedings of the 12th Annual South Florida Education Research Conference SFERC 2013* (pp.149-154). Miami Florida International University. Retrieved November 2, 2014 from http://education.fiu.edu/research_conference/docs/13/SFERC202013Proceedings.pdf#page=168

Oxford University Press. (2013). *Learn about Virtual Learning Environment/Course Management System content*. Retrieved October, 25, 2014, from http://global.oup.com/uk/orc/learnvle/

Palmer, K. D. (2002). *Advanced meta-systems theory for metasystems engineers*. Retrieved November, 2, 2014 from http://holonomic.net/sd01V04.pdf

Pandey, S. K. (2010-2011). *Teacher functions. Operations and activities in teaching*. Retrieved October, 29, 2014 from http://www.slideshare.net/pandeysk/teachers-function-operation-and-activities-in-teaching

Panto, E. & Comas-Quinn, A. (2013). The Challenge of Open Education. *Journal of e-Learning and Knowledge Society*. 9 (1), 11-22.

Papastephanou, M. (2014). *Theory, practice and the philosophy of educational action research in new light. A companion to research in education*. Springer Netherlands.

Papastephanou, M., Christou, M., & Gregoriou, Z. (2013). Globalisation, the challenge of educational synchronisation and teacher education. *Globalisation, Societies and Education*, *11*(1), 61–84. doi:10.1080/14767724.2012.690311

Paquette, G. (2014). Technology-based instructional design: Evolution and major trends. In J. M. Spector, M. D. Merrill, J. Elen, & M. J. Bishop (Eds.), Handbook of research on educational communications and technology (pp. 661-671). Springer New York.

Pask, G. (1968). Final scientific report 1 September 1966 to 30 November 1968. Richmond, UK: System Research. Ltd.

Paxhia, S. (2011). The challenges of higher education digital publishing. *Publishing Research Quarterly*, *27*(4), 321-326.

Peregrin, J. (2014). Rules as the impetus of cultural evolution. *Topoi*, *33*(2), 531–545. doi:10.1007/s11245-013-9219-2

Persaud, N., & Eliot, M. (2014). The development and refinement of student self-regulatory strategies in online learning environments. In M. Horsley, M. Eliot, B. A. Knight, & R. Reilly, (Eds.), Current trends in eye tracking research (pp. 317-336). Springer International Publishing. doi:10.1007/978-3-319-02868-2_25

Peters, O. (2000). Digital Learning Environments: New possibilities and opportunities. Retrieved October, 25, 2014, from http://www.irrodl.org/index.php/irrodl/article/view/3/336

Petrides, L., Jimes, C., Middleton-Detzner, C., Walling, J., & Weiss, S. (2011). Open textbook adoption and use: Implications for teachers and learners. *Open Learning*, *26*(1), 39–49.

Petty, R. E., & Brinol, P. (2014). Emotion and persuasion: Cognitive and meta-cognitive processes impact attitudes. *Cognition and Emotion*. PMID:25302943

Piansi, A. (2010). Learning tasks: Turning a dry subject into an engaging experience. *The Systems Thinker, 21*(2), 2-6.

Pieroni, L., Rossi-Arnaud, C., & Baddeley, A. D. (2011). What can symmetry tell us about working memory? In A. Vandierendonck & A. Szmalec (Eds.), Spatial working memory (pp. 145-158). Hove: Psychology Press.

Pijawka, D., Yabes, R., Frederick, C. P., & White, P. (2013). Integration of sustainability in planning and design programs in higher education: Evaluating learning outcomes. *Journal of Urbanism, 6*(1), 24–36.

Plagiarim.org. (2014). *Glossary*. Retrieved November 21, 2014 from http://www.plagiarism.org/plagiarism-101/glossary

Plagiarism. (2014). *Cyber plagiarism. Plagiarism and the 21st Century Learner*. Retrieved November 21, 2014 http://plagiarism.wiki.westga.edu/Cyber+Plagiarism

Plagiarism.org. (2014). *What is plagiarism?* Retrieved November 21, 2014 from http://www.plagiarism.org/plagiarism-101/what-is-plagiarism/

Plianram, S., & Inprasitha, M. (2012). Exploring elementary Thai teachers' use of mathematics textbook. *Creative Education, 3*(6), 692-695. Retrieved October 25, 2014, from http://www.SciRP.org/journal/ce

Podlasai, I. (2003). *Pedagogies* (in Russian). Moscow: Vlados.

Podlasai, I. (2010). *Information-energetic pedagogy* (in Russian).Moscow: Dern Group.

Price, K. (2013). *Does digital age mean digital textbooks?* Retrieved November 1, 2014 from http://www.hattiesburgamerican.com/article/20130811/NEWS01/308110025/Does-digital-age-mean-digital-textbooks.htm

ProCon.org. (2014). *Should tablets replace textbooks in K-12 schools?* Retrieved November 25, 2014, from http://tablets-textbooks.procon.org/

Pullen, D., & Cole, D. (2010). *Multiliteracies and technology enhanced education: Social practice and the global classroom.* London: Information Science Reference. doi:10.4018/978-1-60566-673-0

Qwen, L. H. (2013). *Google rolls out digital textbooks, to buy and rent — but students should shop around.* Retrieved November 1, 2014 from http://gigaom.com/2013/08/09/google-rolls-out digital-textbooks-to-buy-and-rent-but-students-should-shop-around/

Railean, E. (2006). Concept mapping in the instructional design of the educational software. In Development and Application Systems. *Proceedings of the 8th In. Conf. on Development and Application Systems* (pp. 333-338). Suceava, Romania: Stefan cel Mare University of Suceava.

Railean, E. (2008). Electronic textbooks in electronic portfolio: a new approach for the self-regulated learning. In *Proceedings of 9th International Conference on Development and Application Systems DAS 2008* (pp. 138-141). Suceava: Stefan cel Mare University of Suceava.

Railean, E. (2010). Metasystems approach to research the globalised pedagogical processes. *Annals of Spiru Haret University, Mathematics – Informatics Series* (Special issue), 31-50.

Railean, E. (2013a). In K. K. Patel, & S. Vij (Ed.). enterprise resource planning models for the education sector: Applications and methodologies (pp.77-92). Hershey, PA: IGI Publishing.

Railean, E. (2013b). Metasystems learning design in digital textbook use and development. In *Proceedings of CAIM 2013 Conference on Applied and Industrial Mathematics* (p. 106). Bucharest, Romania: Romanian National Authority for Scientific Research. Retrieved September 2, 2013 from http://www.eapril.org/resources/EAPRIL2013/Book%20of%20abstracts_EAPRIL%202013.pdf

Railean, E. (2013c). Toward metasystems learning design theory for learning environments. In *Proceedings of EAPRIL2013 Conference*, 45. Sweeten: Bienne.

Railean, E. (2014). Instructional dynamic and flexible strategy: integrity of effective methods for engaging all learners in classrooms. In S. Lawrence (Ed.), Critical practice in P-12 education: Transformative teaching and learning (pp. 49-65). Hershey, PA: Information Science Reference.

Railean, E. (2010). Self-regulated learning – condition of adaptation and accommodation of digital native to globalised learning environments achieved through digital textbook[In Romanian]. *Romanian Journal of Education, 1*(2), 27–38.

Railean, E. (2012). Issues and challenges associated with the design of electronic textbook. In B. H. Khan (Ed.), *User Interface Design for Virtual Environments: Challenges and Advances* (pp. 238–256). Hershey, PA: IGI Publishing. doi:10.4018/978-1-61350-516-8.ch015

Railean, E. (2013). Knowledge management model for electronic textbook design. In K. Patel & S. Vij (Eds.), *Enterprise resource planning models for the education sector: Applications and methodologies* (pp. 77–92). Hershey, PA: Information Science Reference. doi:10.4018/978-1-4666-2193-0.ch005

*Rational* reconstruction *II: Identifying* principles. (n. d.). Retrieved September 11, 2014 from http://www.csus.edu/indiv/m/mayesgr/phl4/tutorial/phl4rationalrecon2.htm

Recio-García, J. A., Díaz-Agudo, B., & González-Calero, P. A. (2014). The COLIBRI platform: Tools, features and working examples. In S. Montani & L. C. Jain (Eds.), *Successful case-based reasoning applications-2* (pp. 55–85). Springer Berlin Heidelberg. doi:10.1007/978-3-642-38736-4_5

Reich, Y. (2014). Year closure and a new beginning: Towards better engineering design research. *Research in Engineering Design*, *25*(1), 1–2. doi:10.1007/s00163-013-0167-z

Reid, N. (2014). The learning of chemistry: The key role of working memory. In I. Devetak & S. A. Glažar (Eds.), *Learning with understanding in the chemistry classroom* (pp. 77–101). Springer Netherlands. doi:10.1007/978-94-007-4366-3_5

Reiser, R. A. (2001). A history of instructional design and technology: Part I: A history of instructional media. *Educational Technology Research and Development*, *49*(1), 53–64. doi:10.1007/BF02504506

Resta, P., & Kalk, D. (2012). An ecological approach to instructional design: The learning synergy of interaction and context. In A. Olofsson & J. Lindberg (Eds.), *Informed design of educational technologies in higher education: Enhanced learning and teaching* (pp. 393–411). Hershey, PA: Information Science Reference.

Reynolds, R. (2011). Trends influencing the growth of digital textbooks in US higher education. *Publishing Research Quarterly*, *27*(2), 178–187. doi:10.1007/s12109-011-9216-5

Reys, B. J. (2014). Mathematics curriculum policies and practices in the US: The common core state standards initiative. In Y. Li & G. Lappan (Eds.), *Mathematics curriculum in school education* (pp. 35–48). Netherlands: Springer. doi:10.1007/978-94-007-7560-2_3

Rezat, S. (2006). A model of textbook use. In *Proceedings of the 30th Conference of the International Group for the Psychology of Mathematics Education, 4,* (pp. 409-416).

Risku, M. & Harding, L. (2013). A unified theory. In *Education for tomorrow*: *A biocentric, student-focused model for reconstructing education,* (pp. 113-134).

Rivero, V. (2013). Digital textbooks: Show me the future! *Internet@Schools*, *20*(3), 12-16.

Rix, K. (2013). *Build your own digital textbooks*. Retrieved October 25, 2014, from http://www.scholastic.com/browse/article.jsp?id=3755544

Roberts, T. (2006). *Self, peer, and group assessment in e-learning*. Hershey, PA: Information Science Publishing. doi:10.4018/978-1-59140-965-6

Rockinson- Szapkiw, A. J., Courduff, J., Carter, K., & Bennett, D. (2013). Electronic versus traditional print textbooks: A comparison study on the influence of university students' learning. *Computers & Education*, *63*, 259–266. doi:10.1016/j.compedu.2012.11.022

Rodríguez-Miranda, F. P., Pozuelos-Estrada, F. J., & León-Jariego, J. C. (2014). The role of ICT coordinator. Priority and time dedicated to professional functions. *Computers & Education*, *72*, 262–270. doi:10.1016/j.compedu.2013.11.009

Roncevic, M. (2013). Criteria for purchasing e-book platforms. *Library Technology Reports*, *49*(3), 10–13.

Rowley, J. (2014). Bridging the gap: Improving students' learning experience through shifting pedagogical practices in higher education. *International Journal of Learning and Development*, *4*(1), 28–39. doi:10.5296/ijld.v4i1.4944

Rudic, G. (2013). Modern pedagogy in multi-measured space. In Europe Business Assemble (Ed.), Socrates Almanac "Science and Education", (pp. 74-75). Oxford: Oxford Review

Rudic, G. A. (2013). *The triune aim of educational process in the present conditions, intellect, emotion and energy* [Power Point]. Presented at Republican Scientific and Practical Conference "Development Strategy of spiritual and moral education of personality in the Republic of Kazakhstan. Asthana, 29 November 2013. Retrieved October 1. 2014 from http://www.pedagogiemoderne.ru/blog

Rudic, G. (2013). Modern pedagogy in multi-measured space. In E. B. Assemble (Ed.), *Socrates Almanac "Science and Education"* (pp. 74–75). Oxford: Oxford Review.

Salinas, P., González-Mendívil, E., Quintero, E., Ríos, H., Ramírez, H., & Morales, S. (2013). The development of a didactic prototype for the learning of mathematics through augmented reality. *Procedia Computer Science*, *25*, 62–70. doi:10.1016/j.procs.2013.11.008

Samuel, S., Grochowski, P., & Nicholls, N. (2013). *Students, Vendor Platforms, and E-textbooks: Using E-books as E-textbooks* (ASEE paper). Retrieved October, 25 2014, from http://deepblue.lib.umich.edu/bitstream/handle/2027.42/98430/ASEE%20paper.pdf?sequence=1

Sands, A. & Journal, E. (2013, June 26). Alberta schools prepare to turn the page to digital textbooks. *Edmonton Journal*, A1. Retrieved from eLibrary.

Santacruz-Valencia, L. P., Navarro, A., Aedo, I., & Kloos, C. D. (2010). Comparison of knowledge during the assembly process of learning objects. *Journal of Intelligent Information Systems*, *35*(1), 51–74. doi:10.1007/s10844-009-0088-5

Sawyer, R. K. (Ed.). (2006). *The Cambridge handbook of the learning sciences*, *2*(5). Cambridge: Cambridge University Press. Retrieved September 2, 2014 from http://coseenow.net/exhibit/wp-content/uploads/2009/11/science-of-learning.pdf

Schnotz, W. (2005). An integrated model of text and picture comprehension. In R. E. Mayer (Ed.), *The Cambridge handbook of multimedia learning* (pp. 49–70). New York: Cambridge University Press. doi:10.1017/CBO9780511816819.005

Schwartz, K. (2014). *Bypassing the textbook: Video games transform social studies curriculum*. Retrieved November 25, 2014, from http://blogs.kqed.org/mindshift/2014/01/forget-the-textbook-video-games-as-social-studies-content/

Schwebel, S. L. (2014). Historical fiction, the common core, and disciplinary habits of mind. *Social Education*, *78*(1), 20–24.

Schweppe, J., & Rummer, R. (2014). Attention, working memory, and long-term memory in multimedia learning: An integrated perspective based on process models of working memory. *Educational Psychology Review*, *26*(2), 285–306. doi:10.1007/s10648-013-9242-2

Selby, R. D., Carter, K. P., & Gage, S. H. (2014). Survey concerning electronic textbooks: Assessing student behavior and environmental considerations. *International Journal of Sustainability in Higher Education*, *15*(2), 3–6.

Senger, A. J. (2014). The beneficiation of education. *Knowledge Quest*, *42*(3), 30–34.

Serafimov, L. (2013). *The mobile platforms*. Retrieved October 25, 2014, from http://www.academia.edu/4306384/Mobile_Learning_Platforms

Serafini, F. (2010). Reading multimodal texts: Perceptual, structural and ideological perspectives. *Children's Literature in Education*, *41*(2), 85–104. doi:10.1007/s10583-010-9100-5

Seton Hill University. (2013). *iPad for everyone!* Retrieved October 25, 2014, from http://www-2011.setonhill.edu/techadvantage/

Shafto, P., Goodman, N. D., Gerstle, B., & Ladusaw, F. (2014). *Prior expectations in pedagogical situations*, 2182-2187. Retrieved September 2, 2014 from http://mindmodeling.org/cogsci2010/papers/0514/paper0514.pdf

Sha, L., Looi, C. K., Chen, W., & Zhang, B. H. (2012). Understanding mobile learning from the perspective of self-regulated learning. *Journal of Computer Assisted Learning*, *28*(4), 366–378. doi:10.1111/j.1365-2729.2011.00461.x

Shen, J., Lei, J., Chang, H. Y., & Namdar, B. (2014). Technology-enhanced, modeling-based instruction (TMBI) in science education. In J. M. Spector, M. D. Merrill, J.Elen, & M. J. Bishop (Eds.), Handbook of research on educational communications and technology (pp. 529-540). Springer New York.

Shute, V. J., & Kim, Y. J. (2014). Formative and stealth assessment. In J. M. Spector, M. D. Merrill, J. Elen, & M. J. Bishop (Eds.), *Handbook of research on educational communications and technology*, (pp. 311-321). Springer. doi:10.1007/978-1-4614-3185-5_25

Siame, C. N. (2012). Relativism in Berlin's cultural pluralism. *Theoria*, *59*(130), 42–58. doi:10.3167/th.2012.5913003

Siemens, B. (2004). *Connectivism: A learning theory for the digital age*. Retrieved October 25, 2014, from http://www.elearnspace.org/Articles/connectivism.htm

Siemens, G. (2014). *Connectivism: A learning theory for the digital age*. Retrieved November 1, 2014 from http://er.dut.ac.za/bitstream/handle/123456789/69/Siemens_2005_Connectivism_A_learning_theory_for_the_digital_age.pdf?sequence=1

Simonneaux, L. (2014). Questions socialement vives and socio-scientific issues: New trends of research to meet the training needs of postmodern society. In C. Bruguière, A. Tiberghien, & P. Clement (Eds.), Topics and trends in current science education (pp. 37-54). The Netherlands: Springer.

Simon, R., Acosta, A., & Houtman, E. (2014). "Memeration": Exploring academic authorship in online spaces. In R. E. Ferdig & K. E. Pytash (Eds.), *Exploring multimodal composition and digital writing* (pp. 54–67). Hershey, PA: Information Science Reference.

*Simpson's psychomotor domain.* (n. d.). Retrieved October, 25, 2014 from http://assessment.uconn.edu/docs/LearningTaxonomy_Psychomotor.pdf

Sims, R. (2014). Learning design or design alchemy? In R. Sims (Ed.), *Educational communication and technologies: Issues and innovations* (pp. 79–91). Springer International Publishing.

Skinner, B. F. (1958). Teaching Machines. *The Sciences*, *128*(3330), 969–976. doi:10.1126/science.128.3330.969 PMID:13592277

Smart, C. (2013). *Compare eTextbook.* Retrieved October, 25, 2014, from http://instructors.coursesmart.com/Compare?xmlid=9781605253565&__frompdp=1

Smith, R. S. (2004). *Guidelines for authors of learning objects.* MMC: The New Media Consortium. Retrieved October, 25, 2014, from http://archive2.nmc.org/guidelines/NMC%20LO%20Guidelines.pdf

*Smithsonian Education.* (2014). Retrieved September 2, 2014 from http://www.smithsonianeducation.org/educators/

Soloman, B. A., & Felder, R. M. (2014). *Index of learning styles questionnaire.* Retrieved from http://www.engr.ncsu.edu/learningstyles/ilsweb.html

Song, J. S., Kim, S. J., Byun, G. S., Song, J. H., & Lee, B. G. (2014). Comparing wireless networks for applying digital textbook. *Telecommunication Systems*, *55*(1), 25–38. doi:10.1007/s11235-013-9748-4

St Clair-Thompson, H. (2014). Establishing the reliability and validity of a computerized assessment of children's working memory for use in group settings. *Journal of Psychoeducational Assessment*, *32*(1), 15–26. doi:10.1177/0734282913497344

Stenberg, K., Karlsson, L., Pitkaniemi, H., & Maaranen, K. (2014). Beginning student teachers' teacher identities based on their practical theories. *European Journal of Teacher Education*, *37*(2), 204–219. doi:10.1080/02619768.2014.882309

Streitfeld. (2013, April 13). Smart textbooks monitor student engagement; Data from digital books affects how profs present material - but does it really measure learning? *Montreal Gazette.*

Stiggins, R., Chappuis, S., & Arter, J. (2014). *Classroom assessment for student learning.* Pearson.

Sultan, A. S., & Lim, H. S., MatJafri, M. Z. & Abdullah, K. (2006). Developed of a computer aided instruction (CAI) package in remote sensing educational. *International Archives of the Photogrammetry*, *36*(6), 29–34.

Sweller, J. (2011). Cognitive load theory. In B. N. Ross (Ed.), *The psychology of learning and motivation. Cognition in Education* (Vol. 55). Elsevier Inc.

Tailacova, D. H. (2013). The use of technology for modelling and creating electronic textbook for the course "Mother Tongue" (in Russian). *The Young Scientist*, *5*, 772-775.

Talizina. (1969). *Theoretical problems of programed learning* (in Russian). Moscow: MGU.

Tanriseven, I., & Dilmac, B. (2013). Predictive relationships between secondary school students' human values, motivational beliefs, and Self-Regulated Learning Strategies. *Educational Sciences: Theory and Practice*, *13*(1), 29–36.

Taylor, T. (2014). *Principles of microeconomics.* Retrieved October, 28, 2014, from https://openstaxcollege.org/textbooks/principles-of-microeconomics

Taylor, V. (2014). *Intentional plagiarism: Definition, examples & quiz*. Educational Portal. Retrieved November 21, 2014 from http://education-portal.com/academy/lesson/intentional-plagiarism-definition-examples-quiz.html#lesson

Taylor, T. (2014). Considering complexity in simple solutions: What's so complicated about Skype? *International Journal of Systems and Society, 1*(1), 35–52. doi:10.4018/ijss.2014010104

The Digital Reader. (2014). *Barnes & Noble Launches New e-Textbook App – Yuzu*. Retrieved November 1, 2014 from http://the-digital-reader.com/2014/04/20/barnes-noble-launches-new-e-textbook-app-yuzu/#.VGt-wzSUdQE

*The International Children's National Library*. (2013). Retrieved October 25, 2014, from http://en.childrenslibrary.org/

The Trustees of Princeton University. (2010). *The E-reader pilot at Princeton*. Retrieved October, 25, 2014, from http://www.princeton.edu/ereaderpilot/eReaderFinalReportLong.pdf

*Things you should know about flipped classrooms*. (2015). Retrieved February, 15 2015, from http://net.educause.edu/ir/library/pdf/ELI7081.pdf

Thoermer, A., & Williams, L. (2012). Using digital texts to promote fluent reading. *The Reading Teacher, 65*(7), 441–445. doi:10.1002/TRTR.01065

Thorndike, E. L. (1923). *Education: A first book*. New York: Macmillan Co.

Tintinalli, J. E. (2014). Real textbooks or e-books: What is happening right now? *Emergency Medicine Australasia, 26*(1), 72–75. doi:10.1111/1742-6723.12189 PMID:24495066

Toledano, M. (2002). *Design patterns*. Retrieved November 1, 2014 from http://www.moisesdaniel.com/wri/metapatterns.html

Toppo, G. (2014). *Classroom technology can make learning more dangerous, and that's a good thing*. The Hechinger Report. Retrieved October 25, 2014, from http://hechingerreport.org/content/classroom-technology-can-make-learning-dangerous-thats-good-thing_17755/

Tosun, N. (2014). A study on reading printed books or e-books: Reasons for student-teachers preferences. *The Turkish Online Journal of Educational Technology, 13*(1), 21–28.

Toussaint, E. R., & Toussaint, G. T. (2014). *What is a pattern?* Retrieved November, 21, 2014 from http://m.archive.bridgesmathart.org/2014/bridges2014-293.pdf

Tu, C. H., Sujo-Montes, L., Yen, C. J., Chan, J. Y., & Blocher, M. (2012). The integration of personal learning environments & open network learning environments. *TechTrends: Linking Research & Practice to Improve Learning., 56*(4), 13–19. doi:10.1007/s11528-012-0571-7

Turchin, V., & Joslyn, C. (1993). *The metasystems transition*. Retrieved October 12, 2014 from ftp://ftp.vub.ac.be/pub/projects/Principia_Cybernetica/PCP-Web/MST.html

Tyner, K. (2014). *Literacy in a digital world: Teaching and learning in the age of information*. Routledge Communication Series.

UNESCO. (2014). *Education. Textbook development*. Retrieved May, 24, 2014 from http://www.unesco.org/new/en/education/themes/strengthening-education-systems/languages-in-education/textbooks-development/

UNESCO. (2014). *ICT in education*. Retrieved October, 29, 2014 from http://www.unesco.org/new/en/unesco/themes/icts/

University of Melbourne. (2014). *Academic honesty and plagiarism*. Retrieved November 21, 2014 from https://academichonesty.unimelb.edu.au/plagiarism.html

University of Pittsburgh. (2014). *Plagiarism policy*. Retrieved November 21, 2014 from http://www.frenchanditalian.pitt.edu/undergrad/about/plagiarism.php

van Beek, J. A., de Jong, F., Minnaert, A., & Wubbels, T. (2014). Teacher practice in secondary vocational education: Between teacher-regulated activities of student learning and student self-regulation. *Teaching and Teacher Education, 40*, 1–9. doi:10.1016/j.tate.2014.01.005

Van Meer, E. (2003). PLATO: From computer-based education to corporate social responsibility. *Iterations. An Interdisciplinary Journal of Software History*. Retrieved October 25, 2014, from http://www.cbi.umn.edu/iterations/vanmeer.html

van Merriënboer, J. J., & de Bruin, A. B. (2014). Research paradigms and perspectives on learning. In J. M. Spector, M. D. Merrill, J. Elen, & M. J. Bishop (Eds.), Handbook of research on educational communications and technology (pp. 21-29). Springer New York.

Veenman, M. V., Bavelaar, L., De Wolf, L., & Van Haaren, M. G. (2014). The on-line assessment of metacognitive skills in a computerized learning environment. *Learning and Individual Differences, 29*, 123–130. doi:10.1016/j.lindif.2013.01.003

Veletsianos, G., & Russell, G. S. (2014). Pedagogical agents. In *Handbook of research on educational communications and technology* (pp. 759–769). Springer New York. doi:10.1007/978-1-4614-3185-5_61

Volk, T., & Bloom, J. W. (2007). The use of metapatterns for research into complex systems of teaching, learning, and schooling, Part I: Metapatterns in nature and culture. *Complicity: The International Journal of Complexity and Education, 4*, 25-43. Retrieved July 22, 2014 from http://metapatterns.wdfiles.com/local--files/members:tylervolk/ppr.Volk.Complicity1.2007.pdf

Volk, T., Bloom, J. W., & Richards, J. (2007). Toward a science of metapatterns: Building upon Bateson's foundation. *Kybernetes: The International Journal of Cybernetics, Systems, and Management Sciences, 36*, 1070-1080. Retrieved July 22, 2014 from http://metapatterns.wdfiles.com/local--files/members:tylervolk/Volk.Bateson.27Jul07.pdf

Vollstedt, M., Heinze, A., Gojdka, K., & Rach, S. (2014). Framework for examining the transformation of mathematics and mathematics learning in the transition from school to university. In S. Rezat, M. Hattermann, & A. Peter-Koop, (Eds.), Transformation: A fundamental idea of mathematics education (pp. 29-50). New York: Springer. doi:10.1007/978-1-4614-3489-4_2

Vonderwell, S., & Boboc, M. (2013). Promoting formative assessment in online teaching and learning. *TechTrends: Linking Research & Practice to Improve Learning, 57*(4), 22–27. doi:10.1007/s11528-013-0673-x

Wahl, L., & Duffield, J. (2014*). Using flexible technology to meet the needs of diverse students.* Retrieved November, 22, 2014 from http://www.wested.org/online_pubs/kn-05-01.pdf

Wallace, M. J., & Newton, P. M. (2014). Turnaround time and market capacity in contract cheating. *Educational Studies, 40*(2), 233–236. doi:10.1080/03055698.2014.889597

Walling, D. R. (2014). Framing the learning design approach. In D. R. Walling (Ed.), *Designing learning for tablet classrooms* (pp. 19–24). Springer International Publishing. doi:10.1007/978-3-319-02420-2_4

Walling, D. R. (2014). Who's the learning designer here? In D. R. Walling (Ed.), *Designing learning for tablet classrooms: Innovation and instruction* (pp. 13–18). Springer International Publishing. doi:10.1007/978-3-319-02420-2_3

Walshaw, M., & Duncan, W. (2014). Hermeneutics as a methodological resource for understanding empathy in on-line learning environments. *International Journal of Research & Method in Education*, 1–16. doi:10.1080/1743727X.2014.914166

Walsh, M. (2006). The 'textual shift': Examining the reading process with print, visual and multimodal texts. *Australian Journal of Language & Literacy., 29*(1), 24–37.

Wang, M., & Shen, R. (2012). Message design for mobile learning: Learning theories, human cognition and design principles. *British Journal of Educational Technology, 43*(4), 561–575. doi:10.1111/j.1467-8535.2011.01214.x

Warren, S. J., Lee, J., & Najmi, A. (2014). The impact of technology and theory on instructional design since 2000. In J. M. Spector, M. D. Merrill, D. Elen, & M. J. Bishop, (Eds.), Handbook of research on educational communications and technology (pp. 89-99). Springer New York.

Waters, J. K. (2011). *E-textbooks: 4 keys to going all-digital.* Retrieved October, 25, 2014, from http://campustechnology.com/articles/2011/08/03/e-textbooks-4-keys-to-going-all-digital.aspx

Weller, M. (2007). Learning objects, learning design, and adoption through succession. *Journal of Computing in Higher Education, 19*(1), 26–47. doi:10.1007/BF03033418

Wiek, A., Withycombe, L., Redman, C., & Mills, S. (2011). Moving forward on competence in sustainability research and problem solving. *Environment, 53*(2), 3–13. doi:10.1080/00139157.2011.554496

Wiklund-Hörnqvist, C., Jonsson, B., & Nyberg, L. (2014). Strengthening concept learning by repeated testing. *Scandinavian Journal of Psychology, 55*(1), 10–16. doi:10.1111/sjop.12093 PMID:24313425

Wiley, D. A. (2000). Connecting learning objects to instructional design theory: A definition, a metaphor, and a taxonomy. In D. A. Wiley (Ed.), *The instructional use of learning objects: Online version.* Retrieved from http://reusability.org/read/chapters/wiley.doc

Willey, K., & Gardner, A. (2010). Investigating the capacity of self and peer assessment activities to engage students and promote learning. *European Journal of Engineering Education, 35*(4), 429–443. doi:10.1080/03043797.2010.490577

Williams, M. K., & Donnellon, A. (2014). Personalizing entrepreneurial learning: A pedagogy for facilitating the know why. *Entrepreneurship Research Journal, 4*(2), 167–204.

Wilson, L. (2012). *Apple's iPad textbooks cost 5x more than print.* Retrieved November 25, 2014, from http://tablets-textbooks.procon.org/sourcefiles/print-vs-itext.pdf

Wisse, P. (2008). *Metapattern: Information modelling as enneadic dynamics.* Retrieved November 19, 2014 from http://sprouts.aisnet.org/156/2/R2001-04.pdf

Wogahn, D. (2012). *ISBN essentials: An FAQ for eBook publishers.* SellBox. Retrieved November 2, 2014 from http://www.sellbox.com/isbn-essentials-an-faq-for-ebook-publishers/

Wogahn, D. (2013). *The myth of the eISBN: Why every eBook edition needs a unique number.* Retrieved November 2, 2014 from http://www.sellbox.com/myth-eisbn-every-ebook-edition-needs-unique-number/

Wolf, R. (2014). *Assessing the impact of characteristics of the test, common-items, and examinees on the preservation of equity properties in mixed-format test equating* (Doctoral dissertation). University of Pittsburgh. Retrieved October 25, 2014, from http://d-scholarship.pitt.edu/20130/

Wook, S., Michaels, S., & Waterman, D. (2014). Print vs. electronic readings in college courses: Cost-efficiency and perceived learning. *The Internet and Higher Education, 21,* 17–24. doi:10.1016/j.iheduc.2013.10.004

Wright, M. C. (2002). Same old textbook? An evaluation metric for Web-based supplemental textbooks. *Journal of Computing in Higher Education, 14*(1), 28–49. doi:10.1007/BF02940949

WriteCheck. (2014). *Types of plagiarism.* Retrieved November 21, 2014 from http://en.writecheck.com/types-of-plagiarism

*Writing interactive pages.* (n. d.). Retrieved November 19, 2014 from http://www.conservationphysics.org/appx/writingtec2.php

Wu, W. H., Hsiao, H. C., Wu, P. L., Lin, C. H., & Huang, S. H. (2012). Investigating the learning-theory foundations of game-based learning: A meta-analysis. *Journal of Computer Assisted Learning, 28*(3), 235–280. doi:10.1111/j.1365-2729.2011.00437.x

Xiaoqing, G., Yuankun, Z., & Xiaofeng, G. (2013). Meeting the "Digital Natives": Understanding the acceptance of technology in classrooms. *Journal of Educational Technology & Society, 16*(1), 392–402.

Yu, M., Zhou, C., & Xing, W. (2014). Change towards creative society: A developed knowledge model for IT in learning. In S. Li, Q. Jin, X. Jiang, & J. J. Park (Eds.), Frontier and future development of information technology in medicine and education, Vol. 286 (pp. 3373-3377). Springer Netherlands. doi:10.1007/978-94-007-7618-0_437

Zaiteva, L., & Popco, V. B. (2006). Development and using of electronic textbooks [in Russian]. *Journal of Educational Technology & Society,* 411–421. Retrieved from http://ifets.ieee.org/russian/depository/v9_i1/html/3.html

Zhang, C. X., Zhang, J. S., Ji, N. N., & Guo, G. (2014). Learning ensemble classifiers via restricted Boltzmann machines. *Pattern Recognition Letters*, *36*, 161–170. doi:10.1016/j.patrec.2013.10.009

Zhang, Z., & Fan, L. (2014). *Research on negative influence and strategies of multimedia education in universities.International Conference on Education Reform and Modern Management*. Atlantis Press. doi:10.2991/ermm-14.2014.46

Zhao, K., & Chan, C. K. (2013). Fostering collective and individual learning through knowledge building. *International Journal of Computer-Supported Collaborative Learning*, 1-33.

Zhen, W. (2014). Problems of and reflections on task design in graduate English textbooks. In *Proceedings of the International Conference on Management, Education and Social Science,* (pp. 122-126). Retrieved February 5, 2015, from http://www.atlantis-press.com/php/pub.php?publication=icmess-14&frame=http%3A//www.atlantis-press.com/php/paper-details.php%3Ffrom%3Dauthor+index%26id%3D11159%26querystr%3Dauthorstr%253DW

Zoellner, B., & Cavanaugh, T. (2013). Empowering pre-service science teachers to be active users of eText resources. In R. McBride & M. Searson (Eds.), Proceedings of society for information technology & teacher education international conference (pp. 4085–4091). Chesapeake, VA: AACE; Retrieved from http://www.editlib.org/p/48760

# About the Author

**Elena Railean** has a Ph.D in Pedagogy, and is senior lecturer and vice-chef of Project Management Department at European University of Moldova and senior researcher at Academy of Sciences of Moldova. She is author of two monographs and more than 75 articles in theory and methodology of applied learning theory and design. Her research interests include philosophy of learning, cybernetic pedagogy, computerized assessment, knowledge management, quantum psychology and mathematical modeling. The focus of her research is to investigate the metasystems approach of learning processes, principles of writing and assessment in digital semantic workplaces. Elena is the author of the didactical model for electronic textbooks, which affordance is to develop competence through dynamic and flexible instructional strategy. Her main publications are *Methodology of educational software; The psychopedagogical bases for electronic textbook development; Knowledge Management Model for Electronic Textbook Design; Issues and challenges associated with the design of electronic textbook;* and *Trends, issues and solutions in e-books pedagogy.*

# Index

## T

Taxonomy 35, 99, 112, 114-115, 144, 159, 168, 174, 205, 211, 213, 229
Threshold Concepts (TCs) 247
Transcendental Philosophy 131

## U

Ubiquitous Computing 92
Ubiquitous Learning Materials 109
Ubiquitous Learning (U-Learning) 70, 72, 92, 94-95, 101-102, 104-105, 109
Usability 92, 115, 139, 189, 227, 237, 241

## V

Virtual Learning Environment 34, 46, 153
Visibility 92, 232
Visual Educational Movement 20

## W

Web 2.0 13, 20, 31, 42, 92

Printed in the United States
By Bookmasters